AF885420

SOTHIS PRESS

Sothis Press aims to completely reimagine the public domain book with an emphasis on universal access to captivatingly designed print editions. We believe that technology will enable every single book ever published to be perpetually accessible in beautiful print form. Sothis is beauty in ubiquity.

www.sothis.press
1 Waterhouse Square, London, ECIN 2ST

A Treatise on the Law of Agency in Contract and Tort

Including Special Chapters on Attorneys at Law, Auctioneers, Bank Officers, Brokers, Factors, Insurance Agents, Traveling Salesman, Public Agents and Officers, Master and Servant

George L. Reinhard

SOTHIS PRESS

ISBN 978-1-83548-358-9

A Treatise on the Law of Agency in Contract and Tort is in the public domain.

This edition is published by Sothis Press © 2023. The company is registered in England and Wales. The Company Number is 14900389.

A TREATISE

ON THE

LAW OF AGENCY

IN

CONTRACT AND TORT

INCLUDING SPECIAL CHAPTERS ON

ATTORNEYS AT LAW
AUCTIONEERS, BANK OFFICERS, BROKERS, FACTORS
INSURANCE AGENTS, TRAVELING SALESMEN
PUBLIC AGENTS AND OFFICERS
MASTER AND SERVANT

BY
GEORGE L. REINHARD, A. B., LL. D.
Ex-Justice of Indiana Appellate Court
Dean of the Law Faculty of Indiana University

INDIANAPOLIS
THE BOWEN-MERRILL COMPANY
1902

Copyright 1902
BY
THE BOWEN-MERRILL COMPANY

T
R.[illegible]
1902

THE HOLLENBECK PRESS
INDIANAPOLIS

PREFACE

There is perhaps no branch of the substantive law which is the subject of more constant and rapid development and modification, not to say change, than that which governs the relation of principal and agent; for as Dr. Wharton truly says, "Agency is the creature of usage as established by the courts, and that usage can only be settled by cumulative rulings;" and usage, which is but the result of our habits of business and our methods of dealing, is as evolutionary as is the race itself.

The demand of the present-day lawyer is for the book which presents the law in plain and concise form, supported by an abundance of the most recent and best-considered authorities. It has been the purpose of the author to make a succinct and intelligible exposition of the modern law of Agency as administered in this country and in England. While he has not sought to multiply authorities, he has made the notes sufficiently full to support the text, and also, by quoting liberally from the opinions of judges, to furnish illustrations of the questions involved.

It has been the author's purpose to be accurate rather than original, realizing, from his experience at the bar, on the bench, and in the class-room, that the profession wants books to aid in the search for the law as it is, and not as the author thinks it should be. He has not hesitated, however, where the cases conflict, to give his own opinion as to what is the weight of authority, or the rule resting upon the more reasonable foundation, stating the reasons for his opinion.

The first ten chapters of the work present the general principles and rules of the law of Agency. The succeeding chapters treat sep-

735849

arately the more conspicuous classes of agents, and show the applicability of the general principles contained in the previous chapters to the cases of these special classes of agents.

A chapter on Master and Servant as it affects agency, with an appendix containing the Employers' Liability Acts of England and several of the American states, will be found very useful, from the fact that the two subjects are so closely related that it is impossible to treat intelligently the one without frequent reference to the other.

Among the features to which the author feels warranted in calling special attention is the presentation, in the chapter on the Authority of the Agent, of the subject of filling blanks in written instruments, and the authority which is necessary for that purpose.

Attention may likewise be called to the chapters on Insurance Agents and Traveling Salesmen; for it is believed that these subjects have not hitherto received that special attention in works on Agency which their importance would seem to demand.

GEORGE L. REINHARD.

Bloomington, Ind., November 15, 1902.

CONTENTS

CHAPTER I.

DEFINITIONS AND EXPLANATIONS.

CHAPTER II.

COMPETENCY OF PARTIES.

CHAPTER III.

HOW AGENCY MAY BE CREATED AND PROVED.

I. By Appointment.

II. Termination by Act of Party.

III. Termination by Operation of Law.

CHAPTER V.

AUTHORITY OF AGENT AND THE DELEGATION THEREOF—INTERPRETATION, CONSTRUCTION, AND EXECUTION OF AUTHORITY.

CHAPTER VI.

DUTIES, OBLIGATIONS AND LIABILITIES OF AGENT TO PRINCIPAL, AND RIGHTS OF PRINCIPAL IN REGARD TO AGENT.

CHAPTER VII.

DUTIES, OBLIGATIONS AND LIABILITIES OF PRINCIPAL TO AGENT, AND RIGHTS OF AGENT IN REGARD TO PRINCIPAL.

CHAPTER VIII.

DUTIES, OBLIGATIONS AND LIABILITIES OF AGENT TO THIRD PERSONS, AND RIGHTS OF THIRD PERSONS IN REGARD TO AGENT.

I. On Contract.

II. For Torts.

CHAPTER X.

DUTIES, OBLIGATIONS AND LIABILITIES OF THIRD PERSONS TO AGENT AND TO PRINCIPAL, AND RIGHTS OF AGENT AND PRINCIPAL, RESPECTIVELY, IN REGARD TO THIRD PERSONS.

A. OF THIRD PERSONS TO AGENT.

I. On Contracts.

CHAPTER IX.

DUTIES, OBLIGATIONS AND LIABILITIES OF PRINCIPAL TO THIRD PERSONS, AND RIGHTS OF THIRD PERSONS IN REGARD TO PRINCIPAL.

II. In Tort.

CHAPTER XI.

ATTORNEYS AT LAW.

I. Qualification and Admission to Practice.

CHAPTER XII.

AUCTIONEERS.

CHAPTER XIII.

BANK OFFICERS.

CHAPTER XIV.

BROKERS.

CHAPTER XV.

FACTORS.

CHAPTER XVI.

INSURANCE AGENTS.

CHAPTER XVII.

TRAVELING SALESMEN.

CHAPTER XVIII.

PUBLIC AGENTS AND OFFICERS.

CHAPTER XIX.

MASTER AND SERVANT.

I. Duties, Obligations and Liabilities of Master to Servant.

II. Liability of Master to Third Persons for Acts of Servant.

III. Obligations and Liabilities of Servants.

APPENDIX

EMPLOYERS' LIABILITY ACTS.

TABLE OF CASES.

[*References are to Sections.*]

[*References are to Sections.*]

[*References are to Sections.*]

[*References are to Sections.*]

[*References are to Sections.*]

[*References are to Sections.*]

[*References are to Sections.*]

[*References are to Sections.*]

[*References are to Sections.*]

[*References are to Sections.*]

[*References are to Sections.*]

[*References are to Sections.*]

[*References are to Sections.*]

[*References are to Sections.*]

[*References are to Sections.*]

[*References are to Sections.*]

[*References are to Sections.*]

[*References are to Sections.*]

[*References are to Sections.*]

[*References are to Sections.*]

D

[*References are to Sections.*]

[*References are to Sections.*]

[*References are to Sections.*]

[*References are to Sections.*]

E

[*References are to Sections.*]

[*References are to Sections.*]

F

[*References are to Sections.*]

[*References are to Sections.*]

[*References are to Sections.*]

[*References are to Sections.*]

G

[*References are to Sections.*]

[*References are to Sections.*]

[*References are to Sections.*]

[*References are to Sections.*]

[*References are to Sections.*]

[*References are to Sections.*]

[*References are to Sections.*]

[*References are to Sections.*]

[*References are to Sections.*]

[*References are to Sections.*]

[*References are to Sections.*]

[*References are to Sections.*]

K

[*References are to Sections.*]

[*References are to Sections.*]

[*References are to Sections.*]

[*References are to Sections.*]

[*References are to Sections.*]

[*References are to Sections.*]

[*References are to Sections.*]

[*References are to Sections.*]

[*References are to Sections.*]

[References are to Sections.]

[*References are to Sections.*]

[*References are to Sections.*]

[*References are to Sections.*]

[*References are to Sections.*]

[*References are to Sections.*]

[*References are to Sections.*]

O

[*References are to Sections.*]

P

[*References are to Sections.*]

[*References are to Sections.*]

[*References are to Sections.*]

[*References are to Sections.*]

[*References are to Sections.*]

Q

R

[*References are to Sections.*]

[*References are to Sections.*]

[References are to Sections.]

[*References are to Sections.*]

[*References are to Sections.*]

[*References are to Sections.*]

[*References are to Sections.*]

[*References are to Sections.*]

[*References are to Sections.*]

[*References are to Sections.*]

[*References are to Sections.*]

[*References are to Sections.*]

[*References are to Sections.*]

T

[References are to Sections.]

[*References are to Sections.*]

[*References are to Sections.*]

[*References are to Sections.*]

[*References are to Sections.*]

W

[*References are to Sections.*]

[*References are to Sections.*]

[*References are to Sections.*]

[*References are to Sections.*]

[*References are to Sections.*]

[*References are to Sections.*]

[*References are to Sections.*]

Y

Z

PRINCIPAL AND AGENT.

CHAPTER I.

DEFINITIONS AND EXPLANATIONS.

§ 1. **Importance of this branch of the law.**—In these days of almost unparalleled commercial activity it would be difficult indeed to overestimate the importance of the place occupied by the law of agency in the great body of substantive law, and as a branch of contracts. So extensive have the active business operations everywhere come to be that no one would expect to find in any community any considerable number of business men who have sufficient time and capacity to attend to their affairs without the assistance of agents or servants. Indeed, it is not too much to say that the great bulk of the trade and commerce of the world is carried on through the instrumentality of agents; that is to say, persons acting under authority delegated to them by others, and not in their own right or on their own account. The magnitude of this importance becomes still more manifest when we include also the field covered by the law relating to the subject of torts, which we must do in order to be as thorough as we should be in our consideration.

§ 2. **The maxim "Qui facit per alium facit per se."**—The doctrine of agency is founded upon certain fundamental principles expressed in a few maxims of the law. The most general of these is the maxim *"Qui facit per alium facit per se,"* which, when rendered into English, means, "Whatever a person does through another, he does himself." The proposition meant to be expressed is that, ordinarily, whatever act or business one is capable of doing himself he may empower another to do. The correlative maxim is *"Qui per alium facit, per seipsum facere videtur"*—"He who does an act through the medium of another is, in law, considered as having done it himself." These general statements of the principle that one may act through the instrumentality of another must, however, be received with some qualifications. One of these is that only such persons may act by others as would be capable of acting for themselves in a given transaction; or, to state these maxims somewhat differently, whatever a person *sui juris* and competent may do of himself, he may do by another; and any person *sui juris* and competent who does an act through another is deemed to have done it himself. For it is not every one who is capable, in law, of performing a business transaction or other affair, but only those who are not laboring under some legal disability, such as infancy, coverture, lunacy, idiocy, etc.[1] A further limitation upon the maxims is the statement that the party who is to perform the act must also possess the requisite legal ability, by being free from any incapacity which the law imposes upon him in certain contingencies. But, as we shall hereinafter point out, the incapacities of agents are far less frequent than those of principals. The doctrine may therefore be stated, without further qualification, that whatever a person *sui juris* and competent may do of himself, he may do through another who is not by law incompetent to do it.

[1] Broom Legal Maxims 817; Story Ag., § 2.

§ 3. **The maxim "Respondeat superior."**—Another maxim, standing in near relation to those above quoted, is that of "*Respondeat superior*"—"Let the superior (principal) respond (be held responsible)." It is applicable, however, mostly to actions *ex delicto,* while the others apply more especially to actions growing out of contracts. It is the foundation of the doctrine that the principal is liable for the torts—the wrongful acts—of his agent. This general maxim is likewise subject to qualification, however, in that the principal is not in fact liable in all cases for the torts of his agent or employe, but only for those committed in the course of the agency or employment; while the agent himself is, in such cases, for reasons of public policy, also liable for the same.[2]

§ 4. **Reciprocal rights and obligations of principal, agent and third parties.**—The rights and obligations that grow out of the doctrines that have been established upon these fundamental principles are of a reciprocal nature; for it would not be just or equitable that a person should reap a benefit from a given transaction without at the same time assuming the corresponding burdens incident thereto, or naturally arising out of the same. The result is that if a person would claim the benefits of a transaction performed for him by another, the law casts upon him the duty of conforming to all the requirements involved in such transaction, even though these result in hardship rather than in benefit to him. This is especially true of contracts and of the various incidents involved in their execution and performance. Moreover, from certain considerations of public policy to be hereinafter explained, the law deems it proper and just that one who selects a substitute to act for him, and who is therefore presumed to know his qualifications and to have chosen him with reference thereto, and who has it in his power to remove him for his misconduct, and whose orders such substitute is bound to obey and execute, should be held responsible for his acts; provided, of course, that they have been committed in the performance of the task for which he was employed.[3] Obligations are likewise incurred by those who have dealt with the party to whom authority has been given, usually denominated third persons. Their position is in many respects similar to that of the one in whose behalf the transaction is entered into. If it be a business matter—a contract—the third party

[2] Broom Legal Maxims 843.

[3] Quarman v. Burnett, 6 M. & W. 499, 509; Lane v. Cotton, 12 Mod. 490, per Lord Holt.

acquires certain rights, of course, but the law likewise demands of him that he shall comply with the conditions in consideration of which the rights have accrued to him.

§ 5. **Aim and design of the law of agency.**—To define the relation between those by whom authority is delegated to others and those who receive such authority; to show the effect of such relation, how it may be created and established, and who may and who may not enter into it; to point out what are the rights and liabilities of those who confer and those who undertake to execute such authority, and the rights and liabilities of those with whom dealings are had as a result of such delegation of authority, and how such rights and obligations may be enforced; and to apply the principles to the various classes of agencies,—is the aim and design of the law of agency.

§ 6. **Definition of agency.**—Agency is the jural relation subsisting between two competent parties, one of whom is called principal and the other agent.

§ 7. **Purpose of the relation.**—The purpose for which such a relation is entered into is that the agent may represent and act for the principal in some lawful dealing or transaction of a business character with some third party or parties; and to accomplish this purpose the principal confers upon the agent certain power called the agent's authority.

§ 8. **Nature of the relation.**—The relation thus created between the principal and agent is a contractual one, inasmuch as it usually arises out of the employment of the agent by the principal or out of a contract between them, express or implied; although in certain exceptional cases it results, or is conclusively presumed, as a matter of law; as where the law authorizes a wife to pledge the credit of her husband for necessaries which he has refused or neglected to provide for her.[4]

§ 9. **Authority—How it may be delegated.**—If the contract be express, it may be by mere verbal delegation of authority, or it may be by written instrument under seal or by simple contract not under seal. A written instrument delegating authority to an agent is termed a letter of attorney, or power of attorney. For the delegation of some authority it is required, at least by the rules of the common law, that

[4] Mechem Ag., § 62.

there should be a deed,—that is to say, a sealed instrument, or a power of attorney under seal,—as in cases where power is conferred to convey real estate; while in most other instances a power conferred by simple instrument in writing and not under seal is sufficient. In a very large number of cases no written authority whatever is required, but the express authority may be shown to have been given by mere verbal delegation of the same. In most of the American states the requirement for a seal has been abolished. When the authority has not been expressly delegated, either in writing or verbally, it may be inferred from the nature of the service, the declarations or conduct of the principal, or from other circumstances which the law deems sufficient. To determine either the existence or the extent of the authority the courts will look to the intention of the parties, which may be established by the contract and by the conduct and declarations of the parties, the same as in other contracts. When the relation arises *ex lege* the actual intent of the parties will have but little controlling influence, for they will be presumed to have intended that which is the legal consequence of their personal relation and situation to each other. The agent's authority may also be shown by proof of ratification, or estoppel; but it can hardly be said that in such cases the authority has been "delegated," but rather that it has been assumed by the agent, and the principal is, from considerations of public policy, held to acquiesce in such assumption.

§ 10. **The constituent elements of agency.**—In order to constitute an agency the following elements are essential: 1. There must be a competent principal. 2. There must be a competent agent. 3. There must be a delegation of authority from the principal to the agent, either by contract, express or implied, or authority must be shown to exist by operation of law from the peculiar relation of the parties and the circumstances of the transaction, or by estoppel or ratification. 4. The purpose for which this authority is delegated—the transaction to be performed by the agent—must be a lawful one. It must not be illegal, immoral, or contrary to public policy.

§ 11. **Who is a principal.**—A principal—sometimes otherwise called master, constituent, employer—is a person who, being competent and *sui juris* to do any act for his own benefit, or on his own account, employs another to do it;[5] he is the person from whom authority is derived.[6] He "is the party whom the agent represents and from

[5] Story Ag., § 3.

[6] Evans Pr. & Ag. (Bedford's ed.) 34.

whom he derives his authority; he is the one primarily and originally concerned in the contract of agency."[7]

§ 12. **Who is an agent.**—An agent—sometimes otherwise called servant, representative, delegate, proxy, attorney—is a person who undertakes, by virtue of authority conferred on him in that behalf, or without authority but by some subsequent ratification of the principal, to transact some business or manage some affair for the latter, and to render an account of it. He is a substitute for a person, employed to manage the affairs of another.[8] He is a person duly authorized to act on behalf of another, or one whose unauthorized act has been duly ratified.[9] There are various classes of agents, each of which is known or recognized by some distinctive appellation or name; as factor, broker, etc.

§ 13. **Subagent.**—A subagent is a person selected by an agent to assist him in the performance of his duties as agent, or part of them, or to perform any or all of the acts for which the agency was created.

§ 14. **Other definitions of agency.**—Mechem defines agency as "a legal relation, founded upon the express or implied contract of the parties, or created by law, by virtue of which one party—the agent—is employed and authorized to represent and act for the other—the principal—in business dealings with third persons."[10] Wharton's definition is as follows: "Agency is a contract by which one person, with greater or less discretionary powers, undertakes to represent another in a certain business relation."[11] The popular idea of the term "agency" is that of a relation created by an agreement, express or implied, made between the parties before the performance of the act in question and with reference to it.[12] Chancellor Kent says: "Agency is founded upon a contract, either express or implied, by which one of the parties confides to the other the management of some business to be transacted in his name, or on his account, and by which the other assumes to do the business, and to render an account of it. The authority of the agent may be created by deed or writing, or verbally without writing; and for the ordinary business and commerce the

[7] 1 Am. & Eng. Encyc. L. (2d ed.) 938.

[8] 1 Am. & Eng. Encyc. L. (2d ed.) 938, and note 5.

[9] Evans Pr. & Ag. (Bedford's ed.) 33.

[10] Mechem Ag., § 1.

[11] Wharton Ag., § 1.

[12] 1 Am. & Eng. Encyc. L. (2d ed.) 937, note 2.

latter is sufficient. Though the statute of frauds of 29 Charles II requires, in certain cases, a contract for the sale of goods to be in writing and signed by the party to be charged, or by his authorized agent, the authority to the agent need not be in writing. It may be in parol. The agency may be inferred from the relation of the parties and the nature of the employment, without proof of any express employment. It is sufficient that there be satisfactory evidence of the fact that the principal employed the agent, and that the agent undertook the trust. The statute of frauds does not require that the authority of the agent contracting even for the sale of land should be in writing. But if the agent is to convey or complete the conveyance of real estate or any interests in land, or to make livery of seisin, the appointment must be in writing; and where the conveyance or any act is required to be by deed, the authority to the attorney to execute it must be commensurate in point of solemnity, and be by deed also."[13]

§ **15. Analogy to relation of master and servant.**—Lotz, J., speaking for the appellate court of Indiana, says: "In the primitive conditions of society the things which were the subjects of sale and trade were few in number. There was little occasion for any one to engage in commercial transactions, and when it did become necessary the business was generally transacted by the parties thereto in person. But the strong and powerful had many servants, who were usually slaves. The servants performed menial and manual services for the masters. As civilization advanced the things which are the subjects of commerce increased, and it became necessary to perform commercial transactions through the medium of other persons. The relation of principal and agent is but an overgrowth or expansion of the relation of master and servant. The same rules that apply to the one generally apply to the other. There is a marked similarity in the legal consequences flowing from the two relations. It is often difficult to distinguish the difference between an agent and a servant. This difficulty is increased by the fact that the same individual often combines in his own person the functions of both agent and servant. Agents are often denominated servants, and servants are often called agents. The word 'servant,' in its broadest meaning, includes an agent. There is, however, in legal contemplation, a difference between an agent and a servant. The Romans, to whom we are indebted for many of the principles of agency, in the early stages of their laws

[13] 1 Kent Com., star p. 613.

used the terms *"mandatum"* (to put into one's hands or confide to the discretion of another) and *"negotium"* (to transact business or to treat concerning purchases) in describing this relation.[13a] Agency, properly speaking, relates to commercial transactions, while service has reference to actions upon or concerning things. Service deals with matters of manual or mechanical execution. An agent is the more direct representative of the master, and clothed with higher powers and broader discretion than a servant.[14] The terms 'agent' and 'servant' are so frequently used interchangeably in the adjudications that the reader is apt to conclude they mean the same thing. We think, however, that the history of the law bearing on this subject shows that there is a difference between them. Agency, in its legal sense, always imports commercial dealings between two parties by and through the medium of another. An agent negotiates or treats with third parties in commercial matters for another."[15]

§ **16. Distinction between the relations.**—One of the well recognized distinctions between the two relations is that, in the case of master and servant, the employer always retains the right to direct the manner in which the business shall be done, as well as the result to be accomplished; or, in other words, not only what shall be done, but how it shall be done; whereas, in the case of principal and agent, the latter always has a considerable degree of discretion.[16] It is true that in the relation of master and servant some degree of discretion also exists in most cases on the part of the servant, but the discretion is much more limited than in the case of agency; and there are other points which distinguish the two relations, such as the terms of the employment, the matter of rendering compensation, and the character of the transaction to be performed.[17] Judge Cooley draws the following distinction between the words "agent" and "servant": "The common understanding of the words and the legal understanding is not the same; the latter is broader, and comprehends some cases in which the parties are master and servant only in a peculiar sense and for certain purposes. In strictness, a servant is one who, for a valuable consideration, engages in the service of another, and undertakes to observe his directions in some lawful business. The relation is purely one of contract, and the

[13a] Citing Story Ag., § 4.

[14] Citing Mechem Ag., §§ 1, 2.

[15] Kingan & Co. v. Silvers, 13 Ind. App. 80.

[16] Singer Mfg. Co. v. Rahn, 132 U. S. 518.

[17] Mechem Ag., § 2.

contract may contemplate or stipulate for any services, and any conditions of services not absolutely unlawful."[18] Webster defines a servant as "one who serves or does service voluntarily or involuntarily; a person who is employed by another for menial offices or for other labor, and is subject to his command; a person who labors or exerts himself for the benefit of another, his master or employer; a subordinate helper." An agent is defined to be a person duly authorized to act on behalf of another, or one whose authorized act has been duly ratified.[19] "The word 'servant,' in our legal nomenclature, has a broad significance, and embraces all persons, of whatever rank or position, who are in the employ and subject to the directions and control of another in any department of labor or business. Indeed, it may in most cases be said to be synonymous with 'employe.'"[20] It will be seen from the foregoing observations and citations that the word "servant" is often very difficult to distinguish from the word "agent." In its popular sense, the word "servant" indicates one who is hired by another for wages and is subject to his directions. Such a person Mr. Parsons calls a servant in fact; "but," he says, "the word is also used in many cases to indicate a servant by construction of law; it is sometimes applied to any person employed by another, and is scarcely to be discriminated in these instances from the word 'agent.'"[21]

§ **17. Scope of authority.**—"Scope of authority" is a term used to designate the extent to which an agent may go in representing his principal in a particular transaction. The agent may in many cases involve his principal in liability contrary to his private instructions, or outside of the limit of the actual authority delegated to him; provided he does not exceed the bounds within which agents of his class are permitted to exercise such authority, and the party with whom he deals for his principal does not have knowledge of the limitation of his powers. In such cases he is said to be acting within the *apparent scope* of his authority or employment. If he does not exceed the powers actually delegated to him, he is said to be acting within the *actual scope* of his authority or employment.

§ **18. General and special agents.**—The power or authority of an agent may be general; as when it extends to all acts connected with a certain business, employment or trade; as where a person is authorized

[18] Cooley Torts 531.

[19] Flesh v. Lindsay, 115 Mo. 1, 18.

[20] Hand v. Cole, 88 Tenn. 400, 404, citing Wood Master and Serv., § 1.

[21] 1 Parsons Conts. 101. And see Hand v. Cole, *supra*.

generally to purchase the goods required in a particular trade or business. Such an agent is called a general agent. Or the power or authority may be limited to a single act or single transaction, as the execution of a particular deed, or the purchase of a particular article of merchandise; and in that case the agent is designated a special or particular agent.[22] In *Loudon Savings Fund Society* v. *Hagerstown Savings Bank*,[22a] it was said by Woodard, J., speaking for the court: "By a general agent is understood not merely a person substituted in the place of another, for transacting all manner of business, but a person whom a man puts in his place to transact all his business of a particular kind; as to buy and sell certain kinds of wares, to negotiate certain contracts, and the like. An authority of this kind empowers the agent to bind his employer by all acts within the scope of his employment, and that power can not be limited by any private order or restriction not known to the party dealing with the agent. A special agent is one who is employed about one specific act, or certain specific acts, only, and he does not bind his employer unless his authority be strictly pursued."[23] A general authority, said Lord Ellenborough in *Whitehead* v. *Tuckett*,[24] "does not import an unqualified one, but that which is derived from a multitude of instances." And in *Wood* v. *McCain*,[24a] the supreme court of Alabama said: "The difference between a general and special agent is said to be this: The former is appointed to act in the affairs of his principal generally, and the latter to act concerning some particular object. In the former case, the principal will be bound by the acts of his agent within the scope of the general authority conferred on him, although these acts are violative of his private instructions and directions. In the latter case, if the agent exceeds the special authority conferred on him, the principal is not bound by his acts." It is often difficult to draw the line of demarcation between a general and a special agency. Thus, a person is often spoken of as a general agent whose authority is more limited than in the definition above given; as, for example, a person who has authority in regard to some particular object or thing, such as the purchase or sale of a particular article or parcel of goods, or the execution of a particular contract, his authority not being limited to any special mode of doing it. And so an agent is sometimes said to be a special agent because,

[22] Story Ag., § 17.

[22a] 36 Pa. St. 498.

[23] Paley Ag. 199, *et seq.*

[24] 15 East 408.

[24a] 7 Ala. 800, 42 Am. Dec. 614.

though authorized to act generally in some particular business, his authority is yet limited to some particular territory, or is otherwise qualified and restricted by certain instructions and conditions. In such a case he may be treated by the person dealing with him as a general agent, while, as between him and his principal, he is only a special agent. Hence, a general agency does not always import an unqualified authority, but usually one which is derived from a multitude of instances, or in the general course of an employment or business; whereas a special agency is confined to a particular transaction, and may also be qualified or limited as to the mode or means of performing the same.[25]

§ 19. **Universal agents.**—A universal agent is said to be an agent who is appointed to perform all acts which the principal might himself perform and which he may lawfully authorize another to perform. Such agencies are, however, of very rare occurrence. "And, indeed," says Story, "it is difficult to conceive of the existence of such an agency, practically, inasmuch as it would make such an agent the complete master not merely *dux facti,* but *dominus rerum,*—the complete disposer of all the rights and property of the principal. It is very certain that the law will not, from any general expression, however broad, infer the existence of any such unusual agency, but it will rather construe them as restrained to the principal business of the party, in respect to which, it is presumed, his intention to delegate the authority was principally directed."[26] It must be remembered, moreover, that while these classifications and distinctions are useful and important, they are—all of them—only relatively accurate, and may, if employed indiscriminately, serve to mislead rather than to aid the student. They are to be employed, therefore, with caution. Certain rules of agency have been based upon them, however, and they are well recognized in the terminology of the law of agency.[27]

§ 20. **Other classifications.**—Other classifications are made with reference to the nature of the duties to be performed. Thus, some agents are called brokers, some factors, others attorneys, etc., depending upon the nature of their engagements.

§ 21. **Brokers—Various classes of.**—Brokers are agents who are engaged to negotiate contracts for other persons relative to property,

[25] See Story Ag., §§ 18, 19.
[26] Story Ag., § 21.
[27] Mechem Ag., §§ 7, 284.

with the custody of which they have no concern.[28] Story and Evans say that a broker is an agent employed to make bargains and contracts between other persons in matters of trade, commerce or navigation, for a compensation commonly called brokerage.[29] He is a mere negotiator between the other parties.[29a] It is the duty of a broker to bring the contracting parties together for the purpose of making a contract, or he may, if so authorized, make the contract for them.[30] He is a middle man who brings parties together to bargain, or bargains for them, in private purchase or sale of property of any sort, not ordinarily in possession.[31] There are different classes of brokers; as real estate brokers, merchandise brokers, stock brokers, bill and note brokers, exchange brokers, insurance brokers, brokers for sale, pawnbrokers and ship brokers. There may be other classes to an indefinite extent, depending, of course, upon the demands and necessities of trade and commerce. Those enumerated are among the most important. *Real estate brokers* are those who negotiate between buyers and sellers of real estate. Among the duties most generally performed by them are those of finding purchasers for persons who have property for sale, and finding sellers for those desiring to purchase such property. In many instances they also engage in letting or leasing property and collecting rents, and in negotiating the loans of money on mortgages and other securities.[32] *Merchandise brokers* are those who negotiate the sale of merchandise without having possession or control of it as factors have.[33] *Stock brokers* are brokers employed to buy and sell shares of stock in incorporated companies and the indebtedness of governments.[34] *Bill and note brokers* negotiate the purchase and sale of bills of exchange and promissory notes.[35] *Exchange brokers* negotiate bills of exchange drawn on foreign countries, or on other places in this country.[36] *Insurance brokers* procure insurance and negotiate between insurers and insured.[37] Such a broker usually has a number of insurance companies on his list, and places insurance with them when applied to by his customers who desire to be insured. He is usually also the agent of the insured, while the ordinary insurance agent is usually not so regarded.[38] He

[28] Paley Ag. 13; Bouvier Law Dic., tit. Agency.

[29] Story Ag., § 28; Evans Pr. & Ag. (Bedford's ed.) 36.

[29a] Story Ag., § 28; Evans Pr. & Ag. (Bedford's ed.) 36.

[30] Mechem Ag., § 927.

[31] Bishop Conts., § 1135.

[32] Bouvier Law Dic., tit. Brokers.

[33] *Id.*

[34] *Id.*

[35] *Id.*

[36] *Id.*

[37] *Id.*

[38] Mechem Ag., § 931.

is agent for the assured and also for the underwriter.[39] *Pawnbrokers* lend money in small sums, on the security of personal property, at various rates of interest. They are licensed by the authorities and exempted from the operation of usury laws.[40] Municipal officers usually have authority to license such brokers, and in some states this authority is conferred upon them by their charters or by their general laws, or statutes. A pawnbroker is, strictly speaking, not a broker at all, as he generally makes the loan from his own capital and takes the pledges of security to himself.[41] *Brokers for sale* are persons who undertake to find purchasers for those wishing to sell, and vendors for those wishing to buy, and who negotiate and superintend the making of bargains between them.[42] *Ship brokers* negotiate the purchase and sale of ships and business of freighting vessels.[43] *Marriage brokers* are persons who intervene, for a consideration to be received by them, between a man and woman to negotiate contracts of marriage.[44] The business of marriage brokers, though it may have been recognized as a lawful occupation under the ancient common law, is not now regarded as legitimate in English-speaking countries, and courts of equity will hold such contracts void.[45]

§ 22. **Factors, consignees, commission merchants, del credere factors.**—A factor is an agent who, by virtue of authority delegated to him for that purpose, undertakes to sell goods or merchandise consigned or delivered to him by his principal, for a compensation called a commission or factorage, which is usually a percentum of the proceeds. For these reasons he is also called a "consignee" and "commission merchant," and the goods sent to him at any one time are called a "consignment" of goods.[46] A *del credere* factor or agent is a factor who, for an additional compensation, guarantees the payment of the debt due from the buyer of goods of such agent. The words "*del credere*" are of Italian origin, signifying a guaranty or warranty. The factor is said to be acting or selling upon a *del credere* commission.[47]

[39] Evans Pr. & Ag. (Bedford's ed.) 37.

[40] Bouvier Law Dic., tit. Brokers.

[41] Mechem Ag., § 933.

[42] 4 Am. & Eng. Encyc. L. (2d ed.) 961.

[43] Bouvier Law Dic., tit. Brokers.

[44] 4 Am. & Eng. Encyc. L. (2d ed.) 962.

[45] Bouvier Law Dic., tit. Marriage Brokers.

[46] Story Ag., § 33.

[47] *Id.*

§ 23. **Attorneys—Attorneys at law, advocates, counsellors, barristers,** solicitors, **proctors.**—In the general sense of the word, an attorney is one who is put in the place or turn of another. "It is an ancient English word and signifieth one that is set in the turn, stead or place of another; and of these some be private, * * * and some be public, as an attorney at law, whose warrant from his master is *ponit loco suo talem attornatum suum,* which setteth in his turn or place such a man to be his attorney."[48] Attorneys are of two kinds—attorneys at law and attorneys in fact. An *attorney at law* is an officer in a court of justice, who is employed, and in fact whose profession and business require him, to try cases in court and give legal advice to those who employ him for that purpose.[49] They are known variously by the names advocates, counsellors, barristers, solicitors, proctors, etc. *Advocate.*—In civil and ecclesiastical law, an advocate is an officer of a court, learned in the law, who is engaged by a suitor to maintain or defend his cause.[50] The word is used in Continental Europe to designate practicing lawyers. *Counsellor.*—In the United States supreme court and in some of the state courts the term "counsellor" is used to designate the senior or special counsel in the case, while attorneys carry on the practical and formal parts.[51] *Barrister.*—In English law, "a counsellor admitted to plead at the bar."[52] *Solicitor.*—One who practices in the courts of chancery. In signing pleadings in chancery proceedings an attorney usually styles himself "solicitor" instead of "attorney," as in common-law cases. The distinction arises simply from the two modes of procedure.[53] *Proctor.*—"One appointed to represent in judgment the party who empowers him by writing under his hand called a proxy. The term is used chiefly in the courts of civil and ecclesiastical law."[54] Practitioners in admiralty and probate courts in this country are also called proctors.[55] In England, the term "attorney" is applied to officers who practice in common-law courts, while proctors are those who practice in admiralty and ecclesiastical courts, and solicitors those who practice in chancery. None of them, however, conduct cases in open court, as that is done by advocates or counsel.[56] These distinctions, however, do not prevail to any extent in the United

[48] Coke on Litt., 51b.

[49] Anderson Law Dic. and Bouvier Law Dic., tit. Attorney.

[50] Bouvier Law Dic., tit. Advocate.

[51] 1 Kent Com. 307.

[52] Bouvier Law Dic., tit. Barrister.

[53] Stinson v. Hildrup, 8 Biss. (U. S.) 378.

[54] Bouvier Law Dic., tit. Proctor.

[55] Standard Dic., tit. Proctor.

[56] 1 Am. & Eng. Encyc. L. (2d ed.) 282.

States, the term "attorney" being applied to all who practice law.[57] In this country the term "attorney" or "practicing attorney" means an attorney at law, unless a contrary meaning is indicated by the context.[58] The professional business of attorneys, in this country, is not confined to the preparation and trial of cases in court, but embraces such work as collections of notes and other claims, without suit, the examinations of titles to property, the conduct of negotiations for settlements of estates, compromises of threatened legal controversies, etc.[59] An attorney at law is an officer of the court in which he practices, although not a public officer in the ordinary sense of the term.[60] He is a *quasi* officer, though not perhaps a public officer of the state where justice is administered by the court in which he practices.[61] An attorney in fact is defined as any private or special agent appointed for some particular purpose, not connected with a proceeding at law, by a formal authority called a letter or power of attorney, in which is expressed the particular act or acts for which he is appointed and the extent of his authority.[62] "The term is employed to designate persons who act under a special agency, or a special letter of attorney, in that they are appointed *in factum* for the deed, or special act, to be performed; but in a more extended view it includes all other agents employed in any business or to do any act or acts *in pais* for another."[62a]

§ 24. **Auctioneers.**—An auctioneer is an agent who, for a commission, sells goods or other property at auction.[63] He is agent for both purchaser and seller at a public sale.[64] An auction, in the widest sense of the term, is a sale, however conducted, by which a person obliges himself to transfer property to the highest bidder within the conditions of the sale; it ordinarily denotes such a sale conducted in the usual manner.[65] The sale is usually conducted competitively,

[57] 1 Am. & Eng. Encyc. L. (2d ed.) 282.

[58] Ingram v. Richardson, 2 La. Ann. 839.

[59] See the opinion of Crumpacker, J., in Moore v. Staser, 6 Ind. App. 364.

[60] Ex parte Garland, 4 Wall. (U. S.) 333; Matter of Burchard, 27 Hun (N. Y.) 429.

[61] Matter of Mosness, 39 Wis. 509, 20 Am. Rep. 55.

[62] 3 Am. & Eng. Encyc. L. (2d ed.) 281.

[62a] Bouvier Law Dic., tit. Attorney.

[63] 3 Am. & Eng. Encyc. L. (2d ed.) 489; Story Ag., § 27.

[64] Evans Pr. & Ag. (Bedford's ed.) 60.

[65] Bateman Auctions (1st Am. ed.) 1.

by public outcry, to the highest bidder. An auctioneer differs from a broker in some particulars: A broker can both buy and sell, while an auctioneer can only sell; a broker can not sell at auction, as that is not his function, but that of the auctioneer. An auctioneer can not sell at private sale, but a broker may.[66] In the absence of a statute to the contrary, any person may be an auctioneer. But a state, in the exercise of its police power, may require a license-tax of an auctioneer, and may also authorize municipal corporations to require such tax. This is a common practice in England and many of the states.[67]

§ **25. Bank cashiers.**—Bank cashiers are officers of banks, intrusted with its funds, notes, bills and other choses in action to be used for the ordinary and extraordinary exigencies of the bank. The cashier usually receives, through himself or subordinates, all moneys and notes of the bank; delivers up all moneys and receives in exchange for loans all discounted notes or bills; signs drafts on corresponding banks, and, as an executive officer of the bank, transacts much of its general business. He need not be a stockholder. He is usually required to give security for the faithful performance of his duties. He is required to make a report to designated officers of the state or general government as provided by law, and false statements made by him officially are punished, and render him liable to the injured person for damages.[68]

§ **26. Supercargoes.**—"In maritime law, a person specially employed by the owner of a cargo to take charge and sell to the best advantage merchandise which has been shipped, and to purchase returning cargoes and receive freight as he may be authorized. Supercargoes have complete control over the cargo and everything which immediately concerns it, unless their authority is either expressly or impliedly restrained."[68a] Supercargoes are a variety of factors, being intrusted with both the selling of cargoes accompanied by them on the voyage, and the purchase of new ones for the return trip or other return voyages.[69] A supercargo is a factor authorized to sell a cargo which he accompanies on the voyage.[70]

[66] Story Ag., § 27.

[67] 3 Am. & Eng. Encyc. L. (2d ed.) 489.

[68] Bouvier Law Dic., tit. Cashier.

[68a] Bouvier Law Dic., tit. Supercargo.

[69] Mechem Ag., § 15.

[70] Evans Pr. & Ag. (Bedford's ed.) 35.

§ 27. **Ship's husband.**—A ship's husband is an officer or agent, in maritime law, appointed by the owner of the ship and authorized to make requisite repairs, and attend to the management, equipment and other concerns of the ship. He is the general agent of the owner of the vessel. He may be appointed by writing or parol. He is usually, but not necessarily, a part owner. It is his duty to see that the ship has the proper outfit in the repairs and necessary furniture, and that she is furnished with provisions and stores according to the necessities of the voyage. It is his duty to see to the regularity of the clearances from the customhouse and of the registry. He must settle the accounts against the ship for proper contracts and furnishings. It is his duty to enter into charter parties or engage the vessel for freight or other service. He has all authority incidental to the carrying out of these obligations.[71] His authority does not extend to the procuring of insurance on the vessel without the assent of the owner.[72]

§ 28. **Ships' masters.**—The master of a ship is, in maritime law, the first officer or commander of a merchant vessel,—the captain. A vessel sailing without a competent master is deemed unseaworthy. He is selected by the owners of the ship, and, if he dies or is incapacitated on the voyage, is succeeded by the mate. It is his duty to see that the vessel is seaworthy before she starts on her voyage; that she is provided with all requisite stores and provisions. He makes all contracts with the seamen, if the voyage is a foreign one. He must see that all goods and freight are properly stored. He must obey all instructions of the owners, except in cases of emergency, when it becomes necessary in his judgment to depart from them. It is his duty to take all possible care of the cargo during the voyage, and in case of shipwreck to file a statement of circumstances called a protest. He must do everything reasonably required for the safety of the vessel and cargo in the interests of the owners. For want of reasonable care and skill he is liable to the owners in damages. He has supreme authority on shipboard, but his authority is of a civil character. He may, however, use such force in directing the crew as may be necessary to enforce obedience to his lawful commands. If necessary to suppress a mutiny, he may even take life. He may punish acts of disobedience and such offenses as are dangerous

[71] Bouvier Law Dic., tit. Ship's Husband.

[72] Story Ag., § 35.

to the discipline of the ship; though flogging and other brutal penalties are prohibited in the United States, and render him civilly liable to the injured party and also to the public in a criminal proceeding. In case of necessity he may issue bonds on the credit of the vessel, and may even pledge the cargo to obtain the necessary repairs and supplies. He has a lien on the freight carried by the ship for repairs and supplies for which he has paid; also for wages of the seamen paid by him, but not for his own wages.[73]

§ **29. Partners.**—In partnerships each member of the firm is the general agent of any other member and of the firm as a whole in respect to all the partnership's business. The rules governing the rights and liabilities of partners, when acting in the discharge of their duties as such, are in most respects similar to those pertaining to other agents.[74] "Notwithstanding the fact that every partner is, to a certain extent, a principal, as well as an agent, the liability of his copartners for his acts can only be established on the ground of agency as their agent. He has no discretion, except within the limits set by them to his authority, and the fact that he is himself as one of the firm, a principal, does not warrant him in extending these limits, save on his own responsibility."[75] The power of one partner to bind the others in the firm is confined to the scope of the firm's business, precisely as the power of an agent to bind his principal is limited to the scope of the business for which he is employed. A partner, as the agent of his firm, may thus bind his copartners whenever it is necessary in his judgment to do so, by borrowing money, making, signing, indorsing or accepting paper, selling or pledging partnership property, paying its debts, etc., when he does so in the name of the firm and on account of the partnership.[76] The rule that a partner may thus bind the firm generally applies, however, only to trading partnerships. In cases of non-trading partnerships, no general rule can be laid down, and each case must be determined upon its own facts.[77]

[73] See 3 Kent Com., Lecture XLVI.

[74] Story Ag., §§ 37, 39.

[75] 1 Lindley Part. 239.

[76] Story Ag., § 124; Story Part., §§ 101, 125.

[77] Pooley v. Whitmore, 10 Heisk. (Tenn.) 629, 27 Am. Rep. 733; Lindley Part. 198.

CHAPTER II.

COMPETENCY OF PARTIES.

§ **30. Competency in general.**—It may be stated as a general rule that every person *sui juris* is capable of becoming a principal. The exceptions are those persons who labor under some disability imposed upon them by nature or the law.[1] Of course, before a person can become a principal as to any matter, he must have the right to contract with reference to such matter in his own person, and for himself. If, as the maxim considered in the opening chapter implies, he is capable of performing the act himself, he may perform it by an agent. The converse of the proposition is also true, that if he can not do the act himself, he can not legally authorize an agent to do it for him. One may, for example, authorize another to sell his own goods or land, or any interest he may have in goods or land, for he could do this himself. But he can not authorize another to sell my goods or lands, or goods and lands in which he has no interest, because he could not sell these himself. Hence, we have the rule that any person capable of making a binding business engagement on his

[1] Story Ag., § 5.

own behalf is competent, as to such business engagement, to be a voluntary principal.[2] By "voluntary principal" is meant a person who may voluntarily enter into the relation, as distinguished from one who has assumed the relation by operation of law or the action of a competent court; as when a court appoints a tutor or guardian for an insane person.[3] Conversely, a person who labors under some disability to contract or act in his own behalf is under corresponding disability to make a valid contract for the appointment of an agent.

§ **31. Classes of principals.**—A contract for the appointment or selection of an agent may be made either by an individual or by an aggregation or association of individuals. If the latter, it may be a corporation, a partnership, or an association intermediate between the two, such as an unincorporated stock company, a mining company, etc. If an individual or natural person, he may be an adult or an infant, and may be *compos mentis* or *non compos mentis;* and if a woman, she may be single or married. The question of the competency or incompetency of all of these will be separately considered.

§ **32. Causes of incompetency.**—Incompetency to contract is generally traceable to two kinds of causes; namely: 1. Natural causes; 2. Legal causes. When incompetency is due to some natural cause or causes, it is ordinarily owing to some mental infirmity, such as lunacy, idiocy, habitual drunkenness, etc. When it is the result of a legal cause or causes, it may be traced to the common or statute law of the state in which the incompetency is alleged to exist. The incompetency, from whatever cause it may arise, is either absolute or total, limited or partial, and hence the contract made by such incompetent person may be wholly void or it may be voidable only.[4]

§ **33. Infants as principals.**—One of the causes of incompetency to be a principal is that arising from infancy. This may be said to be partly natural and partly legal; for certainly it could not be maintained that the reason an infant under seven years of age is incompetent to contract is purely a legal one. Such an incompetency, especially before the infant has reached a period in life when he is able to discriminate at all, must be attributable, in part at least, to his mental incapacity. By the Roman law, an infant under seven years of age was absolutely incapable of doing business; while be-

[2] Wharton Ag., § 9.
[3] Wharton Ag., § 10.
[4] Evans Pr. & Ag. (Bedford's ed.) 44.

tween infancy and puberty an infant could do no act prejudicial to his estate without his guardian; and between the ages of puberty and majority he could not alienate his property without the consent of the court. This distinction is believed to be retained in large part, at least in our own jurisprudence, and it has frequently been held that an infant may act through an agent when the act is for his benefit, though it is not conceived that an infant under the age of seven years is capable of committing any judicial act.[5] However that may be, the broad proposition is frequently made, and is doubtless law in most jurisdictions in this country, that an infant, no matter how near the age of majority, can not bind himself by a contract to employ an agent,[5a] and can not legally ratify the acts of such agent after the infant has attained to the age of majority, whether such act was originally authorized by the infant or not.[5b] Indeed, it is held that the only act that an infant can not legally bind himself to perform, at least by subsequent ratification, is the appointment of an attorney or agent.[6]

§ 34. **The soundness of the doctrine in last section questioned.**— The doctrine thus broadly stated does not seem to be founded in logic or reason, and has been subjected to frequent criticism. It is not easy to perceive why the contract of an infant appointing an agent to perform some specific act, especially if made for the infant's benefit, should not rest upon the same fundamental principle upon which other contracts made by him are founded, namely, that they are voidable at his option, and not absolutely void. The reason assigned for the broader doctrine, as gathered from the decisions cited, seems to be that the spirit of the rule by which an infant may avoid his contracts requires that he should be left free to affirm such acts of his agent as he chooses, and to disaffirm all others; but that he can not

[5] Wharton Ag., § 12.

[5a] Fonda v. Van Horne, 15 Wend. (N. Y.) 631.

[5b] Doe v. Roberts, 16 M. & W. 778; Fonda v. Van Horne, *supra;* Trueblood v. Trueblood, 8 Ind. 195; Armitage v. Widoe, 36 Mich. 124.

[6] Oliver v. Woodroffe, 4 M. & W. 650; Lawrence v. McArter, 10 Ohio 37; Trueblood v. Trueblood, 8 Ind. 195; Knox v. Flack, 22 Pa. St. 337; Sadler v. Robinson, 2 Stew. (Ala.) 520; Robbins v. Mount, 4 Rob. (N. Y.) 553; Armitage v. Widoe, 36 Mich. 124; Ware v. Cartledge, 24 Ala. 622; Tapley v. McGee, 6 Ind. 56; Flexner v. Dickerson, 72 Ala. 318; Cole v. Pennoyer, 14 Ill. 158; Bennett v. Davis, 6 Cow. (N. Y.) 393; Wambole v. Foote, 2 Dak. 1; Carnahan v. Allerdice, 4 Harr. (Del.) 99; Hiestand v. Kuns, 8 Blackf. (Ind.) 345; Fetrow v. Wiseman, 40 Ind. 155; Robinson v. Weeks, 56 Me. 102; Fonda v. Van Horne, 15 Wend. (N. Y.) 631.

do this if he is required to affirm the appointment *in toto,* as that would involve the ratification of all the acts done by the agent in the course of the appointment; while, if he disavows the appointment as a whole, he can not, at the same time, sanction some of the acts done by the agent under the appointment. He would thus be prevented from exercising that freedom of choice, after arriving at the age of majority, which the law has always accorded to him in order to secure him against imposition during minority. It may be conceded that if the appointment of the agent involved the performance of a number of different transactions, the reasons given for the rule might have some force. But it is difficult to understand, if an infant should authorize another person to do a single act of business for him, such as buying a horse which he needs in the cultivation of his crops, for example, an act essentially for his benefit, how it would interfere with his freedom of choice if he were permitted to ratify such an act upon reaching the age of majority. Just why an infant is incompetent to bind himself, even for necessaries, when he procures them through the agency of another, it being universally admitted that he would render himself liable if he procured the articles in person, is difficult to explain upon any rational basis of argument. And yet if the rule is to be applied as broadly as the statement of it would seem to indicate, this would be the necessary consequence. That not all of the courts are willing to adhere to this anomalous doctrine is apparent from many decisions of some of the ablest judges. Thus, in *Tucker* v. *Moreland,*[7] Mr. Justice Story, speaking for the supreme court of the United States, holds that an infant might bind himself in appointing an agent to do an act for him unquestionably to his advantage. In a California case,[8] the court decided that an infant might in certain circumstances execute a promissory note by an agent, and that an infant promisee might transfer by indorsement through an agent, the title to a note,—such acts being voidable only, and not void. A similar holding was made by the supreme judicial court of Massachusetts.[9] Professor Huffcut says that the American cases show a decided tendency to confine the rule to cases in which the appointment

[7] 10 Pet. (U. S.) 58.

[8] Hastings v. Dollarhide, 24 Cal. 195.

[9] Whitney v. Dutch, 14 Mass. 457. To the same effect, see Hardy v. Waters, 38 Me. 450. See also, Towle v. Dresser, 73 Me. 252 (appointment of agent—for certain purposes at least—voidable only); Patterson v. Lippincott, 47 N. J. L. 457; Welch v. Welch, 103 Mass. 562; Keegan v. Cox, 116 Mass. 289; Fairbanks v. Snow, 145 Mass. 153.

of the agent was by formal warrant of attorney, and to hold that the appointment of an agent by an infant is generally a voidable and not a void act.[9a] But however unsatisfactory the reasons may seem upon which the rule is founded, it is doubtless true that the great weight of authority in this country holds to the doctrine that an infant can not be a principal, and is incapable also of ratifying any act done in furtherance of such agency, whether the act was done in pursuance of a previous employment of the agent or not. That a formal power of attorney made by an infant is absolutely void seems to be the settled rule, both in England and the United States.[10] It is sometimes said that all contracts of an infant are merely voidable except two; namely: (1) His contract for necessaries, which is valid, and (2) his contract for the appointment of an agent, which is void. By the weight of authority in this country the statement is believed to be correct, although it can not be claimed that the cases are in entire harmony.

§ 35. **Married women as principals.**—Another instance of legal incompetency, at common law, is that of married women. As the wife was generally under disability of making any valid contract whatever, she was, of course, likewise incompetent to employ an agent.[10a] But to the extent that her common-law disabilities have been removed by statute, she has become qualified to enter into such contracts as she is thereby empowered to make. In many of the states, most, though perhaps not all, of her disabilities have been removed; while in others she has full control of and power to contract only as to her separate property, and even then she is generally incapable of conveying her real estate unless her husband join in the deed. It may be regarded as the correct rule, therefore, that in jurisdictions in which she has not been relieved of any of her common-law disabilities she is incapable of appointing an agent; whereas in others she may legally appoint an agent to perform any and all acts that the statutes have enabled her to perform in person. It is, therefore, unnecessary that a statute should confer express authority upon a married woman to become a principal or to appoint an agent. The power to choose an agent or to act through an agent is implied from

[9a] Huffcut Ele. of Ag., § 15.

[10] Oliver v. Woodroffe, 4 M. & W. 650; Ashlin v. Langton, 4 M. & S. 719; Turner v. Bondalier, 31 Mo. App. 582; Knox v. Flack, 22 Pa. St. 337; Bool v. Mix, 17 Wend. (N. Y.) 119; Philpot v. Bingham, 55 Ala. 435.

[10a] Kenton Ins. Co. v. McClellan, 43 Mich. 564; Weisbrod v. Chicago, etc., R. Co., 18 Wis. 40; McLaren v. Hall, 26 Iowa 297; Rowell v. Klein, 44 Ind. 290.

the power conferred upon her to do the act herself. Hence, if the statute empowers her to make contracts with reference to her separate property, she may by force of it make such contracts through an agent, although no statute in terms authorizes her to do so. This is upon the principle of the maxim that whatever one may do himself he may do through another. Her authority to act must be found in the statutes of the state within the jurisdiction of which she resides, or by which the particular act is governed at the time she undertakes to perform it. In those states in which the common law prevails as a fundamental rule of action, the presumption is always against her capacity to act; but this presumption is overcome whenever it appears that the particular disability has been abrogated by legislative enactment, inasmuch as the validity of any contract and the rights and liabilities thereunder depend upon the law of the state in force in which it was entered into.[11]

§ **36. Their acts of a personal nature not capable of delegation.**— It must not be forgotten, however, that the general rule implied in the maxim "*Qui facit per alium facit per se*" admits of a well recognized exception in the principle that wherever the act to be performed is of a personal nature, involving a matter of trust or confidence, or the exercise of some special function authorized by law, the performance of it can not be delegated to another. This question will receive more attention when we come to consider the power of delegation of authority. For the present it is sufficient to show the applicability of the doctrine to the case of persons having specific authority conferred upon them by law to do some act or acts. In such cases, such persons are required to perform the acts so authorized in person, and can not delegate the power to others. Under this rule, where a party is required by statute to perform a certain act as a means of accomplishing some other act, the act constituting such means must be performed in person. Hence, if a married woman be authorized by statute to convey her real estate by means of a deed duly acknowledged by her upon private examination before an officer, she can not make the acknowledgment by an agent.[12] In an early Indiana case in which this question arose, the court said: "A married woman, by the common law, can alien her real estate only by fine and recovery. Our statutes authorize her to sell it by joining with her husband in a deed, and by acknowledging before the proper officer, after having

[11] See 14 Am. & Eng. Encyc. L. (2d ed.) 609-618.

[12] Story Ag., § 12; 1 Bishop Mar. Women, § 602.

been by him examined separate and apart from her husband, and after having its contents made known to her by the officer, that she did voluntarily seal and deliver the deed as her free act, without coercion from her husband. * * * She certainly can not acknowledge a deed by an attorney, because that mode of acknowledgment does not admit of her examination by the officer taking it, in the manner prescribed; and her conveyance, being entirely statutory, is not binding upon her, unless it is acknowledged agreeably to the provisions of the statute."[13]

§ 37. **May appoint husband.**—In cases where the wife has the power to employ an agent she may, of course, authorize her husband to act for her, as well as any other person; and this agency may be proved by circumstances as well as by direct evidence. The mere fact that he is the husband will not warrant an inference of agency, in the absence of other evidence that she has employed him as such.[13a] The agency may be inferred, however, from proof of such relation together with other circumstances,—such as permitting him to manage her estate generally; or that he acted as her agent in similar matters, previously, without objection on her part, etc.[14] Of course, the agency must be established as in other cases, and the rights and liabilities growing out of it are not materially different from those arising in other instances of agency. It is also held by some courts that a married woman can not, at common law, appoint an agent unless she is possessed of an estate of her own.[15] But the same court holds that she may have a servant or servants, and that she and her husband are jointly liable for the negligent acts of such servant or servants.[16]

§ 38. **Persons of unsound mind as principals.**—The question whether a person of unsound mind is capable of appointing an agent and of binding himself by his acts in matters of business depends, as it does in other cases of agency, upon the question as to whether or not the principal, or party assuming to act as such, has the legal capacity of contracting. If a person *non compos mentis* enters into a contract with a person of sound mind, is such contract void or voidable for that reason? This, like all other questions arising in the

[13] Dawson v. Shirley, 6 Blackf. (Ind.) 531. See also, Holladay v. Daily, 19 Wall. (U. S.) 606; Mott v. Smith, 16 Cal. 533; Sumner v. Conant, 10 Vt. 2; Lewis v. Coxe, 5 Harr. (Del.) 401.

[13a] Anderson v. Gregg, 44 Miss. 170, 179.

[14] Barnett v. Gluting, 3 Ind. App. 419; Shafer v. Archibald, 116 Ind. 29; Hunt v. Poole, 139 Mass. 224.

[15] Wilcox v. Todd, 64 Mo. 388, 390.

[16] Flesh v. Lindsay, 115 Mo. 1, 18.

law of agency, depends upon the law of the state or country in which the contract is made. If such person is incapable of binding himself, under the law of the land, to make any contract whatever, he would be necessarily disqualified to make a contract of employing an agent; as he would not be permitted to do by another what he is incapable of doing himself. Story lays down the rule that "idiots, lunatics and other persons not *sui juris* are wholly incapable."[17] This proposition Mr. Evans[18] seems to regard as not wholly tenable, when he says: "Mr. Justice Story lays it down broadly that idiots, lunatics and other person not *sui juris* are wholly incapable of appointing an agent. This can not be accepted without qualification as the law of this country [England], for it has been distinctly laid down by the court of exchequer chamber, after a review of the cases, that when one of the parties to a contract is of unsound mind, and the fact is unknown to the other contracting party, no advantage having been taken of the lunatic, this unsoundness of mind will not vacate a contract, especially where the contract is not merely executory, but executed in whole or in part, and the parties can not be restored altogether to their original position.[19] It is conceived that the same result would take place if the contract were made through another, who acted upon the authority of the lunatic, without having been aware or taken advantage of his state of mind. The principle of the above decision was acted upon in a more recent case."[20] The exception mentioned by Evans is well recognized by the weight of authority in this country. It is now generally held that if the disability was not known or apparent to the other contracting party, and the contract was free from fraud, and the lunatic has received the benefit thereof, it can not be avoided by him unless both parties can be restored to their original position.[21] And a contract made

[17] Story Ag., § 6.

[18] Evans Pr. & Ag. (Bedford's ed.) 44.

[19] Citing Molton v. Camroux, 4 Exch. 17.

[20] Citing Beavan v. M'Donnell, 9 Exch. 309. See, to the same effect, Pollock Conts. 76-84.

[21] Flach v. Gottschalk Co., 88 Md. 368, 71 Am. St. 418. See the elaborate note at p. 425, for a full citation and discussion of the authorities on this subject. See also, to the same effect, Beckroege v. Schmidt, 5 Week. Law Bul. (Ohio) 788, 6 Ohio Dec. R. 994; Matthiessen & Weichers Refining Co. v. McMahon, 38 N. J. L. 536; Beals v. See, 10 Pa. 56, 49 Am. Dec. 573; McCormick v. Littler, 85 Ill. 62, 28 Am. Rep. 610; Copenrath v. Kienby, 83 Ind. 18; Physio-Medical College v. Wilkinson, 108 Ind. 314; Young v. Stevens, 48 N. H. 133, 97 Am. Dec. 592.

by a lunatic during a lucid interval is valid.[22] But contracts made with a lunatic after his mental unsoundness has been established by an inquisition and the appointment of a guardian are absolutely void.[23] Mr. Mechem seems to approve of the general rule as stated by Story, but says that it is "subject to the qualifications quite generally applied to other contracts with persons of this class; that where the unsoundness of mind is unknown to the other party, who has acted in good faith and taken no advantage of it, the contract will not be set aside, where it has been executed in whole or in part and the parties can not be altogether restored to their original situation."[24] In an English case decided in 1892 by the queen's bench division, it was said by Lopes, L. J., that "a defendant who seeks to avoid a contract on the ground of his insanity must plead and prove, not merely his insanity, but also the plaintiff's knowledge of that fact, and unless he proves these two things he can not succeed."[25] The doctrine thus broadly stated by Story can not, therefore, be said to be the prevailing rule in this country, although it must be admitted that the decisions are by no means harmonious. If the statute of the state declares the contracts of persons adjudged insane void, they will, of course, be held not only voidable, but absolutely invalid by the courts.[26] But an insane person not so declared by the judgment of the court may in many instances bind himself by his contract, at least in the absence of a statute making such contract void. The supreme court of Indiana say: "We think it may be safely stated, both on principle and authority, that where a person apparently of sound mind, and not known to be otherwise, and who has not been found to be otherwise by proper proceedings for that purpose, fairly and *bona fide* purchases property and receives and uses the same, whereby the contract of purchase becomes so far executed that the parties can not be placed *in statu quo*, such contract can not be afterward set aside, or payment for the goods refused, either by the alleged lunatic or his representatives."[27] A deed or power of attorney

[22] Lilly v. Waggoner, 27 Ill. 395; Gangwere's Estate, 14 Pa. 417, 53 Am. Dec. 553; Tozer v. Saturlee, 3 Grant (Pa.) 162.

[23] Hughes v. Jones, 116 N. Y. 67, 15 Am. St. 386; Fitzhugh v. Wilcox, 12 Barb. (N. Y.) 235.

[24] Mechem Ag., § 48.

[25] Imperial Loan Co. v. Stone, L. R. (1892) 1 Q. B. 599, 603.

[26] Redden v. Baker, 86 Ind. 191; Carter v. Beckwith, 128 N. Y. 312; Gibson v. Soper, 6 Gray (Mass.) 279; Rogers v. Blackwell, 49 Mich. 192; Hardenbrook v. Sherwood, 72 Ind. 403.

[27] Wilder v. Weakley's Estate, 34 Ind. 181. See also, Fay v. Burditt, 81 Ind. 433.

under seal executed by a lunatic or person *non compos mentis* is held by some courts absolutely void.[28] The court, in the New York case just cited, treats the act of an insane person in making a power of attorney as analogous to a similar act performed by an infant, saying: "The doctrine that a lunatic's power of attorney is void finds confirmation in the analogy there is between the situation and acts of infants and lunatics. Both such classes of persons are regarded as under the protection of the law. But, as already remarked, a lunatic needs more protection than a minor. The latter is presumed to lack sufficient discretion. Reason is wanting in degree. With a lunatic it is wanting altogether. Yet it is universally held, as laid down by Lord Mansfield in *Zouch* v. *Parsons*,[29] that deeds of an infant which do not take effect by delivery of his hand (in which class he places a letter of attorney) are void. We are not aware that any different rule exists in England or in this country. It has repeatedly been determined that a power of attorney made by an infant is void. * * * In fact, we know no case of authority in which the letter of attorney of either an infant or a lunatic has been held merely voidable." As to the extent of the mental unsoundness, it has been held in New Jersey that a deaf-mute, sixty-five years old, who is ignorant and can not read nor write, nor be made to understand an ordinary business transaction, is incapable of appointing an agent to manage her property for her.[30] And that the contract was negotiated for the lunatic or person of unsound mind by an agent will not render such contract binding upon such person, as one who is mentally incapable of making a contract can not have an agent.[31]

§ **39. Same.**—All contracts of lunatics and persons of unsound mind, except for necessaries, are doubtless void if made after such person has been so declared by a competent court, and a guardian appointed, whether the statute so provides or not.[31a] They are likewise void, or at least voidable, if the incompetency is known to the other contracting party or he has reasonable grounds to believe the principal insane.[32] And whenever a statute declares a contract

[28] Dexter v. Hall, 15 Wall. (U. S.) 9. But it is held to be only voidable by other courts: Blinn v. Schwartz, 71 N. Y. Supp. 343.

[29] 3 Burr. 1804.

[30] In re Perrine, 41 N. J. Eq. 409.

[31] Marvin v. Inglis, 39 How. Pr. (N. Y.) 329.

[31a] Wadsworth v. Sharpsteen, 8 N. Y. 388; Redden v. Baker, 86 Ind. 191.

[32] Crawford v. Scovell, 94 Pa. St. 48; Alexander v. Haskins, 68 Iowa 73; Matthiessen v. McMahon's Adm., 38 N. J. L. 536; VanDeusen v. Sweet, 51 N. Y. 378; Rogers v. Blackwell, 49 Mich. 192; Gibson v. Soper, 6

by an insane person void, a contract of agency by such person would be void also. Generally they would be invalid even without such a statute, after an adjudication by an inquest.[33] If not declared void by statute, or if the person had not been adjudged insane by a proper court, when the contract was made, such contract may still be voidable, if the party who contracted with the insane person can be placed *in statu quo,* even though he had no knowledge or notice of the insanity. If the contract was for necessaries, the person will be liable, and it is difficult to perceive why the contract of the lunatic's agent for that purpose, made in his behalf, would not be equally binding. There is still another contingency in which the contract may or may not be binding on the lunatic, and that is in a case in which the principal was of sound mind when the agency was created but became *non compos mentis* afterward. In that case, if the third person was ignorant of the principal's infirmity, the principal, having held the agent out to the world as such, will be bound, whether the agent knew of it or not; and conversely, if the third person was aware of it, the contract would be voidable whether the agent knew of the insanity or not.[34] The reason for the doctrine just enunciated is so aptly stated in an English case, by Brett, L. J., that it is deemed useful to quote a portion of his language: "It is difficult to assign the ground upon which this doctrine, which, however, seems to me to be the true principle, exists. It is said that the right to hold the insane principal liable depends upon contract. I have a difficulty in assenting to this. It has been said also that the right depends upon estoppel. I can not see that an estoppel is created, but it has been said also that the right depends upon representations made by the principal and entitling third persons to act upon them, until they hear that those representations are withdrawn. The authorities collected in Story on Agency[35] seem to base the right upon the ground of public policy; it is there said in effect that the existence of the right goes in aid of public business. It is, however, a better way of stating the rule to say that the holding out of another person as agent is a representation upon which, at the time when it was made, third parties had a right to act, and if no insanity had

Gray (Mass.) 279; Lynch v. Dodge, 130 Mass. 458; Burnham v. Kidwell, 113 Ill. 425; Carter v. Beckwith, 128 N. Y. 312; Teegarden v. Lewis, 145 Ind. 98; Stockmeyer v. Tobin, 139 U. S. 176.

[33] American Trust, etc., Co. v. Boone, 102 Ga. 202; Hovey v. Hobson, 53 Me. 453, 89 Am. Dec. 705; Hughes v. Jones, 116 N. Y. 67.

[34] Davis v. Lane, 10 N. H. 156.

[35] Ch. XVIII, § 481, p. 610 (7th ed.).

supervened would still have a right to act. * * * The defendant became insane and was unable to withdraw the authority which he had conferred upon his wife; he may be an innocent sufferer by his conduct, but the plaintiff who dealt with her *bona fide* is also innocent, and where one of two persons, both innocent, must suffer by the wrongful act of a third person, that person making the representation which, as between the two, was the original cause of the mischief must be the sufferer and must bear the loss."[36]

§ 40. **Drunkards as principals.**—A person who is at the time of the execution of a contract in a state of intoxication may avoid such contract, if at the time of making the same his reason was so far dethroned as to render him incapable of knowing what he was doing.[36a] In such cases the contract is not void, but voidable only, and before the person wishing to avoid it upon that ground can do so he must offer to restore whatever was received in consideration thereof.[37] Intoxication, when it totally incapacitates, will avoid the contract, it being only a species of mental unsoundness. But drunkenness, at the time of the execution of the contract, will not generally avoid it, if the party was not wholly incapacitated and no unfair advantage was taken of him, or if the other party to the contract did not procure the intoxication in order to induce him to make the contract.[38] But if the party was so intoxicated as to render him mentally incapable of contracting, it will be a good defense to an action on the contract.[39] And where the party's mental capacity has been so far impaired from habitual drunkenness as to render him irresponsible, he may avoid the contract.[40] The principle here declared applies to a contract of agency as well as to other contracts. A party making such a contract while in an intoxicated condition may ratify the same when he becomes sober.[41] A person is in a state of intoxication, or drunk, in a legal sense, when he is so far under the influence of intoxicating liquor that his judgment is impaired by the liquor. "Drunkenness is that effect produced on the mind, passions or body by intoxicants

[36] Drew v. Nunn, L. R. 4 Q. B. D. 661.

[36a] See Arnold v. Hickman, 6 Munf. (Va.) 15.

[37] Williams v. Inabnet, 1 Bailey (S. C.) 343; McGuire v. Callahan, 19 Ind. 128; Joest v. Williams, 42 Ind. 565, 13 Am. Rep. 366; Bursinger v. Bank of Watertown, 67 Wis. 77; McClain v. Davis, 77 Ind. 419.

[38] Rodman v. Zilley, 1 N. J. Eq. 320; Campbell v. Ketcham, 4 Ky. 406.

[39] Jenner v. Howard, 6 Blackf. (Ind.) 240; Bush v. Breinig, 113 Pa. St. 310, 57 Am. Dec. 469.

[40] Gates v. Meredith, 7 Ind. 440.

[41] Mansfield v. Watson, 2 Iowa 111; Carpenter v. Rodgers, 61 Mich. 384.

taken into the system, which so far changes the normal condition, as to materially disturb and impair the capacity for health, rational action and conduct; which causes abnormal results, or such as would not ensue in the absence of intoxicants—the changed effect produced by the immoderate or excessive use of intoxicants, as contrasted with normal *status* and conduct."[42] The ratification or disaffirmance of the contract of a lunatic or drunkard may be by the guardian or committee;[43] or, after his death, if a deed, by his heirs.[44] When the guardian of a habitual drunkard has been discharged, it will be presumed that the ward has reformed.[45] If the contract was made during a sober interval, it is binding.[46]

§ 41. **Corporations as principals.**—A corporation is, from its very nature, a competent principal, for it is inconceivable how it could perform any of its functions except through the media of its officers or agents. Usually the charter or general laws under which it is organized provide for the appointment or selection of these; but whether this be true or not, the election of directors, trustees and other suitable officers or agents to govern the affairs of the company and transact its business is a necessary incident of its corporate existence, and may be held without being expressly authorized by the act of incorporation.[47] But when the charter or statute of incorporation provides a certain method of election or appointment of the officers, that method must be substantially pursued, any other rendering the selection void.[48] Where, however, it is provided that the trustees of a corporation shall be elected annually, the words are only directory, and do not take away the incidental power of the corporation to elect afterward, when the annual day has, by some means, free from design or fraud, been passed by.[49] And where the record is silent upon

[42] State v. Savage, 89 Ala. 1, 8.

[43] McClain v. Davis, 77 Ind. 419.

[44] Schuff v. Ransom, 79 Ind. 458.

[45] Makepeace v. Bronnenberg, 146 Ind. 243.

[46] Ritter's Appeal, 59 Pa. St. 9.

[47] Hughes v. Parker, 20 N. H. 58, 65; Kitchen v. Cape Girardeau, etc., R. Co., 59 Mo. 514; St. Andrew's Bay Land Co. v. Mitchell, 4 Fla. 192, 54 Am. Dec. 340; Hayden v. Middlesex Turnpike Corp., 10 Mass. 397, 6 Am. Dec. 143; Kearney v. Andrews, 10 N. J. Eq. 70.

[48] Walseburg Water Co. v. Moore, 5 Colo. App. 144, 38 Pac. 60; In re St. Helen Mill Co., Fed. Cas. No. 12,222, 3 Sawy. (U. S.) 88; Moses v. Tompkins, 84 Ala. 613; People v. New York Infant Asylum, 122 N. Y. 190; State v. McCullough, 3 Nev. 202; Miller v. English, 21 N. J. L. 317.

[49] People v. Town of Fairbury, 51 Ill. 149; Hughes v. Parker, 20 N. H. 58; Beardsley v. Johnson, 1 N. Y. Supp. 608, 49 Hun (N. Y.) 607.

the subject, the presumption will be indulged that the selection was according to the prescribed methods.[50] So, where no particular mode of making the choice is provided, if all having the right to vote have an opportunity and the officers chosen are the choice of the majority of those voting, the election is valid.[51] As a general rule, an agent authorized to make a contract for a corporation must be appointed on the vote of the directors, but the appointment may be implied from the adoption or recognition of the agent's acts by the corporation or the directors.[52] And it is not generally necessary that the vote by which the agent was appointed be recorded or entered on the minutes, but the same may be inferred from the fact that the corporation permitted him to act as such.[53] Nor is it essential that such an agent should be appointed by an instrument under seal.[54] If the acts of an agent of a corporation were unauthorized in the first instance, they may, if within the scope of its corporate powers, be subsequently ratified, and such ratification will cure any defects in the appointment of the agent.[55] In the absence of express provisions to the contrary in the charter of a mutual company, such company possesses the power to appoint such agents as may be necessary to transact its business; and the members of such company are presumed to have consented that it shall be represented by such agents or officers as are reasonably necessary for the conduct of its business.[56] The agent may be a member of the corporation.[57] But a corporation can not be bound by its agents for acts beyond its corporate powers.[58] When the appointment of an agent of a corporation is *ultra vires*, it is void and can not bind the corporation; but where the corpora-

[50] Blanchard v. Dow, 32 Me. 557.

[51] Philips v. Wickham, 1 Paige (N. Y.) 590.

[52] Equitable Gas Light Co. v. Baltimore Coal-Tar & Mfg. Co., 65 Md. 73, 3 Atl. 108.

[53] Alabama, etc., R. Co. v. Kidd, 29 Ala. 221; Wood v. Wiley Const. Co., 56 Conn. 87; Planters' Bank v. Bivingsville Cotton Mfg. Co., 10 Rich. L. (S. C.) 95.

[54] Fleckner v. Bank of U. S., 8 Wheat. (U. S.) 338; St. Andrew's Bay Land Co. v. Mitchell, 4 Fla. 192, 54 Am. Dec. 340.

[55] Fleckner v. Bank of U. S., 8 Wheat. (U. S.) 338; Church v. Sterling, 16 Conn. 388; Home Life Ins. Co. v. Pierce, 75 Ill. 426.

[56] Protection Life Ins. Co. v. Foote, 79 Ill. 368.

[57] Stoddert v. Port Tobacco Parish, 2 Gill & J. (Md.) 227.

[58] Hayden v. Middlesex Turnpike Co., 10 Mass. 397, 6 Am. Dec. 143; Sandford v. McArthur, 18 B. Mon. (Ky.) 411; Gregory Co. v. Raber, 1 Colo. 511; Ryan v. Manufacturers', etc., Bank, 9 Daly (N. Y.) 308.

tion has derived a benefit from the services of such agent, the corporation may, in some cases at least, be liable on a *quantum meruit*.[59]

§ **42. Partnerships as principals.**—The law of partnership is a branch of the law of principal and agent.[60] Each partner is a principal, as well as an agent of the other partners. Besides, each partner has the implied authority to appoint such agents or servants as may be necessary for the proper conduct of the business.[61] An agent thus appointed is an agent of the firm and not an agent of the individual partner merely.[62] Such an agent, when acting within the scope of his authority, may bind the principal firm to the same extent as if such principal were a natural person.[63]

§ **43. Unincorporated societies as principals.**—An unincorporated society, such as a church, lodge or political organization, can not become a competent principal. It is not a legal entity. But if all the members have acted jointly in the appointment of an agent they may be held liable as joint principals for the acts of such agent.[64] Those who appoint the agent will, of course, be liable. The converse of the proposition is also true, that those not joining in the appointment will not be liable.

§ **44. Alien enemies as principals.**—A citizen or subject of a country at war with the United States can not lawfully appoint an agent in the United States during the existence of hostilities.[65] But if the relation of principal and agent already existed, prior to the beginning of the war, it will not be terminated by reason of the breaking out of the war between the two countries, provided it does not involve any communication across the line, and it can be shown that the agency continued by the mutual consent of the parties thereto.[66]

§ **45. Joint principals.**—As shown in the case of unincorporated societies, two or more persons having authority to do so may jointly

[59] Slater Woollen Co. v. Lamb, 143 Mass. 420.

[60] Cox v. Hickman, 8 H. L. Cas. 268.

[61] Paton v. Baker, 62 Iowa 704; Durgin v. Somers, 117 Mass. 55; Harvey v. McAdams, 32 Mich. 472; Tillier v. Whitehead, 1 Dall. (Pa.) 269; Sweeney v. Neely, 53 Mich. 421; Carley v. Jenkins, 46 Vt. 721.

[62] Johnston's Ex. v. Brown, 18 La. Ann. 330; Ayer v. Ayer, 41 Vt. 346.

[63] Henderson v. San Antonio R. Co., 17 Texas 560.

[64] Ray v. Powers, 134 Mass. 22; Newell v. Borden, 128 Mass. 31.

[65] United States v. Grossmayer, 9 Wall. (U. S.) 72.

[66] 1 Am. & Eng. Encyc. L. (2d ed.) 943.

appoint an agent. They are then called joint principals. If two or more persons are jointly interested in a business enterprise, one of them can not appoint an agent for all except by the consent of all.[66a] If the interest is a common one, each being authorized to act for all, as in the case of a partnership,[66b] one may appoint an agent for all, and the act will be binding. If, however, the interests be separate and distinct, one can not bind the others by the appointment of an agent.[67]

§ 46. **Who may be agents—Generally.**—As a general rule, any person may be an agent except a lunatic, imbecile, or child of very tender years. Hence, slaves or villains, persons outlawed or excommunicated, married women, infants, and aliens may become agents for other parties, although incapable of binding themselves by contract.[68] It is obvious that many persons may be agents to carry out the instructions of or to act for others when they would not be competent to do such acts for themselves. Thus, an infant may deliver a deed or an article of personal property for another when he could not bind himself individually by such act. The act to be done in such case may be purely mechanical or ministerial, and it is evident that a much lower degree of competency would be demanded than in cases calling for the exercise of skill and discretion. A mere child may be competent to deliver a deed or money, or perform many other acts of that character involving no particular skill or discretion. Hence, a person, though incompetent to act as a principal, may in many cases take upon himself the duties of an agent; and this is especially so where the duties are more in the nature of those of a servant than of an agent, strictly speaking. So, infants, married women and aliens may be agents.[69] It is not necessary for a person to be *sui juris* in order to be qualified to act as agent for others; and it may be stated as a general rule that all persons of sound mind are capable of becoming agents.[70]

§ 47. **Infants as agents.**—There is no rule of law which prevents an infant from being an agent, and a contract made by such agent is binding upon the principal the same as if the agent were an adult. This is especially true if the infant is above the age of seven years

[66a] Sewall v. Holland, 61 Ga. 608; Reiman v. Hamilton, 111 Mass. 245; Hearsey v. Lambert, 50 Minn. 373.

[66b] Deakin v. Underwood, 37 Minn. 98.

[67] Mechem Ag., § 60.

[68] Lyon v. Kent, 45 Ala. 656.

[69] Story Ag., § 7.

[70] Story Ag., § 7; Evans Pr. & Ag. (Bedford's ed.) 15.

and there is no statutory provision against his being such an agent.[71] The relation between an adult principal and an infant agent can not be said to be a perfect one, however. Of course, the act of the principal to be performed by the infant agent may be as completely accomplished through him as if he were an adult, and, so far as the principal is concerned, his liability to the agent and to third persons would be the same. But the contract between the principal and such infant agent would not be binding on the latter, if he saw proper to avoid it, such a contract being voidable on his part, the same as any other. He would, therefore, not be liable to the principal for failing to meet his obligations as an agent, nor would he be liable to third persons on an implied warranty of authority, as other agents are liable; nor in any other way, except, perhaps, for fraud or other torts committed in the execution of his powers. The agency of an infant or other person *non sui juris* is therefore only a qualified agency.[72]

§ **48. Persons of unsound mind as agents.**—Persons of unsound mind are, as a general rule, as incompetent to be agents as they are incompetent to be principals. A person not possessing sufficient mental discretion to do an act in relation to his own affairs can not be held to have sufficient capacity to perform such an act for another. The appointment of such an agent in a matter in which discretion is required would be void, and so would all the acts performed by him in pursuance of the appointment.[73] Such a person may, however, be a *nuntius*, or messenger, though he can not become a mandatary. A message or package might be delivered through him as well as it could be by means of a wire or a vehicle.[74] Hence, if the act or acts to be performed are merely ministerial or mechanical, such as the delivery of title papers, or of goods and chattels, or other articles, the act performed through a lunatic or idiot will be valid if authorized. In such cases the agent, if such he may be called, is no more than a machine or instrument in the hands of the principal, and when the act is done it is the same as if the principal had done it himself. But if the performance of such act involves the exercise of any discretion, however slight, and the agent does not have the capacity to exercise such discretion, the act is void. Hence, it is believed that while the principal might lawfully deliver a horse to a vendee through

[71] Talbot v. Bowen, 1 A. K. Marsh. (Ky.) 436; Brown v. Hartford Fire Ins. Co., 117 Mass. 479.

[72] Wharton Ag., § 13, *et seq.*

[73] Story Ag., § 7; Evans Pr. & Ag. (Bedford's ed.) 115.

[74] Wharton Ag., § 15.

one who is of unsound mind, he could not effect a valid sale of such horse through such person, as that would require some discretion on the part of the agent. Of course, if the agent did possess sufficient mental discretion to perform the act, though he were otherwise *non compos,* or if the act were subsequently ratified, it would be rendered valid. And if the third party did not know or have reason to believe such agent *non compos,* the principal may be bound.[74a]

§ **49. Married women as agents.**—It may be stated, as a general rule, that a *feme covert* may lawfully be the agent or attorney of her husband and bind him by her act or contract, even at common law,[74b] or she may act as agent for another in a contract with her own husband.[75] But it is not clear that she may, at common law, act as the agent of a third person, as against the express dissent of her husband, as such agency might involve duties and services not consistent with her duties or relations to the husband and family.[75a] But in states in which the legal disabilities of a married woman to make contracts, etc., have been removed by statutes, any restriction of the common law by which she would be prevented from acting as agent is abrogated also. It was said by the supreme court of Indiana: "Where the wife engages in business, with the knowledge and consent of her husband, the business is regarded as that of the husband, the wife as his agent, and he is bound for the performance of contracts which she may make relating to such business."[76] The husband is not liable, however, if the wife obtained the goods on her own credit exclusively, as there can be no presumption in such cases that she was acting for her husband.[77] In cases where the law authorizes the wife to pledge the credit of her husband, it creates a compulsory agency, and he is liable for her acts.[78] The marriage relation alone does not give to the wife any authority to act as agent for her husband, so as to bind him in contracts of a general nature. Her relation in this respect is more nearly analogous to that of a servant to her husband. At least, such was the conception of the common law.[79]

§ **50. Husband as agent of wife.**—The husband may be the agent of his wife in all cases where by law she is competent to appoint an agent.[79a] Such agency may be established by circumstantial evidence; and the fact of the relation of husband and wife, and that the husband openly acted for his wife under circumstances implying a knowledge on her part that he was acting for her, as well as evidence showing that the husband was permitted by the wife to perform other and similar acts for her, may be considered in determining whether

[74a] Mechem Ag., §§ 255, 260.

[74b] Weisbrod v. Chicago, etc., R. Co., 18 Wis. 35.

[75] Story Ag., § 7.

[75a] Story Ag., § 7.

[76] Jenkins v. Flinn, 37 Ind. 352.

[77] Jenkins v. Flinn, *supra.*

[78] Benjamin v. Dockham, 134 Mass. 418.

[79] Selwyn *Nisi Prius* 288.

[79a] Baxter v. Maxwell, 115 Pa. St. 469; Manhattan L. Ins. Co. v. Smith, 44 Ohio St. 156; Brown v. Thompson, 31 S. C. 436.

there was, in fact, an agency.[80] While a husband may, without question, be the agent of his wife, his agency can only come from one source; and that is, the authority conferred by his wife, whether that authority be conferred directly or indirectly. The evidence of the agency, however, should be clear and satisfactory.[81]

§ **51. Corporations as agents.**—A corporation, unless it is authorized to do so by its charter or as an incident of its general powers, can not act as agent for another; but otherwise it has the same power in this respect as a natural person, and the corporation may act as agent for an individual, a firm or another corporation.[82] Thus, a national bank can not act as a broker in the purchase or sale of bonds or stocks on commission;[83] nor can a savings bank act as such broker if it has only the ordinary powers of such corporation;[84] nor has a manufacturing company the power to act as agent for another like corporation in making sale of its product;[85] nor can the corporation act as an attorney at law, although it may be authorized for and be carrying on the business of a collecting agency that may employ attorneys for others and recover fees paid them.[86] National banks, as a general rule, can not act as agents for others in the sale of stocks, notes or other property; but if such a bank holds a note of its debtor as collateral, it may lawfully act as an agent in the sale of such note to a third person, this being an incident of its power to collect the claim.[87] And it has been held that a corporation may under some circumstances execute a conveyance of land as attorney in fact for another.[88]

§ **52. Partnership firms as agents.**—A partnership, like a corporation, may be organized for the express purpose of carrying on an agency, such as real estate brokerage, etc. If not organized for such express purpose, it may not carry on such business, unless the same is incident to its general powers. But when authority is properly delegated to the firm for that purpose, either partner may execute it, and the act of one partner is considered in law the act of the entire partnership for this purpose.[89]

§ **53. Alien enemies as agents.**—What has been said in reference to alien enemies as principals is true of them also as agents. As a general rule, such an agency is invalid during a period of war between

[80] Barnett v. Gluting, 3 Ind. App. 415; Arnold v. Spurr, 130 Mass. 347.

[81] Rowell v. Klein, 44 Ind. 290; McLaren v. Hall, 26 Iowa 297.

[82] Westinghouse Machine Co. v. Wilkinson, 79 Ala. 312.

[83] First Nat'l Bank v. Hoch, 89 Pa. St. 324.

[84] Jemison v. Citizens' Savings Bank, 122 N. Y. 135, 19 Am. St. 482.

[85] Westinghouse Machine Co. v. Wilkinson, 79 Ala. 312.

[86] Snow, Church & Co. v. Hall, 19 Misc. (N. Y.) 655.

[87] Anderson v. Grand Forks First National Bank, 5 N. Dak. 451.

[88] Killingsworth v. Portland Trust Co., 18 Ore. 351, 17 Am. St. 737.

[89] Eggleston v. Boardman, 37 Mich. 14.

the respective countries of the principal and the agent, involving any communication across the line of hostilities.[90] The agency is not discontinued, however, by virtue of the breaking out of hostilities, if it existed prior thereto and the parties consented to its continuation.[91] And payment of debts to the agent of an alien enemy is allowed when the agent resides in the same state with the debtor.[92]

§ **54. Persons having adverse interests as agents.**—One who has an adverse interest to that of the principal in the subject-matter of the agency may not lawfully act as agent therein, and in many instances he can not act as agent for two principals in the same transaction, if his duties require him to do incompatible things; but it is otherwise if he is to act for principals in matters that do not involve a performance of acts that are incompatible, or where both principals have full knowledge of his relation to each.[92a] And a person can not be an agent for a party opposed to himself in the same transaction, such as being an attorney in a cause in which the agent himself is the adverse party.[93]

§ **54a. Joint agents.**—Joint agents, or those appointed to execute the authority of their principal jointly, must act together in the execution of the business for which they have been employed, or it will not be valid.[94] Hence, a joint agent, acting without the co-operation of his fellow agents in such cases, is not a competent agent to execute the will of his principal. This rule, however, applies only to private agents; that is, agents who are appointed by some private person or corporation to perform some act or acts of agency. If the agency be a public one, as in the case of public officers,—for example, a board of county commissioners or a city council or a school board,—in making a contract, if the act is performed jointly by a majority of such public agents or officers it is valid.[95]

[90] Kershaw v. Kelsey, 100 Mass. 561; U. S. v. Grossmayer, 9 Wall. (U. S.) 72.

[91] Ward v. Smith, 7 Wall. (U. S.) 447; Monsseaux v. Uhrquhart, 19 La. Ann. 482; Wharton Ag., § 16; Insurance Co. v. Davis, 95 U. S. 425.

[92] Insurance Co. v. Davis, 95 U. S. 425.

[92a] Morey v. Laird, 108 Iowa 670; Duesman v. Hale, 55 Neb. 577.

[93] Tewksbury v. Spruance, 75 Ill. 187; Taussig v. Hart, 58 N. Y. 425; Hammond v. Bookwalter, 12 Ind. App. 177; Kimball v. Ranney, 122 Mich. 160; McDoel v. Ohio Val. Imp., etc., Co. (Ky.), 36 S. W. 175; Oliver v. Lansing, 48 Neb. 338; Webb v. Marks, 10 Colo. App. 429; In re Watkins' Estate, 121 Cal. 327; Stanley v. Luse, 36 Ore. 25.

[94] Rollins v. Phelps, 5 Minn. 463; Hawley v. Keeler, 53 N. Y. 114.

[95] Loudon Savings Fund Soc. v. Savings Bank, 36 Pa. St. 498, 78 Am. Dec. 390; McNeil v. Chamber of Commerce, 154 Mass. 277; Woolsey v. Tompkins, 23 Wend. (N. Y.) 324.

CHAPTER III.

HOW AGENCY MAY BE CREATED AND PROVED.

I. By Appointment.

§ **55. Appointment and acceptance.**—It has already been shown that an agency may be created between the parties by contract, express or implied. Indeed, this is the normal way in which the relation is formed, and the only way, unless it be shown by proof of ratification, or estoppel, or unless it is created by implication of law. Such contract is usually designated the *appointment* of the agent, and if it be in writing, it is called a letter or power of attorney. An appointment also involves an acceptance thereof on the part of the agent.[1] An agency, like any other contract, presupposes a meeting of the minds. If the parties are present when the contract is entered into, or both parties sign or acknowledge the instrument, if there be one, this will be proof sufficient. If the agent indicates his acceptance by letter, this is equally sufficient. But an acceptance may be presumed or inferred from the acts of the agent; as, by acting upon the appointment. In such case no formal acceptance need be proved.[2]

[1] First Nat'l Bank v. Free, 67 Iowa 11; Cameron v. Seaman, 69 N. Y. 396, 25 Am. Rep. 212.

[2] Delano v. Smith Charities, 138 Mass. 63.

The appointment, however, must be accepted, and until then the contract of agency does not go into effect.[3]

§ 56. **Elements of appointment—Intention.**—As already indicated in a previous chapter, before an agency can be created there must be competent parties to make the contract, there must be a valid consideration, a legal object to accomplish, and in some cases a particular form.[4] It must also appear from the circumstances that there was an intention on the part of the principal to appoint the agent. Unless such intention is real or apparent from the words or actions of the parties, there can be no agency.[5] Thus, a mere correspondence in relation to a transaction, between an owner of real estate and a broker, evincing no intention on the part of the owner to make the broker his agent, would not amount to an appointment; and the words "I will sell," or their equivalent, accompanied by the specifications of the terms of sale by the owner of the land, were held not to constitute an appointment, as there was no intention evinced to make such a party an agent.[6] And where an agent sends a price list of land to a future purchaser, this is not regarded as establishing an agency, if the person addressed merely responds by inquiring as to terms.[7]

§ 57. **The form of the contract—Instruments under seal—Parol authority.**—A contract of agency must of necessity possess all the elements of any other contract enforceable in law. It may be a simple contract in writing or in parol, or it may be a contract under seal, called a specialty. If a simple contract in writing, its form and contents may be simply of the tenor that the party of the first part (the principal) does hereby constitute the party of the second part (the agent) his true and lawful attorney, or agent, to act for him and in his behalf and stead, in the performance of a certain transaction named in the contract. Of course, the purposes of the appointment should be stated explicitly. The appointment may be shown, however, as has been seen, in the form of a correspondence between the parties, such as a proposal by one and an acceptance by the other of the terms of the agency. Where a writing becomes necessary, as

[3] Cameron v. Seaman, 69 N. Y. 396, 25 Am. Rep. 212.

[4] See Anson Conts. (8th ed.) 10, *et seq.*

[5] Felton v. McClave, 46 N. Y. Supr. Ct. 53; Central Trust Co. v. Bridges, 6 C. C. A. 539, 57 Fed. 753.

[6] Bosseau v. O'Brien, 4 Biss. (U. S.) 395.

[7] Stewart v. Pickering, 73 Iowa 652.

when it is required by reason of the provisions of the statute of frauds, the requirement would be met if the agreement were in the form of such a correspondence by letter or by telegram, and if it showed the intention of the parties. In many instances, however, as in other simple contracts, the appointment may be verbal; that is to say, by mere word of mouth, and without any writing. But in some cases the contract, by the rules of the common law, is required to be under seal, as when an agent is appointed to make conveyance of land, and then a greater formality is necessary. In that case the signature and seal of the principal are essential, although the latter requirement has been abolished in many of the states, and the tendency is to do away with the distinction that formerly obtained in the use of seals.[8] If the appointment requires a sealed instrument, the latter should contain an accurate description of the subject-matter of the agency; as, for example, the real estate which the agent is authorized to convey. The rule of the common law as to such an appointment required that if the act were done by the principal himself, instead of being performed for him by an agent, and a sealed instrument were necessary to its performance, the instrument of agency must likewise be a sealed instrument. In other words, the instrument constituting the appointment must be of the same nature, in point of solemnity, as that required by the principal, were he to transact the business in person. But if the instrument be executed by the agent in the immediate presence and under the direction of the principal, express or implied, no written appointment is necessary, and this is true although such instrument is by law required to be in writing, or under seal, such as a negotiable instrument, or a deed.[9] In such cases there is no reason why the name of the attorney should be employed in the instrument which the agent writes by the direction of the principal, and in his presence, such as exists in cases where the instrument is executed in the principal's absence. The principal merely avails himself of the aid of the agent as he would make use

[8] Thus in Indiana and many other states the statutes abolish the requirements of a seal: Burns' R. S. Ind. 1901, §§ 454, 1309, 3421; 21 Am. & Eng. Encyc. L. 888.

[9] Handyside v. Cameron, 21 Ill. 588, 74 Am. Dec. 119; Gardner v. Gardner, 5 Cush. (Mass.) 483; Jansen v. McCahill, 22 Cal. 563; Mutual, etc., Ins. Co. v. Brown, 30 N. J. Eq. 193; Burns v. Lynde, 6 Allen (Mass.) 309; Eggleston v. Wagner, 46 Mich. 610; Meyer v. King, 29 La. Ann. 567; McMurtry v. Brown, 6 Neb. 368; Croy v. Busenbark, 72 Ind. 48; Crow v. Carter, 5 Ind. App. 169; Mackay v. Bloodgood, 9 Johns. (N. Y.) 285; Ball v. Dunsterville, 4 T. R. 313; Harshaw v. McKesson, 65 N. C. 688.

of an inanimate instrument to carry out his purpose. The agent is but an amanuensis. It is immaterial whether the agent thus writes the whole of the instrument or only a portion, such as the signature, or the filling of a blank.[10]

§ **58. Authority to fill blanks in instruments.**—With regard to the filling of blanks by an agent, in the absence of the principal, a somewhat different rule prevails. If the instrument be a simple contract, negotiable or non-negotiable, or a bond, the general rule is that an agent may fill the blank in pursuance of parol authority.[11] As in such instances the principal might have authorized the agent by parol to execute the entire instrument, so he may empower him to execute it in part, by completing or perfecting it. Indeed, the presumption is that when a paper of this character is delivered to an agent with blanks left in it, such agent is authorized to perfect the contract by filling the blanks, for any sum, and upon any terms as to time, place and conditions of payment and name of payee.[12] The principal may, indeed, limit the authority of the person to whom the paper is intrusted, as to the extent to which he may or may not go in filling in the blank spaces, and such limitation of authority will bind the agent, as between him and the principal. But as to *bona fide* transferees of such paper, the principal will be bound by it, even if the authority has been exceeded, unless the transferee had notice of the limitation.[13] The principle underlying the presumption of authority in favor of the agent is that of estoppel on account of the negligence of the party who delivered the paper in blank. Such blanks carry with them, upon the face thereof, an implication of authority to be filled, and if the principal or maker

[10] See Ball v. Dunsterville, 4 T. R. 313; Mackay v. Bloodgood, 9 Johns. (N. Y.) 285; McMurtry v. Brown, 6 Neb. 368; Hudson v. Revett, 5 Bing. 368, 15 E. C. L. 467; Warring v. Williams, 8 Pick. (Mass.) 322.

[11] Boardman v. Gore, 1 Stew. (Ala.) 517, 18 Am. Dec. 73; 2 Starkie Ev. 480, n. 1; Angle v. Northwestern L. Ins. Co., 92 U. S. 330; Greenleaf Ev. (16th ed.), § 568a, notes.

[12] Spitler v. James, 32 Ind. 202; Gillaspie v. Kelley, 41 Ind. 158, 13 Am. Rep. 318; Emmons v. Meeker, 55 Ind. 321; Hepler v. Mt. Carmel Savings Bank, 97 Pa. St. 420, 39 Am. Rep. 813; Redlich v. Doll, 54 N. Y. 234, 13 Am. Rep. 573; Yocum v. Smith, 63 Ill. 321, 14 Am. Rep. 120; South Berwick v. Huntress, 53 Me. 89, 87 Am. Dec. 535; Rainbolt v. Eddy, 34 Iowa 440, 11 Am. Rep. 152; Cronkhite v. Nebeker, 81 Ind. 319.

[13] 1 Daniel Neg. Instr., § 142; Jones v. Pincheon, 6 Ind. App. 460; Frank v. Lilienfeld, 33 Gratt. (Va.) 377; Snyder v. Van Doren, 46 Wis. 602; Johnston Harvester Co. v. McLean, 57 Wis. 258; Eichelberger v. Old National Bank, 103 Ind. 401; Spitler v. James, 32 Ind. 202; Emmons v. Meeker, 55 Ind. 321.

of the paper permits it to pass into the hands of persons thus apparently empowered to perfect it, he ought not to be permitted to deny the authority of such person if the transferee receives it without notice of the facts. The principal should not by his acts, or silence, or negligence, be permitted thus to mislead an innocent person so as to cause injury to such person, but rather should be compelled to bear the loss himself.[14] And whether a person was expressly constituted an agent for the purpose of filling blanks in such paper or not is immaterial; the party to whom the instrument is delivered in blank, though a payee, indorsee or other taker thereof, becomes, *ipso facto,* the agent of the maker, indorser, etc., and has implied authority for that purpose.[15] The presumption of agency does not apply, however, to a case in which the agent or party intrusted with the instrument has made alterations not contemplated and not needed to make a complete instrument,—as, by raising the sum named to a higher one,—although the alteration does not appear on the face of the instrument. In such case the alteration is considered a forgery,[16] and not a mere completion of an imperfect paper, as it would be if the amount or date had been left blank, with authority, express or implied, to fill it up, and it had been accordingly filled up.[17] The right to fill up blanks in negotiable paper may be exercised not only by the first holder of the paper, but by any transferee, who is, in law, regarded as an agent for that purpose.[18]

§ 59. **What authority implied—Material alteration of instrument.**—Even when there is a clear departure from the specified authority of filling such blanks, still, if the matter inserted is no

[14] Garrard v. Haddan, 67 Pa. St. 82, 5 Am. Rep. 412; Blakey v. Johnson, 13 Bush (Ky.) 197; Redlich v. Doll, 54 N. Y. 234.

[15] Violett v. Patton, 5 Cranch (U. S.) 142; Gibbs v. Frost, 4 Ala. 720; Bridgeport Bank v. New York, etc., R. Co., 30 Conn. 231; White v. Alward, 35 Ill. App. 195; Quinn v. Brown, 71 Iowa 376; Abbott v. Rose, 62 Me. 194, 16 Am. Rep. 427; Appeal of Bechtel, 133 Pa. St. 367; Marshall v. Drescher, 68 Ind. 359; Gary v. State, 11 Tex. App. 527; Norwich Bank v. Hyde, 13 Conn. 279; Fullerton v. Sturgis, 4 Ohio St. 529; Holland v. Hatch, 15 Ohio St. 464; Mechanics', etc., Bank v. Schuyler, 7 Cow. (N. Y.) 337; White v. Duggan, 140 Mass. 18, 54 Am. Rep. 437; Boyd v. Brotherson, 10 Wend. (N. Y.) 93; Goodman v. Simonds, 20 How. (U. S.) 343; Bank of Pittsburgh v. Neal, 22 How. (U. S.) 96.

[16] Holmes v. Trumper, 22 Mich. 427, 7 Am. Rep. 661; Luellen v. Hare, 32 Ind. 211. See also, cases cited in notes 12 and 13, *supra.*

[17] Abbott v. Rose, 62 Me. 194; Holmes v. Trumper, 22 Mich. 427, 7 Am. Rep. 661; Luellen v. Hare, 32 Ind. 211.

[18] Page v. Morrell, 33 How. Pr. (N. Y.) 244.

more than is apparently called for to make the paper complete, it will be protected in the hands of an innocent transferee. Thus, where a paper was on its face non-negotiable, and it was expressly agreed that it should not be made negotiable, but the indorsee inserted a provision in a blank space which made it payable in cash, and thus negotiable, and then transferred it, the court held that the transferee could recover.[19] And where the name of the payee is left blank, and the paper thus delivered and sent into the world, such delivery implies authority to fill up the blank with the name of any *bona fide* payee.[20] It is otherwise, however, if the paper is complete upon its face, and an insertion is made which changes the terms or the relations of the parties. In such case, although the alteration may not be apparent on the face of the paper, yet the authority exercised can not be implied, and the alteration will be considered as unauthorized.[21] And where the words "or his order" were inserted in a promissory note, in the space after the name of the payee, the note was thereby rendered invalid in the hands of an innocent holder, although the instrument was on its face free from suspicion, the note being already complete without the words of negotiability.[22]

§ 60. **Filling blanks in sealed instruments.**—As to deeds or instruments required to be under seal at common law, there is still great diversity of opinion among the courts as to whether authority to fill blanks therein may be validly conferred by parol, when it is to be done in the absence of the principal. According to some courts, in jurisdictions where the common-law distinction between specialty contracts and simple contracts is still observed, the authority to fill up the blanks with material provisions in an instrument of such solemnity

[19] Spitler v. James, 32 Ind. 202; Gillaspie v. Kelley, 41 Ind. 158; Orick v. Colston, 7 Gratt. (Va.) 189.

[20] Armstrong v. Harshman, 61 Ind. 52; Brummel v. Enders, 18 Gratt. (Va.) 873; Cruchley v. Clarance, 2 Mau. & Sel. 90; Close v. Fields, 2 Tex. 232; Boyd v. McCann, 10 Md. 118; Townsend v. France, 2 Houst. (Del.) 441.

[21] De Pauw v. Bank of Salem, 126 Ind. 553. Even the insertion of the words "10 per cent." in a blank space in a note, after "interest at," has been held to render the note void: Holmes v. Trumper, 22 Mich. 427.

[22] Bruce v. Westcott, 3 Barb. (N. Y.) 375; Blacknall v. Parish, 59 N. C. 70, 78 Am. Dec. 239; Simms v. Hervey, 19 Iowa 273. And where the drawer of a check intrusted an agent with its delivery to the payee, and the agent forged an indorsement of the check and collected the money from the bank, it was held that the drawer was not bound by the indorsement and could recover the money from the bank: German Savings Bank v. Citizens' National Bank, 101 Iowa 530, 63 Am. St. 399.

as is required in a deed can only be conferred by power of attorney under seal; and parol authority is, therefore, insufficient for the purpose, unless the instrument be redelivered after the blank has been filled.[23] On the other hand, it has long been held, even in jurisdictions where the common law governs as to the subject, that the filling up of a blank in a sealed instrument necessary to make such instrument perfect, will not vitiate it, if authorized by parol.[24] In some jurisdictions, in which the use of seals has been abrogated by statutes, it is held that, by reason of such abrogation, authority to fill blanks in deeds, mortgages and other instruments, such as were formerly required to be under seal, may rest in parol.[25] The tendency of modern decisions generally is to disregard the technical requirements based upon the common law, in this respect, and to hold that parol authority is sufficient to authorize the filling of a blank in a deed, mortgage, and other instruments of that character.[26] And it is

[23] Davidson v. Cooper, 11 M. & W. 778; Hibblewhite v. M'Morine, 6 M. & W. 200; Burns v. Lynde, 6 Allen (Mass.) 305; Gilbert v. Anthony, 1 Yerg. (Tenn.) 69, 24 Am. Dec. 439; Byers v. McClanahan, 6 Gill & J. (Md.) 250; Ayres v. Probasco, 14 Kan. 175; Preston v. Hull, 23 Gratt. (Va.) 600, 14 Am. Rep. 153; Ingram v. Little, 14 Ga. 173, 58 Am. Dec. 549; Upton v. Archer, 41 Cal. 85; Williams v. Crutcher, 5 How. (Miss.) 71, 35 Am. Dec. 422; Cross v. State Bank, 5 Ark. 525; Graham v. Holt, 3 Ired. (N. C.) 300; Moseby v. State, 4 Sneed (Tenn.) 324. In Schintz v. McManamy, 33 Wis. 299, the court held that while the agent might be authorized by parol to insert the name of a specified grantee, he could not, under such authority, insert the name of another grantee.

[24] South Berwick v. Huntress, 53 Me. 89, 87 Am. Dec. 535; Boardman v. Gore, 1 Stew. (Ala.) 517, 18 Am. Dec. 73.

[25] Swartz v. Ballou, 47 Iowa 188, 29 Am. Rep. 470; Threadgill v. Butler, 60 Tex. 599; Lockwood v. Bassett, 49 Mich. 546; McClain v. McClain, 52 Iowa 272; Barton v. Gray, 57 Mich. 622.

[26] Drury v. Foster, 2 Wall. (U. S.) 24; State v. Young, 23 Minn. 551; South Berwick v. Huntress, 53 Me. 89, 87 Am. Dec. 535; Commercial Bank v. Kortright, 22 Wend. (N. Y.) 348, 34 Am. Dec. 317; Bartlett v. Board of Education, 59 Ill. 364; Dunn v. Commercial Bank, 11 Barb. (N. Y.) 580; Whiting v. Daniel, 1 Hen. & M. (Va.) 391; Beery v. Homan's Com., 8 Gratt. (Va.) 48; Sigfried v. Levan, 6 S. & R. (Pa.) 308; Collins v. Welsh, 7 Mart. (La.) 402; Swartz v. Ballou, 47 Iowa 188, 29 Am. Rep. 470; Phelps v. Sullivan, 140 Mass. 36, 54 Am. Rep. 442; Van Etta v. Evenson, 28 Wis. 33, 9 Am. Rep. 486; Field v. Stagg, 52 Mo. 534, 14 Am. Rep. 435; Duncan v. Hodges, 4 McCord (S. C.) 239, 17 Am. Dec. 734; Cribben v. Deal, 21 Ore. 211, 28 Am. St. 746; Owen v. Perry, 25 Iowa 412, 96 Am. Dec. 49; Bridgeport Bank v. New York, etc., R. Co., 30 Conn. 274; Wiley v. Moor, 17 S. & R. (Pa.) 438, 17 Am. Dec. 696; Stahl v. Berger, 10 S. & R. (Pa.) 170, 13 Am. Dec. 666, and note, pp. 669-671; Tisher v. Beckwith, 30 Wis. 55;

to be observed that courts which hold that the authority to fill blank spaces in sealed instruments can not be shown by parol, and those in which it is held that it may be so shown, frequently agree that at all events the principal may estop himself by his acts in delivering sealed instruments, containing blank spaces, to his agent, with authority to fill the blanks, if, when so filled, the document is received in good faith by an innocent grantee or obligee. This is according to the well-known maxim of law that "when one of two innocent persons must suffer by the acts of a third, he by whose negligence it happened must be the sufferer."[27]

§ 61. What are "blanks"—What may be filled in—Ratification of act previously unauthorized.—It is a question of importance, frequently, just what insertions may be regarded as "blanks" so as to be authorized under the holdings of the cases that recognize the sufficiency of parol authority. It is certain, we think, that if the instrument is wanting in everything but the signature and seal of the grantor or obligor, or does not contain the substantial parts, or at least a sufficient portion of the contract to be expressive of the intention, the writing has no validity and can acquire none by the filling in of the missing parts, at least without a redelivery.[28] The blank spaces for the filling up of which parol authority has been held sufficient must be such as leave the instrument merely incomplete in some minor parts. Thus, it is held that a note and mortgage in each of which is left a blank for the name of the payee and mortgagee,

Richmond Mfg. Co. v. Davis, 7 Blackf. (Ind.) 412; Bell v. Kennedy, 100 Pa. St. 215; Allen v. Withrow, 110 U. S. 119; McClung v. Steen, 32 Fed. 373; McNab v. Young, 81 Ill. 11; Farmers' Bank v. Worthington, 145 Mo. 91, 46 S. W. 745; Threadgill v. Butler, 60 Tex. 599; Schintz v. McManamy, 33 Wis. 299; Campbell v. Smith, 71 N. Y. 26. But see *contra*, Upton v. Archer, 41 Cal. 85.

[27] Dolbeer v. Livingston, 100 Cal. 617; Reed v. Morton, 24 Neb. 760, 8 Am. St. 247; Phelps v. Sullivan, 140 Mass. 36, 54 Am. Rep. 442; Campbell v. Smith, 71 N. Y. 26, 27 Am. Rep. 5; Swartz v. Ballou, 47 Iowa 188, 29 Am. Rep. 470; South Berwick v. Huntress, 53 Me. 89, 87 Am. Dec. 535; Tisher v. Beckwith, 30 Wis. 55; Jewell v. Rock River Paper Co., 101 Ill. 57; McNab v. Young, 81 Ill. 11; Pence v. Arbuckle, 22 Minn. 417.

[28] Gilbert v. Anthony, 1 Yerg. (Tenn.) 69, 24 Am. Dec. 439; Lindsley v. Lamb, 34 Mich. 509; Simms v. Hervey, 19 Iowa 273; Ayres v. Harness, 1 Ohio 368, 13 Am. Dec. 629; Ayres v. Probasco, 14 Kan. 175; Duncan v. Hodges, 4 McCord (S. C.) 239, 17 Am. Dec. 734. See note to Woodworth v. Bank of America, 10 Am. Dec. 271.

and which are delivered to an agent to enable him to borrow money thereon, may be validly filled up with the name of such payee and mortgagee, when the money is obtained, by an agent authorized by parol authority for that purpose, without a new execution and delivery.[29] And where a deed duly signed and acknowledged by the grantor was delivered to an agent for the purpose of negotiating a sale of the land therein described, and of delivering the deed in pursuance of such a sale, it was held that if the name of the grantee and the amount of the consideration were by the agent inserted in the blank spaces left for that purpose, the agent was held presumptively to have authority to fill such blanks when the deed was delivered to a third party who had no knowledge of the circumstances.[30] So, also, where a deed was thus executed and acknowledged with a blank left therein for the grantee, the court held that parol authority might validly be given an agent by the grantor to fill the blank with the name of the grantee, and a subsequent delivery of the deed by such agent would make the conveyance a valid one.[31] In *South Berwick* v. *Huntress*,[32] the court ruled that a party executing a bond in blank as to the penal sum, and delivering it to another, must be held as agreeing that the blank may be filled after he has executed it. The court, in discussing the old rule that such authority could not be given by parol, said: "But the rule has never been universally accepted in this country; and however the holding of some courts may be, still the better opinion and the pervading current of authority is that when a deed is regularly executed in other respects, with a blank left therein for the name of the grantee, parol authority is sufficient to authorize the insertion of the name of such grantee, and that when so filled out and delivered, it is a valid deed." And further: "The rule was purely technical, and the outgrowth of a state of affairs and condition of the law which does not now exist. The reason of the law is the life of it, and when the reason fails, the law itself should fail. At the present day the distinctions between sealed and unsealed instruments are fast disappearing, and the courts are gradually doing away with them. As Judge Redfield said: 'But it [the rule] seems to be rather technical than substantial, and to found

[29] Van Etta v. Evenson, 28 Wis. 33, 9 Am. Rep. 486.

[30] Owen v. Perry, 25 Iowa 412, 96 Am. Dec. 49.

[31] Cribben v. Deal, 21 Ore. 211, 28 Am. St. 746.

[32] 53 Me. 89, 87 Am. Dec. 535.

itself either on the policy of the stamp duties or the superior force and sacredness of contracts by deed, both of which have little importance in this country. And the prevailing current of American authority, and the practical instincts and business experience and sense of our people are undoubtedly otherwise.'" But if an agent to whom is intrusted the filling in of the name of a specified grantee and the delivery of the deed to him inserts the name of another grantee and delivers the deed to him at the request of the first grantee, the deed so delivered is invalid, although it would have been sufficient if the party thus receiving it had been ignorant of the facts.[33] Where a surety signed a bond to be delivered as security for a charter party, with the names of the steamer and managing owner left blank, it was held by the supreme court of California that the bond was not void in the hands of an innocent party because the principal had, before the delivery of the bond, filled in the blank spaces with the names of such steamer and managing owner.[33a] The same ruling was made by the Alabama supreme court with regard to the filling of a blank with the name of the obligee of a bond.[34] It remains to be said that in all cases where parol authority is by the law of a particular jurisdiction regarded as insufficient to render valid the act of the agent or person who filled the blank, such act is always capable of being fully ratified by parol.[35] What will be deemed a sufficient ratification of such an act must, of course, be determined by the law of the jurisdiction in which the question arises. However, in those jurisdic-

[33] Schintz v. McManamy, 33 Wis. 299; State v. Matthews, 44 Kan. 596, 10 L. R. A. 308.

[33a] Dolbeer v. Livingston, 100 Cal. 617.

[34] Boardman v. Gore, 1 Stew. (Ala.) 517. For other cases in which the courts follow the rule that parol authority, express or implied, is sufficient to authorize the insertion of the name of the grantee in a deed in which a blank space has been left for that purpose, and that this may be done by an agent or by the grantee himself, see Swartz v. Ballou, 47 Iowa 188, 29 Am. Rep. 470; McCleery v. Wakefield, 76 Iowa 529; Reed v. Morton, 24 Neb. 760, 1 L. R. A. 736. But the contrary was held in DeArguello v. Bours, 67 Cal. 447; and in State v. Matthews, 44 Kan. 596, 10 L. R. A. 308. In the case last cited the grantee had knowledge of the facts.

[35] Emerson v. Opp, 9 Ind. App. 581; Pelton v. Prescott, 13 Iowa 567; Bell v. Mahin, 69 Iowa 408; Conable v. Smith, 61 Hun (N. Y.) 185, 15 N. Y. Supp. 924; Woodbury v. Allegheny, etc., R. Co., 72 Fed. 371; Reed v. Morton, 24 Neb. 760, 8 Am. St. 247, 1 L. R. A. 736; Stanley v. Epperson, 45 Tex. 644; Montgomery v. Crossthwait, 90 Ala. 553, 24 Am. St. 832, 12 L. R. A. 140.

tions in which parol authority in the first instance is held insufficient, a parol ratification is considered as equally insufficient.

§ 62. **The consideration.**—Like every other contract, that of the appointment of an agent must be based upon a favorable consideration, for otherwise the agreement is *nudum pactum* and void.[36] It is not necessary, any more than it is in other contracts, that the consideration should consist of any specified sum of money or article of value; but it may, as in other contracts, consist of a mere promise for an act performed or to be performed. Thus, if the principal employ the agent for a remuneration stipulated in the contract, to be paid upon the performance of the act or acts, it will be sufficient. The remuneration is called the agent's compensation, and consists generally of a sum of money or salary to be paid when the act or acts have been performed in whole or in part. It is not necessary, however, that the promise to pay compensation should be express.[37] Thus, if the principal employ the agent to do the service for him under circumstances warranting an implication of an intention to pay, the inference would be that the principal would pay what the services were reasonably worth. Nor is it essential that the promise for compensation should be stipulated for any definite period of time or any definite amount. It may be a sum in gross for the particular services to be rendered, or it may be a commission on a certain amount of money to be realized on the transaction by the principal; or, as before stated, there may be no stipulated compensation whatever, but it may be left to be shown what the value of it is, in the settlement between the parties, or in the litigation, if such should follow. If there should be an express agreement as to the amount of compensation, it will, of course, control.[38]

§ 63. **Gratuitous agency—Gratuitous promise not enforceable.**—The circumstances, however, may be such as to leave the inference that no compensation is expected or is to be paid. Thus, if a person volunteers to do an act for another, when he is under no obligation to do so, and fails to do it, no compensation can be collected, as in such case it is apparent that none is expected. Thus, where an architect volunteered his services to furnish drawings for a building under circumstances showing that they were to be furnished for the

[36] Balfe v. West, 13 C. B. 466; Elsee v. Gatward, 5 T. R. 143; Thorne v. Deas, 4 Johns. (N. Y.) 84.

[37] Mansell v. Clements, L. R. 9 C. P. 139; Law v. Connecticut, etc., R. Co., 46 N. H. 284.

[38] Wallace v. Floyd, 29 Pa. St. 184.

chances of receiving future employment, no recovery could be had for the services of making such drawings.[39] Nor could the principal in such case recover damages for the failure to perform, if the services so volunteered were not rendered. But if the services are performed, in whole or in part, the agent may render himself liable for damages on account of any negligence in the performance.[40] And, of course, he would be bound to account to the principal for all the receipts on account of the agency.[41] Whether the services are regarded as gratuitous or not must depend on the particular circumstances of the case. Ordinarily, if one man labors for another, or renders him services in his business, from which the latter derives a benefit, and the one who receives the services stands by and sees what is done without making objection, he is estopped to deny that the services were rendered at his request.[42] But the master or principal is bound to pay only when it is his duty to pay, and whether it is his duty or not is a question for the determination of the court and jury.[43] A contract of this character, whether express or implied, must be based upon a sufficient consideration. Thus, where one person agrees to build or repair a house for another by a certain time, nothing being stated as to the consideration, and he fails to do it, he can not be made responsible in damages.[44] In the case just cited it was said by Lord Kenyon: "No consideration results from his [the contractor's] situation as a carpenter, nor from the undertaking is he bound to perform all the work that is tendered to him, and therefore the amount of this is that the defendant has merely told a falsehood, and has not performed his promise; but for his non-performance of it no action can be supported." But if in that or a similar case the contractor had built the house unskillfully, an action would lie against him; for when once he enters upon the performance of his employment, he must perform in the manner proposed.[45]

§ **64. Voluntary and gratuitous services—Presumption of gratuity—Members of same family.**—Where there is an express appointment, and the consideration is stipulated in the agreement, there can

[39] Scott v. Maier, 56 Mich. 554.

[40] Thorne v. Deas, 4 Johns. (N. Y.) 84; Passano v. Acosta, 4 La. Ann. 28, 23 Am. Dec. 470.

[41] Spencer v. Towles, 18 Mich. 9.

[42] Trustees of Farmington Academy v. Allen, 14 Mass. 172; Guild v. Guild, 15 Pick. (Mass.) 129.

[43] Goddard v. Foster, 17 Wall. (U. S.) 123.

[44] Elsee v. Gatward, 5 T. R. 143.

[45] Thorne v. Deas, 4 Johns. (N. Y.) 84. See also, Salem Bank v. Gloucester Bank, 17 Mass. 1.

be no difficulty in determining what the sum is to be, or whether there is in fact a consideration at all upon which the appointment is founded. And when the circumstances of the appointment are such in themselves as to raise a presumption of a promise to pay for the services, the appointment can not be said to be without consideration, but the same will be inferred from such circumstances. This is the case of a *quasi*-contract. The mere fact, however, that services have been rendered by the agent for the principal will not of itself raise a presumption that compensation is to be paid for the same. As was well said in the case of *Chadwick* v. *Knox*:[46] "It is settled that no man can do another an unsolicited kindness, and make it a matter of claim against him; and it makes no difference whether the act was done from mere good will or in the expectation of compensation. Unless the party benefited has done some act from which his assent to pay for the services may be fairly inferred, he is not bound to pay." And "if a man humanely bestows his labor and even risks his life, in voluntarily aiding to preserve his neighbor's house from destruction by fire, the law considers the services rendered as gratuitous, and it therefore forms no ground of action."[47] Of course, the fact that the agent or employe is not entitled to recover compensation in an action by him against the principal may not always be conclusive evidence that the agency was gratuitous in the sense of being without consideration, and void. But as a general rule this fact will be a criterion, and the agency will be considered gratuitous in such cases; so that the principal can not insist upon a performance unless the circumstances indicate a different intention. There are some cases, indeed, in which it is held that there must be an express promise to pay a compensation before it will be presumed that any was intended; as, in dealings between relatives or members of the same family. These are cases in which it is held that the law presumes that the performance of the service was prompted by motives of affection, or other considerations than those of a pecuniary nature; and to rebut this presumption there must be some clear proof of an express promise or agreement to pay for the service rendered.[48] Only enough need be proved, however,

[46] 31 N. H. 226, 64 Am. Dec. 329.

[47] Bartholomew v. Jackson, 20 Johns. (N. Y.) 28, 17 Am. Dec. 237. See also, Seals v. Edmondson, 73 Ala. 295, 49 Am. Rep. 51; Tascott v. Grace, 12 Ill. App. 639; Lange v. Kaiser, 34 Mich. 317; Doane v. Badger, 12 Mass. 65; Keegan v. Malone, 62 Iowa 208; Hall v. Finch, 29 Wis. 278, 1 Am. Rep. 559.

[48] Murdock v. Murdock, 7 Cal. 511; Friermuth v. Friermuth, 46 Cal. 42; Keegan v. Malone, 62 Iowa 208; Brown's Appeal, 112 Pa. St. 18; Morris v. Barnes, 35 Mo. 412; Price v. Jones, 105 Ind. 543.

to show that there was to be compensation, and that the services were not to be gratuitous or without other compensation than that which a member of the family usually received; as, board, clothing, schooling, etc. And so, where there was a promise that if a young girl would live with and render service for a childless couple, they would make her their heir, and, at their death or the death of the survivor, would will her their entire estate, and the girl, in pursuance of such arrangement, carried out her part of the agreement,—although no action would lie for damages for the breach of such contract, it would nevertheless be sufficient to rebut the presumption that the services were to be gratuitously performed; and it was held that she was entitled to recover the value of her services, even though the contract itself could not be literally performed.[49] According to these latter authorities, therefore, an express promise need not be proved to rebut the presumptions of gratuity: such promise may be inferred from the circumstances.

§ 65. **The legality of the subject-matter of the agency—Contracts in violation of positive law—In violation of public policy—What contracts are illegal.**—As pointed out in a previous chapter, the agency must be for a lawful purpose. In this respect a contract of agency stands upon the same footing as a contract for any other purpose. All contracts based upon an illegal consideration, or having for their object the accomplishment of some illegal purpose, are void and can not be enforced. A contract may be illegal because: (1) it is in violation of some positive law; (2) it is contrary to public morals; or (3) it is in violation of public policy. A contract of the first class, as applied to the doctrine of agency, would be where a person employs an agent or servant to commit an assault and battery, or a theft, robbery, arson or other offense; and it is immaterial whether it be *malum prohibitum* or *malum in se*.[50] It is not essential, however, that some public statute be violated or that there should be an

[49] Taggart v. Tevanny, 1 Ind. App. 339; Wallace v. Long, 105 Ind. 522; Jessup v. Jessup, 17 Ind. App. 177; Wood Master and Serv., § 72.

[50] See Gibbs v. Consolidated Gas Co., 130 U. S. 396; Gardner v. Tatum, 81 Cal. 370; Cooper v. Griffin, 13 Ind. App. 212; Clay v. Clay's Heirs, 35 Tex. 509; Puckett v. Alexander, 102 N. C. 95; Holt v. Green, 73 Pa. St. 198, 13 Am. Rep. 737; Friend v. Porter, 50 Mo. App. 89; Penn v. Bornman, 102 Ill. 523; Ingersoll v. Randall, 14 Minn. 400; Seneca Co. Bank v. Lamb, 26 Barb. (N. Y.) 595; Lindsey v. Rottaken, 32 Ark. 619; Snoddy v. Bank, 88 Tenn. 573; Reynolds v. Nichols, 12 Iowa 398; Steele v. Curle, 4 Dana (Ky.) 381; Bensley v. Bignold, 5 B. & Ald. 335, 7 E. C. L. 121; Watts v. Brooks, 3 Ves. Jr. 612.

indictable offense, in order to render such contract void. It would be sufficient if the employment contemplated the perpetration of an act amounting to a civil injury or the commission of a fraud upon some third person, or some act of corruption having an evil tendency.[51] Cases of the character last mentioned, however, would fall more appropriately within the third class above enumerated, as being contrary to public policy. Indeed, it may be truly said that all such contracts, in whatever class we may place them, whether they be in violation of public law, or contrary to public morality, or whether by reason of their natural evil tendency in general they be injurious to the public welfare, are condemned by the courts as being "against public policy;" although it is true that some courts have not hesitated to disapprove, as being "judicial legislation," the authority assumed by judicial tribunals to declare any contract illegal for reasons of public policy, unless it is in plain violation of some positive law.[52] But the great weight of authority, in this country at least, is to the effect that when the upholding of such contracts would undoubtedly tend to result in public injury they will be held illegal and void.[53] If, however, the contract has the positive approval of the legislature by some statutory enactment not unconstitutional, the courts can not declare it illegal as being against public policy; for the policy of the government may be declared in such instances by its legislative branch, and the judicial branch has no power then to interfere with it.[54]

[51] Ray v. Mackin, 100 Ill. 246; Bennett v. Tiernay, 78 Ky. 580; Knight v. Linzey, 80 Mich. 396; Adams v. Outhouse, 45 N. Y. 318; Piatt v. St. Clair, 6 Ohio 227; Buchtella v. Stepanek, 53 Kan. 373; Moody v. Newmark, 121 Cal. 446; Marcy v. Crawford, 16 Conn. 549; Gray v. McReynolds, 65 Iowa 461; St. Mary's Benev. Ass'n v. Lynch, 64 N. H. 213; Harrington v. Victoria Graving Dock Co., L. R. 3 Q. B. Div. 549. Although the act or contract is not declared void in terms, yet where a penalty is prescribed for doing it, this is sufficient to render it illegal: Milton v. Haden, 32 Ala. 30; Wheeler v. Russell, 17 Mass. 258.

[52] Richardson v. Mellish, 2 Bing. 229, 9 E. C. L. 391.

[53] Boardman v. Thompson, 25 Iowa 487; Stanton v. Allen, 5 Den. (N. Y.) 434, 49 Am. Dec. 282; McNamara v. Gargett, 68 Mich. 454; Elkhart County Lodge v. Crary, 98 Ind. 238; Stropes v. Board of Com'rs, 72 Ind. 42; Brown v. First Nat'l Bank, 137 Ind. 655; Teal v. Walker, 100 U. S. 242; Atcheson v. Mallon, 43 N. Y. 147; Richardson v. Crandall, 48 N. Y. 348; Davis v. Commonwealth, 164 Mass. 241; Curran v. Galen, 152 N. Y. 33; Edwards v. Randle, 63 Ark. 318; Richardson v. Scott's Bluff County, 59 Neb. 400.

[54] U. S. v. Trans-Missouri Freight Ass'n, 106 U. S. 290; Davis v. Commonwealth, 164 Mass. 241; Enders v. Enders, 164 Pa. St. 266; Lyman v. Townsend, 24 La. Ann. 625.

§ 66. **The effect of illegality upon the contract—When money illegally paid may be recovered.**—Whether a particular contract is in violation of public policy or not is always a question of law for the decision of the court, if the facts are undisputed.[55] If the contract belongs to a class prohibited by law, as being in violation of public policy, the courts will not hesitate to declare it illegal, because in the particular instance no actual harm or injury would result if the law were upheld. In such cases it is the evil tendency rather than the actual result that forms the test.[56] If, however, the act to be performed is capable of being done in a lawful manner, the fact that one of the parties to the contract violated the law in its performance will not of necessity render the contract illegal, but the breach of the law may be made the subject of an action.[57] If the act or acts to be performed are of a character necessarily involving turpitude, the contract of appointment can not become the basis for a suit by one of the contracting parties against the other.[58] If, in the case of a contract of agency, the agent is apprized of the turpitude of the purpose, as when the act is on its face immoral or unlawful, he can not recover compensation or otherwise enforce the contract against the principal. If, however, the act is on its face not unlawful, and the turpitude depends upon extrinsic facts of which the agent is ignorant, he can not be charged with the turpitude, and as to him the purpose of the agency can not be said to be illegal.[59] "And this doctrine not only applies to suits founded upon matters of account or receipts of money or non-fulfillment of contracts by the agent in

[55] Smith v. DuBose, 78 Ga. 413, 6 Am. St. 260; Tallis v. Tallis, 72 E. C. L. 391.

[56] Brown v. First Nat'l Bank, 137 Ind. 655; Elkhart County Lodge v. Crary, 98 Ind. 238, 49 Am. Rep. 746; Richardson v. Crandall, 48 N. Y. 348; Drexler v. Tyrrell, 15 Nev. 114; Clippinger v. Hepbaugh, 5 W. & S. (Pa.) 315, 40 Am. Dec. 519; Mills v. Mills, 40 N. Y. 543; Fireman's Charitable Ass'n v. Berghaus, 13 La. Ann. 209; Richardson v. Scott's Bluff County, 59 Neb. 400.

[57] Pape v. Wright, 116 Ind. 502; Jones v. Davidson, 2 Sneed (Tenn.) 447; McDearmott v. Sedgewick, 140 Mo. 172.

[58] Thus, a woman can not recover for services performed for a man with whom she lived as his mistress: Walraven v. Jones, 1 Houst. (Del.) 355; McDonald v. Fleming, 12 B. Mon. (Ky.) 285. But the woman may nevertheless recover, in such case, for work and labor done for the man under an express contract: Rhodes v. Stone, 63 Hun (N. Y.) 624, 17 N. Y. Supp. 561. And past illicit cohabitation may form a valid consideration for a deed where the grantee is in possession under the deed: Bivins v. Jarnigan, 50 Tenn. 282.

[59] Wharton Ag., §§ 25, 26.

the course of such illegal transactions or flowing therefrom, but it applies equally to the recovery back of the property which has been intrusted to him when it has been actually employed in such illegal, fraudulent or immoral purposes. Thus, if goods are intrusted to an agent to be smuggled into a country, and sold there against its laws, the principal will be equally disabled to maintain a suit against the agent in the courts of that country, for the goods themselves, as he will be to maintain a suit for the proceeds of the goods if sold. The rule in all such cases is, '*Melior est conditio possidentis.*' "[60] Not only is the appointment for such illegal purposes void, but the act itself when performed, being illegal, can not form the basis for an action thereon. In such cases the law does not so much consider the individual interests of the parties concerned as the effect which such transaction would have upon the public. It leaves the parties in the exact position in which they have placed themselves, and the courts will not lend their aid to extricate them from the situation in which they have thus been placed by their own conduct. Thus, it was said by Devens, J., in a Massachusetts case: "No one can be permitted to found rights upon his wrong, even against another also wrong. A promise made to one in consideration of doing an unlawful act, as to commit an assault or to practice a fraud upon a third person, is void in law; and the law will not only avoid contracts the avowed purpose or express object of which is to do an unlawful act, but those made with a view to place, or the necessary effect of which is to place, a person under wrong influences, and offer him a temptation which may injuriously affect the rights of third persons. Nor is it necessary to show that injury to a third person has actually resulted from such contracts, for in many cases where it had occurred it would be impossible to be proved. The contract is avoided on account of its necessarily injurious tendency."[61] And in a somewhat noted English case the court of common pleas, by Chief Justice Wilmot, decided that a contract by which it is attempted to delegate illegal authority is void by the common law; and the reason why the common law says such contracts are void is for the public good. "You shall not stipulate for iniquity. All writers upon our law agree in this:—no polluted hand shall touch the pure fountains of justice. Whoever is a party to an unlawful contract, if he hath once paid the money stipulated to be paid in pursuance thereof, he shall not have

[60] Story Ag., § 235.

[61] Rice v. Wood, 113 Mass. 133, 18 Am. Rep. 459.

the help of a court to fetch it back again. You shall not have a right of action when you come into a court of justice in this unclean manner to recover it back."[62]

§ 67. **Immoral contracts not enforced on either side.**—If a contract be immoral or illegal, as between the parties to it, at least, it is void and can not be enforced. While it seems inconsistent with honesty and fair dealing to permit a defendant to set up his own wrong, it is now generally allowed in such cases for defendant to plead the illegality. The law does not come to the defendant's relief for his sake, but for the sake of public justice and sound policy, the principle of which is that no court will lend its aid to a man who founds his course of acting upon an immoral or illegal act. If the parties were to change sides the result would be the same. The courts will not assist either of them.[63]

§ 68. **Dealings in "futures," "margins," etc.—Wagering contracts—Agent in pari delicto can not be compelled to account.**—It is well settled by the authorities that a contract for the sale of goods to be delivered in the future is valid, although the seller has not the goods at the time of such contract and has to go into the market to procure them, provided it is the *bona fide* intention of the parties that the goods be actually delivered and paid for. But if such contract be made with a view of speculating in the rise and fall of prices, and there is no intention to deliver the goods, but one party is to pay the other the difference between the contract price and the market price of the goods at the date fixed for executing the contract, the whole transaction is nothing more than a wager, and is null and void.[64] Such a contract being void on the ground of public policy, it follows that an agency created for the purpose of dealing in such "futures,"—as, the purchase and sale of "margins," that is, speculating in the rise and fall of such articles as grain without any intention of an actual delivery of the goods,—is likewise void. Hence, a broker who is privy to the unlawful design of the parties as to the nature of the transaction is *particeps criminis*, especially if he brings them together for the very purpose of entering into such an illegal agreement, and can not recover for his services. But unless it be shown that the broker had knowledge of such unlawful design on the part of the principal

[62] Collins v. Blantern, 2 Wils. 341, 1 Smith Ld. Cas. (9th ed.) 646.

[63] Evans Pr. & Ag. (Bedford's ed.) 77, 78.

[64] Benjamin Sales, §§ 541, 542, and notes to 7th Am. ed., by Bennett; Irwin v. Williar, 110 U. S. 499.

at the time of the negotiations, he may recover his compensation; as, for money advanced by one of the parties at his request. In such a case, the suit not being on the illegal contract itself, the parties are not in the same position as they would be if the suit were on such contract.[65] As a general rule, all wagering contracts are held void by the courts of this country, even at common law, though in England they are not considered illegal.[66] Such contracts as have for their object the purchase and sale of "margins" or "options" are gambling contracts, and can not be enforced in law, nor can damages be recovered for their breach; and no action will lie by an agent to recover for his services if he was a party to the transaction or had knowledge of the unlawful design of such contract.[67] The application of the rule to the law of agency is well recognized. If I employ an agent to assist me in gambling transactions, such as speculating in "futures," and the agent succeeds in making profits out of the transaction, which, if realized in a legitimate enterprise, would belong to me, and for which the agent would then be legally bound to account to me,—if the agent is tainted with the vice of the transaction from the beginning, standing with me *in pari delicto,* and doing the business in his own name, the whole transaction is illegal; and I can not compel the agent to render an account to me of my share of the business any more than he could force me to account to him for commissions or other compensation,—to which he might be entitled were the transaction legitimate. Nor would the courts in such cases compel the agent to perform the unlawful act or acts forming the subject-matter of the agency, or mulct him in damages, any more than they would hold the principal liable in damages for a breach of the contract of agency. In such cases the party sued always has

[65] Roundtree v. Smith, 108 U. S. 269.

[66] Thacker v. Hardy, L. R. 4 Q. B. D. 685. But, even in that country, such contracts have been declared illegal by the statutes of 8 and 9 Vict., ch. 109, § 18.

[67] See Barnard v. Backhaus, 52 Wis. 593; Gregory v. Wendell, 39 Mich. 337; Stewart v. Schall, 65 Md. 299, 57 Am. Rep. 327; Bigelow v. Benedict, 70 N. Y. 202; Whitesides v. Hunt, 97 Ind. 191, 49 Am. Rep. 441; Wolcott v. Heath, 78 Ill. 433; Rumsey v. Berry, 65 Me. 570; Yerkes v. Saloman, 11 Hun (N. Y.) 471; Sampson v. Shaw, 101 Mass. 145; Kirkpatrick v. Bonsall, 72 Pa. St. 155; Flagg v. Baldwin, 38 N. J. Eq. 219, 48 Am. Rep. 308; Plank v. Jackson, 128 Ind. 424; Bishop v. Palmer, 146 Mass. 469; Gibbs v. Consolidated Gas Co., 130 U. S. 396; Embrey v. Jemison, 131 U. S. 336; Sondheim v. Gilbert, 117 Ind. 71; Davis v. Davis, 119 Ind. 511; State v. Tumey, 81 Ind. 559.

the advantage; for the machinery of the law will never be set in motion to redress an alleged wrong based upon so rotten a foundation. The law does not regard one of the parties as being in any better situation than the other, and it will only look to the good of the public.[68] In such cases there is really no agency in contemplation of law, as there can be no such thing as an agency in the perpetration of crimes or unlawful acts, all persons engaged therein being regarded as principals.[69]

§ 69. **When agent must account.**—It is not to be understood, however, that the agent may in all cases involving wagering transactions shield himself from responsibility to the principal for the proceeds or profits received by him, on account of the illegality of the contract out of which said profits or proceeds were derived. Thus, if two parties should enter into a wagering contract, and one of the parties should pay the wager to his agent to be delivered to the other party to such wagering contract, the party for whose benefit the agent received the money could recover from the agent in an action against him. Or, if there has been an honest endeavor to comply with the law, but by mere unintentional omission, and without moral turpitude, the transaction is rendered illegal, and as a result of the transaction money belonging to the principal comes into the hands of the agent, the former may recover it; because to require the agent to account for the money would not in such a case be sanctioning the original illegal transaction, and it would be unconscionable to allow the agent to retain that which does not belong to him.[70]

§ 70. **Lobbying contracts—Corrupt acts of public officers.**—In line with the principles stated in the preceding observations are the declarations of legislatures and courts against the validity of what is known as "lobbying contracts." An agent employed for the purpose of procuring the passage or defeat of legislative enactments by means recognized as being opposed to public policy can not collect compensation for such services; nor can an action be maintained against him for failure to perform such contract.[70a] The same is true of contracts to procure the performance or omission of an act on the part of a public officer. If procured either by the use of corrupt means, or by the exercise of personal influence or persuasion, the contract is condemned by the law. The means by which the result is

[68] Nave v. Wilson, 12 Ind. App. 38; Embrey v. Jemison, 131 U. S. 336.

[69] Pearce v. Foote, 113 Ill. 228.

[70] Nave v. Wilson, 12 Ind. App. 38.

[70a] Richardson v. Scott's Bluff County, 59 Neb. 400.

obtained may in themselves be harmless or void of direct evil; it is sufficient if the employment tends to corruption and is therefore contrary to public policy. The public good requires that even appearances of evil shall be avoided in the public service. Of course, if corrupt or fraudulent methods are employed, and the agent's compensation is contingent upon the success of the enterprise for which he is employed, the evil is so much more flagrant, and the law is that much more emphatic in its condemnation. Within this class of prohibitions fall the awarding of public contracts, such as contracts for the erection of buildings, bridges or other structures of a public nature, to particular individuals; contracts for the location of public offices, such as postoffices, railroad depots, etc.[71]

§ 71. **Contracts rendered void by federal statutes.**—The act of congress of 1853, ch. 81, "to prevent frauds upon the treasury of the United States," annuls all champertous contracts with agents of private claims; it forbids all officers of the United States to be engaged as agents or attorneys for prosecuting claims against the government, and prohibits them from receiving any gratuity or interest in them in consideration of having aided or assisted in the prosecution of them, under penalty of fine and imprisonment in the penitentiary; it forbids members of congress, under like penalty, to act as agents for any claim in consideration of pay or compensation, or to accept any gratuity for the same; it subjects any person who shall attempt to bribe a member of congress to punishment in the penitentiary, and the party accepting the bribe to the forfeiture of his office. The federal supreme court, in commenting upon this act, and in discussing the practice thereby sought to be prohibited, speaking through Mr. Justice Grier, says: "If severity of legislation be any evidence of the practice of the offenses prohibited, it must be the duty of courts to take a firm stand, and discountenance, as against the policy of the law, any and every contract which may tend to introduce

[71] See further, as to the invalidity of "lobbying contracts," Mills v. Mills, 40 N. Y. 543; Clippinger v. Hepbaugh, 5 W. & S. (Pa.) 315; Powers v. Skinner, 34 Vt. 274; Carleton v. Whitcher, 5 N. H. 196; Nichols v. Mudgett, 32 Vt. 546; Haas v. Fenlon, 8 Kan. 601; Martin v. Wade, 37 Cal. 168; Fuller v. Dame, 18 Pick. (Mass.) 472; 1 Story Eq. Jur., § 293; Goodrich v. Tenney, 144 Ill. 422, 36 Am. St. 459; Milbank v. Jones, 127 N. Y. 370, 24 Am. St. 454; Spaulding v. Ewing, 149 Pa. St. 375, 34 Am. St. 608; Houlton v. Nichol, 93 Wis. 393, 37 Am. St. 928.

the offenses prohibited."[72] And in the same opinion it is further said: "Legislators should act from high considerations of public duty. Public policy and sound morality do therefore imperatively require that courts should put the stamp of their disapprobation on every act, and pronounce void every contract, the ultimate or probable tendency of which should be to sully the purity or mislead the judgments of those to whom the high trust of legislation is confided." In the same case the court calls attention to the fact that American courts have steadfastly condemned such contracts by refusing to give relief to the party or parties seeking to profit by them, or to enforce their provisions. "The sum of these cases is," says the learned judge: "1. That all contracts for a contingent compensation for obtaining legislation, or to use personal or any secret or sinister influence on legislators, are void by the policy of the law. 2. Secrecy, as to the character under which the agent or solicitor acts, tends to deception, and is immoral and fraudulent; and where the agent contracts to use secret influences, or voluntarily, without contract with his principal, uses such means, he can not have the assistance of a court to recover compensation. 3. That which, in the technical vocabulary of politicians, is termed 'log-rolling,' is a misdemeanor at common law, punishable by indictment." And in another case, Mr. Justice Swayne, in delivering the judgment of the court, says: "The prohibition of the law rests upon a solid foundation. A private bill is apt to attract little attention. It involves no great public interest, and usually fails to excite much discussion. Not infrequently the facts are whispered to those whose duty it is to investigate, vouched for by them, and the passage of the measure is thus secured. If the agent is truthful, and conceals nothing, all is well. If he uses nefarious means with success, the springhead and the stream of legislation are polluted. To legalize the traffic of such service would open the door at which fraud and falsehood would not fail to enter and make themselves felt at every point. It would invite their presence and offer them a premium. If the tempted agent be corrupt himself, and be disposed to corrupt others, the transition requires but a single step. He has the means in his hands, with every facility and a strong incentive to use them. The widespread suspicion which prevails, and charges openly made and hardly denied, lead to the conclusion that such events are not of rare occurrence. Where the avarice of the agent is inflamed by the hope of a reward

[72] Marshall v. Baltimore, etc., R. Co., 16 How. (U. S.) 314.

contingent upon success, and to be graduated by a percentage upon the amount appropriated, the danger of tampering in its worst form is greatly increased. It is by reason of these things that the law is as it is upon the subject. It will not allow either party to be led into temptation where the thing to be guarded against is so deleterious to private morals and so injurious to the public welfare. In expressing these views we follow the lead of reason and authority."[73]

§ 72. Actual fraud need not be shown—Evil tendency sufficient.— Actual fraud or corruption in procuring the enactment of a law or the performance of a deed by an officer need not be proved in order to invalidate the contract of agency in such a case. It is not even necessary to show that evil was done by the performance of the contract. It is sufficient if it tends to the injury of the public. The courts will not inquire into the motives of those engaged in the transaction. If the contract is contrary to public policy, it can not be enforced in a court of justice. "The law looks to the general tendency of such agreements, and it closes the door to the temptation by refusing them recognition in any of the courts of the country."[74] In a case decided by the supreme court of Indiana, some persons who were the owners of real estate adjacent to a building suitable for a postoffice entered into a combination for the purpose of securing the location of the postoffice in such building, so as to enhance the value of their own properties; and as part of the plan the parties undertook that certain individuals of their number should use their influence with the government officials to effect the purpose of the combination, for which services they were to receive pay in the event of success. The office was located as desired and the parties to whom compensation had been promised, upon failure of the others to pay the same as agreed, brought suit. The trial court decided against the validity of the claim on the ground that such contracts are contrary to public policy. Elliott, C. J., in the course of the opinion affirming the judgment, said: "Where the general public has an interest in the location of an office, a railroad station, or the like, a contract to secure its location at a particular place is held to be against public policy and not enforceable. There are many cases holding that an agreement to locate a railroad station at a designated

[73] Trist v. Child, 21 Wall. (U. S.) 441.

[74] Providence Tool Co. v. Norris, 2 Wall. (U. S.) 45. See also, Clippinger v. Hepbaugh, 5 W. & S. (Pa.) 315; Mills v. Mills, 40 N. Y. 543; Fireman's Charitable Ass'n v. Berghaus, 13 La. Ann. 209.

place is not enforceable because against public policy.[75] The principle upon which these cases proceed is that the public good, and not private interests, should control in the location of railroad depots; and this principle certainly applies with full force to an office of a purely public character, such as a postoffice. We find in these railroad cases, and there are very many of them, a principle which supplies a rule governing such a case as the present. It is true that there is some difference in the views of the courts upon the question whether an agreement for the location of a depot is valid when it does not restrict the location to the place named, and no other, but upon the general principle there is entire harmony. * * * A wholesome rule of law is that the parties should not be permitted to make contracts which are likely to set private interest in opposition to public duty or to public welfare. * * * It is not necessary that actual fraud should be shown, for a contract which tends to the injury of the public service is void although the parties entered into it in good faith. The courts do not inquire into the motives of the parties in the particular case to ascertain whether they were corrupt or not, but stop when it is ascertained that the contract is one which is opposed to public policy. Nor is it necessary that an evil was in fact done by or through the contract. The purpose of the rule is to prevent persons from assuming a position where selfish motives may impel them to sacrifice the public good to private benefit."[76]

§ 73. **Contracts to procure office—To electioneer—To appoint to office.**—All contracts having in view the procurement of office in the public service by methods other than those approved by law are contrary to public policy and void, though they be not intrinsically immoral. Thus, if a candidate for a public office at an election should employ an agent to advocate his claims before the people and otherwise use his influence for him in obtaining the office, in consideration of a promise to share the salary or emoluments with such agent, the promise can not be enforced and no compensation can be

[75] Citing St. Louis, etc., R. Co. v. Mathers, 104 Ill. 257; Williamson v. Chicago, etc., R. Co., 53 Iowa 126, 39 Am. Rep. 206.

[76] Elkhart County Lodge v. Crary, 98 Ind. 238, 49 Am. Rep. 746. See further, on this point, Houlton v. Dunn, 60 Minn. 26; Foltz v. Cogswell, 86 Cal. 542; Burney v. Ludeling, 47 La. Ann. 73, 16 So. 507; Spalding v. Ewing, 149 Pa. St. 375, 15 L. R. A. 727; Bermudez Asphalt Paving Co. v. Critchfield, 62 Ill. App. 221; Fearnley v. De Mainville, 5 Colo. App. 441; Woodman v. Innes, 47 Kan. 26.

collected for the services thus rendered.[77] The same doctrine applies, of course, to an appointive office. All public appointments to office should be made upon considerations of the public interest solely; and all other considerations, involving the one of corrupt means, such as the payment of money or other improper means, are regarded as contrary to public policy, as holding out temptations to appoint persons who are unfit or improper.[78] In a case decided in New York,[79] one of the parties had agreed to withdraw his application for an office and aid the other in securing the appointment, in consideration of which the former was to allow the other one-half of the fees and emoluments of the office as long as he held it. The court said: "I think that this contract was void, because it stipulated that Hook should have a pecuniary compensation for withdrawing his application, by which he had probably driven off all competition and contributed to reduce the number of applicants to himself and Gray. I have no doubt it is void, because it is stipulated that Hook should have pecuniary compensation for aiding Gray to obtain the appointment. And I have no doubt that any agreement between two citizens by which one stipulated to pay the other a portion of the fees and emoluments of a public office which he is seeking, in consideration that the other will aid him in obtaining it, is against public policy and void."[80] And so is an agreement to pay another to work and canvass among the voters in order to secure a nomination or election to an office.[81] This is true also of an agreement by a candidate

[77] Gaston v. Drake, 14 Nev. 175, 33 Am. Rep. 548; Martin v. Wade, 37 Cal. 168.

[78] Robertson v. Robinson, 65 Ala. 610, 39 Am. Rep. 17; Blatchford v. Preston, 8 T. R. 89.

[79] Gray v. Hook, 4 Comst. (N. Y.) 449.

[80] See also, Liness v. Hesing, 44 Ill. 113, 92 Am. Dec. 153; Filson v. Himes, 5 Pa. St. 452, 47 Am. Dec. 422; Outon v. Rodes, 3 A. K. Marsh. (Ky.) 432, 13 Am. Dec. 193; Hager v. Catlin, 18 Hun (N. Y.) 448; Faurie v. Morin, 4 Mart. (La.) 39, 6 Am. Dec. 701; Keating v. Hyde, 23 Mo. App. 55; Foley v. Speir, 100 N. Y. 552; Woodworth v. Wilson, 11 La. Ann. 402; Glover v. Taylor, 38 La. Ann. 634. But there are many items of legitimate expense connected with a public election for which liability may be incurred by one who is a candidate for an office at such election. Thus, it has been held that a promise to compensate one for making speeches and advocating the election of the promisor to office is not void at common law: Murphy v. English, 64 How. Pr. (N. Y.) 362. And that compensation may be recovered for erecting and taking down a tent in which political meetings are held during a campaign: Hurley v. Van Wagner, 28 Barb. (N. Y.) 109.

[81] Keating v. Hyde, 23 Mo. App. 555; Jackson v. Walker, 5 Hill (N.

for office that he will appoint another as his deputy, if elected.[82] All such agreements are against public policy and void.

§ 74. **Contract with attorney to divide fees.**—Where one as the agent and confidential adviser of a business firm agrees with an attorney that, in consideration of a division of fees which the latter may receive of the firm, he, the confidential agent, will procure the discharge of another competent attorney and have him, the attorney who makes the agreement, appointed in his stead, and succeeds in having the old attorney discharged and the new one appointed, public policy forbids the recovery of any portion of such fees by such confidential agent and adviser.[83] An agency to secure a contract from the head of a department of the general government at Washington, in consideration that the agent should receive all the government should pay on such contract above a certain sum, was held to fall within the prohibition of the law.[84]

§ 75. **Claims against government—Contracts to locate buildings at certain points.**—A party has a right, however, to employ legal counsel to assist him in prosecuting claims against the government in any of its departments where the same may be pending; and an attorney or agent thus employed may recover his compensation for pro-

Y.) 27; Robertson v. Robinson, 65 Ala. 610, 39 Am. Rep. 17. In the case last cited the court had under consideration the validity of an agreement between two parties by which one promised the other that if he, the promisor, were elected to the office of tax assessor, he would appoint the other party his chief deputy at a salary of $2,500, to be paid from fees and perquisites of the office, etc. The court held the agreement void, saying: "No judicial tribunal, so far as we can discover, has ever given countenance to any such agreement; and if popular elections are to be kept free from the taint of selfishness and corruption—if public offices are to be dignified as public trusts, and the performance of official duty preserved from the contamination of unlawful and improper influences, all such agreements will be condemned." Indeed, it may be stated as the law that any promise for the appointment of his deputy, by an officer, at a future time, is void, though based on a sufficient consideration: Hager v. Catlin, 18 Hun (N. Y.) 448; Conner v. Canter, 15 Ind. App. 690.

[82] Stout v. Ennis, 28 Kan. 706; Robertson v. Robinson, 65 Ala. 610, 39 Am. Rep. 17; Groton v. Waldoborough, 11 Me. 306, 26 Am. Dec. 530.

[83] Byrd v. Hughes, 84 Ill. 174, 25 Am. Rep. 442.

[84] Providence Tool Co. v. Norris, 2 Wall. (U. S.) 45; Oscanyan v. Winchester Repeating Arms Co., 103 U. S. 261.

fessional services thus rendered for preparing the claim and presenting its merits before the proper officials, if the services be free from any taint of fraud, misrepresentation or unfairness.[85] And no good reason can be conceived of why the employment of an attorney would not be legitimate for the purpose of presenting to the members of a legislative body, or public officials having the measure in charge, the merits of a bill introduced for passage, or the advantages of the location of a building or office, if the agent who is employed for such purpose uses no improper means in making such presentation. If he gives the members or officers to understand the attitude in which he appears; if his compensation does not depend upon the success of the scheme; if he does not bring to bear any corrupt or other improper influences, but employs only open and honorable methods to convince their understandings,—the employment can not be said to violate public policy, and he can recover compensation for such services.[86] In the case of *Beal* v. *Polhemus*,[86a] the Michigan supreme court held that a note given in consideration that the payee would erect a building near the payer's place, to be occupied as a postoffice by a given date, is not void as opposed to public policy, it appearing that the payee used no improper or corrupt means or influence to secure the location. But an agreement very similar to the one upheld in this case was condemned by the Indiana supreme court as being against public policy.[87]

§ 76. Procuring pardons.—The employment of an attorney or agent to procure the pardon of a convict stands upon the same footing. If the means used before the governor or pardoning board are open

[85] Stanton v. Embrey, 93 U. S. 548.

[86] Keating v. Hyde, 23 Mo. App. 555; Oscanyan v. Winchester Repeating Arms Co., 103 U. S. 261. See also, Barber Asphalt Paving Co. v. Botsford, 56 Kan. 532; Russell v. Burton, 66 Barb. (N. Y.) 539; Winpenny v. French, 18 Ohio St. 469. But the rigor of the old doctrine on this subject has been somewhat modified by the more recent decisions, and in Lyon v. Mitchell, 36 N. Y. 235, 93 Am. Dec. 502, the doctrine of the case of Providence Tool Co. v. Norris was expressly disapproved. A distinction, too, is made between cases of interference with legislative action, appointment to office, or executive clemency, where personal and political influenees are brought to bear, on the one hand, and a case of the sale of property to the government, on the other, in which latter case the agent openly professes to be acting upon commercial principles.

[86a] 67 Mich. 130.

[87] Elkhart County Lodge v. Crary, 98 Ind. 238, 49 Am. Rep. 746.

and honest, and if the capacity in which the agent acts is disclosed to the executive or officers of the board, the employment can not be held illegal or in violation of public policy, and the agent may recover proper compensation.[88] "For the purpose of procuring such pardon, the person employed may present the case to the executive with such petitions, memorials, statements of facts and evidence as are suitable to satisfy the pardoning power of the propriety of the relief desired, and we think no censure to any person for his exertions in such a case if the measures adopted are consistent with the facts of the case and with the truth and honesty of all parties concerned, while any effort to obtain such a pardon by falsehood and misrepresentation, or by any species of fraudulent contrivance, or by prostituting the influences resulting from official station, or from personal relation to the pardoning power, is entirely forbidden by law."[89]

§ 77. **Immoral contracts.**—All contracts against public morality, that is to say, those of an immoral tendency or that are based upon an immoral consideration, are void. Hence, the employment of an agent for the purpose of selling or circulating literature of an indecent character is not enforceable, and the agent can not legally recover compensation.[90] Within this rule fall contracts for the procuring of illicit sexual intercourse.[91] The invalidity of such con-

[88] Chadwick v. Knox, 31 N. H. 226, 64 Am. Dec. 329; Thompson v. Wharton, 7 Bush (Ky.) 563, 3 Am. Rep. 306; Bremsen v. Engler, 49 N. Y. Super. Ct. 172; Moyer v. Cantieny, 41 Minn. 242; Timothy v. Wright, 8 Gray (Mass.) 522; Bird v. Meadows, 25 Ga. 251.

[89] Bell, J., in Chadwick v. Knox, *supra*. Where improper or corrupt. means are to be employed to secure the pardon, such as dishonest influences or the suppression of any facts as to the character in which the agent is to appear, etc., the agency is void; that is to say, the agreement can not be enforced on either side: Adams Express Co. v. Reno, 48 Mo. 264; Hatzfield v. Gulden, 7 Watts (Pa.) 152, 32 Am. Dec. 750; Haines v. Lewis, 54 Iowa 301, 37 Am. Rep. 202.

[90] Gale v. Leckie, 2 Stark. 96, 3 E. C. L. 337.

[91] Walker v. Gregory, 36 Ala. 180; Potter v. Gracie, 58 Ala. 303, 29 Am. Rep. 748; Walraven v. Jones, 1 Houst. (Del.) 355; McDonald v. Fleming, 12 B. Mon. (Ky.) 285; Winebrinner v. Weisiger, 3. T. B. Mon. (Ky.) 32; Vincent v. Moriarity, 52 N. Y. Supp. 519, 31 App. Div. (N. Y.) 484; Cusack v. White, 2 Mill (S. C.) 279, 12 Am. Dec. 669. The fact that the man contracts with a third person as trustee for the woman will not render such a contract valid: Benyon v. Nettlefold, 17 Sim. 51, 15 Jur. 209; Smyth v. Griffin, 14 L. J. Ch. 28. But the fact that a man and a woman live together illicitly will not prevent them from entering into contracts with each other which have no connec-

tracts is based upon their immoral tendency, and not upon the theory that illicit sexual intercourse is not a sufficient consideration.

§ 78. **Contracts hindering public justice—To procure false testimony.**—Any and all contracts tending to interfere with the course of public justice, without reference to the motives of the parties entering into such contracts, are inhibited.[92] And likewise, contracts to procure false testimony or to suppress legal evidence in any criminal or civil cause are illegal.[93] Agreements to procure testimony that is true have been upheld, however, and compensation for such services may be recovered in a proper case.[94]

tion with the unlawful intercourse: Winebrinner v. Weisiger, 3 T. B. Mon. (Ky.) 35. And while, as a general rule, there can be no recovery by the woman against the man, on an implied contract for household services or work and labor during the existence of the illicit cohabitation, yet an express contract to pay for such labor or services will be upheld, if the illicit relations do not form a part of the contract or constitute the consideration in whole or in part; but there must be proof of an express contract: Rhodes v. Stone, 17 N. Y. Supp. 561; Cooper v. Cooper, 147 Mass. 370. And it seems that where certain immoral practices are licensed by law, contracts made with reference thereto may be enforced: Baumeister v. Markham, 101 Ky. 122; Lyman v. Townsend, 24 La. Ann. 625; Chateau v. Singla, 114 Cal. 91, 55 Am. St. 63. And a sale of furniture on monthly payments evidenced by notes, the furniture to be used in a house of prostitution, and the title to remain in vendor till price was paid, was held void, and the notes not collectible, being based on an illegal consideration: Reed v. Brewer, 90 Tex. 144, 36 S. W. 99, 37 S. W. 418.

[92] Selz v. Unna, 6 Wall. (U. S.) 327; Brown v. First Nat'l Bank, 137 Ind. 655, 24 L. R. A. 206; Bates v. Cain, 70 Vt. 144; Goodrich v. Tenney, 144 Ill. 422, 36 Am. St. 459, 19 L. R. A. 371.

[93] Haines v. Lewis, 54 Iowa 301; Nicholson v. Wilson, 60 N. Y. 362; Valentine v. Stewart, 15 Cal. 387; Hoyt v. Macon, 2 Colo. 502; Cobb v. Cowdery, 40 Vt. 25; Goodrich v. Tenney, *supra;* Quirk v. Muller, 14 Mont. 467, 43 Am. St. 647; Lyon v. Hussey, 82 Hun (N. Y.) 15, 31 N. Y. Supp. 281. A contract whereby a justice of the peace, with whom a charge for larceny has been filed, agrees to secure the arrest of the thief and the return of the stolen property for a percentage thereof, is against public policy and void: Brown v. First Nat'l Bank, *supra.* And an agreement with an attorney for a certain fee in case he would secure the release from jail of a witness against his client in a criminal case, in order that such witness might be gotten away, discloses an illegal contract on which there can be no recovery: Crisup v. Grosslight, 79 Mich. 380.

[94] Cobb v. Cowdery, 40 Vt. 25; Quirk v. Muller, 14 Mont. 467, 43 Am. St. 647; Willington v. Kelly, 84 N. Y. 543.

§ 79. **Bribery of officers.**—Other contracts for the employment of agents besides those mentioned have been declared invalid by reason of their illegality; such as contracts for services in bribing or attempting to bribe or influence judicial or other officers and others against performing their duties under the law;[95] in influencing or attempting to influence the servants or agents of others in the discharge of their duties;[95a] contracts with agents to sell lottery tickets in violation of law;[95b] to carry on illegal trades, etc. In all such cases, however, the agent must have participated in the unlawful purpose from the beginning, as the contract will not be illegal unless the parties are *in pari delicto.*[96] If, however, the agent transacts the illegal business in his own name without disclosing the agency, and he receives the money in his own right, he can not be compelled to account for it to the principal, for the reason that the principal ought not to be permitted to show his title to the property through the illegal contract.[97]

§ 80. **Marriage brokage contracts.**—Marriage brokage contracts, or contracts with agents having for their purpose the procuring of a husband or a wife for the principal, though recognized as valid by the civil law, are regarded as illegal at common law, and absolutely void in equity.[98]

§ 81. **Defendant may plead illegality.**—As has been seen, the defendant may set up the defense of the illegality of the contract, and thus escape liability; and this is so not from any compassion of the law with one of the wrongdoers any more than the other, but from considerations of public welfare.[99]

[95] Willemin v. Bateson, 63 Mich. 309; Brown v. First Nat'l Bank, 137 Ind. 655; State v. Cross, 38 Kan. 696.

[95a] Morgan v. Ballard, 1 A. K. Marsh. (Ky.) 558.

[95b] Lanahan v. Pattison, 1 Flip. (U. S.) 410.

[96] Daniels v. Barney, 22 Ind. 207; Hovey v. Storer, 63 Me. 486; Willson v. Owen, 30 Mich. 474; Fairbanks v. Blackington, 9 Pick. (Mass.) 93.

[97] Floyd v. Patterson, 72 Tex. 202; Wooten v. Miller, 7 S. & M. (Miss.) 380.

[98] Bispham Eq. Jur., § 224; 1 Story Eq. Jur., § 262. When an agent with knowledge of the illegality of the transaction lays out money for his principal he can not compel the principal to reimburse him for such outlay: Bibb v. Allen, 149 U. S. 481; Leonard v. Poole, 114 N. Y. 371.

[99] See the following further authorities: Mutual Ben. Ass'n v. Hoyt, 46 Mich. 473; Beach v. Kezar, 1 N. H. 184; Hill v. Spear, 50 N. H. 253, 9 Am. Rep. 205; Jacobs v. Mitchell, 46 Ohio St. 601; Ohio Life, etc., Co. v. Merchants', etc., Co., 11 Humph. (Tenn.) 1, 53 Am. Dec. 742; Sprague v. Rooney, 104 Mo.

§ 82. **Defense of illegality can not be waived.**—It has been held that a party to an illegal contract can. not, at the time of entering into it or afterwards, waive the defense of illegality, as this would be, like the contract itself, an infringement of public policy. Nor will he be estopped to plead such illegality in any case.[100] Under this rule it is likewise held that the defendant need not plead the illegality specially, and that the court is in duty bound to take notice of it whenever it is made to appear by the evidence.[101] The courts also hold that oral evidence may be introduced to prove the illegality of the contract. This rule is not a violation of the doctrine that parol evidence is not admissible to vary or contradict a written contract, but it is founded upon the principle that an illegal contract being held void *ab initio,* it is the same as if no contract had ever been entered into.[102]

II. By Implication of Law.

§ 83. **Assent of principal generally required—Fiction of a quasi-contract.**—As a general rule, all contracts, to be valid and binding on the parties, must receive their assent in the manner required by

349; Eldorado County v. Davison, 30 Cal. 521; Hertz v. Wilder, 10 La. Ann. 199; Ellsworth v. Mitchell, 31 Me. 247; Worcester v. Eaton, 11 Mass. 368; Hanauer v. Doane, 12 Wall. (U. S.) 342; Collins v. Blantern, 2 Wils. C. P. 341; Lightfoot v. Tenant, 1 B. & P. 551; Holman v. Johnson, 1 Cowp. 341.

[100] Embrey v. Jemison, 131 U. S. 336; Dunham v. Presby, 120 Mass. 285; Cardoze v. Swift, 113 Mass. 250; Shenk v. Phelps, 6 Ill. App. 612; Brown v. First Nat'l Bank, 137 Ind. 655; Pullman's Palace Car Co. v. Central Transp. Co., 171 U. S. 138; Faircloth v. DeLeon, 81 Ga. 158; Oscanyan v. Winchester Repeating Arms Co., 103 U. S. 261; Tyler v. Larimore, 19 Mo. App. 445. In some of the states, however, the courts, perhaps by reason of statutory provisions, hold that the defense of illegality will not avail a party unless it be specially pleaded: Riech v. Bolch, 68 Iowa 526; McDermott v. Sedgwick, 140 Mo. 172; Collier v. Davis, 94 Ala. 456.

[101] Libby v. Downey, 5 Allen (Mass.) 299; Johnson v. Hulings, 103 Pa. St. 498; Wright v. Rindskopf, 43 Wis. 344; Scott v. Brown, L. R. (1892) 2 Q. B. 724; Oscanyan v. Winchester Repeating Arms Co., 103 U. S. 261; Schmidt v. Barker, 17 La. Ann. 261, 87 Am. Dec. 527; Prost v. More, 40 Cal. 347; Morrill v. Nightingale, 93 Cal. 452; Richardson v. Buhl, 77 Mich. 632; Fowler v. Scully, 72 Pa. St. 456; Keith v. Fountain, 3 Tex. Civ. App. 391.

[102] Martin v. Clarke, 8 R. I. 389; Bell v. Leggett, 7 N. Y. 176; Brown v. Brown, 34 Barb. (N. Y.) 533; Sprague v. Rooney, 82 Mo. 493, 52 Am. Rep. 383; Newsom v. Thighen, 30 Miss. 414; Murphy v. Trigg, 1 T. B. Mon. (Ky.) 73; First Nat'l Bank v. Oskaloosa Packing Co., 66 Iowa 41; Paxton v. Popham, 9 East 408; Cooper v. Southgate, 63 L. J. Q. B. 670.

law. Without such assent the act has no efficacy whatever.[102a] This doctrine is applicable to the law of agency; for it has been truly said that "it is a rule of law that no one can become the agent of another except by the will of the principal;"[103] to which might be added, that no one can become the principal of another except by the will of the agent. But while these propositions are true, as general rules, they are subject to some well-known qualifications. There are jural relations between parties in which they are held to certain liabilities and to have certain rights of a contractual nature without any express or even implied contract. The remedies afforded in these instances are the same as in cases of contracts, although in point of fact no agreement was ever entered into between the parties. Persons laboring under legal or natural disabilities, such as married women, infants and insane persons, may not be capable of making express contracts that will bind them, and yet it is but justice that their estates or those upon whom they are legally dependent should be responsible for those necessaries of life that are essential to their physical and moral welfare. In some instances, moral obligations exist between parties which public policy requires they should not be permitted to escape. In such cases, the law or equity has invented the fiction of a contract to secure remuneration to those who have, under proper circumstances, furnished them the articles necessary to supply their reasonable wants. These fictitious contracts are distinguished from ordinary contractual agreements by the name of contracts created by law, or *quasi*-contracts.[103a] The doctrine just stated applies with equal force to the law of agency, which, in its contractual aspects, is but a portion of the law of contracts. Agencies of this kind are spoken of and have come to be regarded as agencies arising by implication of law.

[102a] Great Western R. Co. v. Grand Trunk R. Co., 25 U. C. Q. B. 37; Barber v. Burrows, 51 Cal. 404; Girard v. St. Louis Car Wheel Co., 123 Mo. 358, 45 Am. St. 556.

[103] Evans Pr. & Ag. (Bedford's ed.) 30.

[103a] Keener *Quasi*-Conts., Ch. I. "The term 'contract implied in law,'" says that learned author, "is used, however, to denote, not the nature of the evidence by which the claim of the plaintiff is to be established, but the source of the obligation itself. It is a term used to cover a class of obligations where the law, though the defendant did not intend to assume an obligation, imposes an obligation upon him, notwithstanding the absence of intention on his part, and in many cases in spite of his actual dissent:" *Ibid.*, p. 5.

§ 84. **Wife's agency to purchase necessaries on husband's account.**—The best illustration of an agency of this character is the case of a wife purchasing necessaries for herself and children, in case the husband fails to supply them himself. If the goods are purchased by the wife on the husband's account by his consent, the agency will be of the class created by the agreement of the parties. But in the absence of such consent, and even in the face of his direct and positive opposition, the wife may successfully pledge his credit and render him liable for her necessaries. The theory upon which this liability is generally based by the courts is that of a compulsory agency, or agency by implication of law.[104] The liability is, however, sometimes based upon the broader ground of his marital obligations,[105] although the theory of a compulsory agency is the one generally accepted by the courts.

§ 85. **Medical and surgical assistance in cases of personal injuries.**—Another class of cases, to which the doctrine of agency by implication of law may be properly applied, is that of medical or surgical assistance in cases of injuries received in railroad accidents. If a servant or passenger of a railroad company sustain an injury in such an accident which requires immediate attention at the hands of a medical practitioner, and the general superintendent, or other highest official of the railroad there present, call a physician or surgeon to render necessary professional aid to the injured party, such medical attendant can, under this rule, recover the reasonable value of his services from the railroad company, although there be no evidence that such officer had any express authority to make such employment, it being conclusively presumed to be within the scope of his powers as such officer. While the courts generally adopt the view that those superior officers and agents of such a company who possess a general power of making contracts for it may bind the company by the employment of a physician or surgeon, it can not be assumed that the inferior officers of a railroad corporation are clothed with sufficient general authority to employ medical or surgical aid and bind the company. But there may be special cases of great emergency when the dictates of both justice and humanity will so extend the scope of the temporary power of an agent or servant in charge, though he occupy an inferior rank, as to authorize him to employ a physician or surgeon to care

[104] Benjamin v. Dockham, 134 Mass. 418; Johnston v. Sumner, 3 Hurl. & N. 261; Lane v. Ironmonger, 13 M. & W. 368; Eiler v. Crull, 99 Ind. 375; Watkins v. DeArmond, 89 Ind. 553.

[105] Keener *Quasi*-Conts. 22, 23.

for the servant injured in the employment of the company, or even a passenger who was injured while traveling on the company's train.[105a] Such a duty, however, can only arise with such an emergency, and will not continue after it has ended. The authority does not extend to a case of protracted illness or suffering, though incurred in the company's service or on its train, and the company could be rendered liable in such case only by a ratification of the employment. There must, however, be a request by some officer or agent of the company to perform the services, as there is no duty resting on the company to pay for such services when rendered without any authority from them whatever.[106] In the case of *Toledo, etc., R. Co.* v. *Rodrigues,* just cited, a brakeman in the employment of the road was run over and injured by a locomotive engine; and the station agent at the point where the injury occurred employed a nurse to care for the injured person, and assured him that the company would pay him for the services. The station agent informed the general superintendent of the road by letter, making a full statement of what had been done, although there was no evidence that the superintendent had ever received the letter. The superintendent subsequently, upon receiving the bill for the services, said he would pay the amount if the charges were reasonable, and made no objection at the time. It was insisted that these agents had no authority to bind the company, and that the latter was not bound, nor indeed authorized by the terms of its charter, to pay for such services. The court, however, held the company liable, saying: "If, from the necessary hazards of the employment, a person devoting his energies in promoting the interests of the company at a moderate compensation, without fault on his part, is severely injured, and for a length of time wholly disabled, humanity, if not strict justice, would say that when the company have employed others to take the care and incur the expense of his cure, they should be compelled to observe their contract, and meet the expense." And later on, the opinion says: "Whether the station agent had such power or not, the general superintendent was clothed, and necessarily must be, with large specific as well as discretionary powers. As his title implies, he has a general superintendence of the business affairs of the road, and we deem it but a reasonable inference to conclude

105a 1 Thompson Neg. (2d ed.), §§ 546-548.

106 1 Elliott Railroads, § 222; Toledo, etc., R. Co. v. Rodrigues, 47 Ill. 188. It seems that the doctrine here under consideration is applicable only to railroad corporations: Chaplin v. Freeland, 7 Ind. App. 676; New Pittsburgh Coal, etc., Co. v. Shaley, 25 Ind. App. 282.

that this was within the scope of these powers, and when exercised, that the company must be held liable. The company is governed, within the limits of its charter, by the adoption of rules and regulations for the purpose. These regulations govern the actions of its officers. By them they confer powers and impose duties on their various agents and officers, and by these means they exercise their franchises. These regulations are private and not accessible to the public, and hence the difficulty of other persons showing, except by inference or circumstantial evidence, that an officer performs any act within the scope of his authority. That fact must be left to proof as in other cases. And when it is known that the general superintendent arranges all the business of the road within his department, and binds the company by contracts on its behalf, in regard to its general business, it may be safely inferred that such a contract as this was within the scope of his authority." Although this case seems to place the liability of the company on the ground of actual authority presumed in the absence of proof to the contrary, other cases go still further and hold that the presumption of such agent's authority is conclusive.[107] The Indiana cases place the liability of the company on the emergency of the situation and the conclusive presumption of the employment of the surgeon by the highest officer in charge at the time of the accident on the authority of the company. It must be remembered, however, that the employment of a surgeon by a minor officer of the company is warranted only in cases of great emergency, and in such a case the highest officer present alone can act.[108] Even when there is not an emergency, and the employment of the surgeon is general, it is not *ultra vires* if made by the general officers of the company.[109]

[107] See Indianapolis, etc., R. Co. v. Morris, 67 Ill. 295; Terre Haute, etc., R. Co. v. Stockwell, 118 Ind. 98; Terre Haute, etc., R. Co. v. McMurray, 98 Ind. 358; Evansville, etc., R. Co. v. Freeland, 4 Ind. App. 207; Swazey v. Union Mfg. Co., 42 Conn. 556.

[108] Terre Haute, etc., R. Co. v. McMurray, 98 Ind. 358; Louisville, etc., R. Co. v. McVay, 98 Ind. 391; Terre Haute, etc., R. Co. v. Stockwell, 118 Ind. 98; Cincinnati, etc., R. Co. v. Davis, 126 Ind. 99, 9 L. R. A. 503; Louisville, etc., R. Co. v. Smith, 121 Ind. 353. The power of employing surgeons to attend their employes when injured by accident in the course of employment is inherent in corporations that carry on a hazardous business: 1 Thompson Corps., § 58; 1 Thompson Neg. (2d ed.), §§ 544-548.

[109] Bedford Belt R. Co. v. McDonald, 17 Ind. App. 492. It is generally held, however, that the doctrine of the power of employment of surgical aid, in an emergency, to at-

§ 86. The doctrine in England—Supreme court of Michigan divides evenly on doctrine.—The doctrine of the liability of a corporation in such cases for the services of a surgeon employed in an emergency by the superintendent of the company to attend an injured employe, whose injuries were received in the course of his employment, is upheld by the courts of England.[110] In Michigan the judges were evenly divided as to the soundness of the doctrine that an agent of even the highest rank may render a railroad corporation liable in an emergency for the services of a surgeon employed by such agent to attend an employe who sustained a severe injury in the service incident to such employment, Gray and Campbell, JJ., taking the

tend an injured employe of the corporation, is limited to railroad corporations, and does not apply to other corporations. Thus, it was held in Godshaw v. Struck (Ky.), 58 S. W. 781, 51 L. R. A. 668, that it does not apply to the employment of a physician or surgeon by the foreman of a building in process of erection to treat an employe who was injured by the falling of a brick from the building. Nor does it apply to a laundry business: Holmes v. McAllister, 123 Mich. 493, 48 L. R. A. 396. Nor to a factory: Chaplin v. Freeland, 7 Ind. App. 676. Nor to a milling plant: Swazey v. Union Mfg. Co., 42 Conn. 556. In the following recent cases the highest officer or representative of the railroad company present was held to have sufficient authority to employ a surgeon and bind the company in case of great emergency: Chicago, etc., R. Co. v. Davis, 98 Ill. App. 54; Arkansas, etc., R. Co. v. Loughridge, 65 Ark. 300, 45 S. W. 907; Toledo, etc., R. Co. v. Mylott, 6 Ind. App. 438; Toledo, etc., R. Co. v. Rodrigues, 47 Ill. 188; Ohio, etc., R. Co. v. Early, 141 Ind. 73; Terre Haute, etc., R. Co. v. Brown, 107 Ind. 336; Louisville, etc., R. Co. v. Smith, 121 Ind. 353. Contrary holding: Sevier v. Birmingham, etc., R. Co., 92 Ala. 258, 9 So. 405. See also, the elaborate note to Ohio, etc., R. Co. v. Early, 141 Ind. 73, in 28 L. R. A. 546. See also, Union Pacific R. Co. v. Beatty, 35 Kan. 265; Hanscom v. Minneapolis St. R. Co., 53 Minn. 119, 54 N. W. 944. It is the master's duty to procure medical assistance, at the ports where ship touches, for injured seamen: The Vigilant, 30 Fed. 288; Scarff v. Metcalf, 107 N. Y. 211. In Cairo, etc., R. Co. v. Mahoney, 82 Ill. 73, the Illinois supreme court decided that while a railroad company is not legally bound ordinarily to furnish medical attendance to its employes in case of injury, "yet where a day laborer has, by an unforeseen accident, been rendered helpless, when laboring to advance the property and success of the company, honesty and fair dealing would seem to demand that it should furnish medical assistance;" and slight evidence of ratification was held sufficient to bind the company.

[110] See Walker v. Great Western R. Co., L. R. 2 Exch. 228. A railroad company is not bound to furnish medical and surgical aid to a passenger injured through its fault: Cox v. Midland, etc., R. Co., 3 Exch. 268.

view that the power of the superintendent to make such employment must be proved, and Cooley, J., and Christiancy, C. J., holding that "it is within the general scope of the employment of a railroad superintendent to make such a contract" with a surgeon, "and that no evidence to prove a special authority is requisite."[111] In the Illinois case just cited, the station agent employed the surgeon and reported the case to the superintendent. The court said that "although a railway company is under no legal obligation to provide medical attendance for persons injured in its service, yet this would be so reasonable a thing to do, where the wounded employe is dependent upon his daily labor for support, that a jury will generally find, even upon somewhat slight evidence, that the act of the station agent in employing the surgical skill necessary to save human life was ratified by his superior."[112] It is believed that the weight of authority is in favor of the doctrine, although there is respectable authority against it.[113]

§ 87. **Master of ship—His implied authority.**—The master of a ship has much authority not expressly conferred upon him. This may, perhaps, be properly said to arise from custom long acquiesced in, but there are incidents in the course of his employment when he can act only in cases of the highest emergency. Thus he may, while in a foreign port, hypothecate the vessel for her necessaries or for the money with which to purchase such necessaries; and such authority thus arbitrarily assumed is said to be confirmed by necessity, and binds the owner. But if the goods or money can be otherwise obtained, as by consent of the owner, an agency by necessity will not be deemed to have been established.[114] The authority of the master is likewise extended, in cases of great emergency, to the cargo carried on his vessel, although he is ordinarily a mere stranger to such cargo. In "cases of instant and unforeseen emergency the character of agent and supercargo is forced upon him, not by the immediate act and appointment of the owner, but by the general policy of the law."[115] And so he may, in case of a jettison becoming necessary, order a por-

[111] Marquette, etc., R. Co. v. Taft, 28 Mich. 289. See also, Toledo, etc., R. Co. v. Prince, 50 Ill. 26.

[112] See also, Sloan v. Central Iowa R. Co., 62 Iowa 728; Fox v. Chicago, etc., R. Co., 86 Iowa 368; Atlantic, etc., R. Co. v. Reisner, 18 Kan. 458; Atchison, etc., R. Co. v. Reeeher, 24 Kan. 228.

[113] Tucker v. St. Louis, etc., R. Co., 54 Mo. 177; Sevier v. Birmingham, etc., R. Co., 92 Ala. 258.

[114] Story Ag., § 116.

[115] Story Ag., § 118.

tion or all of the cargo thrown overboard, he being the sole judge as to which of such goods will be selected for that purpose, and how many, in order to save the ship and the lives of the passengers and crew. He may also sacrifice a portion or all of the cargo for the ransom of the ship, and may even sell the ship and cargo, or hypothecate the same, for repairs, or to enable the ship to perform the voyage. If there is an abandonment of the ship or cargo to the underwriters for a total loss during the voyage, "the master becomes the agent of the underwriters by the operation of law, with the same general rights and authorities as he would have in regard to the owner."[116]

§ 88. **Father's liability for necessaries of children.**—Some of the American courts place the liability of a father for necessaries furnished his infant child of tender years upon the theory of agency by necessity or operation of law, as in the case of a husband's liability for necessaries of the wife.[117] Whether the liability in such cases rests upon the theory of an agency on the part of the child or upon the legal obligation of the parent to support the child seems not to have been clearly settled by the authorities, nor is it a matter of much consequence. In England and many of the American states, in the absence of any actual authority in the child to pledge the father's credit, or statutory obligation on the part of the parent, it is held that there can be no liability whatever.[118] In cases of extreme emergency, as where the father drives his infant children of tender age away from home, and they are cared for by another, the legal liability of the father seems to be clear, although in instances where there is no such emergency, according to some of the cases, the obligation may be a moral one.[119]

[116] Story Ag., § 188. See also, Gaither v. Myrick, 9 Md. 118; Pike v. Balch, 38 Me. 302; Butler v. Murray, 30 N. Y. 88.

[117] Watkins v. DeArmond, 89 Ind. 553; Gilley v. Gilley, 79 Me. 292; Cromwell v. Benjamin, 41 Barb. (N. Y.) 558; Porter v. Powell, 79 Iowa 151; Pidgin v. Cram, 8 N. H. 350; Allen v. Jacobi, 14 Ill. App. 277; 1 Parsons Conts. 306; Keener *Quasi*-Conts. 23. It is said to be a principle of natural law: 1 Blackstone Com. 447; 2 Kent Com. 189.

[118] Motimore v. Wright, 6 M. & W. 482; Kelley v. Davis, 49 N. H. 187; Carney v. Barrett, 4 Ore. 171; Freeman v. Robinson, 38 N. J. L. 383, 20 Am. Rep. 399. The authority, however, is often inferred from very slight circumstances: Jordan v. Wright, 45 Ark. 237.

[119] Watkins v. DeArmond, 89 Ind. 553; Freeman v. Robinson, 38 N. J. L. 383, 20 Am. Rep. 399; Pidgin v. Cram, 8 N. H. 350; Allen v. Jacobi, 14 Ill. App. 277.

§ 89. **Vendee of goods failing to receive them—Vendor's authority as agent to sell.**—Another instance of agency by implication of law is found in the case of one who has sold goods to another when the latter fails or refuses to receive and pay for them. In that event the vendor, if the title of the goods has passed to the purchaser, but the goods are in possession of the vendor by force of the relation between him and the purchaser, may act as the agent of the purchaser and sell the goods to satisfy, in whole or in part, the equitable lien which the law gives him for the purchase money. True, the seller in such case may retain the goods for the benefit of the purchaser and sue him for the entire purchase price, but he is not compelled to adopt this remedy. He may treat the property as that of the vendee and resell it as his agent, having first given him notice of his intention to do so. When he elects to resort to this latter remedy, he is entitled, as the purchaser's agent, to reimburse himself out of the proceeds of the resale to the extent of the price agreed upon between him and the original purchaser; and if on the resale the property does not bring enough to pay such original purchase price, he may recover the balance in an action for damages against the defaulting purchaser.[120] "Such resale," says Mr. Sutherland, "is made on the theory that the property is that of the vendee, retained by the vendor as a means of realizing the contract price; he acts as the agent of the vendee, and deducts from the proceeds all the expenses incurred."[121]

III. By Estoppel.

§ **89a. What is an estoppel.**—In discussing the subject of agency by implication of law, we found that the relation may sometimes be formed without the actual assent of the principal.[122] In addition to the instances there mentioned, such a relation will often be implied from the acts or conduct of the principal. This rule is founded on the well-known doctrine of estoppel. By force of this doctrine a person is precluded from asserting a fact which he has previously denied or from denying what he has previously admitted, either expressly or by implication, and whereby he has induced another, to his

[120] Dustan v. McAndrew, 44 N. Y. 72; Pittsburgh, etc., R. Co. v. Heck, 50 Ind. 303, 19 Am. Rep. 713; Ridgley v. Mooney, 16 Ind. App. 362; Benjamin Sales (Corbin's Amer. ed., 1889), § 1165, and note 3; Pollen v. LeRoy, 30 N. Y. 549; Westfall v. Peacock, 63 Barb. (N. Y.) 209; Young v. Mertens, 27 Md. 114; Bagley v. Findlay, 82 Ill. 524; 1 Sutherland Dam. (2d ed.), § 647.

[121] 1 Sutherland Dam., § 647.

[122] *Ante*, § 83.

prejudice, to believe and act or to rely upon the truthfulness of the matter that he now denies.[123]

§ 90. **Holding out as agent—Illustration.**—If one person hold another out as his agent, and thus induce a third person to deal with him as such, to the prejudice of such third person, the person holding him out as such agent should not, and will not, in justice and equity, be heard to say that there really was no agency. In other words, he is estopped to deny the existence of the agency, and that without reference to what may have been the fact as to whether there really was such an agency or not. The holding out may have been by express language, written or oral, admitting that there was such a relation; or by words unquestionably capable of such construction; or by acts and conduct calculated to induce a reasonable man to believe in the existence of such agency. "The rule of law is clear," says Lord Denman, "that where one, by his words or conduct, willfully causes another to believe the existence of a certain state of things, and induces him to act on that belief, so as to alter his previous position, the former is concluded from averring against the latter a different state of things as existing at the same time."[124] Doubtless the most convincing illustration of holding one out as an agent is where the assumed principal, by letter or other writing, introduces the bearer as his agent for a certain purpose, or informs a third party that such a relation exists. Such instances, however, are not numerous, for ordinarily a person who has gone thus far in admitting his principalship will not afterwards deem it probable that he may be able to overcome the presumption arising from such an admission. The holding out of the party as his agent is generally committed by the conduct of the supposed principal and not by his express admission.[125] And the liability of the party who thus holds another out as his agent is not based upon the theory of an intention to create an agency, but he is held liable without reference to the question of his intention. It must be shown, however, that the principal knew that the party was

[123] Bigelow Estoppel, Ch. XVII; Reynolds v. Collins, 78 Ala. 94; Burke v. Taylor, 94 Ala. 530; Hubbard v. Tenbrook, 124 Pa. St. 291, 10 Am. St. 585; Hoppe v. Saylor, 53 Mo. App. 4; Collins v. Cooper, 65 Tex. 460; Western Land Ass'n v. Banks, 80 Minn. 317.

[124] Pickard v. Sears, 6 Ad. & E. 469.

[125] Pittsburgh, etc., R. Co. v. Berryman, 11 Ind. App. 640; Gilbraith v. Lineberger, 69 N. C. 145; Story Ag., §§ 54, 55; Wharton Ag., §§ 40, 44.

undertaking to act in his behalf, and intended that he should so act.[126]

§ 91. Estoppel by silence—Third person's knowledge of want of authority of alleged agent—Illustrations of estoppel.—The mere silence of the assumed principal may in certain circumstances be sufficient to create an estoppel. It is the duty of a person who knows that another is acting for him as agent in any given transaction to notify the party with whom the supposed agent is dealing that he does not represent him; and if he fails to do this, when occasion demands it, he will be held liable as principal.[127] Thus, if I allow one, in my presence, to sell my property, as my agent, and raise no objection, the purchaser will receive a good title, and I will be estopped to deny the authority of the one who has sold it to represent me, for it was my duty to speak and not to stand by and suffer the innocent purchaser to be imposed upon.[128] But in such cases, if the third person had knowledge of the want of authority of the person acting as agent, and could not, therefore, have believed in the existence of the agency, or relied upon it, there will be no estoppel. The person who claims that he was imposed upon must himself have acted in good faith.[129] If one carries on a business in the name of another in order to avoid the payment of the debts of the real owner, the latter is estopped to deny the ownership of the former as against a third party, who deals with the person in possession in good faith. And the circumstance of allowing one's name to stand over the door of a shop, or permitting his name to be used on letter-heads, bill-heads, etc., may be considered in determining the question of whether the one in charge of the business transacted there is the agent of him who thus allows his name to be used, or is himself the principal.[130] Where the son of a grocer and saloon keeper was allowed by his father to order a lot of cigars and ale in the father's name, but which the son himself used, it was held that the father was estopped to deny that his son was his agent for the purpose.[131] An agency may sometimes be presumed from a single transaction.[132] But the law will not raise an inference from a special agency, involving but a single transaction,

[126] Bigelow Estoppel, 528–552, 555' 556, 573.

[127] Story Ag., §§ 89, 91; Bigelow Estoppel, 500–527.

[128] 1 Story Eq. Jur., §§ 385–395.

[129] Norton v. Richmond, 93 Ill. 367.

[130] Gilbraith v. Lineberger, 69 N. C. 145.

[131] Thurber v. Anderson, 88 Ill. 167.

[132] Story Ag., § 94.

that the agency extends to other transactions, occurring years afterwards.[133] The most numerous instances of estoppel, however, arise from a series of transactions, or "from the usual habits of dealing between the parties."[134] Thus, where a husband generally managed the business affairs of his wife, she living in the country and giving the matter no attention, while he was transacting business in the city where the real estate was located, and he had previously sold portions of her property with her consent, this was held sufficient evidence to warrant a conclusion that he was her agent for the purpose of employing a real estate broker who effected a sale of her property.[135] Where an insurance company had provided one with blanks and papers relating to the business, and approved his acts in giving permits of removal, and paid his rents, the company was held liable as his principal.[136] In all such cases, however, the principal is liable only for acts within the real or apparent scope of authority of the assumed agent. The party who deals with the agent may safely act upon appearances, but beyond that any confidence placed in him must be upon his own credit and at the peril of the third party. This is especially true if the act performed is in violation of the law, as there can be no presumption that authority was delegated for such purpose.[137] The doctrine of estoppel as applying to agency may, therefore, be summarized that where a party holds out another as his

[133] Malburn v. Schreiner, 49 Ill. 69; Reed v. Baggott, 5 Ill. App. 257.

[134] Story Ag., § 95; 2 Kent Com. (12th ed.) 613–615; Bryan v. Jackson, 4 Conn. 288; Smith v. White, 5 Dana (Ky.) 376; Weaver v. Ogletree, 39 Ga. 586; Anderson v. Supreme Council, 135 N. Y. 107; Doan v. Duncan, 17 Ill. 272.

[135] Barnett v. Gluting, 3 Ind. App. 415; Parker v. Freeman, 11 Colo. 576.

[136] Hardin v. Alexandria Ins. Co., 90 Va. 413. And that one is the agent or servant of a railroad or steamship company may be inferred from his dress as well as from the services performed by him: Hughes v. New York, etc., R. Co., 36 N. Y. Super. Ct. 222; Sevenson v. Atlantic Mail Steamship Co., 57 N. Y. 108; McCoun v. New York, etc., R. Co., 66 Barb. (N. Y.) 338. And where the principal allows the wife of an authorized agent to receive payment on its behalf, such principal is estopped to deny that she was authorized to receive such payments: Anderson v. Supreme Council, 135 N. Y. 107. And a father is bound by the acts of his son, as clerk, when he allows the latter to stand behind the counter in his (the father's) shop, and deal with the customers, such acts being binding on the father so long as they are in the line of his duty: Elsner v. State, 30 Tex. 524.

[137] Owings v. Hull, 7 Pet. (U. S.) 607; Empire State Nail Co. v. Faulkner, 55 Fed. 819.

agent, or has knowingly allowed such person to act for him in one or more similar transactions without objection, he will, as a general rule, be estopped to deny the agency, whether it in fact existed or not, if a third party, without knowing the real state of the matter, and acting in good faith, and as a reasonable man would act from the appearance of things as created by the supposed principal, relies upon the existence of the agency and deals with the supposed agent as such, if the transaction be within the real or apparent scope of the authority exercised.[138]

§ 92. **Third party must exercise prudence and care.**—It must not be forgotten, however, that the third party, in order to be entitled to the protection afforded by this rule, must exercise the care of an ordinarily prudent man, and hence must not rely too implicitly upon mere surface appearances. Where he is in a position to ascertain the exact truth and does not avail himself of the opportunity, he will not be protected.[139] Nor will the mere acceptance of the benefits of an unauthorized agency warrant the presumption of the continuation of the relation as to future transactions. Much depends upon the nature of the act or acts relied upon. It has been held that if a friend or near relation merely gives some information or advice in a land trade, this will not make him the agent of the one to whom the information or advice is given.[140]

§ 93. **Principal not responsible for agent's acts outside of scope of apparent authority.**—Of course, if the assumed agent goes outside the apparent scope of authority, the principal will not be responsible for his acts. Thus, if one should hold out another as his agent whose business it was to sign receipts for goods actually received at a wharf boat, the principal could not be held responsible for the act of the agent in signing a receipt for goods before they were received.[141] Here the party dealing with the supposed agent must have known that he had no authority to sign receipts in advance of the delivery of the goods, as this is not the usual manner of conducting business of this character, and could not, therefore, be said to be within the

[138] Commonwealth v. Holmes, 119 Mass. 195; Croy v. Busenbark, 72 Ind. 48; Thurber v. Anderson, 88 Ill. 167; Farmers', etc., Bank v. Butchers', etc., Bank, 16 N. Y. 125; Bronson v. Chappell, 12 Wall. (U. S.) 681.

[139] Pole v. Leask, 33 L. J. Eq. 155.

[140] McNamara v. McNamara, 62 Ga. 200.

[141] Coleman v. Riches, 24 L. J. C. P. 125.

apparent scope of the agent's authority. The third party may safely rely upon the acts of the agent, if within the apparent scope of authority, though they be beyond his real authority or his private instructions. So, where it is a rule of a railroad company not to check the baggage of a passenger until he has procured a ticket, yet if a baggage master, whose duty it is to receive and check the baggage of passengers, does so in violation of such rule, and the baggage is lost, the company will be liable, if the passenger was ignorant of the rule or regulation referred to, especially if baggage had been previously received from the passenger under like circumstances.[142] In this kind of a case, the receiving of baggage is the duty for the performance of which the agent is held out by the company to the public, and this is the general scope of his authority. Persons dealing with him in his especial employment may assume, in the absence of knowledge to the contrary, that he may receive baggage both before and after tickets have been purchased by the passenger, as certainly the company would have the right so to receive and check the baggage. It is, therefore, within the apparent scope of the agent's authority to receive baggage before the fare has been paid, and the company can not be heard to say that the rules and regulations were binding upon the passenger under the circumstances.

§ **94. Estoppel manifest by external indicia.**—In like manner an estoppel may arise from the external *indicia* of property; as, where a broker has possession of goods, with the owner's consent, for the apparent purpose of brokerage, a purchaser would be protected in buying them in due course of trade whatever might be the private instructions of the broker.[143]

§ **95. The burden of proof.**—Inasmuch as the burden of proof is always upon him who seeks to hold another responsible for the acts of an alleged agent to establish such agency, it follows that the *onus* is likewise upon him who seeks to establish the relation by an estoppel, to prove the facts relied upon as constituting such estoppel. The reason for this rule is clearly stated by Lord Cranworth in an English house of lords case, where he says: "Unless this principle is strictly acted upon, great injustice may be the consequence, for any one dealing with a person assuming to act as agent for another can always

[142] Lake Shore, etc., R. Co. v. Foster, 104 Ind. 293.

[143] Evans Pr. & Ag. (Bedford's ed.) 200.

save himself from loss or difficulty by applying to the alleged principal to learn whether the agency does exist, and to what extent. The alleged principal has no similar mode of protecting his interest; he may be ignorant of the fact that any one is assuming to act for him, or that any other persons are proposing to deal with another under the notion that the other is his agent. It is, therefore, important to recollect constantly where the burden of proof lies."[144]

IV. By Ratification.

§ **96. Assent may be obtained after act of agency performed.**—It has been heretofore stated that there can be no agency except with the assent of the principal, unless the relation has been created by implication of law or by estoppel. It is not necessary, however, that the principal's assent or sanction be given in advance of the performance of the transaction which constitutes the subject-matter or purpose of the agency. If his assent be obtained after the transaction by a confirmation of the assumed relation, it is equally binding and efficacious. Such a confirmation of the authority of the supposed agent is called a ratification.

§ **97. Definition of ratification.**—"To ratify is to give sanction and validity to something done without authority."[145] It means to confirm.[146] To ratify the authority of an agent is to adopt the act or contract entered into by the alleged agent on behalf of the alleged principal without previous authority.[147] When the party on whose behalf an act has been done by another without previous authority is informed of the same, he may either repudiate or affirm it. If he chooses the former course, he can not be held as a principal, and as to him the act will be null. If he elects to adopt the act as his own, he will be bound by it the same as if he had authorized it prior to its performance.

(*a*) *Essential Elements of Ratification.*

§ **98. Acts that may be ratified.**—An act, to be capable of ratification, must be voidable or defeasible only, and not void. That an act which could not have been authorized in the first instance can not

[144] Pole v. Leask, 33 L. J. Eq. 155. See also, Johnson v. Hurley, 115 Mo. 513.

[145] Evans Pr. & Ag. (Bedford's ed.) 90.

[146] Evans Pr. & Ag. (Bedford's ed.) 90.

[147] Negley v. Lindsay, 67 Pa. St. 217.

be ratified seems clear, and upon this point the adjudications are in full accord. It is a pertinent question, then, What is a void act? or, When is an act void and when is it only voidable? In the first place, it may be stated, truly, we think, that an act which is illegal, in the sense of being an indictable offense, or as being opposed to the public welfare, and therefore to public policy, is void; and as such an act, for reasons heretofore mentioned, could not have been authorized, it can not be ratified. "Two rules," says Evans, "may be laid down with certainty. In the first place, there can be no ratification of an indictable offense, or an offense against public policy; in the second place, the doctrine of ratification is only applicable to cases where the conduct of the parties on whom it is to operate, not being referable to any agreement, can not in the meantime depend on whether there is subsequent ratification. The rules which determine whether an act is void or not for the purposes of ratification have been summed up by a learned writer in terms consistent with the above statement of the law, in *Fisher* v. *Cuthell*.[147a] Where an act is beneficial to the principal and does not create an immediate right to have some other act or duty performed by a third person, but remains simply to the assertion of a right on the part of the principal, the maxim '*Omnis ratihabitio retrotrahitur et mandato priori aequiparatur*' applies.[148] But if the act done by such person would, if authorized, create a right to have some act or duty performed by a third person so as to subject him to damages or losses for the non-performance of that act or duty, or would defeat a right or an estate already vested in the latter, there the subsequent ratification or adoption of the unauthorized act by the principal will not give validity to it so as to bind such third persons to the consequences."[149]

§ **99. Illegal contracts.**—We have heretofore seen that a contract to create an agency for a purpose in itself illegal, as being contrary to public policy, or as being in violation of some known law, is void, and not voidable merely. We need not repeat here what we said in respect to illegal contracts. It is sufficient to remark here that no such contract is capable of being vitalized by ratification. Among

147a 5 East 491.

148 The import of the maxim is that if a person assents to what has been done by another in his name it is equivalent to a prior command. This is true, however, only to the extent that it does not prejudice intervening rights: Broom Legal Maxims 866; Fleckner v. Bank of U. S., 8 Wheat. (U. S.) 338.

149 Evans Pr. & Ag. (Bedford's ed.) 91, 92.

this class of cases may be mentioned such indictable crimes as that of forgery. To forge a note or other written instrument is not only a crime for which the forger may subject himself to punishment, but the act is, so far as creating any liability of the feigned maker is concerned, an absolute nullity. It would, therefore, seem that no validity could be given to such an act by a subsequent ratification. The English and American cases are a unit in holding that no ratification can in any way serve to condone the offense so as to give the offender immunity from punishment.[150]

§ 100. **Can a forgery be ratified?**—On the question, however, as to whether the person whose name has been forged can make himself civilly liable by ratification the authorities are not agreed. On the one hand, it is held that if the party whose signature has been forged, knowing all the circumstances and evincing an intention to be bound thereby, adopts or acknowledges it as his own, there is no good reason why he should not thereby make himself liable, the same as if the instrument had been executed by his authority, even if the conduct constituting the ratification does not amount to an estoppel, unless the ratification is made on condition that the forger is not to be prosecuted criminally.[151] On the other hand, there are many cases in England and the United States which take the position that if the act is a forgery it could not be rendered valid by a subsequent ratification, as this would be in plain conflict with public policy.[152]

§ 101. **Estoppel to deny forged instrument.**—But whichever of these divergent views may be regarded as the correct one, it is certain that the alleged maker of the note or other instrument may render

[150] McKenzie v. British Linen Co., L. R. 6 App. Cas. 82; Brook v. Hook, L. R. 6 Exch. 89; Henry v. Heeb, 114 Ind. 275; Workman v. Wright, 33 Ohio St. 405; Union Bank v. Middlebrook, 33 Conn. 95; Greenfield Bank v. Crafts, 4 Allen (Mass.) 447.

[151] Commercial Bank v. Warren, 15 N. Y. 577; Bartlett v. Tucker, 104 Mass. 336; Hefner v. Vandolah, 62 Ill. 483; Cravens v. Gillilan, 63 Mo. 28; Union Bank v. Middlebrook, 33 Conn. 95; McKenzie v. British Linen Co., L. R. 6 App. Cas. 82; Greenfield Bank v. Crafts, 4 Allen (Mass.) 447. See also, Forsyth v. Day, 46 Me. 176; Lysle v. Beals, 27 La. Ann. 274; Emerson v. Opp, 9 Ind. App. 581.

[152] See Owsley v. Philips, 78 Ky. 517; Brook v. Hook, L. R. 6 Exch. 89; Henry v. Heeb, 114 Ind. 275; Shisler v. Vandike, 92 Pa. St. 447; McHugh v. County of Schuylkill, 67 Pa. St. 391; Workman v. Wright, 33 Ohio St. 405; Negley v. Lindsay, 67 Pa. St. 217; Clark v. Peabody, 22 Me. 500.

himself liable by an estoppel *in pais*. And the person whose name has been forged may so estop himself by the same acts and conduct which might, in other cases, constitute a ratification.[153] The estoppel may, of course, arise as in other cases, by conduct and acts, or by silence when the party is required to speak.[154] The distinction made in many well considered cases seems to be this: "Where the act of signing constitutes the crime of forgery, while the person whose name has been forged may be estopped by his admissions, upon which others may have changed their relations, from pleading the truth of the matter to their detriment, the act from which the crime springs can not, upon considerations of public policy, be ratified without a new consideration to support it."[155]

§ 102. Corporations—Ratification of ultra vires acts—Can shareholders ratify?—English and American cases.—Another class of acts that can not be ratified are acts performed by an assumed agent of a corporation which the corporation could not have validly performed or authorized originally. Corporations act only by and through agents. Such agents may act, of course, either with or without authority. If the act, to perform which the agent has been duly authorized, is legal and within the corporate powers of the society, it will, of course, be the act of the corporation, and the liability is clear. If, however, the act is unauthorized, but within the scope of the corporate powers of the company, it may be subsequently ratified by the adoption thereof by the company.[156] An act is not necessarily void because it is *ultra vires*. It may be voidable merely. There is a distinction also between acts *ultra vires* and acts that are illegal. But an act may be both *ultra vires* and illegal, and then it is absolutely

[153] Mather v. Maidstone, 18 C. B. 273, 86 E. C. L. 373; President, etc., of Bank v. Bank of Ga., 10 Wheat. (U. S.) 333; VanDuzer v. Howe, 21 N. Y. 531; Dodge v. National Exch. Bank, 20 Ohio St. 234; Workman v. Wright, 33 Ohio St. 405; Mayer v. Old, 57 Mo. App. 639; Third Nat'l Bank v. Butler Colliery Co., 59 Hun (N. Y.) 627, 14 N. Y. Supp. 21; Woodruff v. Munroe, 33 Md. 146; First Nat'l Bank v. Parsons, 19 Minn. 289; Forsyth v. Day, 46 Me. 176; National Bank v. Fassett, 42 Vt. 432; Henry v. Heeb, 114 Ind. 275, 5 Am. St. 613; Kuriger v. Joest, 22 Ind. App. 633 (this case presents an exhaustive discussion of the doctrine of estoppel, as applicable to such cases); Campbell v. Campbell, 133 Cal. 33, 65 Pac. 134.

[154] Reg. v. Smith, 3 F. & F. 504; Corser v. Paul, 41 N. H. 24, 77 Am. Dec. 713; Bank v. Keene, 53 Me. 103; Lewis v. Hodapp, 14 Ind. App. 111.

[155] Mitchell, J., in Henry v. Heeb, 114 Ind. 275, 5 Am. St. 613.

[156] Evans Pr. & Ag. (Bedford's ed.) 94.

void and can not be ratified.[157] Of course, an act that is illegal, and therefore void, can not become the legitimate subject of ratification, whether done in the name of a corporation, municipal or private, or an individual. But if the act is *ultra vires* by reason of being in violation of the charter of a private corporation, it may be ratified by the shareholders.[158] The question has arisen whether those acts that are expressly forbidden the corporation by statute can be ratified by the subsequent approval of the shareholders of the corporation. The question has received consideration in the English house of lords, the prevailing opinion there being that no such ratification could

[157] Martin v. Zellerbach, 38 Cal. 300; Whitney Arms Co. v. Barlow, 63 N. Y. 68; Smith v. Newburgh, 77 N. Y. 130; Highway Commissioners v. Van Dusan, 40 Mich. 429; Green v. City of Cape May, 41 N. J. L. 45; City of Indianapolis v. Wann, 144 Ind. 175. But the plea of *ultra vires* can not be set up by a corporation as long as it retains the benefits of the contract or transaction in reference to which it claims its want of authority: Wright v. Hughes, 119 Ind. 324; Louisville, etc., R. Co. v. Flanagan, 113 Ind. 488; Kelley v. Newburyport, etc., R. Co., 141 Mass. 496. And neither can it be invoked by the party who has contracted with the corporation and refuses to comply with the contract because of the absence of authority on the part of such corporation. When the latter has complied with its part of the contract, the other contracting party can not complain of its want of authority to make the contract: Chicago, etc., R. Co. v. Derkes, 103 Ind. 520; Holmes, etc., Mfg. Co. v. Holmes, etc., Mfg. Co., 127 N. Y. 252. But if the act was illegal and void, retaining the benefits thereof will not render a municipal corporation liable: State v. City of Pullman, 23 Wash. 583, 63 Pac. 265; Arnott v. Spokane, 6 Wash. 442.

[158] Kent v. Quicksilver Mining Co., 78 N. Y. 159; Sheldon, etc., Co. v. Eickemeyer, etc., Co., 90 N. Y. 607; Phosphate of Lime Co. v. Green, L. R. 7 C. P. 43; Evans v. Smallcombe, L. R. 3 H. L. 249; Ohio, etc., R. Co. v. McPherson, 35 Mo. 13; Des Moines Gas Co. v. West, 50 Iowa 16. The power of ratification, however, is not confined to the shareholders. If the act is such as could have been authorized by the directors in the first place the directors have the power to ratify such act: Fleckner v. Bank of U. S., 8 Wheat. (U. S.) 338; Darst v. Gale, 83 Ill. 136; Reichwald v. Commercial Hotel Co., 106 Ill. 439; Sherman v. Fitch, 98 Mass. 59; Lyndeborough Glass Co. v. Massachusetts Glass Co., 111 Mass. 315; Kelsey v. National Bank, 69 Pa. St. 426. Moreover, the company may estop itself by acquiescence in the unauthorized act without express ratification: Morawetz Priv. Corp., § 628. A majority of the shareholders is generally sufficient for ratification, if a majority could have authorized the act originally: Aurora Agr., etc., Soc. v. Paddock, 80 Ill. 263; Bank of Columbia v. Patterson, 7 Cranch (U. S.) 299; Arlington v. Peirce, 122 Mass. 270.

take place. Lord Cairns, in an elaborate judgment, emphatically concludes that the shareholders of a corporation have no power to ratify such an act. He reasons that if only the rights of the present shareholders were involved there might be ground for the contention that they could make the society responsible for the unauthorized act. But the law takes cognizance not only of the rights of the present shareholders, but of those also who might become such by succession; and second, of the rights of the outside public, and more particularly of those who might become creditors of the company.[159] There are some acts, however, which, though not within the scope of authority which is expressly conferred upon the directors by the charter of the company, or by the general law under which it was organized, may yet be binding upon it. Acts of this class are included in the powers incident to the existence of the corporation. The rule is that a corporation, unless restricted by its charter, has the power to enter into contracts that may be necessary or usual in the course of the business for which it was created and that are reasonably incident thereto. This power, unless excluded by the charter or general law, is always implied. Such an act, when performed by an agent without authority, may become valid by ratification.[160]

§ 103. **Acts restricted by charter—Incidental powers—Rights of innocent third persons.**—There is another class of acts which, though within the scope of the franchises granted the corporations, are still beyond the authority granted the officers thereof. Thus, the directors of a company may by the charter be prevented from the performance of certain acts, or it may require the votes of three-fourths or some other proportion of such directors before such act can be per-

[159] Ashbury, etc., Co. v. Riche, L. R. 7 H. L. 653. It seems, however, that many, if not the majority of the cases, hold that any contract made on behalf of a corporation, if not originally authorized, may be subsequently ratified, except such as are illegal or *malum prohibitum:* Phosphate of Lime Co. v. Green, L. R. 7 C. P. 43; Sheldon, etc., Co. v. Eickemeyer, etc., Co., 90 N. Y. 607; Bissell v. Michigan, etc., R. Co., 22 N. Y. 258; Kent v. Quicksilver Mining Co., 78 N. Y. 159. But other cases, as we have seen, do not indorse this doctrine, and take the position that such acts can not legitimately become the proper subjects of ratification: Ashbury, etc., Co. v. Riche, L. R. 7 H. L. 653, per Lord Cairns; Hazlehurst v. Savannah, etc., R. Co., 43 Ga. 13; Cozart v. Georgia, etc., Co., 54 Ga. 379; Barton v. Port Jackson, etc., Co., 17 Barb. (N. Y.) 397; Martin v. Zellerbach, 38 Cal. 300.

[160] Pittsburgh, etc., R. Co. v. Keokuk, etc., Co., 131 U. S. 371.

formed. These acts, being within the incidental powers of such corporations, may be ratified by the shareholders, and, it seems, can not be avoided when acted upon by third persons in good faith, though not formally ratified.[161]

§ 104. Acts of assumed agents before incorporation.—It may well be doubted whether an act performed on behalf of a corporation before it has acquired a corporate existence can subsequently be ratified by the corporation. It is a familiar doctrine that there can be no agency without an existing principal, whose identity must be fixed at the time of the performance of the act sought to be ratified.[163] It is true that a corporation subsequently acquiring an existence may make itself liable for acts done on its behalf before the incorporation by adopting or retaining the benefits of such acts, etc.; but this liability is based upon the theory of a new contract rather than upon that of ratification of the precedent act.[164] Whether, strictly speaking, the adoption by the corporation of an act done for it prior to its incorporation might more properly constitute an estoppel or a new contract is of little consequence. Certainly the company may render itself liable for such an act by its subsequent adoption or approval and the retention of the benefits arising therefrom.[165]

§ 105. Promoters of projected corporations.—Perhaps the most frequent instances of acts performed on behalf of an intended corporation before it is organized occur in cases in which the promoters of such corporation undertake by their acts to make it liable for some

[161] Kent v. Quicksilver Mining Co., 78 N. Y. 159; Hazlehurst v. Savannah, etc., R. Co., 43 Ga. 13; Cozart v. Georgia, etc., Co., 54 Ga. 379; Lucas v. White Line Transfer Co., 70 Iowa 541; Taylor v. South, etc., R. Co., 4 Woods (U. S.) 575; Sheldon, etc., Co. v. Eickemeyer, etc., Co., 90 N. Y. 607; Hollins v. St. Paul, etc., R. Co., 9 N. Y. Supp. 909; Phosphate of Lime Co. v. Green, L. R. 7 C. P. 43; Poole v. West Point, etc., Ass'n, 30 Fed. 513.

[163] Foster v. Bates, 12 M. & W. 226; Bullard v. DeGroff, 59 Neb. 783; O'Shea v. Rice, 49 Neb. 893. The promoters are not the agents of the corporation, as the latter had no existence when the act was committed. The corporation is, therefore, not liable for their torts: Rockford, etc., R. Co. v. Sage, 65 Ill. 328; Bell's Gap R. Co. v. Christy, 79 Pa. St. 54; New York, etc., R. Co. v. Ketchum, 27 Conn. 170; Frost v. Belmont, 6 Allen (Mass.) 152.

[164] See Whitney v. Wyman, 101 U. S. 392; Gent v. Manufacturers', etc., Ins. Co., 107 Ill. 652; Western Screw, etc., Co. v. Cousley, 72 Ill. 531; Little Rock, etc., R. Co. v. Perry, 37 Ark. 164; Bommer v. American, etc., Co., 81 N. Y. 468.

[165] McArthur v. Times Printing Co., 48 Minn. 319.

contract entered into between the promoters and third persons. In such cases, there being no existing principal when the contract was entered into, the company would not be liable in the first instance and could not be made so by ratification.[166] But, though the company might not render itself liable by the ratification of the acts of the promoters, it may nevertheless, for reasons already stated, incur responsibility for them after the organization is effected, if within the corporate powers, by entering into a new contract relative to the same matter. Upon the original contract the promoter or promoters would doubtless be liable individually. If by an agreement, amounting to novation, the corporation should assume the obligation of such contract, the third party discharging the agent from liability, the agreement would doubtless become valid between the parties. What may be done by express agreement may also be accomplished by implication. Should the corporation, for example, act upon the assumption of its responsibility as the real principal and accept the profits of the contract, it would incur also the corresponding liabilities, for no one can take the benefit of a contract without, at the same time, assuming its burdens.[167] The power of a corporation to render itself subsequently liable by the adoption of the acts of its projectors performed prior to its incorporation is sometimes said to be asserted in courts of equity, but denied by common-law tribunals.[168] The courts of this country recognize and enforce the rule that a corporation may assume liability for the acts of its promoters, prior to incorporation, if within the corporate powers of the society, upon the theory of a new contract, express or implied.[169]

[166] Bell's Gap R. Co. v. Christy, 79 Pa. St. 54; Western Screw, etc., Co. v. Cousley, 72 Ill. 531; Paxton Cattle Co. v. First Nat'l Bank, 21 Neb. 621; New York, etc., R. Co. v. Ketchum, 27 Conn. 170; Franklin Fire Ins. Co. v. Hart, 31 Md. 59; McArthur v. Times Printing Co., 48 Minn. 319, 31 Am. St. 653; Gent v. Manufacturers', etc., Ins. Co., 107 Ill. 652.

[167] See cases cited *supra*.

[168] Evans Pr. & Ag. (Bedford's ed.) 99–103.

[169] A corporation may be rendered liable for the acts of its promoters by the provisions of its charter or the law under which it is incorporated: Tilson v. Warwick Gas Light Co., 4 B. & C. 961. In this country an express agreement after the incorporation will render the company liable: Wood v. Whelen, 93 Ill. 153; Whitney v. Wyman, 101 U. S. 392; Western Screw, etc., Co. v. Cousley, 72 Ill. 531; Rochford, etc., R. Co. v. Sage, 65 Ill. 328; Franklin Fire Ins. Co. v. Hart, 31 Md. 59; MacDonough v. Bank of Houston, 34 Tex. 309. In England, however, the courts hold that such a contract (by the promoters) is void as to the company and can not be ratified or

§ 106. **Contracts made on Sunday.**—Under the common law, a contract entered into on Sunday was as valid as if it had been entered into on any other day.[170] Such contracts have, however, been prohibited by statutes in England.[171] In America similar statutes have been enacted by the various states. These statutes being in derogation of the common law, it is held in some states that they must be specially pleaded when relied upon. According to this view, a party sued on a Sunday contract may waive the defense allowed by the statute, and does so waive it if he fails to plead it. A complaint declaring on a contract entered into on Sunday is, in those jurisdictions, not open to demurrer.[172] It may be truly said, therefore, that, in the states holding to this construction, a Sunday contract is not void, but voidable only.[173] According to this line of decisions, a contract entered into on Sunday, being voidable merely, may be ratified on a secular day thereafter.[174] In many jurisdictions it is held, however, that a contract made on Sunday is absolutely void, and, therefore, incapable of ratification. The contract, having been declared illegal by statute, can not be legalized by subsequent agreement of the parties; what the law has made illegal the parties can not make legal.[175]

adopted without a new consideration: Kelner v. Baxter, L. R. 2 C. P. 174; Melhado v. Porto Alegre, etc., R. Co., L. R. 9 C. P. 503. Even there it is held, however, that the original consideration may be a sufficient one in equity: In re Empress Eng. Co., L. R. 16 Ch. D. 125.

[170] Rex v. Brotherton, Stra. 702; Story v. Elliot, 8 Cow. (N. Y.) 27; Johnson v. Day, 17 Pick. (Mass.) 106; Kepner v. Keefer, 6 Watts (Pa.) 231; Bloom v. Richards, 2 Ohio St. 387.

[171] The principal English statute on the subject was that of 29 Car. II, ch. 7, § 1.

[172] Heavenridge v. Mondy, 34 Ind. 28; Chlein v. Kabat, 72 Iowa 291; Nason v. Dinsmore, 34 Me. 391; O'Shea v. Kohn, 33 Hun (N. Y.) 114. Sunday laws are constitutional and valid as police regulations: State v. Nesbit, 8 Kan. App. 104.

[173] Heavenridge v. Mondy, 34 Ind. 28; Western U. Tel. Co. v. Eskridge, 7 Ind. App. 209.

[174] Williamson v. Brandenberg, 6 Ind. App. 97; Sargent v. Butts, 21 Vt. 99; Sumner v. Jones, 24 Vt. 317; Russel v. Murdock, 79 Iowa 101; McKinney v. Denby, 44 Ark. 78; Evansville v. Morris, 87 Ind. 269; Kuhns v. Gates, 92 Ind. 66; Smith v. Case, 2 Ore. 192; Perkins v. Jones, 26 Ind. 499; Van Hoven v. Irish, 3 McCrary (U. S.) 444; Saginaw, etc., R. Co. v. Chappell, 56 Mich. 190; Wilson v. Milligan, 75 Mo. 41; Clough v. Davis, 9 N. H. 500; Harrison v. Colton, 31 Iowa 16; King v. Fleming, 72 Ill. 21. Where one party to a Sunday contract performs his part during week days, and the other party accepts what is done, he must pay for what he receives: Bollin v. Hooper (Mich.), 86 N. W. 795.

[175] Day v. McAllister, 15 Gray (Mass.) 433; Vinz v. Beatty, 61 Wis.

As a contract appointing an agent is, in this respect, the same as any other contract, it follows that in jurisdictions where it is held that such contracts are absolutely void, an agency contract entered into on Sunday is not capable of ratification. But wherever the courts declare such contracts voidable only, then they may be ratified the same as contracts concerning matters other than agencies, and the ratification may be made in the same way as that of other contracts. It is true, however, that in all jurisdictions, contracts that have been entered into on Sunday may be adopted by the parties on a future secular day, as new contracts, and this may be done by implication as well as expressly. It seems that retaining the benefits of the property forming the subject-matter of a contract will not render the promisor liable.[176]

§ 107. **Must have been existing principal when act was performed.**—As we learned in considering the question of ratification by corporations of the acts of their promoters, there must be an existing principal at the time of the commission of the act subsequently ratified. Therefore, it would seem that if A, as agent, undertake to perform an unauthorized act for B, who is dead, the personal representative of B can not validify the act of A, for it is well established that the person ratifying must be ascertained at the time the act is done; but if the act is done in behalf of the estate of the intestate, even prior to the appointment of an administrator, the latter may legally

645; Cranson v. Goss, 107 Mass. 440; Reeves v. Butcher, 31 N. J. L. 224; Gwinn v. Simes, 61 Mo. 335; Shippey v. Eastwood, 9 Ala. 198; Merriweather v. Smith, 44 Ga. 541; Pope v. Linn, 50 Me. 83; Tucker v. Mowrey, 12 Mich. 379; Kountz v. Price, 40 Miss. 341; Steffens v. Earl, 40 N. J. L. 137; Bishop Conts. (enlarged ed.) 542; Hare Conts. 296-297. See also, Finn v. Donahue, 35 Conn. 216; Parker v. Pitts, 73 Ind. 597; Myers v. Meinrath, 101 Mass. 366; Bryan v. Watson, 127 Ind. 42; Pillen v. Erickson (Mich.), 83 N. W. 1023; Riddle v. Keller (N. J.), 48 Atl. 818; Acme Electrical, etc., Co. v. Vanderbeck (Mich.), 86 N. W. 786; Ryne v. Darby, 20 N. J. Eq. 231; Bradley v. Rea, 103 Mass. 188; Allen v. Deming, 14 N. H. 133; Durant v. Rhener, 26 Minn. 363.

176 Catlett v. Methodist Epis. Church, 62 Ind. 366; Rogers v. Western U. Tel. Co., 78 Ind. 169. And where this is the defense relied upon, the answer or plea should allege not only that the note was signed on Sunday, but that it was delivered on that day: Conrad v. Kinzie, 105 Ind. 281. An indorser of a note, when sued, can not set up a defense that the note was made on Sunday, as he warrants its legality: Prescott Nat'l Bank v. Butler, 157 Mass. 548.

ratify such act; as the title of the administrator relates back to the time of the death of the intestate.[177]

§ 108. **Party ratifying must have been competent as principal.**—A party undertaking to ratify an act or contract made in his behalf by another must be competent to perform such act or enter into such contract to the same extent that a principal must be competent to confer the authority upon the agent in the first instance.[178] Thus, as we have already had occasion to observe, an infant, by the great weight of authority, is not competent to be a principal to a contract entered into by him by which he undertakes to confer authority upon an agent, and such contract would be not voidable merely, but absolutely void; and as a void contract can never become valid by ratification, it follows that an infant can not ratify an act done for him by any one assuming to act as his agent.[179] And as an agent has no authority, as a general rule, to delegate the power conferred upon him by a principal, the agent could not in such case legally ratify an act which was performed for him without authority. Having no power to delegate authority conferred upon him, he has not the power to ratify that which he could not have authorized.[180] Likewise an idiot, lunatic or other person of unsound mind, and a *feme covert*, under the common law, could not, while laboring under such disability, render an act done for him or her valid by ratification; though such incompetent person might ratify the act after the removal of the incompetency and disability.

§ 109. **Party ratifying must know all the facts or willfully or carelessly ignore them.**—It is further essential to a valid ratification that the party undertaking to ratify must have knowledge of all the material facts concerning the performance of the act to be ratified,

[177] Foster v. Bates, 12 M. & W. 226. But if the decedent was *non compos mentis*, though not judicially so declared, his contracts, being only voidable, may be disaffirmed or ratified after his death by his representatives, either personal or real, according to whether the contract concern real estate or personal property: Schuff v. Ransom, 79 Ind. 458; Fay v. Burditt, 81 Ind. 433; Ashmead v. Reynolds, 127 Ind. 441; Louisville, etc,. R. Co. v. Herr, 135 Ind. 591; Campbell v. Kuhn, 45 Mich. 513.

[178] Taymouth v. Koehler, 35 Mich. 22.

[179] Armitage v. Widoe, 36 Mich. 124; Trueblood v. Trueblood, 8 Ind. 195, 65 Am. Dec. 756. But see *contra*. Whitney v. Dutch, 14 Mass. 457, 7 Am. Dec. 229; Patterson v. Lippincott, 47 N. J. L. 457, 54 Am. Rep. 178.

[180] O'Conner v. Arnold, 53 Ind. 203.

or must ratify with an intention to assume the risk, notwithstanding the want of such knowledge.[181] Unless the party undertaking to ratify knew that he was not liable without such ratification, he will not be bound.[182] The principle recognized by the authorities cited was clearly set forth in an English case decided by the court of exchequer in 1845. In that case a landlord had authorized his bailiffs to distrain for rent, but instructed them to take only such articles as they might find on the demised premises. The bailiffs, in violation of their instructions, took certain cattle found by them beyond the boundaries of the premises. The cattle were sold and the money was paid over to the landlord. In an action of trover against the landlord, the court decided that he could not be held liable in this action unless he had ratified the seizure of the cattle with knowledge that they were taken beyond the boundaries, "or unless he meant to take upon himself, without inquiry, the risk of any irregularity which they might have committed, and to adopt all their acts."[183] If the assumed principal makes a deliberate ratification upon such facts as are within his knowledge, without caring to make further inquiry, he will be bound.[184] If the act performed by the agent consisted of entering into a contract for the assumed principal, the party ratifying must, in order to become liable, have knowledge of the nature and consideration of the contract made for him.[185] But deliberate, or even careless ignorance, will not excuse.[186] It is not necessary that, in addition to a knowledge of all the facts, the principal should also have knowledge of the legal effect of such facts.[187]

[181] Lewis v. Read, 13 M. & W. 834; Smith v. Cologan, 2 T. R. 188, n.; Ritch v. Smith, 82 N. Y. 627; Combs v. Scott, 12 Allen (Mass.) 493; Thacher v. Pray, 113 Mass. 291; Proctor v. Tows, 115 Ill. 138; Bannon v. Warfield, 42 Md. 22; Bryant v. Moore, 26 Me. 84; Wright v. Burbank, 64 Pa. St. 247; Spooner v. Thompson, 48 Vt. 259; Pittsburgh, etc., R. Co. v. Gazzam, 32 Pa. St. 340; King v. MacKellar, 109 N. Y. 215; Manning v. Leland, 153 Mass. 510.

[182] Pittsburgh, etc., R. Co. v. Gazzam, 32 Pa. St. 340.

[183] Lewis v. Read, 13 M. & W. 834. See also, to the same point, Freeman v. Rosher, L. R. 13 Q. B. 780; Gauntlett v. King, 3 C. B. N. S. 59.

[184] Kelley v. Newburyport, etc., R. Co., 141 Mass. 496.

[185] Dickinson v. Conway, 12 Allen (Mass.) 487; Mathews v. Hamilton, 23 Ill. 417; Woodbury v. Larned, 5 Minn. 339; Pittsburgh, etc., R. Co. v. Gazzam, 32 Pa. St. 340; Manning v. Gasharie, 27 Ind. 399; Bank of Owensboro v. Western Bank, 13 Bush (Ky.) 526, 26 Am. Rep. 211.

[186] Miller v. Board of Education, 44 Cal. 166; Lewis v. Read, 13 M. & W. 834.

[187] Kelly v. Newburyport, etc., R. Co., 141 Mass. 496.

§ 110. Assumed agent must have acted for ratifying party.—Another confirmed rule in relation to the doctrine of ratification is that the person assuming to act as agent must have acted in behalf of the person undertaking to ratify, and not on his own or some other person's account.[188] This doctrine is as old as the year books. And it was consequently held that if a bailiff took a heriot in which he claimed property himself, the subsequent adoption by the lord of his act would not amount to a ratification; but if he should take it as the bailiff of the lord, the subsequent assent of the latter would amount to a ratification of the bailiff's act. The same doctrine holds good in the case of goods distrained without authority.[189] Therefore, if a person purchase goods in his own behalf, the transaction can not be adopted by another as principal; and the relation of agency and its usual consequences can not result from such transaction.[190]

§ 111. Mistake or fraud.—The doctrine enunciated in the cases referred to is based upon the fundamental principle that a contract can not be enforced if it be tainted with fraud or entered into through a mistake as to the facts out of which such contract arises. Courts of equity will always relieve a person from liability when such contract was obtained by means of fraud or by reason of mistake which proper care could not have guarded against.[191]

§ 112. Ratification must be in toto.—Another essential requisite of a valid and binding ratification is that the act must be ratified *in toto,* and not in part only. This is but another statement of the doctrine that a person can not avail himself of the benefits of a contract without at the same time taking upon himself its corresponding burdens.[192]

[188] Crowder v. Read, 80 Ind. 1; Wilson v. Tumman, 6 M. & G. 236; Roby v. Cossitt, 78 Ill. 638.

[189] Evans Pr. & Ag. (Bedford's ed.) 96, 97.

[190] Ballock v. Hooper, 6 Mackey (D. C.) 421; Fellows v. Commissioners, etc., of Oneida Co., 36 Barb. (N. Y.) 655.

[191] Combs v. Scott, 12 Allen (Mass.) 493; Owings v. Hull, 9 Pet. (U. S.) 607.

[192] Billings v. Mason, 80 Me. 496; Brigham v. Palmer, 3 Allen (Mass.) 450; Hutchings v. Ladd, 16 Mich. 493; Krider v. Trustees of Western College, 31 Iowa 547; Eberts v. Selover, 44 Mich. 519; Widner v. Lane, 14 Mich. 124; Crans v. Hunter, 28 N. Y. 389; Crawford v. Barkley, 18 Ala. 270; Bristow v. Whitmore, 9 H. L. Cas. 391; Smith v. Hodson, 4 T. R. 211; Rader v. Maddox, 150 U. S. 128; Cornwal v. Wilson, 1 Ves. Sr. 509; 1 Parsons Conts. (7th ed.) 49-52; Burke Land, etc., Co. v. Wells, Fargo & Co. (Idaho), 60 Pac. 87; Loomis Milling Co. v. Vawter, 8 Kan.

§ **113. Different aspects of ratification—Question for jury.**—It is important to note the different aspects in which the doctrine of ratification may be considered. The party acting as agent may be wholly unauthorized,—that is, he may be a mere volunteer; or the relation of principal and agent may in reality exist between him and the person for whom he acts, but the agent may, in performing the act, exceed his authority. In the latter case, it always being presumed that the agent promptly informs his principal of what has been done in connection with all matters concerning the agency, not as much evidence would be required in order to constitute a ratification as where the relation did not already exist. Hence, in case the unauthorized act is merely in excess of the authority actually conferred, mere silence on the principal's part may be sufficient to authorize an inference of ratification.[193] The question of ratification is, however, one of fact for the jury, and the burden of proof is upon the party alleging it. But if the facts are uncontradicted, ratification may become a question of law solely.[194]

(*b*) *Manner of Ratification.*

§ **114. May be express or implied.**—A ratification may be either express or implied. An express ratification is made with the same degree of solemnity and formality with which an express appointment of an agent is made. An implied ratification is shown by proof of acquiescence on the part of the principal, which is usually inferred from the conduct of the latter. Whether the ratification be express or implied, however, it must not rest upon mere probability or conjecture, but must be shown to have been made deliberately.[195]

§ **115. Form of express ratification.**—Where a written instrument is relied upon to furnish the proof of express ratification, the form of such instrument, except as hereinafter stated, is of little consequence. It may, as in case of express appointment, consist of cor-

App. 437; Martin v. Humphrey, 58 Neb. 414, 78 N. W. 715; German Nat'l Bank v. First Nat'l Bank, 59 Neb. 7, 80 N. W. 48; Citizens' State Bank v. Pence, 59 Neb. 579, 81 N. W. 623.

[193] Evans Pr. & Ag. (Bedford's ed.) 111.

[194] See Lewis v. Read, 13 M. & W. 834; Gimon v. Terrell, 38 Ala. 208; Heath v. Paul, 81 Wis. 532; Burr v. Howard, 58 Ga. 564; Robinson v. Chapline, 9 Iowa 91; Storkes v. Mackay, 140 N. Y. 640; Bryant v. Moore, 26 Me. 84, 45 Am. Dec. 96; Garrett v. Gonter, 42 Pa. St. 143.

[195] Evans Pr. & Ag. (Bedford's ed.) 106.

respondence between the parties or simply a letter of memorandum from the principal. The exception referred to is in cases in which a particular form of authority was required in the first instance. In such cases, under the rules of the common law, the ratification must be in the same form and manner as were required of the original instrument. At common law, authority to execute a deed could only be conferred in writing, under seal, and hence the unauthorized execution of such a deed by an agent could only be ratified by an instrument under seal.[196]

§ **116. Ratification of sealed instrument by parol.**—In some cases it is held, however, that a sealed instrument executed without previous authority may be ratified by parol. This ruling has generally been confined to those cases in which one partner, without previous authority from his copartners, executed a deed in the name of the firm. It is held that such act, though unauthorized originally, may be ratified by the remaining partners orally.[197]

§ **117. The Massachusetts rule.**—In Massachusetts the courts apply the rule governing in partnerships to other cases. In that state it is held that an unauthorized instrument under seal, executed by an agent, may be legally ratified by parol in any case.[198] The rule thus extended seems to be applied in Indiana.[199] In Indiana and many other states, however, the requirement of the common law for a seal has been abolished. In those states, of course, no seal is necessary in the ratifying instrument, and, generally, the ratification may be by

[196] Despatch Line v. Bellamy Mfg. Co., 12 N. H. 205, 37 Am. Dec. 203; Spofford v. Hobbs, 29 Me. 148; Blood v. Goodrich, 9 Wend. (N. Y.) 68; Taylor v. Robinson, 14 Cal. 396; Pollard & Co. v. Gibbs, 55 Ga. 45; Ragan v. Chenault, 78 Ky. 545.

[197] McIntyre v. Park, 11 Gray (Mass.) 102; Swan v. Stedman, 4 Metc. (Mass.) 548; Holbrook v. Chamberlin, 116 Mass. 155, 17 Am. Rep. 146; Smith v. Kerr, 3 N. Y. 144; Skinner v. Dayton, 19 Johns. (N. Y.) 515, 10 Am. Dec. 286; Drumright v. Philpot, 16 Ga. 424, 60 Am. Dec. 738; Peine v. Weber, 47 Ill. 41; Pike v. Bacon, 21 Me. 280, 38 Am. Dec. 259; McDonald v. Eggleston, 26 Vt. 154, 60 Am. Dec. 303; McNaughten v. Partridge, 11 Ohio 223, 38 Am. Dec. 731; Fichthorn v. Boyer, 5 Watts (Pa.) 159, 30 Am. Dec. 300; Deckard v. Case, 5 Watts (Pa.) 22, 30 Am. Dec. 287; Robinson v. Crowder, 4 McCord (S. C.) 519, 17 Am. Dec. 762; Hart v. Withers, 1 P. & W. (Pa.) 285, 21 Am. Dec. 382.

[198] McIntyre v. Park, 11 Gray (Mass.) 102; Swan v. Stedman, 4 Metc. (Mass.) 548; Holbrook v. Chamberlin, 116 Mass. 155, 17 Am. Rep. 146; Cady v. Shepherd, 11 Pick. (Mass.) 400, 22 Am. Dec. 379.

[199] Fouch v. Wilson, 59 Ind. 93; approved in Fitzgerald v. Goff, 99 Ind. 28.

parol, or by implication. The courts are growing more disposed constantly to disregard the useless formalities implied in the employment of seals, and the tendency doubtless is toward more liberality in the requirements for ratification of what are known as sealed instruments executed by agents without formal authority under seal.[200]

§ **118. Ratification of deed by estoppel.**—It does not always require a specific ratification of an unauthorized sealed instrument, even in jurisdictions where a seal is required, to render it binding on the principal; for he may estop himself to deny its execution by his acts and conduct. It has consequently been decided that where an agent undertakes to make a sale of land which is unauthorized, and the principal, with a full knowledge of the facts, adopts the sale and accepts the purchase money, he is estopped from denying the agent's authority.[201] But before the party will be estopped it must be shown that he had been informed of the facts and that the purchaser was misled to his prejudice.[202] And one who accepts rent as the proceeds of an unauthorized lease will be estopped to deny the authority of the agent to execute such lease.[203] An instrument executed in the presence of the principal, and with his assent or by his direction, need not be authorized in writing under seal.[204]

§ **119. Statute of frauds.**—A contract required to be in writing, by virtue of the statute of frauds, must be authorized in writing, where the statute is so framed as to render the contract invalid unless signed by the party or his agent thereunto legally authorized. This being true, such a contract made by an agent, it is held by some courts, requires a written ratification in order to be binding.[205] According to this rule, an unauthorized lease for nine years made by parol was declared invalid as such, and it was held that such lease could be ratified only in writing, but that a parol ratification would give the tenant an estate at will. In a case decided by the supreme court of Illinois, the facts were that the agent had written authority to sell certain lots belonging to his principal at a fixed price and upon certain terms. The agent sold the lots at a less price and on terms

[200] Adams v. Power, 52 Miss. 828; Hammond v. Hanniu, 21 Mich. 374; Dickerman v. Ashton, 21 Minn. 538.

[201] Grove v. Hodges, 55 Pa. St. 504.

[202] Palmer v. Williams, 24 Mich. 328.

[203] Hyatt v. Clark, 118 N. Y. 563.

[204] Gardner v. Gardner, 5 Cush. (Mass.) 483; King v. Longnor, 4 B. & Ad. 647; Jansen v. McCahill, 22 Cal. 563.

[205] M'Dowell v. Simpson, 3 Watts (Pa.) 129.

more favorable to the purchaser, and informed the principal of these facts, who assented to the same and verbally directed the agent to execute the contract, which he did. The court ruled that, as the agent's authority to sell on these terms was not in writing, the sale was invalid and the principal was not bound by it. A new writing was necessary to constitute a valid ratification.[206] In a Michigan case, however, the supreme court of that state, in an opinion by its distinguished Judge Cooley, decided that a parol ratification of such contract is binding.[206a] In that case the plaintiff sought to recover damages from the defendant for breach of contract to sell and convey to the plaintiff a parcel of land. The contract was in writing and was signed and sealed on behalf of the defendant, a married woman, by her husband, who had oral authority to do so. The contract being for the sale of an interest in land, it was insisted that it was void under the statute of frauds. A parol ratification was, however, held to be sufficient, and the plaintiff was awarded judgment. The court, in support of its ruling, cites some English cases, a New York case, and a decision of the United States supreme court.[207] In these cases, the doctrine that a contract required to be in writing by the statute of frauds, when made in writing by an agent, without authority from his principal, may be ratified by parol, is adhered to. The statute requires that the contract be signed by the party or his duly authorized agent. How the agent shall be authorized is not stated; a resort must therefore be had to the common law. The signing by the agent takes the contract out of the statute; and the parol sanction of his act by the principal is a valid ratification, the same as in the case of any other instrument.[208] These cases seem to be in direct opposition to each other. The better rule appears to us to be enunciated in those cases which hold that no writing is necessary, either to make a valid appointment of an agent to execute such a written instrument, or to ratify the execution of a written instrument by the agent without previous authority. In either case the statute is satisfied when the agent has made the instrument in writing, and signed his principal's name to the same. The statute only requires that, in case the instrument is executed by an agent, he shall be "thereunto legally authorized." That authority, it appears to us,

[206] Cozell v. Dearlove, 144 Ill. 23.

[206a] Hammond v. Hanniu, 21 Mich. 374.

[207] Maclean v. Dunn, 4 Bing. 722; Hunter v. Parker, 7 M. & W. 322; Worrall v. Munn, 5 N. Y. 229; Bank of Metropolis v. Guttschlick, 14 Pet. (U. S.) 19.

[208] See also, Evans Pr. & Ag. (Bedford's ed.) 54, n. 1, 55.

may be legally conferred by parol; and if this may be done, the act of the agent may be ratified by parol also.

§ **120. Ratification of written instruments.**—In just what particular form an instrument, sealed or unsealed, may be ratified, when ratification is required to be in writing or under seal, can not be determined by any unvarying rule. It has been held that the unauthorized execution of a bond for a principal, by an attorney appointed by parol, may be ratified by a power of attorney being dated back to a time before the execution of the bond.[209] And in another case, where a sale of land, in which a party to a suit in chancery had an interest, was claimed to have been ratified, the court held that where the answer filed in the suit by such person admitted the sale of the land, such an admission was a sufficient ratification of the sale, as to the interest of such person.[210] But in Kentucky it was held that an agent, without written authority to do so, can not bind his principal as surety for another, and the principal's ratification of such an act is not binding upon him unless it is in writing.[211] In other states also, the courts hold that an agent's unauthorized act in executing a bond or other sealed instrument can be ratified only by a written instrument under seal.[212]

§ **121. Implied ratification—Intention.**—But the most common instances of ratification are those arising by implication from the conduct of the supposed principal. The ratification of an act is but a retroactive grant of authority, and this, as we have seen, may be effected in the same manner as the granting of authority prior to the act. Hence, as the delegation of authority may be proved by circumstances from which an inference may be drawn that such authority had in fact been bestowed, an inference may likewise be gathered from circumstances from which the ratification is commonly implied, or the acts and conduct of the principal with reference to the transaction performed for him. One who conducts himself in such a manner as to lead an ordinarily prudent man to believe to his prejudice that an act, though done without authority, has received the approval of him for whom it was performed, can not in justice and good conscience be permitted to say that he really never assented to the act,

[209] Milliken v. Coombs, 1 Greenl. (Me.) 343, 10 Am. Dec. 70.

[210] Stoney v. Shultz, 1 Hill Ch. (S. C.) 465, 21 Am. Dec. 429.

[211] Ragan v. Chenault, 78 Ky. 545.

[212] Ingraham v. Edwards, 64 Ill. 526; Pollard v. Gibbs, 55 Ga. 45.

or that he did not intend his words and conduct to have the effect of such assent. It is not material, therefore, what the actual intention of the ratifying party may have been, as to whether he would affirm the act or reject it. The old and familiar rule that a person must be held to have intended the natural and ordinary consequences of his act is fully applicable; and if his language, his silence or his acts were such as would naturally cause another to believe that he had assented, and to act upon such belief, it will be conclusively presumed that his intention was consistent with his conduct, and he will be held responsible the same as if he had manifested his assent by express ratification.

§ **122. What will amount to ratification.**—No positive rule can be laid down by which the fact that an implied ratification has taken place may be established. If one man write to another, "I have this day sold your wife a set of diamonds for five hundred dollars and charged them to your account," the silence of the person thus addressed may be taken as conclusive evidence of the approval of the act of the wife by the husband; and in such case the silence would be sufficient to warrant the inference that the wife was the agent of the husband for the purpose of the sale; or, in other words, it would be sufficient proof of the ratification, even if the act had not been authorized originally. Under different circumstances, however, the silence of the husband might not be any evidence whatever of the ratification. Thus, if the wife had been dealing with the merchant on her own account, and he had simply notified the husband that he had shipped to him a bill of goods purchased by the wife, the failure of the husband to disaffirm liability would not of itself amount to the ratification of a sale to the husband through the wife. In all such cases, where there is a conflict in the testimony, the question of ratification, implied as well as expressed, is for the jury; but in the absence of any dispute as to the facts, the question is one of law for the court. In the first supposed case the circumstances were undoubtedly such that an ordinarily prudent man would naturally infer from the mere silence of the principal that he approved of the act done for him, and, in the absence of other facts, it would be conclusive upon him as a matter of law. In the latter case, however, the jury would have no right from the mere silence of the husband to infer a ratification; for the circumstances would not warrant an ordinarily prudent man in concluding that it was the husband's contract, instead of that of the wife. And so every case must of necessity stand upon its own merits, and be determined by its own peculiar circumstances. Only general rules can be laid down in such cases, and not rules that will fit every case. A few of the most common illustrations may, indeed, be given, in which the courts have held that certain acts or conduct on the part of the principal is sufficient to constitute a ratification. But there are numerous other cases where the line of demarcation is so finely drawn that it would be a matter of greatest difficulty to determine upon which side of the line the cases should fall.

§ **123. Accepting benefits.**—It is an invariable rule that if one accepts the benefits of an unauthorized contract made in his behalf by another, he is bound by its terms the same as if he had entered into the contract in person or had expressly ratified it; provided, of course, that he had full knowledge of all the facts. Hence, if an agent has procured from a third person a note payable to his principal on condition that the note is to be used for a certain purpose, the acceptance of the note by the principal amounts to a ratification of the terms and conditions upon which it was given, and the maxim "*Qui sentit commodum sentire debet et onus*"—"He who receives the benefit ought also to bear the burden"—applies.[213]

§ **124. Corporations—Stockholders receiving benefit of loan.**—Even though the directors of a private corporation have not authority to borrow money and execute a mortgage on its real estate to secure the loan, yet if the stockholders acquiesce therein, by approving the minutes of their proceedings before the loan was effected, and afterward receiving the benefit of such loan and paying interest thereon, the company can not be heard to say that the directors had no authority to mortgage the property for the loan.[214]

[213] Wheeler v. Aughey, 144 Pa. St. 398. See also, Strasser v. Conklin, 54 Wis. 102; Hyatt v. Clark, 118 N. Y. 563; Fairchild v. McMahon, 139 N. Y. 290; Murray v. Mayo, 157 Mass. 248; Pattison v. Babcock, 130 Ind. 474; Wilder v. Beede, 119 Cal. 646; Avakian v. Noble, 121 Cal. 216; Witcher v. Gibson (Colo. App.), 61 Pac. 192; Marks v. Taylor (Utah), 63 Pac. 897, 65 Pac. 203; Owens v. Swanton (Wash.), 64 Pac. 921; Burlingtou, etc., R. Co. v. City of Columbus Junction, 104 Iowa 110; Blakley v. Cochran, 117 Mich. 394; Henry, etc., Co. v. Halter, 58 Neb. 685; Piano Mfg. Co. v. Millage (S. D.), 85 N. W. 594; State Bank v. Kelly, 109 Iowa 544; Bissell v. Dowling, 117 Mich. 646; Wright v. Vineyard M. E. Church, 72 Minn. 78; Moody, etc., Co. v. Trustees of M. E. Church, 99 Wis. 49; Hassard v. Tomkins, 108 Wis. 186, 84 N. W. 174; Des Moines Nat'l Bank v. Meredith (Iowa), 86 N. W. 46.

[214] Aurora Agr., etc., Soc. v. Paddock, 80 Ill. 263. See *ante*, § 102, n. 157.

§ 125. Wife accepting benefit of husband's contract made for her.—Where a wife had authorized her husband to sell her property, but upon different terms from those agreed upon between him and the purchaser, and she accepted the benefits of same, she must be presumed to have ratified the transaction.[215]

§ 126. Corporation retaining benefits.—A corporation sent its employe with an officer to find property of one of its debtors to attach upon a note it held against him. The employe settled the claim with the debtor by taking a horse at an agreed price and a bill of sale to himself of the wagon, which he was to sell, retain a certain amount to extinguish the balance of the debt out of the proceeds of such sale, and turn the remainder over to the debtor. The employe informed the president of the company of the particulars of the arrangement, and the latter expressed no disapproval, but withdrew the suit against the debtor and turned the note over to the employe. The wagon proved to be the property of a stranger, who demanded it of the corporation, and, having met with a refusal, brought suit against it in trover for the value of the wagon. The court held that the acts of the employe would be regarded as ratified by the company, and his possession of the wagon regarded as that of the company.[216]

§ 127. Agent's act in excess of authority.—If an agent acts in excess of the authority delegated to him, and the principal, with the knowledge of all the facts, receives and retains the advantages of such act, he thereby ratifies the transaction.[217]

§ 128. Accepting services of attorney at law.—Where parties knowingly accept the services of an attorney and act upon and enjoy the fruits thereof, they will be held liable for the fee of such attorney, such acceptance and enjoyment of the benefits of the services being a sufficient ratification of the employment in their behalf of

[215] Parish v. Reeve, 63 Wis. 315. See also, Barnett v. Gluting, 3 Ind. App. 415.

[216] Dunn v. Hartford, etc., Horse R. Co., 43 Conn. 434.

[217] Bacon v. Johnson, 56 Mich. 182. See also, Wright v. Vineyard M. E. Church, 72 Minn. 78; Fleishman v. Ver Does, 111 Iowa 322; State Bank of Tabor v. Kelly, 109 Iowa 544; Brong v. Spence, 56 Neb. 638; Sokup v. Lettelier, 123 Mich. 640; Fairchild v. McMahon, 139 N. Y. 290; Murray v. Mayo, 157 Mass. 248; Avakian v. Noble, 121 Cal. 216; Pattison v. Babcock, 130 Ind. 474; Dort v. Nicken, 130 N. Y. 637; Witcher v. Gibson (Colo. App.), 61 Pac. 192; Marks v. Taylor (Utah), 63 Pac. 897, 65 Pac. 203.

the attorney by other clients jointly liable in the litigation or transaction in which the services were rendered.[218]

§ 129. **Unauthorized warranty by agent for principal.**—Upon the same principle, if one accepts the proceeds of a sale made by an agent employed to make such sale, but not authorized to make a warranty, the principal will be bound by the warranty upon the ground of ratification.[219] But this rule will not hold in a case where the agent had a mere special authority to sell a certain kind of property which is not usually sold with a warranty. In this latter case the principal will not be bound by the mere receipt of the proceeds of the sale, unless he had knowledge of the nature of the undertaking at the time of the receipt of the money.[220]

§ 130. **Bringing action on unauthorized contract.**—If an assumed principal, with full knowledge of the facts, brings an action on a contract made for him by the agent without authority, there is a sufficient ratification to warrant the jury or court in holding the principal liable, and that without reference to whether the action is against the third person on the contract, or against the agent for the proceeds collected by him and arising out of the contract.[221] And where an agent sold a piano for his principal at an agreed price, to be paid for in services to the agent by the purchaser, and the principal, with full knowledge of the facts, sued the purchaser for the agreed price, it was held that he thereby affirmed the contract, both as to the sale and as to the mode of payment.[222] After suit and judgment for the

[218] Hauss v. Niblack, 80 Ind. 407. See also, Viley v. Pettit, 96 Ky. 576; Felker v. Haight, 33 Wis. 259; Hogate v. Edwards, 65 Ind. 372; Shelton v. Johnson, 40 Iowa 84; McCrary v. Ruddick, 33 Iowa 521; 2 Parsons Conts. 46. But the mere performance by an attorney of a service resulting in a benefit to the one for whom it is performed is not sufficient, in itself, to render such party liable for the services: Roselius v. Delachaise, 5 La. Ann. 481, 52 Am. Dec. 597; Chicago, etc., R. Co. v. Larned, 26 Ill. 218; Savings Bank v. Benton, 2 Metc. (Ky.) 240; Jones v. Woods, 76 Pa. St. 408; In re Borkstrom, 71 N. Y. Supp. 451.

[219] Cochran v. Chitwood, 59 Ill. 53. See Andrews v. Kneeland, 6 Cow. (N. Y.) 354; Cooley v. Perrine, 41 N. J. L. 322.

[220] Smith v. Tracy, 36 N. Y. 79.

[221] Bank of Beloit v. Beale, 34 N. Y. 473; Benson v. Liggett, 78 Ind. 452; Frank v. Jenkins, 22 Ohio St. 597; Ogden v. Marchand, 29 La. Ann. 61.

[222] Shoninger v. Peabody, 57 Conn. 42, 14 Am. St. 88. See, on the point that suit on the unauthorized contract is a ratification of its execution, Bailey v. Pardridge, 134 Ill. 188; Bissell v. Dowling, 117 Mich. 646; Osborn Co. v. Jordan, 52 Neb. 465, 72 N. W. 479.

purchase money, in such case, the principal can not disavow the agency and sue in replevin for the possession of the goods.[223]

§ 131. **Giving unauthorized contract in evidence.**—Even the giving of an unauthorized contract in evidence by the principal may be construed as a ratification, when it is introduced as a defense in a suit brought contrary to its terms.[224]

§ 132. **Unauthorized sale of goods and embezzlement of proceeds—Accepting satisfaction.**—In a Louisiana case, an agent had effected an unauthorized sale and embezzled the money. The principal afterward accepted from the agent something in satisfaction of the wrong; and it was held that he could not, after such acceptance, follow up the property and take the same in satisfaction of his claim, inasmuch as the acceptance was a ratification of the sale.[225]

§ 133. **Compromise of suit.**—Where an attorney at law effects a compromise in a suit, without authority of his client, the principal or party in whose behalf the compromise was made may, of course, proceed with the suit at his pleasure and thereby repudiate the settlement; but if he abandon the suit, the abandonment may be taken as a ratification of the compromise.[226]

§ 134. **Assenting to alteration of terms of written contract.**—Where a party had signed a subscription paper, in which he agreed to contribute a certain sum to the building of a church, and the paper was subsequently altered in a material respect, but at a meeting of the congregation the paper as altered was read and the subscribers asked whether any one of them did not intend to pay his subscription, and, if so, to give his reasons for not paying, the objecting subscriber being then present and making no objection, it was held that the failure to object to the alteration was a sufficient ratification of the contract in its changed state.[227]

§ 135. **Promise to pay unauthorized note.**—The mere oral promise, after maturity, to pay an unauthorized note without knowledge of the material facts in relation thereto, when made without consid-

223 Marsh v. Pier, 4 Rawle (Pa.) 273.

224 Smith v. Plummer, 5 Whart. (Pa.) 89.

225 Ogden v. Marchand, 29 La. Ann. 61.

226 McClure v. Evartson, 14 Lea (Tenn.) 495.

227 Landwerlen v. Wheeler, 106 Ind. 523.

eration, and without injury to the holder, is not a sufficient ratification to render the alleged maker liable; neither does it create an estoppel; although, if the alleged maker had adopted the note before maturity and thus assisted in its negotiation, he might be estopped from setting up forgery.[228]

§ **136. Ratification by silent consent.**—Where a young man, eighteen years of age, exchanged his father's horse for another, and after the exchange took the horse obtained by the exchange home to his father's barn, informing his father of the exchange, who neither approved nor forbade the act, but retained the horse received in exchange for two or three months, and then tendered him back, demanding his own horse in return, the court held that the jury were fully justified in treating the father's silence, under the circumstances, as a ratification. "An old and just legal maxim may well be applied to the plaintiff here," said the court, "which says, 'If he keeps silent when duty requires him to speak, he shall not be allowed to speak when duty requires him to keep silence.' "[229]

§ **137. Promise to make loss good.**—Where a broker sold the stock of a customer without authority, and afterwards presented an account to the customer showing the sale and the resultant loss, and the customer, without objection, promised to pay the balance shown to be due, thus making good the loss, it was held to be a ratification of the unauthorized sale.[230]

§ **138. Retaining fruits of compromise.**—Where an agent without authority accepted a conveyance of land, in payment of a debt, the creditor, by retaining the land, was held to have ratified the arrangement.[231] And where an agent without authority, professing to act for another, buys goods for him, and the goods come to the principal, and the latter, after being notified of the facts, retains the goods, the seller may maintain an action against the principal for the price of the goods, the latter having ratified the transaction by the retention.[232]

228 Barry v. Kirkland (Ariz.), 40 L. R. A. 471.

229 Hall v. Harper, 17 Ill. 82.

230 Gillett v. Whiting, 141 N. Y. 71.

231 Miles v. Ogden, 54 Wis. 573, 24 Am. Rep. 617.

232 Ketchum v. Verdell, 42 Ga. 534. But where a lease was made by an agent of the landlord to a tenant, without authority, and the landlord so notified the agent, and repudiated the lease, but authorized the tenant to remain in possession of the premises as tenant from month to month, the acceptance of rent from the tenant by the landlord, at the rate specified in the lease, was held not to constitute a ratification of the

§ **139. Ratification after express repudiation.**—Even after a transaction of this kind has been expressly repudiated by the alleged principal, he may still render himself liable by his subsequent conduct.[233]

§ **140. Ratifying party's knowledge of facts.**—Of course, in all such cases, where ratification is claimed by reason of receiving the benefits of the transaction, it must appear that the principal had knowledge of the facts constituting the transaction, or that he had failed or refused to inform himself when he had opportunity to do so. If not so informed, he will not be bound by the receipt of the property, if he makes timely restitution as far as possible.[234] Where an agent sold goods and warranted them, when he had authority to sell, but not to warrant, the mere fact that the owner, in ignorance of the warranty, received the proceeds of the sale, would not amount to a ratification, as the owner would have a right to the proceeds without the warranty.[235] And where one without authority sold the plaintiff's chattel, receiving in payment a bank check which the holder indorsed to the plaintiff in satisfaction of the debt he owed him, and the agent collected the money on the check, and applied it to the extinguishment of the debt, the court, in an action against the defendant for the value of the chattel, held that the receipt of the proceeds of the sale was not an indorsement thereof, inasmuch as the plaintiff was not in possession of the facts under which the check was received.[236]

§ **141. Accepting proceeds of salĕ of land.**—Where the owner of real estate makes a power of attorney to an agent to sell the land of the owner, but does not by such power of attorney authorize the agent to make conveyance thereof, and the agent, in excess of his authority, makes such a conveyance thereof, as well as sale,—the principal, upon being informed, may reject such sale; but if he approves what has been done in his name, and accepts notes and mortgage given by the

lease: Owens v. Swanton (Wash.), 64 N. W. 921.

[233] City of Findlay v. Pertz, 66 Fed. 427.

[234] Schutz v. Jordan, 32 Fed. 55. The ratifying party must know or understand the contract he is approving: Williams v. Hamilton, 104 Iowa 423. And in case of the ratification of a contract, the execution of which was secured by duress, it must be clearly the intention of the principal to ratify such contract: Kennedy v. Roberts, 105 Iowa 521. But if the principal sign a contract for the sale of land previously unauthorized, without reading over such contract, he will be bound by its provisions: Liska v. Lodge, 112 Mich. 635.

[235] Smith v. Tracy, 36 N. Y. 79.

[236] Thacher v. Pray, 113 Mass. 291.

purchaser, and insists upon their payment after being informed of the conveyance, he thereby ratifies the conveyance and the effect of the power of attorney to convey as executed by the agent.[237] And upon the same principle, where a third person sold land in the name of the owner, but without authority, the transaction was held to be ratified by showing that the landowner accepted without objection installments of the purchase money, and gave his receipts in which he acknowledged that such installments were made in part payment of the land in question.[238]

§ **142. Silence when speech required.**—It is a familiar rule, as we have seen, that where one who ought to speak remains silent, he may be held responsible for the consequences. If, by his silence, he permits third persons to become involved so that they would suffer loss, which they would not have incurred but for his inaction, he ought not to be heard to say that he did not authorize the transaction which he has failed to disavow, and which will cause the loss to such third person, if permitted. In such a case, it is his duty to give notice of the repudiation of the act that was performed without his assent, and such notice must be given within a reasonable time, and upon his failure so to give it he will be held to have ratified the act.[239] What is a reasonable time within which the act should be repudiated is to be determined by the surrounding circumstances of each case.[240] Some courts hold that the principal must act at once as soon as knowledge of the matter comes to him.[241] In this, as in all other matters in which the rights of third persons are involved, the parties concerned must act with proper diligence. They must not sleep upon their rights, lest others suffer loss through their negligence.[242]

(*c*) *Effects of Ratification.*

§ **143. Purpose.**—Having now considered the essential requirements of a valid ratification, and the manner in which it may be

[237] Delano v. Jacoby, 96 Cal. 275, 31 Am. St. 201.

[238] Murray v. Mayo, 157 Mass. 248.

[239] Parish v. Reeve, 63 Wis. 315; Hamlin v. Sears, 82 N. Y. 327; Meyer v. Morgan, 51 Miss. 21, 24 Am. Rep. 617; Gold Mining Co. v. National Bank, 96 U. S. 640; Mobile, etc., R. Co. v. Jay, 65 Ala. 113; Wright v. Boynton, 37 N. H. 9.

[240] Philadelphia, etc., R. Co. v. Cowell, 28 Pa. St. 329, 70 Am. Dec. 128.

[241] Ward v. Williams, 26 Ill. 447, 79 Am. Dec. 385; Foster v. Rockwell, 104 Mass. 167; Kelsey v. National Bank, 69 Pa. St. 426; Hart v. Dixon, 5 Lea (Tenn.) 336; Kehlor v. Kemble, 26 La. Ann. 713.

[242] Saveland v. Green, 40 Wis. 431; Kent v. Quicksilver Mining Co., 78 N. Y. 137.

brought about, it is proper to notice the effects that will result from such ratification, both upon the immediate and upon third parties.

§ 144. **Relates back to time of performance of act.**—And first, it may be laid down as a well established general rule that one of the most sweeping effects of a ratification, and one which changes at once the entire relationship from one of mere usurpation to one of authorized representation, is that it relates back to the time of the performance of the unauthorized transaction, and gives to it the same sanctity and character that it would have had if authorized in the inception. This general rule is subject to the single exception that if the rights of innocent third persons would be injuriously affected by the ratification, it will not be permitted to operate. As between the assumed principal (the ratifying party) and the third person (the one with whom the assumed agent has dealt) the effect is in all respects as if the agent had received full authority in the beginning. Here the maxim applies: *"Omnis ratihabitio retrotrahitur et mandato priori aequiparatur"*—"Every ratification relates back and is equivalent to a prior authority."[243]

§ 145. **No locus poenitentiae.**—It is an equally well established rule that the moment a principal ratifies or adopts as his own the unauthorized act of an agent done in his, the principal's, behalf, he is bound by it. He can not afterward recant, as it were, and avoid the results of his ratification. In other words, there is no *locus poenitentiae*. The ratification can never afterward be revoked, so far as the principal is concerned.[244] As already remarked, the revocation relates back to the commission of the act, and is the same as though it had been expressly authorized at that time. If, after the revocation, some new rights are acquired by reason of the same, third parties to whom such rights have accrued can not be deprived of the benefits thereof.

§ 146. **Ratification disturbing vested rights.**—On the other hand, if, between the time of the performance of an unauthorized act and that of ratification, third parties have acquired rights based upon the assumption that the act was unauthorized, a ratification can not be invoked to serve as a divestment of such rights or to disturb the

[243] Lynch v. Smith, 25 Colo. 103. When a contract, though unauthorized, was subsequently ratified by the principal, all that was said and done at the making of the contract becomes proper evidence as of the *res gestae:* Marks v. Taylor (Utah), 63 Pac. 897, 65 Pac. 203.

[244] Evans Pr. & Ag. (Bedford's ed.) 107; Smith v. Cologan, 2 T. R. 188, n.; Brock v. Jones, 16 Tex. 461.

same in any particular; nor will it, to the extent of its interference with such vested rights, relate back to the performance of the unauthorized act. Thus, the subsequent ratification of a deed of conveyance made to a creditor by a debtor through the agent of the creditor, and in payment of a debt, will not relate back to the time of the conveyance so as to defeat the lien of attachment levied on the property after the conveyance but before the ratification, although the deed was recorded before the levy of attachment.[245] And if an agent without authority should make a sale and conveyance of land for another, the principal could not, by ratification, defeat the results of another sale made by himself between the time of the agent's unauthorized act and the time of the sale made by himself.[246]

§ **147. Superior equities.**—While it is true, as a general rule, that the ratification can not be given effect as against intervening rights of third persons, it will nevertheless be applied to cases in which the equities of the party claiming the benefit of the ratification are superior to those of the opposing party. So, where persons, on the faith of an apparent partnership, give credit to the concern, though in fact the formation of such alleged partnership was but the result of the unauthorized act of the agent of one of the parties to it, if the transaction is subsequently ratified, the act of forming the partnership becomes valid from the time of its performance; and creditors having claims against the firm will be preferred to individual creditors of the other partner, although execution had been levied for the individual debts when the act of ratification occurred.[247]

(d) Parties Affected by Ratification.

§ **148. Effect as between principal and agent.**—The unauthorized act, when ratified by the principal, becomes his own act the same as if he had previously authorized it.[248] He now becomes a principal, and the relation is as fully established as though it had been entered into by express agreement. And it is immaterial whether the ratified act is a benefit or detriment to the ratifying party: he will be bound by it just the same; nor is it material whether it be founded on contract or tort.[249]

[245] Kempner v. Rosenthal, 81 Tex. 12; United States Express Co. v. Rawson, 106 Ind. 215.

[246] McCracken v. San Francisco, 16 Cal. 591, 624.

[247] Williams v. Butler, 35 Ill. 544.

[248] U. S. Express Co. v. Rawson, 106 Ind. 215; Drakely v. Gregg, 8 Wall. (U. S.) 242.

[249] Wilson v. Tumman, 6 M. & Gr. 236; Hovil v. Pack, 7 East 164.

§ 149. **Public agents—Ratification by state and general governments.**—As a general rule, a public agent can act only within the scope of authority conferred upon him by statute. But the unauthorized act of such an agent may be ratified by the enactment of a statute for that purpose, and the effect of such an enactment will be the release of the agent as in other cases of ratification.[250] In case of ratification of a trespass or other tort by the crown, the party injured can no longer sue the trespasser, but must look for redress to the crown, if he has any remedy at all. Thereafter the trespassing party is exempt from all liability.[251]

§ 150. **Position of agent after ratification.**—If the principal has ratified the unauthorized act with a full knowledge of the facts, he is bound by the act, as we have seen, to the same extent as if he had originally authorized it. The agent is thereafter discharged from all liability, unless, indeed, he would have been liable had the act been done by authority of the principal originally. The agent may still be liable, however, to the principal in damages, if he has misled the latter as to the true condition of the matter ratified. If the agent informed the principal wrongly, he will be accountable to him in damages whether the information was given fraudulently or in good faith.[252]

§ 151. **Deviation from instructions—Ratification of.**—If the agent has deviated from his principal's instructions he will be liable for the consequences primarily. Thus, if a collecting agent, contrary to his principal's direction to remit money by express, purchases exchange of parties then in good standing, and the principal endeavors to collect the exchange, but it is dishonored, the drawers having become insolvent meanwhile, the agent is liable to the principal for the loss; and the attempt of the principal to collect it before he discovers the insolvency is not a ratification of the act of sending the money by exchange.[253]

§ 152. **Liability for torts.**—Where a tort has been committed by the agent, either by authority of the principal previously conferred, or without such authority, but subsequently ratified, the agent will be

[250] State v. Torinus, 26 Minn. 1.

[251] Buron v. Denman, 2 Exch. 167.

[252] Bank of Owensboro v. Western Bank, 13 Bush (Ky.) 526.

[253] Walker v. Walker, 5 Heisk. (Tenn.) 425.

liable as well as the principal. The effect of ratification in such case is not the substitution of the principal's liability for that of the agent, but it renders the principal liable to third parties in addition to the agent.[254]

[254] Perminter v. Kelly, 18 Ala. 716; Richardson v. Kimball, 28 Me. 463; Burnap v. Marsh, 13 Ill. 535. Mr. Justice Holmes, in the case of Dempsey v. Chambers, 154 Mass. 330, in discussing the doctrine of the ratification of torts, speaking for the court says:

"If we were contriving a new code to-day we might hesitate to say that a man could make himself a party to a bare tort, in any case, merely by assenting to it after it had been committed. But we are not at liberty to refuse to carry out to its consequences any principle which we believe to have been part of the common law simply because the grounds of policy on which it must be justified seem to us to be hard to find, and probably to have belonged to a different state of society.

"It is hard to explain why a master is liable to the extent that he is for the negligent acts of one who at the time really is his servant, acting within the general scope of his employment. Probably master and servant are feigned to be all one person, by a fiction which is an echo of the *patria potestas* and of the English frankpledge: Byington v. Simpson, 134 Mass. 169, 170; Fitz. Abr., Corone, pl. 428. Possibly the doctrine of ratification is another aspect of the same tradition. The requirement that the act should be done in the name of the ratifying party looks that way: New England Dredging Co. v. Rockport Granite Co., 149 Mass. 381, 382; Fuller & Trimwell's Case, 2 Leon. 215, 216; Sext. Dec. 5, 12, De Reg. Jur., Reg. 9; D. 43, 26, 13; D. 43, 16, 1, § 14, glossary. See also cases next cited.

"The earliest instances of liability by way of ratification in the English law, so far as we have noticed, were where a man retained property acquired through the wrongful act of another: Y. B. 30 Ed. I, 128 (Rolls ed.); 38 Lib. Ass. 223, pl. 9, s. c. 38 Ed. III, 18, Engettement de Garde. See Plowd. 8, *ad fin.*, 27, 31; Bract., fol. 158b, 159a, 171b; 12 Ed. IV, 9, pl. 23. But in these cases the defendant's assent was treated as relating back to the original act, and at an early date the doctrine of relation was carried so far as to hold that, where a trespass would have been justified if it had been done by the authority by which it purported to have been done, a subsequent ratification might justify it also: Y. B. 7 Hen. IV, 34, pl. 1. This decision is qualified in Fitz. Abr., Bayllye, pl. 4, and doubted in Bro. Abr., Trespass, pl. 86; but it has been followed or approved so continuously, and in so many later cases, that it would be hard to deny that the common law was as there stated by Chief Justice Gascoigne: Godbolt, 109, 110, pl. 129, s. c. 2 Leon. 196, pl. 246; Hull v. Pickersgill, 1 Brod. & Bing. 282; Muskett v. Drummond, 10 B. & C. 153, 157; Buron v. Denman, 2 Exch. 167, 188; Secretary of State in Council of India v. Kamachee Boye Sahaba, 13 Moore P. C. 22, 86; Cheetham v. Mayor, etc., of Manchester, L. R. 10 C. P. 249; Wiggins v. United States, 3 Ct. of Cl. 412.

"If we assume that an alleged

§ 153. **Can third party recede?**—After the ratification the third party may enforce the contract against the principal the same as if the latter had authorized or entered into it on his own behalf.[255] Suppose, however, that the third party desires to recede from the agreement before the ratification by the supposed principal. As to whether this may be done or not the authorities are not fully agreed.

principal, by adopting an act which was unlawful when done, can make it lawful, it follows that he adopts it at his peril, and is liable if it should turn out that his previous command would not have justified the act. It never has been doubted that a man's subsequent agreement to a trespass done in his name and for his benefit amounts to a command, so far as to make him answerable. The *ratihabitio mandato comparatur* of the Roman lawyers and the earlier cases (D. 46, 3, 12, § 4; D. 43, 16, 1, § 14; Y. B. 30 Ed. I, 128) has been changed to the dogma *aequiparatur* ever since the days of Lord Coke: 4 Inst. 317. See Bro. Abr., Trespass, pl. 113; Co. Lit. 207a; Wingate's Maxims 124; Com. Dig., Trespass, C, 1; Eastern Counties R. Co. v. Broom, 6 Exch. 314, 326, 327, and cases hereafter cited. Doubts have been expressed, which we need not consider, whether this doctrine applied to the case of a bare personal tort: Adams v. Freeman, 9 Johns. (N. Y.) 117, 118; Anderson and Warberton, JJ., in Bishop v. Montague, Cro. Eliz. 824. If a man assaulted another in the street out of his own head, it would seem rather strong to say that, if he merely called himself my servant, and I afterwards assented, without more, our mere words would make me a party to the assault, although in such cases the canon law excommunicated the principal if the assault was upon a clerk: Sext. Dec. 5, 11, 23. Perhaps the application of the doctrine would be avoided on the ground that the facts did not show an act done for the defendant's benefit: Wilson v. Barker, 1 Nev. & Man. 409, s. c. 4 B. & Ad. 614, *et seq.*; Smith v. Lozo, 42 Mich. 6. As in other cases, it has been on the ground that they did not amount to such a ratification as was necessary: Tucker v. Jerris, 75 Me. 184; Hyde v. Cooper, 26 Vt. 552.

"But the language generally used by judges and text-writers, and such decisions as we have been able to find, is broad enough to cover a case like the present when the ratification is established: Perley v. Georgetown, 7 Gray (Mass.) 464; Bishop v. Montague, Cro. Eliz. 824; Sanderson v. Baker, 2 W. Bl. 832, s. c. 3 Wils. 309; Barker v. Braham, 2 W. Bl. 866, 868; s. c. 3 Wils. 368; Badkin v. Powell, Cowper 476, 479; Wilson v. Tumman, 6 M. & G. 236, 242; Lewis v. Read, 13 M. & W. 834; Buron v. Denman, 2 Exch. 167, 188; Bird v. Brown, 4 Exch. 786, 799; Eastern Counties R. Co. v. Broom, 6 Exch. 314, 326, 327; Roe v. Birkenhead, etc., R. Co., 7 Exch. 36, 41; Ancona v. Marks, 7 H. & N. 686, 695; Condit v. Baldwin, 21 N. Y. 219, 225; Exum v. Brister, 35 Miss. 391; Galveston, etc., R. Co. v. Donahoe, 56 Tex. 162; Murray v. Lovejoy, 2 Clif. (U. S.) 192, 195. See Lovejoy v. Murray, 3 Wall. (U. S.) 1, 9; Story Ag., §§ 455, 456."

[255] Szymanski v. Plassan, 20 La. Ann. 90, 96 Am. Dec. 382.

The American courts generally hold that the third party is at liberty to recede at any time before the ratification by the principal, inasmuch as there is, up to the period of ratification, no mutuality between the principal and the third party.[256] After ratification by the assumed principal the third person will not be bound unless he does some act signifying his affirmance; as, by bringing suit or otherwise attempting to enforce the contract. The right to repudiate the transaction, unless it be a case where he is required to speak and has not done so, remains in the third party until he has by his express or implied affirmation signified his intention to abide by it.[257]

§ **154. The English doctrine.**—But the English doctrine is that the third party can not recede, but is bound by the contract the same as if it had been originally authorized by the principal. According to this rule the element of mutuality is not wanting when there is a ratification. If the contract does not originally bind the principal, it does bind the one who has undertaken to act for him, the latter and the third person being mutually liable *inter sese*. If the agent's act is ratified by the person for whom it was done, the ratification relates back to the time of the performance, and the principal's liability becomes a substitute for the liability of the agent, while the third party has no greater than he assumed in the beginning.[258] The third person may, indeed, be released from liability by the agent, but this must be done before ratification.[259] Thus, in the case cited in the note, a person assuming to act as agent for another paid a portion of a debt for him, expecting to be reimbursed by the debtor. Afterwards the money was returned to the person who paid it, and the trial court held that the debtor could avail himself of the benefit of the payment made for him, and, when sued for the debt, plead payment by his agent. But the court of exchequer decided otherwise. The debtor might have ratified the payment, even after suit against him, by pleading the payment as a defense, had the money been retained by the creditor. But if, before such ratification, the creditor and the assumed agent, apart from the debtor, agree to cancel what had been done between them, and the money is refunded,

[256] Atlee v. Bartholomew, 69 Wis. 43; Dodge v. Hopkins, 14 Wis. 686; Townsend v. Corning, 23 Wend. (N. Y.) 435.

[257] Dodge v. Hopkins, 14 Wis. 686. See also, State v. Torinus, 26 Minn. 1.

[258] In re Portuguese, etc., Mines, L. R. 45 Ch. D. 16.

[259] Walter v. James, L. R. 6 Ex. 124.

it is competent for them to do so, and the transaction between the debtor and the agent becomes a nullity. "When a payment is not made by way of a gift for the benefit of the debtor, but by an agent who intended that he be reimbursed by the debtor, but who had not the debtor's authority to pay, it is competent for the creditor and the person paying to rescind the transaction at any time before the debtor has affirmed the payment and repaid the money, and thereupon the payment is at an end and the debtor again responsible."[260]

§ 155. Discharge of agent from liability except in cases of tort.— As has already been stated, and as we shall have occasion to discuss more fully hereafter,[261] one who, without authority, undertakes to perform an act for another becomes personally liable to him with whom he deals for his alleged principal. But when the act has been ratified by the party on whose account it has been performed, the agent is discharged from any liability to the person with whom the transaction has been had. This is for the sufficient reason that the agent has performed all he engaged to perform. He entered into the contract—if such it was—not on his own behalf, but for another. This assumption of authority he has fully made good by procuring the principal's approval. He is now no longer a factor in the transaction. He could only be liable, in the event of having no authority, for assuming to act without it. He can not become liable for this because the authority has become real. And, having no personal interest in the matter, he can not himself assert any right of action.[262] If, however, the matter ratified is a trespass, or other tort, the rule is different. In that case, as we have seen, both the principal and the agent are responsible to the third party. What was previously the wrong of one is now the wrong of both. The agent and the principal become joint tort-feasors, and are jointly and severally responsible for the injury done.[263]

[260] Per Martin, B., in Walter v. James, *supra*.

[261] *Post*, § 309.

[262] Story Ag., § 244.

[263] Perminter v. Kelly, 18 Ala. 716, 54 Am. Dec. 177; Burnap v. Marsh, 13 Ill. 535; Thorp v. Burling, 11 Johns. (N. Y.) 285; Josslyn v. McAllister, 22 Mich. 300.

CHAPTER IV.

HOW AGENCY MAY BE TERMINATED.

§ **155a. General statement of the law.**—Mr. Evans mentions three general methods by either of which an agency may be determined: (1) By agreement; (2) by act of party; (3) by operation of law. These general heads, however, may be subdivided. Thus, under the term "agreement" may be included the time during which, according to the stipulation of the contract, the agency is to continue, and also the happening of some event upon which it is to be terminated, as well as the matter of performance of the object or objects for which the agency was created. And under the head of "act of party" may be brought the method of revocation of the agency by the principal or its renunciation by the agent. In the term "operation of law" may be included termination by death of the principal, by death of the agent, by bankruptcy of the principal, by bankruptcy of the agent, by marriage (under the common-law rules) of a *feme sole* principal, by insanity of the principal, by insanity of the agent, and by destruction of the subject-matter.[1]

I. Termination by Agreement of Parties in Original Contract.

§ **156. By expiration of time or happening of event.**—An agency, being generally but the condition or relation created by a contract between the parties to it, will, of course, become dissolved by its own terms whenever the time expires for which it has been created or the event happens at which it was to end. In this particular a contract of agency is precisely like any other contract. If by its terms it is to remain in force for a year, it will expire at the end of that period; and so as to any other time. Hence, if A employ B as a commercial traveler to sell goods for him, or as a clerk in his store, or in any other capacity, the relation will cease to exist with the expiration of the term of employment; unless, indeed, the employe should continue to act without any new arrangement, in which case the presumption would be that he continued upon the old terms.[2] This question often becomes important where a bond is given, with sureties, by an agent or employe, for the faithful performance of his duties; or where the question arises whether the agent has earned his compensation. In case a bond is given by the agent, with sureties, conditioned upon the faithful discharge of the agent's duty, the sureties are, of course, discharged from liability for any act done by him after the period of employment expires, and are no longer liable for the conduct of the agent thereafter.[3] In this class of contracts there can be but little difficulty when once the time is determined for which the employment is to continue, or the event is

[1] Evans Pr. & Ag. (Bedford's ed.) 119, 120.

[2] Standard Oil Co. v. Gilbert, 84 Ga. 714; Sines v. Superintendent of Poor, 58 Mich. 503; Tatterson v. Suffolk Mfg. Co., 106 Mass. 56.

[3] Gundlach v. Fischer, 59 Ill. 172.

ascertained at the happening of which it is to cease. If the agency is to terminate upon the happening of some event, as, for example, the return of the principal to the place where the business is to be transacted or the subject of the agency is located, and from which the principal was about to depart, leaving certain business management to his agent during his absence, the agency is limited to the time of the principal's absence.[4] And so, the parties may also provide in their agreement that the agency may be terminated at the will of either party, or by giving the other party written notice to that effect, or by giving such notice for a certain length of time; and the employment will terminate, of course, when the event happens, or the notice has been given for the length of time provided for, and the agent can not, generally, recover compensation thereafter.[5] If the agency is to be terminated at the option of either party, or if no time has been agreed upon when it shall expire, the principal has the right, as well as the power, to revoke the appointment at any time. Thus, in the case of an insurance agency, where the contract contained no limitation as to the time during which it was to continue, but did contain a stipulation that it might be terminated upon the neglect or refusal of the agent to account for moneys of the company, or for dishonesty, or noncompliance with the rules and instructions of the company, it was held that the company might discontinue the agency at any time and for any reason it deemed proper, there being nothing in the contract to prevent.[6] An agreement for the employment of an agent for a certain time, provided

[4] Danby v. Coutts, L. R. 29 Ch. D. 500.

[5] Doyle v. Phœnix Ins. Co., 25 N. Sc. 436; Witherell v. Murphy, 147 Mass. 417. Where, according to the original contract, the principal had given the agent three months' written notice of revocation, which was explicit and unequivocal, the agency was at an end; and the mere fact that the agent continued to do business for the principal, such as he had done before, did not necessarily amount to a waiver or withdrawal of such notice: Clover Condensed Milk Co. v. Cushman Bros. Co., 52 N. Y. Supp. 769. But where it was provided that the authority might be revoked at the principal's written request, a written demand for securities coming into the hands of the agent by reason of the agency, made by a party claiming to be an attorney of the principal, without a written order or other evidence of authority, was held not sufficient proof of revocation to enable the principal to maintain a suit for the securities: Tingley v. Parshall, 11 Neb. 443.

[6] Stier v. Imperial Life Ins. Co., 58 Fed. 843; Willcox, etc., Co. v. Ewing, 141 U. S. 627.

he prove satisfactory, may be terminated at the will of the principal.[7] Such a contract is in the nature of an unilateral agreement, being an agreement on the one hand to serve or perform, but no agreement on the other to employ for any definite time. Such contracts terminate whenever the principal chooses to withhold employment.[8] The fact that an agent or servant was hired at so much per year might constitute proof that he was employed for a year, but not necessarily so, if circumstances indicate the contrary intention.[9] Of course, much must be left to be determined from the circumstances of each individual case, it being impossible to lay down any definite rule for deciding the question as to when the employment was to end where the terms of the contract are not explicit. The general rule applicable to all classes of contracts, that the courts will aim to ascertain, from all the facts and circumstances of the transaction, what were the intentions of the parties, will, of course, govern here also.

§ 157. **By accomplishment of object for which agency was created.**—If, however, no specific time has been fixed, but the agency is created simply for the accomplishment of some particular object,—as, for example, the sale of certain lands, or the purchase of a horse, or the collection of a debt,—the relation will terminate with the accomplishment of the object; that is to say, with the sale of property, or the purchase of the animal, or the collection and payment of the debt.[10] Therefore, where the owner of a parcel of land employed a broker to sell the same, under an agreement that if the agent would obtain a purchaser the owner would pay him a certain sum of money for his services, the court ruled that the agency came to an end as soon as the purchaser was procured.[11] And the duties of the agent are discharged and the relation is ended with the delivery of the title papers and the payment of the purchase price, when the agent was employed to sell the property.[12] Where a real estate broker was

[7] Tyler v. Ames, 6 Lans. (N. Y.) 280.

[8] See Burton v. Great Northern R. Co., 9 Exch. 507; Aspdin v. Austin, L. R. 5 Q. B. 671; Dunn v. Sayles, L. R. 5 Q. B. 685. Where an attorney employed by the state fund commissioners to prosecute claims against the United States was to receive commissions for his services, the state could revoke the agency at its will by a repealing act: Walker v. Walker, 125 U. S. 339.

[9] Tatterson v. Suffolk Mfg. Co., 106 Mass. 56. For a more extended discussion of this subject, see *post*, § 278.

[10] Ahern v. Baker, 34 Minn. 98; Walker v. Derby, 5 Biss. (U. S.) 134; Moore v. Stone, 40 Iowa 259.

[11] Short v. Millard, 68 Ill. 292.

[12] Walker v. Derby, 5 Biss. (U. S.) 134.

employed to find a purchaser for land owned by the principal, at a certain price, it was held that when this service was performed the agent was at liberty to engage in the service of the purchaser in securing a conveyance for the same land, and that there was no longer any conflict between these services.[13] Generally, whenever a real estate broker, employed for the purpose of selling land, has found a purchaser ready, willing, and able to buy, upon the terms specified in his employment, his duties have been fully performed, and the agency is ended.[14] Where the owner of property placed the same in the hands of a real estate broker for sale upon certain terms, agreeing that the broker should be the exclusive agent for the next six months, and that the agency should not be revoked except upon payment of commission, it was held that the agency expired at the end of six months, and that the agent was not entitled to collect commissions when, long after the expiration of the six months, the owner sold the property himself without consulting the agent, and that the clause as to the revocation of authority must be held to mean a cancellation within six months from the time the contract was entered into.[15] And if no terms are stipulated, the duties of a real estate agent are ended when he has produced a purchaser to whom a sale is actually made by the principal.[16] In an Illinois case, where an agent was employed to secure a debt due the principal, and the agent in settlement took notes indorsed by the debtor to the principal, the court decided that the agency did not cease until the notes had been delivered to and accepted by the principal, and that until then the declarations of the agent were competent testimony against the principal.[17] Where an agent is employed to accomplish a certain object, and the object is accomplished otherwise than by his instrumentality, the agency is at an end. So, where a town treasurer was authorized to borrow money for the payment of a certain tax, and the tax was paid by other means, it was held that the agent's authority to borrow money ceased when the tax was paid.[18]

[13] Short v. Millard, 68 Ill. 292.

[14] Fischer v. Bell, 91 Ind. 243; Neilson v. Lee, 60 Cal. 555; Monroe v. Snow, 131 Ill. 126; Duclos v. Cunningham, 102 N. Y. 678.

[15] Learned v. McCoy, 4 Ind. App. 238, 30 N. E. 717.

[16] Coleman v. Meade, 13 Bush (Ky.) 358; Desmond v. Stebbins, 140 Mass. 339; Sibbald v. Bethlehem Iron Co., 83 N. Y. 378.

[17] Wallace v. Goold, 91 Ill. 15.

[18] Benoit v. Inhabitants of Conway, 10 Allen (Mass.) 528.

II. Termination by Act of Party.

§ **158. By subsequent agreement of parties.**—The parties may, of course, agree at any time to dissolve the relation between them, and thus end it, whatever may have been their contract as to its duration.[19] This may amount to a rescission of the original contract by agreement, or it may be only a construction of its terms as to the time of expiration. It would be rescission if, by its terms, the original contract had not expired, and the agreement to dissolve were based upon a sufficient consideration. If the original contract is ambiguous as to its duration, the parties can agree to dissolve the relation, and thus give a construction to its meaning which the courts will uphold.

§ **159. By revocation of principal or renunciation of agent.**—Either party to such a contract also has the power, though not always the right, to revoke or renounce it before the expiration of the time during which it is to run. Thus, the principal may at any time revoke the authority of the agent, unless it is coupled with an interest, or unless it is necessary to effectuate any security.[20] True, this would constitute a breach of the contract, for which, if the agent were not in default, the principal would be liable to him in

[19] Wharton Ag., § 93.

[20] Evans Pr. & Ag. (Bedford's ed.) 126; Story Ag., § 463; Montague v. McCarroll, 15 Utah 318, 49 Pac. 419. See Woods v. Hart, 50 Neb. 497, 70 N. W. 53; Kolb v. Bennett Land Co., 74 Miss. 567, 21 So. 233; Marbury v. Barnet, 40 N. Y. Supp. 76; Smith v. Dare, 89 Md. 47, 42 Atl. 909. It is not always easy to determine what is an authority coupled with an interest. The subject will be fully considered in a subsequent portion of this book. See *post*, § 181, *et seq.* Where the interest was merely contingent upon the sale the agent was to make, it was not such as would prevent a revocation: Hall v. Gambrill, 88 Fed. 709. Under the rule that an authority is irrevocable when coupled with an interest, it has been held that an authority to sell personal property to satisfy a claim is irrevocable, and it is not necessary that the authority be given in writing: Terwilliger v. Ontario, etc., R. Co., 149 N. Y. 86, 43 N. E. 432. To the same effect, see American Loan, etc., Co. v. Billings, 58 Minn. 187, 59 N. W. 998. But an agreement to pay an attorney a *percentum* on collections to be made by him for the client is not irrevocable as being an authority coupled with an interest: Burke v. Priest, 50 Mo. App. 310. And where a power of attorney was given an agent to collect rents of a farm, with directions to "advance no rents before due," it was held this implied that there was no obligation to make any advances to the principal, and hence, that the latter could revoke the power at will despite the fact that such advances had been made: Smith v. Dare, 89 Md. 47, 42 Atl. 909.

damages. The question of remedy for a wrongful revocation will be more fully considered hereafter, when we come to discuss the duties of the parties to each other. On the other hand, the agent may renounce the contract, and thus terminate the relation, and he may do so without cause. This, too, is but a naked power, without a right. It is not the policy of the law to force the parties to continue in the relation contrary to their own volition. There is, therefore, no power anywhere by which the parties may be kept together in the relation. They are not without remedy, however, as we shall hereafter see.[21] As we have observed, the authority of the agent may be terminated at any time by the principal's act of revocation. The authority, being predicated upon the assent of the principal, is at an end when he withdraws it, unless it be coupled with an interest or is necessary for the purposes above mentioned, and this is true although it is stipulated in the contract of appointment that the authority is irrevocable.[22]

§ 160. **Revocation may be express or implied.**—The authority may be revoked expressly or by implication. If done expressly, the revocation may be in writing under seal, by an instrument in writing not under seal, or by parol. If by implication, it may be inferred from the conduct of the principal. In the absence of a statute, or a stipulation in the contract of appointment to that effect, no writing or other formality is necessary, although the appointment was made by a

[21] *Post*, § 269. See Chambers v. Seay, 73 Ala. 372; Blackstone v. Buttermore, 53 Pa. St. 266; MacGregor v. Gardner, 14 Iowa 326; Ætna Life Ins. Co. v. Nexsen, 84 Ind. 347. An agent or employe can not enforce specific performance of a contract of employment, though wrongfully discharged, unless his agency was coupled with an interest: Elwell v. Coon (N. J. Eq.), 46 Atl. 580.

[22] Chambers v. Seay, 73 Ala. 372; Walker v. Denison, 86 Ill. 142; Hunt v. Rousmanier, 8 Wheat. (U. S.) 174, 201. But an agency can not be revoked when it is done for the sole purpose of depriving a court of jurisdiction, so as to enable a foreign insurance company to avoid the effects of prospective judgment against it for a loss of which it has been notified, as such a proceeding savors of bad faith: Michael v. Nashville Mut. Ins. Co., 10 La. Ann. 737. Where a person is appointed agent to sell the principal's property and apply the proceeds to the payment of his debts, the arrangement being subject to the approval of the principal's creditors, it was held that until such acceptance the creditors have no legal interest in the matter, and the principal may revoke the direction without their consent. A demand of the property by the principal, in such case, operates as a revocation: Comley v. Dazian, 114 N. Y. 161. An agency may be made irrevocable by special contract, if based upon a good consideration: Wharton Ag., § 95.

sealed instrument.[23] If the conduct of the principal is such as to lead clearly to the inference that he intended a revocation, it will be implied. This may be done by his delegation of authority to another agent when the first appointment was exclusive.[24] Thus, where the owner of land employs a broker to negotiate a sale of the land, and the appointment is exclusive, the subsequent appointment of another broker to sell the same land may be taken as a revocation of the authority of the first. But if the authority is not exclusive it will not be deemed revoked by the subsequent appointment of another agent to do the same thing. Custom has much to do with this. If it is customary, for instance, among real estate brokers, to give the property to be sold into the hands of several agents or brokers, it will be implied that such conduct is to be pursued in the given instance. If the principal, after conferring such authority upon the agent, sells the property himself, or if it is destroyed by fire or otherwise, the agent's authority is revoked.[25] But an employment to collect a sum of money is not necessarily revoked by the

[23] Brookshire v. Brookshire, 8 Ired. (N. C.) 74, 47 Am. Dec. 341. Where an agent was appointed by two joint principals, it was held that upon a severance of the joint interest of the principals the agency was terminated, even though the object of his appointment was not yet fully accomplished: Rowe v. Rand, 111 Ind. 206. The marriage of a *feme sole* also has the effect of revoking an agency by her to another to lease her lands; and a lease by the agent subsequent to such marriage is void: Linton v. Minneapolis, etc., Co., 2 N. D. 232, 50 N. W. 357.

[24] Copeland v. Mercantile Ins. Co., 6 Pick. (Mass.) 198. Where the agent has employed a subagent, the revocation of the agent's authority carries with it the revocation of the authority of the subagent: Jackson Ins. Co. v. Partee, 9 Heisk. (Tenn.) 296. But it is otherwise if the subagent derived his authority from the principal: Smith v. White, 5 Dana (Ky.) 376. Where an old lady had authorized the defendant in her suit to dismiss the same, but afterward, and before such dismissal, had executed a power of attorney to her counselor to prosecute the action to its conclusion, it was held that the power of attorney constituted a revocation of the authority to dismiss: Aiken v. Taylor (Tenn.), 62 S. W. 200. And so, where a power of attorney was executed to convey lands, but the principal conveyed the land by subsequent deed to the agent as trustee of his son, it was held that the deed from the principal to the agent, as trustee, was a revocation of the power of attorney, and a conveyance by the agent under such power of attorney was void: Chenault v. Quisenberry (Ky.), 56 S. W. 410, 57 S. W. 234.

[25] Bissell v. Terry, 69 Ill. 184; Gilbert v. Holmes, 64 Ill. 548.

engagement of another agent to do the same thing.[26] Instances of revocation by implication are too numerous to warrant an attempt at specification of any considerable number in this treatise. Where the principal himself disposes of the subject-matter,[27] or where there is a dissolution of a partnership which has an agent who had been previously appointed,[28] or where the agent was appointed by the joint act of two principals and there is a severance of their interests,[29]—any of these or similar instances will be sufficient to authorize the conclusion that the principal has terminated the authority of his agent. In some of the states, statutes provide how an authority conferred in writing shall be revoked.

§ 161. Consequences of revocation—Between principal and agent.—Having considered some of the methods by which an agency may be revoked by the principal, it is proper that we should ascertain what are the consequences that may flow from such revocation. And first, as between the principal and the agent. When a principal discharges his agent, he may do so for several reasons: 1. He may dissolve the relation because the agent was employed for no specific period, but only during the will of the principal, until he should see proper to discharge him. 2. He may revoke the authority because of the misconduct of the agent, although by the contract the period of service has not yet expired. 3. He may discharge the agent without any good reason, and in violation of his contract; but in the latter case a distinction must be made, as we have already seen, between the power of the principal to discharge his agent and the right to do so. If the revocation is prompted by the first and second causes above enumerated, the principal has the right as well as the power to revoke; and the agent has no remedy unless it be the recovery of compensation up to the time of his discharge, if any be due him. But if the principal revoke the authority without cause, he will be liable to the agent for all damages that the latter may sustain by reason of the wrongful act of the principal.[30]

[26] Davol v. Quimby, 11 Allen (Mass.) 208.

[27] Ahern v. Baker, 34 Minn. 98. Thus, the assignment of a judgment has been held to be a revocation of the authority of plaintiff's attorney to control it: Trumbull v. Nicholson, 27 Ill. 149; Wilson v. Harris, 21 Mont. 374, 54 Pac. 46. And where property is placed in the hands of a broker, but is subsequently sold by the principal, the sale is a revocation of the broker's authority: Walker v. Denison, 86 Ill. 142; Torre v. Thiele, 25 La. Ann. 418. See also, Hale v. Kumler, 85 Fed. 161, 166, 167.

[28] Whitworth v. Ballard, 56 Ind. 279.

[29] Rowe v. Rand, 111 Ind. 206.

[30] Lewis v. Atlas, etc., Ins. Co., 61 Mo. 534.

§ 162. When either party may terminate relation as of right.— As has been seen, when the contract of employment contains no stipulation or provision that the agent shall continue in the principal's employment for a definite time, the relation may be dissolved, as of right, by either party, at any time.[31] The contract of employment may provide, as heretofore stated, that either party shall have the right to dissolve the relation at any time he becomes dissatisfied with it. When such is the contract, the dissatisfaction is a sufficient cause for termination of the relation.[32] Under the second specification given in the preceding section, the principal may revoke the authority when the agent is unfaithful in performing the services or executing the authority conferred upon him; for it is the duty of the agent to serve his principal with fidelity and diligence, and to perform properly the services for which he is employed.[33]

[31] Kirk v. Hartman, 63 Pa. St. 97.

[32] Adriance v. Rutherford, 57 Mich. 170.

[33] Dieringer v. Meyer, 42 Wis. 311. In this case it was said by Lyon, J., speaking for the court: "It is well settled that if a servant, without the consent of his master, engage in any employment or business for himself or another which may tend to injure his master's trade or business, he may lawfully be discharged before the expiration of the agreed term of service. This is so because it is the duty of the servant not only to give his time and attention to his master's business, but, by all lawful means at his command, to protect and advance his master's interests. But when the servant engages in a business which brings him in direct competition with his master, the tendency is to injure or endanger, not to protect and promote, the interests of the latter. It was said by Lord Ellenborough, in a discussion of this subject in Thompson v. Havelock, 1 Camp. 527, that 'no man shall be allowed to have an interest against his duty.' Manifestly, when a servant becomes engaged in a business which necessarily renders him a competitor and rival of his master, no matter how much or how little time and attention he devotes to it, he has an interest against his duty. It would be monstrous to hold that the master is bound to retain the servant in his employment after he has thus voluntarily put himself in an attitude hostile to his master's interests. The fact may be, in certain cases, that, notwithstanding the servant has engaged in a rival business, still he has given his whole time and attention to the business of his master. An attempt was made to show that this is such a case. But the existence of that fact will not take a case out of the rule above stated, for the reason that the servant would yet have an interest against his duty. The cases which sustain or tend to sustain the doctrine here laid down are very numerous. For convenience we cite a few of them: Singer v. M'Cormick, 4 W. & S. (Pa.) 265; Jaffray v. King, 34 Md. 217; Adams Express Co. v. Trego, 35 Md. 47; Lacy v. Osbaldiston, 8 C. & P. 80; Read v. Dunsmore,

§ 163. Consequences of dissolution as between principal and third persons—Notice.—The effect of the dissolution of the relation between the principal and agent would naturally be the same upon third persons as upon the immediate parties, provided such third party received timely notice of the dissolution. But as the scope of authority of some agents is often very extensive, and the persons with whom they deal for their principals are very numerous, it frequently happens that without some action on the part of the principal or agent apprising them of the fact that the relation has ceased, third persons remain in ignorance of the change, and are in danger of becoming injured by it, unless protected by the law. If a third party should continue to deal with an agent in ignorance of the dissolution and in continued reliance upon the credit of the principal, it is obvious that he should not be made to suffer from the result of the condition in the creation of which he had no part. Such a person should, from considerations of justice and equity, have a right to expect that if any change occur in the situation between the principal and the agent, and the former desire to be no longer responsible for the acts of the latter done in his behalf, due and sufficient notice of such change will be given him by the principal, in order that he may be placed upon his guard as to any further dealings with the agent. Hence, the courts have ruled that when it is established that general authority has been delegated to the agent, the party who has been dealing with him upon such authority may justly presume that the relation still exists, and that if a revocation takes place the principal will give him timely notice thereof; and if, without such notice, and

9 C. & P. 588; Nichol v. Martyn, 2 Esp. 732; Gardner v. M'Cutcheon, 4 Beav. 534; Ridgway v. Hungerford Market Co., 3 A. & E. 171; Amor v. Fearon, 9 A. & E. 548; Horton v. McMurtry, 5 Hurl. & N. 667. See also, Wood on Master and Servant, § 116, and cases cited in notes. If the plaintiff became engaged in a business which necessarily made him a competitor of his employer in the purchase of wood at New Cassel, or in selling the same at Fond du Lac, such business had a direct tendency to raise the price at the former place and depress it at the latter, as well as to decrease the defendant's business interests. And it was equally hostile, even though the plaintiff conducted it entirely by agents, and gave his whole time and attention to the business of the defendant." That the agent eats morphine, which tends to incapacitate him for the performance of his duties, is not a sufficient ground to give the principal the right to discharge him in the absence of a showing that it actually incapacitates him: Jakowenko v. Des Moines Life Ass'n, 21 Ohio C. C. 199, 11 Ohio C. D. 576.

in good faith, he continues to deal with the agent as such, the acts of the agent in behalf of the principal will bind the latter.[34]

§ 164. **Termination by act of agent—Renunciation.**—The relation between the principal and agent may be terminated, as has been seen, by the agent's act of renouncing or abandoning the service of the principal. A distinction must be observed here also, as in the case of revocation by the principal, between the power of the agent to renounce or abandon and his right to do so. His power to dissolve the relation is as ample as that of the principal; for, as before stated, it is not the policy of the law to coerce the parties to continue the relation, and specific performance will not generally be decreed in order to continue the agency. Hence, even though the agency was, by the contract, to continue for a definite time, and the contract was based upon a sufficient consideration, the agent has the power to renounce it before the expiration of the time; subject, of course, to the rights of the principal accruing to him by reason of the wrongful renunciation.[35] If the relation was, by the terms of the con-

[34] Fellows v. Hartford, etc., Co., 38 Conn. 197; Hatch v. Coddington, 95 U. S. 48; Rowe v. Rand, 111 Ind. 206; Murphy v. Ottenheimer, 84 Ill. 39; Rice v. Barnard, 127 Mass. 241; Tier v. Lampson, 35 Vt. 179; McNeilly v. Continental Life Ins. Co., 66 N. Y. 23; Baltimore v. Eschbach, 18 Md. 276; Perrine v. Jermyn, 163 Pa. St. 497, 30 Atl. 202. Where a power of attorney to sell and convey land is duly recorded, a purchaser without notice from the attorney named in such instrument obtains a better title than does a purchaser from the grantor, whose deed was executed before that of the attorney, though not recorded: Gratz v. Land and River Imp. Co., 82 Fed. 381, 40 L. R. A. 393. See also, Johnson v. Christian, 128 U. S. 374; Quinn v. Dresbach, 75 Cal. 159, 7 Am. St. 138; Murphy v. Ottenheimer, 84 Ill. 39, 25 Am. Rep. 424; Fanning v. Cobb, 20 Mo. App. 577; Ætna Life Ins. Co. v. Hanna, 81 Tex. 487; Smith v. Watson, 82 Va. 712; Foellinger v. Leh, 110 Ind. 238. The notice may be by oral or written statement, or by course of dealing: Perrine v. Jermyn, *supra*.

[35] U. S. v. Jarvis, 2 Daveis (U. S.) 278; Story Ag., § 478. If the agency is based upon a valuable consideration, the agent can not renounce it without subjecting himself to liability for such damages as the principal may sustain: See White v. Smith, 6 Lans. (N. Y.) 5; Case v. Jennings, 17 Tex. 661. If the authority of the agent is based upon a sufficient consideration, the principal will have his remedy in damages. In case of a purely gratuitous agency no damages can be collected by the principal. If, however, the agency were in part executed and then renounced, the principal would be entitled to such damages as might be sustained by him. In all cases of renouncement, however, the agent is bound to give notice to the princi-

tract, to continue at the will of the parties, or either of them, or of the agent alone, the latter may, as of right, terminate it at any time by giving reasonable notice.[36]

§ 165. **How renunciation may be effected.**—The renunciation, like the revocation, may be express or implied. It is express when the agent informs the principal, orally or in writing, that he will not continue longer in his service, or uses words tantamount to these. But the agent may accomplish the same result by his conduct, without any express declaration. Thus, he may abandon the agency, in which case the principal may treat the act as a renunciation and appoint a new agent.[37] The acts and conduct of an agent which may authorize the principal to regard the agency as abandoned are too numerous to justify the statement of more of them than will be sufficient to serve as an illustration. Thus, if the agent write to the principal threatening to leave his work or sell out the subject-matter of the agency, or do acts inconsistent with the faithful discharge of his duties, this may be treated by the principal as an abandonment of the agency.[38]

III. Termination by Operation of Law.

§ 166. **Derivative authority expires with the original authority.**—"A revocation by operation of law," says Story, "may be by a change of condition or of state, producing an incapacity of either party. This proceeds upon a general rule of law, that the derivative authority expires with the original authority, from which it proceeds. The power of constituting an agent is founded upon the right of the principal to do the business himself; and when that right ceases, the right of creating an appointment, or of continuing the appointment of an agent already made, for the same purpose, must cease also. In short, the derivative authority can not generally mount higher or exist longer than the original authority."[39]

pal: Story Ag., § 478; Barrows v. Cushway, 37 Mich. 481; Hitchcock v. Kelley, 18 Ohio C. C. 808, 4 Ohio C. D. 180. When the principal breaks his contract with the agent the latter is generally justifiable in abandoning the agency: Duffield v. Michaels, 97 Fed. 825.

[36] Barrows v. Cushway, 37 Mich. 481; Conrey v. Brandegee, 2 La. Ann. 132.

[37] Stoddart v. Key, 62 How. Pr. (N. Y.) 137.

[38] Stoddart v. Key, *supra*. Where one who was authorized to sell a slave attempted to run him off and conceal him, it was held that the agent's conduct warranted the principal in treating the agency as abandoned: Case v. Jennings, 17 Tex. 661.

[39] Story Ag., § 481.

§ 167. **Death of principal—Is notice of required?**—A naked authority, by which is meant an authority not coupled with an interest, is always revoked by the death of the principal.[40] Hence, the power of a married woman to bind her husband for necessaries is not continued after the demise of the husband so as to bind his estate.[41] And the death of the principal likewise terminates the authority of the substitute, if there be one.[42] The rule of the common law, that the death of the principal terminates the agency unless the authority is coupled with an interest, is too well settled to admit of controversy, and it is not necessary even that the party who deals with the agent should have notice of the fact. At least this is the weight of authority. Those who deal with the agent do so at the risk that his authority may be terminated by death without notice to them.[43]

§ 168. **The rule of civil law and in equity—Holdings in some states.**—By the civil law the rule is different, and the authority of the agent, as in the case of revocation by act of party, ceases only from the time of notice. The civil law rule was followed in a Pennsylvania case, where it was held that an act done by an attorney, after the death of his principal, and in ignorance thereof, is binding upon the parties.[44] In some states the rule of the common law has

[40] Long v. Thayer, 150 U. S. 520, and note in 37 L. ed. 1167; Connor v. Parsons (Tex.), 30 S. W. 83; Soltau v. Goodyear Vulcanite Co., 33 N. Y. Supp. 77; Krumdick v. White, 107 Cal. 37, 39 Pac. 1066; In re Kern's Estate, 176 Pa. St. 373, 35 Atl. 231; Tusch v. German Sav. Bank, 46 N. Y. Supp. 422; Pacific Bank v. Hannah, 90 Fed. 72; Brown v. Cushman, 173 Mass. 368, 53 N. E. 860; Duckworth v. Orr, 126 N. C. 674, 36 S. E. 150; Triplett v. Woodward, 98 Va. 187, 35 S. E. 455; Tuttle v. Green (Ariz.), 48 Pac. 1009. See Daggett v. Simonds, 173 Mass. 340, 46 L. R. A. 332; Farmer v. Marvin (Kan.), 65 Pac. 221. If, however, the subject-matter of the agency is the collection of a note, and the agent has the same in his possession at the time of the principal's death, the agency is not revoked by the death of the principal: Deweese v. Muff, 57 Neb. 17, 42 L. R. A. 789.

[41] Blades v. Free, 9 B. & C. 167.

[42] Peries v. Aycinena, 3 W. & S. (Pa.) 64, 79.

[43] Story Ag., § 488; Hunt v. Rousmanier, 8 Wheat. (U. S.) 174; Johnson v. Wilcox, 25 Ind. 182; Lincoln v. Emerson, 108 Mass. 87; Weber v. Bridgman, 113 N. Y. 600; Clayton v. Merrett, 52 Miss. 353; Farmers' Loan, etc., Co. v. Wilson, 139 N. Y. 284, 34 N. E. 784, 19 N. Y. Supp. 142; Jenkins v. Atkins, 1 Humph. (Tenn.) 294, 34 Am. Dec. 648; Rigs v. Cage, 2 Humph. (Tenn.) 350; Lewis v. Kerr, 17 Iowa 73; Galt v. Galloway, 4 Pet. (U. S.) 332, 334; Peries v. Aycinena, 3 W. & S. (Pa.) 64.

[44] Cassiday v. M'Kenzie, 4 W. & S.

been modified by statute.[45] Sometimes the right of a third person to notice of the death of the principal is asserted upon equitable grounds, the general rule at law that death terminates the agency being conceded.[46] But by the great weight of authority the death of the principal immediately terminates the agency, and all dealings with the agent thereafter are void, though the parties are at the time ignorant of the principal's death.[47]

§ 169. Exception—Where principal is a partnership firm.—An apparent exception to the rule that death revokes the agent's authority may be found in cases where the principal was a partnership firm, and only one of the partners died. In such cases the authority of the agent continues in qualified form after the death of the principal.[48] But, generally speaking, the death of one of two or more joint principals revokes the agency.[49] The fact that the power of attorney or instrument of appointment expressly provides that the power is irrevocable makes no difference, unless the power is coupled with an interest. Such a stipulation would doubtless prohibit the principal from revoking the authority if he were alive, but death will have the opposite effect.[50]

§ 170. A further exception—Where agency is coupled with interest.—The rule that the death of the principal revokes the agency

(Pa.) 282, 39 Am. Dec. 76. See also, Carriger v. Whittington, 26 Mo. 311, 72 Am. Dec. 312. And where the matter to be done is *in pais*, and not by deed, and where it need not be done in the name of the principal, it has been held that if done by the agent after the principal's death, if within the apparent scope of his authority, and in ignorance of the principal's death, it is valid; and the representatives of the principal are estopped to deny such apparent authority: Ish v. Crane, 8 Ohio St. 520. Where an agent, in pursuance of authority, ordered goods for his principal by mail, and the principal died the next day, and before the order was filled, and the third party filled the order in ignorance of the principal's death, the contract was held binding as of the day on which the order was deposited in the mail: Davis v. Davis, 93 Ala. 173, 9 So. 756.

[45] See Weber v. Bridgman, 113 N. Y. 600, 605.

[46] See Cassiday v. M'Kenzie, 4 W. & S. (Pa.) 282, 39 Am. Dec. 76.

[47] Davis v. Windsor Sav. Bank, 46 Vt. 728; Companari v. Woodburn, 15 C. B. 400; Saltmarsh v. Smith, 32 Ala. 404; Travers v. Crane, 15 Cal. 12; Carriger v. Whittington, 26 Mo. 311; Lincoln v. Emerson, 108 Mass. 87; Houghtaling v. Marvin, 7 Barb. (N. Y.) 412. See cases in note 40, *supra*.

[48] Bank of New York v. Vanderhorst, 32 N. Y. 553; Merry v. Lynch, 68 Me. 94; Primm v. Stewart, 7 Tex. 178; Fereira v. Sayres, 5 W. & S. (Pa.) 210, 40 Am. Dec. 496.

[49] Rowe v. Rand, 111 Ind. 206.

[50] Story Ag., § 488.

does not apply to agencies in which an authority is coupled with an interest, or in which the act may be performed in the name of the agent himself. "Where the act, notwithstanding the death of the principal, can and may be done in the name of the agent, there seems to be a sound reason why his death should not be deemed to be a positive revocation under all circumstances, and the subsequent execution of it may be valid."[51]

§ **171. Death of agent.**—The consequences resulting from the death of the principal upon the relation between the parties are the same in case of the death of the agent. To constitute an agency there must be both an existing principal and an existing agent, and the agent must be the person designated by the principal or his duly authorized substitute. Moreover, it must be assumed that the agent was selected by the principal on account of his peculiar fitness and ability to perform the duties involved in the authority delegated to him. The contract between the parties is a personal one, and can be performed, as a general rule, only by the person appointed. There is, therefore, no right of inheritance of the agent's position by the representatives of the latter.[52] To this rule there is, however, the usual exception existing in other cases of revocation, that the authority is not revoked by the agent's death if it be coupled with an interest in the subject-matter. Hence, it has been held that when a mortgage has been executed which contains a power to sell the mortgaged property, the death of the mortgagee does not necessarily revoke the authority to sell, but it may be executed by his representatives or assigns.[53]

§ **172. Death or severance of interest of one of two or more joint principals or agents.**—When there is a severance of the interest of one of two or more joint principals in the subject-matter of the agency, the authority of the agent is terminated. The same is true when one of the joint principals dies: the death of the one has the effect

[51] Story Ag., § 495; Ish v. Crane, 8 Ohio St. 520, 13 Ohio St. 574, 576, 611. See also, Dick v. Page, 17 Mo. 234; Hunt v. Rousmanier, 8 Wheat. (U. S.) 174; Davis v. Windsor Sav. Bank, 46 Vt. 728. If the authority is coupled with an interest it is not revoked by the principal's death: Kelly v. Bowerman, 113 Mich. 446; Hennessee v. Johnson, 13 Tex. Civ. App. 530, 36 S. W. 774; Carleton v. Hausler, 20 Tex. Civ. App. 275, 49 S. W. 118; Grapel v. Hodges, 112 N. Y. 419, 20 N. E. 542.

[52] Adriance v. Rutherford, 57 Mich. 170.

[53] Collins v. Hopkins, 7 Iowa 463.

of severing the joint interest; and hence the agency becomes revoked.[54] And, likewise, the death of one of two or more joint private agents has the effect of terminating the relation. The reason for this rule is found in the requirement that a joint commission of a private agency must be jointly executed, and the absence of one of the agents renders it impossible to fulfil this requirement.[55]

§ **173. Insanity of principal.**—As a general rule it may be stated that whenever the principal is rendered incapable of exercising an intelligent control over his affairs, his capacity to appoint an agent ceases; and, being thus incapable of making such an appointment, he likewise becomes incapable of maintaining such a relation as that of principal by his after-occurring insanity. But it is a more serious question as to whether or not the insanity in itself will bring about a dissolution of the relation, or whether it must be first established by an inquest of lunacy. Chancellor Kent has indeed given it as his opinion that the better rule would be that the existence of lunacy must first be established by inquisition before it could control the operation of the power.[56] But "by the weight of authority, as well as sound reasoning, we would conclude that the after-occurring insanity of the principal operates, *per se,* as a revocation or suspension of agency, except in cases where a consideration has previously been advanced in the transaction of the subject-matter of the agency, so that the power became coupled with an interest, or where a consideration of value is given by a third person, trusting to the apparent authority in ignorance of the principal's incapacity."[57] In an early New York case the court held that the lunacy of a person who has executed a power of attorney does not operate to revoke, at least

[54] Rowe v. Rand, 111 Ind. 206; Travers v. Crane, 15 Cal. 12; Marlett v. Jackman, 3 Allen (Mass.) 287. See also, Bank of New York v. Vanderhorst, 32 N. Y. 553; Tasker v. Shepherd, 6 Hurl. & N. 575.

[55] Hartford Fire Ins. Co. v. Wilcox, 57 Ill. 180; Story Ag., § 42. But where the principal recognized the surviving agent as the proper person to execute the authority, without objection, it was held the case was taken out of the rule that the death of one joint agent terminates the agency: Davidson v. Provost, 35 Ill. App. 126. Misconduct of an agent in conspiring with one of several joint principals against the others will have the effect to revoke his agency, though nothing was done pursuant to the conspiracy: Cotton v. Rand, 93 Tex. 7, 51 S. W. 538.

[56] 2 Kent Com. 645.

[57] Per Depue, J., in Matthiessen, etc., Co. v. McMahon, 38 N. J. L. 536. See also, Hill v. Day, 34 N. J. Eq. 150; Bunce v. Gallagher, 5 Blatchf. (U. S.) 481; Hunt v. Rousmanier, 8 Wheat. (U. S.) 174.

until the fact has been established by an inquisition.[58] The fact that a principal was put under guardianship for insanity was held in Vermont not necessarily sufficient proof that an agency previously created by him had been terminated. To prove this it would have to be shown by other evidence that the principal was disqualified.[59] It is believed to be the general rule, however, that the lunacy operates, *ipso facto,* as a suspension of authority until the recovery of the lunatic, the burden being on the third party to show he had no notice of it; and if the latter then fails to dissent when informed of the acts of his agent, his assent to the same may be inferred.[60] In accordance with this general rule, the supreme court of New Hampshire, in a case where a party, previous to his death, held a note against another, and on the day of his death, and when he was entirely senseless and no hopes were entertained of his recovery, his wife, who had been his general agent for years past, and who had been authorized to settle this concern in the manner she did, turned the note over in settlement of a debt owing by the husband,—held that the agency of the wife was revoked by the situation; the court saying: "An authority to do an act for and in the name of another presupposes a power in the individual to do the act himself, if present. The act to be done is not the act of the agent, but the act of the principal; and the agent can do no act in the name of the principal which the principal might not himself do, if he were personally present. The principal is present by his representative, and the making or execution of a contract or acknowledgment of a deed, is his act or acknowledgment. But it would be preposterous, where the power is in its nature revocable, to hold that the principal was, in contemplation of law, present, making a contract or acknowledging a deed, when he was in fact lying insensible on his deathbed, and this fact well known to those who undertook to act with and for him. The act done by the agent, under a revocable power, implies the existence of volition on the part of the principal. He makes the contract,—he does the act. It is done through the more active instrumentality of another, but the latter represents his principal and uses his name. Farther, upon the constitution of an agent or attorney to act for another, where the authority is not coupled with an interest and not irrevocable, there exists at all times a right of supervision in the principal, and the power to terminate the authority

[58] Wallis v. Manhattan Co., 2 Hall (N. Y.) 495.

[59] Motley v. Head, 43 Vt. 633.

[60] Hill v. Day, 34 N. J. Eq. 150; Bunce v. Gallagher, 5 Blatchf. (U. S.) 481; Hunt v. Rousmanier, 8 Wheat. (U. S.) 174.

of the agent at the pleasure of the principal. The law secures to the principal the right of judging how long he will be represented by the agent and suffer him to act in his name. So long as, having the power, he does not exercise the will to revoke, the authority continues. When, then, an act of Providence deprives the principal of the power to exercise any judgment or will on the subject, the authority of the agent to act should thereby be suspended for the time being; otherwise the right of the agent would be continued beyond the period when all evidence that the principal chose to continue the authority had ceased; for after the principal was deprived of the power to exercise any will upon the subject, there could be no assent, or acquiescence, or evidence of any kind to show that he consented that the agency should continue to exist. And, moreover, a confirmed insanity would render wholly irrevocable an authority, which, by the original nature of its constitution, it was to be in the power of the principal at any time to revoke."[61] Seemingly at variance with the generally accepted rule is the decision of the queen's bench division in a case where a husband, who had held out his wife as his agent to a tradesman and others, subsequently became insane, and during the insanity the wife ordered goods of the tradesman, the latter being ignorant of the husband's insanity. The court ruled that the husband's insanity did not dissolve the agency, and that his estate was liable for the goods.[62] The turning-point in this case, however, was the third party's want of knowledge of the insanity.

§ **174. Insanity of agent.**—As was stated in a previous chapter, an idiot, lunatic, or other person *non compos mentis,* is generally incapable of becoming an agent.[63] The after-occurring insanity, if of such nature as to render the agent incapable of performing the duties imposed upon him, would seem to operate as a termination, *per se,* of the relation, whether there has been a judicial declaration of insanity or not; for in such a case the principal can not be presumed to have authorized the act done for him by one incapable of performing it, the exercise of sound judgment and discretion being required at all times, it would seem, as preliminaries to the due execution of the authority conferred.[64]

§ **175. Notice of agent's insanity.**—If, however, the insanity be of such a character as not to be readily apparent, and the third party

[61] Davis v. Lane, 10 N. H. 156.

[62] Drew v. Nunn, L. R. 4 Q. B. D. 661.

[63] *Ante,* § 38.

[64] Story Ag., § 487.

deal with the agent in good faith, and in ignorance of the mental unsoundness, and the parties can not be restored to their original situation, an executed transaction will not become invalid by reason of the agent's mental unsoundness.[65] A judicial determination of the agent's lunacy, however, will be sufficient notice to third parties; and subsequent dealings with him will be at their peril.

§ **176. Insanity of one of two or more joint agents.**—A joint private agency must be executed by the agents jointly; and hence, if one of them becomes incompetent by insanity or otherwise, the authority will thereby be revoked, the same as in case of the death of the joint agent.[66]

§ **177. Bankruptcy of principal.**—A party who has been adjudged a bankrupt is thereby rendered incompetent, until discharged, to apply the funds or property in his hands to the payment or adjustment of his obligations, that power being transferred to his trustee. Being incapacitated to transact such business himself, he could not legally authorize an agent to do so for him, as otherwise the derivative and implied authority would be stronger and more extensive than the original and principal authority of the party himself, which can not be. The consequence is that the bankruptcy of the principal revokes the power of the agent, and such power ceases with the transfer of the principal's effects to the trustee in bankruptcy.[67] This rule does not apply, however, to cases in which the agent's authority is coupled with an interest.[68] While the proceedings in bankruptcy are pending, the power of the agent to act is suspended, but third persons dealing with the agent in good faith will not be affected by such proceedings until after the adjudication in which the bankruptcy is judicially declared.[69] Nor is an agency affected by the bankruptcy where it does not involve the bankrupt's control over the subject-matter of the agency.[70]

§ **178. Bankruptcy of agent.**—Whether or not the bankruptcy of an agent will revoke his authority depends on the nature of the agency. When the agency is such as to render the agent's solvency

[65] Mechem Ag., § 260.

[66] Salisbury v. Brisbane, 61 N. Y. 617.

[67] Parker v. Smith, 16 East 382; Minett v. Forrester, 4 Taunt. 541; Rowe v. Rand, 111 Ind. 206; Story Ag., § 482.

[68] Hall v. Bliss, 118 Mass. 554.

[69] Ex parte Snowball, L. R. 7 Ch. App. 548.

[70] Dixon v. Ewart, Buck 94.

necessary to a due and faithful performance of the act, as where he is authorized to receive the principal's money, or to sell his property, the authority will generally be terminated by the agent's bankruptcy.[71] Other and mere formal acts, passing no interests, such as the execution and delivery of a deed, may still be performed by the agent when he has obtained the previous authority to do so from his principal.[72]

§ **179. Breaking out of war.**—Another cause for the termination of the relation is the occurrence of war between the country of the principal and that of the agent. When hostilities break out between two states, all commercial intercourse between them is, by the rules of international law, forbidden.[73] But, as was observed in the chapter on competency of parties, when the agency existed prior to the breaking out of hostilities, and the parties consent to its continuation, it will not necessarily be dissolved by reason thereof, unless the agency involves communications across the line of hostilities.[74] Another exception to the general rule that war terminates the agency is in cases where debts are paid to the agent of the alien enemy, when such agent resides in the state of the debtor, and the principal and agent assent in good faith that this may be done.[75]

§ **180. Marriage of feme sole.**—If the principal be an unmarried female, under the common law she will become incompetent when she contracts marriage, and a power of attorney executed by her while a *feme sole* will be revoked by the marriage. This rule is still in force in some jurisdictions to the extent that the common-law disabilities of a married woman have not been removed by statute.[76] In some instances the power of attorney of a man executed while single will become inoperative by his marriage. Thus, where an unmarried man had executed a power of attorney to an agent to sell his homestead, is was held to be revoked by his marriage; inasmuch as the

[71] Audenried v. Betteley, 8 Allen (Mass.) 302; Hudson v. Granger, 5 B. & Ald. 27.

[72] Audenried v. Betteley, 8 Allen (Mass.) 302; Story Ag., § 486; 2 Kent Com. (4th ed.) 644, 645, Lect. XLI.

[73] Kershaw v. Kelsey, 100 Mass. 561; U. S. v. Grossmayer, 9 Wall. (U. S.) 72; Lyon v. Kent, 45 Ala. 656; Insurance Co. v. Davis, 95 U. S. 425.

[74] Kershaw v. Kelsey, *supra.* See also, Clark v. Reeder, 158 U. S. 505; Williams v. Paine, 169 U. S. 55.

[75] Insurance Co. v. Davis, 95 U. S. 425; New York Life Ins. Co. v. Statham, 93 U. S. 24.

[76] Wambole v. Foote, 2 Dak. 1.

wife, by virtue of the marriage, became entitled to an inchoate interest in the homestead, of which she could not be deprived without her consent, manifested by joining her husband in a conveyance.[77]

§ 181. **Authority coupled with interest.**—It has been seen that an agency can not be revoked by the act of the principal, nor will it be revoked by operation of law, where the authority of the agent is coupled with an interest. Just what is such an interest is sometimes difficult to determine. As a general rule, we think it may be safely stated that when the interest is merely in the power, and not in the subject of the agency, it is not sufficient to prevent a revocation.

§ 182. **Illustrations of insufficient interest.**—The interest must be such as to survive the principal in case of death, or in that and other cases of revocation, must be such as the agent is authorized to execute in his own name and not in the name of the principal. Thus, if the interest is merely by way of compensation out of the proceeds of the sale of property forming the subject of the agency, no matter how great the proportion to the principal sum, it is not sufficient to prevent a revocation.[78] The power and interest must coexist. If the interest be only in the proceeds collected under the power, and the exercise of the power would operate as an extinguishment of the power, it is not a sufficient interest to satisfy the rule.[79] A bare power is always revocable. Hence, if a debtor deposit money with another to be paid by him to a creditor, the money deposited will remain the property of the debtor until paid over to the creditor, and the agency will be revoked either by the act of the parties or by operation of law. A power of attorney may indeed be irrevocable by its terms, but to uphold such an agreement there must be a consideration or independent compensation to be rendered for the services to be performed.[80] If there is merely a power to a creditor to receive a debt expressly for the purpose of liquidating the claim of the creditor, unaccompanied by an actual assignment of the debt, or by any security to which the power might have been ancillary, it is revoked

[77] Henderson v. Ford, 46 Tex. 627.

[78] Chambers v. Seay, 73 Ala. 372. To constitute a power of agency coupled with an interest, both the agency and the interest must be derived from the same source: Black v. Harsha, 7 Kan. App. 794, 54 Pac. 21. See *ante*, § 159, note.

[79] Hartley & Minor's Appeal, 53 Pa. St. 212; Blackstone v. Buttermore, 53 Pa. St. 266; Frink v. Roe, 70 Cal. 296.

[80] Blackstone v. Buttermore, *supra*.

by the death of the principal.[81] And a power of attorney to confess judgment in favor of a third person, unless based upon some special consideration or given to secure a debt, may be revoked at the will of the principal.[82] Where authority is conferred to sell land and apply the proceeds to the extinguishment of a debt owing to the principal, it has been held that the interest is in the proceeds merely, and not in the subject, the land; and the power is, therefore, revocable.[83] But in other cases such an interest as that has been sufficient to render the power irrevocable.[84]

§ 183. **Illustrations of sufficient interest—Revocation where agent would suffer loss.**—Generally speaking, if the interest of the agent is in the thing itself that constitutes the subject of the agency, and not merely in the proceeds or avails thereof,—that is, "a power engrafted on an estate in the thing,"—it is sufficient to render the power irrevocable.[84a] Some instances of this kind are:—Where the power conferred is that the agent may reimburse himself for advances made in the course of the agency;[85] where it is given to secure a debt or demand;[86] or to reimburse a factor for prior advances;[87] or to indemnify a surety against loss;[88] or where a note has been indorsed and delivered by the principal to the agent for collection, thus transferring the legal title and enabling the agent to sue in his own name;[89] or where a mortgagor has empowered the mortgagee to sell the property for the purpose of paying an indebtedness.[90] In all such cases the agent or party to whom the power is delegated acquires not merely the right to exercise that power, but also a *quasi* title in the thing itself concerning which the agency is formed. It is not merely an interest in that which has to be produced by the exercise of power, but an interest in the thing out of which it is to be produced.[91] It is sometimes stated that an agency is irrevocable where the revocation would result in injury or loss to the agent by way of damages to third persons. Thus, where a debtor intrusts money to his agent to deliver to

[81] Houghtaling v. Marvin, 7 Barb. (N. Y.) 412.

[82] Evans v. Fearne, 16 Ala. 689, 50 Am. Dec. 197.

[83] Frink v. Roe, 70 Cal. 296.

[84] Gaussen v. Morton, 10 B. & C. 731; Barr v. Schroeder, 32 Cal. 609; Watson v. King, 4 Camp. 272.

[84a] Hunt v. Rousmanier, 8 Wheat. (U. S.) 174; Smart v. Sandars, 5 C. B. 895.

[85] Posten v. Rassette, 5 Cal. 467.

[86] Hunt v. Rousmanier, 8 Wheat. (U. S.) 174; Beecher v. Bennett, 11 Barb. (N. Y.) 374, 380.

[87] Raleigh v. Atkinson, 6 M. & W. 670.

[88] Hynson v. Noland, 14 Ark. 710.

[89] Moore v. Hall, 48 Mich. 143.

[90] Conners v. Holland, 113 Mass. 50.

[91] Hunt v. Rousmanier, *supra*.

a creditor, in payment of a debt, and the agent promises the creditor to pay the debt, the agent is liable to the creditor for the payment of the debt to the extent of the funds received, and in case of failure to pay, the agent will be liable in damages. The agency can not, therefore, be revoked by the act of the principal or by operation of law in such a case, as that would render the agent personally liable without being reimbursed by the principal; hence, such an agency becomes irrevocable by reason of the receipt of money by the agent and his promise to pay the same.[92] This is, however, after all, nothing but an authority coupled with an interest.[93]

[92] Goodwin v. Bowden, 54 Me. 424. [93] Anson Conts. (7th ed.) 358.

CHAPTER V.

AUTHORITY OF AGENT AND THE DELEGATION THEREOF—INTERPRETATION, CONSTRUCTION, AND EXECUTION OF AUTHORITY.

§ **184. Purpose of this chapter.**—We have heretofore seen that the power which is delegated to an agent by his principal, or is exercised by him, is denominated the agent's authority; that it may be express,—as when conferred by a writing under seal, or by a writing not under seal, or by word of mouth; that it may be implied from the surrounding circumstances and the acts, declarations and conduct of the principal; or that it may simply be assumed by the agent without any previous appointment, and subsequently ratified by the principal; or that it may exist by operation of law.[1] We have also seen that such authority may be universal, general or special; thus constituting a universal agency, a general agency or a special agency.[2] It is the purpose of this chapter to ascertain what authority may and what authority may not be delegated; the nature and extent of the agent's authority; how such authority is determined, interpreted and construed in particular cases; its effect, generally, and by custom and usage of trade; its operation on various classes of agencies; and how such authority is executed by the agent.

§ **185. Delegation of authority.**—And first it will be proper to give a somewhat more extended presentation of the subject of the delegation of authority than that already given. "'Delegation,' in the sense assigned to the term at the common law," says Evans, "means the act of investing one or more persons with authority to do some act or acts. The term is applicable not only to cases where

[1] *Ante*, § 9.

[2] *Ante*, §§ 18, 19.

the person who delegates has himself authority in his own right to do the act the performance of which he delegates to another, but also to those cases where the person who delegates has only a delegated and not an original authority to do that which he delegates to another. In other words, the appointment of a subagent by an agent, no less than that of an agent by a principal, involves a delegation of authority. An authority or power, then, is either original or it is delegated. Where the authority is original, the general maxim of the law of England applies, that whatever a person may do of his own right he may do by another. Where, on the other hand, the authority in question is a delegated authority, the well known rule is that such authority can not be delegated."[3]

§ **186. What acts can not be performed for one by another.**—The maxim just stated implies that even original authority is not always capable of being delegated; for one may not legally delegate authority to do what one can not himself legally perform. Therefore, as we have heretofore explained, a person can not legally delegate the performance of an illegal or immoral act. But there are some things which a man may do himself and yet can not do by another. Thus, he can not delegate authority to perform an act of a personal nature; that is, an act which, to be valid, must be performed by the party himself. Therefore, a person could not render homage or fealty by another, as such service was personal. "So the lord might beat his villain, and if it were without cause the villain had no remedy; but the lord could not authorize another to beat him without cause."[4] And a married woman can not delegate to another person the power to acknowledge an instrument for her, as that comes within the class of acts that must be personally performed.[5]

§ **187. Delegated authority can not be delegated.**—It is a well established general rule, though not without its exceptions, that delegated authority can not be redelegated. The maxim is, "*Delegatus non potest delegare.*" The rule is founded upon solid grounds. An

[3] Evans Pr. & Ag. (Bedford's ed.) 75–76; Kohl v. Beach, 107 Wis. 409, 50 L. R. A. 600, 83 N. W. 647; Springfield, etc., Ins. Co. v. DeJarnett (Ala.), 19 So. 995; Ladonia Dry Goods Co. v. Conyers (Tex. Civ. App.), 58 S. W. 967; Dingley v. McDonald, 124 Cal. 682, 57 Pac. 574; Fargo v. Cravens (S. D.), 70 N. W. 1053.

[4] Evans Pr. & Ag. (Bedford's ed.) 78; Combe's Case, 9 Co. 75a.

[5] Dawson v. Shirley, 6 Blackf. (Ind.) 531; Holladay v. Dailey, 19 Wall. (U. S.) 606.

agent, or one to whom is intrusted the performance of an act by another, is supposed to be selected by the principal with reference to his peculiar fitness for and adaptation to the principal's business. The undertaking may require a certain kind of ability, skill, judgment and discretion; and the person whom the principal selects as his agent is supposed to possess these qualities. He is, therefore, *delectus personae,* and he alone can legally perform the business intrusted to him; unless, indeed, the principal's assent be obtained to the appointment of a substitute.[6] Hence, we have the further rule that, in the absence of any authority, either express or implied, to employ a subagent, the trust committed to the agent is personal, and can not be delegated by him to another so as to affect the rights of the principal. In such cases, if the agent employs a substitute, he does it at his own risk and upon his own responsibility.[7] The principle enunciated above is well illustrated in a recent case decided by the supreme court of Indiana.[8] In that case, a party had made application for a license to sell intoxicating liquors at retail, under a statute of that

[6] Lynn v. Burgoyne, 13 B. Mon. (Ky.) 400; Warner v. Martin, 11 How. (U. S.) 209; Darling v. St. Paul, 19 Minn. 389; Alexander v. Alexander, 2 Ves. Sr. 640; McClure v. Mississippi Valley Ins. Co., 4 Mo. App. 148; Titus v. Cairo, etc., R. Co., 46 N. J. L. 393; Connor v. Parker, 114 Mass. 331; Emerson v. Providence Hat Co., 12 Mass. 237; Planters', etc., Bank v. First Nat'l Bank, 75 N. C. 534; Waldman v. North British, etc., Ins. Co., 91 Ala. 170, 24 Am. St. 883; Fairchild v. King, 102 Cal. 320; Tynan v. Dullnig (Tex. Civ. App.), 25 S. W. 465; Atlee y. Fink, 75 Mo. 100, 43 Am. Rep. 385; Hunt v. Douglass, 22 Vt. 128; Locke's Appeal, 72 Pa. St. 491, 13 Am. Rep. 716; Loeb v. Drakeford, 75 Ala. 464. Duties of public officers which are judicial or discretionary, or governmental in their nature, can not be delegated: Maxwell v. Bay City Bridge Co., 41 Mich. 454; People v. Bank of North America, 75 N. Y. 547; Commonwealth v. Smith, 143 Mass. 169; Bradley Fertilizer Co. v. Taylor, 112 N. C. 141; Seymour Woollen Factory Co. v. Brodhecker, 130 Ind. 389; Pressley v. Lamb, 105 Ind. 171; McGuffie v. State, 17 Ga. 497; Jackson v. Buchanan, 89 N. C. 74; Lyon v. Jerome, 26 Wend. (N. Y.) 485, 37 Am. Dec. 271.

[7] Appleton Bank v. McGilvray, 4 Gray (Mass.) 518. See also, McCroskey v. Hamilton, 108 Ga. 640, 34 S. E. 111; Springfield, etc., Ins. Co. v. DeJarnett (Ala.), 19 So. 995. But in some cases,—where, for example, from the nature of the business it is apparent that subagents are required,—the power to appoint these is often inferred from the character of the duties and general authority of the agent: McKinnon v. Vollmar, 75 Wis. 82, 17 Am. St. 178; Lingenfelter v. Phœnix Ins. Co., 19 Mo. App. 252.

[8] Cochell v. Reynolds, 156 Ind. 14, 58 N. E. 1029.

state. It was provided in the statute that if a majority of the legal voters of a township or ward of a city should sign a remonstrance and file it with the county auditor, it should be unlawful for the county board to grant the license.[9] It was shown that a remonstrance was filed in this particular case to which a number of names had been signed by an agent under a power of attorney authorizing him to sign the names of the principals to any remonstrance against the granting of a license to any person *he might see fit* to remonstrate against receiving such license, and to file the same in the auditor's office at any time he might see fit; such power to cover a period of two years from the time it was granted to such agent. Unless the names signed by the agent under this power of attorney could be legally counted, it was agreed that the remonstrance did not contain the required number of signatures. The court held that the power to remonstrate in such a case was one that had been delegated by the legislature to the voters of the townships and wards, thus committing to each voter the right to decide whether or not he would approve any or all applications; that the right of the voter to remonstrate, being a delegated right, could not be redelegated by him unless such power to redelegate had been expressly conferred by the legislature, which had not been done in this instance.[9a]

§ 188. **Exceptions to the rule.**—There are, however, certain well known exceptions to the general rule. One of these is that when the act to be performed by the agent is purely mechanical or ministerial in its nature, and does not require the exercise of judgment, discretion or skill, or has in it no element of trust, the agent may lawfully authorize another to perform it.[10] Illustrations of agencies requiring the performance of mere mechanical or ministerial acts are found in

[9] Burns' R. S. Ind. 1901, § 7283i.

[9a] But where no discretion was conferred upon the agent, but he was instructed to remonstrate against "any applicant," such delegation of power to sign the remonstrance was held valid: Ludwig v. Cory (Ind.), 64 N. E. 14. See also, White v. Furgeson (Ind. App.), 64 N. E. 49.

[10] Johnson v. Osenton, L. R. 4 Exch. 107; Page v. Hardin, 8 B. Mon. (Ky.) 648, 662; Achorn v. Matthews, 38 Me. 173; Chase v. Ostrom, 50 Wis. 640; People v. Bank of North America, 75 N. Y. 547; Star Line v. Van Vliet, 43 Mich. 364; Drum v. Harrison, 83 Ala. 384; Grinnell v. Buchanan, 1 Daly (N. Y.) 538; McEwen v. Mazyck, 3 Rich. (S. C.) 210; Yates v. Freckleton, 2 Doug. 623; Crooke v. Kings County, 97 N. Y. 421; Kohl v. Beach, 107 Wis. 409, 50 L. R. A. 600, 83 N. W. 647; McCroskey v. Hamilton, 108 Ga. 640, 34 S. E. 111; Dingley v. McDonald, 124 Cal. 682, 57 Pac. 574; McConnell v. Mackin, 48 N. Y. Supp. 18, 22 App. Div. (N. Y.) 537; and cases cited in note 9a, *supra*.

cases in which an agent is authorized by his principal to bind him by signing accommodation paper, acceptances, etc. In such cases the agent, having first made up his mind as to the propriety of the act, may delegate the writing or signing of the paper or papers to another.[11] And an agent appointed to sell land may authorize a subagent to find a purchaser.[12] The same principle is applicable to cases where agents are authorized to issue insurance policies, the authority to do the mere clerical part, such as filling out, and even signing the policies, being such as may be exercised by subagents or clerks.[13] And likewise, an insurance agent may employ clerks, authorizing them to contract for risks, deliver policies and renewals, and collect premiums; and the acts of such clerks are regarded as the acts of the company and will bind the latter.[14]

§ **189. When authority to redelegate will be implied—Banks and their correspondents—Conflict in the decisions.**—When custom or usage sanctions the redelegation of authority to subagents or assistants, the power to redelegate will be implied; and it is not necessary that express power to do so be shown.[15] Instances of this kind occur where paper is intrusted to banks for collection. Thus, if a note or a draft payable at a distant point is left with a local bank for collection, it can not, according to one line of cases, be required of the bank that collection be made by it or its employes directly, it being deemed permissible in such cases that the bank only send the paper to one of its correspondents for that purpose, and the owner or depositor of the paper is presumed to have assented thereto. Necessity, it would seem, prompts this course of dealing; for it might be a matter of extreme hardship, if not of impossibility,

[11] Commercial Bank v. Norton, 1 Hill (N. Y.) 501.

[12] Renwick v. Bancroft, 56 Iowa 527.

[13] Grady v. American, etc., Ins. Co., 60 Mo. 116, 120. See Insurance Co. v. Thornton (Ala.), 30 So. 614; Springfield, etc., Ins. Co. v. DeJarnett (Ala.), 19 So. 995.

[14] Bodine v. Exchange Fire Ins. Co., 51 N. Y. 117; Eclectic Life Ins. Co. v. Fahrenkrug, 68 Ill. 463; Lingenfelter v. Phœnix Ins. Co., 19 Mo. App. 252; Indiana Ins. Co. v. Hartwell, 123 Ind. 177; German Fire Ins. Co. v. Columbia Encaustic Tile Co., 15 Ind. App. 623; May v. Western Assur. Co., 27 Fed. 260; Arff v. Star Fire Ins. Co., 125 N. Y. 57, 21 Am. St. 721; McGonigle v. Susquehanna, etc., Ins. Co., 168 Pa. St. 1; Phœnix Ins. Co. v. Ward, 7 Tex. Civ. App. 13; Goode v. Georgia Home Ins. Co., 92 Va. 392, 53 Am. St. 817.

[15] Combe's Case, 9 Co. 75a; Wilson v. Smith, 3 How. (U. S.) 763; Mayer v. McLure, 36 Miss. 390; Lynn v. Burgoyne, 13 B. Mon. (Ky.) 400; Lamson v. Sims, 48 N. Y. Super. 281; Buckland v. Conway, 16 Mass. 396; Smith v. Sublett, 28 Tex. 163.

for the bank in such a case to be required to do the collecting in person or become an insurer thereof, for the small commission usually charged. And as an agent's authority generally includes the power of employing all the means that are usual and necessary to execute the trust, the agent bank should have the implied authority in such cases to send the paper to a correspondent, without whose assistance it could not effectually carry out its employment.[16] On the other

[16] Harralson v. Stein, 50 Ala. 347; Strong v. Stewart, 9 Heisk. (Tenn.) 137; Bank of Washington v. Triplett, 1 Pet. (U. S.) 25; Siner v. Stearne, 155 Pa. St. 62; Masich v. Citizens' Bank, 34 La. Ann. 1207; East-Haddam Bank v. Scovil, 12 Conn. 303; Kavanaugh v. Farmers' Bank, 59 Mo. App. 540; Daly v. Butchers', etc., Bank, 56 Mo. 94, 17 Am. Rep. 663; Planters', etc., Bank v. First Nat'l Bank, 75 N. C. 534; Second Nat'l Bank v. Cummings, 89 Tenn. 609; Ætna Ins. Co. v. Alton City Bank, 25 Ill. 221; Guelich v. National State Bank, 56 Iowa 434; Jackson v. Union Bank, 6 Harr. & J. (Md.) 146; Bank of Louisville v. First Nat'l Bank, 8 Baxt. (Tenn.) 101; Stacy v. Dane Co. Bank, 12 Wis. 629; Fabens v. Mercantile Bank, 23 Pick. (Mass.) 330; Dorchester, etc., Bank v. New England Bank, 1 Cush. (Mass.) 177; Drovers' Nat'l Bank v. Anglo-American, etc., Co., 117 Ill. 100; Merchants' Nat'l Bank v. Goodman, 109 Pa. St. 422; Bedell v. Harbine Bank (Neb.), 86 N. W. 1060; Davis v. King, 66 Conn. 465; Planters', etc., Bank v. First Nat'l Bank, 75 N. C. 534; Blakeslee v. Hewett, 76 Wis. 341. Where this view prevails it is made applicable only to such collections as require to be sent to a distance; it does not apply to collections at the home of the bank. See also, American Exch. Nat'l Bank v. Thuemmler, 94 Ill. App. 622. The general holding of these cases is that where the first bank has used due diligence in selecting a correspondent and forwarding the claim to it, it has done all that it is required to do. Thus, in the case of East-Haddam Bank v. Scovil, 12 Conn. 303, it was said by Huntington, J., speaking for the court: "The plaintiff's place of business was East-Haddam. The bill was payable in New York. It was necessary that it should be transmitted to the latter place for collection. These facts were known to the defendant, who must also have known that the plaintiffs could do no more than transmit it to the city of New York, to a reputable correspondent, according to their usual course of business, to be collected. All this was done by the plaintiffs. Under such circumstances it can not justly be claimed that the plaintiffs should have become insurers against the defaults of their correspondents. Such a doctrine would be as inequitable as it might be oppressive and ruinous to banks, who are merely the medium through which the holders of bills and drafts payable in other states transmit them for collection. If they act in good faith, in the selection of an agent to protect the interests of the holder of the bill, in cases where it is obvious an agent must be selected for such purpose, what principle of justice or commercial policy requires that they should be held liable for any neglect of duty on the part of

hand, there is a strong line of cases holding that in such a contract there is no privity between the depositor of the collection and the correspondent bank, and that the latter is but the servant or agent of the bank to whom the paper has been intrusted, that bank occupying the position of a principal that is responsible for the acts of its agents or servants. According to this view, the first bank must account to the owner or depositor of the paper, and is responsible for the conduct of its correspondent without reference to the question as to whether or not it exercised diligence in the selection of such correspondent. This view is based upon the theory of public policy, and that the consideration paid to the first bank will warrant the presumption that such bank has undertaken to do the collecting and can not shift the responsibility upon any one else. "The distinction," said the supreme court of the United States, "between the liability of one who contracts to do a thing and that of one who merely receives a delegation of authority to act for another is a fundamental one, applicable to the present case. If the agency is an undertaking to do the business, the original principal may look to the immediate contractor with himself, and is not obliged to look to inferior or distant under-contractors or subagents, when defaults occur injurious to his interest." Whether the paper is to be collected in the place where the bank is situated or elsewhere, the court says is immaterial. "In either case, there is an implied contract of the bank that the proper measures shall be used to collect the draft, and a right, on the part of its owner, to presume that proper agents will be employed, he having no knowledge of the agents. There is, therefore,

such agent? To impose this liability would make a special contract excluding it necessary in all cases, or it would render the collection of bills of this description extremely difficult. It would tend very much to destroy the facilities which at present exist, of making collections through the agency of banks, and subject the holders of bills to inconvenience, and expense, and probably, in many cases, to serious loss. The mode now adopted and in general use is well calculated to insure collections with promptitude, at a trifling expense, and without trouble to the holder. It is highly reasonable he should assume the risk of the defaults of the collecting agent, rather than the bank, who merely transmits its bills and selects the agent, with the consent of the holder, and with a perfect knowledge on his part that such selections must be made; and when the power is exercised in good faith, and with reasonable care, and according to general usage. The views we have thus expressed, so eminently just, and so well calculated to protect the rights of all concerned, are sanctioned by many adjudications of high authority."

no reason for liability or exemption from liability in the one case which does not apply in the other. And while the rule of law is thus general, the liability of the bank may be varied by consent, or the bank may refuse to undertake the collection. It may agree to receive the paper only for transmission to a correspondent, and thus make a different contract and become responsible only for good faith and due discretion in the choice of an agent. If this is not done, or there is no implied understanding to that effect, the same responsibility is assumed in the undertaking to collect foreign paper and in that to collect paper payable at home. On any other rule, no principal contractor would be liable for the default of his own agent, where, from the nature of the business, it was evident he must employ subagents. The distinction recurs, between the rule of merely personal representative agency and the responsibility imposed by the law of commercial contracts. This solves the difficulty and reconciles the apparent conflict of decision in many cases. The nature of the contract is the test. If the contract be only for the immediate services of the agent and for his faithful conduct as representing his principal, the responsibility ceases with the limits of the personal services undertaken. But where the contract looks mainly to the thing to be done, and the undertaking is for the due use of all proper means to perform it, the responsibility extends to all necessary and proper means to accomplish the object, by whomsoever used."[17]

[17] Per Blatchford, J., in Exchange Nat'l Bank v. Third Nat'l Bank, 112 U. S. 276. The English cases support the doctrine of the liability of the first bank for the acts or omissions of the correspondent bank: Mackersy v. Ramsays, 9 Cl. & F. 818; Van Wart v. Woolley, 3 B. & C. 439, 10 E. C. L. 145, 5 D. & R. 374; Cobb v. Becke, 6 Q. B. 930, 51 E. C. L. 930. This doctrine is recognized in the federal courts of the United States and the courts of New York, Michigan, Minnesota, New Jersey, Ohio, Montana, Colorado, Indiana, and perhaps other states: Hoover v. Wise, 91 U. S. 308; Dodge v. Freedman's, etc., Co., 93 U. S. 379; Montgomery Co. Bank v. Albany City Bank, 7 N. Y. 459; St. Nicholas Bank v. State Nat'l Bank, 128 N. Y. 26; Commercial Bank v. Union Bank, 11 N. Y. 203; Ayrault v. Pacific Bank, 47 N. Y. 570; Allen v. Merchants' Bank, 22 Wend. (N. Y.) 215; Corn Exch. Bank v. Farmers' Nat'l Bank, 118 N. Y. 443; Castle v. Corn Exch. Bank, 148 N. Y. 122; Simpson v. Waldby, 63 Mich. 439; Streissguth v. National, etc., Bank, 43 Minn. 50, 19 Am. St. 213; Davey v. Jones, 42 N. J. L. 28, 36 Am. Rep. 505; Titus v. Mechanics' Nat'l Bank, 35 N. J. L. 588; Reeves v. State Bank, 8 Ohio St. 465; Power v. First Nat'l Bank, 6 Mont. 251; German Nat'l Bank v. Burns, 12 Colo. 541, 13 Am. St. 247; Tyson v. State Bank, 6 Blackf. (Ind.) 225, 38 Am. Dec. 139; American Express Co. v. Haire,

§ **190. Express contract governs—Collecting agencies.**—Of course, if the parties have expressly contracted that the first bank shall be responsible for the collection, even if undertaken by its foreign agents or correspondents, the courts will hold such bank liable.[18] Or if the first bank has been guilty of negligence in the selection of its correspondent, it will undoubtedly be liable.[19] The solution of the question may, however, depend upon the usage or custom of banks in the place where the first bank is situated. "If the law has not been already settled by judicial determination, so as to exclude any subsequent evidence of usage to subvert it, the bank may absolve itself from liability for the acts of agents other than itself, or the customer may fix such liability upon the bank, by showing, respectively, that such is the established usage and understood custom in the place where the bank, the extent of whose duty and liability is in question, is situated. But the evidence must show a usage having the strictly legal traits; it must be a real, *bona-fide* usage, an actual practice, a general understanding, not the mere opinion of either merchants or bankers."[19a] The circumstances of each particular case must, of course, be consulted before determining whether it comes under any particular rule of law of those above stated and discussed. It can not be denied, however, that, as to the main question,—the liability of the first bank for negligence or other misconduct of its correspondents or other agents,—there is a hopeless conflict in the decisions. We can only refer the reader to the cases. It seems to us, however, that the better rule is to treat the bank as the agent of the owner or depositor of the paper. Considering that when the collection is to be made at a distant place the immediate agents or employes of the bank, at the place of its own locality, could not give the matter the attention that would be expected of them in case of a

21 Ind. 4, 83 Am. Dec. 334. While Indiana is generally classed as among the states holding that the first bank is liable, the cases cited do not seem to support the doctrine fully, as the exact point does not seem to have been presented. See also, Citizens' Nat'l Bank v. Third Nat'l Bank, 19 Ind. App. 69. And in Irwin v. Reeves Pulley Co., 20 Ind. App. 101, the appellate court holds that the first bank is only bound to exercise reasonable care and skill in selecting the correspondent. The supreme court of that state does not seem to have passed upon the precise question; nor is the appellate court unanimous in the position it assumes: See the dissenting opinions of Robinson, C. J., and Comstock, J.

[18] Mechanics' Bank v. Earp, 4 Rawle (Pa.) 384.

[19] Fabens v. Mercantile Bank, 23 Pick. (Mass.) 330; Ætna Ins. Co. v. Alton City Bank, 25 Ill. 221.

[19a] 1 Morse Banks and Banking, § 270.

collection at its home place, it appears to us that when the deposit is made, if nothing was said upon the subject, the depositor contracts with a view to the custom of the bank to send the paper to a correspondent at or near the place of residence of the debtor. In other words, the implication is that the creditor consents that the collection may be made by others than the home officers and employes of the first bank, just as an insurance company tacitly consents that a large portion of the business intrusted to its general agents may be transacted by subagents. The small compensation collected for the labor of collecting such claims can not be supposed to cover the risk of insuring the conduct of the bank's agents or correspondents at distant points. As to collecting agencies other than banks,—agencies which hold themselves out as specially engaged in that business, and who advertise "Collections made in all parts of the United States," etc., as their special business, exacting a special compensation therefor in proportion to the risk,—they are doubtless to be held liable as having undertaken the risk by their contract. However, even upon this question there seems to be a conflict of authority.[20]

§ 191. **From what the power to appoint subagents may be inferred.**—From the character of the transaction for which an agency has been established it may often be inferred that a general agent has the power to employ subagents. Thus, the person employed to charter a ship may employ a ship broker to assist him in the performance of his duty.[21] An auctioneer may employ an assistant under his immediate direction to make outcry and use the hammer.[22] Much depends, of course, upon the usages of trade. If custom or usage sanctions the practice to employ a subagent, the principal will usually be bound by such appointment.[23] These cases serve sufficiently to illustrate the rule that an authority, though not original, may sometimes be delegated.

§ 192. **Principal bound by apparent as well as implied and incidental authority—Special and general authority.**—The authority which an agent exercises in the performance of an act or acts may

[20] See 1 Morse Banks & Banking, §§ 267, 270.

[21] Saveland v. Green, 40 Wis. 431.

[22] Commonwealth v. Harnden, 19 Pick. (Mass.) 482.

[23] Trueman v. Loder, 11 Ad. & E. 589, 39 E. C. L. 178; Wallace v. Bradshaw, 6 Dana (Ky.) 383; Bilsborrow v. James, 25 Hun (N. Y.) 18; Nugent v. Martin, 1 Tex. App. Civ. Cas., § 1175; Laussatt v. Lippincott, 6 S. & R. (Pa.) 386, 9 Am. Dec. 440.

have been actually conferred, or it may be apparent only. If actually conferred, third persons will, of course, be justified in dealing with the agent, and the principal will be liable for his acts. But if the authority is only apparent, or was not conferred to the full extent to which it was exercised, the question often arises how far third persons will be protected in relying upon appearances. If authority of some kind has been conferred, but not to the extent exercised, the question occurs whether the agent has acted within the apparent scope of his authority. In such cases the principal will be bound—if the agent has been held out to possess general powers—by all the acts done within the apparent scope of such power, though in fact the agency was limited by private instructions. In other words, the principal will be held to the performance of such of the agent's contracts as he permitted him to appear to possess authority to make.[23a] But if the agency be special, it is said to be the duty of a third party to inquire into the nature and extent of the authority conferred by the principal and to deal with the agent accordingly.[24] It would

[23a] Merchants' Bank v. Central Bank, 1 Ga. 418, 44 Am. Dec. 665; Towle v. Leavitt, 23 N. H. 360, 55 Am. Dec. 195; Munn v. Commission Co., 15 Johns. (N. Y.) 44, 8 Am. Dec. 219.

[24] Towle v. Leavitt, 23 N. H. 360, 55 Am. Dec. 195; Denning v. Smith, 3 Johns. Ch. (N. Y.) 332, 344; Snow v. Perry, 9 Pick. (Mass.) 539, 542; Fenn v. Harrison, 3 T. R. 757; Congar v. Galena, etc., R. Co., 17 Wis. 477; Luse v. Isthmus Trans. R. Co., 6 Ore. 125; Cairo, etc., R. Co. v. Mahoney, 82 Ill. 73; Stewart v. Woodward, 50 Vt. 78; Davis v. Talbot, 137 Ind. 235; Gaar, Scott & Co. v. Rose, 3 Ind. App. 269; Robinson v. Anderson, 106 Ind. 152; Blackwell v. Ketcham, 53 Ind. 184; Metzger v. Huntington, 139 Ind. 501; Reed v. Ashburnham R. Co., 120 Mass. 43; Holt v. Schneider, 57 Neb. 523, 77 N. W. 1086. Thus, an agent who has power to sell property for his principal may be presumed to have authority to warrant the same, although, in fact, he is expressly prohibited by his instructions from so doing, unless the third party has notice of such instructions: J. I. Case Threshing Machine Co. v. McKinnon, 82 Minn. 75, 84 N. W. 646. And so, where an agent was authorized on one occasion to accept part payment of a mortgage debt before it was due, the mortgagors were warranted in believing he had authority to accept the balance before it was due: Harrison v. Legore, 109 Iowa 618, 80 N. W. 670. But where one was authorized to lease property it does not warrant the lessee in assuming that such person was authorized to cancel such lease: Faville v. Lundvall, 106 Iowa 135, 76 N. W. 512. And authority to collect a debt does not carry with it authority to accept the debtor's note: Holt v. Schneider, 57 Neb. 523, 77 N. W. 1086. Neither does a traveling salesman, in the absence of custom, have implied authority to collect money: Brown v. Lally, 79

thus seem that the effect of the apparent scope of authority is different in the case of a special agency from what it is in that of a general agency. In the former case, the principal has only held out the agent as possessing the authority that agents of a like class usually exercise. The very nature of the power exercised by a special agent is supposed to be such as should place the party dealing with him on his inquiry, and it will be no great hardship for him to ascertain the real authority; whereas, in the case where an agent is held out as possessing extended powers, the appearance of things is such as will warrant the implication of the principal's assent to its exercise. But the difference is more apparent than real; for it may be truly said that in either a general or special agency there is a scope of authority beyond which third parties can not safely go, and that, in either case, they will be confined to appearances rather than the actual power conferred.[25] And whenever, in either case, the agent acts within the limits in which he is held out to third parties by his principal, or in which it is usual for agents of that class to act, he will, in the absence of notice to such third parties of his real powers, bind his principal, notwithstanding he acted without authority or exceeded that which he possessed; for it is well settled that, in such a case, where one of two innocent persons must suffer, he ought to suffer who misled the other by holding out the agent as competent to act, and as apparently enjoying his confidence.[26]

Minn. 38, 81 N. W. 538. In such cases the third party can not assume the existence of authority which is not necessarily included in that actually conferred. An agent employed to drive stock from place to place would have no authority to sell such stock in case it become foot-sore and unable to travel: Reitz v. Martin, 12 Ind. 306. "The general rule is," said the court in this case, "that the authority of the agent, of whatever description, must be strictly pursued; otherwise the principal, if his agent be a special one, will not be bound. . . . And if the principal has never held the agent out as having any authority whatever in the premises it is the duty of one purchasing from him to inquire, and if he trusts without inquiry, he trusts to the good faith of the agent and not of the principal:" Citing Story Ag., § 133. So, where a party authorizes another to sign his name to a note for a specific sum, the authority is a special one, and the payee of the note is chargeable with knowledge of the extent of the authority: Blackwell v. Ketcham, 53 Ind. 184.

[25] Hodge v. Combs, 1 Blatchf. (U. S.) 192; Lister v. Allen, 31 Md. 543.

[26] Story Ag., § 443. The principal is bound by the exercise of all the authority necessarily implied by and incident to that actually conferred; and an authority always carries with it the requisite means for its exercise, except such as are express-

§ **193. Custom or usage.**—In every agency the law presumes, furthermore, that the authority was conferred in contemplation of the usage that prevails in such matters; and hence, persons dealing with the agent in good faith will be protected if the power has been exercised in accordance with such usage, unless the limitations of power were known to those who dealt with the agent.[27] The particular custom or usage must, however, be a reasonable one, and must have existed long enough to have become generally known, so that the parties must have acted with a view to it.[28] If the usage is a mere local one, and not generally known, the presumption that otherwise prevails as to the principal's knowledge of the same may be overcome by him, by proving that he had in fact no notice or information of the same.[29] But the mere fact that the principal had no actual knowledge of the custom or usage, if general, does not excuse him from being charged with notice thereof.[30] It would be difficult, if not impossible, for the parties to an agency contract to provide for every contingency that may arise in the execution thereof. Many questions may come up as to which no provision has been or can well be made in the specification of the power conferred by the principal. In all such cases the usage of trade is the criterion by

ly forbidden: Adams v. Pittsburgh Ins. Co., 95 Pa. St. 348, 40 Am. Rep. 663.

[27] Wharton Ag., §§ 134, 676; Greeves v. Tegge, 12 Exch. 642; Russell v. Hankey, 6 T. R. 12; Brady v. Todd, 9 C. B. (N. S.) 592, 99 E. C. L. 591; Sutton v. Tatham, 10 Ad. & E. 27, 37 E. C. L. 25; Young v. Cole, 3 Bing. N. C. 724, 32 E. C. L. 334; Frank v. Jenkins, 22 Ohio St. 597; Randall v. Kehlor, 60 Me. 37, 11 Am. Rep. 167; Willard v. Buckingham, 36 Conn. 395; American Cent. Ins. Co. v. McLanathan, 11 Kan. 533; Taylor v. Bailey, 169 Ill. 181; McKee v. Wild, 52 Neb. 9, 71 N. W. 158; Gehl v. Milwaukee Produce Co., 105 Wis. 573, 81 N. W. 666; McMasters v. Pennsylvania R. Co., 69 Pa. St. 374, 8 Am. Rep. 264; Talcott v. Smith, 142 Mass. 542; Bailey v. Bensley, 87 Ill. 556; Samuels v. Oliver, 130 Ill. 73.

[28] Knowles v. Dow, 22 N. H. 387, 35 Am. Dec. 163; Buyck v. Schwing, 100 Ala. 355, 14 So. 48. Whether a custom is reasonable or not is a question of law for the decision of the court; while usage, which is the evidence of custom, is a question of fact for the jury: Bourke v. James & Kneeland, 4 Mich. 336; Chicago Packing Co. v. Tilton, 87 Ill. 547; Randall v. Smith, 63 Me. 105, 18 Am. Rep. 200.

[29] Barnard v. Kellogg, 10 Wall. (U. S.) 383; Walls v. Bailey, 49 N. Y. 464, 10 Am. Rep. 407.

[30] Bailey v. Bensley, 87 Ill. 556; Samuels v. Oliver, 130 Ill. 73; Union Stock Yard, etc., Co. v. Mallory, etc., Co., 157 Ill. 554, 41 N. E. 888; Sleght v. Hartshorne, 2 Johns. (N. Y.) 531; Cole v. Skrainka, 37 Mo. App. 427; Blin v. Mayo, 10 Vt. 56, 33 Am. Dec. 175.

which the agent's authority is to be measured; and this is so, as we have observed, although the principal and agent have agreed in their contract that things are to be done which are directly in conflict with the usages and customs of trade, provided the usage is general and reasonable, and the third party had no information concerning the agent's limitations.[31] Thus, the ordinary usages and customs of the officers of a bank in the transaction of their business are so well and generally known that the parties to a contract of this nature are always presumed to have contracted with reference to them; and in the absence of knowledge of contrary instructions on the part of third parties, the bank will be bound by the acts of such officers, if the authority exercised by them was within the scope of such usage or course of business.[32] Accordingly, the courts will give effect to the customs of shipmasters in charge of vessels at river ports to insure their vessels and give premium notes therefor, and such notes will bind the owners of such boats.[33] Upon the same principle, where a customer had given a broker an order for a quantity of stock, the broker, it was held, might, in accordance with custom, direct his correspondents in another state to purchase the stock.[34] Of course, as between principal and agent, the latter will never be justified by custom or usage in departing from his plain instructions.[34a] Moreover, usage can never be relied upon to violate a positive law;[35] nor can it be invoked to change the intrinsic character of a contract as between the parties thereto.[36]

[31] See Upton v. Suffolk Co. Mills, 11 Cush. (Mass.) 586, 589.

[32] Minor v. Mechanics' Bank, 1 Pet. (U. S.) 46.

[33] Adams v. Pittsburgh Ins. Co., 95 Pa. St. 348, 10 Am. Rep. 662.

[34] Rosenstock v. Tormey, 32 Md. 169.

[34a] Day v. Holmes, 103 Mass. 306; Hutchings v. Ladd, 16 Mich. 493.

[35] Healey v. Mannheimer, 74 Minn. 240, 76 N. W. 1126; McKee v. Wild, 52 Neb. 9, 71 N. W. 958; Hopper v. Sage, 112 N. Y. 530, 8 Am. St. 771. No custom or usage which will relieve a party from a just legal obligation will be recognized by the courts; and this being true, evidence tending to prove such custom is properly excluded: Western Union Cold Storage Co. v. Winona Produce Co., 94 Ill. App. 618; Barnes v. Zettlemoyer (Tex. Civ. App.), 62 S. W. 111. Nor can the existence of a custom be established by evidence of a single act, custom being the result of a series of acts; or, in other words, custom is the result of usage, and must be proved by usage: Shields v. Kansas City, etc., R. Co., 87 Mo. App. 637.

[36] Mollett v. Robinson, L. R. 5 C. P. 646, 7 C. P. 84, 7 H. L. 802; Brown v. Foster, 113 Mass. 136; Meloche v. Chicago, etc., R. Co., 116 Mich. 69, 74 N. W. 301; Burnham v. City of Milwaukee, 100 Wis. 55, 75 N. W. 1014; McKee v. Wild, 52 Neb. 9, 71

§ 194. Custom or usage, how established—Summary of authority agent may exercise.—Whether a custom or usage exists or not is a question of fact to be proved as any other fact is proved; courts do not take judicial notice of customs or usages.[37] To summarize, then, the nature and extent of the authority an agent may exercise and bind his principal by, it may be stated that the authority may consist of: 1. Such as has been expressly delegated to him by the act of the principal; 2. Whatever powers are reasonably implied in those actually conferred and are reasonably necessary to carry into effect the powers actually delegated; 3. Such powers as the principal has by his conduct led third persons to believe he has conferred; 4. Such powers as the usage or custom of the country or community adopts or sanctions with reference to the transaction of the business for the performance of which the agent is actually employed; 5. Such powers as, though not delegated originally, are subsequently approved by ratification on the part of the principal.

§ 195. Interpretation and construction of authority.—The authority of an agent, except where established by implication of law, being contained in the contract between him and the principal, whether such contract be express or implied, it is obvious that the rules as to interpretation and construction of contracts generally must be looked to in cases involving the interpretation and construction of contracts by which authority is conferred upon agents.[38] The student should not lose sight of the distinction between the interpretation of the words, phrases and sentences in a contract, and its construction. This distinction is thus lucidly expressed by Dr. Lieber: "Interpretation is the act of finding out the true sense of any form of words; that is, the sense which the author intended to convey. * * * Construction is the drawing of conclusions respecting subjects that

N. W. 958; Swadling v. Barneson, 21 Wash. 699, 59 Pac. 506; Allen v. Dykers, 3 Hill (N. Y.) 593, 7 Hill (N. Y.) 497; Hopper v. Sage, 112 N. Y. 530, 8 Am. St. 771; Pickering v. Weld, 159 Mass. 522.

[37] Sullivan v. Jernigan, 21 Fla. 264; Chicago Packing, etc., Co. v. Tilton, 87 Ill. 547; Pardridge v. Bailey, 20 Ill. App. 351; Haas v. Hudmon, 83 Ala. 174; Eager v. Atlas Ins. Co., 14 Pick. (Mass.) 141, 35 Am. Dec. 363; Ward v. Everett, 1 Dana (Ky.) 429; Bentley v. Doggett, 51 Wis. 224; Stanton v. Embrey, 93 U. S. 548; Ahern v. Goodspeed, 72 N. Y. 117; Talmage v. Bierhause, 103 Ind. 270. The burden of proving a custom or usage is upon him who asserts it: The John H. Cannon, 51 Fed. 46; Thomas v. Hooker, etc., Pump Co., 28 Mo. App. 563; Hall v. Storrs, 7 Wis. 253.

[38] Wharton Ag., § 221.

lie beyond the direct expressions of the text, from elements gathered from and given in the text—conclusions which are in the spirit though not within the letter of the text."[39] In general, questions of interpretation are for the jury, while questions of construction are for the court. There may be instances, however, where a question as to the proper construction of a contract becomes a mixed question of law and fact, to be determined by the jury, under the instructions of the court. Questions of this character usually arise when the contract is in parol, or partly in writing and partly in parol. When the contract is entirely in writing, its construction is for the court; unless there is such a latent ambiguity as to require parol evidence in explanation, when it may become a mixed question of law and fact. Where there is, in a written contract of agency, no such ambiguity as to require parol testimony to explain, or where the contract is oral and undisputed, the court is the proper tribunal for its construction.[40] In such case, if there be ambiguity, the court should charge the jury hypothetically, as to the true interpretation.[41] When written words are illegible or in a foreign language, the questions as to what they are and what they mean is generally one of fact to be submitted to the jury. When the language of the contract is unwritten, that is, rests in parol, and there is any dispute as to what the language really is, the question is for the jury to decide,—it being a question of interpretation. In other words, the question is as to what the contract really is or whether there is in fact one at all or not. When the jury has once found the language of the contract, then its construction will be for the court.

§ **196. Intention of parties.**—As the authority of an agent rests mainly upon the assent of the parties, the court will aim to ascertain the character of the contract by their intention as manifested by the language of the contract. As in all other contracts, the intention must govern; and if that may be ascertained by the text of the instrument or the language of the authority, in whatever form it may exist, the court will give it effect. The intention of the principal, therefore, as to the nature and extent of the powers to be conferred upon the agent, is an all-important factor, where the existence of such au-

[39] See Wharton Conts., § 628, n. 1.

[40] Loudon Savings Fund Society v. Savings Bank, 36 Pa. St. 498, 78 Am. Dec. 390; Gulick v. Grover, 33 N. J. L. 463, 97 Am. Dec. 728; Claflin v. Continental Jersey Works, 85 Ga. 27; Dobbins v. Etowah Mfg., etc., Co., 75 Ga. 238, 243; Millay v. Whitney, 63 Me. 522.

[41] 1 Beach Conts., § 743

thority depends upon the contents of the contract solely.[42] The powers conferred must be construed with a view to their object and design, as gathered from the contract; or if there was no express contract, or none was known to the party affected, the intention must be gathered from the circumstances of the case.[43]

§ 197. **Authority in writing—Construction of.**—When the authority of the agent is conferred by written power of attorney, and the question of the extent of the agent's authority arises in a controversy between the principal and agent, or between the principal and a third party,—provided the latter had knowledge of the written contract,—the construction must, as a general rule, be limited to the contents of the written instrument. In such cases the construction of the contract, as to the nature and extent of the authority conferred, is always a question of law and must be made by the court.[44] And the instrument itself must be introduced in evidence, or its absence accounted for.[45] And while the court will not, as a general rule, permit such instrument to be varied or explained by parol testimony, if additional authority has been conferred subsequently to the execution of the power of attorney, it may be proved by evidence *aliunde*.[46] Thus, where an agent was authorized by power of attorney to sell or procure a purchaser for certain real estate at a fixed price, in cash, and execute a contract of such sale; and the agent made the sale at the price named, but partly on credit,—it was held that parol testimony was properly admitted to prove that the agent, subsequently to the execution of the power of attorney, was authorized by parol to make the sale in the manner in which it was executed by him.[47]

[42] Marr v. Given, 23 Me. 55, 39 Am. Dec. 600; Holladay v. Daily, 19 Wall. (U. S.) 606; Spect v. Gregg, 51 Cal. 198; Brantley v. Southern Life Ins. Co., 53 Ala. 554.

[43] Vanada v. Hopkins, 1 J. J. Marsh. (Ky.) 285, 19 Am. Dec. 92.

[44] Loudon Savings Fund Society v. Savings Bank, 36 Pa. St. 498, 78 Am. Dec. 390; Berry v. Harnage, 39 Tex. 638; McCreery v. Garvin, 39 S. C. 375; Claflin v. Continental Jersey Works, 85 Ga. 27; Equitable Life Assur. Soc. v. Poe, 53 Md. 28; Millay v. Whitney, 63 Me. 522. It is the duty of one who deals with an agent whose authority is in writing to inspect it, and he is chargeable with knowledge of its legal effect: North River Bank v. Aymar, 3 Hill (N. Y.) 262. If the authority is by parol he must learn its language as best he can: North River Bank v. Aymar, 3 Hill (N. Y.) 262.

[45] Stadleman v. Fitzgerald, 14 Neb. 290.

[46] Williams v. Cochran, 7 Rich. (S. C.) 45; Hartford Fire Ins. Co. v. Wilcox, 57 Ill. 180.

[47] McGill v. Stoddard, 70 Mo. 75.

§ **198. Rules of construction.**—"When an authority is conferred upon an agent by a formal instrument, as a power of attorney, there are two rules of construction to be carefully attended to: 1. The meaning of general words in the instrument will be restricted by the context, and construed accordingly. 2. The authority will be construed strictly, so as to exclude the exercise of any power which is not warranted, either by the actual terms used, or as a necessary means of executing an authority with effect."[48] The authority given an agent by power of attorney is never extended by intendment or construction beyond that which is given in terms or is absolutely necessary to carry such authority into effect.[49] The construction, however, must not be such as to defeat the intention of the parties in the accomplishment of the object, if such intention fairly appears from the language used.[50] Under the rules of construction above stated it has been held that a power of attorney under seal, authorizing an agent to sign the principal's name to a contract, authorizes him to execute a contract under seal;[51] and that authority to cite a principal confers authority to defend suit brought by or against the principal;[52] but that a power of attorney to execute an injunction bond according to the order of the court does not authorize the execution of a bond that the principal will pay the damages that may be awarded against him on the dissolution of the injunction, where that is not required by the statute;[53] nor will an authority to confess a judgment described authorize the confession of another judgment, at a different time from that authorized in the instrument;[54] but he may confess judgment with a stay of execution;[55] and a general power of attorney has been held sufficient to authorize the agent to execute a general release in the principal's name.[56] The words of an instrument should always be construed with reference to the object to be accomplished; and where a power is given to do some particular

[48] Evans Pr. & Ag. (Bedford's ed.) 203; Gouldy v. Metcalf, 75 Tex. 455, 16 Am. St. 912.

[49] Gilbert v. How, 45 Minn. 121, 22 Am. St. 724; Ashley v. Bird, 1 Mo. 640, 14 Am. Dec. 213; Brantley v. Southern Life Ins. Co., 53 Ala. 554; Bissell v. Terry, 69 Ill. 184; Craighead v. Peterson, 72 N. Y. 279, 28 Am. Rep. 150.

[50] Hemstreet v. Burdick, 90 Ill. 444.

[51] Wickham v. Knox, 33 Pa. St. 71.

[52] Miller v. Marmiche, 24 La. Ann. 30.

[53] Dehart v. Wilson, 6 T. B. Mon. (Ky.) 577.

[54] Rankin v. Eakin, 3 Head (Tenn.) 229.

[55] Calwells v. Sheilds, 2 Rob. (Va.) 305.

[56] Quesnel v. Mussy, 1 Dall. (Pa.) 449.

act, followed by general words, such words will not be extended beyond what is necessary for the accomplishment of such act.[57] Thus, a power of attorney to collect debts due, and to compromise, settle and arrange them, either in law or otherwise, as the attorney may see fit, does not authorize such attorney to forgive the debt or postpone or discharge the security, except in fulfillment of some arrangement for its satisfaction.[58] And a power of attorney to transact all business of the principal, with certain books and accounts for professional services "for settlement," was held not to authorize the transfer of such books and accounts to the surety of the principal to indemnify him for being such surety.[59] Nor will an authority constituting another the principal's "general and special agent to do and transact all manner of business," authorize the agent to sell stocks or other property.[60]

§ 199. **Ambiguity in authority of agent.**—Where the authority conferred is ambiguous and capable of more than one construction, it should be construed according to the usual course of dealing in such matters.[61] If, however, the agent has in good faith done an act upon one construction, the principal will be bound.[62] A power to collect a note does not include authority to bind the principal by an expression of the agent's opinion as to the correct reading of a doubtful word.[63] Authority to draw a bill of exchange does not authorize the agent to bind the principal by receiving notice of dishonor;[64] nor will a power of attorney authorizing an agent to represent the principal's interest in the settlement of certain claims authorize the attorney to bind the principal for the debts of third persons;[65] nor will an authority to negotiate an exchange of

[57] Luke v. Griggs, 4 Dak. 287; Wood v. Goodridge, 6 Cush. (Mass.) 117, 52 Am. Dec. 771; Craighead v. Peterson, 72 N. Y. 279, 28 Am. Rep. 150; Rountree v. Denison, 59 Wis. 522; Billings v. Morrow, 7 Cal. 171, 68 Am. Dec. 235.

[58] Chilton v. Willford, 2 Wis. 1, 60 Am. Dec. 339.

[59] Wood v. McCain, 7 Ala. 800, 42 Am. Dec. 612.

[60] Hodge v. Combs, 1 Blatchf. (U. S.) 192.

[61] Pole v. Leask, 28 Beav. 562; Ireland v. Livingston, L. R. 5 H. L. 395; Mattocks v. Young, 66 Me. 459; Mann v. Laws, 117 Mass. 293.

[62] See Brown v. McGran, 14 Pet. (U. S.) 479; Mechanics' Bank v. Merchants' Bank, 6 Met. (Mass.) 13.

[63] Van Vechten v. Smith, 59 Iowa 173.

[64] Hockaday v. Skeggs, 2 Phila. (Pa.) 268.

[65] Hart v. Dixon, 5 Lea (Tenn.) 336.

lands authorize a binding contract to exchange or receive a deed to be given the principal on exchange;[66] nor will an authority to exchange a mule for other property bind the principal to the payment of a sum of money as the estimated difference in value;[67] nor will an authority to receive money authorize the agent to pay it out.[68]

§ 200. **How intention of parties is ascertained.**—The intention of the parties to such a contract, as in the case of any other, is to be sought in the language used by them, if that be possible. The parties will be held to the legal effect of their written agreement, although their real intention may have been otherwise; unless, indeed, there has been a mutual mistake, in which case the court will give relief by the reformation of the instrument. But courts will not usually relieve parties from their mistaken views of the law; and hence, if the legal effect of a contract is different from that contemplated by one of the parties, he will nevertheless be bound by it.[69] In ascertaining the intention of the parties, the courts will consider the instrument as an entirety, and not in single isolated portions, and will take into account every word and sentence and the situation and surrounding circumstances of the parties at the time of the making of the contract, so as to place itself as nearly as may be in their position and probable frame of mind, in case the words and phrases chosen by them are at all ambiguous or doubtful. Instruments under seal are always strictly construed with reference to the subject-matter, and in powers of attorney the same rule is applied. No enlarged meaning beyond the subject-matter will be given the general words employed, unless it expressly appears from the instrument that such was their unquestionable intention. Thus the term "to transact all business" is construed to mean only all such business as is necessary to perform the task that has been intrusted to the agent.[70] And so, where a bond was executed to secure the faithful performance of all

[66] Swain v. Burnette, 89 Cal. 564.

[67] McMillan v. Wooten, 80 Ala. 263.

[68] Knowlton v. School City of Logansport, 75 Ind. 103. Authority to collect the principal and interest of a debt is not authority to receive either the principal or the interest before it becomes due: Park v. Cross, 76 Minn. 187, 78 N. W. 1107. An agent authorized to receive money (such amounts as the debtor may be able to pay) has authority to receive an order for money about to become due to the debtor: Ruthven v. Clarke, 109 Iowa 25, 79 N. W. 454.

[69] Loudon Savings Fund Society v. Savings Bank, 36 Pa. St. 498, 78 Am. Dec. 390.

[70] Hay v. Goldsmidt (Eng. K. B.), mentioned in Hogg v. Snaith, 1 Taunt. 349.

the official duties of an office, the condition of the bond is held to refer only to the term of office for which the officer was chosen, and will not cover loss resulting from failure to perform duties subsequently to the expiration of the term.[71] But the liability on an official bond continues until the officer's successor is appointed and qualified, where the statute provides that the officer shall so long continue in office.[72] A power of attorney "to negotiate, compromise, determine, settle and arrange all differences between them [partners] and the bank of Vincennes and all persons whatever; to execute and sign their names to any lease, covenant, or conveyance of all or any part of their joint estate, whether real or personal; and to give and receive discharges, receipts," etc., was held not to authorize the agent to confess judgment.[73] Neither will a power of attorney to "demand, sue for, recover, and receive all moneys, debts, and dues, and to give discharges," authorize the agent to indorse paper in the name of the principal.[74]

§ **201. Collateral writings, when may enter into construction.**— The court, in determining what the authority of the agent is in a given case, may resort to collateral writings between the parties in reference to the same matter, such as letters, memoranda, agreements, etc., as all these together may constitute but one contract, or may serve at least to disclose the real intention of the parties as to the particular matter in dispute.[75]

§ **202. Interpretation as distinguished from construction.**—It must be remembered, however, that these rules apply only to the *construction* of contracts. Words themselves may have an ambiguous or even an unknown meaning, and may require, therefore, not construction, but interpretation. When this is the case, witnesses may be called who are familiar with the meaning of the words to interpret the same. A foreign word or phrase may be used in a contract, and a linguist may be required to translate it; terms of art may be explained by specialists; terms of business by evidence of business usage; technical terms may be explained by competent witnesses; ciphers, abbreviations, signs, informal memoranda, etc., may be ex-

[71] Lord Arlington v. Merricke, 2 Wms. Saunders 403, 411a. See also, Rooke v. Lord Kensington, 2 K. & J. 753; Jenner v. Jenner, L. R. 1 Eq. 361; Moore v. Magrath, 1 Cowp. 9.

[72] Akers v. State, 8 Ind. 484.

[73] Lagow v. Patterson, 1 Blackf. (Ind.) 252.

[74] Murray v. East India Co., 5 B. & Ald. 204.

[75] Bishop Conts., § 382.

plained by parol testimony, and their interpretation should always be with reference to the purpose for which, as well as the time when and locality where, they were employed. The rule with reference to the construction of an ambiguous contract, that where it is capable of more than one construction, that construction which the agent or third party has adopted will be enforced, is applicable also to some cases of interpretation. In such cases the interpretation which the parties have adopted and acted upon as the true meaning will be adopted by the court. But while latent ambiguities may thus be explained by parol, there is no rule of law that permits a party to show that he understood a word or sentence to mean something out of the ordinary or accepted signification, unless there was a mutual mistake between the parties or a fraud perpetrated by one of them upon the other. Rules of interpretation are, therefore, not to be confounded with rules of construction. The former appeal solely to the critical, the latter to the logical faculties. But the rules of interpretation are nevertheless important in dealing with the work of construction, both because there can be no construction without previous interpretation of the elemental parts, and because the rules of interpretation also bear more or less directly upon those applicable to construction.[76]

§ **203. Construction of unwritten authority—What authority, written or oral, carries with it.**—When the authority of the agent is unwritten, it may be an express oral authority or it may be implied from the acts and circumstances, in which latter case it is called authority by implication. When it is unwritten, but express, the same general rules of construction are applicable that apply to written authority, provided the contract has been duly established. When authority is to be determined by implication or inference from the facts and circumstances surrounding the transaction, the rules of construction are necessarily more liberal; since, in such cases, it is just to innocent persons dealing with the agent, and who may possibly be misled by appearances, to give such persons the benefit of any doubt that may arise, and construe the authority most strictly against the principal, who had it in his power to set a limit to it by conferring it only in positive terms. However the authority may have been conferred, it always carries with it the necessary and usual means to execute it effectually.[77] Thus, if an

[76] See 2 Wharton Conts., Ch. XIX.

[77] Pole v. Leask, 28 Beav. 562; Howard v. Baillie, 2 H. Bl. 618; Shackman v. Little, 87 Ind. 181; Michigan Slate Co. v. Iron Range, etc., R. Co., 101 Mich. 14; Craighead

agent has authority to issue policies of insurance, he may bind his principal by any act, agreement, representation or waiver within the ordinary scope and limit of the insurance business not known by the insured to be outside of the authority actually granted the agent.[78] And where the agent of a building and loan association had authority to solicit applications for stock and to effect loans, he was held to have the implied power to bind the association by an agreement that the money advanced to a borrower should be used in improving the mortgaged premises.[79] So, it has been held that an agent having authority to deliver policies and collect premiums has incidental power to waive a cash payment of the premium, even though there is a stipulation in the policy to the contrary, unless it is avoided by bad faith or collusion.[80] But an architect, who is the agent of

v. Peterson, 72 N. Y. 279, 28 Am. Rep. 150; McAlpin v. Cassidy, 17 Tex. 449; Rogers v. Kneeland, 10 Wend. (N. Y.) 218; Banner Tobacco Co. v. Jenison, 48 Mich. 459; Bridenbecker v. Lowell, 32 Barb. (N. Y.) 9; Baldwin v. Garrett, 111 Ga. 876, 36 S. E. 966; Smith v. Droubay, 20 Utah 443, 58 Pac. 1112. An authority to an agent to sell flour to be manufactured for the purchaser carries with it authority to warrant its equality to certain described brands, adopted as a sample for the purpose of such sale: Loomis Milling Co. v. Vawter, 8 Kan. App. 437, 57 Pac. 43. An agent who is authorized to collect a certificate of deposit when due has implied authority to procure a confession of judgment for the same: Briggs v. Yetzer, 103 Iowa 342, 72 N. W. 647. One who superintends a stock farm owned by a nonresident, and who has authority to sell a horse on such farm, has authority to warrant such horse: Belmont v. Talbot (Ky.), 51 S. W. 588. And an agent employed to sell property has implied authority to make any declaration regarding the property necessary to effect a sale, and which is usually incidental thereto; and his principal is bound by his declarations, though the sale was not concluded until a subsequent day: Reynolds v. Mayor, Lane & Co., 57 N. Y. Supp. 106, 39 App. Div. (N. Y.) 218. An agent buying and shipping horses for his principal has the incidental authority to borrow money to purchase feed for such horses, since the exercise of such authority is necessary to the conduct of the business: Rider v. Kirk, 82 Mo. App. 120. See also, John Spry Lumber Co. v. McMillan, 77 Ill. App. 280, in which it is held that authority to build a house implies authority to purchase the lumber. See further on this subject, Singer Mfg. Co. v. McLean, 105 Ala. 316, 16 So. 912; Keim v. Lindley (N. J.), 30 Atl. 1063; Union Pacific, etc., R. Co. v. McCarty, 3 Colo. App. 530, 34 Pac. 767; Jones v. New York, etc., R. Co., 38 N. Y. Supp. 284, 3 App. Div. 341.

78 American Cent. Ins. Co. v. McLanathan, 11 Kan. 533.

79 Wayne, etc., Ass'n v. Moats, 149 Ind. 123.

80 Western Assur. Co. v. McAlpin, 23 Ind. App. 220; Insurance Co. v. Colt, 20 Wall. (U. S.) 560; Painter v. Industrial Life Ass'n, 131 Ind. 68.

the owner of a building in process of construction under such architect's supervision and direction, has no power to waive an agreement by the owner as to the terms on which payment is to be made.[81] The power to sell and convey lands for cash carries with it authority to receive the purchase money.[82] And the authority to purchase grain is held to include the power to modify or waive a contract made by the agent in respect to grain.[83] The authority, however, can not be extended by implication beyond what is fairly warranted by the facts of the particular transaction and the purpose of the agency. The authority should never be construed as extending beyond this legitimate scope. The authority being inferred from the acts of the agent, passively assented to by the principal, it should be limited to acts of a like nature; and where the power is inferred from the general custom of dealing between the parties, it must be confined to dealings of like character; while if it arises from the fact of previous employment in a particular business, it should be limited to such business. Hence, authority of the agent to loan money for his principal and take security on unincumbered land does not authorize the loan with security on incumbered land; and the agent will be liable in damages to the extent of the loss to the principal by reason of such incumbrance.[84]

§ **204. Implied authority of auctioneer to pay duty on goods.**— The agent is presumed to have authority to perform every act and obligation incident to the purpose of the employment. Thus, where the law imposes a duty upon goods and makes it incumbent upon an auctioneer into whose possession the goods may come to pay such duty, it is held that the auctioneer has full authority to pay such duty upon goods left with him for sale, and that he may recover such expenditure of the owner of the goods, as being a necessary consequence of and incident to the end for which he is employed, whether the owner knows of such payment or wishes to have it made or not.[85]

§ **205. Execution of authority by agent—Manner of.**—Having now discussed in a general way the nature and extent of the authority of an agent, it becomes proper to notice for a time the manner in which

[81] Leverone v. Arancio (Mass.), 61 N. E. 45.

[82] Peck v. Harriott, 6 S. & R. (Pa.) 146; Rice v. Groffmann, 56 Mo. 434.

[83] Anderson v. Coonley, 21 Wend. (N. Y.) 279.

[84] Welsh v. Brown, 8 Ind. App. 421.

[85] Brittain v. Lloyd, 14 M. & W. 762; Brown v. Hodgson, 4 Taunt. 189.

such authority may be executed by him. The main purpose of the agent in entering into all contracts for his principal which he is authorized to make is so to frame the contract as to carry out the will of the principal, and not that of himself, and to make the contract binding, not only upon the third party, but upon the principal as well, as otherwise he might render himself personally liable on such contract. The transactions which an agent is usually called upon to perform in the business world for his principal consist mainly of the execution of contracts or of bringing together for that purpose the minds of his principal and the third party or parties with whom the agent deals for such principal; and such contracts may consist: 1. Of simple contracts not in writing; 2. Of simple contracts in writing, such as evidences of debt and other contracts not negotiable by the law merchant; 3. Of bills of exchange and other instruments negotiable by the law merchant; 4. Of instruments under seal, or specialties. We shall consider these in their order.

§ **206. Contracts between agent and third person.**—If it be the purpose of the agent, for and on behalf of his principal, to enter into a simple contract, not in writing, to do which he is duly authorized, he may do so without making himself personally liable by informing the person with whom he deals of the nature and extent of the authority possessed by him for such purpose, and of the nature of the transaction about to be performed. A safe way for the agent to do in such cases is always to disclose the relations between him and his principal fully, and to explain the character of the contract or agreement desired to be entered into. When this is done, no difficulty can arise out of any consequences that may follow such transaction. The contract or agreement to be entered into between the agent and third party may be express or implied, as contracts between other persons may be; and an implied contract between the agent and third party, if duly authorized, or, if not authorized, subsequently ratified by the principal, will bind the latter as effectually as if entered into by him personally, and in express language. The difficulty in proving unwritten contracts consists mainly in the fact that frequently they are not fully expressed, or not expressed at all, but left to inferences. Hence, the rules of construction applied to such contracts are usually more liberal than to those that are reduced to writing,—the main object being to get at the intention of the parties. If, however, the exact language of the parties can be established by the proof, and it is unambiguous, thus constituting an express contract, though unwritten, the same rules of construction apply as in simple contracts in writing: it is for the court to construe, and not for the jury.[86] But usually, if not always, when an unwritten contract is in litigation, there is a disagreement between the parties as to just what was said and done. If this be the case, it of course devolves upon the party alleging the existence of the contract to establish it by evidence as a question of fact; and such a question is always for the jury, or the court sitting as such. Of course, the best method for the agent to pursue in such cases is to reduce the contract to writing, but this is not always practicable or perhaps desirable; and as trouble is scarcely ever anticipated, the necessity for a written agreement is not always apparent. When courts come to deal with such agreements, they must do the best they can with them. When the terms of such a contract are in dispute, or are obscure or equivocal, it is for the jury to determine their meaning, from all the circumstances of the transaction; although the effect of the agreement, when once established, is for the court as a matter of law.[87] If the contract was partly oral and partly written, as occasionally happens when negotiations are carried on by correspondence, the questions of whether there is a contract and what are its terms, are for the jury.[88] The intention of the parties being the chief purpose of construction in such and similar cases of unwritten agreements, all the facts and circumstances surrounding the transaction may be inquired into in order to determine what was the intention.

§ 207. **Contracts in writing between agent and third person.**—If the agent is authorized to enter into a written contract for his principal, he may easily do so, and bind the latter without binding himself personally. A simple mode of doing this is by putting himself in the place of the principal and letting the latter speak by and through him. This he may do by signing the contract in the name of his principal first and then adding his own signature as agent or attorney; thus: "John Doe, by Richard Roe, his attorney (or agent)." He may accomplish the same result by adopting the form, "Richard Roe, agent for John Doe;" or simply, "Richard Roe, for John Doe."[89] While it may be desirable for the sake of double clearness to indicate who is the principal in the body of the contract also,

[86] Norton v. Higbee, 38 Mo. App. 467.

[87] Spragins v. White, 108 N. C. 449.

[88] Scanlan v. Hodges, 52 Fed. 354.

[89] Story Ag., §§ 274, 278; 1 Parsons Notes & B. 91; Bank of Genesee v. Patchin Bank, 19 N. Y. 312, 315.

it is by no means essential if one of the forms above given be observed in the signature. Thus, one may write, "I, John Doe, by Richard Roe, agent (or attorney), promise to pay;" but it would be equally as good a promise to state simply, "I promise to pay," concluding with one of the forms of signature above given.

§ 208. **Apt words required to bind principal—Mere descriptive words insufficient.**—It must not be supposed, however, that in all cases in which one promises simply as agent, or signs his name to a contract followed by the word "agent," or "agent of John Doe," the principal is bound and the agent is not. Such added words as "agent," "trustee," "treasurer," "president," etc., are generally regarded as merely descriptive of the person of the signer, and will not exonerate the agent from personal liability unless the agency is otherwise revealed.[89a] By reason of this doctrine, which is called the doctrine of *"descriptio personae,"* or *"descriptio personarum,"* persons duly authorized as agents and intending to enter into contracts for and on behalf of their principals frequently render themselves personally liable on such contracts when it was their real intention to charge only their principals. Thus, it is well established that a note running, "I promise to pay," and signed, "Richard Roe, agent," or "Richard Roe, agent of John Doe," purports to be the note of Richard Roe, and not that of John Doe; for the word "agent," or the words "agent of John Doe," are merely descriptive of the person of Richard Roe, and do not absolutely indicate that he signed the instrument for and on behalf of John Doe, or as his representative.[90] To make such a promise, on its face, binding upon the principal, it should purport to be made by the principal, as "John Doe, by Richard Roe, agent;" although the word "agent," and indeed the name of the agent also, may be altogether omitted after the name of the principal.[91] If the agent's name is used in the signature, it need not stand first in position, if it can be legally determined from it that the contract is being executed for the principal or on his behalf. Thus, a note will bind the principal, and not the agent, if signed, "Richard Roe, agent for John Doe;" or simply, "Richard Roe, for John Doe;" or "For John Doe, Richard Roe," with or without the word "agent" added.[92]

[89a] See *post*, § 302.

[90] Kenyon v. Williams, 19 Ind. 44; Hobbs v. Cowden, 20 Ind. 310; Haverhill Ins. Co. v. Newhall, 1 Allen (Mass.) 130; Tucker Mfg. Co. v. Fairbanks, 98 Mass. 101; Hays v. Crutcher, 54 Ind. 260.

[91] 1 Daniel Neg. Instr., § 300.

[92] Story Ag., § 154; Mechem Ag., § 432.

It would thus seem that the simple change of the word "of" to "for" will render the obligation that of the principal, where before such change it was only that of the agent. But even the use of "for" instead of "of," is not always conclusive, unless it be contained in the signature; for, as held in Massachusetts, where the note runs, "We, ..., promise to pay .... for," etc., and the note is signed by the agent without qualifying words, it is, *prima facie* at least, the note of the agent alone.[93] As a general rule, however, the word "for" standing after the agent's signature and appellation, if any be used, and before the name of the principal, is held sufficient to make it the obligation of the principal, on its face; provided, of course, that the agent have sufficient authority.

§ **209. Construction of simple contracts in writing—Intention of parties.**—In determining who shall be liable on simple contracts in writing, not negotiable by the law merchant, it is a cardinal rule that the court will endeavor to ascertain the intention of the parties; and, when it can be done, such intention will always be gathered from the face of the instrument itself, by considering it in all its parts, as an entirety.[94] When this can be done, parol evidence can not be introduced to explain who is the real contracting party. But a simple contract may be ambiguous as to the real parties. When it is so, the court will solve the ambiguity, if possible, from the instrument itself, taking into consideration not only the words and figures in the body thereof, and the signatures and additions thereto, but any printed or written headings, memoranda in the margin, or other *indicia* which may serve to throw light upon the question of intention.[95] If the ambiguity can not be thus solved, and does not arise from the meaning to be given to the words employed, but from the question as to what claims or persons are embraced within the meaning of certain words or phrases, parol evidence may be introduced to show what the intention of the parties was with regard to it.[96] And generally, where there is ambiguity as to whether the principal or agent was intended to be bound, the courts will admit parol testimony as to such intention.[97]

[93] Bradlee v. Boston Glass Manufactory, 16 Pick. (Mass.) 347.

[94] Bishop Conts., § 384.

[95] Hitchcock v. Buchanan, 105 U. S. 416; Carpenter v. Farnsworth, 106 Mass. 561; Scanlan v. Keith, 102 Ill. 634; 1 Beach Conts., § 743.

[96] Ginnuth v. Blankenship (Tex. Civ. App.), 28 S. W. 828; Barbre v. Goodale, 28 Or. 465, 43 Pac. 378.

[97] Lerned v. Johns, 9 Allen (Mass.) 419; Getchell v. Foster, 106 Mass. 42; Cutler v. Ashland, 121 Mass. 588; Bean v. Pioneer Mining Co., 66 Cal.

§ 210. **Rules applied to sealed and negotiable instruments less liberal.**—A more liberal rule obtains in the construction of simple contracts than in that of sealed instruments, owing to the fact that contracts under seal, or specialties, under the common law, are regarded as of such a solemn character that only the parties named or described therein can sue or be sued upon them.[98] In simple contracts, however, as we have seen, the principal question is as to the intention of the parties, however informally expressed; and whatever that intention may be found to be, the courts will ascertain and adopt.[99] Parol evidence will never be received, however, as to any written contract, to prove a different intention from that which plainly appears upon a fair construction from the face of the instrument itself, except in case of fraud or mutual mistake. Hence, if such an instrument, on its face, discloses an absolute undertaking by one party, it can not be proved by extrinsic evidence that it was in fact intended to bind another.[100] Negotiable instruments, as we shall presently see, under the law merchant, by reason of their superior character as a circulating medium, also require a stricter construction than other evidences of debt not under seal. But whatever the character of the contract, whether sealed or unsealed, negotiable or non-negotiable, the agent may easily accomplish the purpose by the employment of apt words, and thus bind his principal without making himself personally liable, as suggested with reference to simple contracts.[101]

§ 211. **Personal liability of agent on contract entered into for principal.**—On the other hand, an agent may undoubtedly render himself personally liable by entering into a written contract, although it is his purpose to bind only the principal; and this he may do by neglecting to observe the doctrine of *descriptio personae*. It is very clear that if the agent simply contracted in his own name, with-

451; Ogden v. Raymond, 22 Conn. 379; Post v. Pearson, 108 U. S. 418; Whitney v. Wyman, 101 U. S. 392; Swarts v. Cohen, 11 Ind. App. 20; McNeil v. Shober, etc., Lith. Co., 144 Ill. 238; LaSalle Nat'l Bank v. Tolu, 14 Ill. App. 141; Haile v. Peirce, 32 Md. 327; Hardy v. Pilcher, 57 Miss. 18; Metcalf v. Williams, 104 U. S. 93; Shaffer v. Hohenschild, 2 Kan. App. 516, 43 Pac. 979; Barbre v. Goodale, 28 Ore. 465, 43 Pac. 378.

[98] Briggs v. Partridge, 64 N. Y. 357.

[99] Merchants' Bank v. Central Bank, 1 Ga. 418, 44 Am. Dec. 665.

[100] Hypes v. Griffin, 89 Ill. 134; American Ins. Co. v. Stratton, 59 Iowa 696; Williams v. Second Nat'l Bank, 83 Ind. 237.

[101] *Ante*, § 207.

out using the suffix "agent," he would bind himself; for certainly in such case he has not bound the principal; and no other promisor appearing in the paper, it must be construed either as his own obligation, or as being a mere nullity.[102] But suppose he styles himself "agent," what effect will this appellation have upon the question as to whether he is or is not the promisor? The rule is, as we have seen, that the addition of such word, or of similar words, such as "president," "treasurer," "trustee," etc., is a mere *descriptio personae,* and will be disregarded as surplusage, unless it serves as an earmark of the transaction.[103]

§ **212. Negotiable instruments.**—In cases of bills of exchange and other instruments negotiable by the law merchant, a more stringent rule is applied with regard to construction than in other simple contracts in writing. In such cases, parties whose names do not appear on the face of the instrument can not, as a general rule, be introduced into the contract by parol. Such instruments are, in many particulars, on an equality with bank bills and other securities passing as money; and the rules of the law merchant demand that persons receiving them in due course of business must be presumed to take them on the credit of the parties whose names appear thereon as obligors. "It is a general principle of commercial law that a negotiable instrument must wear no mask, but must reveal its character upon its face. And it extends to the liability of parties thereto, who must appear as distinctly as the terms of the instrument itself, in order to be bound by those terms."[104]

§ **213. Extrinsic evidence to explain negotiable instruments—Conflicting decisions.**—All the decisions agree that when a party to a negotiable instrument has by apt words, on the face of the instrument, made himself a promisor or obligor, he will be bound thereby, and that extrinsic evidence can not be admitted to show that in fact such party executed the instrument for another and not for himself. On the other hand, there is equally unanimous agreement that when the words of the instrument are sufficiently clear to show that the contract was in fact made by an agent for and on behalf of his principal, extrinsic evidence is also inadmissible to prove that the

[102] Stackpole v. Arnold, 11 Mass. 27.

[103] Kenyon v. Williams, 19 Ind. 44; Hall v. Bradbury, 40 Conn. 32; Collins v. Buckeye State Ins. Co., 17 Ohio St. 215; Toledo Agricultural Works v. Heisser, 51 Mo. 128; Avery v. Dougherty, 102 Ind. 443.

[104] 1 Daniel Neg. Instr., § 300. See *post,* § 224.

contract was the personal obligation of him who purports to be an agent only. The authorities are not harmonious, however, as to whether certain recitals in the body of the instrument and certain forms of signature are to be construed as purporting to be the contract of the principal or the personal obligation of the agent. Moreover, some of the authorities are to the effect that the courts will look only to the recitals in the body of the contract proper, and to the signature at the foot; while in others these have been construed in connection with other *indicia*,—such as words and phrases contained in the headings or margins, the corporate seal, etc., printed, written, or impressed upon the same paper. Still other cases find in such recitals, headings and other *indicia* sufficient data to adjudge that ambiguity exists, which is to be solved either with or without the introduction of extrinsic evidence, according to the nature of such ambiguity. While it is impossible to reconcile these conflicting views, it may not be unprofitable to review some of the leading cases bearing on the points as to which there is this disagreement.

§ 214. Construction from recitals and signature alone—Illustrative cases.—The first class of cases we shall notice are those in which the question of the liability of a particular party has been determined by the construction of the recitals in the body of the instrument in connection with the form of the signature, without the aid of extrinsic evidence.

In an action on a promissory note, in which the recitals were: "We, two of the directors of the Ark, etc., Assurance Society, by and on behalf of said society, do hereby promise to pay," and the paper was signed by two persons, without any addition indicating an agency, the contract was held to be that of the society and not of the persons signing the same.[105] Substantially the same conclusion was reached in an Iowa case, where the action was on a note reading: "We, the undersigned, directors," etc., "promise," etc., and the signatures of three persons were appended without any addition to the same. It was held that the signers were not personally liable.[106] But where the trustees of a masonic lodge executed to a bank their promissory note reading: "We promise to pay," the note being signed: "A, B, C, trustees D lodge," it was held to be the contract of the signers individually, and not that of the lodge; and extrinsic evidence to show that the note was in fact that of the lodge

[105] Aggs v. Nicholson, 1 H. & N. 165.

[106] Baker v. Chambles, 4 Greene (Iowa) 428.

was held improper. The court said: "Knowing the law, they [the trustees] must be held to have known that the note, in the form in which it was executed, purported to be the note of the appellants, and not the note of the lodge. What the parties in fact understood, supposed, or believed as to the legal effect or meaning of the form in which they contracted is immaterial. The intention which the law imputes to their contracts must, in the absence of fraud or mistake of fact, be held to be the intention of the parties. They can not avoid the contract by averring an intention or purpose opposed to that which the law attaches to their agreement."[107]

In another case in Indiana, the supreme court has held that where a party is sued upon a promissory note, and desires to escape liability because he executed such note merely as agent, he should plead *non est factum*, thus denying the execution of the note under oath; and that upon failure to do so, he can not succeed in the defense that the note sued upon is not his personal contract.[108] In the same state, a note showing on its face that it was given for money of which the principal, a civil township, received the benefit, and providing that it was "to be paid out of the township's funds," and signed by the maker as "trustee of X township," was held on its face to be the note of the township, and not of the trustee, personally.[109]

A similar ruling was made by the court of appeals of Kentucky in a case in which the plaintiff brought suit on a bill reading as follows:

"Thos. B. Posey, Tr., Grand Division of Kentucky, pay to the order of A. W. Elder three hundred and twenty dollars, in full of copies of Kentucky New Era, ordered to be sent D. G. W. Patricks at January session of G. Division.

"Geo. W. Williams, G. W. P.

"Attest: L. Hord, G. S."

The answer alleged that the defendant (Williams) drew the order sued on as the presiding officer of the grand division of the Sons of Temperance of Kentucky, as grand worthy patriarch, which was sig-

[107] Williams v. Second Nat'l Bank, 83 Ind. 237.

[108] Fulton v. Loughlin, 118 Ind. 286.

[109] Wallis v. Johnson School Township, 75 Ind. 368. As to this case it should be noted also that the principal was a public school corporation, which would bring the trustee within the rules governing cases of public agents. Such an agent is not liable personally on a contract attempted by him to be made in favor of his principal, as it would be against public policy to hold him liable thereon: See Knight v. Clark, 48 N. J. L. 22, 57 Am. Rep. 534.

nified by the letters "G. W. P." annexed to his signature; and that it was drawn upon the grand treasurer of said grand division, and attested by L. Hord, the grand scribe, which was signified by the letters "G. S." annexed to his signature; and that the consideration was for copies of the New Era, a newspaper, as expressed in the instrument; that the said grand division was a corporation, and that the order was drawn in conformity to the rules of the said grand division, and was drawn by the defendant in his official character, and not as an individual, etc. The lower court overruled a demurrer to this answer, and this ruling was affirmed on appeal. The court of appeals said: "The doctrine is well established that, in a case like the present, if it can, upon the whole instrument, be collected that it was intended to bind the principal, courts of justice will adopt that construction of it, however informally it may be expressed."[110]

In Massachusetts, where a note contained a promise in this form: "I, the subscriber, treasurer of the D. T. Corporation, promise," etc., which was signed: "G. L. C., treasurer of the corporation," the supreme court decided that it was on its face the note of the corporation and not that of the treasurer personally.[111]

Some of these holdings apparently support the proposition that where the consideration, on the face of a promissory note, purports to move to the principal, and the note is signed by one of its officers, the corporation alone is liable on the contract.

The following forms of notes have been held sufficient to bind the principal, and not the agent, when construed in connection with the signatures:

"We, the trustees of the X Society, promise," etc.; signed, "Trustees of the X Society,—A, B, C, D."[112]

"The pastor and deacons of X church promise to pay;" signed, "S. D. Y., for X church."[113]

"The trustees of the X church of Y, as such trustees," etc., "promise to pay;" signed, "A, B, C, D," etc., "as trustees of the X church of Y."[114]

[110] Taylor v. Williams, 17 B. Mon. (Ky.) 489.

[111] Mann v. Chandler, 9 Mass. 335. See, to the same effect, McHenry v. Duffield, 7 Blackf. (Ind.) 41; Richmond, etc., R. Co. v. Snead, 19 Gratt. (Va.) 354, 100 Am. Dec. 670.

[112] New Market, etc., Bank v. Gillet, 100 Ill. 254, 29 Am. Rep. 39.

[113] Jetts v. York, 4 Cush. (Mass.) 371, 50 Am. Dec. 791.

[114] Little v. Bailey, 87 Ill. 239.

"I, as treasurer of the X Society, or my successors in office, promise to pay;" signed, "S. R., treasurer."[115]

"The X Association, who execute this note by her directors, A, B," etc., "promise to pay;" signed, "A. B., secretary," and others, "directors X Assn."[116]

"We promise to pay;" signed, "A. B., Pres. X Co., C. D., Sec. *pro tem.*"[117]

"We, or either of us, promise to pay in behalf of school district No. 6," etc.; signed, "A. B., president, C. D., secretary, E. F., treasurer."[118]

Where the recital was, "We, *as* directors," etc., only the corporation was held liable, the word "as" excluding the idea of individual liability.[119]

"The H. County Agricultural Association, who execute this note by her directors, do promise to pay," etc.; signed "T. M. K., A. L. S., secretary, S. F. B. (and ten others), directors H. County Agricultural Association. ————, sureties."[120]

"We promise to pay;" signed, "Warrick Glass Works, J. Price Warrick, Pres."[121] In this case the court said: "I do not perceive any significance in the use of the words 'we promise to pay,' instead of 'the company promises to pay.' The contention was that the use of these words raised an implication that it was the joint note of the corporation and of Warrick. But, as has been remarked in more than one of the cases cited in which the notes contained a promise in like form, the word 'we' is often used by a corporation aggregate." The form of the signature in this case was considered equally as significant as if it had been written "Warrick Glass Works, per J. Price Warrick, agent." A similar ruling was made in Wisconsin in a case in which the form of the promise was, "We promise to pay;" and that of the signature, "X, etc., Milling Company, F. K., president."[122]

[115] Barlow v. Congregational Soc., 8 Allen (Mass.) 460.

[116] Armstrong v. Kirkpatrick, 79 Ind. 527.

[117] Farmers', etc., Savings Bank v. Colby, 64 Cal. 352.

[118] Harvey v. Irvine, 11 Iowa 82.

[119] Sanborn v. Neal, 4 Minn. 126, 137.

[120] Armstrong v. Kirkpatrick, 79 Ind. 527.

[121] Reeve v. First Nat'l Bank, 54 N. J. L. 208.

[122] Liebscher v. Kraus, 74 Wis. 387, 17 Am. St. 171. For further rulings to the effect that such a contract is the obligation of the principal, a corporation, see Rendell v. Harriman, 75 Me. 497; Carpenter v. Farnsworth, 106 Mass. 561.

"We promise to pay;" signed, "I. Mfg. Co., B. I. B., Pres., D. B. S., Sec'y."[123]

"I promise to pay," etc.; signed, "B., Treas. St. Paul's Parish."[124]

A note reading, "We promise to pay," signed, "The P. G. Co., by B. F. A., president, C. B. O., vice-president, C. H. R., secretary, A. B. T., B. R., J. R. B., directors," was held in Indiana to be, *prima facie,* the joint obligation of the makers in their individual capacity, the word "directors" subjoined to the three last names being but *descriptio personarum.*[125]

Where an agreement was entered into for the building of a church "by and between the trustees, and building committee of ——— Church,—J. M., president, F. L., secretary, J. B., L. X., R. S., members, all of the city of D., by authority of the Right Rev. J. S. F., bishop of the diocese of D., parties of the first part, and the mason, M. L., of the same place, party of the second part," providing that "the parties of the first part herewith promise and agree for themselves, their heirs, executors and administrators," etc.,—it was held that the persons designated as "parties of the first part" were individually liable.[126]

And a note reading as follows: "We promise to pay to the order of C. & C. I. Co. $7,500, at M. bank, value received;" signed, "E. H. C., Treas., J. C., Prest.," the words "R. C. Co." being printed across the face of the note, was held, in New York, to be the personal and individual obligation of the signers.[127] The court said: "The note does not purport to bind the company. If the addition of the official character of the signers had not been added, the words 'R. C. Co.' printed on the side of the note would not bind that company. The makers expressly promise to pay the note jointly, and if they are not liable upon the note, there is no maker who is liable.[128] The note must show on its face that it was signed for the principal and in some way in his name; where an agent fails to designate a principal, he will be personally liable."[129]

[123] Heffner v. Brownell, 70 Iowa 591, 75 Iowa 341.

[124] Sturdivant v. Hull, 59 Me. 172, 8 Am. Rep. 409.

[125] Taylor v. Reger, 18 Ind. App. 466. See also, Albany Furniture Co. v. Merchants' Nat'l Bank, 17 Ind. App. 531.

[126] Landyskowski v. Lark, 108 Mich. 500, 66 N. W. 371.

[127] Casco Nat'l Bank v. Clark, 18 N. Y. Supp. 887.

[128] Citing DeWitt v. Walton, 9 N. Y. 571.

[129] Citing Pentz v. Stanton, 10 Wend. (N. Y.) 271. See Casco Nat'l

§ 215. **Construction from recitals, together with signatures, headings, marginal notes, etc.**—The cases in which the courts have taken into account, in construing the contract upon the question whether the principal or the agent was bound, the headings, marginal notes, corporation seal, etc., on the paper upon which the contract was written, are not so numerous, but they are sufficiently so to constitute a distinct class. These are cases in which the ambiguity, if there could be said to be such, was solved by the court itself, without receiving parol evidence. Thus, in New Hampshire, it was held that a note signed "A. G., secretary," with the official seal of the corporation attached, was a corporate and not an individual note.[130] And so it has been held in Illinois.[131] According to the decisions of some courts, the impression of the corporate seal has the same effect as if the name of the corporation had been written under the contract.[132] A bill of exchange, headed, "Office of the Belleville Nail Co.," and concluding, "Charge same to account of the Belleville Nail Co., A. B., Prest., C. D., Sec'y," was held to bind the company, and not the signers.[133] And a bill dated at the office of a corporation, signed by the president with the addition of the title of his office abbreviated, and directing the sum to be charged "to motive power and account," according to the decision of the New York court of appeals, purports to be the contract of the corporation only.[134] How-

Bank v. Clark, 139 N. Y. 307, affirming the decision of the supreme court. See further, in this class of cases, Day v. Ramsdell, 90 Iowa 731, 52 N. W. 208, holding that a note reciting, "We, the T. P. Co., promise to pay," and signed, "J. R., Pres.," and "H. E. R., Sec.," is the obligation of J. R. and H. E. R. individually. See also the following cases: Chase v. Pattberg, 12 Daly (N. Y.) 171; McClellan v. Reynolds, 49 Mo. 312; Merchants' Nat'l Bank v. Clark, 139 N. Y. 314; Tama Water Power Co. v. Ramsdell, 90 Iowa 747, 52 N. W. 209.

[130] Dow v. Moore, 47 N. H. 419.

[131] Scanlan v. Keith, 102 Ill. 634. In this case (p. 644) the court said: "Dealing with the corporation and taking a note made by its officers, with its corporate seal attached, it is most improbable the plaintiff supposed he was obtaining the individual note of the officers. Had it been so the note would no doubt have been executed without attaching to the signatures of the makers the name of the corporation. It is still more unusual that persons making an individual note or other obligation would cause it to be attested by the seal of the corporation with which they were connected." But a contrary ruling was made by the English queen's bench: Dutton v. Marsh, L. R. 6 Q. B. 361.

[132] Miller v. Roach, 150 Mass. 140; Means v. Swormstedt, 32 Ind. 87.

[133] Hitchcock v. Buchanan, 105 U. S. 416.

[134] Olcott v. Tioga R. Co., 27 N. Y. 546.

ever, in this case, no special significance seems to have been attached to the circumstance that the bill was dated at the office of the company, further than that given in the opinion of the court, that "there was clearly sufficient upon the face of the bill to indicate an intention to bind the company." In a case decided in Massachusetts[135] the suit was against the acceptor upon two drafts, one of which ran as follows:

"Office of Portage Lake Manufacturing Co.,
"Hancock, Mich., June 5, 1861.

"E. T. Loring, Agent, 39 State St., Boston:

"At four months' sight, pay to the order of J. H. Slawson, four hundred dollars, and charge the same to account of this company.

"$400.00 L. R. Jackson, Agt."

Written across the face of the draft were these words: "Accepted June 15. E. T. Loring, Agent." The question arose whether Loring was personally liable as acceptor, and the court held that he, and not the company, was bound. The court, speaking through Bigelow, C. J., said: "Being negotiable paper, all evidence *dehors* the drafts is to be excluded. It is wholly immaterial that the defendant was in fact the agent of the company named on the face of the drafts, and that the plaintiff knew he was so, and that the defendant had no personal interest in the company.[136] The rule excluding all parol evidence to charge any person as principal, not disclosed on the face of a note or draft, rests on the principle that each person who takes negotiable paper makes a contract with the parties on the face of the instrument, and with no other person. Taking the signature of the defendant as acceptor written across the face of the drafts by itself, without reference to other parts of the instruments, it is clear that it would bind him personally."[137] A bill headed with the name of the office of an express and banking house, directed to be charged to "account of this office," and signed by a person as agent, was held by

[135] Slawson v. Loring, 87 Mass. 340.

[136] Citing Fuller v. Hooper, 3 Gray (Mass.) 334; Bank of British North America v. Hooper, 5 Gray (Mass.) 567; Draper v. Massachusetts Steam Heating Co., 87 Mass. 338.

[137] It should be noted that in this case it was a question of the liability of the acceptor, and not the drawer. Had the suit been against the drawer a different result might have been reached, as in that event the court might properly have considered the headings of the paper as a part of the contract. Here the headings had already served their purpose as explanatory of the signature of the drawer, and could not be used again to qualify that of the acceptor.

the supreme court of California not to be the personal obligation of the agent, but that of the house.[138] This ruling has been followed by the courts of Montana and Nevada.[138a] A draft headed "Pompton Iron Works," directing that the amount of such draft be placed "to the account of the Pompton Iron Works," and signed, "W. Burtt, Ag't," was held by the supreme judicial court of Massachusetts to be the draft of the company, and not of the agent.[139] And by the same court a bank check having the words "Ætna Mills" printed in the margin, and signed "I. D. Farnsworth, treasurer," was declared to be the check of the Ætna Mills, and not that of Farnsworth.[140] And so, a draft headed "New England Agency of the Pennsylvania Fire Insurance Company," with the words "Foster and Cole, general agents for the New England states," printed in the margin, appearing on its face to be drawn upon such company in payment of a claim against it, and signed "Foster and Cole," without any addition to the signature, was adjudged by the same court to be the draft of the company, and not of Foster and Cole.[141]

§ 216. **Ambiguity in instruments—Parol evidence.**—A third class of cases are those in which it is held that where, upon the face of a negotiable instrument, there is a doubt or ambiguity as to whether the contract is that of the principal or of the agent, parol testimony may be introduced to show what was the intention of the parties with reference to the matter. A leading case upon this question is that

[138] Sayre v. Nichols, 7 Cal. 535, 68 Am. Dec. 280.

[138a] Gerber v. Stuart, 1 Mont. 172, 177; Gillig v. Lake Bigler Co., 2 Nev. 214, 223.

[139] Fuller v. Hooper, 3 Gray (Mass.) 334.

[140] Carpenter v. Farnsworth, 106 Mass. 561.

[141] Chipman v. Foster, 119 Mass. 189. But a contrary conclusion was reached by the court of appeals of New York, where an action was brought on a note containing in the margin the printed words, "Bridgewood Ice Co.," and running, "We promise to pay," and which was signed "John Clark, Prest.," and "E. H. Close, Treas.," although the note was given for the debt of the ice company, a corporation. The court held that as the note was negotiable and in the hands of an innocent holder, it must be regarded as the agreement of the ostensible maker, and that the appearance in print, upon the margin, of the name of the corporation was not a fact carrying with it any presumption that the note was intended to be that of the company; hence the signers were held liable personally: Casco Nat'l Bank v. Clark, 139 N. Y. 307.

of *Mechanics' Bank* v. *Bank of Columbia.*[142] It was an action of *assumpsit* on a check running as follows:

"Mechanics' Bank of Alexandria,
"June 25, 1817.

"Cashier of the Bank of Columbia:
"Pay to the order of P. H. Minor, Esq., ten thousand dollars.
"$10,000.00 (Sig.) Wm. Paton, Jr."

The margin of the paper upon which the check was printed and written contained the printed words "Mechanics' Bank of Alexandria." The supreme court held that it appeared doubtful on the face of the check whether it was an official or a private act, and that parol evidence was, therefore, admissible to show that it was the official act of Paton, he being the cashier of the Mechanics' Bank. "The appearance of the corporate name of the institution on the face of the paper," said the court, "at once leads to the belief that it is a corporate, and not an individual transaction; to which must be added the circumstances that the cashier is the drawer, and the teller the payee [facts which had been given in evidence *dehors* the check]; and the form of ordinary checks deviated from by the substitution of *to order* for *to bearer.* The evidence, therefore, on the face of the bill, predominates in favor of its being a bank transaction. * * * But it is enough for the purposes of the defendant to establish that there existed, on the face of the paper, circumstances from which it might reasonably be inferred that it was either one or the other. In that case, it became indispensable to resort to extrinsic evidence to remove the doubt." In Maryland, the court held, in conformity to this rule, that where a bill, drawn by a corporation, was addressed to its treasurer, and accepted by him by signing his name as treasurer of the corporation after the word "accepted" written across the face of the instrument, parol evidence was admissible to show that the acceptance was designed to be only in his official capacity.[143] In a New Jersey case, a bill of exchange signed by one as "President Elizabethtown and Somerville R. R. Co.," there being nothing in the body of the instrument to show the nature of the obligation, was held to be ambiguous, and parol evidence was decided admissible to determine whether it was the obligation of the company or of the president individually.[144] In a suit by the payee against the drawer

[142] 5 Wheat. (U. S.) 326.

[143] Laflin v. Sinsheimer, 48 Md. 411, 30 Am. Rep. 472.

[144] Kean v. Davis, 21 N. J. L. 683, 47 Am. Dec. 182.

of a bill headed "Wetumpka, etc., R. Co., President's Office," and signed by one as "Pres't," parol evidence was held proper to show that the company was the real principal.[145] Similarly, the supreme court of Mississippi ruled that a bill of exchange drawn by H. and accepted by B., "agent of H.," was ambiguous, and that, as between the parties to the bill, parol evidence was competent to show that the intent was not to charge B. personally, but to charge H., whose funds were in B.'s hands. "Ordinarily," said Chalmers, J., "no extrinsic testimony of any kind is admissible to vary or explain negotiable instruments. Such paper speaks its own language, and the meaning which the law affixes to it can not be changed by any evidence *aliunde.* One of the few exceptions to this rule is where anything on the face of the paper suggests a doubt as to the party bound, or the character in which any of the signers acted in affixing his name, in which case testimony may be admitted between the original parties to show the true intent. Thus, where one has signed as agent of another, while the *prima facie* presumption is that the words are merely *descriptio personae,* and that the signer is individually bound, yet it may be shown, in a suit between the parties, that it was not so intended, but that, on the contrary, the true intention was that the payee should look to the principal whose name was disclosed in the signature of his agent, or who was well known to be the true party to be bound."[146] In Texas a note which ran: "We, the trustees of C. H. College, promise to pay," signed by several persons with their own names merely, was held to be *prima facie* the note of the signers; but extrinsic evidence to show an intention to bind the corporation was held admissible.[147] And in Colorado, where the action was by the drawee against the acceptor of certain drafts, accepted by "F. D. H., treasurer," drawn on "S. A. R.," and directed to be charged to account of "S. L. S. N. Co.," a corporation, it was held that the trial court erred in sustaining a demurrer to the plea which alleged that the defendant was the treasurer of the company; that the bill was given for an indebtedness of the company to the plaintiff; that it was his duty as treasurer to pay out all moneys of the company in his hands on the order of the company, and to accept, as its treasurer, all orders or bills drawn by the company on

[145] Wetumpka, etc., R. Co. v. Bingham, 5 Ala. 657.

[146] Hardy v. Pilcher, 57 Miss. 18, 34 Am. Rep. 432.

[147] Traynham v. Jackson, 15 Tex. 170, 65 Am. Dec. 152.

its treasurer and pay the same when due if he had sufficient funds in his hands, belonging to the company, to do so; that he accepted the bill as treasurer of the company and not otherwise; that when the bill became due there was no money of the company in his hands, and that the plaintiff had knowledge of all the facts before set out. Said the court: "If a bill of exchange is complete in itself, free from any latent ambiguity, obviously carrying its passport upon its face, there is no need of oral testimony to aid in its exposition. The clear and intelligible terms of such an instrument may not be explained by extrinsic evidence. This is a familiar rule of constant application in the interpretation of written contracts. Can it be said that the drafts in question belong to this class? That upon their face it is proclaimed to the world that Hayer was acting in his individual capacity in accepting them? Or rather, would not the more natural construction be that these drafts were drawn by the principal, the company (whose name appears on the face of the instrument), by its president, upon its treasurer, as such? Giving to each word its appropriate meaning, considering each instrument in every part, and as a whole, and having reference to well established commercial usage, as to the mode of drawing bills of exchange by a corporation upon itself, we do not hesitate in our conclusion that the drafts in controversy must have been understood, especially if the averments in the third plea are true, as having been accepted by the treasurer as such, and not as an individual."[148] In a recent Indiana case, the supreme court of that state, contrary to many of its previous decisions, held that a note dated at the office of a corporation, running "We promise to pay," and signed, "R. J. Beatty, president," was not conclusively the obligation of Beatty, but that it could be shown by extrinsic evidence that it was a corporate note.[149]

[148] Hager v. Rice, 4 Colo. 90, 34 Am. Rep. 68.

[149] Second Nat'l Bank v. Midland Steel Co., 155 Ind. 581, 58 N. E. 833, 52 L. R. A. 307. And this seems to be the tendency of the more modern decisions: See 4 Thompson Corp., § 5141, *et seq.* See also, Bean v. Pioneer Min. Co., 66 Cal. 451, 56 Am. Rep. 106; Baker v. Gregory, 28 Ala. 544, 65 Am. Dec. 366; Brockway v. Allen, 17 Wend. (N. Y.) 40; Smith v. Alexander, 31 Mo. 193; Hovey v. Magill, 2 Conn. 680; Haile v. Peirce, 32 Md. 327, 3 Am. Rep. 139; Richmond, etc., R. Co. v. Snead, 19 Gratt. (Va.) 354, 100 Am. Dec. 670; Newman v. Greeff, 101 N. Y. 663; Bank of Genesee v. Patchin Bank, 19 N. Y. 312; Gillig v. Lake Bigler Co., 2 Nev. 214; Musser v. Johnson, 42 Mo. 74, 97 Am. Dec. 316; Keidan v. Winegar, 95 Mich. 430; Webb v. Burke, 5 B. Mon. (Ky.) 51; Paige v. Stone, 10 Metc. (Mass.) 160; Barlow v. Congregational Soc., 8 Allen (Mass.)

§ 217. Illustrative cases in which parol evidence was excluded.— In the list of cases in which parol evidence to explain an alleged ambiguity has been excluded we note the following:—In *Conner* v. *Clark*[150] it was decided that one who signs a promissory note with the addition of the word "trustee" to his name is personally liable thereon; and testimony can not be admitted to show a contemporaneous parol agreement that the signer should not personally be liable, but that the note was to be paid out of a trust fund. This decision was, however, based largely upon the principle mentioned by Story, that trustees, guardians, executors, etc., are generally held personally liable on notes, because they have no authority to bind, *ex directo,* the persons for whom or for whose benefit or estates they act, although even they might exempt themselves from personal liability by using clear and explicit words to show that intention.[151] In *Wing* v. *Glick*[151a] the contract was phrased, "We promise to pay," and was signed by two persons with the additions, "president school board" and "secretary school board," but without any reference in the body to any particular school district. It was held to be the personal contract of the signers, and not variable by parol. In *Bartlett* v. *Hawley*[152] and *Tucker Mfg. Co.* v. *Fairbanks,*[153] where bills of exchange were directed to be paid to "A. B., agent," and indorsed by "A. B., agent," it was held that the agent was personally liable; and parol evidence to show that the indorsers were agents of the drawers was excluded, on the ground that the defendants appeared on the face of the bills to be themselves the payees and indorsees, the word "agent" in each case being treated as *designatio personarum.* In *Webster* v. *Wray*[154] the supreme court of Nebraska decides that where a person executes a negotiable instrument in his own name, without disclosing his principal or his own character as agent, if in point of fact he was acting as agent for another, the signer will be personally liable on such instrument, and evidence to show the agency will not be received.[155] This case does not contravene the proposition, however, that such evidence might be admitted if the word "agent" or something equivalent had been added to the signature, and the controversy were between the original parties.[156]

460; Pratt v. Beaupre, 13 Minn. 187; Peterson v. Homan, 44 Minn. 166, 20 Am. St. 564; Baldwin v. Bank of Newbury, 1 Wall. (U. S.) 234.

[150] 12 Cal. 168.

[151] Story Prom. Notes, § 63.

[151a] 56 Iowa 473.

[152] 120 Mass. 92.

[153] 98 Mass. 101.

[154] 19 Neb. 558, 56 Am. Rep. 754.

[155] Citing 1 Daniel Neg. Instr., § 284.

[156] See further, in this line of cases, Hayes v. Matthews, 63 Ind.

§ 218. **Cases holding that principal is liable in equity.**—Still another class of cases hold that although such an instrument, signed by one as "agent" without revealing the name of the principal on the face thereof, would, in an action at law, bind the agent only, yet that in a suit in equity it might be enforced against the principal,[157] or that the instrument might be reformed, in a proper proceeding for that purpose.[158]

§ 219. **Construction of negotiable instruments as between original parties—When in hands of innocent third party.**—The courts in this country are disposed to apply the rule against the admission of parol evidence more strictly in cases where the instrument before maturity has passed into the hands of an innocent holder for value than in actions between the original parties, or between the original maker or drawer on the one hand and a third party who acquired it with notice on the other.[159] These decisions and others holding to the same doctrine have been criticised upon the ground that the right to introduce parol evidence depends, not upon the actual knowledge that the interested parties may have of the transaction upon which the contract is founded, but upon the fact that there is an ambiguity on the face of the instrument; and that the ambiguity, if it exists, will continue until the paper has come into the possession of the third party, and must be as obvious to him as it is to the judge who pronounces it ambiguous.[160] However cogent this reasoning may appear, we think it must be admitted that the preponderance of authority in this country is against it. It would seem that there is

412, 30 Am. Rep. 226; Williams v. Second Nat'l Bank, 83 Ind. 237; Prather v. Ross, 17 Ind. 495; Pentz v. Stanton, 10 Wend. (N. Y.) 271, 25 Am. Dec. 558; Anderton v. Shoup, 17 Ohio St. 125, 93 Am. Dec. 612; Robinson v. Kanawha Valley Bank, 44 Ohio St. 441; Hypes v. Griffin, 89 Ill. 134; Scanlan v. Keith, 102 Ill. 634, 40 Am. Rep. 624.

157 Kenyon v. Williams, 19 Ind. 44; Thomson v. Davenport, 2 Smith Lead. Cas. 377, and notes; Board of Com'rs v. Butterworth, 17 Ind. 129; Davison v. Davenport Gas-Light Co., 24 Iowa 419; Clarke's Ex'r v. Van Riemsdyk, 9 Cranch (U. S.) 153; Baker v. Gregory, 28 Ala. 544, 65 Am. Dec. 366.

158 Lee v. Percival, 85 Iowa 639.

159 Metcalf v. Williams, 104 U. S. 93; Casco Nat'l Bank v. Clark, 139 N. Y. 307; Mechanics' Bank v. Bank of Columbia, 5 Wheat. (U. S.) 326; Smith v. Alexander, 31 Mo. 193; Brockway v. Allen, 17 Wend. (N. Y.) 40; Hardy v. Pilcher, 57 Miss. 18, 34 Am. Rep. 432; Martin v. Smith, 65 Miss. 1, 3 So. 33; Haile v. Peirce, 32 Md. 327, 3 Am. Rep. 139; Roberts v. Austin, 5 Whart. (Pa.) 313.

160 Huffcut Ele. of Ag., § 190.

no valid reason for applying a more rigid rule of construction to negotiable instruments than to other simple contracts in writing, except that by reason of their negotiable character such instruments become a kind of circulating medium, and public policy demands their protection while in the hands of innocent holders. After all, the question to be decided in construing any simple contract is, What was the intention of the parties? and if that is not clear, upon the face of the instrument, or if there are suggestions giving rise to doubt, parol evidence should be admitted to solve the doubt. This is the undisputed rule governing informal instruments not negotiable by the law merchant. A different rule applies with regard to negotiable instruments, it is true, but only when such instruments are sought to be enforced by third parties who acquire title thereto before dishonor, in good faith, and for a valuable consideration.[161] As Dr. Wharton expresses it, "So far as concerns persons taking such paper before maturity, for a valuable consideration, we must sweep aside all questions as to whether those signing the paper occupy other relations than those which the paper states. The courts must determine the question of liability by an examination of the terms used, taking them in their ordinary commercial sense."[162] This is doubtless a correct statement of the rights of innocent holders of such paper, but as the language of the author plainly imports, it does not apply to the immediate parties. As to them, the paper is no more sacred than any other simple contract. Third parties who acquire such an instrument in the course of business may, of course, also be affected by an ambiguity upon the face thereof, but it must be so obvious and apparent as to put them upon inquiry. For example, in England it is a custom with some agents to sign, "C. D., by procuration of A. B.;" but this is ambiguous, and the words "by procuration" are held to be an express intimation of special and limited authority, and sufficient to place the person taking an instrument so drawn, accepted, or indorsed, upon his inquiry as to the extent of the agent's authority.[163] The arbitrary doctrine of *descriptio personarum* ought not to be extended so as to fasten obligations upon those who in fact never assumed them, unless absolutely required by the rules of law. As was well said by the supreme court of Michigan: "The rule that rejects words added to the signature is an arbitrary one. Its reason is not so much that the words are not,

[161] 1 Parsons Notes & B. 274.
[162] Wharton Ag., § 290.
[163] 1 Daniel Neg. Instr., § 299, and cases cited.

or may not be, suggestive, but that they are but suggestive, and the instrument, as a whole, is not sufficiently complete to point to other parentage. The very suggestiveness of these added words has given rise to an irreconcilable conflict in the authorities as to the legal effect of such an instrument. Extrinsic evidence, therefore, is admissible in such cases, between the immediate parties, to explain a suggestion contained on the face of the instrument, and to carry out the contract actually entered into as suggested, but not fully shown by the note itself. The presumption that persons dealing with negotiable instruments take them on the credit of the parties whose names appear should not be absolute in favor of the immediate payee, from whom the consideration proceeds, who must be deemed to have known all the facts and circumstances surrounding the inception of the note, and with such knowledge accepted a note containing such a suggestion."[164] The competency of extrinsic evidence in such cases, as between the immediate parties, is sustained by other high authority.[165] It is a very difficult task, in view of what has been shown as to the conflicting decisions, to extract from them a satisfactory rule upon the subject under discussion. It is always safest for the practitioner to consult the rulings of the courts in the particular jurisdiction in which the controversy has arisen.

§ 220. Summary of the most approved doctrine as to negotiable instruments.—The most approved, though by no means universal doctrine upon this subject may, we think, be stated as follows:—1. A negotiable instrument may be drawn, accepted, or indorsed by an authorized agent so as to bind only his principal when, either by the recitals or the signature, he discloses the principal and makes it appear that he, the agent, is "the mere scribe who applies the executive hand as his instrument;"[166] or that the principal but speaks through him; as, for example, by employing the form "John Doe, by Richard Roe, his agent (or attorney);" or "Richard Roe, agent for John Doe;" or "John Doe, per Richard Roe, agent (or attorney)," or any equivalent words; or other words clearly showing that it is the intention that the person for whom the agent is professing to act be bound, and not the agent himself personally. 2. A negotiable instrument attempted to be drawn by an authorized agent for his principal will bind the agent personally, if neither in the recitals thereof, nor in the signa-

[164] McGrath, J., in Keidan v. Winegar, 95 Mich. 430.

[165] 1 Daniel Neg. Instr., § 418; Mechem Ag., § 443.

[166] 1 Daniel Neg. Instr., § 298.

ture or elsewhere, the principal is named or referred to, although the signer has described himself by adding to his own name such appellations as "agent," "trustee," "president," "treasurer," etc., such words being regarded merely as *descriptio personae;* and extrinsic evidence is not admissible to show that another is the real obligor. 3. If a negotiable instrument of the description last above given, in addition thereto contain upon its face, or in the headings or marginal memoranda, the name of the principal, so as to indicate that it was the intention to bind the principal and not the agent, the court will, by construing the various recitals, memoranda, headings, etc., together, and without extrinsic evidence, declare it to be the obligation of the principal only, when the controversy is between the original parties. 4. If a negotiable instrument of the description given in summary 2, in addition thereto contain upon its face, or in the headings or marginal memoranda, some suggestion that the signer may have been acting merely as the agent or representative of another, whether his name appear or not, the instrument, while still *prima facie* the personal obligation of the agent, will generally be regarded as sufficiently ambiguous, if the controversy be between the immediate parties, or between the drawer or maker and a holder thereof with notice or knowledge of the facts, to warrant the admission of parol evidence to show such facts, in order to exonerate the agent. 5. As to all negotiable instruments in which the paper, on its face, in respect of the question as to which of two persons is the real obligor, shows such ambiguity as to put an ordinarily prudent business man upon his inquiry, parol evidence is admissible to solve the ambiguity even as against an otherwise innocent holder, who acquired the paper before maturity and for a valuable consideration. 6. In the case stated in summary 5, even though there be no ambiguity, yet if it be asserted that the principal was in the habit of transacting that class of business in the name of the agent, or that the name of the agent was the principal's trade name, parol evidence is admissible to prove such fact, either between the immediate parties, or against a third party who took the paper with notice or knowledge thereof; and to prove that fact it may be shown that in the course of dealing between the original parties the name adopted in the particular contract under dispute had become the common name by which the obligation of the principal was expressed.[167]

[167] Bank of Rochester v. Monteath, 1 Denio (N. Y.) 402, 43 Am. Dec. 681; Metcalf v. Williams, 104 U. S. 93; Hovey v. Magill, 2 Conn. 680;

§ 221. **Acceptances—Construction of indorsements.**—What has been said in the preceding sections regarding the execution of negotiable instruments and the liabilities of the parties thereon had reference mainly to the makers or drawers of such instruments, although in some of the cases cited and reviewed the question of liability concerned the acceptors and indorsers of such paper. As to acceptors, we think it may be stated that there is no appreciable distinction, in point of liability on their contracts, between them and the makers or drawers. As a general rule, the doctrine of *descriptio personarum* is as applicable to the one as to the other. Whether, in construing the signature of an acceptor, the court will look to the entire instrument together with the *indicia* of the paper, such as headings and marginal remarks, is not definitely established. In one case, as we have seen, the court ruled that the acceptance and the signature thereto alone could be considered, without reference to other parts of the instrument, it being a separate and independent contract; that while headings and other earmarks of the paper might serve to explain the signature of the maker or drawer, they could not also be used to qualify that of the acceptor.[168] This rule, however, can not be deemed of universal application, we apprehend, for it would be absurd to disregard wholly the nature of the instrument which the party accepts, in the construction of the contract of acceptance. If a bill is drawn on John Doe and accepted "John Doe, by Richard Roe, his agent," it can not be said that the court may disregard the bill itself; for without looking to its several parts it will be unable to determine whether the acceptance is valid or not. And when a bill is drawn on John Doe and accepted by "Richard Roe, agent," it would seem that the court would determine the validity of the acceptance by construing the acceptance and signature thereto in connection with the whole instrument; and that, when so construed, the only rational meaning to be given to the appellation after the signature of Richard Roe must be "agent for John Doe;" for as John Doe is the drawee, and he alone can legally accept the bill, there would be no room for other construction; and this is believed to be the true rule.[169] But where an instrument, in the form of a bill of exchange, was drawn by

Pease v. Pease, 35 Conn. 131; Gerber v. Stuart, 1 Mont. 172; Milligan v. Lyle, 24 La. Ann. 144; Melledge v. Boston Iron Co., 5 Cush. (Mass.) 158; Rumsey v. Briggs, 139 N. Y. 323, 34 N. E. 929.

[168] Slawson v. Loring, 87 Mass. 340; *ante*, § 215.

[169] See Souhegan Nat'l Bank v. Boardman, 46 Minn. 293.

H. W. Harding and accepted by "William S. Bolling, agent of H. W. Harding," parol evidence was held admissible between the parties to show that the intent was not to charge Bolling personally, but to charge Harding, whose funds were in the hands of Bolling.[170] In this case, it will be noted, the acceptance was not by a drawee of a bill, but by the agent of the drawer, which is of course unusual, and at once suggests an ambiguity, the instrument, though in form a bill of exchange, being really a promissory note, and Bolling being an apparent indorser rather than an acceptor. It was held proper, therefore, to admit extrinsic evidence to show that Bolling had funds in his hands belonging to Harding, and that the intention was merely to dedicate such funds *pro tanto* to the security of the note, and not to hold Bolling personally liable in any manner. A similar ruling was made by the supreme court of Tennessee. There the suit was on a note. The mother of the plaintiffs, then infants, loaned a sum of money belonging to them to Partee and Harbut, a firm composed of C. C. Partee and B. F. Harbut, taking therefor two notes of the firm payable to John Harbut and H. Partee, and indorsed by them severally, and by James H. French. The suit was against all the parties to the paper. The court held that the doctrine of *descriptio personae* was applicable to indorsers, but that when the indorsement was irregular, as in this case, parol evidence was admissible, as between the parties, to prove the real attitude of the apparent indorser to the paper.[171] That an apparent indorser may thus explain his relation by parol evidence, when the suit is between the original parties and there is ambiguity, has been decided in other cases.[172] And when the indorsement is in blank, parol evidence may be received to annex a condition or qualification to the indorsement when the controversy is between the immediate parties;[173] but not when the action is by a remote indorser, who purchased *bona fide*, for full value and without notice.[174] In suits against indorsers of notes and bills payable to a corporation by its corporate name and indorsed by an authorized agent or official, with the suffix of his office or position, it is generally regarded that the agent or official acted for the corporation, which can

[170] Hardy v. Pilcher, 57 Miss. 18.

[171] Taylor v. French, 2 Lea (Tenn.) 257, 31 Am. Rep. 609.

[172] Cole v. Smith, 29 La. Ann. 551, 29 Am. Rep. 343; Babcock v. Beman, 11 N. Y. 200.

[173] Davis v. Morgan, 64 N. C. 570.

[174] Hill v. Shields, 81 N. C. 250, 31 Am. Rep. 499; Rodney v. Wilson, 67 Mo. 123, 29 Am. Rep. 499; Doolittle v. Ferry, 20 Kan. 230, 27 Am. Rep. 166.

only act by an agent, and can transfer title only in that manner.[175] Indeed, the courts are manifesting a disposition to hold that such words as "agent," "treasurer," "president," "cashier," etc., added to the signature of an apparent indorser, or even maker or drawer, indicate that the indorsement or execution is as agent of the payee or principal maker or drawer, and may be so construed *prima facie,* if warranted by the appearance of the paper; or that parol evidence may be adduced to show that such is the case.[176] Even where the note was payable to "R. B., treasurer," and indorsed "R. B., treasurer," it was held that this indorsement did not necessarily create a personal liability against R. B., and that parol evidence was proper to show that the indorsement was made in behalf of the corporation of which R. B. was treasurer.[177]

§ **222. Bank cashiers—Rule of descriptio personarum not applicable to.**—In respect of bank cashiers it is now generally held that one who indorses or accepts a negotiable instrument by adding to his signature the suffix "cashier," or "cash.," or "cas.," is presumed to be acting for the bank of which he is cashier, and that a note, bill, or other instrument payable to a person as cashier is payable to his bank.[178] Such added word is not regarded as a mere descriptive appellation, but as a valid substitute for the name of the principal, which may not be disclosed on the face of the paper.[179]

§ **223. Undisclosed principal—Parol evidence to hold liable.**—While extrinsic evidence, except in the instances heretofore pointed out, will not generally be received to vary or contradict the contents of a written instrument, such evidence is always admissible to charge with liability an undisclosed principal, or one who, though disclosed, is not named in the instrument. The purpose of such evidence is

[175] 1 Daniel Neg. Instr., § 416.

[176] Falk v. Moebs, 127 U. S. 597; Scanlan v. Keith, 102 Ill. 634, 40 Am. Rep. 624; Merchants' Bank v. Central Bank, 1 Ga. 418, 44 Am. Dec. 665.

[177] Babcock v. Beman, 11 N. Y. 200. See also, Vater v. Lewis, 36 Ind. 288.

[178] Nave v. First Nat'l Bank, 87 Ind. 204; Erwin, etc., Co. v. Farmers' Nat'l Bank, 130 Ind. 367; Hodge v. Farmers' Bank, 7 Ind. App. 94; Bank of Genesee v. Patchin Bank, 19 N. Y. 312; Folger v. Chase, 18 Pick. (Mass.) 63; Houghton v. First Nat'l Bank, 26 Wis. 663; Pratt v. Topeka Bank, 12 Kan. 570; Stamford Bank v. Ferris, 17 Conn. 259; Watervliet Bank v. White, 1 Denio (N. Y.) 608; 1 Daniel Neg. Instr., § 417; Morse Banks & Banking, §§ 158h, 170; Garland v. Dover, 19 Me. 441.

[179] 1 Daniel Neg. Instr., § 417.

not, however, to exonerate the agent, but to hold the principal in addition. This subject will be fully dealt with hereafter.[180]

§ 224. **Sealed instruments—How must be executed to bind principal—Illustrative cases.**—Instruments under seal were, by the common law, regarded as the highest class of written instruments; and although the requirement of a seal has in many states of the Union been abrogated by statutes, and in those and in many other jurisdictions the importance attached to such instruments has been greatly diminished by the decisions of the courts, it is still true that deeds and instruments that were required to be under seal by the rules of the common law are regarded as being of a much more solemn and important character than simple contracts, and that many of the common-law rules as to these are still in force; and as to these the rule against the admission of parol testimony to vary the writing is still generally applicable. An agent who is duly authorized to execute an instrument of this character must be careful to execute it so as not to render himself personally liable. It is possible that the execution of such an instrument by an agent may have one of the following consequences: 1. It may bind the principal and not himself. 2. It may bind himself and not the principal. 3. It may be void as to both himself and the principal.[181] Assuming that the agent was properly authorized to execute such an instrument on behalf of his principal, he may do so, without binding himself, by using the name of the principal as the grantor, or party who contracts, and stating that the act is done by him as his agent; thus: "Know all men by these presents that John Smith, by William Jones, his attorney (or agent), does hereby grant, convey," etc. This is the granting clause, and must purport to be made by the principal. The same is true of the covenants in the deed, which may be expressed as follows: "And the said John Smith, by his attorney (or agent) aforesaid, does hereby covenant, warrant and defend," etc. Then follows the *testimonium* clause, which should likewise be executed in the name of the principal; thus: "In testimony whereof, the said John Smith, by his said attorney (or agent), has hereunto set his hand and affixed his seal, this," etc., giving the date of the execution of the deed. Lastly comes the signature, which must purport to be that of the principal, and may or may not be followed by that of the attorney or agent; thus: "John Smith (seal)," or "John Smith (seal), by

[180] See *post*, § 303.

[181] Evans Pr. & Ag. (Bedford's ed.) 231.

William Jones, his attorney (or agent)."[182] This will clearly be binding upon the principal, and him only. It must not be understood, however, that the deed or sealed instrument must be in the exact form of words above given. It is believed that this form is most to be commended, but it is by no means the only one that will stand the test. As said in an English case, "Whether the attorney put his name first or last can not affect the validity of the act done."[183] And in the same case it was said by Lawrence, J.: "But here the bond was executed by Wilks, for and in the name of his principal, and this is distinctly shown by the manner of making his signature. Not that even this was necessary to be shown; for if Wilks had sealed and delivered it in the name of Browne, that would have been enough without stating that he had so done. * * * There is no particular form of words to be used, provided the act be done in the name of the principal." "For A. B., by C. D.," is sufficient; and the order of the words is not material, if the deed purports on its face to be the deed of the principal. If the mode of execution, however informal, is not repugnant to such purport, it will be construed to be the deed of the principal, provided the *testimonium* clause is that the principal has thereunto set his hand and seal.[184] In a Missouri case the form was "that the A. B. Co., by S. H., president, and T. S. C., secretary, has granted," etc. "In witness whereof we hereunto subscribe our names and affix our seals." The acknowledgment was that the president and secretary, by name, acknowledged that they executed and delivered the deed as their voluntary act and

[182] Story Ag., § 153.

[183] Per Grose, J., in Wilks v. Back, 2 East 142.

[184] Story Ag., § 153. See also, Ball v. Dunsterville, 4 T. R. 313; Bohannons v. Lewis, 3 T. B. Mon. (Ky.) 376; Wilburn v. Larkin, 3 Blackf. (Ind.) 55; Berkey v. Judd, 22 Minn. 287; Spencer v. Field, 10 Wend. (N. Y.) 88. The following form was held sufficient to bind the principal in Butterfield v. Beall, 3 Ind. 203: "This indenture, made ...... between J. C. W., ..., attorney in fact for A. B. and R. B., ..., parties of the first part, and J. B., ..., of the second part, witnesseth, that the said J. C. W., party of the first part, ..., hath granted," etc. "In witness whereof the said J. C. W., attorney, hath hereunto set their hands and seals," etc. "A. B. (seal). ...... R. B. (seal). ...... By J. C. W. (seal), their attorney in fact." The court said that the deed, "while very inartificially drawn, we have determined, not, however, without a good deal of hesitation, should be held operative to the extent of the power that had been legally conveyed to him. It was Wright's intention to act under the power granted him, and justice will be promoted and litigation, perhaps, saved, by holding the deed operative."

deed. Each of the names had a seal attached to it, and there was a fourth seal attached not opposite to any name. The court ruled that the deed was that of the corporation.[185] One Daniel King and one Zachariah King were joint owners of a piece of land; and Daniel King executed a deed thereto in the following terms: "I, Daniel King, as well for myself as attorney for Zachariah King, doth (*sic*) for myself and the said Zachariah, remise, release and forever quit-claim the premises described in the deed, together with all the estate, right, title, interest, use, property, claim, and demand whatsoever of me, the said Daniel, and said Zachariah, which we now have, or heretofore had at any time, in said premises. And we, the said Daniel and Zachariah, do hereby for ourselves, our heirs, and executors, covenant that the premises are free of all incumbrance, and that the grantee may quietly enjoy the same without any claim or hindrance from us, or any one claiming under us, or either of us. In witness whereof, we the said Daniel for himself, and as attorney aforesaid, have hereunto set our hands and seals," etc. Signed, "Daniel King;" and also, "Daniel King, attorney for Zachariah King, being duly authorized as appears of record," with seals attached to each signature. It was held that the covenants of the deed were clearly those of the principal; that from the terms used the grant purported to be that of the principal; and that the deed, as executed, passed the title of both Daniel and Zachariah King. The court in the course of the opinion said: "The deed of the attorney, to be valid, must be in the name and purport to be the act and deed of the principal; * * * but whether such is the purport of an instrument must be determined from its general tenor, not from any particular clause. Such construction must be given, in this as well as in other questions arising on conveyances, as shall make every part of the instrument operative as far as possible; and where the intention of the parties can be discovered, such intention should be carried into effect, if it can be done consistently with the rules of law."[186] It has been repeatedly held that no particular set of words is necessary, if the intention to bind the principal is clearly manifest from the writing. Thus, it was said by the court of appeals of Kentucky: "The attorney should act in the name of his principal, and not in his own name merely. There is no inflexible rule as to the mode in which this is to be done; and when both names are to be used both in the caption or body and

[185] City of Kansas City v. Hannibal, etc., R. Co., 77 Mo. 180.

[186] Hale v. Woods, 10 N. H. 470, 34 Am. Dec. 176.

signature of the instrument, it is a question of intention and construction, whether the act is done, or the engagement made, in the name of the principal or of the agent. The terms of the covenant itself are commonly decisive as to intention. The description in the caption and the mode of signature are referred to, either as aids in discovering the intention, or as determining whether the form of the instrument corresponds with this intention, so that it may be carried out. If, in view of all its parts, the instrument can be regarded as the deed or covenant of the party intended to be bound, it must, on principle, be so regarded. There is, we believe, no difference of opinion with regard to the propriety of these positions, though there doubtless may be in their application."[187] And a lease in which "Edward F. Lawrence, president of the Northwestern Distilling Company," described himself as the party of the second part, and in which the *testimonium* clause was as follows: "In testimony whereof the said parties have hereunto set their hand and seals," and which was signed "Northwestern Distilling Company (seal), by Edward Lawrence, president,"—was held well executed, and binding on the company, and not on Lawrence personally.[188] But an agent or attorney-in-fact can not convey land or otherwise execute authority in his own name, even though he describe himself as "agent" of the person for whom he professes to act; the words "agent of" being construed, in such a case, as merely descriptive of the person of the signer. Thus, a conveyance which reads: "Know all men by these presents that I, A. B., as agent of C. D., do hereby grant, sell, convey," etc., is the deed of A. B. and not of C. D.; and this is true, Story says, although he sign the instrument "A. B., for C. D.;" for while, in such cases, the *testimonium* clause and the signature and seal purport to be those of the principal, the granting clause not purporting to be that of the principal, it is only the deed of the agent, and not that of the principal.[189] And where a deed recited, "Know all men by these presents that the N. England Silk Co., a corporation, by C. C., their treasurer," etc., "do hereby grant," etc., and the *testimonium* clause was, "In witness whereof, I, the said C. C., in behalf of said company, and as their treasurer, do hereunto set my hand and seal. C. C., treasurer of N. England Silk Co.,"—such deed was held not properly

[187] Hunter v. Miller, 6 B. Mon. (Ky.) 612. See also, Carter v. Doe, 21 Ala. 72; Magill v. Hinsdale, 6 Conn. 464, 16 Am. Dec. 70.

[188] Northwestern Distilling Co. v. Brant, 69 Ill. 658, 18 Am. Rep. 631.

[189] Story Ag., § 148.

executed and as not being the deed of the corporation.[190] The reason for the requirement that the deed must purport to be executed in the name of the principal is obvious. It is not sufficient that the agent have authority to execute the instrument. If he has such authority and attempts to execute it in his own name, he does not execute it at all; for it must be the deed of the principal that is executed, and not the deed of the agent, for the agent can not convey a thing which he himself does not have. In many jurisdictions short forms of deeds of conveyance and mortgages have been adopted by statute, and where this is the case, these forms may, of course, be used.

§ **225. Consequences of defective execution.**—If the agent fail to execute properly the authority of the principal, one of two consequences will follow: 1. The deed may be absolutely void; 2. The deed may be valid so as to bind the agent, but void as to the principal. The result depends altogether on the legal effect of the contract. The only way in which it can bind the agent, of course, is to render him personally liable in damages; unless his authority be coupled with an interest, in which case it may have the effect of an alienation of the subject-matter of the agency *pro tanto*. If an agent undertakes to execute a deed of conveyance for his principal, to do which he has been duly authorized, and fails to make an effectual conveyance of the land, it is apparent that the deed is entirely void so far as conveying anything by it is concerned. The title of the land being in the principal, the personal deed of the agent would not convey it, of course. Such a deed is therefore void.[191] However, if the agent should himself have an interest in the land, it is easily seen that by his personal deed he would convey at least his own interest, and to that extent the deed would be a valid conveyance, as to such interest, but no further. Or if the instrument be a bond for the payment of money, and the agent has bound himself by apt words, the bond will be valid so as to bind the agent, as an obligor, although void as to the principal. Thus, where an agent undertakes to execute a bond on behalf of his principal, and in the body of the instrument writes, "I promise to pay," etc., and signs himself "John Smith, agent of William Jones,"—William Jones, the principal, incurs no liability, as no one purports to act for him; but John Smith is liable on the

[190] Brinley v. Mann, 2 Cush. (Mass.) 337.

[191] Fowler v. Shearer, 7 Mass. 14; McNaughten v. Partridge, 11 Ohio 223, 30 Am. Dec. 731.

bond, for he has promised to pay.[192] And the agent may incur liability upon a deed if the same contain covenants of warranty in his own name, whether the descriptive words "agent of ———" be added or not. If the deed of conveyance in such instrument contain such covenant, the agent will be individually liable thereon, and an action in covenant will lie against him individually.[193]

§ 226. **Tendency of courts to relax strict rules of common law as to sealed instruments—Statutes.**—The American courts are constantly evincing a disposition to relax the rigid rules of the common law in relation to the execution of sealed instruments, even independently of statutes. Thus, a deed signed "A. B., by C. D., his attorney in fact," has been held by the supreme court of Minnesota to be a sufficient execution, without reciting the grant in the body of the deed.[194] And it has been held that though an agreement under seal is inoperative in law to convey title for want of a formal execution in the name of the principal, yet if the agent or attorney was duly authorized to make the conveyance, it is binding in equity.[195] Such a deed, when executed by an agent, though defective and inoperative to convey title, will be specifically enforced in equity as an agreement to convey.[196] By virtue of statutes in many states the rule is less rigorously applied.[197] But in Alabama it is held that the fact that the common-law requirement of seals on deeds of conveyance of lands has been abolished does not change the rule as to the execution of such instruments by agents.[198] Of course, where an instrument is executed under seal when none is required, the rules applicable to sealed instruments do not apply, and the seal will be treated as surplusage.[199]

§ 227. **Rules prevailing in local jurisdictions should be ascertained.**—Finally, it is proper to state that the rule of construction

[192] Fowler v. Shearer, 7 Mass. 14; Elwell v. Shaw, 16 Mass. 42.

[193] Mitchell v. Hazen, 4 Conn. 495, 10 Am. Dec. 169; Ogden v. Raymond, 22 Conn. 379, 58 Am. Dec. 429.

[194] Tidd v. Rines, 26 Minn. 201.

[195] Love v. Sierra Nevada, etc., Co., 32 Cal. 639, 91 Am. Dec. 602; McNaughten v. Partridge, 11 Ohio 223, 38 Am. Dec. 731; Daughtrey v. Knolle, 44 Tex. 450; Johnson v. Johnson, 1 Dana (Ky.) 364.

[196] Salmon v. Hoffman, 2 Cal. 138, 56 Am. Dec. 322; Welsh v. Usher, 2 Hill Eq. (S. C.) 167, 29 Am. Dec. 63.

[197] See Simpson v. Garland, 72 Me. 40, 34 Am. Rep. 297; Warner v. Mower, 11 Vt. 385; Bryan v. Stump, 8 Gratt. (Va.) 241, 56 Am. Dec. 139; Gibbs v. Dickson, 33 Ark. 107.

[198] Jones v. Morris, 61 Ala. 518.

[199] Stowell v. Eldred, 39 Wis. 614; Kirschbon v. Bonzel, 67 Wis. 178; Steele v. McElroy, 1 Sneed (Tenn.) 341.

applicable to all contracts is that which prevails in the jurisdiction where the contract is entered into.[200] This is, of course, true of a contract of agency or a contract made by an agent on behalf of his principal. If the authority is conferred in one place and executed in another, the presumption, in the absence of any expression to the contrary, is that it is to be executed according to the law of the place where it is to be performed; and of all this the principal is presumed to have knowledge.[201]

[200] 1 Wharton Conts., § 20.

[201] Mechem Ag., § 305.

CHAPTER VI.

DUTIES, OBLIGATIONS AND LIABILITIES OF AGENT TO PRINCIPAL, AND RIGHTS OF PRINCIPAL IN REGARD TO AGENT.

§ 228. **Purpose of this chapter.**—Growing out of the relation between the principal and the agent, and the execution of the authority placed in the hands of the latter by the former, are certain reciprocal duties, obligations, rights and liabilities between the principal and the agent, which it is our purpose, in due course, to consider. And first, as to the duties and obligations an agent owes to his principal, and the corresponding rights accruing from these to the principal, on the part of the agent. These will be discussed in the present chapter.

§ 229. **Duty of agent to enter upon performance of trust.**—The first duty devolving upon an agent after he has assumed the relation with his principal is to enter upon the performance of the task intrusted to him and which he has agreed to perform; unless, indeed, the time for such performance is postponed to some future date; or unless he has been released by a new contract, or the principal has revoked the agency; or unless the agreement is either illegal, immoral, contrary to public policy, or impossible.[1] It is immaterial that the commission is a hard one, or that it would subject him to losses. If the agency is created upon a sufficient consideration, the agent is bound to execute it, and for failure to do so is guilty of non-feasance, and is liable to the principal for all damages that the latter may sustain by reason of such failure. Thus, if an agent whose duty it is to procure insurance neglects to do so and there is a loss to his principal, the agent is liable for the full amount of the loss that he should have insured against.[2] The agent must perform the duty intrusted to him, and accepted by him, at the time and place and in the manner which his contract and instructions demand; and upon failure to do this, he will be liable to the principal for negligence, in such damages as the principal may sustain.[3]

[1] Evans Pr. & Ag. (Bedford's ed.) 253; Rechtscherd v. Accommodation Bank, 47 Mo. 181; Williamsburg, etc., Ins. Co. v. Frothingham, 122 Mass. 391.

[2] Story Ag., § 218; Vickery v. Lanier, 1 Metc. (Ky.) 133. Of course, the undertaking must be founded on a good consideration. In the case cited the court said: "There must have been an undertaking or promise to insure, made at the time, and intended as such by the parties. The party making the request must have had some assurance on which he had the right to rely, and from which he had the right to expect the other party would insure; or, in other words, there must, in the language of all the books, have been an undertaking to that effect. Without it no liability attaches. Such promise or undertaking is implied where the course of dealing has been such that the agent has been used to effect insurances, or where he has funds or effects on hand, or even where the bill of lading from which he derives his authority contains an order to insure; and *in such case he is bound at his peril to insure.*" Where an insurance company has directed its agent to cancel a policy and he fails to use diligence in doing so, and the company sustains a loss thereby, the agent is liable to the company for the damages: Phœnix Ins. Co. v. Frissell, 142 Mass. 513.

[3] Wilson v. Wilson, 26 Pa. St. 393. Hence, if an agent to whom a collection of negotiable paper has been intrusted, before maturity, fails to

§ 230. **For what losses of principal agent is liable.**—The next question that naturally arises is, For what losses is the agent liable in such cases? In the first place, it may be truly stated that the agent is responsible to the principal only for the real loss or actual injury sustained by him by reason of the non-feasance, and not for merely a probable or possible one. Hence, if, in the case supposed in the previous section, the agent had undertaken to procure insurance in a designated company and the company had become insolvent before the loss, or the principal had no insurable interest, or the voyage (if marine insurance), as described in the order, would not have covered the risk,—there could be no responsibility attaching to the agent, as there would be no actual injury or real loss resulting from the neglect.[4] But loss or injury will always be presumed in such cases, if a casualty has occurred, and the burden is on the agent to show that no injury has accrued to the principal by reason of the breach, and even then the latter will be entitled to nominal damages.[5] The principal is entitled to recover such damages as are the proximate results of the agent's non-feasance, or omission. The damages need not be the direct or immediate consequences of the agent's negligence, though it will not be sufficient if they be merely a remote result, or an accidental mischief, the maxim being applicable: *"Causa proxima, non remota, spectatur."* If the injury is a natural result of, or is fairly attributable to, the agent's failure or negligence, it is

present the same in due time for acceptance, he is guilty of negligence; and if the collection is thereby lost, he will be liable to the principal in damages for the amount of such loss: Allen v. Suydam, 20 Wend. (N. Y.) 321; First Nat'l Bank v. Fourth Nat'l Bank, 77 N. Y. 320, 33 Am. Rep. 618; Merchants', etc., Bank v. Stafford Bank, 44 Conn. 565; Warren Bank v. Suffolk Bank, 10 Cush. (Mass.) 582; Bank of Delaware Co. v. Broomhall, 38 Pa. St. 135; Flint v. Rogers, 15 Me. 67. And if specific directions be given as to the method of collection, these must, of course, be followed, at the peril of the agent in case of loss: Johnson v. New York, etc., R. Co., 33 N. Y. 610, 88 Am. Dec. 416.

[4] Story Ag., § 222.

[5] It is, however, the duty of the principal, when he has ascertained that the agent has failed to procure the insurance, to take steps himself to effect such insurance; and if, after he has acquired knowledge of the agent's failure to take out sufficient insurance to cover any probable loss, he fails to do so himself, provided he have time and opportunity, he can not recover for the loss he may sustain by reason of the agent's negligence. This is on the principle that it is the duty of one who has suffered a wrong at the hands of another to use proper diligence in preventing loss from such wrong: Brant v. Gallup, 111 Ill. 487.

sufficient to render him liable.[6] Hence, if an agent is directed to purchase for the principal and forward to him a certain article, and the agent fails to do so, the principal can recover what loss he has sustained, including the profits which he could have obtained on the sale of the article directed to be purchased.[7] But speculative profits or gains that might possibly arise in the future can not be allowed.[8] And if an agent whose duty it is to collect money for his principal has failed to do so, he can not be held responsible for all the profits the principal might have made out of such money, in some speculation or business into which he was prevented from entering owing to the negligence of his agent. Nor would he be liable if by reason of such failure to collect, on the part of the agent, the principal should become embarrassed in the payment of his debts, or fail in business, or be injured in his credit, for these are but remote or accidental consequences of the agent's negligence.[9] Nor is the agent always liable

[6] Willard v. Pinard, 44 Vt. 34; Gilson v. Collins, 66 Ill. 136; Whitney v. Merchants', etc., Co., 104 Mass. 152.

[7] Bell v. Cunningham, 3 Pet. (U. S.) 69. But it is held (and this seems to be the weight of authority) that mere delay in forwarding, though due to negligence of a carrier, can not be regarded as the proximate cause of an injury resulting from a storm, fire, or other causes which could not have been anticipated and for which the agent is not responsible, although the injury might not have occurred if the carrier had been diligent in forwarding: Hoadley v. Northern Trans. Co., 115 Mass. 304, 15 Am. Rep. 106; Dubuque Wood, etc., Ass'n v. Dubuque, 30 Iowa 176; Michigan, etc., R. Co. v. Burrows, 33 Mich. 6; McClary v. Sioux City, etc., R. Co., 3 Neb. 44, 19 Am. Rep. 631; Daniels v. Ballantine, 23 Ohio St. 532, 13 Am. Rep. 264; Morrison v. Davis, 20 Pa. St. 171, 57 Am. Dec. 695; Lamont v. Nashville, etc., R. Co., 9 Heisk. (Tenn.) 58; Davis v. Central Vermont R. Co., 66 Vt. 290, 44 Am. St. 852; Reid v. Evansville, etc., R. Co., 10 Ind. App. 385; Memphis, etc., R. Co. v. Reeves, 10 Wall. (U. S.) 176; Scott v. Baltimore, etc., Steamboat Co., 19 Fed. 56; McCarthy v. Louisville, etc., R. Co., 102 Ala. 193, 48 Am. St. 29; O'Brien v. McGlinchy, 68 Me. 552, 557. The holding of the courts in some states is, however, directly the opposite of this view. It is there ruled that the carrier is liable in such cases, the negligent delay being regarded as the proximate cause of the injury: Pruitt v. Hannibal, etc., R. Co., 62 Mo. 527; Wolf v. American Express Co., 43 Mo. 421, 97 Am. Dec. 406; Bostwick v. Baltimore, etc., R. Co., 45 N. Y. 712; McGraw v. Baltimore, etc., R. Co., 18 W. Va. 361; Deming v. Grand Trunk R. Co., 48 N. H. 455. See also, Ruppel v. Allegheny Valley R., 167 Pa. St. 166, 46 Am. St. 666; St. Clair v. Chicago, etc., R. Co., 80 Iowa 304.

[8] Bell v. Cunningham, 3 Pet. (U. S.) 69.

[9] Story Ag., § 220; Evans Pr. &

for failure to perform his agreement. No man can be compelled to perform an illegal or immoral act, or one that is contrary to public policy or that is impossible to be performed; nor can the principal recover any damages for the agent's failure to perform such act. We have already discussed the classes of contracts that are illegal, immoral, and opposed to public policy, in another chapter of this work, to which the student is referred.[10] We need only say here that if the contract of agency belongs within the category of any of these inhibited transactions, the agent need not, indeed he should not, perform it; and he will not be liable to the principal in damages for his failure to execute the agreement. The first duty of the parties is to obey the law, and the law will not permit either party to violate any moral or legal duties. If, for example, the agent's contract requires him to smuggle goods into a country, in violation of its laws, and he fails or refuses to do so, no recovery can be had by the principal for such failure to perform, any more than the agent could recover compensation from the principal if he had performed the illegal contract. The law will leave the parties in such cases precisely as it finds them, and will not interfere in behalf of either of them.[11]

§ 231. **Gratuitous services.**—These observations as to the duty of the agent to act apply, however, only to agents for hire or compensation. If the agency is entirely gratuitous, and the agent does not enter upon the performance of the duty intrusted to him, he will not incur any liability to his principal for such failure to perform. In such case, there is no consideration for the promise to perform, and hence no liability.[12] An agent is liable, however, if he undertakes to execute the business in whole or in part, and any loss or injury results to the principal from his negligence or from failure to complete the business or to perform it in accordance with his instructions. No man can be compelled against his wishes to perform for another

Ag. (Bedford's ed.) 253; Davis v. Barger, 57 Ind. 54; City of Indianapolis v. Wann, 144 Ind. 175.

[10] *Ante*, §§ 61–76.

[11] Armstrong v. Toler, 11 Wheat. (U. S.) 258; Brown v. Howard, 14 Johns. (N. Y.) 119. See also, Rechstscherd v. Accommodation Bank, 47 Mo. 181; Mills v. Mills, 40 N. Y. 543, 100 Am. Dec. 535; Byrd v. Hughes, 84 Ill. 174; Pearce v. Foote, 113 Ill. 228.

[12] Morrison v. Orr, 3 S. & P. (Ala.) 49, 23 Am. Dec. 319; Spencer v. Towles, 18 Mich. 9; Balfe v. West, 13 C. B. 466, 22 Eng. L. & Eq. 506; Thorne v. Deas, 4 Johns. (N. Y.) 84; Benden v. Manning, 2 N. H. 289.

any act of friendship or service of any kind without compensation; yet if he undertake the business and fail to perform it in compliance with his agreement or the instructions of his principal, he will be liable for the loss occasioned by his negligence, and a relinquishment of his commission will not release him from damages.[13] In other words, a gratuitous agent is not responsible for non-feasance, but he is responsible for misfeasance.[14] When the party undertakes to perform the business intrusted to him, he becomes an agent, whether he does so gratuitously or for pay. His previous promise for a gratuitous service was not binding upon him, for it was not supported by any consideration, and was, therefore, *nudum pactum*. But by the voluntary undertaking and entering upon the service, such party becomes subject to the ordinary and usual rules pertaining to an agency, and is then under obligations to execute the business of his principal, or suffer the consequences for any injury caused by his negligence.[15]

§ 232. Gratuitous bailees and bank directors—Negligence—Degrees of.—The question then arises, When does a gratuitous agent become liable to his principal for negligence in the performance of the latter's business? The classes of agents most generally affected by this branch of the law of agency are gratuitous bailees and directors of banks, though these are by no means the only ones. A bailment, according to Blackstone, is a delivery of goods in trust, upon a contract, express or implied, that the trust shall be duly executed on the part of the bailee.[16] The party who thus delivers the goods for bailment is called the bailor, while he who receives them for the purpose is the bailee. There are three kinds of bailments; namely: (1) those which are solely for the benefit of the bailor; (2) those which are solely for the benefit of the bailee; (3) those which are for the benefit of both the bailor and bailee.[17] In the first, only slight care is said to be required of the

[13] Walker v. Smith, 1 Wash. (U. S.) 152; Watson v. Union Iron, etc., Co., 15 Ill. App. 509; Spencer v. Towles, 18 Mich. 9; Passano v. Acosta, 4 La. 28, 23 Am. Dec. 470; Gill v. Middleton, 105 Mass. 477, 7 Am. Rep. 548.

[14] Thorne v. Deas, 4 Johns. (N. Y.) 84.

[15] Spencer v. Towles, 18 Mich. 9.

[16] 2 Bl. Com. 395, 451; Swentzel v. Penn Bank, 147 Pa. St. 140; Hammond v. Hussey, 51 N. H. 40, 12 Am. Rep. 41; Grant v. Ludlow, 8 Ohio St. 1; Eddy v. Livingston, 35 Mo. 487.

[17] Story Bailm., § 23; Schouler Bailm., § 15.

bailee; in the second, it is said that great care and diligence are required; while in the third, ordinary care is the standard.[18] It is only the first kind of bailment above mentioned with which we are here concerned. Bailments solely for the benefit of the bailor being gratuitous bailments, the bailee is generally required to use but slight diligence or care; and the only kind of negligence for which he is said to be liable to the bailor is "gross" negligence.[19] Special deposits in banks come within this class of bailments. They are generally, if not universally, without hire or compensation. The bailment is for the sole benefit and accommodation of the bailor. Still, there is an implied contract that the deposit shall be safely kept and the identical thing returned when the bailment is ended.[20] Such a deposit is a naked bailment, without recompense, and the bailee is liable only for "gross negligence."[21] Just what is meant by "gross" negligence is not always easy to determine. One may be guilty of such negligence in one case when under the same or similar circumstances in another case he would be guilty only of ordinary or slight negligence. The general rule is that the care must be proportioned to the business undertaken by the agent or bailee,[22] and the nature of the

[18] Story Bailm., § 23; Schouler Bailm., § 15.

[19] Story Bailm., *supra;* 1 Thompson Neg. (2d ed.), §§ 18-26; 1 Shearman & Redf. Neg., §§ 47-49; Persch v. Quiggle, 57 Pa. St. 247; Shiells v. Blackburne, 1 H. Bl. 158; Beardslee v. Richardson, 11 Wend. (N. Y.) 25, 25 Am. Dec. 596; Grant v. Ludlow, 8 Ohio St. 1; Hibernia Bldg. Ass'n v. McGrath, 154 Pa. St. 296, 26 Atl. 377, 35 Am. St. 826; Burk v. Dempster, 34 Neb. 426, 51 N. W. 976; Ray v. Bank of Kentucky, 10 Bush (Ky.) 344; Singer Mfg. Co. v. Tyler, 54 Ill. App. 97; Tancil v. Seaton, 28 Gratt. (Va.) 601.

[20] State v. Clark, 4 Ind. 315.

[21] Whitney v. Brattleboro Bank, 55 Vt. 154, 45 Am. Rep. 598; Patterson v. McIver, 90 N. C. 493; Dunn v. Branner, 13 La. Ann. 452; First Nat'l Bank v. Rex, 89 Pa. St. 308; Eldridge v. Hill, 97 U. S. 92; Ray v. Bank of Kentucky, 10 Bush (Ky.) 344; Henry v. Porter, 46 Ala. 293. A leading case upon the subject under discussion is Foster v. Essex Bank, 17 Mass. 479. It is there held that a bailee or mere depositary of goods, without any special undertaking and without reward, is not liable for loss of the goods by theft or otherwise, without proof of "gross negligence." See the note to this case in 9 Am. Dec., at p. 183.

[22] Eddy v. Livingston, 35 Mo. 487; Mariner v. Smith, 5 Heisk. (Tenn.) 203; Kirtland v. Montgomery, 1 Swan (Tenn.) 452. It is sometimes said that where persons volunteer to render mere friendly services, or give aid, advice and counsel in cases of illness or other trouble without expecting any reward, that only "gross negligence" will give the injured party a right of action. See Mechem Ag., § 497. But it is not necessary, even in these instances, to employ an epithet with which to

goods bailed.[23] Many cases hold that a mandatary or bailee who undertakes without hire or recompense to care for goods intrusted to his custody, or to perform some duty affecting the subject of the bailment,—as, by carrying the goods from place to place,—is required to use such care as men of common sense and prudence, who are not experts, ordinarily take of their own affairs of that nature, and that he is guilty of gross negligence only when he fails to do this.[24] But it has been held that if a mandatary who undertakes to carry money fails to use the ordinary care called for under the particular circumstances, and the money is lost in consequence of such carelessness, he is liable to the owner for such loss.[25] It is also held that money requires more care at the hands of a mandatary than common articles of property.[26] But the distinction between gross negligence and ordinary negligence has come to be regarded as most unsatisfactory to rely upon, doubtless tending to produce confusion. Negligence of whatever kind is but the absence of such care as one is in duty bound to exercise.[27] The court, in *Wilson* v. *Brett*,[28] declined to recognize the legal distinction between negligence and gross negligence, except that the latter has a vituperative epithet added. "'Gross negligence,'" said the supreme court of the United States, "is a relative term. It is doubtless to be understood as meaning a greater want of care than is implied by the term 'ordinary negligence;' but, after all, it means the absence of the care that was requisite under the circumstances."[29] In cases of gratuitous bailments the law re-

characterize the negligence of which a party rendering these services may be guilty. It is, after all, only a question as to whether or not his conduct would amount to negligence for which an action would lie. The care required to be exercised in such circumstances must be determined by the duty the one who renders the service owes to his friend or neighbor whom he volunteers to assist. And this is the rule in all cases where negligence is charged.

[23] Tracy v. Wood, 3 Mason (U. S.) 132.

[24] Kemp v. Farlow, 5 Ind. 462; First Nat'l Bank v. Ocean Nat'l Bank, 60 N. Y. 278; Conner v. Winton, 8 Ind. 315; Fulton v. Alexander, 21 Tex. 148; Dudley v. Camden, etc., Ferry Co., 42 N. J. L. 25; Lobenstein v. Pritchett, 8 Kan. 213; Tompkins v. Saltmarsh, 14 S. & R. (Pa.) 275.

[25] Jenkins v. Motlow, 1 Sneed (Tenn.) 248; Delaware Bank v. Smith, 1 Edm. Sel. Cas. 351; Colyar v. Taylor, 41 Tenn. 372.

[26] Storer v. Gowen, 18 Me. 174; Anderson v. Foresman, Wright (Ohio) 598; Graves v. Ticknor, 6 N. H. 537.

[27] Per Willes, J., in Grill v. General Iron Screw Collier Co., L. R. 1 C. P. 600.

[28] 11 M. & W. 113.

[29] Milwaukee, etc., R. Co. v. Arms, 91 U. S. 489, 494. And see Preston v. Prather, 137 U. S. 604; Isham v. Post, 141 N. Y. 100. While there are

quires the bailee or mandatary, as we have seen, to use such care as a man of common prudence, not an expert or specialist, ordinarily exercises over his own affairs in like cases. Whether or not he has used such care is a question of fact for the jury.[30] In the case of bank directors who serve without pay, the same rule is generally applied. They, too, are said to be liable only for "gross negligence."[31] But the same degree of care is not required, according to the rulings of the courts, in all cases of gratuitous bailments. Thus, it was said in a New York case: "Trustees of savings banks, though receiving no compensation, are bound to exercise great diligence in the discharge of their duties. The degree of care required depends upon the subject to which it is to be applied. Slight care is not enough. One who voluntarily undertakes the position of director and invites confidence in that relation undertakes, like a mandatary, with those whom he represents or for whom he acts, that he possesses at least ordinary knowledge and skill, and that he will bring them to bear in the discharge of his duty. Such is the rule applicable to public officers, professional men and mechanics, and must be applicable to every one who undertakes to act for another in a situation or employment requiring skill or knowledge; and it matters not that the service was gratuitous. Hence, trustees of a savings bank are deemed to undertake to exercise the ordinary skill and judgment requisite for the discharge of their delicate trust."[32]

doubtless different degrees of care required in different relations, and where the duties and obligations are different, the current of modern law recognizes but one kind of negligence; namely, actionable negligence. Whenever there has been an absence of the exercise of that degree of care—usually denominated due care—which the law requires in a particular case, whether it be slight, ordinary, or great care, then there is actionable negligence: See 1 Thompson Neg. (2d ed.), §§ 18–26; Beven Neg. 16, *et seq.;* Grill v. General Iron Screw Collier Co., L. R. 1 C. P. 600, 612, per Willes, J.; Smith v. New York, etc., R. Co., 24 N. Y. 222; McAdoo v. Richmond, etc., R. Co., 105 N. C. 140; Lane v. Boston, etc., R. Co., 112 Mass. 455; Mariner v. Smith, 5 Heisk. (Tenn.) 203; Steamboat New World v. King, 16 How. (U. S.) 469; Storer v. Gowen, 18 Me. 174.

[30] Preston v. Prather, 137 U. S. 604; Rowland v. Jones, 73 N. C. 52; Griffith v. Zipperwick, 28 Ohio St. 388; Fulton v. Alexander, 21 Tex. 148; and see Isham v. Post, 141 N. Y. 100; Eddy v. Livingston, 35 Mo. 487, 88 Am. Dec. 122.

[31] Dunn v. Kyle, 14 Bush (Ky.) 134; United Soc. of Shakers v. Underwood, 9 Bush (Ky.) 609; Batchelor v. Planters' Nat'l Bank, 78 Ky. 435; Brinckerhoff v. Bostwick, 88 N. Y. 52; German, etc., Bank v. Auth, 87 Pa. St. 419.

[32] Hun v. Cary, 82 N. Y. 65.

§ 233. **Gratuitous agents holding themselves out as possessing professional skill, etc.**—However, where persons hold themselves out to the world as possessing the peculiar skill and knowledge of a profession or occupation which requires such skill or knowledge, they will be held to the exercise thereof, though the service be rendered gratuitously, the same as if they received pay therefor.[33] If they profess to be experts, they will be so treated, and held responsible as such. Thus, a gratuitous agent who undertakes to loan money must use reasonable prudence in the selection of the security, the examination of the title to the property by which the loan is to be secured. the making of the necessary records, conveyances and documents required, etc.[34] In case of loss by a banker, it is his duty to account for the same, the burden being upon him to show that he exercised proper diligence and care in connection with the loan.[35] And so, a physician, or one who holds himself out as such, will be required to possess and exercise the skill and diligence of such profession.[36] As no definite rule can be established by which the negligence is to be measured with exactness, it follows, as observed above, that each case must be decided upon its own peculiar circumstances and requirements. Thus, in the case of gratuitous bank directors, it is held that they must exercise that care and prudence which the ordinarily prudent bank director exercises.[37] Such an agent must exercise that degree of prudence and care which a man prompted by such interest generally exercises in his own affairs.[38] And so, an agent to collect a debt, it was held in Pennsylvania, must likewise exercise that degree of prudence which an ordinarily prudent man would exercise under the circumstances; and if he takes a note payable to himself, he thereby makes himself liable to the principal for the entire debt.[39]

[33] McNevins v. Lowe, 40 Ill. 209; Shiells v. Blackburne, 1 H. Bl. 158; Landon v. Humphrey, 9 Conn. 209; Gill v. Middleton, 105 Mass. 477, 7 Am. Rep. 548; Williams v. McKay, 40 N. J. Eq. 189, 53 Am. Rep. 775; Isham v. Post, 141 N. Y. 100.

[34] Isham v. Post, *supra*.

[35] Isham v. Post, *supra*.

[36] McNevins v. Lowe, 40 Ill. 209; Landon v. Humphrey, 9 Conn. 209. One who agrees to loan money without charge and then to collect it, with interest, must use due and proper care in doing so, or he will be liable for negligence: Samonset v. Mesnager, 108 Cal. 354, 41 Pac. 337. See also, Ehmer v. Title, etc., Co., 89 Hun (N. Y.) 120, 34 N. Y. Supp. 1132.

[37] Briggs v. Spaulding, 141 U. S. 132; Swentzel v. Penn Bank, 147 Pa. St. 140.

[38] Hun v. Cary, 82 N. Y. 65.

[39] Opie v. Serrill, 6 W. & S. (Pa.) 264.

§ 234. Duty of agent to act in principal's name.—As has been shown in the preceding chapter, the agent, in order to bind his principal, should transact the business in the latter's name. He should do this so as to avoid confusion relative to the respective rights of the parties growing out of the contract into which the agent has entered for the principal. If he fail to do so, and by reason thereof the principal suffer any injury, the agent will be liable to him for damages resulting therefrom. The agent is but a medium for transferring to his principal all rights acquired by virtue of any contract he may make for the principal.[40]

§ 235. Agent must generally act in person.—The next rule is that which requires the agent to execute his authority in person. As stated and fully explained elsewhere in this work, authority that has been delegated can not, as a general rule, be redelegated.[41] The agent has been selected, perhaps, on account of the special confidence or trust of the principal in the agent, or of his peculiar skill or fitness to perform the act in question. But whether this be so or not as an actual fact, such is the presumption; and in the absence of countervailing proof, or circumstances indicating a contrary intention, he will be held responsible for any injury that results which may be traced to the fact that he did not give the business his personal attention. But if the circumstances are such as to make it appear that the principal had authorized such redelegation, even though, in fact, he had not, while the principal might by his conduct have bound himself to a third party, the agent will be responsible to the principal for such unauthorized proceeding, if any loss has been sustained by the latter. The common instances where the agent is

[40] Sullivan v. Ross, 39 Mich. 511.

[41] See *ante*, § 187. Thus, an agent employed to loan money for the principal can not employ a subagent to do the essential parts of such work; though he may appoint such subagents to assist him in the merely ministerial or unimportant details: Kohl v. Beach, 107 Wis. 409, 81 Am. St. 849; and a subagent in such a case can not legally collect the money thus loaned; and if the debtor pay such subagent the amount due on such loan, or any portion thereof, such subagent not being in possession of the note and mortgage relating to the loan, the payment of the money does not constitute a payment to the principal or payee of the note: Kohl v. Beach, *supra*. See also, Bartel v. Brown, 104 Wis. 493; Murphy v. Barnard, 162 Mass. 72, 44 Am. St. 340; Joy v. Vance, 104 Mich. 97; Wilson v. Campbell, 110 Mich. 580; Bacon v. Pomeroy, 118 Mich. 145; Dexter v. Morrow, 76 Minn. 413, 79 N. W. 394; Hollinshead v. Stuart, 8 N. Dak. 35, 77 N. W. 89.

liable to the principal for a redelegation of the authority are those in which, the appointment of the subagent being unauthorized, a loss or injury has accrued to the principal from the unskillful or negligent execution of the power on the part of such subagent. There being in such case no privity between the principal and subagent, the agent is responsible to the principal for the manner in which the business of the agency has been transacted.[42]

§ 236. **Must obey instructions and act within scope of authority.**— It is also the duty of the agent to obey the instructions of his principal, and to observe, generally, the terms of the authority under which he acts. If he disobey, or if he go beyond the scope of the authority conferred upon him, he will be liable to the principal for all damages actually sustained on account of the misfeasance. He must follow the directions given him by his principal; and this he must do in good faith and not merely in a perfunctory manner.[43] Thus, where an agent is directed to forward to a person named a claim for collection, and he forwards it to another, he is liable for any loss that results from such disobedience.[44] And an agent who failed to return promptly a draft upon nonpayment, as instructed to do, was held liable for the amount of the draft.[45] So, where the agent's instructions required him to accept in payment nothing but "undoubted paper" or "first-class collectible paper," and he made no effort to ascertain the solvency of the parties, or took paper which he knew to be worthless, he was held chargeable with any loss that might occur, or he might be held as a guarantor.[46] And an agent instructed to remit money by express, but who remits by draft, is liable for the loss if the drawers afterward become insolvent beforé payment.[47] If instructed to remit by draft and he remits by letter, he does

[42] Barnard v. Coffin, 141 Mass. 37, 55 Am. Rep. 443; Loomis, etc., Co. v. Simpson, 13 Iowa 532; Ledoux v. Goza, 4 La. Ann. 160; Sexton v. Weaver, 141 Mass. 273; Exchange Nat'l Bank v. Third Nat'l Bank, 112 U. S. 276.

[43] Loeb v. Hellman, 45 N. Y. Super. 336; Sawyer v. Mayhew, 51 Me. 398; Scott v. Rogers, 31 N. Y. 676; Holbrook v. McCarthy, 61 Cal. 216; Amory v. Hamilton, 17 Mass. 103; Laverty v. Snethen, 68 N. Y. 522, 23 Am. Rep. 184; Whitney v. Merchants' Union Express Co., 104 Mass. 152, 6 Am. Rep. 207; Butts v. Phelps, 79 Mo. 302; United States Mortgage Co. v. Henderson, 111 Ind. 24.

[44] Butts v. Phelps, 79 Mo. 302.

[45] Fahy v. Fargo, 17 N. Y. Supp. 344, 61 Hun (N. Y.) 623.

[46] Osborne v. Rider, 62 Wis. 235; Clark v. Roberts, 26 Mich. 506.

[47] Walker v. Walker, 5 Heisk. (Tenn.) 425.

so at his peril.[48] He must strictly follow the methods of remitting which he is instructed to pursue; otherwise he acts at his own risk and peril.[49] But an agent is only required to use ordinary and reasonable care and diligence in making remittances to his principal, unless he has received instructions to remit in a certain way; and when not so instructed specially, he may remit by mail; as there is no rule of law that a postoffice is a less safe or appropriate means of conveyance than a private carrier or banker.[50] An insurance agent who was directed by his company to cancel a policy of insurance, but, without sufficient reason, delayed doing so for several days, during which time the property insured was destroyed by fire, and the company suffered loss, was held liable to the company for the loss.[51] And an agent who is instructed to sell for cash only will be liable for any loss occurring if he sell on credit, or accept a check in payment, should the drawer become insolvent before presentation and payment.[52] In all such cases the agent will be protected if he obey the instructions of his principal; but it is no defense for him to say that he used proper care and prudence in performing the duty intrusted to him, if he failed to follow his principal's directions: he can not exercise discretion or choice of means when they are pointed out to him by his instructions. Whether the motive of the agent is good or bad is entirely immaterial: he may believe, in good faith, that his methods are the best, but this will not excuse him.[53]

§ 237. **Principal's remedies against agent for violating instructions.**—It sometimes becomes important to know in what kind of an action the agent is liable to his principal for the consequences of his disobeying instructions. This, of course, depends upon the nature of the wrong done to the principal. Generally speaking, the action is upon the contract of agency; but he may be liable in tort, in an action on the case; or in trover for the conversion of the goods of the principal, if there has been a conversion. Trover is a proper remedy if the agent does such acts as in law amount to a conversion or appropriation of the property to himself.[54] In *Laverty* v.

[48] Foster v. Preston, 8 Cow. (N. Y.) 198.

[49] Kerr v. Cotton, 23 Tex. 411.

[50] Buell v. Chapin, 99 Mass. 594, 97 Am. Dec. 58.

[51] Phœnix Ins. Co. v. Frissell, 142 Mass. 513.

[52] Hall v. Storrs, 7 Wis. 217; Harlan v. Ely, 68 Cal. 522.

[53] Laverty v. Snethen, 68 N. Y. 522, 23 Am. Rep. 184.

[54] Farrand v. Hurlbut, 7 Minn. 477; McMorris v. Simpson, 21 Wend. (N. Y.) 610; Wells v. Collins, 74 Wis.

Snethen,[55] the agent disposed of the principal's goods contrary to his instructions, and the court held that he was liable for the resulting loss in an action of trover as for a conversion. But where the agent is guilty of a mere breach of duty in violating his instructions,—as, where he is instructed to sell for a certain price, but sells for less,—the remedy is an action on the case for damages.[56]

§ 238. When agent may deviate from instructions—Ambiguous instructions.—It is to be observed that there may be instances of unforeseen emergency when an agent will be justified in deviating from his instructions; unless, indeed, such emergency is attributable to the agent's own default.[57] Thus, as pointed out in a preceding portion of this work,[58] the master of a ship may, in cases of instant necessity, acquire an authority over the ship, and even the cargo, which he does not ordinarily possess; as, in case of a jettison becoming necessary on the voyage, when he may order any or all of such cargo thrown overboard.[59] And so, a factor or other agent having the control of perishable goods may, in cases of extraordinary emergency, sell the goods contrary to his instructions, so as to prevent a total or greater loss.[60] In these and kindred instances, the agent becomes, *ex necessitate,* excused from the strict performance of the duties devolving upon him, owing to the impossibility of communicating with his principal concerning the emergency; and the rule of the particular agency is, for the time being, suspended by a special contract created by the law.[61] It is proper to observe, moreover, that substantial compliance with his instructions is all that the law requires of an agent; and a mere circumstantial departure, which does not materially affect the result, will not involve the agent in damages of a substantial nature.[62] The burden of proof in such cases is, however, upon the agent to show that no material injury resulted from the deviation from instructions; as the presumption is always against him

341; Bostwick v. Dry Goods Bank, 67 Barb. (N. Y.) 449; McNear v. Atwood, 17 Me. 434; McCrillis v. Allen, 57 Vt. 505; Lindley v. Downing, 2 Ind. 418.

[55] 68 N. Y. 522, 23 Am. Rep. 184.

[56] McDermid v. Cotton, 2 Ill. App. 297; Sarjeant v. Blunt, 16 Johns. (N. Y.) 74.

[57] Evans Pr. & Ag. (Bedford's ed.) 253-254; Harter v. Blanchard, 64 Barb. (N. Y.) 617; Dusar v. Perit, 4 Binn. (Pa.) 361.

[58] *Ante,* § 87.

[59] Story Ag., § 118.

[60] Story Ag., § 141.

[61] Evans Pr. & Ag. (Bedford's ed.) 254.

[62] Parker v. Kett, 1 Salk. 95; Huntley v. Mathias, 90 N. C. 101, 47 Am. Rep. 516.

in such case.[63] When the agent's instructions are ambiguous,—that is to say, when they are susceptible of two or more constructions, and the agent construes them in one of these ways,—the principal can not recover damages of the agent if the latter has pursued the directions, in good faith, according to his own construction. The principal had it in his power to make the directions clear and specific, and he can not be heard to say that he meant a construction different from that placed upon it by the agent.[64]

§ 239. **Agent's duty to observe good faith.**—It is also the duty of the agent to act in the utmost good faith in executing the authority of his principal.[65] The agent's position being one of trust and confidence, he must pursue his principal's directions and do everything necessary and conducive to fairness and honest dealing between himself and his principal. He can not speculate on the property of the latter, nor take advantage of his position to profit by the relation[66] beyond the legitimate profits or income derived from the relation, and with the full knowledge of his principal. And if any knowledge or information come to the agent which the interest of the principal may require that he should know, the agent will be liable in such damages as the principal may sustain from the agent's failure to

[63] Milbank v. Dennistoun, 21 N. Y. 386; Greenleaf v. Moody, 13 Allen (Mass.) 363.

[64] Ireland v. Livingston, L. R. 5 H. L. 395; Shelton v. Merchants', etc., Co., 59 N. Y. 258; Minnesota Linseed Oil Co. v. Montague, 65 Iowa 67.

[65] Evans Pr. & Ag. (Bedford's ed.) 255.

[66] Sterling v. Smith, 97 Cal. 343, 32 Pac. 320. In this case the court quotes approvingly the following extract from Pomeroy's Equity Jurisprudence, § 959: "Equity regards and treats this relation in the same general manner, and with nearly the same strictness, as that of the trustee and beneficiary. The underlying thought is, that an agent should not unite his personal and his representative characters in the same transaction; and equity will not permit him to be exposed to the temptation, or brought into a situation where his own personal interests conflict with the interests of his principal. In dealings without the intervention of his principal, if an agent, for the purpose of selling property of the principal, purchases it himself, or an agent for the purpose of buying property for the principal buys it from himself, either directly or through the instrumentality of a third person, the sale or purchase is voidable; it will always be set aside at the option of the principal; the amount of consideration, the absence of undue advantage, and other similar features are wholly immaterial; nothing will defeat the principal's right of remedy, except his own confirmation after full knowledge of all the facts."

impart to him such knowledge or information.[67] In the transaction of his principal's business, the interest of the agent is the interest of the principal,—he can have no other; and he must perform the duties intrusted to him with the strictest fidelity, with that end in view. Thus, one can not legally purchase property on his own account which his duty or trust requires him to sell on account of another, nor purchase on account of another that which he sells on his own account. The two interests are antagonistic, and he can not unite them both in one.[68] Neither can an agent, as a general rule, act for two principals who have an adverse interest in the same matter, unless he have the consent of both.[69] If any advantage accrues from the business in which he is engaged, it inures to the benefit of the principal, and not to that of the agent, and he can not use the authority conferred upon him to further his own pecuniary interest in any manner.[70] It makes no difference whether his motive be good or evil in such matters. Good faith does not mean simply an honest intention; it means that all of the agent's acts in furtherance of the business intrusted to him shall be in the principal's interest and for his benefit, and that the results shall inure to the latter's benefit. Public policy forbids that one acting as the trustee of another should be permitted to enrich himself out of the proceeds of the trust, even though there be no loss to the principal; and in no case will the law protect an agent in transactions out of which he may derive a personal advantage.[71] The law will not tolerate that an agent shall place himself in a position where there are such abundant opportunities to profit by his wrongs. Though the agent may have the best of intentions, the evil tendencies still remain, and these the law will not in any manner encourage.[72]

§ **240. Resulting trust in favor of principal—Statute of frauds.**— If the agent fails to perform a duty imposed upon him by his trust,

[67] Devall v. Burbridge, 4 W. & S. (Pa.) 305; Hegenmyer v. Marks, 37 Minn. 6.

[68] Michoud v. Girod, 4 How. (U. S.) 503.

[69] Walker v. Osgood, 98 Mass. 348; Meyer v. Hanchett, 39 Wis. 419; Raisin v. Clark, 41 Md. 158. Nor can he act for the principal in the same transaction in two inconsistent capacities,—one favorable to his wishes and interest, and the other hostile to them: Pittsburgh, etc., Iron Co. v. Kirkpatrick, 92 Mich. 252.

[70] Bunker v. Miles, 30 Me. 431.

[71] Michoud v. Girod, 4 How. (U. S.) 503.

[72] Taussig v. Hart, 58 N. Y. 425; Florance v. Adams, 2 Rob. (La.) 556, 38 Am. Dec. 226; Ely v. Hanford, 65 Ill. 267.

he can not profit by such remissness. Thus, where a principal has intrusted money to an agent with which to pay the taxes on the principal's property, and the agent neglects to do so, the latter can not purchase the property at a tax sale and hold the title in his own name, but in such case he will be held to be a trustee for the principal.[73] And so, where an agent, in violation of his trust, uses the money of his principal intrusted to him for any purpose, and invests it in property, the law creates a trust in favor of the principal. In such a case, even a purchaser from the agent who is either a volunteer or a fraudulent grantee will be liable to a suit in equity to have such property subjected to the principal's claim.[74] And where a husband had money intrusted to him by his wife, out of her separate means, with which to purchase land for her, and in the performance of the trust he did purchase lands with such money, but took the title in his own name, it was held that a trust resulted in favor of the wife that would be enforced in equity.[75] Neither is it material that the principal has not been damnified by such transactions. "Actual injury is not the principle the law proceeds on in holding such transactions void. Fidelity in the agent is what is aimed at; and as a means of securing it, the law will not permit the agent to place himself in a situation in which he may be tempted by his own private interests to disregard those of his principal."[76] But a trust in land will not always be decreed in favor of the principal simply because the agent took the title to the property in his own name, when commissioned to purchase for the principal. To satisfy the statute of frauds in such case, the evidence of the purchaser must either be in writing, or the property must have been paid for with the principal's money.[77]

[73] Barton v. Moss, 32 Ill. 51. Where an agent purchased land for his principal and represented to him that it cost more than it really did, the agent thereby making a profit off of his principal, the court held that it was a breach of good faith for which the agent would be liable to the principal to the extent of the profit so received by him: Rorebeck v. Van Eaton, 90 Iowa 82, 57 N. W. 694. To the same effect, see Duryea v. Vosburgh, 138 N. Y. 621. And so, it was held to be bad faith for an agent to buy hay for his principal, and with his principal's money, and then sell it to another than the principal, at a profit, in order to obtain a larger commission for making a profit out of it: Rundell v. Kalbfus, 125 Pa. St. 123.

[74] Riehl v. Evansville, etc., Ass'n, 104 Ind. 70.

[75] Goldsberry v. Gentry, 92 Ind. 193.

[76] People v. Township Board, 11 Mich. 222.

[77] Burden v. Sheridan, 36 Iowa 125, 14 Am. Rep. 505; Kendall v. Mann, 11 Allen (Mass.) 15.

Where a part of the purchase-money is paid by the principal, and there is no written agreement, the principal can not compel a conveyance of the title to himself.[78] But where even a portion of the purchase-money has been paid by the principal, and the whole title is taken by the agent, a resulting trust *pro tanto* may under some circumstances be created.[79] Whether the money was in fact paid by the principal in person or not is immaterial: if his money was used in the purchase, it is sufficient;[80] but this fact must be made to appear clearly.[81]

§ 241. **Want of good faith is fraud upon principal.**—"It may be correctly said, with reference to Christian morals," says Story, "that no man can faithfully serve two masters whose interests are in conflict."[82] The principal reposes confidence in the agent that he will act with sole regard to the interests of the principal as far as he lawfully may. He does not bargain for impartiality, even if such could be conceived to exist on the part of the agent where the agent's interests are concerned. Impartiality may frequently be the last thing he would want. Thus, a seller of property must be presumed to desire the highest price he can fairly obtain therefor; while the purchaser must be presumed to desire to buy it as low as possible.[83] What the principal naturally demands of the agent in such case is to assist him in obtaining that which he most desires, and not to act impartially between him and the third party. Good faith requires that the agent should at all times act with a view to the benefit and advantage of the principal, and not of himself. A departure from this fundamental rule will be regarded as a fraud upon the rights of the principal; and the latter may, as between himself and the agent, always have the transaction set aside, or sue the agent for damages in case that is not practicable.[84] According to this rule, an agent will not be permitted to assume an attitude of antagonism to his principal, nor perform any acts or discharge any duties incompatible

[78] Sugden Vendors (14th ed.) 703.

[79] McGowan v. McGowan, 14 Gray (Mass.) 119.

[80] Page v. Page, 8 N. H. 187.

[81] Davis v. Wetherell, 11 Allen (Mass.) 19, note.

[82] Story Ag., § 210.

[83] *Ibid.*

[84] Lamb v. Evans, 2 Rep. 189, L. R. (1893) 1 Ch. 218; Keighler v. Savage Mfg. Co., 12 Md. 383, 71 Am. Dec. 600; Young v. Hughes, 32 N. J. Eq. 372; Persch v. Quiggle, 57 Pa. St. 247; Moore v. Moore, 5 N. Y. 256; Sterling v. Smith, 97 Cal. 343; Palmer v. Pirson, 24 N. Y. Supp. 333; Hammond v. Bookwalter, 12 Ind. App. 177.

with those implied in his agency.[85] All dealings between him and his principal will be closely scrutinized; and this is especially true of a fiduciary, who is in a position to take undue advantage of those for whom he is acting, or to overreach them. In all such cases nothing but the highest good faith will excuse the agent. Thus, if by unfair means he has exchanged his own land for that of his principal of greater value, he is liable for such damages as the principal has sustained.[86]

§ 242. **Skill required of agent—Members of learned professions.**—The agent is furthermore required to possess and exercise reasonable skill in the execution of his powers. If he is not possessed of the skill and capability that he holds himself out as possessing, or if he possesses and does not exercise such skill, he violates his obligation to his principal, and is guilty of such negligence as will render him liable to the latter. What is the degree of skill an agent is required to possess is a question not always easy to answer. The skill required is not necessarily the highest class, but it is reasonable skill under the circumstances: it is the skill which men engaged in the same profession, occupation, or business usually exercise. One who holds himself out as possessing the peculiar skill and ability of a profession, business, or calling of any kind is required to possess and exercise such skill as those engaged in such profession, etc., ordinarily possess and exercise.[87] "Every person who enters into a learned profession," says Chief Justice Tindal, "undertakes to bring to the exercise of it a reasonable, fair and competent degree of skill."[88] Says Story, in regard to bailments: "In all cases where skill is required, it is to be understood that it means ordinary skill in the business or employment which the bailee undertakes; for he is not presumed to engage for extraordinary skill, which belongs to a few men only, in his business or employment, or for extraordinary endowments or acquirements. Reasonable skill constitutes the measure

[85] Hughes v. Washington, 72 Ill. 84; Knabe v. Ternot, 16 La. Ann. 13; Pittsburgh, etc., Iron Co. v. Kirkpatrick, 92 Mich. 252.

[86] Palmer v. Pirson, 24 N. Y. Supp. 333; Brooke v. Berry, 2 Gill (Md.) 83; Rubidoex v. Parks, 48 Cal. 215. "A confidential relation gives cause of suspicion, and the circumstances under which a deed is made during such a relation must be closely scanned; and if a reasonable suspicion exists that confidence has been abused where reposed, the deed should be set aside:" Uhlich v. Muhlke, 61 Ill. 499, per Breese, C. J.

[87] McNevins v. Lowe, 40 Ill. 209.

[88] Lanphier v. Phipos, 8 C. & P. 475.

of the engagement, in regard to the thing undertaken."[89] This is doubtless the common-law doctrine as applicable to the ordinary practitioner in the professions of medicine and law. But just what is meant by "ordinary" or "reasonable skill" is not always clear. It must be true that the standard can not always be the same.[90] In large cities and thickly settled older communities, where the facilities are far greater for acquiring knowledge and carrying it into execution, there is always found a much larger number of practitioners of a very high degree of skill and knowledge, and they impliedly contract to do more than the ordinary members of the profession who are not so pretentious. In smaller towns and in sparsely settled or new communities, where the opportunities are not so great as those enjoyed in the metropolitan places, the members of the profession can not be expected to exercise that high degree of skill and practical knowledge possessed by those having greater opportunities and facilities.[91] The standard of skill ordinarily applied to physicians and surgeons is that degree of knowledge and science which the leading authorities have pronounced as the result of their researches and experiences up to the time or within a reasonable time before the question to be determined arose.[92] As to the degree of skill and knowledge required of attorneys at law or legal practitioners of various kinds, the requirement is the same in England as in America. The rule as to such a practitioner is thus stated by Tindal, C. J.: "He is liable for the consequences of ignorance, for unobservance of the rules of practice of the courts, for want of care in the preparation of the cause for trial, or of attendance thereon with his witnesses, and for the mismanagement of so much of the conduct of a cause as is usually and ordinarily allotted to his department of the profession; whilst, on the other hand, he is not answerable for error in judgment

[89] Story Bailm., § 433.

[90] Bishop Non Contr. Law, § 439; Cooley Torts (2d ed.) 794. "What is ordinary care in some cases would be gross carelessness in others. The law regards the circumstances surrounding each case. . . . Greater care is required to be taken of a stallion than of a mare; so, in the management of a steam engine, greater care is necessary than in the use of a plow. Yet it is all ordinary care; such care as a prudent, careful man would take under like circumstances. The degree of care is always in proportion to the danger to be apprehended." Meredith v. Reed, 26 Ind. 334, 336. See also, 1 Thompson Neg. (2d ed.), §§ 18-26.

[91] Pitt v. Yalden, 4 Burr. 2060; Laidler v. Elliott, 3 B. & C. 738; Varnum v. Martin, 15 Pick. (Mass.) 440; Crooker v. Hutchinson, 1 Vt. 73; Holmes v. Peck, 1 R. I. 242; 2 Greenl. Ev. 120.

[92] Elwell Malpr. 55.

upon points of new occurrence, or of nice or doubtful construction."[93] Negligence on the part of a practicing attorney is always redressible in damages. What is negligence in such a case is not always easy to determine, however. The adjudicated cases are to the effect that an attorney must exercise ordinary skill and care in managing the business of his client.[94] Thus, it is held that he is liable for losing valuable papers, such as a deed, when injury results;[95] and for negligence in collecting a debt, if there is a loss to the client.[96] It is said that one who holds himself out as a practitioner of one of the learned professions, by implication warrants his possession of the ordinary and reasonable skill required in the particular case.[97] Thus, it is required of a physician and surgeon that he possess and exercise the average degree of skill and care possessed and exercised by members of his profession practicing in the same vicinity.[98] But if the patient is also guilty of negligence contributing to the injury, he can not recover.[99] This rule does not apply, however, where the party who employs the agent has knowledge of the want of skill of such person; for in such case he can not be presumed to have relied upon such warranty; and if a principal deems it proper to employ such an agent, he can blame no one but himself.[99a]

[93] Godefroy v. Dalton, 6 Bing. 460.

[94] Humboldt Bld'g Ass'n Co. v. Ducker (Ky.), 64 S. W. 671.

[95] Reeve v. Palmer, 5 C. B. (N. S.) 84.

[96] Wilson v. Coffin, 2 Cush. (Mass.) 316. See also, as to attorneys, Varnum v. Martin, 15 Pick. (Mass.) 440; Marsh v. Whitmore, 21 Wall. (U. S.) 178.

[97] Wilson v. Brett, 11 M. & W. 113; Leighton v. Sargent, 27 N. H. 460, 59 Am. Dec. 388; Howard v. Grover, 28 Me. 97, 48 Am. Dec. 478. An attorney at law is required to possess to a reasonable extent the knowledge and skill requisite to a proper performance of the duties of his profession, and is liable for injuries to the client resulting as a proximate consequence from the lack of such knowledge or skill or the failure to exercise the same, but is not liable for mere errors or mistakes: Malone v. Gerth, 100 Wis. 166, 75 N. W. 972. See also, Humboldt Bldg. Ass'n Co. v. Ducker (Ky.), 64 S. W. 671.

[98] Kelsey v. Hay, 84 Ind. 189; Becknell v. Hosier, 10 Ind. App. 5.

[99] Young v. Mason, 8 Ind. App. 264; Lower v. Franks, 115 Ind. 334. The law does not require of a surgeon the utmost degree of skill and care, but he is required to possess and exercise that degree of knowledge, skill and care ordinarily possessed and exercised by members of his profession: Van Skike v. Potter, 53 Neb. 28, 73 N. W. 295. The requirement for the qualifications relates to the time of his practice and not to times prior thereto: McCracken v. Smathers, 122 N. C. 799, 29 S. E. 354.

[99a] Felt v. School District, 24 Vt. 297.

§ 243. **Agent must exercise due care and diligence.**—According to the rule enunciated in the last section, the agent must not only possess the requisite skill and knowledge, but he must use a degree of care and diligence commensurate with the situation. It is not sufficient that he should know what and what not to do, but he must do that which is reasonably necessary, and refrain from doing what is apparently detrimental and injurious.[100] Hence, an agent whose duty it is to bring suit or take an appeal in order to have redress from illegal assessments or duties, is liable in an action for damages if he allows the time to go by within which suit could be brought to recover the illegal assessments.[101] And an agent who is employed to keep a highway in repair is liable to the town for any damages sustained by it by having to pay for an injury to one who was injured by reason of the negligence of the agent in making such repair.[102] Banks, brokers, and collecting agents are liable for negligence in the exercise of the business of their respective agencies. So, a bank is liable if it accepts depreciated currency in payment of a collection;[103] or fails promptly to present a draft for payment, if injury results.[104] And so, a loan agent is liable for accepting insufficient security.[105] The agent is not, however, an insurer, and is only required to use ordinary care in placing the loan on what reasonably appears to be adequate security.[106] When an agent undertakes to loan money for his principal on first mortgage security, it is his duty to have an abstract of title prepared or to have the title of the property examined before he places the loan, or otherwise to ascertain the condition of the property as to incumbrances, or he will be guilty of actionable negligence.[107] And an agent who undertakes to loan money has no right to use it himself and pay the principal with the note of a third party, given for another consideration, without the principal's agreement to that effect.[108] So, a factor whose duty it was to collect cotton for his principal was held liable for failure to do so, for the value of the cotton, with interest.[109]

[100] Long v. Morrison, 14 Ind. 595.

[101] Bowerman v. Rogers, 125 U. S. 585.

[102] Wilson v. Greensboro, 54 Vt. 533.

[103] Waterhouse v. Citizens' Bank, 25 La. Ann. 77.

[104] Meadville First Nat'l Bank v. Fourth Nat'l Bank, 77 N. Y. 320.

[105] Bank of Owensboro v. Western Bank, 13 Bush (Ky.) 526, 26 Am. Rep. 211; Bronnenburg v. Rinker, 2 Ind. App. 391; Welsh v. Brown, 8 Ind. App. 421.

[106] Kennedy v. McCain, 146 Pa. St. 63.

[107] Hardwick v. Ickler, 71 Minn. 25, 73 N. W. 519.

[108] Scott v. Turley, 9 Lea (Tenn.) 631.

[109] Dickson v. Screven, 23 S. C. 212.

A collecting agent who fails to use due care in pressing the claim, making the collection, and remitting the proceeds, is liable for a loss of any or all of the debt through his negligence.[110] He is, however, required to use ordinary care and diligence only.[111] When an agent has a note for collection, he should at once make a demand of the debtor at the proper place, and if payment is refused, give immediate notice to the principal in order that the latter may take the necessary steps for his security.[112] And if the collection be a bill of exchange, payable at a certain day and place, the agent is held to a strict vigilance in making presentation of the bill for acceptance.[113] The burden of proof in such cases is on the principal to show negligence on the part of the agent.[114] But where a confidential agent or one occupying a fiduciary relation to the principal has purchased property of the latter, the burden is on such agent or person to show that the bargain was fair and equitable and that there was no suppression or concealment of facts which might have influenced the principal's conduct.[115] As to the kind of payment a collecting agent may receive, it is generally held that he may take only lawful money, or such as is generally received by prudent business men for similar purposes.[116] If the agent accepts a draft or check in payment, the latter is valid if the drawer has money in bank to cover the amount represented by it. In such case, the principal is bound by the payment and can not fall back upon the debtor to collect again.[117] As a general rule, however, an agent or officer can accept in payment money only.[118] And where an agent accepted Confederate treasury notes, without showing any necessity therefor, or without making any effort to dispose of them to the best advantage, he was compelled to bear the loss.[119] The same rule as to diligence applies to agents employed to sell property: they are required not only to make reasonable efforts to effect a sale, but they must use due diligence to secure a fair price.[120] But

[110] Mechanics' Bank v. Merchants' Bank, 6 Metc. (Mass.) 13, 26; Reed v. Northrup, 50 Mich. 442.

[111] Lawrence v. McCalmont, 2 How. (U. S.) 426.

[112] Bank of Mobile v. Huggins, 3 Ala. 206.

[113] Allen v. Suydam, 20 Wend. (N. Y.) 321, 32 Am. Dec. 555.

[114] Rand v. Johns (Tex. App.), 15 S. W. 200.

[115] Rochester v. Levering, 104 Ind. 562.

[116] Baird v. Hall, 67 N. C. 230.

[117] Indiana Bond Co. v. Bruce, 13 Ind. App. 550.

[118] Armsworth v. Scotten, 29 Ind. 495.

[119] Webster v. Whitworth, 49 Ala. 201.

[120] Montgomery v. Pacific Coast Land Bureau, 94 Cal. 284; Bigelow

the agent can only be required to act fairly and use his best judgment under all the circumstances.[121] It is a difficult matter to find illustrative cases for every variety of negligence. It has been held that no greater diligence is required of an agent than would have been exercised under similar circumstances by his principal.[122] And wherever the matter in question has been left to the agent's discretion, he can not be held responsible for a mere error of judgment.[123] In all such cases he is liable only for the actual loss sustained by reason of his negligence.[124] As to the form of action that may be maintained against the agent by the principal, it may be stated that the usual remedy for negligence in such cases is either *assumpsit* on the contract,[125] or an action on the case for tort.[126] The action of trover may also lie, but not unless there has been a conversion by the agent of money or property of the principal, either actual or constructive.[127] The requirements as to the exercise of proper care and diligence apply with peculiar force to agents who occupy a fiduciary relation; such as executors, administrators, guardians, etc.[128]

v. Walker, 24 Vt. 149, 58 Am. Dec. 156.

[121] Betts v. Planters', etc., Bank, 3 Stew. (Ala.) 18; James v. Borgeois, 4 Baxt. (Tenn.) 345.

[122] Blight v. Ashley, 1 Pet. (C. C.) 15.

[123] Page v. Wells, 37 Mich. 415; Steele v. Taylor, 4 Dana (Ky.) 445.

[124] Ryder v. Thayer, 3 La. Ann. 149.

[125] Washington v. Eames, 6 Allen (Mass.) 417; Greentree v. Rosenstock, 61 N. Y. 583; Paul v. Grimm, 165 Pa. St. 139.

[126] McMorris v. Simpson, 21 Wend. (N. Y.) 610.

[127] McMorris v. Simpson, *supra*. "The most usual remedies of a principal against his agent," said Bronson, J., speaking for the supreme court of New York in this case, "are the action of *assumpsit* and special action on the case; but there can be no doubt that trover will sometimes be an appropriate remedy. That action may be maintained whenever the agent has wrongfully converted the property of his principal to his own use, and the fact of conversion may be made out by showing either a demand and refusal or that the agent has, without necessity, sold or otherwise disposed of the property contrary to his instructions. When an agent wrongfully refuses to surrender the goods of his principal or wholly departs from his authority in disposing of them, he makes the property his own, and may be treated as a tort-feasor."

[128] Executors, administrators, and other trustees are generally held to the requirement of exercising ordinary care in managing the trust confided to them. Thus, an administrator or executor must adopt such precautions against loss by fire as ordinarily prudent men are accustomed to exercise under similar circumstances against casualties: Rubottom v. Morrow, 24 Ind. 202, 87 Am. Dec. 324. He is liable for whatever of the assets in his hands may

§ 244. **In what matters agent must keep principal advised.**—The next duty of an agent to his principal that we shall consider is that of making full disclosure of all matters that come to his knowledge pertaining to the subject-matter of the agency. What has been said as to the agent's duty to act in good faith applies in a large measure to this subject also. An agent, whatever his class may be, must deal fairly and openly with his principal. Under no circumstances is he permitted to overreach him by withholding information which might, if given, lead the principal, who has placed confidence in him, to regard the transaction in a different light from that in which he does view it. "Whenever two persons stand in such relation that while it continues confidence is abused, or the influence is exerted to obtain an advantage at the expense of the confiding party, the party so availing himself of his position will not be permitted to retain the advantage, although the transaction could not have been impeached if no such confidential relation had existed."[129] Whenever the point is reached, in the relation between the two, that the agent's duty and his interest come in conflict, the agent can with propriety adopt but one of two courses: he must either sever the relation between him and his principal, or yield implicitly to the demands of duty, making a full disclosure. As heretofore stated, he is not permitted, in any case, to make a secret profit out of his dealings as agent. Hence, he can neither sell to the principal for a higher price than he gave, nor purchase of him at a lower price than the full value; and in all such transactions the court will scrutinize with the utmost vigilance the conduct of the agent. "Where the known and defined relation exists, the conduct of the party benefited must be such as to sever the connection and to place him in the same circumstances in which a mere stranger would have stood, giving him no advantage, save only whatever kindness or favor may have arisen out of the transaction. Where,

be lost through his negligence or mismanagement; and the fact that they were lost will be no excuse if such loss was occasioned by his own default: Vreeland v. Schoonmaker, 16 N. J. Eq. 512; Harris v. Parker, 41 Ala. 604; Succession of Stone, 31 La. Ann. 311; Lindsley v. Dodd, 53 N. J. Eq. 69. Good faith and ordinary care, however, are all that are required of him,—he is not an insurer: McCabe v. Fowler, 84 N. Y. 314; Deberry v. Ivey, 55 N. C. 370; Nelson v. Hall, 58 N. C. 32; In re Calhoun's Estate, 6 Watts (Pa.) 185; State v. Meagher, 44 Mo. 356, 100 Am. Dec. 298. If, however, he retains money after the law requires him to distribute it, he is liable for it if stolen: Black v. Hurlbut, 73 Wis. 126.

[129] Evans Pr. & Ag. (Bedford's ed.) 256.

on the other hand, the only known relation between the parties is that of friendly habits or habitual reliance on advice and assistance, accompanied with partial employment in doing some sort of business, care must be taken that no undue advantage shall be made of the influence thus acquired."[130] A principal may, in a proper case, indeed, waive the protection which the law affords him as such, and he may deal with the agent as if the relation did not exist; but in order that the agent may be justified in relying upon such waiver, he must show to the satisfaction of the court or jury that the principal had been fully apprised of the facts. Thus, an agent employed to sell will not be allowed to become purchaser unless he make known to his principal that he intends to become such and obtain his consent; and if he purchase without such knowledge and consent, he will become a trustee of such property for the benefit of the principal.[131] Nor can an agent represent two parties having adverse interests in a transaction; and if he does, his acts in that behalf may be avoided by either principal.[132] But when he is acting for both principals with their consent, or when each principal knows that the agent is also acting for the other, and does not object, it has been held that the agent may properly act for both.[133] Hence, if the agent would act in conformity with his obligations in such cases, he must inform both parties for whom he purposes to act and obtain their consent; to conceal the fact that he is acting in the double capacity of agent for both parties would be a fraud upon both.[134] The rule under discussion is intimately related to, if not identified with, the one that he must act with fidelity to his principal or employer. He can not serve two masters, whose interests are adverse, at the same time: each relies or is presumed to rely upon his judgment and discretion; and when their

[130] Evans Pr. & Ag. (Bedford's ed.) 256.

[131] Story Ag., § 211; Audenreid v. Walker, 11 Phil. (Pa.) 183; Bain v. Brown, 56 N. Y. 285.

[132] Story Ag., § 31.

[133] Alexander v. Northwestern Christian Univ., 57 Ind. 466; Rowe v. Stevens, 53 N. Y. 621; Cox v. Haun, 127 Ind. 325; Helmer v. Krolick, 36 Mich. 371. It is not in every case, however, that the agent is forbidden to act for two principals to the same transaction. If their interests do not conflict, and loyalty to the one is not a breach of duty to the other, the maxim that "no man shall serve two masters" does not apply: Nolte v. Hulbert, 37 Ohio St. 445. And in Fitzsimmons v. Southern Express Co., 40 Ga. 330, 2 Am. Rep. 577, the court ruled that if a principal employs the agent knowing that he is also acting for another, who is adversely interested, he is estopped from pleading the agent's adverse employment.

[134] Story Ag., § 31.

interests are antagonistic he can not faithfully discharge his duty to each.[135] This rule is particularly applicable to brokers. The rule is founded upon public policy. It is immaterial that the transaction was a fair one.[136] Nor is it any excuse that it is the custom of brokers to do business in this manner, as such a custom would be invalid as against public policy.[137] But if the broker simply acts as a middleman between the purchaser and seller, to bring them together, taking no part in the negotiations between them, the rule does not apply, and it is immaterial whether each party had knowledge of the employment by the other or not.[138] The doctrine is, however, not confined to brokers; the law never tolerates double dealing by agents of any class; courts of equity will always severely scrutinize a transaction in which the agent has not dealt openly and fairly with his principal, and will relieve the latter of the consequences if timely application be made. If the agent wishes to escape the avoidance of such dealings, he must make full disclosure of the facts involved and must act in perfect good faith. When he does this, there is no reason why he may not deal with a competent principal the same as any other person may deal with him.[139] When the relation of guardian and ward subsists, the guardian who contracts with the ward will take the burden of showing that he dealt fairly and took no advantage from the contract.[140] But whether the trustee be a guardian, executor, or administrator, a surviving partner, or any party whatever standing in a fiduciary relation to the other party, the law will not tolerate that he deal with him upon an unequal footing. "Such transactions," as was said by an able judge, "are poisonous in their tendencies, and violative of the principles of public policy. They are declared void, not for the purpose of affording a remedy against actual mischief, but to prevent the possibility of wrong."[141] As to the matters of which the agent should give notice to the principal, it may be stated that it is his duty to keep the principal advised not only as

[135] Farmsworth v. Hemmer, 1 Allen (Mass.) 494; Scribner v. Collar, 40 Mich. 375.

[136] Cannell v. Smith, 142 Pa. St. 25; Scribner v. Collar, *supra*.

[137] Farmsworth v. Hemmer, *supra*.

[138] Cox v. Haun, 127 Ind. 325; Green v. Robertson, 64 Cal. 75; Rupp v. Sampson, 16 Gray (Mass.) 398, 77 Am. Dec. 416; Knauss v. Krueger Brewing Co., 142 N. Y. 70.

[139] Rochester v. Levering, 104 Ind. 562.

[140] Wainwright v. Smith, 106 Ind. 239.

[141] Mitchell, J., in Valentine v. Wysor, 123 Ind. 47.

to those in which the agent has an adverse interest, but of everything in connection with the agency which pertains to the interest of the principal and of which he should be apprised, so that he be enabled to take such steps as he may deem necessary to protect himself.[142] Thus, if the agent has undertaken to insure property and has failed to do so, he should notify the principal.[143] And if he has taken a note in payment of goods sold by him, and the note is not paid at maturity, it is his duty to inform the principal.[144] If his commission be to sell land for a certain price, he should inform the principal of any rise in the market price thereof; and a sale without such notice upon the basis of the old price, without informing the principal, is a fraud upon the latter.[145]

§ **245. Duty of agent to keep and render account.**—Another duty devolving upon an agent by reason of the relation is to keep and render to his principal an account of all receipts and disbursements.[146] The matters to be accounted for include not only the money and property received from the principal directly, but all assets, profits and interests that come into the agent's hands in the course and as a result of the agency.[147] The agent may be required to keep accounts by his contract, but it is his duty to do so whether this is true or not. When the circumstances admit of it, he should keep regular book accounts of his receipts and disbursements, preserving all vouchers and papers that cast any light upon his dealings.[148] Of course, it is not required in all cases of agency that book accounts be kept; for there are classes of agents—notably those between whom and their principal a strictly fiduciary relation does not subsist—where book accounts would not be necessary, for generally such agents do not engage in monetary transactions. But when the relation is a fiduciary one, the

[142] Norris v. Tayloe, 49 Ill. 17; Clark v. Bank of Wheeling, 17 Pa. St. 322.

[143] Callander v. Oelrichs, 5 Bing. N. C. 58, 35 E. C. L. 29.

[144] Harvey v. Turner, 4 Rawle (Pa.) 223.

[145] Hegenmyer v. Marks, 37 Minn. 6, 5 Am. St. 808.

[146] Evans Pr. & Ag. (Bedford's ed.) 293; Topham v. Braddick, 1 Taunt. 572; Monitor, etc., Ins. Co. v. Young, 111 Mass. 537; Hancock v. Gomez, 58 Barb. (N. Y.) 490; Tupper v. Rider, 61 Vt. 69; Wooster v. Neville, 73 Cal. 58; Haas v. Damon, 9 Iowa 589; McVeigh v. Bank of the Old Dominion, 26 Gratt. (Va.) 188; Coquillard v. Suydam, 8 Blackf. (Ind.) 24; Lindley v. Downing, 2 Ind. 418.

[147] Mechem Ag., § 522; Story Ag., § 203.

[148] Haas v. Damon, 9 Iowa 589; Clarke v. Tipping, 9 Beav. 284; Clark v. Moody, 17 Mass. 145.

agent should keep his accounts in such manner as to be able to make a full showing of his standing with his principal at all times.[149] No designated standard of bookkeeping is demanded, but there should be no suppression or concealment of anything.[150] Every case must, of course, stand on its own merits; and what is or is not a substantial compliance with the rules depends wholly upon the particular nature of the transaction or business of the agency.[151] The duty of keeping accurate accounts, moreover, includes an obligation on the part of the agent to render an account to his principal upon proper occasions. If his contract, or usage, or the peculiar circumstances, require this to be done at regular periods, the agent will be obliged to comply with such requirement without any previous demand. Or if no regular periods for the accounting be thus provided for, then the agent must render such accounts at all reasonable times, and when an accounting is reasonably demanded by the principal.[152] In this, too, the circumstances must govern. If the agent is a factor, for instance, and goods are consigned to him for sale by the principal, he must render an account within a reasonable time. Such accounting must always follow a reasonable demand; but when the demand is impracticable or extremely inconvenient, the agent will be required to render an account without demand.[153] And in cases of unreasonable delay, the principal will even be entitled to collect interest of the agent, whether the latter has actually received it or not.[154] But if there has been no demand, and the agent has dealt fairly and is free from fraud, or if the negligence consists merely in failure to deliver accounts, the agent is not chargeable with interest.[155] The proper tribunal for instituting an action for an accounting, when the relation between the parties is strictly fiduciary, is a court of chancery. This is especially true when the accounts are so complicated as to bring the case peculiarly within the jurisdiction of equity, and when fraud is charged in connection with the failure to account. In such case the suit for the accounting or a bill of discovery may be maintained in a court of chancery.[156] But the mere existence of the relation of principal and agent is not sufficient in itself to make such a case cognizable by a

149 Evans Pr. & Ag. (Bedford's ed.) 293.

150 Story Ag., § 203.

151 Makepeace v. Rogers, 34 L. J. Ch. 396.

152 Leake v. Sutherland, 25 Ark. 219.

153 Mechem Ag., § 530.

154 Story Ag., § 204.

155 Turner v. Burkinshaw, L. R. 2 Ch. App. 488.

156 Coquillard v. Suydam, 8 Blackf. (Ind.) 24.

court of chancery, and a court of law will usually grant an accounting. If the declaration or complaint charges such misconduct upon the agent as to amount to a conversion of the property or money, the action may be in assumpsit, as for a breach of contract, or in trover, as for a conversion;[157] and in a proper case, where the goods are still in the agent's possession, an action of replevin will lie in favor of the principal for the recovery of the specific goods, upon a proper tender being made to the agent for his commission and charges.[158]

§ 246. **Agent need account to principal only—Agent can not dispute principal's title.**—There are a few rules subordinate to the general rule in reference to an accounting, which may well be mentioned here. In the first place, the agent is never obliged to account to any one but his principal.[159] Whatever may have been the delinquencies of the agent, he is not accountable for them in such action, except to the party who has sustained the direct injury. There is in such case no privity between him and any third person regarding the relation; and no one but the principal himself can maintain an action, whether it be at law or in chancery. Another well recognized rule is that in relation to any property constituting the subject-matter of the agency, the agent will not be permitted to dispute the principal's title.[160] Thus, if an agent has been intrusted with the collection of money by the principal, he is estopped to deny that the money belongs to the principal, or to assert that some other person has a better title to it. The very fact that he accepted the commission for such collection from the principal is sufficient to bring about such estoppel. He may, however, show in his defense that the principal has been divested of his title to the property by a paramount title.[161]

§ 247. **Agent can not plead illegality of agency, when.**—It is also a general rule that an agent, in a suit by the principal against him for an accounting in relation to money or other property that came

[157] Colt v. Stewart, 50 N. Y. 17; Coleman v. Pearce, 26 Minn. 123; Seidel v. Peschkaw, 27 N. J. L. 427; English v. Devarro, 5 Blackf. (Ind.) 588; Coquillard v. Suydam, 8 Blackf. (Ind.) 24; Knotts v. Tarver, 8 Ala. 743.

[158] Terwilliger v. Beals, 6 Lans. (N. Y.) 403.

[159] Attorney - General v. Chesterfield, 18 Beav. 596; Tripler v. Olcott, 3 Johns. Ch. (N. Y.) 473; Lake Erie, etc., R. Co. v. Eckler, 13 Ind. 67.

[160] Von Hurter v. Spengeman, 17 N. J. Eq. 185; Farrow v. Edmundson, 4 B. Mon. (Ky.) 605; Collins v. Tillou, 26 Conn. 368, 68 Am. Dec. 398.

[161] Burton v. Wilkinson, 18 Vt. 186; Doty v. Hawkins, 6 N. H. 247, 25 Am. Dec. 459.

into his hands for the benefit of the principal, or for a balance due the principal, or for a conversion, as to any transaction in which he and the principal were not *in pari delicto,* will not be permitted to set up the illegality of the transaction to defeat the principal's claim.[162] In a previous chapter we discussed at some length the doctrine pertaining to illegal contracts and how the principal and agent are affected by the same.[163] It was there shown that neither party to an illegal contract can invoke the aid of the law to reap the benefit of its provisions: the principal can not sue the agent for having failed to keep the contract; and the agent can not recover compensation for its execution; nor will he even be permitted to recover for advancements and disbursements incurred by him in the carrying out of such illegal transaction. The maxim is, *"In pari delicto potior est conditio defendentis."* The courts will leave the parties to such transaction in the dilemma in which they have placed themselves. If, therefore, the agent receive money or property from his principal which he is to use for him in gambling transactions, and he does so use it, the principal can not generally recover for profits made out of the transaction, if the parties are *in pari delicto.*[164] But where the agency is not tainted with the original illegal contract or undertaking, and the money or property for which the agent is called upon to account came into his hands in some transaction collateral to the illegal one, though remotely connected with it, the defense of illegality will not avail the agent; as in the latter case the contract is said to be in a degree removed from the original illegal agreement, being in itself an independent contract which ought not to be tainted by the illegality of the original transaction, notwithstanding the agent had knowledge of it.[165] And the rule is well established that an agent who has received money from some third party for his principal can not successfully defend a suit for an accounting on the ground that the principal had no right to engage in the transaction which yielded the money.[166] And so, where a tax collector was sued for money collected by him for taxes, it was held that he could not be heard to say in his defense that the tax which he had collected was illegally levied, and that he would therefore refuse to pay it over.[167] Likewise, where a county

[162] Kiewert v. Rindskopf, 46 Wis. 481; Peters v. Grim, 149 Pa. St. 163, 34 Am. St. 599.

[163] *Ante,* § 65, *et seq.*

[164] Story Ag., § 344.

[165] Story Ag., § 347.

[166] Wilson v. Town of Monticello, 85 Ind. 10.

[167] Placer County v. Astin, 8 Cal. 304; Clark v. Moody, 17 Mass. 145.

treasurer had received from his predecessor United States bonds belonging to the county, which had been held as county property, having been purchased by the county board, it was ruled that the treasurer must, on sale of such bonds, account for all the proceeds, and that he could not question the county's power to make such purchase on the ground that it was illegal to do so.[168] Where the illegal act has not yet been fully consummated, either party may invoke the power of the courts to prevent its consummation. Many of the American states have enacted statutes enabling the principal to recover money or other property placed with the agent in furtherance of gambling contracts; but even in the absence of such statutes, the principal may revoke such agency and recover the money or property, if the agent has not paid or turned it over on the principal's loss or losses.[169] It must be admitted, however, that the authorities are not entirely in harmony upon this question; some courts holding that the agent may set up the illegality of the transaction in defense, either before or after he has paid out the money or turned over the property upon the loss.[170]

§ **248. Stakeholders.**—A person selected by the parties to a wager to hold the money or property wagered, and turn it over to the winner, is denominated a stakeholder.[171] The stakeholder is a mere depositary or bailee, and is not regarded as a party to the gambling contract; nor is he, strictly speaking, an agent: he can not plead in defense of a suit for the stake money that he received it in a gambling contract.[172] Either party to a wager may disaffirm the contract at any time before the event is determined upon which the wager is laid, and recover his deposit; and in such case the stakeholder is bound to return it, upon demand.[173] But if, after the determination of the event, and before demand is made upon the stakeholder, he pay the wager to the winner in good faith, the deposit can not generally be recovered.[174] But a demand is generally necessary before suit.[175]

[168] Nixon v. State, 96 Ind. 111.

[169] Dauler v. Hartley, 178 Pa. St. 23; Walker v. Johnson, 59 Ill. App. 448; Crandell v. White, 164 Mass. 54.

[170] Connor v. Black, 132 Mo. 150; Sowles v. Welden Nat'l Bank, 61 Vt. 375; Cunningham v. Fairchild (Tex. Civ. App.), 43 S. W. 32. See also, Bingham v. Scott, 177 Mass. 208, 58 N. E. 687; Lyons v. Coe, 177 Mass. 382, 59 N. E. 59.

[171] See Dauler v. Hartley, 178 Pa. St. 23.

[172] Jones v. Cavanaugh, 149 Mass. 124.

[173] Taylor v. Moore, 20 Ind. App. 654.

[174] Goldberg v. Feiga, 170 Mass. 146; Trenery v. Goudie, 106 Iowa 693.

[175] Jones v. Cavanaugh, 149 Mass. 124.

Even after the event, if notice had been given the stakeholder before the wager was paid to the winner, he would be bound to return the deposit.[176] Strictly speaking, the law of agency does not apply to parties engaged in gambling transactions, and they are only treated under this head for the sake of convenience. A person who assists in making or executing a gambling contract is not an agent, but a *particeps criminis*.[177] Where parties are jointly interested in a gambling contract, neither of them can generally enforce any rights arising out of the same; as no party can, strictly speaking, have any legitimate rights which arise out of such contract.[178] In some jurisdictions, however, it is held that an action may be maintained against the party who has collected the winnings, on an express contract to pay to his associates their share of the common gains.[179]

§ 249. Failure to keep and render account—Effect of upon construction of agent's rights.—It may be stated as a final proposition regarding the agent's duty to keep and render accounts to his principal, that a failure on the agent's part to perform this branch of his obligation will always result in an unfavorable construction of his rights, in order that the principal may not be made to suffer by the negligence or fraud of such agent.[180] Thus, while a factor may,

[176] Lewis v. Bruton, 74 Ala. 317, 49 Am. Rep. 816; Petillon v. Hipple, 90 Ill. 420; Alexander v. Mount, 10 Ind. 161; Morgan v. Beaumont, 121 Mass. 7; Hampden v. Walsh, L. R. 1 Q. B. Div. 189; Frybarger v. Simpson, 11 Ind. 59; Storey v. Brennan, 15 N. Y. 524. Under a statute of Massachusetts a party who has paid money on a bet or gambling contract may sue for and recover "from the other party any payment so made thereon." By virtue of this statute, the loser may, of course, sue the winner after the money has been paid to the latter, and recover the amount paid from him. In such case, however, it is held that one who received the money as agent and paid it over can not be made to repay it to the original owner, as the "other party" referred to in such statute clearly means the other principal: Bingham v. Scott, 177 Mass. 208, 58 N. E. 687. But under a somewhat similar statute in Illinois the supreme court of that state decides that the agent or broker who receives the money and pays it over to the winner is himself the winner, and may be compelled to repay the same: Kruse v. Kennett, 181 Ill. 199, 54 N. E. 965; Pearce v. Foote, 113 Ill. 228; Jamieson v. Wallace, 167 Ill. 388, 47 N. E. 762.

[177] Fortenbury v. State, 47 Ark. 188; Cunningham v. National Bank, 71 Ga. 400, 51 Am. Rep. 266, 75 Ga. 366.

[178] Shaffner v. Pinchback, 133 Ill. 410, 38 Am. St. 624; Sampson v. Shaw, 101 Mass. 145.

[179] Terry v. Olcott, 4 Conn. 442.

[180] Beaumont v. Boultbee, 11 Ves. 358; Clarke v. Moody, 17 Mass. 145.

especially if usage sanctions such a course, take from a purchaser one note for goods sold for different persons, payable to himself, and procure the note to be discounted in his own name; yet the result of such a course would be that the agent could be held to have made the note his own, and he might be made liable to the principal for the proceeds of the goods sold, whether the maker was solvent or not.[181] And where the agent fails to keep a separate account of stock purchased with his principal's money, but keeps it standing in his own name, he will be required by a court of equity to make a clear showing under oath as to what portion of the stock was purchased with the principal's money and what portion with his own; and upon failure to do so, the court may restrain him from disposing of any of the stock thus standing in the agent's name.[182] Another consequence of the agent's failure to keep correct accounts clearly demonstrating his standing with his principal will be to deprive the agent of his right to commissions or other compensation otherwise due him in consideration of the services performed, and in cases of loss will be to subject the agent to a suit for damages to make the principal whole. In such case every doubtful circumstance is construed unfavorably to the agent.[183]

§ 250. **Duty of agent to keep principal's property separate from his own.**—Finally, it is the duty of an agent having in his hands money and goods of his principal, to keep them separate from his own, so that at any time when he may be called upon to do so, he will be able to show the state of accounts between them correctly.[184] This is but a branch of the rule requiring agents to keep and render accounts of their receipts and disbursements; for it is obvious that if an agent commingle the property of his principal with his own, it will make it more difficult, if not impossible, at times, to render a satisfactory account, and thus bring about confusion detrimental to his trust.[185] To such an extent has this doctrine been carried that if an agent allows his property and that of his principal to become so confused as to render them indistinguishable, the courts will hold the agent liable to turn over all of such property, or will adjudge that the agent has no interest in the same whatever.[186] And so, where an

[181] Johnson v. O'Hara, 5 Leigh (Va.) 456.

[182] Story Eq. Jur., § 468.

[183] Story Ag., §§ 332–333.

[184] Evans Pr. & Ag. (Bedford's ed.) 253.

[185] Clarke v. Tipping, 9 Beav. 284; Greene v. Haskell, 5 R. I. 447.

[186] Story Ag., § 205; Darke v. Mar-

administrator was ordered to sell the land of his decedent for the payment of the debts of the estate, and the administrator purchased the land himself, and afterward sold it at an advanced price, he was held liable to account to the heirs for the profits. The court ruled that if uncertainty arise in such case, as to what profits were really made by the agent, the uncertainty will be resolved in favor of the heirs, and the trustee will be chargeable with the largest amount which, from the circumstances, he can be presumed to have realized; the court saying: "The rule both in law and equity is, that if a person having charge of the property of another so confounds it with his own that it can not be distinguished, he must bear all the inconveniences of the confusion. If it be a case of damages, damages will be given against him for the utmost value of the articles."[187] It is the duty of an agent who has in his hands trust money collected for his principal, if impracticable to remit at once, to keep such money in some solvent bank or other depository, making the deposit either in the principal's name, or in his own as agent or trustee, or in some other way to "earmark" such money.[188] Money collected by an agent for his principal is a trust fund: it belongs to the principal and not to the agent. The relation of debtor and creditor is not necessarily created by the receipt of such money; but the agent may, by his conduct, establish such a relation, at the option of the principal.[189] If the agent preserve the money in its trust character and exercise due care and caution in respect of depositing it, etc., he will be protected in case a loss occur by reason of the failure of the bank or other depository, or by theft or other mishap. But such agent or trustee must not so deposit the fund as to authorize him or his assignee or legal representative to claim it as his own; and if he does, he can not

tyn, 1 Beav. 525; Safford v. Gallup, 53 Vt. 292; Lupton v. White, 15 Ves. 432; Atkinson v. Ward, 47 Ark. 533; Hart v. Ten Eyck, 2 Johns. Ch. (N. Y.) 62; National Bank v. Insurance Co., 104 U. S. 54.

[187] Brackenridge v. Holland, 2 Blackf. (Ind.) 377. The whole amount is in such cases taken to be the property of the principal, and the burden is on the agent to show how it may be distinguished: Lupton v. White, 15 Ves. 432. See also, Atkinson v. Ward, 47 Ark. 533; National Bank v. Insurance Co., 104 U. S. 54.

[188] Robinson v. Ward, 2 C. & P. 60, 12 E. C. L. 29; Commercial, etc., Bank v. Jones, 18 Tex. 811; Naltner v. Dolan, 108 Ind. 500, 58 Am. Rep. 61; Mason v. Whitthorne, 2 Coldw. (Tenn.) 242; Norris v. Hero, 22 La. Ann. 605.

[189] Strickland v. Burns, 14 Ala. 511; Jones v. Gregg, 17 Ind. 84; Coit v. Stewart, 50 N. Y. 17; Gordon v. Camp, 2 Fla. 422; Anderson v. First Nat'l Bank, 5 N. Dak. 80.

throw such loss upon the principal, but it will be his own; and this is true without reference to any good or bad intention on his part.[190] Such an agent is not an insurer; all he is required to do is to use due and proper diligence in preserving the fund in its trust character; and if the money is lost through no fault or negligence of his own, the loss is the principal's and not the agent's.[191] The fact that the agent deposits the money in his name will be treated as a conversion thereof by the agent; and if the bank becomes insolvent, the agent can not set up the insolvency as a defense to a suit for the money.[192] In a New York case, where the agent had so intermingled the money of his principal with his own as to make it impossible to determine to whom the money actually belonged, and a portion of it was stolen, it was held that the loss must fall upon the agent as a penalty for not keeping the principal's and his own funds separate.[193] And the same result will follow if there be a depreciation of the money or currency collected by the agent: the loss will in all such cases fall upon the agent and not upon the principal, unless the fund is kept separate.[194] And where an agent commingles the principal's and his own money, and the whole can be reached by legal process, the whole may be taken, in the absence of a showing by the agent as to which portion belongs to him and which to the principal.[195]

§ **251. Fiduciaries.**—Where a strictly fiduciary relation subsists between two parties,—as, that of guardian and ward,—these rules are most strictly enforced. Thus, if a guardian would exonerate himself from liability on account of an insolvent note taken in the course of the administration of the ward's estate, which he turned over in settlement with the ward, he must show that he kept the funds of his ward and those of his own separate, and exercised at least ordinary care in loaning such funds of his ward by taking adequate security.[196] "A guardian," said the court, "it is true, is not an insurer of the safety of investments made by him, nor is he to be held to an extraordinary degree of care; but in order that he may be exonerated from loss on account of insolvent securities, taken in the course of the guardianship, it is

[190] Naltner v. Dolan, 108 Ind. 500; Norwood v. Harness, 98 Ind. 134.

[191] Mowbray v. Antrim, 123 Ind. 24.

[192] Cartmell v. Allard, 7 Bush (Ky.) 482; Mason v. Whitthorne, 2 Coldw. (Tenn.) 242, 245.

[193] Massachusetts Life Ins. Co. v. Carpenter, 2 Sweeney (N. Y. Super.) 734.

[194] Marine Bank v. Fulton Bank, 2 Wall. (U. S.) 252.

[195] Atkinson v. Ward, 47 Ark. 533.

[196] Line v. Lawder, 122 Ind. 548.

his duty to keep the trust estate separate from his own funds, and to act in good faith, and observe that sound discretion and prudence usually exercised by diligent men about their own business. In making loans of the trust funds it is his duty to take security. A loan made in good faith, and in the exercise of ordinary care and prudence, upon security which seemed ample at the time, will not be at the personal risk of the guardian if, on account of changed circumstances or depreciation in values, loss subsequently occurs.[197] Where adequate care is observed, and the condition of the estate and the character of investments are truthfully reported to the court, as the law requires, a guardian may relieve himself and his sureties by turning over the estate to his ward, who has attained his majority, in the condition in which it actually exists at the time a settlement is made. Where a settlement is thus made, and it afterward turns out that securities so taken and turned over were worthless, in order to justify a cancellation of the settlement there must appear to have been negligence or bad faith on the part of the guardian.[198] Where, however, unsecured notes, the makers of which are of doubtful solvency, have been taken in the individual transactions of the guardian, in the manner already described, and where these have been accepted in lieu of money, upon the faith that they were available solvent securities, it requires a degree of assurance to insist that the receipt and release of the ward should be a bar to the opening up of the final settlement."[199] The fact that a guardian takes a note for his ward's property payable to himself has been held to be a sufficient proof of conversion of such property to his own use.[200] It has been decided, however, on the other hand, that this fact is but *prima facie* evidence of conversion, and may be rebutted by proof.[201] And there are exceptional cases, no doubt, when a guardian may leave the money of his ward temporarily with his own papers and money in a separate package; and in case it is stolen from him, and he uses proper diligence to recover it, he will not be liable as for a conversion.[202] An administrator who deposited the funds of the estate in his own name was held to be liable therefor on failure of the bank, even though he

[197] Citing State, etc., v. Slevin, 93 Mo. 253, 3 Am. St. 526.

[198] Citing Hardin v. Taylor, 78 Ky. 593.

[199] Citing Breneman's Appeal, 121 Pa. St. 641.

[200] State v. Greensdale, 106 Ind. 364.

[201] Sanders v. Forgasson, 3 Baxt. (Tenn.) 249; Slauter v. Favorite, 107 Ind. 291.

[202] Schouler Dom. Rel., § 352.

had no other deposit in the bank.[203] And generally, an executor or administrator is held to the same requirement as to keeping the funds of the estate separate as is a guardian or other fiduciary; and if he commingles them with his own he is individually liable therefor, as for a conversion, in case they are lost or he fails to account for them satisfactorily.[204]

[203] Williams v. Williams, 55 Wis. 300, 42 Am. Rep. 708. But see Hale v. Wall, 22 Gratt. (Va.) 424.

[204] McElroy v. Thompson, 42 Ala. 656; Henderson v. Henderson, 58 Ala. 582; Raines v. Raines, 51 Ala. 237; Norwood v. Duncan, 10 Mart. (La. O. S.) 708. But see State v. Cheston, 51 Md. 352.

CHAPTER VII.

DUTIES, OBLIGATIONS AND LIABILITIES OF PRINCIPAL TO AGENT, AND RIGHTS OF AGENT IN REGARD TO PRINCIPAL.

§ 252. **Purpose of this chapter.**—It is our purpose in this chapter to set forth and consider the duties and obligations the principal owes to his agent, and the liabilities growing out of the same, as well as the corresponding rights and remedies of the agent as against the principal; the duties and obligations of both principal and agent to subagents, and their reciprocal rights and remedies; and the duties and obligations of the principal to unauthorized agents, and such rights and remedies as these may have against him. Such duties, obligations and liabilities and the rights and remedies incident thereto have reference to: 1. The compensation of the agent for services rendered his principal; 2. Reimbursement of the agent for all necessary and legitimate outlays and expenditures in the course of the agency; 3. Indemnity of the agent for losses sustained by him in the course of the agency; 4. Compensation, reimbursement and indemnity of subagents; 5. Compensation, reimbursement and indemnity of unauthorized agents; 6. Remedies of agents against their principals; including 7. Liens.

§ 253. **Compensation of agent—Classification of.**—The agent's compensation may consist of a "salary" or a "commission" or an "honorarium" or of "wages." "Salary" is a term used to denote a reward or recompense for services performed, and is usually applied to public officers with reference to their pay for the performance of official duties. It is not confined to these, however, and is often employed to designate the compensation of ordinary agents or employes who are paid periodically; as, for example, the salary of a salesman, or bookkeeper, or other employe of a mercantile house; or of the conductor or engineer of a railroad. An "honorarium" is a reward given to the most elevated professions for services performed.[1] It is in the nature of a gratuity given for services rendered by a physician, counsellor, advocate, or barrister. These were considered services of such an exalted character that it was deemed inconsistent with their dignity to give a remedy for them in a judicial forum. Such services were considered purely honorary, and whatever compensation was given for them was regarded as a voluntary gift on the part of the one benefited by the services. In England the common-law rule still governs, and a barrister or counsellor at law can not recover compensation from his client in a court of justice; he must be satisfied with whatever compensation the client voluntarily renders.[2] This rule does not apply, however, even in England, to ordinary attorneys at law, conveyancers, and others, who discharge some of the duties devolving upon attorneys in this country.[3] While an advocate or counsel could not, under the common law, recover compensation for services in an action for that purpose, an ordinary attorney was entitled to such recovery.[4] The distinction between attorneys and barristers, etc., was never generally recognized in the United States; and here the rule is, generally, that practicing lawyers may contract with their clients for compensation and compel payment by an action in court, the same as other agents;[5] or they may recover on a *quantum meruit*.[6] In Pennsylvania the rule was formerly as in England, at least as to all charges in excess of the fees fixed by statute;[7] but the cases so holding have been overruled, and the law in that state now permits practicing lawyers to recover compensation.[8] In New Jersey the parties may agree upon a specific fee for counsel, and this may be enforced by an action at law; but no fee can be collected in the absence of such agreement.[9] In the British provinces, generally, counsel fees may be collected as in the states.[10]

[1] Bouvier Law Dic.

[2] Moor v. Row, 1 Ch. Rep. 21; 3 Bl. Com. 28; Kennedy v. Brown, 13 C. B. (N. S.) (106 E. C. L.) 677.

[3] See authorities in last note.

[4] Van Atta v. McKinney, 16 N. J. L. 235.

[5] Stevens v. Monges, 1 Harr. (Del.) 127; Lorilard v. Robinson, 2 Paige (N. Y.) 276; Thurston v. Percival, 1 Pick. (Mass.) 415.

[6] Quint v. Ophir Mining Co., 4 Nev. 305.

[7] Mooney v. Lloyd, 5 S. & R. (Pa.) 411.

[8] Balsbaugh v. Frazer, 19 Pa. St. 95.

[9] Hopper v. Ludlum, 41 N. J. L. 182; Zabriskie v. Woodruff, 48 N. J. L. 610.

[10] Paradis v. Bosse, 21 Can. S. C. 419; McDougall v. Campbell, 41 U. C. Q. B. 332. See Mowat v. Brown, 19 Fed. 87.

Even in this country it has been held that the presumption obtains that the common-law rule is in force; and hence, where a suit is instituted for such a fee for services rendered by an attorney for his client, in a state other than that in which he sues, he must allege and prove that under the laws of such other state the action for such services will lie.[11] But even in jurisdictions where counsel fees can not be collected by suit, an action will lie on a promissory note or bill of exchange given for such services.[12] It has been held that where a lawyer enters into a contract with his client for counsel fees before the fiduciary relation between him and the client has commenced, the contract will govern as to the amount to be paid; but where the agreement is made after the relation has been entered into and during its continuance, no more than reasonable compensation can be collected, whatever may have been the contract.[13] The question of what is a fair and reasonable fee of counsel in a given case may be a question of law for the court to determine, when the services were performed in the presence of the court which is to fix the compensation;[14] otherwise it is a question of fact depending on the proof, unless the amount is fixed by the contract.[15] But in no event can more be collected than the sum agreed upon, if an agreement was entered into.[16] "Commissions" is a term employed to denote the compensation allowed to agents, factors, trustees, receivers and others who manage the affairs of others, in recompense for their services. The amount of such commissions is generally a percentage on the sums paid out or received, and is regulated either by special contract or by the usage in the particular business, if such there be.[17] A factor sometimes guarantees the debt growing out of a sale made by him for his principal, and he is then paid a higher compensation called a *del credere* commission.[18] "Wages" is compensation given to a hired person for his or her services.[19] The term "wages" is used to denote the pay received by manual laborers at a certain sum per day, week or month.[20]

[11] Williams v. Dodge, 28 N. Y. Supp. 729, 8 Misc. (N. Y.) 317.

[12] Mowat v. Brown, 19 Fed. 87.

[13] White v. Tolliver, 110 Ala. 300, 30 So. 97.

[14] Succession of Rabasse, 51 La. Ann. 590, 25 So. 326.

[15] Wyant v. Pottorff, 37 Ind. 512.

[16] Montgomery v. Ætna Life Ins. Co., 97 Fed. 913.

[17] 3 Chitty Com. L. 221; Story Ag., § 326.

[18] Paley Ag. 88, *et seq.* See *ante*, § 22.

[19] Bouvier Law Dic.

[20] Standard Dic.

§ 254. Compensation, how measured—Special contract—Quantum meruit.—The compensation or reward of an ordinary agent, servant or other employe may, of course, be fixed by the terms of the contract of employment, if there be such a contract; and when this is the case, the amount stipulated will form the exclusive basis of the recovery.[21] Where there is no express contract, or the compensation is not fixed in the contract, the agent will generally be entitled to receive such an amount as is reasonable and warranted by the custom of the trade or business in the community where the services were rendered, or on a *quantum meruit*;[22] that is, the value of the particular services as it may be established by the testimony of witnesses who are competent to give their opinion upon the subject.[23] As a general rule, where one performs services for another at the latter's request, or under circumstances indicating an expectation of compensation on the one hand and an intention to pay on the other, the law will imply a promise to pay what the services are reasonably worth.[24] But it is not always essential that the principal should expect the agent to charge for his services.[25]

§ 255. Contingent compensation—Rule in England and America.—The agent's compensation may also be made to depend upon the happening or not happening of some contingency,—as, that the agent for the sale of goods realize a certain amount for them, or that no loss accrue to the principal, etc.; and if that be the agreement, the agent can recover no compensation unless the contingency has or has not happened, according to the agreement, or unless the agent was prevented, through the fault of the principal.[26] In a case decided in Massachusetts, the plaintiff, one Zerrahn, sued the members of an executive committee for services rendered by him in conducting and

[21] Bower v. Jones, 8 Bing. 65, 21 E. C. L. 224.

[22] Masterson v. Masterson, 121 Pa. St. 605; Lockwood v. Robbins, 125 Ind. 398; Krekeler's Succession, 44 La. Ann. 726; Spearman v. Texarkana, 58 Ark. 348; Baxter v. Knox, 19 Ky. L. Rep. 1973; Ruckman v. Bergholz, 38 N. J. L. 531; Wadleigh v. McDowell, 102 Iowa 480.

[23] Bowen v. Bowen, 74 Ind. 470.

[24] Martin v. Roberts, 36 Fed. 217; Lewis v. Trickey, 20 Barb. (N. Y.) 387; Roberts v. Swift, 1 Yeates (Pa.) 209, 1 Am. Dec. 295.

[25] Morrison v. Flournoy, 23 La. Ann. 593.

[26] Walker v. Tirrell, 101 Mass. 257, 3 Am. Rep. 352; Hinds v. Henry, 36 N. J. L. 328; Lewis v. Trickey, 20 Barb. (N. Y.) 387. See Nixon v. Cutting Fruit Pack. Co., 17 Mont. 90, 42 Pac. 108.

superintending the musical performance of the "World's Peace Jubilee," at Boston. The defendants answered, setting up a special contract contained in the correspondence between Zerrahn and S. P. Gilmore, the agent of the management. In his letter to Zerrahn, Gilmore guaranteed that the former should receive the sum of five thousand dollars, provided "that the profits of the festival, including my own benefit, will result in the aforesaid amount being placed to my credit and under my control; but it must be distinctly understood that neither the executive committee nor any person or persons shall be held responsible for the fulfillment of this contract, which is made this day in good faith, with an earnest desire that it shall be fulfilled to the letter and to the entire satisfaction of you and I [*sic*], who are the sole contracting parties. It is further understood that, should the festival result in a loss, you will hold no demand against myself or anybody else connected with it." To this letter Zerrahn replied his acceptance. The finding of the court upon trial showed that the Jubilee enterprise was not pecuniarily successful, but resulted in a heavy loss to the defendants who carried it on. The court, speaking by Morton, J., said: "We are of opinion that, in this case, as plaintiff has stipulated that in the contingency which has happened he shall have no demand against the defendants, the law does not imply a promise by them to pay him any compensation for his services, and, therefore, that the superior court correctly ruled that he could not maintain this action."[27] In England and some of the states of the Union, agreements for contingent fees for professional services, such as counsel fees depending on the success of a law suit, are held void for champerty or maintenance; but the courts in a great majority of the American states have ruled otherwise. While such contracts are closely scrutinized, they are generally upheld, if made in good faith.[28]

[27] Zerrahn v. Ditson, 117 Mass. 553.

[28] See Moore v. Campbell Academy, 9 Yerg. (Tenn.) 115; Fowler v. Callan, 102 N. Y. 395; Coughlin v. New York, etc., R. Co., 71 N. Y. 443, 27 Am. Rep. 75; Reece v. Kyle, 49 Ohio St. 475; Perry v. Dicken, 105 Pa. St. 83, 51 Am. Rep. 181; Hilton v. Woods, L. R. 4 Eq. 432, 36 L. J. Ch. 491, 15 W. R. 1105; In re Masters, 1 H. & W. 348; Robertson v. Furness, 43 U. C. Q. B. 143; Jenkins v. Bradford, 59 Ala. 400; Gilman v. Jones, 87 Ala. 691; Nixon v. Cutting Fruit Pack. Co., 17 Mont. 90, 42 Pac. 108; Trist v. Child, 21 Wall. (U. S.) 441; Wright v. Tebbitts, 91 U. S. 252; Stanton v. Embrey, 93 U. S. 548; Duke v. Harper, 66 Mo. 51; Manning v. Sprague, 148 Mass. 18, 1 L. R. A. 516; Bayard v. McLane, 3 Harr. (Del.) 139; Flower v. O'Conner, 7 La. 194; Martinez v. Succession of Vives, 32 La. Ann. 305; Moody v.

§ 256. **Champerty and maintenance.**—Champerty is defined by Blackstone as "a bargain with a plaintiff or defendant *campum partire,* to divide the land or other matter sued for between them, if they prevail at law, whereupon the champertor is to carry on the party's suit at his own expense."[29] Coke says that it is champerty "to maintain to have part of the land or anything out of the land or part of the debt or other thing in plea or suit."[30] It will be noticed that in Coke's definition it is not made an essential ingredient of champerty that the champertor shall maintain the suit or plea at his own expense, as in Blackstone's. These seemingly inconsistent definitions have apparently given rise to diversities of ruling on the part of the courts; some holding that to constitute champerty it is essential that the champertor must carry on the suit at his expense, while others rule that this is not essential, since the contingent agreement for a fee out of the recovery is itself a contribution toward carrying on the suit or plea.[31] But it is held in many jurisdictions that in order to constitute champerty, if champerty avoids the contract at all, the ingredient of an agreement by the attorney or agent to pay the expenses of litigation, in whole or in part, must be present also.[32] The difference, however, between the respective

Harper, 38 Miss. 599; Chester County v. Barber, 97 Pa. St. 455; Perry v. Dicken, 105 Pa. St. 83, 51 Am. Rep. 181; Nickels v. Kane, 82 Va. 309; Sussdorff v. Schmidt, 55 N. Y. 319. *Contra,* Scobey v. Ross, 13 Ind. 117; Ackert v. Barker, 131 Mass. 436; Butler v. Legro, 62 N. H. 350; McLimans v. City of Lancaster, 63 Wis. 596, 23 N. W. 689.

[29] 4 Bl. Com. 135.

[30] Co. Litt. 368b.

[31] The following are some of the cases holding that an agreement between an attorney and his client that the attorney is to prosecute or defend the action for a part of the recovery, without reference to the fact that the attorney is to pay the expenses of the litigation, in whole or in part, is champertous and void: Scobey v. Ross, 13 Ind. 117; Thurston v. Percival, 1 Pick. (Mass.) 415; Davis v. Sharron, 15 B. Mon. (Ky.) 64; Brown v. Beauchamp, 5 T. B. Mon. (Ky.) 413; Rust v. Larue, 4 Litt. (Ky.) 412; Poe v. Davis, 29 Ala. 676; Elliott v. McClellan, 17 Ala. 206; Dumas v. Smith, 17 Ala. 305; Hayney v. Coyne, 10 Heisk. (Tenn.) 339; Butler v. Legro, 62 N. H. 350, 13 Am. St. 573; Backus v. Byron, 4 Mich. 535. Also the following English cases: Stanly v. Jones, 5 M. & P. 193, 7 Bing. 369, 20 E. C. L. 165; Reynell v. Sprye, 21 L. J. Ch. 633; Sprye v. Porter, 7 El. & Bl. 58, 90 E. C. L. 80, 26 L. J. Q. B. 64.

[32] Duke v. Harper, 66 Mo. 51, 27 Am. Rep. 314, affirming 2 Mo. App. 1; Coleman v. Billings, 89 Ill. 183; Bayard v. McLane, 3 Harr. (Del.) 139; Allard v. Lamirande, 29 Wis. 502; Dockery v. McLellan, 93 Wis. 381, 67 N. W. 733; Orr v. Tanner, 12 R. I. 94; Benedict v. Stuart, 23 Barb. (N. Y.) 421; Scott v. Harmon, 109

holdings in these cases is not as great as might appear upon first view. While the definition given by Blackstone is generally followed by the courts of the present day, it is believed that an agreement to pay the attorney a portion of the recovery is equivalent to an agreement to pay the expenses, or a portion of the expenses, to carry on the suit or defense. As Bouvier says: "When it is considered that champerty is á species of maintenance, it is clear that all these definitions import that the party bargaining for an interest in the thing in dispute undertakes to aid in the prosecution of the suit for its recovery, and whether such aid is furnished in money by a layman, who pays the expenses of the suit, or by an attorney or solicitor, in services rendered in its prosecution, it is the same, and each alike in effect, and in contemplation of law, is a maintainer of the suit, and prosecutes it, in whole or in part, at his own expense. The consideration paid in the latter case would be equally as valuable as in the former, and the inducement to prosecute a doubtful or unconscionable claim would be the same, and the evil, if any, the same. It is equally champerty, whether the contract be for one-half, one-quarter or one-eighth of the thing in dispute; and it would be strange, indeed, if the validity or invalidity of the contract of this character were made to depend upon the

Mass. 237, 12 Am. Rep. 685; Park Commissioners v. Coleman, 108 Ill. 591; Moody v. Harper, 38 Miss. 599; Wheeler v. Pounds, 24 Ala. 472; Aultman v. Waddle, 40 Kan. 195; Moses v. Bagley, 55 Ga. 283; Jewel v. Neidy, 61 Iowa 299; Quigley v. Thompson, 53 Ind. 317; Ware v. Russell, 70 Ala. 174, 45 Am. Rep. 82; Blaisdell v. Ahern, 144 Mass. 393, 59 Am. Rep. 99; McPherson v. Cox, 96 U. S. 404; Atchison, etc., R. Co. v. Johnson, 29 Kan. 218; Phillips v. South Park Com'rs, 119 Ill. 626; North Chicago St. R. Co. v. Ackley, 171 Ill. 100, 49 N. E. 222; Martin v. Clarke, 8 R. I. 389. Where, however, the attorney does agree to pay the costs or expenses of litigation, in whole or in part, the contract will generally be held void: Coquillard v. Bearss, 21 Ind. 479; McPherson v. Cox, 96 U. S. 404; Jeffries v. Mutual Life Ins. Co., 110 U. S. 305; Peck v. Heurich, 167 U. S. 624; Belding v. Smythe, 138 Mass. 530; Low v. Hutchinson, 37 Me. 196; Hyatt v. Burlington, etc., R. Co., 68 Iowa 662, 32 N. W. 330; Thompson v. Reynolds, 73 Ill. 11; Taylor v. Hinton, 66 Ga. 743; Martin v. Clarke, 8 R. I. 389, 5 Am. Rep. 586; Wildey v. Crane, 63 Mich. 720; Kelly v. Kelly, 86 Wis. 170; Key v. Vattier, 1 Ohio 132; Coughlin v. New York, etc., R. Co., 71 N. Y. 443, 27 Am. Rep. 75; Lancy v. Havender, 146 Mass. 615; Pince v. Beattie, 32 L. J. Ch. 734; Earle v. Hopwood, 9 C. B. (N. S.) (99 E. C. L.) 566, 30 L. J. C. P. 217; Hilton v. Woods, L. R. 4 Eq. 432, 36 L. J. Ch. 491.

amount of the consideration to be paid; or, in other words, upon the payment of a part or the whole of the expenses of the suit."[33]

§ 257. **Division of spoils the offensive ingredient.**—The offensive ingredient in such a contract is the division of the spoils,—the agreement that the agent or attorney shall receive a portion of the money or thing that may be recovered. This is no less a contribution of a portion of the expenses of the litigation by the agent or attorney than it would be if he were to agree to pay a portion or all of the costs in the case. But it is also held that an agent or attorney may contract for a fee in a sum equal to one-half or one-fourth, or any other portion of the recovery, and that this is not a champertous agreement. Thus in Kentucky, where a client agreed to pay his attorney, in case of the success of the litigation, an amount equal to one-half of the value of the property recovered, the court ruled that the agreement was not champertous, but valid and enforceable, saying: "It is as competent for the litigant to regulate the amount of his attorney's fee by the value or half the value of the property in contest, as to regulate it by the value or half the value of any other piece of property. Whether he regulates it by the one or the other or agrees to pay a contingent fee in money, agreed upon by the parties at the time, he is not subject to the denunciation of the statute; provided that he is not to give a part of the profit or the thing in contest."[34] And in the same state a contract between an attorney and client that the latter should pay the former a sum equal to one-half (or other fractional part) of the amount recovered, was held not to be void for champerty.[35] The question of champerty

[33] Bouvier Inst. Am. L., vol. 4, p. 236.

[34] Wilhite v. Roberts, 4 Dana (Ky.) 172.

[35] Evans v. Bell, 6 Dana (Ky.) 479. See also, Ramsey v. Trent, 10 B. Mon. (Ky.) 336; Omaha, etc., R. Co. v. Brady, 39 Neb. 27, 57 N. W. 767; Christie v. Sawyer, 44 N. H. 298. The rule was thus stated by the Massachusetts court: "Where the right to compensation is not confined to an interest in the thing recovered, but gives a right of action against the party, though pledging the avails of the suit, or a part of them, as security for payment, the agreement is not champertous:" Blaisdell v. Ahern, 144 Mass. 393, 59 Am. Rep. 99. This would, of course, be analogous to an assignment of part of the claim. And so, an agreement between an attorney and client to prosecute a claim before a *quasi*-court, such as a commission appointed by the president of the United States, in pursuance of a treaty, is held by the supreme court of the United States not to be champertous nor illegal because it stipulates for an amount equal to one-tenth of the sum re-

can only be raised by a party to the contract.[36] In those states and jurisdictions in which contingent fees are held to be illegal, there can, of course, be no recovery on a contract in which the principal or client agrees to pay his agent or attorney a fee only in case of success, though there may still be a recovery in some cases on a *quantum meruit.*[37] In some of the states statutes have been enacted permitting attorneys and clients to make such contracts relative to compensation as may seem best to them.[38]

§ 258. **The common-law doctrine of champerty.**—The common-law doctrine of champerty is founded upon the principle enunciated by Coke. "Nothing," says that author, "in action, entry or re-entry, can be granted over; for so under color thereof, pretended titles might be granted to great men, whereby right might be trodden down, and the weak oppressed."[39] The rule applied to officers, attorneys and individuals alike: no one was permitted to take upon him any business in suit in any court, or to have a part of the thing in demand, and every agreement thereto was declared void.[40] Champerty is a species of maintenance and punishable in the same manner.[41] "The distinction between maintenance and champerty seems to be this: where there is no agreement to divide the thing in suit, the party intermeddling is guilty of maintenance only; but where he stipulates to receive part of the thing in suit, he is guilty of champerty."[42]

§ 259. **Harshness of doctrine criticized by the courts.**—Under the common-law rule, a chose in action could not be assigned, such an assignment being void for maintenance.[43] The doctrine was otherwise carried to great extremes. "The peculiar state of society out

covered by way of compensation, especially if the agreement to pay the compensation be made after the services have been rendered, in whole or in part: Wright v. Tibbitts, 91 U. S. 252; Wylie v. Coxe, 15 How. (U. S.) 415; Taylor v. Bemiss, 110 U. S. 42. By these rulings it seems that claims against the United States government may be prosecuted by an attorney for part of the recovery as his compensation. See also, Manning v. Sprague, 148 Mass. 18, 1 L. R. A. 516.

[36] Hart v. State, 120 Ind. 83.

[37] Goodman v. Walker, 20 Ala. 482, 68 Am. Dec. 134; Stearns v. Felker, 28 Wis. 594; Merritt v. Lambert, 10 Paige (N. Y.) 352.

[38] See, for example, Howell's Comp. Stat. of Mich., § 9004.

[39] Co. Litt. 114a.

[40] 4 Kent Com. (8th ed.) 449, note *a*.

[41] 4 Bl. Com. 135.

[42] 4 Cooley Bl. 134, note.

[43] Master v. Miller, 4 T. R. 320.

of which the law grew," said the supreme court of Alabama, "carried it to the most absurd degrees; men were held indictable for aiding a litigant to find a lawyer, for giving friendly advice to a neighbor as to his legal rights, for lending money to a friend to vindicate his known legal rights, for offering voluntarily to testify in a pending suit, and other like offices of charity and friendship."[44] The doctrine, as was well said by the federal court, "has come to be regarded as something belonging to the past, and not suited to the circumstances of this age."[45] In an Indiana case,[46] Elliott, J., speaking for the supreme court, says of the doctrine of champerty and maintenance as prevailing in that state: "It is settled that the rule of the common law upon the subject of champertous contracts prevails in this state.[47] It is clear, however, that the rule does not, and can not, prevail in this state in its full extent since the code of 1852, for it makes radical changes in the common-law rule upon the subject of the assignment of choses in action. The common-law rule is limited in its operation by several provisions of the code, but we deem it unnecessary to notice them. Many of the courts where the code system prevails have denied its force altogether, and the tendency of modern decisions in America is to restrict rather than to enlarge the operation of the rule.[48] The rule has often been criticised by the English courts; even as early as *Master* v. *Miller*[49] unfavorable criticism was made. But our decisions, as we have seen, declare the rule to be in force in this state, although the extent to which it prevails has not been defined. It may, however, be safely assumed that the rule is narrowed rather than extended, since to hold otherwise would be to oppose the letter and spirit of our code, as well as the general principles of what Austin calls our 'judge-made law.'"[50]

§ 260. Tendency of modern decisions toward a more liberal rule.—There can be no doubt that the tendency of modern decisions,

[44] Gilman v. Jones, 87 Ala. 691.

[45] Hickox v. Elliott, 10 Sawy. (U. S.) 415, 429.

[46] Board of Com'rs v. Jameson, 86 Ind. 154.

[47] Citing Stotsenburg v. Marks, 79 Ind. 193; Greenman v. Cohee, 61 Ind. 201; Quigley v. Thompson, 53 Ind. 317; Scobey v. Ross, 13 Ind. 117.

[48] Citing Mathewson v. Fitch, 22 Cal. 86; Cain v. Monroe, 23 Ga. 82; Allard v. Lamirande, 29 Wis. 502; Bentinck v. Franklin, 38 Tex. 458; Roberts v. Cooper, 20 How. (U. S.) 467; Stoever v. Whitman, 6 Bin. (Pa.) 416; Coughlin v. New York, etc., R. Co., 71 N. Y. 443, 27 Am. Rep. 75; Orr v. Tanner, 12 R. I. 94, 17 Am. L. Reg. (N. S.) 759.

[49] 4 T. R. 320, *vide* p. 340.

[50] Citing Patterson v. Nixon, 79 Ind. 251. See also, Hart v. State, 120 Ind. 83; Brown v. Ginn (Ohio), 64 N. E. 123.

both in England and America, is away from the old and stringent doctrine toward a more liberal rule which is in harmony with modern conditions of society. "It is curious, and not altogether useless," says Buller, J., "to see how the doctrine of maintenance has, from time to time, been received in Westminster Hall. At one time, not only he who laid out money to assist another in his cause, but he that by his friendship or interest saved him an expense which he would otherwise be put to, was guilty of maintenance. * * * Nay, if he officiously gave evidence, it was maintenance; so that he must have had a subpena or suppressed the truth. That such doctrine, repugnant to every honest feeling of the human heart, should be soon laid aside, must be expected."[51] That champerty or maintenance has long since ceased to be prosecuted as a crime in England is sufficiently evidenced by the fact, as stated by Stephen, that no person has been criminally punished for it in that country within the memory of living man.[52] In California, Delaware, Nebraska and New Jersey the law of champerty and maintenance has never been in force.[53] In Utah the statute has so modified the common law that the parties are permitted to make any contract as to compensation for services which would formerly have been champertous.[54] In Michigan, though the common-law doctrine was declared to prevail in that state at one time,[55] it seems to have been abolished by statutes subsequently to the rendition of that decision.[56] And in New York, it is said that no vestige of the law of maintenance, including that of champerty, now remains, except what is contained in the revised statutes with reference to some matters connected with the transfer of real estate.[57] The appellate court of Illinois says that the doctrine "has been so pruned away and exceptions so grafted upon it that there is nothing of the substance left of it in this state.[58] In Indiana, as

[51] Master v. Miller, 4 T. R. 340.

[52] 3 Stephen Hist. Crim. L. of Eng. 234.

[53] Mathewson v. Fitch, 22 Cal. 86; Hoffman v. Vallejo, 45 Cal. 564; Ballard v. Carr, 48 Cal. 74; Bayard v. McLane, 3 Harr. (Del.) 139; Omaha, etc., R. Co. v. Brady, 39 Neb. 27; Schomp v. Schenck, 40 N. J. L. 196, 29 Am. Rep. 219.

[54] Croco v. Oregon, etc., R. Co., 18 Utah 311, 54 Pac. 985.

[55] Backus v. Byron, 4 Mich. 535.

[56] Wildey v. Crane, 63 Mich. 720.

[57] Sedgwick v. Stanton, 14 N. Y. 289; Coughlin v. New York, etc., R. Co., 71 N. Y. 443.

[58] Dunne v. Herrick, 37 Ill. App. 180. But see Geer v. Frank, 179 Ill. 570, 45 L. R. A. 110, where it is held that if both the elements of contingency and agreement to pay part of the costs of the suit are present the contract will not be enforced.

we have just seen, the doctrine has been greatly modified by the codes and the decisions.[59] In most of the other states of the Union, it seems that the law of champerty is recognized as being in force, either by statute or the common law, but in greatly modified form. And we think it may be stated as the prevailing rule, deducible from the current of modern decisions, that contracts for contingent fees between attorney and client for services, are valid and enforceable, if made in good faith; that such contracts are not rendered illegal by reason of their contingent character; that is, that they are not void for champerty simply because the compensation is to be measured by the *quantum* of recovery, and the avails of the suit are pledged as security; provided, of course, the suit or defense is not to be carried on, in whole or in part, at the attorney's expense, and there is to be no division of such avails.[60] But while this is doubtless the prevailing rule, there are jurisdictions in which contingent fees can not be collected at all, and others in which contracts are held champertous upon the sole ground that the amount of compensation is to depend upon the question and amount of recovery, or is to be paid out of the avails of the suit. It may be added that other states have departed so far from the doctrine of champerty and maintenance that almost any kind of contingent compensation agreed upon is collectible; provided, of course, there be no overreaching or unfair advantage taken of the principal or client, and the agreement be otherwise free from bad faith.[61]

[59] See note 46, *supra*.

[60] Taylor v. Bemiss, 110 U. S. 42; Greenhalgh v. The Alice Strong, 57 Fed. 249; In re Hynes, 105 N. Y. 560; Reece v. Kyle, 49 Ohio St. 475, 16 L. R. A. 723; County of Chester v. Barber, 97 Pa. St. 455; Perry v. Dicken, 105 Pa. St. 83, 51 Am. Rep. 181; Rickel v. Chicago, etc., R. Co., 112 Iowa 148, 83 N. W. 957; Wallace v. Chicago, etc., R. Co., 112 Iowa 565, 84 N. W. 662; Croco v. Oregon, etc., R. Co., 18 Utah 311, 54 Pac. 985; Courtright v. Burns, 13 Fed. 317; Zeigler v. Mize, 132 Ind. 403. And a plea of champerty or maintenance must be specially pleaded: Croco v. Oregon, etc., R. Co., *supra*. In California it has been held that, the law of champerty and maintenance not being in force, an attorney is not prohibited from making a contract with his client by which the attorney is to receive as his compensation a portion of the recovery in the suit, and is to pay a part or all of the costs of such suit: Hoffman v. Vallejo, 45 Cal. 564. See also, Potter v. Ajax Mining Co., 22 Utah 273, 61 Pac. 999.

[61] Lytle v. State, 17 Ark. 609; Davis v. Webber, 66 Ark. 190, 49 S. W. 822; Courtright v. Burnes, 13 Fed. 317; Geer v. Frank, 179 Ill. 570, 45 L. R. A. 110.

§ 261. **Recovery on quantum meruit.**—When the contract for compensation is void on the ground of champerty or because it is contingent, it does not necessarily follow that no compensation can be collected by the agent or attorney. The general rule upon the subject is unquestionably to the effect that the agent or attorney may still recover for his services, upon a *quantum meruit,* the same as if the champertous or contingent contract had never been made, and the agreement to pay were an implied one.[62]

§ 262. **Contingent compensation—When enforceable—Condition precedent.**—If the compensation of the agent is a contingent one, and collectible by the law of the jurisdiction, he will be entitled to collect it, if the contingency has happened and he has fulfilled his part of the engagement, whether the principal avails himself of the benefits of the agent's services or not. And so, when a real estate broker has, according to his agreement, produced a purchaser who is able, ready and willing to buy on the terms upon which the broker was authorized to sell, he is entitled to receive his commission, even though the owner refuses to execute the deed of conveyance or otherwise to carry out the contract of sale according to its terms.[63] But if the contingency have not come to pass, the agent will not be entitled to compensation, no matter how much work he may have done or effort he may have made to bring it about. Thus, in the case of the employment of a broker to find a customer, he is not entitled to his commissions unless the customer is found, ready, able and willing to purchase or sell, as the case may be. He can not recover on a *quantum meruit.* If the principal fails to fulfill his part of the engagement,—as, for example, where the broker was employed to sell real estate on certain terms, and has found a customer, but the owner of the real estate is unwilling or unable to carry out the contract,—the broker's commission is earned, and his remedy is to sue for the commission, and not on the *quantum meruit.*[64] The employment of a broker on commissions is not like

[62] Merritt v. Lambert, 10 Paige (N. Y.) 352; Stearns v. Felker, 28 Wis. 594; Rust v. Larue, 4 Litt. (Ky.) 412, 14 Am. Dec. 172; Elliott v. McClelland, 17 Ala. 206; Caldwell v. Shepherd, 6 T. B. Mon. (Ky.) 389; Holloway v. Lowe, 7 Port. (Ala.) 488; Goodman v. Walker, 30 Ala. 482, 500, 68 Am. Dec. 134.

[63] Moses v. Bierling, 31 N. Y. 462; McFarland v. Lillard, 2 Ind. App. 160; Duffy v. Hobson, 40 Cal. 240; Lockwood v. Rose, 125 Ind. 588.

[64] Fitzpatrick v. Gilson, 176 Mass. 477.

the ordinary case of employment of labor, but more in the nature of an offer which can be accepted at any time before it is withdrawn. Whenever the terms are complied with, it amounts to an acceptance; and if withdrawn before acceptance, it is not a contract, and no compensation can be recovered.[65] The same is true where the agent is employed to procure a loan of money for the principal. When the agent has found a lender who is able, ready and willing to furnish the money, the agent has earned his fee and is entitled to it, whether the loan be accepted by the principal or not.[66] In all such cases the basis of the right of recovery of the agent is the performance of the condition upon which he agreed to perform the service. Having done what he agreed to do, it is immaterial whether the principal comes up to his part of the agreement or not; but if the agent has not fully complied with his agreement, he is not entitled to his compensation. These are cases where the right of recovery of the agent depends upon the fulfillment of a condition precedent. If this condition is not fulfilled, it is immaterial what services the agent has performed: he will not be entitled to receive compensation. Thus, where the condition was that the agent should sell at a stipulated price, it was held that he was not entitled to his commissions unless he sold for such price.[67] And the same rule holds when the condition requires him to sell within a stipulated time.[68] On the other hand, the agent's claim can not be defeated or forfeited by any default of the principal. The principal may indeed revoke the agent's authority or take away from him the subject-matter of the agency before the contract is carried into execution by the agent; but he can not thereby defeat the agent's right to recover for his services if the conditions have been fulfilled.[69] Nor is it material that the principal has realized no profits from the transaction or that he has incurred a loss thereby. The agent does not undertake to insure profits to his principal or to keep him harmless from loss; his undertaking only requires him to fulfill the terms of his contract or to comply with the conditions therein stipulated. When he has done that he is entitled to compensation. It must be kept in mind, however, that the element of contingency, while not in itself sufficient to render the contract for compensation void, in most jurisdictions, is yet sufficient to lay such contract open to

[65] Cadigan v. Crabtree (Mass.), 61 N. E. 37.

[66] Vinton v. Baldwin, 88 Ind. 104.

[67] Jones v. Adler, 34 Md. 440.

[68] Irby v. Lawshe, 62 Ga. 216.

[69] Attrill v. Patterson, 58 Md. 226.

close scrutiny; and if there be in it any element of illegality or violation of public policy, the agent will not be entitled to collect the contingent fee for which the parties have stipulated.[70] Of this character are contracts for lobbying and the performance of services in procuring offices, gambling and other contracts that are void as being against public policy.[71]

§ **263. No compensation when purpose of agency is illegal.**—Of course, in cases in which the agency is an illegal one—that is, where the agent is employed to perform some illegal transaction, of which he has knowledge—he can not collect compensation for the service except such as the principal is disposed to pay voluntarily. Thus, a broker is not entitled to commissions for procuring a charter party if the contemplated voyage is illegal. But if the illegality is not apparent on the face of the contract, or if, though the general subject-matter appears to be illegal, the contract is susceptible of being legally performed, and is so performed, the agent is entitled to his compensation.[72] And a note given to a broker for his commission and to cover loss in stock-gambling operations is void.[73] If, however, the broker simply brings the parties together for the purpose of a purchase and sale of property, and, after his services are performed, they enter into a contract which is immoral and against public policy,—as, a wagering contract,—he may recover his commissions, although the broker has knowledge of the character of the contract, he not being a party to it.[74] And practitioners in the learned professions can not legally recover fees for their services unless they have been licensed or otherwise qualified as required by law.[75] But it is otherwise if a physician is called to render services in case of pressing emergency, where the physician is otherwise qualified, but has not yet procured the proper license.[76]

§ **264. Nature of agent's compensation—No compensation for useless services.**—When an agent has rendered the service undertaken by him and has in all respects fulfilled the conditions of his contract

[70] Fowler v. Callan, 102 N. Y. 395; Geer v. Frank, 179 Ill. 570, 45 L. R. A. 110.

[71] See *ante*, § 65, *et seq.*

[72] Haines v. Busk, 5 Taunt. 521.

[73] Fareira v. Gabell, 89 Pa. St. 89.

[74] Crane v. Whittemore, 4 Mo. App. 510.

[75] Howarth v. Brearley, L. R. 19 Q. B. D. 303; Turner v. Reynall, 14 C. B. (N. S.) 328; Orr v. Meek, 111 Ind. 40.

[76] Board of Com'rs v. Cole, 9 Ind. App. 474.

with the principal, he is entitled to his recompense. If the remuneration was not to be contingent, the agent is entitled to receive payment according to the express contract, if the latter contains stipulations controlling the compensation; if the contract contains no stipulation as to compensation, the law implies a promise to pay what the services are reasonably worth.[77] What is a reasonable compensation depends largely upon the nature of the service to be performed, the skill and reputation of the agent, the dangers and responsibilities involved, the expense incurred, if any, and the time consumed in its performance. Custom also may largely influence the question of compensation; the evidence of what is usually charged for such services under similar circumstances may be introduced, but evidence of what was paid for similar services in another case is ordinarily inadmissible.[78] If, however, the agent's work is entirely useless, owing to his want of skill or to his failure to exercise due care and diligence, he can not recover anything for his services.[79] It is the duty of the agent to exercise reasonable skill and diligence in the performance of the task he has undertaken; and if he be incompetent or negligent, he will be not only liable for any damages that his principal may sustain, but may forfeit his entire compensation. If, however, the services be not wholly worthless, he will be entitled to claim on a *quantum meruit;* unless the special contract between him and his principal provide for such contingency, in which case the contract will control.[80] Thus, in a New Jersey case, it was held that if an agent who has been employed to perform certain services at a regular salary, neglects to keep proper accounts of the money received by him in the course of the agency, as a result of which considerable sums of money previously received by him are omitted to be credited to the principal, the salary for the year in which the omissions occurred is properly disallowed.[81] And where an attorney employed to conduct a suit is guilty of negligence rendering all previous steps useless in the result, he can not recover for any por-

[77] Cranmer v. Building and Loan Ass'n, 6 S. D. 341, 61 N. W. 35; Van Arman v. Byington, 38 Ill. 443.

[78] Mechem Ag., §§ 605, 606.

[79] Denew v. Deverell, 3 Camp. 451; Shaw v. Arden, 9 Bing. 287; Fisher v. Dynes, 62 Ind. 348; Hart v. Ten-Eyck, 2 Johns. Ch. (N. Y.) 62; Story Ag., § 331.

[80] Evans Pr. & Ag. (Bedford's ed.) 403-404; Farnsworth v. Garrard, 1 Camp. 38; Rochester v. Levering, 104 Ind. 562.

[81] Ridgeway v. Ludlam, 7 N. J. Eq. 123.

tion of his services in connection therewith.[82] Slight negligence, however, will not work a forfeiture of all the agent's compensation, but may go to reduce the amount of the demand.[83] A mere error of judgment or omission, which does not amount to misconduct or culpable negligence on the part of the agent, does not work a forfeiture of his right to compensation.[84] The agent's right to compensation may likewise be forfeited by him by perpetrating a fraud upon his principal in relation to the business of the agency. This may be done by withholding valuable information from the principal, resulting in loss to the latter.[85] And an agent can not sell the principal's property to himself and recover compensation for his services.[86] And so, where an agent sold his principal's land to a company in which the agent was a shareholder and a director, without disclosing such fact to the principal, he was adjudged to have forfeited his commissions.[87] And where he purchases property for his principal and receives from the principal much more than he himself has paid for it, he forfeits his right to compensation.[88] Where the agent takes advantage of his position to promote his own interest, which is inimical to that of the principal, he can not recover for services in connection therewith.[89] The same result as to the forfeiture of compensation ensues where a broker undertakes to represent two principals having conflicting interests.[90] But the acceptance of conflicting agencies will not work a forfeiture of his commissions, if the agent has previously apprised both principals of the fact, or if they are otherwise aware of the same, and make no objections thereto.[91] And a mere middleman employed simply to bring the parties together, without taking any part in the contract between them, may recover a commission from

[82] Bracey v. Carter, 12 A. & E. 373, 40 E. C. L. 74.

[83] Rochester v. Levering, 104 Ind. 562.

[84] Rochester v. Levering, 104 Ind. 562.

[85] Wadsworth v. Adams, 138 U. S. 380.

[86] McGar v. Adams, 65 Ala. 106.

[87] Salomons v. Pender, 3 H. & C. 639.

[88] Blair v. Shaeffer, 33 Fed. 218.

[89] Salomons v. Pender, 3 H. & C. 639.

[90] Cleveland, etc., R. Co. v. Pattison, 15 Ind. 70; Hunsaker v. Sturgis, 29 Cal. 142; Sumner v. Reicheniker, 9 Kan. 320; Jones v. Hoyt, 25 Conn. 374; Hannan v. Prentiss, 124 Mich. 417, 83 N. W. 102; Marshall v. Eggleston, 82 Ill. App. 52; Duesman v. Hale, 55 Neb. 577, 76 N. W. 205; Lewis v. Denison, 2 App. D. C. 387; Smith v. Tyler, 57 Mo. App. 668; Sessions v. Payne, 113 Ga. 955, 39 S. E. 325; In re Evans, 22 Utah 366, 62 Pac. 913.

[91] Stewart v. Mather, 32 Wis. 344. See Ferguson v. Gooch, 94 Va. 1, 40 L. R. A. 234.

each, although they were both ignorant of the adverse employment of the agent.[92] So, an agent who was authorized to sell land for two distinct parties, and who brought about an interview between both principals, which ended in the exchange of such lands by the principals, was held entitled to recover his customary commission from each; the court saying: "The plaintiff was not an agent to buy or to sell, but only to act as a middleman to bring the parties together in order to enable them to make their contract. He stood entirely indifferent between them, and held no such relation in consequence of his agency as to render his action adverse to the interests of either party."[93]

§ **265. Compensation by way of commissions.**—Ordinary commercial agents employed to buy and sell goods are usually paid a commission on purchases or sales made by them, unless the contract of agency stipulates for a salary or other kind of compensation. A commission is an allowance of a percentage on the sums paid out or those realized on the sale, or on the value of the goods purchased or sold. Auctioneers, brokers, and factors usually receive such commissions; and, where they are not fixed in the contract, they are ordinarily regulated by usage.[94] Thus, where an owner of real estate employs a broker to sell it for him, and nothing is said as to his compensation, he will be entitled to recover such commission upon the amount realized as may be established by evidence of what is usually paid real estate brokers for such services.[95]

§ **266. Implied contract to pay for services.**—Where commissions are not the appropriate mode of compensation, and there is no fixed recompense agreed upon, and the services are performed under circumstances implying a promise to pay for them, the agent will be entitled to receive such compensation as he may be able to show the services were reasonably worth. The law usually implies a promise to pay for such services, when they are performed at the request of the party receiving the benefit thereof; but if the services are performed gratuitously, or without request, or the circumstances under which they were performed do not indicate an intention to pay for them, or do indicate a contrary intention, no such promise can be

[92] Rupp v. Sampson, 16 Gray (Mass.) 398.

[93] Rupp v. Sampson, *supra.*

[94] Story Ag., § 326.

[95] Ruckman v. Bergholz, 38 N. J. L. 531.

inferred, and the agent will not be entitled to receive compensation.[96] As has been well said, "all persons engaged in commerce called upon to perform services in the due course of business are *ex necessitate* entitled to compensation as growing out of and inseparably connected with the contract of their employment."[97] The intention to compensate an agent may likewise be implied from the beneficial nature of the service.[98] Thus, where a party knows that services are being performed for him by another, and makes no objection thereto, and receives the benefit thereof, he will be compelled to pay for such services what they are reasonably worth.[99] The mere fact, however, that the services are of benefit to the principal, is not necessarily conclusive of the fact that they were to be paid for, if the circumstances indicate a different intention;[100] such fact will be treated as a circumstance from which a request may be presumed, but it is not conclusive evidence.[101] But an agent can not rightly claim compensation for mere gratuitous services, or for services performed voluntarily, either with or without the expectation of compensation.[102]

§ **267. Gratuitous services.**—Whether the services are gratuitous or not depends, of course, either upon the express contract between the parties, or, in the absence of such contract, upon the particular circumstances of the case. Thus, not only the character of the services rendered, but the relation which the parties sustain to each other, will often exert a controlling influence in determining the question whether or not it was intended that the services should be paid for. It is not probable, for instance, that members of the same family, and those who are nearly related, will expect compensation for the performance of services usually rendered by and between such parties with the expectation of no reward save that of love and affection. In such cases courts and juries will be guided largely by probabilities: if from all the circumstances it does not appear probable that an intention to pay was present, none will be implied.[103]

[96] Van Arman v. Byington, 38 Ill. 443; Waterman v. Gibson, 5 La. Ann. 672; Roberts v. Swift, 1 Yeates (Pa.) 209, 1 Am. Dec. 295; Mangum v. Ball, 43 Miss. 288, 5 Am. Rep. 488.

[97] Martin v. Roberts, 36 Fed. 217.

[98] Hatch v. Purcell, 21 N. H. 544.

[99] Bartlett v. Sparkman, 95 Mo. 136, 6 Am. St. 35; Garrey v. Stadler, 67 Wis. 512, 58 Am. Rep. 877; Scully v. Scully, 28 Iowa 548.

[100] Muscott v. Stubbs, 24 Kan. 520.

[101] Westgate v. Munroe, 100 Mass. 227.

[102] Scott v. Maier, 56 Mich. 554; Seals v. Edmondson, 73 Ala. 295, 49 Am. Rep. 51.

[103] Hinds v. Henry, 36 N. J. L. 328; Hertzog v. Hertzog, 29 Pa. St. 465;

Nor is it always necessary that a request to perform the services be shown. Thus, if an attending physician call in a consulting physician, who renders services to the patient, the consulting physician may recover from the patient the reasonable value of his services, although the regular attending physician had agreed to pay for such services himself, of which fact the consulting physician was, however, ignorant.[104] And the same rule is applied in the case of attorneys. If an attorney who is conducting a suit for his client call in assistant counsel, who render services of which the client receives a benefit, although it be done without the express consent of the client, but without objection from him, such client may render himself liable for the reasonable fee of such assisting counsel.[105] But where one of several clients employs an attorney for himself, and the benefit of his services, from the nature of the case, inures to the others, who merely stand by and accept such benefit without objection, such other clients do not thereby become liable for any fees of such attorney.[106] If, however, such parties are aware of the fact that the attorney employed to assist intends to look to them for pay, and they do not interpose timely objection or declare their unwillingness to become liable, they may render themselves responsible to him for pay.[107] Services are sometimes rendered by architects and mechanics which are of a mere preliminary character, preparatory to the erection of houses or other buildings, for which the person employed may not be entitled to compensation. If an architect is called upon to furnish the plans and specifications for a-building, and nothing is said as to paying for the same, he will generally be entitled to recover the reasonable value of such services. But there may be circumstances under which he would not be entitled to recover anything. If, for example, the evidence shows that such services were voluntarily performed, with the chances of future employment, or the sketches and estimates were not accepted, there could be no recovery whatever.[108]

Pew v. First Nat'l Bank, 130 Mass. 391; St. Jude's Church v. Van Denberg, 31 Mich. 287; Palmer v. Haverhill, 98 Mass. 487; Taggart v. Tevanny, 1 Ind. App. 339.

[104] Garrey v. Stadler, 67 Wis. 512, 58 Am. Rep. 877.

[105] McCrary v. Ruddick, 33 Iowa 521; Muscot v. Stubbs, 21 Kan. 521; Ector v. Wiggins, 30 Tex. 55; Yerger v. Aiken, 7 Baxt. (Tenn.) 539.

[106] Jones v. Woods, 76 Pa. St. 408; Simms v. Floyd, 65 Ga. 719. But see Hauss v. Niblack, 80 Ind. 407.

[107] Savings Bank of Cincinnati v. Benton, 2 Metc. (Ky.) 240; McCrary v. Ruddick, 33 Iowa 521; Weston v. Davis, 24 Me. 374.

[108] Scott v. Maier, 56 Mich. 554.

§ 268. **Services by members of common family.**—One of the most frequent instances in which the question of compensation for services arises, and whether such services are to be classed as gratuitous or otherwise, is in cases where the services have been performed by members of a common family residing together. The circumstances of near relatives by blood or marriage living together in the same family, and one furnishing board, lodging, clothing, or other necessaries or comforts of life, and the other rendering services in return, are held to raise a presumption that such relatives are not to be compensated in money; and no recovery can be had therefor, in the absence of evidence showing an agreement to pay for the same. The presumption arising from such circumstances may indeed be rebutted; but the burden is upon the party alleging that compensation was to be made to prove a contract or agreement, express or implied, that the services were to be paid for.[109] Thus, where a child, after arriving at the age of majority, continued to reside in the father's family and render services, receiving in return his board, lodging and other maintenance, as before, without any understanding that the services were to be paid for, it was held that the child could not collect pay for such services.[110] If the relation is not that of parent and child, but some other near relation, as that of uncle and niece,[111] or brother and sister,[112] the rule is the same. But the relation of cousins or that of granddaughter is not sufficient in itself to raise the presumption that pay was not expected.[113] But aside from the matter of relationship, if it be shown that the party claiming for the services was living with the defendant as a member of his family, and receiving from him his maintenance and support, it is generally sufficient to raise the presumption that other remuneration was not intended.[114] So, where a person from whom compensation

[109] Hill v. Hill, 121 Ind. 255; Smith v. Denman, 48 Ind. 65; Wallace v. Long, 105 Ind. 522; Curry v. Curry, 114 Pa. St. 367; Walls' Appeal, 111 Pa. St. 460; Taggart v. Tevanny, 1 Ind. App. 339; Hays v. McConnell, 42 Ind. 285; James v. Gillen, 3 Ind. App. 472.

[110] Miller v. Miller, 16 Ill. 296. See also, Hertzog v. Hertzog, 29 Pa. St. 465; Allen v. Allen, 60 Mich. 635; Kaye v. Crawford, 22 Wis. 320; Richards v. Humphreys, 15 Pick. (Mass.) 133; Curry v. Curry, 114 Pa. St. 367, 371.

[111] Hays v. McConnell, 42 Ind. 385.

[112] Carpenter v. Weller, 15 Hun (N. Y.) 134.

[113] Gallaher v. Vought, 8 Hun (N. Y.) 87; Hauser v. Sain, 74 N. C. 552.

[114] Gallaher v. Vought, *supra;* Neal v. Gilmore, 79 Pa. St. 421; Hays v. McConnell, 42 Ind. 285.

was claimed had taken a child into his family to live with him until he arrived at the age of twenty-one years, and the child continued to reside in the family after the time had expired, the party benefited by the services was held not to be liable for the same.[115] But where an aged and infirm woman requested her son-in-law to take her to his home and care for her, and he did so, and it was shown that he gave her such care and attention as she in her helpless condition stood in need of, it was held that she was not residing with him as a member of his family, and that he was entitled to collect from her estate the value of the services so rendered.[116] If a child is not living with its parent, having been emancipated by him, or having arrived at the age of majority, there is no binding obligation on the child to render services for the parent gratuitously; and the child will have a valid claim against the parent for any services it may render for him, the same as if the parties were strangers.[117] And where an aged pair took into their home a young girl to live with them and serve them until the death of both, upon an agreement that she was to be compensated out of the estate of the survivor, who would make a will providing for her, it was held that an action would lie against the estate of the survivor for a reasonable compensation for such services.[118] But the mere promise or expectation of a legacy is not always sufficient to show that it was intended to pay the servant the value of the services, particularly where the claim has no equity.[119] The best evidence with which to overcome the presumption that services were to be gratuitous is, of course, that of an express contract.[120] But it is not essential that there should be proof of an express stipulation for a salary or wages: the claimant may prove the claim by circumstances proving to the jury's satisfaction that the services were rendered in expectation of pay by the claimant and that it was the intention of the defendant to make compensation therefor.[121] In *Fisher* v.

[115] Brush v. Blanchard, 18 Ill. 46; Andrus v. Foster, 17 Vt. 556; Medsker v. Richardson, 72 Ind. 323.

[116] Wence v. Wykoff, 52 Iowa 644.

[117] Hall v. Hall, 44 N. H. 293; Ulrich v. Ulrich, 136 N. Y. 120; Parker v. Parker, 33 Ala. 459.

[118] Taggart v. Tevanny, 1 Ind. App. 339; Davison v. Davison, 13 N. J. Eq. 246; Martin v. Wright, 13 Wend. (N. Y.) 460, 28 Am. Dec. 468.

[119] Grandin v. Reading, 10 N. J. Eq. 370; Hartman's Appeal, 3 Grant's Cas. (Pa.) 271.

[120] Medsker v. Richardson, 72 Ind. 323; Hall v. Hall, 44 N. H. 293; Wilson v. Wilson, 52 Iowa 44; Faloon v. McIntyre, 118 Ill. 292; Hertzog v. Hertzog, 29 Pa. St. 465.

[121] Faloon v. McIntyre, *supra;* Morton v. Rainey, 82 Ill. 215, 25 Am. Rep. 311; Green v. Roberts, 47 Barb.

Fisher,[122] the court said that "the plaintiff might have shown to the satisfaction of any jury that by the course of dealing between him and the defendant,—as, for instance, that they kept books of account, or had had settlements, or acts of this kind,—the relation of debtor and creditor subsisted between them, and that it was not intended or expected that these services should be rendered gratuitously." Facts showing that parties only remotely related are living together in one family do not of themselves necessarily raise the presumption of gratuitous services; and where in such a case there is evidence showing that the party claiming pay for services, though living in the family for some years as a minor, and performing services for his board, clothing and medical attendance, continued to reside there after becoming of age, but furnished his own clothes and paid his own medical bills, it was held sufficient to establish an implied contract to pay what the services were reasonably worth.[123] True, no invariable rule can be laid down as to the exact nature and *quantum* of evidence necessary to prove the existence of a contract to compensate the servant or agent for the services rendered: every case must be determined largely upon its own peculiar facts and circumstances. When the relationship is such as to raise the presumption of gratuitous services, there can be no recovery in any case without positive proof of a contract, either express or implied, that compensation other than the benefits incidentally derived from the living in the family was to be paid the claimant. The probative force of the evidence introduced to overcome the presumption of gratuity is always for the jury or the court trying the cause. Moreover, a promise to pay for gratuitous services, made after they were rendered, can not form the basis of an action to recover the same. If such services were really gratuitous, the promise is a mere *nudum pactum*, being without any consideration, and, therefore, void.[124]

§ **269. Compensation when agency is revoked.**—The principal has the power, though not always the right, as has been seen,[125] to revoke the agent's authority at any time, unless it be coupled with an interest. But if the principal exercises the power without the right, the agent can not be deprived of his compensation. Where the parties have provided by their agreement what the agent's com-

(N. Y.) 521; Fisher v. Fisher, 5 Wis. 472; Taggart v. Tevanny, 1 Ind. App. 339.

[122] 5 Wis. 472.

[123] Morton v. Rainey, 82 Ill. 215, 25 Am. Rep. 311.

[124] Allen v. Bryson, 67 Iowa 591.

[125] *Ante*, §§ 159, 161, 164.

pensation shall be in case the principal sees fit to revoke the authority prematurely, such agreement will form the basis of the agent's recovery. But if there be no provision of that character in the contract, the question arises, What will be the agent's remedy as to the matter of compensation? In that case, if the employment was for a definite period and the agent was wrongfully discharged before the expiration thereof, or was prevented by the wrongful act of the principal from performing his undertaking, the law gives him a choice of remedies: he may elect to treat the contract as rescinded, and sue upon a *quantum meruit* for the services performed by him, less the amount already received; or he may sue immediately for a breach of the contract and recover all probable damages resulting from such breach; or he may wait until the expiration of the term and recover the actual damages sustained by him.[126] He must, however, make his election between these remedies: he can not resort to all: if he pursues the one, he thereby abandons the other. Neither can he elect to treat the contract as being still in force and sue for the various portions or installments of his salary as they become due: he is not permitted thus to split his remedies. Formerly, it seems, the law was construed differently; it was then held that the agent or servant might recover for "constructive wages" for those portions of the term during which he was turned out of employment; but the so-called constructive wages are now included under the head of damages resulting from the breach, and it is held that there can be but a single demand for such breach.[127] As said by Mitchell, J., in a case decided by the Indiana supreme court: "A party will not be permitted to present by piecemeal, in successive suits, claims which grow out of an indivisible, entire contract, and which might have been litigated and determined when the first suit was brought. In such a case, the judgment in the first suit will be a conclusive merger of all the plaintiff's rights under the contract."[128] And in the same case the court quote approvingly the following statement of the law from Freeman: "Where the action is upon a contract, it merges all amounts due under or arising out of the contract, prior to the suit. They constitute a single, indivisible demand.

126 Colburn v. Woodworth, 31 Barb. (N. Y.) 381; Cutter v. Powell, 2 Smith Ld. Cas. (9th ed.) 1220, note; Gandell v. Pontigny, 4 Camp. 375; Planchè v. Colburn, 8 Bing. 14.

127 Richardson v. Eagle Machine Works, 78 Ind. 422, 41 Am. Rep. 584.

128 Indiana, etc., R. Co. v. Koons, 105 Ind. 507.

The plaintiff can not be allowed to split up the various covenants or promises contained in one contract and to recover upon each separately."[129]

§ **270. Doctrine of constructive services.**—The doctrine of constructive services is still adhered to in some jurisdictions.[130] If, under that doctrine, the agent or servant was unjustly discharged by the master or principal before the end of his term, and his compensation was payable in installments, he might, whenever an installment fell due, bring his action therefor, in the meantime holding himself in readiness to serve the master or principal according to the requirements of the contract. But he was also required, by another rule of law, to accept employment elsewhere, if offered, thus doing everything within his power to make the master's loss no greater than was reasonably necessary. He was thus placed in the dilemma of remaining idle, so as to be ready to serve the master, and, at the same time, of accepting other employment whenever opportunity offered. A doctrine so repugnant to correct principle could not well continue to receive the approbation of the courts, and it is now generally repudiated.[131]

§ **271. Modern rule.**—Under the modern, and what is believed to be the better rule, the agent, as we have seen, can have but one recovery for any and all breaches of the contract by the principal. The measure of damages, if he elect to treat the contract as still in force, whether the suit be brought before or after the expiration of the term of service, is, *prima facie,* the amount of compensation stipulated in the contract of employment for the entire time, not exceeding the amount that would have been due him had he completed his undertaking.[132]

[129] Freeman Judgm., § 240. See also, Henderson v. Henderson, 3 Hare Ch. 100, 115.

[130] Strauss v. Meertief, 64 Ala. 299; Gardenhire v. Smith, 39 Ark. 280; Jones v. Jones, 2 Swan (Tenn.) 605; Armfield v. Nash, 31 Miss. 361.

[131] Goodman v. Pocock, 15 A. & E. (N. S.) (69 E. C. L.) 576; Howard v. Daly, 61 N. Y. 362, 19 Am. Rep. 285; Richardson v. Eagle Machine Works, 78 Ind. 422, 41 Am. Rep. 584; Smith v. Hayward, 7 A. & E. 544; Chamberlin v. McCalister, 6 Dana (Ky.) 352; James v. Allen County, 44 Ohio St. 226, 58 Am. Rep. 821; Willoughby v. Thomas, 24 Gratt. (Va.) 521.

[132] Howard v. Daly, 61 N. Y. 362, 19 Am. Rep. 285; Hunt v. Crane, 33 Miss. 669, 69 Am. Dec. 381; Richardson v. Eagle Machine Works, 78 Ind. 422, 41 Am. Rep. 584; Pennsylvania Co. v. Dolan, 6 Ind. App. 109; Hinchcliffe v. Koontz, 121 Ind. 422.

§ 272. **Agent's duty to seek other employment.**—But the agent, upon his discharge, is bound to use reasonable diligence to secure employment elsewhere; and if he succeed in doing so, or if he could, by the exercise of proper efforts, have secured other employment, the compensation will be reduced in accordance with the amount received or that would have been received for such other employment.[133] The principal will, of course, be permitted to deduct, also, any amount he may have paid the agent by way of compensation, from the whole sum; and the remainder will be the damages the agent will be entitled to receive. The kind of employment the agent is required to use diligence in attempting to procure is employment of the same general nature as that from which he was wrongfully dismissed.[134] The agent or servant wrongfully discharged by the principal or master can not be required to accept any and all kinds of employment that he may be offered or have the opportunity of receiving; he is not supposed to be skilled in other matters than those in which he was employed when discharged. Thus, if he be an actor, he can not be required to accept employment as a singer; and if he had been engaged as a clerk or bookkeeper, he would not be compelled to accept employment as a farm laborer.[135] Nor does the rule require the agent or servant to go beyond the locality of his original employment to seek or accept other work.[136] Whether the agent made reasonable efforts to secure such other employment in the locality, and whether he might have found such employment or not, are questions for the jury to determine. The burden of proof in such cases is always upon the principal: it devolves upon him to establish to the satisfaction of the jury or court trying the cause that the agent has accepted or could have found other employment of the same general character in the locality, the same as in the case of any other defense upon which he chooses to rely.[137] As has been seen, the agent should

[133] Fain v. Goodwin, 35 Ark. 109; Williams v. Chicago Coal Co., 60 Ill. 149; Williams v. Anderson, 9 Minn. 39; Kirk v. Hartman, 63 Pa. St. 97; Sutherland v. Wyer, 67 Me. 64; Howard v. Daly, 61 N. Y. 362, 19 Am. Rep. 285; Perry v. Simpson, etc., Mfg. Co., 37 Conn. 520.

[134] Wolf v. Studebaker, 65 Pa. St. 459; Costigan v. Mohawk, etc., R. Co., 2 Denio (N. Y.) 609, 43 Am. Dec. 758; Strauss v. Meertief, 64 Ala. 299, 38 Am. Rep. 8.

[135] Mechem Ag., § 623.

[136] Harrington v. Gies, 45 Mich. 374; Costigan v. Mohawk, etc., R. Co., 2 Denio (N. Y.) 609, 43 Am. Dec. 758; Strauss v. Meertief, 64 Ala. 299, 38 Am. Rep. 8.

[137] Howard v. Daly, 61 N. Y. 362, 19 Am. Rep. 285; Ricks v. Yates, 5 Ind. 115; Pennsylvania Co. v. Dolan, 6 Ind. App. 109.

be ready and willing to continue in the service of his principal at the time of his dismissal;[138] but there is no rule of law that requires him to make a formal tender of his services to the principal, after he has been discharged by him. Whether or not he held himself in readiness to perform at the time of the dismissal is a question of fact for the jury, and may be established by the circumstances of the case, the same as any other fact that the party is required to prove; and when the agent has once indicated his readiness to serve the principal or master, there is no further obligation upon him to hold himself in readiness to perform such services.[139]

§ 273. No compensation after death or insanity of principal—Exceptions.—Death or insanity of the principal, as has been heretofore shown, operates as a revocation of the agency by force of law, unless the agency was coupled with an interest. In such cases the agent is not entitled to recover compensation beyond the period at which the death or insanity occurred; nor would he be entitled to damages for a wrongful discharge.[140] But this rule will not apply in case of the bankruptcy of the principal. Although such bankruptcy operates as a revocation, it is not considered to be such an unavoidable occurrence as that of death or insanity. The bankruptcy of the principal, therefore, does not furnish any defense to an action brought by an agent for the refusal or neglect of his principal to employ such agent after the bankruptcy.[141] And an agent who consents to the principal's discharge, or evinces an acquiescence therein by his acts and conduct, can not recover damages for a breach of the contract.[142] And where a corporation, on account of its insolvency, has passed into the hands of a receiver, an agent previously employed by such company, at a stipulated salary, and whose term of service has not expired when the receiver is appointed, is not entitled to recover damages out of the funds in the hands of the receiver, in the absence of any default of the company during its life.[143]

§ 274. Death, insanity, sickness, etc., of agent.—In case of the death of the agent before the completion of the service for which

[138] Howard v. Daly, 61 N. Y. 362, 19 Am. Rep. 285.

[139] Howard v. Daly, 61 N. Y. 362, 19 Am. Rep. 285.

[140] Yerrington v. Greene, 7 R. I. 589, 84 Am. Dec. 578.

[141] Lewis v. Atlas, etc., Ins. Co., 61 Mo. 534.

[142] Patnote v. Sanders, 41 Vt. 66; Boyle v. Parker, 46 Vt. 343.

[143] People v. Globe, etc., Ins. Co., 91 N. Y. 174.

he was employed, the agency is terminated, and his estate may recover the value of his services to the time of his death.[144] The old rule seems to have been that in case of an entire contract there could be no division or apportionment of the compensation, notwithstanding the failure to perform was through no fault of the agent.[145] But the rule now generally enforced is to the effect that where the agent is prevented by death, insanity, sickness or other disability from performing the contract, though it be a special, entire contract, and the agent professes to act under it, and has done for and delivered to the other party something of value to him, which he has accepted,—although no action will lie on the special contract for the work done or thing delivered, yet the party who has been thus benefited by the labor and performance of the other will be liable on an implied promise arising out of the circumstances, to the extent of the value received by him.[146] But it has been held that where sickness was the cause of the revocation, and the sickness could have been foreseen, but was not provided against, no recovery can be had, even upon a *quantum meruit*.[147]

§ **275. Renunciation of agency by agent—Rule as to compensation in case of.**—When the agent himself dissolves the relation between him and his principal, by a renunciation of the same, it may be under circumstances furnishing a justification for his doing so or it may not. If the agent has in his contract reserved the right of renunciation at his will, he will doubtless be entitled to recover compensation to the time of the dissolution, according to the terms of the contract, whether he have good reasons for breaking off the relation or not.[148] And if the parties have provided in their contract that in case of the renunciation or abandonment of the agency by the agent he shall forfeit a certain amount or all of his compensation, such provision will be enforced, unless it be an un-

[144] Coe v. Smith, 4 Ind. 79, 58 Am. Dec. 618; Wolfe v. Howes, 20 N. Y. 197, 75 Am. Dec. 388.

[145] Cutter v. Powell, 6 T. R. 320, 2 Smith Ld. Cas. (9th ed.) 1212.

[146] Lomax v. Bailey, 7 Blackf. (Ind.) 599; Milnes v. Vanhorn, 8 Blackf. (Ind.) 198; Fenton v. Clark, 11 Vt. 557; Britton v. Turner, 6 N. H. 481; Ryan v. Dayton, 25 Conn. 188, 65 Am. Dec. 560; Fuller v. Brown, 11 Metc. (Mass.) 440; Lakeman v. Pollard, 43 Me. 463, 69 Am. Dec. 77; Riddle v. Gilbert, 21 Wis. 395; Hillyard v. Crabtree, 11 Tex. 264, 62 Am. Dec. 475.

[147] Jennings v. Lyons, 39 Wis. 554. See also, Leopold v. Salkey, 89 Ill. 412; Hunter v. Waldron, 7 Ala. 763.

[148] Provost v. Harwood, 29 Vt. 219; Evans v. Bennett, 7 Wis. 351.

reasonable or oppressive exaction on the part of the principal.[149] Provisions of this character are now frequently inserted in contracts with the employes of manufacturing companies, including also a stipulation that the employe will give notice a certain time before abandonment of his intention to do so; and where such stipulations are not unreasonable and oppressive, the courts will enforce them. Such stipulations may be made by express contract between the employer and the individual employe or servant, or may constitute a portion of the rules and regulations of the company or firm, agreed to by the employes generally. If the employe sign such regulations or enter into the employment with knowledge of them, he will be bound by them.[150] But the mere fact that the employe had been informed of the regulations, and continued to work for the company without objection, is not necessarily conclusive, as matter of law, that he assented to them.[151] And whether or not there has been an abandonment by the employe of his work is a question for the jury, under all the circumstances of the case;[152] a mere temporary absence, for example, would not justify the conclusion of an abandonment and a consequent forfeiture of accrued wages.[153] In the absence of any stipulation for a forfeiture of accrued wages unless notice of abandonment be given, there can be no such forfeiture; unless the agent is otherwise at fault, as we shall presently see. And even where there is such a stipulation, if the absence of the agent or employe is not attributable to his own default, but rather to some unavoidable cause, such as illness or other visitation of Providence, there will be no forfeiture, although notice has not been given.[154]

§ 276. When agent abandons undertaking without just cause—Entirety or divisibility of contract—Rule in equity.—A very important question, and one upon which there appears to be some

[149] Richardson v. Woehler, 26 Mich. 90; Walsh v. Walley, L. R. 9 Q. B. 367; Pottsville Iron, etc., Co. v. Good, 116 Pa. St. 385, 2 Am. St. 614.

[150] Harmon v. Salmon Falls Mfg. Co., 35 Me. 447, 58 Am. Dec. 718; Walsh v. Walley, L. R. 9 Q. B. 367; Pottsville Iron, etc., Co. v. Good, 116 Pa. St. 385, 2 Am. St. 614; Bradley v. Salmon Falls Mfg. Co., 30 N. H. 487.

[151] Collins v. New England Iron Co., 115 Mass. 23; Preston v. American Linen Co., 119 Mass. 400.

[152] Partington v. Wamsutta Mills, 110 Mass. 467.

[153] Herber v. U. S. Flax Mfg. Co., 13 R. I. 303.

[154] Fuller v. Brown, 11 Metc. (Mass.) 440; Hughes v. Wamsutta Mills, 11 Allen (Mass.) 201.

conflict in the decisions, is whether the agent forfeits the compensation already earned by him, if he leaves his principal's employment before the expiration of the term of service, and without any just cause. Much depends, in such cases, upon whether the contract of employment is an entire one, in point of time, or whether it is divisible. If the contract be for an entire, indivisible undertaking, the prevailing doctrine in England and America is to the effect that the agent who, without any just cause, voluntarily abandons his undertaking, forfeits his entire compensation, and is liable to the principal in damages besides.[155] This was the common-law rule, and it is still in force in many jurisdictions. It is applicable, however, only in cases where the entirety of the contract is so plain and evident as to render full performance a condition precedent. In such case it was said that no recovery could be had upon a *quantum meruit,* for the plain reason that there was an express contract by which the parties must be guided; and that there could be no recovery upon the special contract, because the agent had failed to comply with his part of it. The parties having made the contract, the courts could not relieve them.[156] Whether the contract is entire or not depends upon the intention of the parties as expressed in the contract, and such intention must be gathered from all its terms when construed together.[157] A contract is entire when it is the intention of the parties that the whole undertaking is to be completed before any portion of the consideration can be demanded. Payment in such cases is in one specified amount of money or in some specific article. Thus, where the contract was for the complete repair of certain chandeliers, and they were returned incompletely repaired, the court held that there could be no recovery for what had been done on them.[158] The full performance in such cases is a condition

[155] Waddington v. Oliver, 2 B. & P. N. R. 61; Ellis v. Hamlen, 3 Taunt. 52; Spain v. Arnott, 2 Stark. 227, 3 E. C. L. 400; Diefenback v. Stark, 56 Wis. 462, 43 Am. Rep. 719; Dover v. Plemmons, 10 Ired. (N. C.) 23; Clark v. Gilbert, 26 N. Y. 279, 84 Am. Dec. 189; Preston v. American Linen Co., 119 Mass. 400; Word v. Winder, 16 La. Ann. 111; Jewell v. Thompson, 2 Litt. (Ky.) 52; Caldwell v. Dickson, 17 Mo. 575; Thrift v. Payne, 71 Ill. 408; Miller v. Goddard, 34 Me. 102, 56 Am. Dec. 638; Martin v. Schoenberger, 8 W. & S. (Pa.) 367; Mack v. Bragg, 30 Vt. 571; Cutter v. Powell, 6 T. R. 320, 2 Smith Ld. Cas. (9th ed.) 1212.

[156] Stark v. Parker, 2 Pick. (Mass.) 267, 13 Am. Dec. 425.

[157] Ritchie v. Atkinson, 10 East 295; More v. Bonnett, 40 Cal. 251.

[158] Sinclair v. Bowles, 4 M. & R. 1, 9 B. & C. 92.

precedent, unless performance was prevented by the fault of the principal; and if the requirement entail a hardship upon one of the parties, he can justly blame no one but himself for having entered into it. The rule was formerly much more rigorously applied than now. Thus, it was held in an English case, where a sailor had accepted a promissory note from his employer for the services to be performed by him, and it was provided by the agreement between the two that he should "proceed, continue and do his duty on board for the voyage," and he died before the arrival of the ship, that there could be no recovery on the note, nor on a *quantum meruit*.[159] This iron rule of the common law has, however, been much relaxed in modern times, by the application of the principles of equity. As we have already seen, an employe will be relieved from the forfeiture of wages already earned; and this is true even where full performance is a condition precedent to the collection of compensation, if the abandonment of the service is not due to the fault or wrongful act of the employe. Hence, it has been held that where an attorney failed to complete his contract for the rendition of professional services, on account of his election to the bench, he could recover on a *quantum meruit* for that portion of the services already performed by him.[160] And where a servant was called away as a witness, the same ruling was made.[161]

§ 277. **Application of equity rule in some of the states.**—In many of the states of the Union the courts have applied a more equitable rule to the construction of indivisible, entire contracts, though the failure to perform is due to the fault or wrongful act of the agent or servant. In those states it is held that if the employer has received and accepted a substantial benefit from the services of the employe, the latter may recover on a *quantum meruit;* the amount of compensation being limited, however, to the contract price, after deducting all damages sustained by the employer by reason of the servant's abandonment or wrongful act.[162] Under this rule the

[159] Cutter v. Powell, 6 T. R. 320, 2 Smith Ld. Cas. (9th ed.) 1212.

[160] Baird v. Ratcliff, 10 Tex. 81.

[161] Melville v. De Wolf, 4 E. & B. 844.

[162] Britton v. Turner, 6 N. H. 481; Coe v. Smith, 4 Ind. 79; Ricks v. Yates, 5 Ind. 115; Adams v. Cosby, 48 Ind. 153; Everroad v. Schwartzkopf, 123 Ind. 35; Gastlin v. Weeks, 2 Ind. App. 222; Lincoln v. Schwartz, 70 Ill. 134; Dobbins v. Higgins, 78 Ill. 440; Dover v. Plemmons, 10 Ired. (N. C.) 23; Wilson v. Adams, 15 Tex. 323; Powers v. Wilson, 47 Iowa 666; Robinson v. San-

principal is entitled to recover from his agent all damages that the former may have sustained by reason of the wrongful abandonment. Such damages may be recovered in a separate action by the principal, or he may recoup the agent's claim in an action by the latter for the compensation, by way of defense. If recoupment is resorted to, the claim for it must grow out of the same contract or transaction sued upon by the agent, and the principal can not recover judgment over, for damages in excess of what is found to be due the agent, the principal being relegated to a separate action. Recoupment is a common-law proceeding or defense, and goes to reduce the plaintiff's damages.[163] But if the suit be in equity, or in a state where the code provides for a counterclaim, the defendant principal may file such counterclaim and recover judgment over, if the defendant's claim exceed that of plaintiff.[164]

§ 278. Further as to severable and indivisible contracts.—Of course, if the contract is severable, the agent is entitled to recover for any compensation falling due at any period, and a subsequent abandonment by him of the service does not operate as a forfeiture of salary or wages already earned.[165] A contract is severable if by its terms it is the duty of one of the parties to perform several and distinct items, and of the other to pay the price apportioned to each item, or the price to be paid is left to be implied by law. And the same rule holds where the price to be paid is clearly and distinctly apportioned to different parts of what is to be performed, although the latter is in its nature single and entire.[166] But if the consideration to be paid is single and entire, the contract must be regarded as entire; although the subject of the contract may consist of several distinct and independent items.[167] A divisible contract is one that, in respect of the things contemplated and embraced by it, may be divided into two or more parts not necessarily dependent on each other nor intended by the parties that they should be.[168] Thus, a contract to perform some specific service is entire, and the price

ders, 24 Miss. 391; Allen v. McKibbin, 5 Mich. 449; Wolf v. Gerr, 43 Iowa 339; Parcell v. McComber, 11 Neb. 209, 38 Am. Rep. 366; Duncan v. Baker, 21 Kan. 99; Downey v. Burke, 23 Mo. 228; Wood Master and Serv. 240.

[163] Mechem Ag., § 647.

[164] Pomeroy Rem., § 736; Woodruff v. Garner, 27 Ind. 4; Standley v. Northwestern, etc., Ins. Co., 95 Ind. 254.

[165] Taylor v. Laird, 1 H. & N. 266.

[166] 2 Parsons Conts. (5th ed.) 517.

[167] 2 Parsons Conts. (5th ed.) 519.

[168] Wooten v. Walters, 110 N. C. 251.

can not be demanded until it is fully performed.[169] So, if a builder engage to erect a house within a specified time, and at a specified price, he to furnish all the materials and labor, the contract is entire; and if the part of the house which has been constructed be destroyed by fire, the loss will be that of the builder, and not that of the other party. If in such case the party contracting with the builder has advanced money to the latter, he may recover the same in an action for that purpose, and also the damages caused by the failure to complete the building according to contract.[170] And where one was employed to serve for a year at so much per month, the contract was adjudged to be entire.[171] And so, a contract to teach school for a school term, consisting of so many days, is entire; and if the teacher is prematurely discharged, he or she may recover for the entire term, if otherwise entitled to recover; and this is true even though the teacher fail to serve during the entire term, unless such failure be due to the fault of such teacher.[172] But a contract to perform a specified service for a given sum, of which service the other party receives the benefit, and to pay for the same in installments as the performance progresses, is divisible, and the installments may be sued for as they mature.[173] And a contract made by one person with three others not in any way connected, that he will represent them in the sale of their coal, taking the same from them in equal quantities from their respective mines, is a severable contract, especially where all the parties have so treated it.[174] In Massachusetts, in an action by the plaintiff growing out of an agreement to work for the defendant seven months, at twelve dollars per month, the court was of opinion that the contract was entire, and that the plaintiff, who had left the defendant's service before the time had expired, could not recover for partial services performed. The plaintiff contended that it was a contract for seven months, at twelve dollars per month, to be paid at the end of each month; but the court refused to give it that construction, saying that it was not the contract proved. As there was no time fixed in the contract for payment, the law fixed the time at the period when the services were com-

[169] Rockwell v. Newton, 44 Conn. 333; Hulse v. Bonsack Mach. Co., 65 Fed. 864.

[170] Tompkins v. Dudley, 25 N. Y. 272.

[171] Reaf v. Moor, 19 Johns. (N. Y.) 337.

[172] School Town of Carthage v. Gray, 10 Ind. App. 428; Charlestown School Tp. v. Hay, 74 Ind. 127.

[173] Cunningham v. Morrell, 10 Johns. (N. Y.) 203, 6 Am. Dec. 332.

[174] Shipman v. Straitsville Central Mining Co., 158 U. S. 356.

pleted. The fixing of the rate of payment at so much per month was regarded by the court as simply a convenient rating in case the contract should be terminated by consent, or death, or other casualty, before its expiration.[175] In Mississippi the court declined to follow the rule enunciated in *Britton* v. *Turner*,[176] which seems to be the leading case in which the right of an agent who has abandoned the service of his principal to recover on a *quantum meruit* for services actually rendered is asserted. "The decided weight of authority," says Cooper, J., "is to the contrary."[177] "And it was decided at an early day, in this state," continues the same learned judge, "that an entire contract of this character could not be apportioned, and that, under the circumstances named, no recovery could be had by the party guilty of the breach of contract; that he could not recover on the special contract because he himself had not performed, nor upon *quantum meruit*, because of the existence of the special contract."[178]

§ 279. Agent's right to reimbursements—Manner of proving disbursements.—"Another right of agents is to be reimbursed all their advances, expenses and disbursements made in the course of the agency on account of, or for the benefit of their principal. This is naturally, nay necessarily, implied from the very character of every agency to which such advances, expenses and disbursements are incident, whenever they fall within the appropriate duty of the agent. Hence, all the incidental charges and expenses incurred for warehouse room, duties, freight, lighterage, general average, salvage, repairs, journeys and other acts done to preserve the property of the principal, and to enable the agent to accomplish the objects of the principal, are to be fully paid by the latter. So, if an agent has, at the express or the implied request of his principal, necessarily incurred expenses in carrying on or defending suits for the benefit of his principal, those expenses must be borne by the latter, and the agent will be entitled to recover them from him."[179] The doctrine here stated rests upon the implication that the expenditures for which the agent asks to be reimbursed are paid at the principal's express or implied request, or are such as the principal is liable for by implication of law. Of course, where the authority is express, there

[175] Davis v. Maxwell, 12 Metc. (Mass.) 286.

[176] 6 N. H. 481.

[177] Citing Lawson Conts., § 470, n. 4.

[178] Timberlake v. Thayer, 71 Miss. 279.

[179] Story Ag., § 335.

can be no difficulty in determining the fact and extent of the principal's liability, for in such a case the contract is the best and only evidence. Being requested to make such payments, the agent is clearly entitled to be reimbursed, the law always implying a duty and promise to refund on the part of the principal.[180] On the contrary, where the contract provided that the agent should pay charges and expenditures, it was held that there could be no reimbursement, and evidence of a different custom in the community was held not admissible.[181] But even where the agent has not been requested to make such advances, if properly incurred, and reasonably and in good faith paid, without any default on the part of the agent, he will be entitled to reimbursement by the principal.[182] On the other hand, the agreement may clearly imply that there is to be no reimbursement. After all, the right of the agent to be reimbursed depends upon the agreement, express or implied.[183] Thus, in cases of real estate brokers, rental agents, etc., the agent may incur expenses for advertising, etc., for which, in case of failure to sell or rent, he is not entitled to be reimbursed, and is, therefore, subjected to a loss. This is true even if he succeeds in selling or renting the property. In such cases the commissions of the agent to which he is entitled in case of success are deemed adequate to cover such expenditures as are incident to the services.[184] The doctrine that renders principals liable for the proper and necessary expenditures of their agents is founded upon necessity and justice. Thus, if an agent be sued on a contract made in pursuance of authority, though the suit be without cause and he eventually succeeds, the law implies that the principal will indemnify him and refund the expense.[185] Usage, too, is not without a controlling influence. When usage sanctions it, an agent may, if he act in good faith concerning it, and there is an emergency, insure a cargo, and collect the premium from the principal.[186] Where an attorney, under implied authority, indemnifies an officer for making a levy, and sustains a loss, he may recover the loss from

[180] Sutherland Dam. (2d ed.), § 789.

[181] Champion Mach. Co. v. Ervay (Tex. App.), 16 S. W. 172.

[182] Story Ag., § 336.

[183] Sentance v. Hawley, 13 C. B. (N. S.) 458.

[184] Simpson v. Lamb, 17 C. B. 603, 25 L. J. C. P. 603; Martin v. Silliman, 53 N. Y. 615. See also, Gillespie v. Wilder, 99 Mass. 170; Sibbald v. Bethlehem Iron Co., 83 N. Y. 378, 38 Am. Rep. 441.

[185] Stocking v. Sage, 1 Conn. 518.

[186] Wolff v. Horncastle, 1 B. & P. 316.

the client.[187] And where a general business agent for an individual person is also the agent of an insurance company, and in that capacity writes insurance on the property of his principal, but under circumstances that make the policy valid, or at most only voidable, he is entitled to be reimbursed for the premiums paid by him.[188] As to the manner of proving disbursements and advances, not much need be said. Common-law evidence is always proper in such cases; but the receipts and vouchers of the persons who received the money are always competent, if such payments were legitimate. In such case, if the undertaking be the supervising of the building of a house, for example, it is not essential that the supervisor furnish proof of the actual delivery of the material, or the number of days workmen were employed, but the receipts and vouchers are sufficient *prima facie* evidence of payment, and, in the absence of evidence to the contrary, will entitle the supervisor to recover expenses thus incurred.[189] It should be remembered, however, that the agent can not recover disbursements unnecessarily incurred, or such as might by the exercise of reasonable diligence have been avoided.[190] The agent in this, as in all other branches of his undertaking, must exercise proper care and diligence in the execution of his trust, and the principal can not be made answerable to the agent for money paid out uselessly or carelessly; and the same is true of acts that are unauthorized by the express or implied agreement between the parties.[191]

§ 280. **Agent's right to be indemnified.**—Besides the duty of reimbursing the agent for necessary outlays in the course of the agency, the principal is likewise compelled, under the law, to indemnify the agent against the consequences of all acts done by the latter in the exercise of his authority, provided such acts are not illegal.[192] That the rule which enables an agent to recover indemnity from the principal is grounded in justice and fair dealing is well illustrated by the

[187] Clark v. Randall, 9 Wis. 135.

[188] Rochester v. Levering, 104 Ind. 562.

[189] Blazo v. Gill, 143 N. Y. 232.

[190] Brown v. Clayton, 12 Ga. 564.

[191] Clamagaran v. Sacerdotte, 8 Mart. N. S. (La.) 538.

[192] Saveland v. Green, 36 Wis. 612; Powell v. Newburgh, 19 Johns. (N. Y.) 284; Howe v. Buffalo, etc., R. Co., 37 N. Y. 297; Otter Creek Lumber Co. v. McElwee, 37 Ill. App. 285; Flower v. Downs, 6 La. Ann. 538; Beach v. Branch, 57 Ga. 362; Greene v. Goddard, 9 Metc. (Mass.) 212; Bibb v. Allen, 149 U. S. 481; Betts v. Gibbins, 2 A. & E. (29 E. C. L.) 57; Stocking v. Sage, 1 Conn. 518; Avery v. Halsey, 14 Pick. (Mass.) 174.

statement of Mr. Story, that as on the one hand the agent is not permitted to reap any of the profits of his agency properly belonging to his principal, so on the other hand the agent is entitled to be indemnified against all losses which have been innocently sustained by him, on the same account, except those sustained by his own fault or negligence.[193] The losses must, however, be the proximate results,—the natural consequences of the execution of the agency. If they be merely the results of casualty or accident, or if the agency be only the occasion, and not the cause of the losses or damages, the agent can not recover them from the principal.[194] Hence, if the agent unnecessarily expose himself to injury while engaged in the execution of his authority, he can not recover damages of the principal. If, however, the thing done was properly conducive to the discharge of the duties of the agency, the principal is liable.[195] The business in which the agent is employed must be the cause and not merely the occasion or condition of the same.[196] Hence, if an agent, under direction of his principal, has by mistake cut timber partly from the land of another, which his principal has received and disposed of, he is entitled to recover from the principal the damages he was bound to pay on account of the trespass.[197] And a like remedy is open to the agent where he has been compelled to pay damages for a false representation of the quality of his principal's goods, made innocently in pursuance of directions from the principal, and in consequence of a deception practiced by him; or for converting the property of a third person by his principal's direction, claiming to be the owner, the agent having no notice of any adverse title; or to pay the price of property purchased for his principal and the expenses of a suit consequent upon the purchase.[198] But the agent must not have exceeded his authority in the incurring of the loss. Hence, where the principal had employed the agent, who was skilled in the management of horses, to take two horses to Richmond, Va., to exhibit them at the state fair, and sell them at the best price he could obtain for them, and the agent sold one of the horses, but, being unable to sell the other, after ineffectual efforts to do so, and without consulting his principal, took the remaining horse to Charles-

[193] Story Ag., § 346.

[194] Story Ag., § 341; Duncan v. Hill, L. R. 8 Ex. 242.

[195] Saveland v. Green, 36 Wis. 612.

[196] Wharton Ag., § 346.

[197] Drummond v. Humphreys, 39 Me. 347.

[198] Sutherland Dam. (2d ed.), § 793.

ton, S. C., where he finally succeeded in selling it, his expenses amounting to $445.23, it being impossible for the agent, after he reached Wilmington, N. C., owing to the unsettled state of the country, to bring back the horse, it was held by the supreme court of Vermont that the agent exceeded his instructions and was not entitled to pay for his expenses after he left the place to which his instructions directed him to go.[199] Illustrations of losses not the proximate results of an agency are given in an early Pennsylvania case—*D'Arcy* v. *Lyle;*[200] namely, where the agent, while on a journey for his principal, and on his business, is robbed of his own money, or receives a wound, or his horse is taken lame, the agent furnishing his own horse. In the first illustration it was not necessarily a part of the agent's business to carry the money. In the case where the agent was wounded, the principal was not bound for the cure of the wound, for it was one of the risks which the agent took upon himself. In the last example, that of the horse becoming lame, the court said it depended upon the contract: if the contract required the agent to carry a letter for the principal and deliver it at a certain place, the agent would be bound to furnish his own horse, and the principal would not be liable for an injury that might befall the animal. This case of *D'Arcy* v. *Lyle* is itself an apt illustration of a loss incurred in the execution of the agency. There the agent had been employed by the principal to recover goods of the latter from a firm at Cape Francis, San Domingo. He succeeded in securing the goods by judicial proceedings, and accounted for them to the principal. In the meantime, the agent having executed a bond to one Richardson, who had attached the goods to satisfy an alleged claim, Richardson brought suit against the agent D'Arcy to recover the value of the goods. D'Arcy was again successful in court; but the matter was now taken in hand by Christophe, who had succeeded by revolution in becoming president of Hayti, and he issued an arbitrary order that D'Arcy and Richardson should engage in combat, and that the victor should have judgment in the suit. The result of the fight being uncertain, Christophe decreed that they should fight again, whereupon D'Arcy attempted to flee the country. Having been intercepted and brought before the president, D'Arcy consented to confess judgment for the $3,000, and subsequently paid the same. He then sued his principals and obtained a verdict. Upon a review of the case, the court decided that the verdict ought to stand, it

[199] Fuller v. Ellis, 39 Vt. 345.

[200] 5 Binney (Pa.) 441.

being regarded by the court as a determination of the question whether the proceedings at the Cape were in consequence of D'Arcy having received possession of his principal's goods there. The court held that damages incurred by an agent under such circumstances should be borne by the principal; and the objection that, at the time the judgment was rendered against the agent, "he was no longer an agent, having long before made up his accounts, and transmitted the balance to the defendant," was declared to have no weight, the judgment being but the consummation of the proceedings which were commenced during the agency. It was further objected that no man would be safe if he were to be responsible, to an unknown amount, for any sums which his agent might consent to pay, in consequence of threats of unprincipled tyrants in foreign countries; but the court refused to suppose extreme cases, which it would be time enough to decide when they occurred. The amount paid by the agent under the circumstances was not more than the estimated value of the property. Had it been far in excess of that, the court intimated that a different conclusion might have been reached, as to the excess. The mere fact that the principal had no title to the property in dispute in such a case would not be sufficient to defeat the agent's claim for indemnity, for it was this want of title that occasioned the agent's loss. If the agent has reasonable grounds to believe that the principal is the owner of the property, and he is duly authorized to take it, and does so without knowing at the time that such taking is a trespass or a tort, a promise of indemnity will be implied, although it subsequently turn out that the principal's title was not good and that the act of taking was a trespass.[201]

§ 281. **Agent can not recover for** illegal outlays.—But if the act performed by the agent, and on account of which he suffered the loss or outlay, was illegal on its face, or he had knowledge of the illegality, the law does not give him the right of indemnity.[202] In such case the law will not lend its aid to change the result which the agent produced by his wrongful act, any more than it will interfere between wrongdoers in other cases; and this is true without reference to the question whether the principal expressly promised to indemnify

[201] Moore v. Appleton, 26 Ala. 633; Avery v. Halsey, 14 Pick. (Mass.) 174.

[202] Bibb v. Allen, 149 U. S. 481; Jacobs v. Pollard, 10 Cush. (Mass.) 287, 57 Am. Dec. 105; Cumpston v. Lambert, 18 Ohio 81, 51 Am. Dec. 442; Howe v. Buffalo, etc., R. Co., 37 N. Y. 297; Harvey v. Merrill, 150 Mass. 1.

the agent in his wrongdoing or not.[203] If, however, the principal appears to have a right to authorize the act to be done, but the agent, fearing that the act may prove to be unlawful, requires indemnity, which is given, the agent is entitled to recover it.[204] If the principal and the agent are both wrongdoers there can be neither indemnity nor contribution. This is the general rule. The exception is where the act is not clearly illegal in itself.[205] And a further qualification of the rule is that the parties must know at the time that it is a wrong.[206] The agent's right to receive indemnity from his principal applies not only to the recovery for losses already sustained by the former, but includes the right to retain funds or securities in his hands so as to protect himself against outstanding liabilities not yet matured or that have not been enforced.[207]

§ 282. **Agent may pay loss without waiting to be sued.**—When the agent becomes satisfied that he has rendered himself liable in damages to a third party on account of an act done for his principal, in good faith, he is not required to wait until he is sued before he will be permitted to pay such damages, in order that he may recover them from his principal; as soon as he becomes assured of his liability, he may pay such third person and then proceed against the principal, if the latter refuses to reimburse him. But in such case, he can recover only such amount as he was legally bound for, without regard to the fact that he may have paid more.[208]

§ 283. **Rights and remedies of subagents.**—A subagent is entitled to all the rights and remedies against his employer that an agent is entitled to. The law of principal and agent applies to him as it does to the principal and the chief agent. The only difficulty is in determining when the relation subsists between him and the principal, and when between him and the chief agent. We have already seen that in some instances the selection of the subagent may be by the express or implied appointment of the principal, and that, by the usages of trade, he may sustain the same relation to the principal as that occupied by the chief agent; while in other instances, when not so appointed, or when usage does not sanction it, he becomes the ap-

203 Story Ag., § 339.

204 Adamson v. Jarvis, 4 Bing. 66. See also, Coventry v. Barton, 17 John. (N. Y.) 142; Howe v. Buffalo, etc., R. Co., 37 N. Y. 297.

205 Betts v. Gibbins, 2 A. & E. 57.

206 Story Ag., § 339.

207 Sutherland Dam. (2d ed.), § 793.

208 Saveland v. Green, 36 Wis. 612; Clark v. Jones, 16 Lea (Tenn.) 351.

pointee of the agent solely.[209] Where his employment is effected without the express or implied assent of the principal, or is not sanctioned by usage, there is no privity between the two, and there can be no reciprocal rights or obligations subsisting between them; unless, indeed, his acts in the course of the undertaking are duly ratified by the principal with a full knowledge of all the facts. But wherever there is such privity between them, the subagent will have a personal claim against the principal for his compensation, and for disbursements and indemnity, the same as the real agent; and, if the principal knowingly adopts his acts, the subagent will be entitled to pay, and to a lien upon property in his hands for commissions, disbursements and indemnity, the same as the agent would have been.[210] And while ordinarily he will have no general lien if he knows or has reason to believe that the agent is acting for another and not for himself in the particular undertaking, yet he may avail himself of a general or special lien against the principal to the extent that the agent himself has such lien at the same time against the principal, unless the acts of the superior agent or his own are tortious.[211] But the mere fact that the principal knows of the employment of the subagent, and that he is acting as such, will not render the principal liable for the services of the subagent, even though the principal has accepted benefits resulting from such employment, in the absence of the element of privity between the principal and the subagent.[212] Nor can a principal be held liable on a special contract for compensation entered into between the agent and subagent, unless he has ratified it.[213] Where there is no evidence to show that the principal employed the subagent or in any way agreed to the agent's employment of him, the subagent can not recover from the principal upon the contract for services. He can at best only recover for work and labor, on the *quantum meruit*.[214] But if A employ B to effect a policy of insurance for his benefit, and B, without A's knowledge, employ C to effect the policy, representing himself to C as the principal, C will have a lien on the policy against A for the general balance due to him from B.[215] And where a contract for services was made on behalf of an insurance company by its agent with a subagent, providing that

[209] *Ante*, § 188, *et seq.*

[210] Story Ag., §§ 388-390.

[211] Story Ag., § 389; McKenzie v. Nevius, 22 Me. 138, 38 Am. Dec. 299.

[212] Homan v. Brooklyn Life Ins. Co., 7 Mo. App. 22.

[213] 1 Am. & Eng. Encyc. L. (2d ed.) 984, n. 1, citing Beyers v. Hodge, 1 Misc. (N. Y.) 76.

[214] Johnson v. Pacific Mail S. S. Co., 5 Cal. 408.

[215] Westwood v. Bell, 4 Camp. 349.

as part compensation for such services the subagent should receive a specified percentage of the amount paid by the principal for the services of the agent so making the contract, it was held that the contract was that of the principal and not that of the agent, the latter being estopped to claim of the company the share of his profits contracted to be paid to another, and that in such case the subagent could recover such percentage from the company upon performing the services.[216]

§ 284. **Rights and remedies of employes of agents in cases of emergency—Application of doctrine of agency by implication of law.**—The power of an agent or employe of a company or corporation to procure the services of another employe, such as a physician or surgeon, to attend upon one injured in the service of the company, etc., has already been discussed under the head of agency by necessity.[217] It need only be said, in addition, that where the doctrine of an agency by implication of law is recognized in such cases, the sub-employe can recover from the principal the value of his services rendered in emergencies pertaining to the hazardous business in which such company is engaged, provided the agent had express or implied authority to make such employment, or occupied such a position in the company's service that the law will presume he had such authority.[217a] Thus, where that doctrine is recognized, the courts will presume that the "general manager" of a railroad company has the general direction and control of the company's affairs, and that this includes the authority to bind it by contracts for the services of surgeons, nurses, etc., to persons injured on the line of its railway.[218] But it must appear, either from the nature of the duties imposed upon the officer making such employment, or from such duties being known, or from other evidence, that he had such authority; and in the absence of such proof, the presumption will not be indulged.[219] As a general rule, "neither a roadmaster, section agent, yardmaster nor station master will be presumed to have authority to employ a physician to attend a servant of the company injured in the line of his duties.

[216] Ætna Ins. Co. v. Church, 21 Ohio St. 492.

[217] *Ante*, §§ 85, 86.

[217a] See 1 Thompson Neg. (2d ed.), §§ 544-548.

[218] Louisville, etc., R. Co. v. McVay, 98 Ind. 391.

[219] Pierce Railroads 277; Williams v. Cammack, 27 Miss. 209; Louisville, etc., R. Co. v. McVay, 98 Ind. 391. See also, McCarthy v. Missouri R. Co., 15 Mo. App. 385; Walker v. Great Western R. Co., L. R. 2 Ex. 228.

So, also, it is held that there is nothing in the duties of the company's solicitor, or surgeon, or engineer, or conductor, from which such authority can be presumed. But an emergency calling for immediate action in order to save life or prevent suffering may be sufficient to confer authority upon the subordinate to employ necessary surgical aid, if he is the highest representative of the company on the ground. * * * The authority of such a subordinate agent, however, arises only with the emergency which makes it necessary for him to possess it, and ends with such emergency."[220] Hence, the company is not bound by the act of such subordinate officer in continuing the employment of nurses and the purchase of medicines, after the emergency has ceased to exist. And if the company employ a physician or surgeon regularly, and he be conveniently at hand, there can be no presumption that a subordinate agent of the company has the authority to employ another. Even the regularly employed surgeon of the company has no such authority. And in the absence of an express contract entered into by some one authorized to represent the company, a physician can have no claim against the company for services rendered to an injured employe or passenger. The service must be rendered upon the credit of the company.[221] An agent, as a general rule, has no authority to employ a subagent; and unless express or implied authority is proved, or the act of appointment or the acts of the subagent done in behalf of the principal are ratified by the latter, the agent alone will be liable to the subagent for any claim he may have for services, etc.[222]

§ 285. **Rights of unauthorized agent whose acts are subsequently ratified.**—When the agent undertakes to act without authority conferred expressly or by implication, or by operation of law, his acts are absolutely void, and he is not entitled to recover compensation, or to be reimbursed or indemnified by the principal. But if the principal ratifies the acts of the agent, and accepts the benefits thereof, he is liable to the agent the same as if the acts had been authorized by him originally. And this, as we have seen, may be done expressly or by implication. The principal is bound by the act, even though it results to his detriment: he adopts the agent's acts as his own and takes his agency *cum onere*.[223] By such ratification the principal

[220] Elliott Railroads, § 222.

[221] Elliott Railroads, § 222.

[222] Wilkins v. Duncan, 2 Litt. (Ky.) 168; Taylor v. Nostrand, 134 N. Y. 108.

[223] Hovil v. Pack, 7 East 164.

impliedly agrees to pay the agent not only his commissions, but his necessary outlays, and to indemnify him against losses incurred in the assumed agency. Thus, where the master of a ship entered into a charter party whereby he was himself to receive the freight, and as a consideration therefor was to convey troops and to fit the vessel for that purpose, and he advanced money out of his own pocket and drew bills on the owner for the rest of the expenses to enable the ship to earn the freight, and the owner ratified the contract, it was held by the house of lords that the master, when sued by the owner for the freight, as money had and received, had a right at law to deduct the money so advanced without pleading a set-off, and that he had a right in equity to be reimbursed out of the freight so earned; such a case not falling within the rule that the master has not, in ordinary circumstances, a lien on the freight for wages and disbursements.[224] And if the agent improperly appoint a subagent under him, and such unauthorized act be subsequently ratified by the principal, the latter will be bound by the ratified acts of the subagent in the same manner and to the same extent as if he had originally given to the agent a power of substitution.[225] The assumed agent is entitled to recover the expenses incurred in such case the same as if he had acted with full authority.[226] If, however, there are intervening rights in favor of third parties, which had accrued prior to the time of the vesting of the agent's rights by reason of the ratification, or, in other words, prior to the ratification itself, the latter will not have a retrospective effect, so as to divest the rights of such third parties.[227] Thus, where goods are stopped *in transitu* by an unauthorized person, a purchaser in good faith can not be divested of his rights in them by a subsequent ratification of the unauthorized stoppage.[228] And so, where a debtor's books and accounts are assigned to a surety for indemnity by the act of an unauthorized agent, and the assignment is subsequently ratified by the owner, the ratification does not relate back to the time of the assignment, as would be the case if no rights intervened; and if, before such assignment is ratified, a party holding a claim against the owner of the accounts garnish the claim in the hands of the party owing it, the garnishor can not be deprived of the

[224] Bristow v. Whitmore, 9 H. L. Cas. 391, 31 L. J. Ch. 467.

[225] Story Ag., § 249.

[226] Hovil v. Pack, 7 East 164; Frixione v. Tagliaferro, 10 Moore P. C. 175.

[227] Story Ag., §§ 245, 246; Wharton Ag., §§ 77, 78.

[228] Bird v. Brown, 4 Exch. 786.

lien thus acquired by the ratification of the assignment.[229] And the same rule holds where property conveyed to satisfy a debt was accepted by an agent without authority: where, prior to the ratification of such acceptance, an attachment had been levied on such property, the holder of the attachment lien could not be deprived of his rights thereunder; the ratification not being retroactive so as to carry it back to the time of the commission of the unauthorized act.[230]

§ **286. Remedies of agent against principal.**—We are next to inquire, in a general way, what are the remedies by which an agent or representative may enforce against his principal the duties and obligations which the latter owes to him, in case the principal fails or refuses to discharge these voluntarily. If the claim of the agent is for compensation for services performed, whether the same be commissions, wages, salary, or fees, it is quite obvious that the ordinary common-law remedies of *assumpsit* and debt are open to him. The most usual remedies, unless suit be upon a special contract, are the common counts for work and labor done or services rendered.[231] He may also, in a proper case, maintain a suit in equity.[232] If the action is for indemnity, whether in contract or tort, the law implies a promise on the part of the principal, and the agent may sue in *assumpsit;* or, if the act was a tort, he may bring an action on the case.[233] We have already pointed out the remedy for a wrongful discharge of the agent by the principal.[234] Of course, if the forum is in a code state, the agent will have his remedy in the ordinary civil action for work and labor or services, or on the special contract; or, if in tort, for damages. In addition to these remedies the agent may withhold from moneys in his hands belonging to his principal such amounts as may be justly owing to him by the latter for advances, expenses, disbursements and loans arising in the course of the agency, whenever the amounts are definite and certain and do not merely sound in damages; and this may be done by recoupment, counterclaim, or set-off, in any action instituted against him by the principal for any balance in his hands.[235] And in certain cases—as, where a consignment has been made to the order of a factor—he has also the right of stoppage *in transitu,* and a lien for his general balance.[236]

229 Wood v. McCain, 7 Ala. 800, 42 Am. Dec. 612.

230 Kempner v. Rosenthal, 81 Tex. 12.

231 16 Encyc. of Pl. & Pr. 917.

232 Story Ag., § 350.

233 16 Encyc. of Pl. & Pr. 916, and notes.

234 *Ante,* §§ 269–271.

235 Story Ag., § 350; Pomeroy Rem., § 777, *et seq.*

236 Story Ag., § 350.

§ **287. Agent's lien for compensation, expenses, etc.**—In addition to these personal remedies by which the agent may enforce the duties and obligations due him from the principal, the law in many cases gives the agent a special remedy, by way of a right to hold the property, money or effects of the principal that may be in the agent's hands, in order to secure himself in any just claim he may have against the principal for compensation, expenses, disbursements, indemnity, etc. This right is called a "lien." The word "lien" is French, and means a tie or bond or band, being derived from the Latin *"ligare,"* to bind. A lien, in its legal sense, is a tie that binds property to a debt or claim for its satisfaction.[237] "In its most extensive signification, the term includes every case in which real or personal property is charged with the payment of any debt or duty; every such charge being denominated a lien on the property. In a more limited sense, it is defined to be a right of detaining the property of another until some claim is satisfied."[238] Liens may be either: (1) of common-law origin, or (2) of statutory creation, or (3) they may be the results of contracts. Many kinds of liens have been given to agents and employes by statutory enactments; it is also true that many more may be and are created by contracts between the parties. While a large portion of statutory and contract liens may be made applicable between principals and agents, it is our purpose to notice these only incidentally; what we have to say on the subject of liens will have reference more especially to common-law liens. The liens of agents are of common-law origin, though they have often been enlarged upon by statutes, in cases of particular classes of agents. The lien which an agent is entitled to, therefore, as a general rule, is the right to retain that which is in his possession belonging to his principal, until his demands have been satisfied.[239]

§ **288. General and particular liens—Illustrations of each.**—Agent's liens are divisible into two classes; namely, (1) specific or particular liens, and (2) general liens. A specific or particular lien is a lien upon some particular article of another in the hands of one who has bestowed labor upon it or performed services or incurred expenses with reference to it. "A particular lien is usually defined to be the right to retain a thing for some charge or claim growing out of or connected with that identical thing; such as for labor or

[237] Anderson Law Dic., citing Stephani v. Bishop of Chicago, 2 Ill. App. 249.

[238] Bouvier Law Dic.

[239] Story Ag., § 352; 2 Kent's Com., Lect. XLI.

services or expenses bestowed upon that identical thing."[240] A general lien, on the other hand, "is a right to retain a thing not only for charges and claims specifically arising out of, or connected with, the identical thing, but also for a general balance of accounts between the parties, in respect to other dealings of a like nature."[241] A particular lien extends not only to goods and chattels, but to money which constitutes the fruits of the agency and which remains in the hands of the agent, or has not so far gone out of his possession as to constitute delivery to another.[242] Thus, where one employs another to obtain for him a loan of money for a stipulated commission, the agent procuring the loan has a lien upon and is entitled to retain the money in his hands for the amount of his commission, until the same is paid.[243] A particular or specific lien can arise only in one of four ways: (1) by an express contract; (2) by a usage or custom of trade; (3) by implication of law; (4) by a statute.[244] When the lien arises by implication of law, it results from the relation of the parties and their acts, independently of any contract. From this source are believed to come the particular liens of innkeepers, common carriers, farriers, blacksmiths, tailors, shipwrights, and other artisans.[245] As was said in an English case: "The principle seems to be well laid down * * * that where a bailee has expended his labor and skill in the improvement of a chattel delivered to him, he has a lien for his charge in that respect. Thus, the artificer to whom the goods are delivered for the purpose of being worked up into form, or the farrier by whose skill the animal is cured of a disease, or the horsebreaker by whose skill he is rendered manageable, have liens on the chattels in respect of their charges. All such specific liens being consistent with the principles of natural equity, are favored by the law, which is construed liberally in such cases."[246] Particular liens have been declared to exist at common law in favor of the following classes of agents:—those who keep and train horses under contract with their owners;[247] auctioneers for their commissions and expenses,—and these may be retained out of any deposits

[240] Story Ag., § 354.
[241] Story Ag., § 354.
[242] Muller v. Pondir, 55 N. Y. 325; Nagle v. McFeeters, 97 N. Y. 196.
[243] Vinton v. Baldwin, 95 Ind. 433.
[244] 13 Am. & Eng. Encyc. L. (1st ed.) 576, citing Fergusson v. Norman, 5 Bing. (N. C.) 76.
[245] Story Ag., § 355.
[246] Scarfe v. Morgan, 4 M. & W. 270.
[247] Scott v. Mercer, 98 Iowa 258, 60 Am. St. 188.

or proceeds of sale received by them on account of their principals;[248] common carriers for the price of carriage or freight upon particular goods;[249] masters of ships on their vessels for wages and disbursements,—and the lien is to be preferred to that of a mortgagee;[250] brokers, when in a position to exercise the right,—as in case of insurance brokers, on policies and the proceeds for commissions due them and premiums paid by them;[251] artisans and mechanics on the specific property bailed to them, on the theory that such property has been enhanced in value by the services of such artisans and mechanics bestowed upon the property.[252] General liens are liens for a general balance of account due from the owner of the property to which it attaches to the one having it in possession.[253] General liens are not favored in law or equity. Such a lien can, in the absence of express contract, be claimed only as arising from dealings in a particular trade or line of business in which the existence of a general lien has been judicially proved and acknowledged, or upon express evidence being given that according to the established custom a general lien is claimed and allowed.[254] General liens have been declared to exist in favor of attorneys at law;[255] of factors or commission merchants on the goods consigned to them or the proceeds thereof or securities for the same;[256] and of banks, upon all funds and securities of depositors for the balance of their accounts.[257] Banks also have liens on paper which they hold for collection from other banks, whether it is the property of such other banks or not, unless it is so earmarked as to show other ownership.[258]

§ 289. **Possession essential to maintain lien.**—Whether a common-law lien be general or particular, it is an essential element of its existence that there should be possession and the right to possession of the property upon which it is asserted.[259] If the party claiming the

[248] Hammond v. Barclay, 2 East 227; Beller v. Block, 19 Ark. 566.

[249] Butler v. Woolcott, 2 N. R. 64.

[250] The Mary Ann, L. R. 1 A. & E. 8.

[251] McKenzie v. Nevius, 22 Me. 138, 38 Am. Dec. 299.

[252] Quimby v. Hazen, 54 Vt. 132; Oakes v. Moore, 24 Me. 214, 41 Am. Dec. 379.

[253] Evans Pr. & Ag. (Bedford's ed.) 428.

[254] Evans Pr. & Ag. (Bedford's ed.) 428.

[255] Bowling Green Sav. Bank v. Todd, 52 N. Y. 489.

[256] McKenzie v. Nevius, 22 Me. 138, 38 Am. Dec. 299; Nagle v. McFeeters, 97 N. Y. 196; Martin v. Pope, 6 Ala. 532.

[257] 13 Am. & Eng. Encyc. L. 97, and authorities cited.

[258] 13 Am. & Eng. Encyc. L. 97.

[259] 3 Parsons Conts. 234; Paley Ag.

lien never had possession of the property, or, having had such possession, has relinquished it, the lien either never attached or has been lost. Nor will any lien, whether general or particular, attach to goods on account of a debt or debts accruing before the relation of agent commenced.[260] But by possession is not necessarily meant the actual custody of the property, for that may be in a servant or employe whose duty it is to care for it; and the possession may be constructive,—as, where the property is at sea and bills of lading for it have been indorsed or delivered. Such possession is sufficient to authorize a lien.[261] So where a consignment of goods was made to a creditor, and they were set apart in the factory and given into the custody of a special bailee of the consignor, who had control over them, and gave notice of the lien to attaching creditors, the lien of the creditor for advances, etc., was not defeated for want of sufficient possession.[262]

§ 290. **Who may exercise right of lien and against whom.**—It is furthermore essential to the validity of a lien that, on the one hand, the right to it must be exercised by the bailee of the property, and, on the other, against one who has the general or special ownership of it. The lien never inures—in the absence of a statute—to one who is merely an agent or employe of the bailee. "It exists not in favor of a journeyman or day laborer, whose possession is that of the employer, and who has no other security for his wages than the employer's personal responsibility on the contract of hiring; and he who claims it, therefore, must be a bailee under the contract which the civilians call *locatio operis faciendi*."[263] That it can not, as a general rule, be asserted against one who has not the right to exercise ownership over it is self-evident; for if the rule were otherwise, a stranger who might wrongfully have acquired the custody of the property would then be in position to incumber it to an extent that would render it valueless, in whole or in part, to the owner. There is, however, a well recognized exception in favor of those whose duty to the public requires them to receive the property and care for it. Thus it was said in a Massachusetts case: "Again, a lien is a proprietary interest, a qualified ownership, and, in general, can only be

(Lloyd's ed.) 137; 3 Chitty Com. Law 547; Story Ag., § 361.

260 2 Kent's Com. 638; Story Ag., § 361.

261 Story Ag., § 361.

262 Sumner v. Hamlet, 12 Pick. (Mass.) 76.

263 Per Gibson, C. J., in McIntyre v. Carver, 2 W. & S. (Pa.) 392.

created by the owner, or by some person by him authorized. In case of innholders and a few others who are by law bound to give credit for the keeping of horses, etc., it may well be held that the person putting up the horse at the innkeeper's stable shall be deemed the agent of the owner, whoever he is, so far as the providing for his sustenance, and, therefore, that the innkeeper may have a lien, though the horse be left by a person other than the owner."[264] Originally, indeed, the common law only gave a lien to those who were thus required by the nature of their occupation to receive property delivered to them, and to be at trouble and expense in regard to it. These vocations were regarded as a necessity or convenience to the public; and it was deemed but just and salutary that those who were thus in duty bound should have the privilege of retaining possession of the property until their just charges were paid.[265] This privilege has been since extended to every bailee for hire who, by his skill or labor, has imparted additional value to the particular property delivered into his custody, whether he is required by law to receive the same or not; and he is entitled, the same as in the other cases, to hold the property until his charges are paid.[266]

§ 291. **Innkeeper's lien.**—An innkeeper has a right to a lien upon all the property of his guest placed under the protection of the inn for the full amount of his bill.[267] But the lien does not extend to the person of the guest, though this is said to have been formerly his privilege;[268] nor does it extend to the wearing apparel on his person.[269] The common-law right to such a lien does not exist unless the person against whom such right is asserted is a guest of the innkeeper. The latter is an insurer of the property of his guests, and for this extraordinary responsibility the law accords to him the extraordinary privilege of holding such property for his charges; so, before he can exercise that privilege, it is essential that it be shown that the goods were brought under protection of the inn by a person in the character of guest.[270]

[264] Hollingsworth v. Dow, 19 Pick. (Mass.) 228.

[265] Naylor v. Mangles, 1 Esp. 109.

[266] 2 Kent's Com. 635.

[267] Mulliner v. Florence, L. R. 3 Q. B. D. 484.

[268] Newton v. Trigg, 1 Show. 268; Grinnell v. Cook, 3 Hill (N. Y.) 485, 38 Am. Dec. 663.

[269] Sunbolp v. Alford, 1 Horn & H. 13, 3 M. & W. 248; Grinnell v. Cook, 3 Hill (N. Y.) 485.

[270] Elliott v. Martin, 105 Mich. 506, 55 Am. St. 461; Grinnell v. Cook, 3 Hill (N. Y.) 485; Smith v. Dearlove, 6 C. B. 132, 9 C. & P. 208, 38 E. C. L. 82.

§ 292. Boarding-house keepers have no common-law lien.—A boarding-house keeper or lodging-house keeper is not an innkeeper, and hence has no lien under the common law on the property of his boarders or lodgers.[271] In many states, however, statutes have been enacted extending to boarding-house and lodging-house keepers the same responsibilities and privileges that apply to innkeepers; and when there is such a statute the proprietor of such a place is entitled to a lien the same as an innkeeper. It frequently happens, however, that the proprietor is engaged in keeping both a hotel or inn and a boarding and lodging-house. When this is the case, and there is no statute giving the proprietor a lien, his only rights are to be found at the common law. In such instances, if the liability of the debtor was incurred as a mere boarder or lodger, or in some other way besides that of guest, the proprietor has no lien.[272]

§ 293. Relation of host and guest.—As the relation of host and guest determines both the liability and the right of the proprietor, it is of great importance to be able to determine when that relation subsists. The mere fact that a party takes meals and lodging at a hotel or an inn does not necessarily constitute such relation. A guest is generally a traveler, one away from home, who receives the accommodations of the inn.[273] Parsons says a guest is one who comes "without any bargain for time, remains without one, and may go when he pleases."[274] While a guest must be a traveler, it is not material that he should travel any distance. "A townsman or neighbor may be a traveler, and, therefore, a guest at an inn, as well as he who comes from a distance or from a foreign country. If he resides at the inn, his relation to the innkeeper is that of a boarder; but if he resides away from it, whether far or near, and comes to it for entertainment as a traveler, and receives it as such, paying the customary rates, we know no reason why he should not be subjected to all the duties of a guest, and entitled to all the rights and privileges of one."[275] Nor does the mere fact that one is staying at a hotel or inn in pursuance of a previous special arrangement as to the time he expects to remain, the price to be paid, etc., necessarily ren-

[271] Southwood v. Myers, 3 Bush (Ky.) 681; Queen v. Askin, 20 U. C. Q. B. 626; Cochrane v. Schryver, 12 Daly (N. Y.) 174.

[272] Pollock v. Landis, 36 Iowa 651; Reed v. Teneyck, 19 Ky. L. 1690, 44 S. W. 356.

[273] Pullman Palace Car Co. v. Lowe, 28 Neb. 239, 26 Am. St. 325.

[274] Parsons Conts. 151.

[275] Pullman Palace Car Co. v. Lowe, *supra*.

der the party a boarder instead of a guest.[276] And whether the party is a guest or a boarder is always a question of fact to be determined from all the evidence before the trial court or jury.[277] We have said that a lodger is not a guest in the sense of the common law relating to innkeeper's liabilities and rights: a lodger is one who, for the time being, makes his home at his lodging place.[278] This home or lodging place may be at a hotel or an inn; but the fact that lodgings have been taken at such place does not render the occupant a guest or entitle the proprietor to an innkeeper's lien.

§ **294. Not essential that guest have title to property in order that lien may attach.**—As to the title to the property upon which the lien attaches, it is not necessary, as we have seen, that it be in the guest's name, but it is sufficient if the property was brought to the inn by him, and received by the innkeeper on the faith of the innkeeping relation.[279] Under this rule, even stolen property becomes the subject of a lien, unless the innkeeper has ground for suspicion that would justify a refusal on his part to receive it. The rigid requirement of the law which compels the landlord not only to receive but to insure the safety of all property of his guests would render a refusal on his part to receive such property extremely hazardous; and it is only just that the law should accord him this summary method of enforcing compensation for the extreme risks that he assumes. Hence, whether the property be that of the guest or not, if it is brought by him to the inn and receives its protection, the host may, under the law, claim his lien upon it to the extent of the accommodation supplied; and even if the property has been stolen, the owner is not entitled to its possession until he has paid the charges.[280] And the lien attaches even to property exempt from execution, when it has been given by statute for a boarding-house keeper's lien.[281] The

[276] Bershire Woollen Co. v. Proctor, 7 Cush. (Mass.) 417; Fay v. Pacific Imp. Co., 93 Cal. 253, 27 Am. St. 198.

[277] Magee v. Pacific Imp. Co., 98 Cal. 678, 35 Am. St. 199.

[278] Pullman Palace Car Co. v. Lowe, 28 Neb. 239, 26 Am. St. 325.

[279] Manning v. Hollenbeck, 27 Wis. 202; Hollingsworth v. Dow, 19 Pick. (Mass.) 228.

[280] Black v. Brennan, 5 Dana (Ky.) 310.

[281] Swan v. Bournes, 47 Iowa 501, 29 Am. Rep. 492. See also, Proctor v. Nicholson, 7 C. & P. 67, 32 E. C. L. 503, where it was held that the sheriff under a *fi. fa.* against the guest could only levy upon the guest's property subject to the lien of the innkeeper for accommodations, including wine sup-

innkeeper, however, has no right to detain the property of one guest for the debt of another, though they be in the same company.[282]

§ 295. **For what supplies innkeeper may have lien.**—The innkeeper's privilege of a lien is generally limited to the usual accommodations furnished a guest at an inn, such as food, drink, lodging, horse-feed and stabling, etc. But it has been held that an innkeeper may acquire a lien upon the goods of his guest for money loaned him, if there was an agreement between them that the goods should stand good for the amount of the loan.[283]

§ 296. **What guests innkeeper bound to receive.**—An innkeeper is legally bound to receive and entertain all guests apparently responsible and of good conduct who may come to his house. The mere fact that the guest is an infant does not justify a refusal to receive him; and unless the innkeeper, from the conduct of such infant guest, has some reason to believe that he is acting contrary to the wishes of his guardian, he is justified in entertaining him, and is entitled to a lien upon his goods for such entertainment, and even for money furnished him if used in the purchase of necessaries.[284] An infant may, however, be of such tender years, or there may be such other circumstances, as to indicate that he is not properly a guest at an inn, in which case the innkeeper may be justified in not receiving him; and he would probably not have a lien on the infant's effects if he did.

§ 297. **Agisters and livery-stable keepers—Horse trainers.**—Agisters and livery-stable keepers have no common-law lien on stock received by them for feed and care. Here again the statutes have in many states extended the rights and privileges of agents' liens to where they did not exist before. In all such cases the student or practitioner should fully acquaint himself with the statutes of his state, before determining in his mind whether the lien exists or not. A horse trainer, however, has a common-law lien upon the horse trained by him, upon the theory that the training has imparted additional value to the animal, by reason of the services bestowed upon it.[285]

plied to the guest's order, without regard to the quantity thereof.

[282] Kennedy v. Muller, 1 W. N. C. (Pa.) 445.

[283] Proctor v. Nicholson, 7 C. & P. 67, 32 E. C. L. 503.

[284] Watson v. Cross, 2 Duv. (Ky.) 147.

[285] Bevan v. Waters, 3 Car. & P. 520.

§ 298. **Nature of common-law lien—Remedies thereunder.**—A common-law lien, as we have seen, is a mere right to hold the property for the payment of the charges, and can not be enforced by any legal proceedings. The privilege of a lien is lost when the property on which it is claimed passes out of the possession of the lienor. The lien is not property nor a right to property. It is neither *jus ad rem* nor *jus in re,* but a mere personal right of retainer. It is not assignable, nor is it subject to attachment or other legal process of the creditors of the lienor, as a chose in action would be.[286] The common law gives the holder of such a lien no means of enforcing it, except to sue the lienee on the debt and obtain execution against him, in which case the property may, of course, be levied upon to satisfy such debt, provided the debtor own it or have an interest in it. The only other remedy is the retaining of the property, unless the statute of the particular state has provided a method of enforcing the lien either by sale or by legal proceedings. The case of a factor is an exception; for a factor has the power to sell and may reimburse himself out of the proceeds.[287] In case of a pledge of the property, too, the agent or pledgee may sell the property at public sale after demand and reasonable notice have been given the owner.[288] It has indeed been held in a few states that the lien of an innkeeper or common carrier might be enforced in equity, without a statute. Thus, in Kentucky, it was decided by the court of appeals that an innkeeper may go into a court of chancery and obtain a decree enforcing his lien upon the horse of his guest.[289] Mr. Jones, in his valuable work on Liens, denies the general power of courts of equity to enforce such liens; saying: "Generally, a court of equity has no jurisdiction to enforce a common-law lien by sale merely because there is no remedy at law, or because the retaining of possession under a passive lien involves expense or inconvenience. Generally, a lien at law or by statute can be enforced only under express statutory provisions. An equitable form of procedure may be expressly provided; but in the absence of such provision, a lien can not be enforced in equity unless jurisdiction is acquired under well established rules."[290] It seems that, where an accounting is involved, a court of equity has jurisdic-

[286] Lovett v. Brown, 40 N. H. 511.

[287] 2 Kent's Com. 642; Shaw v. Ferguson, 78 Ind. 547; Parker v. Brancker, 22 Pick. (Mass.) 40.

[288] Parker v. Brancker, *supra;* Potter v. Thompson, 10 R. I. 1.

[289] Black v. Brennan, 5 Dana (Ky.) 310. See also, Cairo, etc., R. Co. v. Fackney, 78 Ill. 116.

[290] Citing Thames Iron Works Co. v. Patent Derrick Co., 1 J. & H. 93, 97.

tion.[291] By the great weight of authority also, the lienholder has no power to sell the property to satisfy his lien.[292] Possibly a sale will be justified if the property be a horse that has eaten its full value, or some perishable article. Such seems to be the custom of London and Exeter, if not the general rule.[293] The lien of an agent is generally a particular lien, and does not extend to claims beyond the scope of the agency. There are some classes of agents, however, who, as we have already seen, are entitled to general liens.

[291] Jones Liens, § 1038.

[292] Briggs v. Boston, etc., R. Co., 6 Allen (Mass.) 246; Bailey v. Shaw, 24 N. H. 297, 55 Am. Dec. 241.

[293] Thames Iron Works Co. v. Patent Derrick Co., *supra;* Bacon Abridg. "Liens," D, cited in Jones Liens, § 1038, n. 3.

CHAPTER VIII.

DUTIES, OBLIGATIONS AND LIABILITIES OF AGENT TO THIRD PERSONS, AND RIGHTS OF THIRD PERSONS IN REGARD TO AGENT.

§ 299. **Public and private agents—Distinction between.**—In treating of the relation of agents to third parties it has been found convenient to divide agents into two classes; namely, public and private agents. A public agent is one who represents the government, whether national, state or municipal,—a public officer.[1] By a private

[1] State v. Stanley, 66 N. C. 59, 8 Am. Rep. 488; State v. Judges, 21 Ohio St. 1. In Ogden v. Raymond, 22 Conn. 379, 58 Am. Dec. 429, the

agent is meant one who acts for an individual, or a firm, or a private corporation. Concerning the duties, obligations and liabilities of these respective classes of agents to third persons, and the rights of third persons as against agents, a marked distinction must be observed. The authority of a public agent is generally conferred by statute or other public law, of which every one is bound to take notice; and the government or other public authority can not be bound by the acts of its agents, unless they be performed according to the power thus conferred, or unless the agent is held out as possessing such power, or is employed thus to represent his government or that division thereof for which he assumes to act. In cases of private agencies, on the other hand, the authority is not generally conferred by statutes or other public law, but by private contract, of which third parties can not be presumed to have actual knowledge; and the principals of such private agents are therefore held responsible, not only for the exercise of authority actually conferred, but for such also as they hold out their agents to appear to possess. This is so, as stated by Story, "in order to guard the public against losses and injuries arising from the fraud or mistake, or rashness and indiscretion of their agents. And there is no hardship in requiring from private persons, dealing with public officers, the duty of inquiry, as

court, by Elsworth, J., speaking to the question of who are public agents and whether or not a school trustee is such agent, said: "We do not readily apprehend why the defendant [the school trustee], deriving his public and official character from the general law and the election of the people of a given district, under the law, may not be held to be a public agent as much as if he were the agent of the state immediately, or of a county, town, society or school district. Wherein is the difference? All derive their power from the same source, parceled out, only to be exercised in different jurisdictions and for different purposes." But while every public office may be said to embrace, in a sense, the idea of an agency, a civil officer is something more than a mere agent, he being a part of the governmental machinery: State v. Vallé, 41 Mo. 29. And an officer, in the sense in which that word is used in the constitution of the United States, is a public functionary appointed either by the president, by the heads of the departments, or by the courts of law; no other appointee is an officer within the meaning of that instrument. Hence, it has been held that an examining surgeon appointed by the commissioner of pensions is not an officer liable to indictment under section 12 of the act of 1825 (4 Stat. 118) for extortion, though he may properly be called an agent or employe: United States v. Germaine, 99 U. S. 508.

to their real or apparent power and authority to bind the government."[2]

§ 300. **Private agent owes duty to principal only.**—And first as to private agents. Strictly speaking, the duty such an agent owes is to his principal, and to him only, and third persons acquire no rights whatever against the agent which arise out of the agency, as such. There is between him and the general public no contractual relation whatever, and as long as he enters into no such relation on behalf of himself he can incur no liability. If he fail to perform the undertaking he has assumed for his principal, he will, of course, be responsible to the latter for such failure; but with this the public have no concern; as long as he remains inactive no one but his principal can complain; the agent is not liable to any one but him for his non-feasance or mere omission or nonperformance of his duties.[3] Hence, if the principal has engaged with some third party to perform an act, and he employs an agent for the purpose of performing such act and the agent fails to do so, the principal, and not the agent, is liable to such party. The agent has entered into no agreement except with his principal; he, therefore, owes no one any duty but him, and the law imposes none upon him with reference to outsiders.[4] It is otherwise, of course, if he undertakes to act for the principal: the very moment he does so, he necessarily comes in contact with others; he then assumes an obligation to those also with whom he acts as the representative of him whose authority he undertakes to execute; if he directly inflicts an injury upon the stranger with whom he deals for his principal, he may render himself liable to such stranger.[5] One of the most common instances of this kind is where the agent acts without authority.[6]

I. On Contract.

§ 301. **Agent not liable if he discloses principal and acts in his name.**—A private agent may assume duties and obligations and incur liabilities that will result in his being subjected either to an action

[2] Story Ag., § 307a.

[3] Dean v. Brock, 11 Ind. App. 507; Brown Paper Co. v. Dean, 123 Mass. 267; Labadie v. Hawley, 61 Tex. 177, 48 Am. Rep. 278.

[4] Delaney v. Rochereau, 34 La. Ann. 1123, 44 Am. St. 456.

[5] Delaney v. Rochereau, *supra.*

[6] Terwilliger v. Murphy, 104 Ind. 32; Cochran v. Baker, 34 Ore. 555, 52 Pac. 520, 56 Pac. 641; De Remer v. Brown, 55 N. Y. Supp. 367.

upon contract or an action in tort. We shall first inquire into his liability upon contracts. As has been seen, an agent may, in contracting with a third party for his principal, act entirely within the scope of his authority, or partly or entirely outside of the same. If he acts wholly within the limits of his authority, and the principal is known or disclosed, and the agent acts for him only, the agent is not personally liable to the third party for a breach of the contract.[7] In such case the contract is wholly that of the principal and the third party, and the agent is but the medium of bringing the parties together; and after the contract has been entered into, the agent is entirely eliminated from it and can not be rendered liable thereon. "If a different rule were to prevail," says Story, "it would greatly embarrass all the transactions of parties, and especially those of a commercial nature, through the instrumentality of agents, since the latter could never escape a personal responsibility in the execution of mere authority, by any precautions whatever."[8] And Chancellor Kent, speaking upon the same subject, says: "Every contract made with an agent in relation to the business of his principal is a contract with the principal, entered into through the instrumentality of the agent, provided the agent acts in the name of the principal. * * * It is a general rule, standing on strong foundations, and pervading every system of jurisprudence, that where an agent is duly constituted, and names his principal, and contracts in his name, and does not exceed his authority, the principal is responsible and not the agent."[9]

§ 302. General presumption that agent intended to bind principal —How agent may render himself personally liable.—And inasmuch

[7] Whitney v. Wyman, 101 U. S. 392; Newman v. Sylvester, 42 Ind. 106; Ogden v. Raymond, 22 Conn. 379, 58 Am. Dec. 429; Lewis v. Harris, 4 Metc. (Ky.) 353; Maury v. Ranger, 38 La. Ann. 485, 58 Am. Rep. 197; American Nat'l Bank v. Wheelock, 82 N. Y. 118; Humes v. Decatur Land Imp., etc., Co., 98 Ala. 461; Gulf City Const. Co. v. Louisville, etc., R. Co., 121 Ala. 621, 25 So. 579; Thilmany v. Iowa Paper Bag Co., 108 Iowa 357, 79 N. W. 261; Merrill v. Williams, 63 Cal. 70; Green v. Kopke, 18 C. B. (86 E. C. L.) 549; Newland Hotel Co. v. Lowe Furniture Co., 73 Mo. App. 135.

[8] Story Ag., § 261.

[9] 2 Kent's Com. 629, 630. See also, Green v. Kopke, 18 C. B. (86 E. C. L.) 549; American Nat'l Bank v. Wheelock, 82 N. Y. 118; Merrill v. Williams, 63 Cal. 70; Rosenthal v. Myers, 25 La. Ann. 463; Comer v. Bankhead, 70 Ala. 493; Tuttle v. Ayres, 3 N. J. L. 257; Anderson v. Timberlake, 114 Ala. 377, 62 Am. St. 105; Robeson v. Chapman, 6 Ind. 352.

as the law always presumes that every person will do his duty, when an agent has undertaken to contract for or on behalf of his principal, speaking the language of the latter and not his own, and having authority to do so, there is a presumption that he intended to bind his principal and not himself.[10] This presumption will prevail until overcome by evidence to the contrary. The agent may, however, render himself personally responsible, either in addition to making the principal liable, or independently thereof. In the former case, he may do so by pledging his own credit in addition to that of the principal; as, by becoming for him a surety, guarantor or co-contracting party of any kind.[11] He may purposely and intentionally incur the liability; as where, by express contract, he personally warrants an article.[12] Or he may render himself liable without any actual intent to do so, but by employing such terms in the contract as will preclude him from denying such intent. Illustrations of the latter character are found in cases in which the agent denominates himself as agent, trustee, or by some other description, but still binds himself as an individual.[13] This rule has already been discussed in a preceding portion of this work.[14] It is immaterial, in such cases, whether the term "agent" is used in the body of the instrument or in the signature or in both. Thus, where the lessees in the caption of a lease were described as "trustees of Q. Lodge, No. 139, I. O. of G. Templars, or their successors in office," and such lessees in the body of the instrument covenanted to pay the rent, without using any words indicating that they were acting for another, the words "trustees," etc., were regarded as simply *descriptio personarum*.[15] And the following agreement, "I, G. W. C., land agent of the O. & M. R. Co., hereby agree to pay," etc., signed "G. W. C., land agent," was held to be the personal agreement of G. W. C.[16] So, where two parties entered into a contract for the sale and purchase of real estate, and the purchaser was designated in the body of the contract as "President," and signed as "President of B. C. Institute," the con-

[10] Hall v. Lauderdale, 46 N. Y. 70; Johnson v. Smith, 21 Conn. 627; Story Ag., § 264.

[11] Armstrong v. Stokes, L. R. 7 Q. B. 598; Hall v. Lauderdale, *supra;* Shordan v. Kyler, 87 Ind. 38.

[12] Wilder v. Cowles, 100 Mass. 487; Hull v. Brown, 35 Wis. 652.

[13] Dayton v. Warne, 46 N. J. L. 659.

[14] See *ante*, § 207, *et seq.*

[15] Stobie v. Dills, 62 Ill. 432.

[16] Prather v. Ross, 17 Ind. 495. To the same effect are the cases of Hobbs v. Cowden, 20 Ind. 310; Inhabitants, etc., v. Weir, 9 Ind. 224; Hayes v. Matthews, 63 Ind. 412.

tract being made on condition that the "B. C. Institute will accept and approve of this purchase and its terms and agreement" within a stated time, and the purchaser agreed to pay and to secure the purchase-money by his bond and mortgage on the premises, the contract was decided to be that of the individual purchaser and not that of the corporation, the words "President," etc., being held as *descriptio personae* merely.[17] In all such cases, the agent, in order to bind his principal and not himself, must execute the instrument in the name and on behalf of the principal,—as, "John Doe, by Richard Roe, his agent, promises," or "Richard Roe, for John Doe, agrees," or "Richard Roe, agent for John Doe, covenants," etc.; and must sign the instrument in the name or on behalf of the principal,—as, "John Doe, by Richard Roe, agent," or "Richard Roe, agent for John Doe," or "*Pro* John Doe, Richard Roe, agent," or simply "John Doe," without any words to show that the signature was made or the instrument executed by an agent.[18]

§ 303. **Where principal is undisclosed.**—It must be quite clear, then, that an agent may render himself personally liable on a contract attempted to be executed by him for and on behalf of his principal, if he has employed language that the law regards as that of the agent, personally, and not that of the principal. His liability is, however, not confined to that class of contracts. "There are three cases," said the supreme judicial court of Massachusetts, "in which the agent becomes personally liable: (1) where the principal is not known; (2) where there is no responsible principal; (3) where the agent becomes liable by any undertaking of his own."[19] The last of these heads was briefly considered in the preceding section, and was more fully elaborated in Chapter V, under the head of Execution of Authority.[20] It remains to consider the agent's liability in cases where the principal is undisclosed, and in cases where there is no responsible principal. And first, as to contracts in which the agent fails to disclose his true relation. In making a contract the agent may disclose the fact that he is acting for another without disclosing the name of such other person; or he may disclose neither the name of the principal nor the fact that he, the agent, is acting for another instead of for himself. If he disclose neither the fact of the agency

[17] Buffalo Catholic Institute v. Bitter, 87 N. Y. 250.

[18] See *ante*, § 207, *et seq.*

[19] Hastings v. Lovering, 2 Pick. (Mass.) 214, 13 Am. Dec. 420; citing Paley Pr. & Ag. 255.

[20] See *ante*, § 205, *et seq.*

nor the name of the principal, he will be clearly liable as principal.[21] If he disclose the fact of the agency, but not the name of the principal, and use terms in themselves sufficient to bind himself, he will be liable at the election of the third party, the same as if he were the real principal. The mere fact that he professes to act as agent for another, or to execute the contract as such, is not sufficient in itself to prevent responsibility from attaching to him.[22] If he would escape personal liability he must name the principal in the contract, and employ such language as on its face purports to be the obligation or undertaking of the principal, and renders him liable *ex vi termini*.[23] If the contract be in writing, much depends, of course, upon its wording. "If the form of the contract is such that the agent personally covenants, and then adds his representative character, which he does not in truth sustain, his covenant remains personal and in force, and binds him as an individual; but, if the form of the contract is otherwise, and the language, when fairly interpreted, does not contain a personal undertaking or provision, he is not personally liable; for it is not his contract and the law will not force it upon him. He may be liable, it is true, for tortious conduct if he has knowingly or carelessly assumed to bind another without authority; or, when making the contract, has concealed the true state of his authority, and falsely led others to repose in his authority; but as we have said, he is not of course liable on the contract itself, nor in any form of action whatever."[24] Where the contract is not in writing, and the agent does not disclose the fact that he is acting for another, together with the name of the principal, the same rule applies, and he can not escape liability on the ground that he contracted merely as agent. And the fact that the third party had knowledge of the agency is not in itself sufficient to exempt the agent from personal responsibility. The duty is upon the agent to disclose the principal, and not upon those with whom he deals to

[21] Boyd v. L. H. Quinn Co., 40 N. Y. Supp. 370; Pierce v. Johnson, 34 Conn. 274; Jones v. Johnson, 86 Ky. 530; Bartlett v. Raymond, 139 Mass. 275; Argersinger v. Macnaughton, 114 N. Y. 535, 11 Am. St. 687; Johnson v. Armstrong, 83 Tex. 325.

[22] Per Byles, J., in Kelner v. Baxter, L. R. 2 C. P. 174, 180.

[23] Ex parte Hartlep, 12 Ves. 349; Irvine v. Watson, L. R. 5 Q. B. D. 414; Welch v. Goodwin, 123 Mass. 71, 25 Am. Rep. 24; Merrill v. Wilson, 6 Ind. 426; Bartlett v. Raymond, 139 Mass. 275.

[24] Per Ellsworth, J., in Ogden v. Raymond, 22 Conn. 379, 58 Am. Dec. 429. See also, Paice v. Walker, L. R. 5 Ex. 173; Higgins v. Senior, 8 M. & W. 834; Story Ag., § 269.

discover it, and if he fails to do so, and deals with persons unaware of his agency, he must answer personally for the debts he contracts.[25] Dr. Wharton expresses the view that the doctrine that agents are personally liable when they disclose the fact of the agency, but not the name of the principal, applies primarily only to auctioneers and factors, and that the cases in which other agents are held liable rest partly on the usage of trade and partly on the fact that the parties charged acted without authority;[26] and there is other respectable authority for thus limiting the rule.[27] Whatever classes of agents the rule applies to, however, it is certain that such agent is liable unless he discloses both the fact of the agency and the identity of the principal. And in all contracts other than specialties, when there is an undisclosed principal, either the agent or the principal—when the latter is discovered—may be held liable; the third party having the right to elect which he will pursue.[28] In such cases, parol evidence is not admissible to exonerate the agent; for if, by the terms of the contract, he has bound himself individually, the admission of parol evidence to show that he contracted only as agent would be a violation of the rule that the terms of a written instrument can not be contradicted or varied by parol proof.[29] We shall hereafter discuss, as fully as may be, the liability of the undisclosed principal in such cases.[30] For the present it will be sufficient to say that parol evidence is admissible in this class of cases to charge the undisclosed principal, now discovered, and that this is held not to be in violation of the rule which forbids the introduction of parol evidence to contradict a written instrument.[31] Such a contract binds not only the

[25] Per Steele, J., in Baldwin v. Leonard, 39 Vt. 260, 94 Am. Dec. 324. See to the same effect, also, Bickford v. First Nat'l Bank, 42 Ill. 238, 89 Am. Dec. 436; Story Ag., § 266; Argersinger v. Macnaughton, 114 N. Y. 535, 11 Am. St. 687; Kain v. Humes, 5 Sneed (Tenn.) 610.

[26] Wharton Ag., § 502.

[27] Hutchinson v. Tatham, L. R. 8 C. P. 482; Fleet v. Murton, L. R. 7 Q. B. 126; Dale v. Humfrey, El. B. & E. (96 E. C. L.) 1004, 27 L. J. Q. B. 390.

[28] Kingsley v. Davis, 104 Mass. 178; Taintor v. Prendergast, 3 Hill (N. Y.) 72, 38 Am. Dec. 618; Merrill v. Kenyon, 48 Conn. 314, 40 Am. Rep. 174; Higgins v. Senior, 8 M. & W. 834.

[29] Higgins v. Senior, *supra;* Cream City Glass Co. v. Friedlander, 84 Wis. 53; Evans Pr. & Ag. (Bedford's ed.) 362.

[30] *Post*, §§ 328–334.

[31] Briggs v. Partridge, 64 N. Y. 357; Higgins v. Senior, 8 M. & W. 834; Byington v. Simpson, 134 Mass. 169; Waddill v. Sebree, 88 Va. 1012; Chandler v. Coe, 54 N. H. 561.

agent, but the principal also, unless it be under seal and required to be so; because the act of the agent is the act of the principal, or, as said in some cases, because the principal "is taken to have adopted the name of the agent as his own, for the purpose of the contract."[32] Some of the New York cases seem to hold that when the agent describes himself as such in the contract, but does not sign the contract with the name of the principal, the latter can not be held liable, and the agent alone is bound.[33] But whether the principal is liable or not, the agent certainly is. Unless the agent, on the face of the contract, in some manner discloses the principal, and acts on his behalf and in his name, or evinces an intention to do so, he will generally be precluded from showing that the contract was that of another and not of himself; unless the contract is ambiguous, so as to admit of parol evidence. "A man has a right to the character, credit and substance of the person with whom he contracts; if, therefore, he enters into a contract with an agent, who does not give his principal's name, the presumption is that he is invited to give credit to the agent; still more, if the agent does not disclose his principal's existence."[34]

§ 304. **Contract by agent in behalf of nonexisting principal.**— An agent is furthermore liable on the contract into which he has entered for and on behalf of an assumed principal when the latter has no existence in fact at the time of the making of such contract.[35] But if the agent, in good faith, makes a contract in behalf of his principal, who has died without his knowledge, the agent is not liable personally.[36] No distinction is to be observed between a non-

[32] Byington v. Simpson, *supra;* Higgins v. Senior, *supra;* Thomson v. Davenport, 9 B. & C. 78, 3 Smith Ld. Cas. (9th ed.) 1648, and notes; Cothay v. Fennell, 10 B. & C. 671; Hunter v. Giddings, 97 Mass. 41, 93 Am. Dec. 54; Bickford v. First Nat'l Bank, 42 Ill. 238, 89 Am. Dec. 436.

[33] Barker v. Mechanic Ins. Co., 3 Wend. (N. Y.) 94; Spencer v. Field, 10 Wend. (N. Y.) 87; Stone v. Wood, 7 Cow. (N. Y.) 453; Bank of Genesee v. Patchin Bank, 19 N. Y. 315. See, *per contra*, besides the cases cited in note 32, *supra*, Hopkins v. Lacouture, 4 La. 64; Carlisle v. Steamer Eudora, 5 La. Ann. 15.

[34] Anson Conts. 345. See also, 2 Kent's Com. 630; Rendell v. Harriman, 75 Me. 497; Casco Nat'l Bank v. Clark, 139 N. Y. 307; Souhegan Nat'l Bank v. Boardman, 46 Minn. 293; Higgins v. Senior, 8 M. & W. 834.

[35] Kelner v. Baxter, L. R. 2 C. P. 174; Lewis v. Tilton, 64 Iowa 220; Patrick v. Bowman, 149 U. S. 411; Washburn v. Frank, 31 La. Ann. 427.

[36] Smout v. Ilbery, 10 M. & W. 1.

existing or purely fictitious principal and one that may have an existence, in a sense, and yet not be recognized as possessing a distinct legal entity, sometimes called an irresponsible principal; such as a married woman, who, under the common law, could not be sued; or an unorganized society,—such as a social club, or a political meeting. In either case, the one who assumes to represent such supposed person is personally liable. A very common illustration of a fictitious or nonexistent principal is that of the promoters of an intended railway or other company before incorporation; here there is no existing principal when the contract is made, for there is no corporation; and if incorporation never takes place the promoters are personally liable on contracts made or for debts incurred by them.[37] The contract may, of course, be so worded as to exempt the promoters from personal responsibility; or it may be so framed that no suit could be maintained upon it, as such, and an action on the original undertaking might become necessary in order to render the promoters liable. But unless this be true, they will generally be personally bound on the contract; and if subscriptions to stock have been paid to them, the subscribers may recover the money so paid from the person to whom such payments were made, if the company is not incorporated.[38] The contracts of the promoters in behalf of the projected corporation will not bind the latter after organization, unless the company subsequently adopt the acts as its own.[39] Whether the company, subsequently to its becoming a chartered organization, can ratify the acts of the promoters, in the technical sense of the term, seems to be very doubtful, as there must be an existing principal at the time of the unauthorized contract entered into by the agent before a valid ratification can take place.[40] There is no doubt, however, that the contracts or agreements of the promoters may be adopted by the corporation when it comes into existence, although this would amount to a new contract; and such an adoption may be implied from the circumstances; as, for example, from knowingly accepting the benefits of the engagements made by the promoters.[41]

[37] Kelner v. Baxter, L. R. 2 C. P. 174; Hurt v. Salisbury, 55 Mo. 310; Johnson v. Corser, 34 Minn. 355; Sproat v. Porter, 9 Mass. 300; Nockels v. Crosby, 3 B. & C. 814.

[38] 1 Elliott Railr., § 13.

[39] Kelley v. Newburyport, etc., Horse R. Co., 141 Mass. 496; Oakes v. Cattaraugus Water Co., 143 N. Y. 430; 1 Elliott Railr., § 14.

[40] 1 Morawetz Corp., § 549.

[41] *Ibid.*

§ 305. **Unincorporated associations, clubs and meetings.**—A common illustration of an irresponsible principal is the case of an unincorporated association; such as a social club, acting by a committee. In such case the debts contracted by such committee are the personal obligations of the members of the committee, and they are liable therefor. "One professing to act as agent," to quote the language of the supreme court of Wisconsin, "if he does not bind his principal, binds himself. And it can make no difference that the reason why he does not bind his principal is because the principal for whom he professes to act has no existence."[42] In the case referred to, the court went so far as to hold that where such a committee acts by an agent all the members of the committee are liable. "Such a rule is salutary," say the court, "and tends to the promotion of justice, by preventing the procurement of services from too incautious and confiding laborers, by putting forward an irresponsible committee to act for an irresponsible public gathering."[43] Of course, in this class of cases, as in those of promoters of intended corporations, it may be shown in defense that the credit was extended only to the society and not to the agent, in which case there would be no liability on the part of the agent. Thus, where an unincorporated post of the Grand Army of the Republic duly authorized and subsequently ratified a contract made by a committee of such post, with a third party, for the giving of a number of performances of a spectacular entertainment, the profits to go to the post, and there was nothing to show that such post could not render itself liable, as such, for the expenses incurred by virtue of such contract, it was held by the supreme court of Pennsylvania that the members of the committee were not individually liable upon such contract.[44] But in the same state it was decided that the members of a committee of a political meeting, appointed to give a free public dinner for the party, were personally liable for the bill, there being no responsible principal, and the creditor being presumed to have relied upon the responsibility of the persons who gave the order.[45] Of course, an unincorporated society, such as a club, can not, as such, generally become a party to a contract; but the members thereof who contract in the name of the organization may render themselves personally liable as principals, when they themselves create the debt or obliga-

[42] Per Paine, J., in Fredendall v. Taylor, 23 Wis. 538.

[43] *Ibid.*

[44] Pain v. Sample, 158 Pa. St. 428.

[45] Eichbaum v. Irons, 6 W. & S. (Pa.) 67, 40 Am. Dec. 540.

tion, or ratify it, or when they hold themselves out as agents for a principal having no legal existence. In such a case no member can bind another,—as a partner binds his copartners, for example; but his own liability is predicated upon the theory that he himself entered into or ratified the contract, or represented himself to be acting for an alleged principal, and that the latter would do and perform certain things.[46] Even if the credit is extended to the supposed principal, if the latter has no legal existence, and certainly if the third party is without knowledge of that fact, the pretended agent is liable.[47] If, however, the third party is fully aware of the fact that there is no responsible principal, and yet is willing to deal with the agent, not upon his personal credit, but in the full confidence that he will be repaid by the person whom the agent assumes to represent, though no obligation may rest upon such person to do so, the agent will not be personally liable.[48] And it is incumbent upon one who alleges that credit was extended to such principal, and him only, to establish that fact by the evidence.[49] But an unincorporated society may, by statutory enactment, become a legal entity in such a way as to bind itself by its contract; and, when this is the case, it may, of course, be bound by the contract of its authorized agent, or by a ratification of such contract, if unauthorized originally.[50] That the members of a society or club having no corporate existence authorized the contract or debt in such a way as to render themselves personally accountable may be shown by the constitution or by laws or by the vote of a meeting in which they acquiesced. Thus, where a college class, at a meeting of the members, voted for the publication of a book, and selected one of their number as "business manager of the publication," who made a contract for such publication, the members of the class who thus voted or assented to the result of the vote were held personally liable in an action by the publisher for work done and materials furnished.[51]

§ 306. **Nature of action against agent in such case.**—Whether a person holding himself out as agent and contracting for an assumed principal having no legal existence is liable upon the contract directly, or whether the suit must be in the nature of an action in tort for damages, for contracting without authority, are important questions that

[46] Per Seevers, J., in Lewis v. Tilton, 64 Iowa 220.

[47] *Ibid.*

[48] Story Ag., § 287.

[49] Comfort v. Graham, 87 Iowa 295.

[50] See Lewis v. Tilton, 64 Iowa 220.

[51] Wilcox v. Arnold, 162 Mass. 577.

often arise in practice. The rule is that an agent so contracting is ordinarily liable directly upon the contract; for in such cases the law presumes that he contracts upon his own responsibility, and intends to bind himself, and it so holds him, for in no other way could the contract have any validity.[52] Accordingly, in a case where the mayor of a city officially offered a reward for the arrest of a fugitive municipal officer, such mayor having no authority to bind the municipality or any of its departments by such an offer, the supreme court of New Jersey held—applying the rule applicable to private agents—that the mayor was personally liable for the reward; the law presuming that he contracted upon his own responsibility.[53] The presumption that the agent intended to bind himself renders him liable on the contract directly; unless, indeed, there is something in its terms which makes it necessary that the plaintiff proceed specially against the agent for contracting without authority.[54] So, in a case decided in Missouri, where the captain of a military company had signed an instrument on behalf of the company, it was held by the supreme court of that state that the captain was liable upon the instrument.[55] Where the contract is in writing, therefore, and is executed on behalf of an assumed principal having no legal existence or authority to execute it, it is the general rule that the person assuming to act as agent will be held liable on the instrument directly, as the real principal. Where the contract is not in writing, it will be governed by similar rules; the facts, of course, depending upon the evidence. It must be remembered, moreover, that in such cases the presumption that the agent intended to bind himself is only a *prima facie* presumption, and may be overcome by evidence showing that the credit was in reality not extended to him; and when this is shown, the agent is not liable, either upon the contract or in tort. And this, in cases of unwritten contracts, may be shown by the circumstances of the case. Thus, it was held that the members of a building committee of an unincorporated church society were not personally liable, for services rendered in building a meeting-house, to one jointly concerned with them as shareholders in the building, where it was shown they had no funds in their hands to pay for such services, and where it did not appear that any express promise was made by them, or that their

[52] Booth v. Wonderly, 36 N. J. L. 250.

[53] Timken v. Tallmadge, 54 N. J. L. 117. See also, Kelner v. Baxter, L. R. 2 C. P. 174.

[54] Booth v. Wonderly, *supra*.

[55] Blakely v. Bennecke, 59 Mo. 193.

individual credit was pledged to the payment of such services; it also appearing that they were appointed by the body of the subscribers to the shares of the building fund to execute a mere trust, and were acting under the direction and control of such subscribers, and subject to their orders and to removal by them.[56] And, generally, the trustees of a voluntary association are not liable personally for its debts, unless made so by statute, or unless they have rendered themselves so by contract.[57] Whether the credit was extended to the agent individually or not is, therefore, a question of fact to be determined by the jury, or the court sitting as such. If, however, the contract be a written one, its construction is solely for the court; and evidence to show a contrary intention from that apparent on its face is not generally admissible, unless such contract is ambiguous.[58]

§ 307. **Nature of liability of agent acting without authority.**—One who assumes to act as agent for another in a given transaction may do so wholly without authority, or he may act in excess of the authority actually possessed by him. If he enter into a written contract on behalf of another without authority, the question may, and frequently does arise, whether he is liable on such contract personally, or whether he must be sued in another kind of an action. Some of the authorities hold that, in all written contracts except specialties, if the pretended agent has so worded the instrument as to make it appear that he is acting for or on behalf of another, and not himself,—having no authority to do so,—he binds himself personally, and will be liable in an action on the contract itself, for the reason that he must have intended to bind some one; and if he was unauthorized to bind the principal, he is estopped to deny that he intended to bind himself, as in that case no one whatever would be bound.[59] But the objection to this doctrine is that it would require the court to make a new contract for the parties, or one into

[56] Cheeny v. Clark, 3 Vt. 431, 23 Am. Dec. 219.

[57] Wolf v. Schleiffer, 2 Brew. (Pa.) 563; Hall v. Siegel, 7 Lans. (N. Y.) 206.

[58] See *ante*, § 216.

[59] Palmer v. Stephens, 1 Denio (N. Y.) 471; Richardson v. Crandall, 47 Barb. (N. Y.) 335; Rossiter v. Rossiter, 8 Wend. (N. Y.) 495, 24 Am. Dec. 62; White v. Skinner, 13 Johns. (N. Y.) 307, 7 Am. Dec. 381; Sinclair v. Jackson, 8 Cow. (N. Y.) 543; Richie v. Bass, 15 La. Ann. 668; Levy v. Lane, 38 La. Ann. 252; Keener v. Harrod, 2 Md. 63; Dale v. Donaldson, 48 Ark. 188; Terwilliger v. Murphy, 104 Ind. 32; Andrews v. Tedford, 37 Iowa 314; Coffman v. Harrison, 24 Mo. 524; Weare v. Gove, 44 N. H. 196.

which they have not themselves entered; and the courts now generally repudiate it. While the decisions are not uniform, the great weight of modern authority is that the agent is not personally bound on the contract itself, and can not be held liable in an action thereon.[60] The agent may indeed be liable *ex contractu* when he executes a written contract for another without authority. If the contract is in writing, and the agent himself did not receive the consideration upon which it is based, he may yet be liable *ex contractu*. In that case, his liability is on an implied warranty of his authority to act, although he intended no wrong, but honestly believed himself to be in possession of authority to enter into the contract.[61] In such case, he has inflicted an injury upon another; and as he has held himself out as having competent authority to do the act, it is but just that he should be personally responsible for the consequences of the wrongful assertion; for, "where one of two innocent persons must suffer a loss, he ought to bear it who has been the sole means of producing it, by inducing the other to place a false confidence in his acts, and to repose upon the truth of his statements."[62]

§ 308. **Agent not liable when third party knew facts—Death of principal—Fraudulent misrepresentation of authority.**—But if the party with whom the agent has contracted knew that the agent had no authority, or was cognizant of all the facts upon which the assumption of authority was based,—as, for example; where both parties labored under a mistake of law with reference to the liability of the principal,—the agent is not liable either in tort or upon the contract.[63] And if the principal is dead at the time the contract is en-

[60] Lewis v. Nicholson, 18 Q. B. 503; Duncan v. Niles, 32 Ill. 532, 83 Am. Dec. 293; McCurdy v. Rogers, 21 Wis. 199, 91 Am. Dec. 468; Ogden v. Raymond, 22 Conn. 379, 58 Am. Dec. 429; Harper v. Little, 2 Me. 14, 11 Am. Dec. 25; Abbey v. Chase, 6 Cush. (Mass.) 54; Bartlett v. Tucker, 104 Mass. 341, 6 Am. Rep. 240; Hall v. Crandall, 29 Cal. 567, 89 Am. Dec. 64; Cole v. O'Brien, 34 Neb. 68; Dung v. Parker, 52 N. Y. 494; Simmons v. More, 100 N. Y. 140; Fleet v. Murton, L. R. 7 Q. B. 126; Pitman v. Kintner, 5 Blackf. (Ind.) 251, 33 Am. Dec. 469; Trust Co. v. Floyd, 47 Ohio St. 525, 12 L. R. A. 346; Delius v. Cawthorn, 2 Dev. (N. C.) 90.

[61] Cochran v. Baker (Ore.), 56 Pac. 641; Trust Co. v. Floyd, 47 Ohio St. 525, 12 L. R. A. 346; Campbell v. Muller, 43 N. Y. Supp. 233.

[62] Story Ag., § 264; Collen v. Wright, 8 E. & B. 647; Smout v. Ilbery, 10 M. & W. 1; Kroeger v. Pitcairn, 101 Pa. St. 311; Baltzen v. Nicolay, 53 N. Y. 467; Simmons v. More, 100 N. Y. 140; Boston, etc., R. Co. v. Richardson, 135 Mass. 473.

[63] Newport v. Smith, 61 Minn. 277; Newman v. Sylvester, 42 Ind. 106;

tered into, and there is consequently no principal who is bound, still the agent will not be liable, if the fact of the principal's death was unknown to both parties.[64] Death, it is true, revokes the agency in that case, and it is to be assumed that an injury has resulted to the third party; but such injury can not be said to have been wrongfully inflicted by any act of the agent, it being regarded as the act of God; neither can there be said to be any implied warranty, as the agent was acting in perfect good faith and could not by the exercise of ordinary prudence have anticipated such injury. If the pretended agent fraudulently represented himself as such when he was really not, he will, as we shall hereafter see, be liable in an action *ex delicto* for a deceit, for the damages caused by his wrongful act.[65] But even here the injured party might waive the tort and sue on the implied contract, if the agent received the benefit of the consideration involved in the contract entered into by him for the supposed principal.[66]

§ 309. **Liability of agent for money had and received.**—An agent is also liable for money had and received, if money has been paid to him by mistake and he has turned it over to his principal after notice of such mistake; but if it was paid voluntarily, and the agent paid it over to the principal before notice, the agent is not liable in any form of action.[67] And where the party who contracted with the agent under a mistake of fact had no notice of the agency, the payment of the money by the agent to the principal, even before demand

Murray v. Carothers, 1 Metc. (Ky.) 71; Snow v. Hix, 54 Vt. 478; Hall v. Lauderdale, 46 N. Y. 70; Abeles v. Cochran, 22 Kan. 406; Barry v. Pike, 21 La. Ann. 221; Humphrey v. Jones, 71 Mo. 62; Western Cement Co. v. Jones, 8 Mo. App. 373.

[64] Story Ag., § 265a; Smout v. Ilbery, 10 M. & W. 1; Carriger v. Whittington, 26 Mo. 311, 72 Am. Dec. 212.

[65] Noyes v. Loring, 55 Me. 408; Taylor v. Shelton, 30 Conn. 122; Sheffield v. Ladue, 16 Minn. 388, 10 Am. Rep. 145; Hancock v. Yunker, 83 Ill. 208; Bartlett v. Tucker, 104 Mass. 341, 6 Am. Rep. 240. As to the agent's liability for torts, see *post*, § 312, *et seq.*

[66] Russell v. Koonce, 104 N. C. 237.

[67] Cabot v. Shaw, 148 Mass. 459; Herrick v. Gallagher, 60 Barb. (N. Y.) 578; Ashley v. Jennings, 48 Mo. App. 142; Hobensack v. Hallman, 17 Pa. St. 154; Shepard v. Sherin, 43 Minn. 382; Upchurch v. Norsworthy, 15 Ala. 705; Smith v. Binder, 75 Ill. 492; Wallis v. Shelly, 30 Fed. 747; Cox v. Prentice, 3 M. & S. 344; Jefts v. York, 10 Cush. (Mass.) 392; Jetts v. York, 12 Cush. (Mass.) 196; Elliott v. Swartwout, 10 Pet. (U. S.) 137.

upon the agent, will be no defense to an action against such agent by the third party to recover the money.[68]

§ 310. **Unauthorized agent not liable if principal would not have been liable.**—If an agent, without authority, enter into a contract for an assumed principal with a third party upon which the principal would not be liable if he had authorized its execution, there can be no liability of the agent. To illustrate: if one person should undertake to make a contract for another which would be void by the statute of frauds, the party on whose behalf the contract was entered into would of course not be bound; but neither would the other person, the one who assumed to act as agent; for the third party could not be said to have been injured by the act of the pretended agent in going through the idle ceremony of making a void contract; and having sustained no injury, the third party could recover nothing in any form of action.[69]

§ 311. **Public agents not generally liable.**—We now come to consider the rule as to public agents. Upon this subject, Story says: "But a very different rule, in general, prevails in regard to public agents; for, in the ordinary course of things, an agent, contracting in behalf of the government, or of the public, is not personally bound by such a contract, even though he would be by the terms of the contract, if it were an agency of a private nature. The reason of the distinction is that it is not to be presumed either that the public agent means to bind himself personally, in acting as a functionary of the government, or that the party dealing with him in his public character means to rely upon his individual responsibility. On the contrary, the natural presumption in such cases is, that the contract was made upon the credit and responsibility of the government itself. * * * This principle not only applies to simple contracts, both oral and written, but also to instruments under seal, which are executed by agents of the government in their own names, and purporting to be made by them on behalf of the government; for the like presumption prevails in such cases, that the parties contract, not personally, but merely officially, within the sphere of their appropriate duties. * * * So, an indenture, executed between A. B., describing himself as 'secretary of war,' of the one part, and C. D. of the other part, for a demise of certain buildings for public pur-

[68] Newall v. Tomlinson, L. R. 6 C. P. 405.

[69] Dung v. Parker, 52 N. Y. 494; Baltzen v. Nicolay, 53 N. Y. 467.

poses, and for a certain period, and containing a covenant, on the part of A. B., to pay the stipulated rent during that period, has been held not to bind A. B. personally, but to bind the government alone. The same principle applies to cases, where public officers, contracting for a public purpose, afterwards, upon a settlement of accounts with the other contracting party, strike a balance, and in writing promise to pay that balance on a specific day, signing their names, with their official designations annexed,—as, for example, as commissioners; for such a written document is quite consistent with an intention not to incur any personal responsibility, but merely to apply the public funds, which might be in their hands at the time prescribed, towards the discharge of the public debt."[70] The rule as to public agents being deemed to act only for the public and not for themselves is, however, one of presumption merely, which is always subject to rebuttal by proper evidence showing that it was in fact the intention to charge the agent personally.[71] Notwithstanding the general rule as stated, there are cases in which the distinction between the liability of public and private agents to third persons seems not to have been observed. Thus, where a paper was headed, "State of Iowa, County of Jones, Township of Hale," and signed, "W. H. Glick, Pres. School Board," and "I. B. Southrich, Sec'y School Board," ordering the delivery of certain school supplies, and containing a promise to pay, it was held to be the personal obligation of the signers and not of the school corporation, there being no terms used in the contract showing any design to bind such corporation, and the additions to the names of the signers being held merely descriptive.[72] But in accordance with the rule mentioned it was held that notes headed "Monticello, Ind.," and reading, "We promise to pay," and "the subscribers promise to pay," and signed respectively by the subscribers as "Trustees of Monticello School," and "School Trustees," were the obligations of the school corporation, and not of the signers personally, and that the additions, "Trustees of Monticello School," and "School Trustees," were not mere *descriptio personarum*, but showed

[70] Story Ag., § 302, *et seq.* See also, Hodgson v. Dexter, 1 Cranch (U. S.) 109; Fox v. Drake, 8 Cow. (N. Y.) 191; Tutt v. Hobbs, 17 Mo. 486; Simonds v. Heard, 23 Pick. (Mass.) 120, 34 Am. Dec. 41; Walker v. Swartwout, 12 Johns. (N. Y.) 444, 7 Am. Dec. 334; Belknap v. Reinhart, 2 Wend. (N. Y.) 375, 20 Am. Dec. 621.

[71] Story Ag., § 306.

[72] Wing v. Glick, 56 Iowa 473. See also, Fowler v. Atkinson, 6 Minn. 579; Village of Cahokia v. Rautenberg, 88 Ill. 219.

an intention to charge the school town. Judge Woods, who delivered the opinion of the court, said: "Contracts made by public agents stand upon a different footing [with regard to the rule of *descriptio personae*] from those made by agents of persons or of private corporations."[73] When the instrument is negotiable by the law merchant, and there is enough indicated in the body and signatures to show that it is the contract of a public agent, as such, it is believed that it will not bind the agent personally, even when the instrument is held by an innocent third person; and certainly this is true when the controversy is between the original parties.[74]

II. For Torts.

§ **312. Agent's liability for torts generally.**—An agent, whether public or private, is liable to third persons in many cases for his torts; that is to say, for the wrongs done by him to such persons in the course of his agency. An agent, like a servant, is only liable to third persons for acts of misfeasance and malfeasance, but not for acts of nonfeasance;[75] his obligations are to his principal, and not to other parties. As to his principal, the agent must not fail to act, for this is but a part of his agreement. As to third parties, he is under no obligation to act, for he has not engaged to do so with them; all he is required to do with reference to third parties is that when he does act for his principal he shall act so as not to injure them; or that he shall not act at all, if to do so would injure them. Nonfeasance is the failure to do a thing which it is the duty of a person to do. Misfeasance is the doing of a thing one ought to do, but doing it in a wrong way. Malfeasance is the doing of a thing which the law directs one ought not to do at all.[76] Now, an agent owes his principal the duty of doing what he has undertaken to do for him; but he owes no such duty to third persons. Hence, if an agent engage to sell goods for his principal, he may render himself liable to the latter for failing to make sales when opportunity offers;

[73] School Town of Monticello v. Kendall, 72 Ind. 91, 37 Am. Rep. 139. And to the same effect, see Wallis v. Johnson School Township, 75 Ind. 368; Pine Civil Township v. Huber Mfg. Co., 83 Ind. 121.

[74] Mechem Ag., § 440.

[75] Delaney v. Rochereau, 34 La. Ann. 1123, 44 Am. Rep. 456; Block v. Haseltine, 3 Ind. App. 491; Baird v. Shipman, 132 Ill. 16, 22 Am. St. 504, and elaborate note at p. 512; Osborne v. Morgan, 130 Mass. 102, 39 Am. Rep. 437.

[76] Coit v. Lynes, 33 Conn. 109; Wright v. Spencer, 1 Stew. (Ala.) 576; Bell v. Josselyn, 3 Gray (Mass.) 309, 63 Am. Dec. 741.

but he will not be liable to third persons for such failure, because he owes them no such duty. If the agent should undertake to make a sale, however, and in the course of the same should make a misrepresentation or false warranty or be guilty of other fraudulent conduct to the injury of the other contracting party,—the purchaser,—the agent would be liable to him for the damages sustained. The one is a case of nonfeasance, the other of misfeasance. Hence, if the agent once undertakes to perform the work of his principal for which he was employed, he owes to third persons as well as to his principal the duty of exercising proper care and diligence so as not to cause injury to them by his acts; and having undertaken the work, he is in duty bound to complete it, if the failure to do so would cause injury to any person. His failure to complete the work undertaken is not nonfeasance.[77] Thus, if an agent or servant whose duty it is to handle gunpowder or other explosives, after doing so, leaves the same exposed so as to cause an explosion from which an injury results, he is liable in damages to the person who sustains the injury.[78] This is not because he is an agent, but because he is a wrongdoer; it is an act of negligence, and not a mere negligent omission. Had he not undertaken to handle the explosives at all, although in duty bound to his principal to do so, he could not be held accountable to third parties for injury resulting from the omission. And if a blacksmith, whose duty it is to shoe the horse of his customer, imposes that task upon his servant, who had agreed to perform it, but fails entirely to do so, and in consequence thereof the horse becomes lame and is injured, the servant is not liable to the owner of the horse for injury. Or if the servant has undertaken to shoe the horse, and by his mere negligence a consequential injury results to the owner, there is no liability on the part of the servant. "But if the servant, in shoeing the horse, has pricked him, or has maliciously or wantonly lamed him, an action will lie personally against the agent himself."[79] The former are instances of nonfeasance, the latter of misfeasance and malfeasance, respectively. A good illustration of the distinction is found in a Massachusetts case, where the manager of a building had caused the water to be turned into the water pipes of the building without first inspecting such pipes as to

[77] Osborne v. Morgan, 130 Mass 102, 39 Am. Rep. 437.

[78] Jenne v. Sutton, 43 N. J. L. 257, 39 Am. Rep. 578.

[79] Story Ag., § 310; Story Bailm., §§ 402, 409.

their condition. It was held that he was liable to a tenant in a lower story for an injury caused by the water coming into the pipes when the latter were out of repair. The failure to examine the pipes was a mere nonfeasance, but the turning in of the water when the pipes had not been examined was an act so negligently done as to amount to a misfeasance.[80] The distinction was illustrated by Lord Holt in the case of *Lane* v. *Cotton*.[81] "If a bailiff," said his lordship, "who has a warrant from the sheriff to execute a writ, suffer his prisoner by neglect to escape, the sheriff shall be charged for it, and not the bailiff; but if the bailiff turn the prisoner loose, the action must be brought against the bailiff himself; for then he is a kind of wrongdoer, or rescuer; and it will lie against any other that will rescue in like manner."

§ **313. No defense that principal is also** liable.—It is not material that the principal may also be liable for the same tort. If the principal has directed the agent or servant to do the wrongful act, it is no excuse for the agent: they are simply tort-feasors, and either or both are liable, as other tort-feasors are; the agent can not shield himself behind his principal and say that he acted upon the latter's authority to commit a wrong. Therefore, an auctioneer employed by a sheriff to sell goods wrongfully taken upon execution is liable to the injured party for the conversion, the same as the sheriff.[82] And the agent can not exonerate himself by showing that he committed the act innocently or in ignorance of the rights of the third party, and in the full belief that his principal had ample authority; the agent must know the law, and the law does not permit that one person confer authority upon another to perpetrate a wrong upon the person or property of a third party; indeed, in matters of tort there can be no such relation as that of principal and agent.[83] Thus, a person who sells intoxicating liquors in violation of law—such as selling without a license, or to infants, or on forbidden days—can not shield himself behind the person for whom he is doing business and say that he is only acting as the agent of the owner of the saloon; and the same is true with reference to other business prohibited except by license.[84] As to the commission of any illegal

[80] Bell v. Josselyn, 3 Gray (Mass.) 309, 63 Am. Dec. 741.

[81] 12 Mod. 472, 488.

[82] Story Ag., § 312.

[83] Berghoff v. McDonald, 87 Ind. 549; Josselyn v. McAllister, 22 Mich. 300.

[84] Winter v. State, 30 Ala. 22; Hays v. State, 13 Mo. 246; Wason v. Underhill, 2 N. H. 505; Temple v.

act, it may be stated that each person is responsible for his own and not for his neighbor's affairs; hence, if an agent do an act in violation of law and injury result to another, he can not excuse himself by showing that he was acting for another.[85]

§ 314. **Agent's liability for fraud in executing principal's contract.**—An agent may be guilty of fraud in the execution of his principal's authority; and if injury result from it to the party with whom he has dealt, he will be liable *ex delicto* in an action for the damages resulting from the wrongful act, as will also the principal; or, if the transaction result in a benefit to the agent personally, he may be sued *ex contractu* for money had and received.[86] The rule applies to directors and other officers of corporations as to fraud, negligence, mismanagement, etc.[87]

§ 315. **Agent's liability for personal injuries.**—An agent may be liable for a personal injury resulting to another through his negligence. Keeping in mind the doctrine that mere nonfeasance will not, as a general rule, subject an agent to liability, it is nevertheless true, as we have heretofore seen, that when the agent has once entered upon the performance of his undertaking, he must do everything reasonably necessary to its performance with due regard for the safety of others. Thus, where one who is employed to superintend the erection of a building fails to provide suitable scaffolding to prevent bricks from falling to the ground, he is liable to one injured by the falling of a brick from the building.[88] Some of the decisions are difficult to reconcile. Thus, it is held in some cases that an agent who has the possession and control of the real estate of another,—who is a nonresident,—and who is bound to keep the premises in repair, and fails to do so, or to take proper care of the same, will be liable to a third party for any injury sustained by reason of such

Sumner, 51 Miss. 13, 24 Am. Rep. 615.

[85] Swaggard v. Hancock, 25 Mo. App. 596; Duluth v. Mallett, 43 Minn. 204; Bennett v. Bayes, 5 H. & N. 391.

[86] Moore v. Shields, 121 Ind. 267; Campbell v. Hillman, 15 B. Mon. (Ky.) 508, 61 Am. Dec. 195; Salmon v. Richardson, 30 Conn. 360, 79 Am. Dec. 255; Hedden v. Griffin, 136 Mass. 25, 49 Am. Rep. 25; Kroeger v. Pitcairn, 101 Pa. St. 311, 47 Am. Rep. 718.

[87] Salmon v. Richardson, *supra;* Hodges v. New England Screw Co., 1 R. I. 312, 53 Am. Dec. 624.

[88] Mayer v. Thompson, etc., Bldg. Co., 104 Ala. 611, 16 So. 620; Baird v. Shipman, 132 Ill. 16, 22 Am. St. 504; Campbell v. Portland Sugar Co., 62 Me. 552, 16 Am. Rep. 503; Ellis v.

failure;[89] while in others this is said to be a nonfeasance, for which such agent is not liable.[89a] The difficulty which seems to have led to the conflict between these and other decisions upon this subject obviously lies in the failure of some of the courts to observe the distinction between nonfeasance and misfeasance, and the further failure to observe the principle that when a person commits an act which amounts to a malfeasance he violates a duty which he owes to third parties; not because he is an agent of some one, but because he is a member of society and must so conduct himself as not to inflict injury upon others, whether he do so in the performance of his engagements as an agent or in any other capacity.[90]

§ **316. Agent's liability for conversion.**—A conversion of the property of another subjects the wrongdoer to an action. If the case is clearly one of a conversion, no difficulty can be encountered in coming to a proper conclusion. The fact that he is an agent will furnish no justification for the conversion; for, as the Indiana supreme court said, "in torts, the relation of principal and agent does not exist; they are all wrongdoers."[91] But suppose the agent is himself ignorant of the title of the real owner, acting merely on behalf of another, and under his direction; he would still be liable, under the decisions, for the conversion of the property. "A person is guilty of a conversion who intermeddles with any property and disposes of it," says Lord Ellenborough, "and it is no answer that he acted under authority from another, who had himself no authority to dispose of it. And the court is governed by the principle of law, and not by the hardship of any particular case."[92] Cases of this character frequently occur in the transactions of auctioneers, factors and brokers

McNaughton, 76 Mich. 237, 15 Am. St. 308; Shearman & Redf. Neg., § 244.

[89] Baird v. Shipman, 132 Ill. 16, 22 Am. St. 504; Campbell v. Portland Sugar Co., 62 Me. 552, 16 Am. Rep. 503; Ellis v. McNaughton, 76 Mich. 237, 15 Am. St. 308.

[89a] Dean v. Brock, 11 Ind. App. 507. Compare also, Delaney v. Rochereau, 34 La. Ann. 1123, 44 Am. Rep. 456; Feltus v. Swan, 62 Miss. 415.

[90] Shearman & Redf. Neg., § 244; Berghoff v. McDonald, 87 Ind. 549; Bennett v. Ives, 30 Conn. 329; Blue v. Briggs, 12 Ind. App. 105.

[91] Berghoff v. McDonald, *supra*.

[92] Stephens v. Elwall, 4 M. & S. 259, cited in 14 M. & W. 270; Lee v. Mathews, 10 Ala. 682, 44 Am. Dec. 498; Marks v. Robinson, 82 Ala. 69; Robinson v. Bird, 158 Mass. 357, 35 Am. St. 495; McPheters v. Page, 83 Me. 234, 23 Am. St. 772; Koch v. Branch, 44 Mo. 542, 100 Am. Dec. 324.

with persons with whom they have dealings for their principals. So, an auctioneer who sells the property of another without his consent is liable to the owner for conversion, though he acts on the authority of another who has no title to it, and though he is innocent of any intentional wrong, and ignorant of the title of the owner.[93] And a stockholder who received from the thief stolen certificates of stock and sold them was held liable to the true owner for the value of the stock, though he acted in good faith about the matter, believing that his principal was the owner thereof.[94] So, a cotton factor who sold the crop of the tenant was held liable to the landlord for the conversion of the crop without having satisfied the landlord's lien.[95] And a sewing machine agent who took from a married woman a sum of money and a machine, belonging to her husband, in exchange for another machine, without the husband's consent, was held liable to the husband for the conversion.[96]

§ 317. **Agent's liability on implied warranty of authority.**—An agent is liable, as we have had occasion to observe, for a false warranty or representation of his authority.[97] If the warranty was not express, but arose simply by implication from the exercise of the authority, and the agent honestly believed himself to be in possession of such authority, although he was not, it is generally held that he is not liable *ex delicto,* but may be sued on the implied contract of warranty.[98] But if the misrepresentation be fraudulent, or if the business transaction be under such circumstances as will show that he had knowledge of his want of authority, but assumed to act as if he possessed it, he will be liable in an action *ex delicto* for the damages sustained by the misrepresentation or false warranty. Thus, where a person without any authority signs a promissory note or other contract as agent of another person, falsely representing himself to be authorized to do so, he is liable to the injured party in a special action in tort.[99]

[93] Robinson v. Bird, *supra.*

[94] Swim v. Wilson, 90 Cal. 126, 25 Am. St. 110.

[95] Merchants', etc., Bank v. Meyer, 56 Ark. 499.

[96] Rice v. Yocum, 155 Pa. St. 538. But see Lenthold v. Fairchild, 35 Minn. 99, where it is held that an agent acting solely for his principal and under his directions, who disposes or assists the principal in disposing of property belonging to a third person, in ignorance of the title of the true owner, is not thereby rendered liable for a conversion.

[97] *Ante,* §§ 307, 308.

[98] See cases cited in note 61, *supra.*

[99] Ballou v. Talbot, 16 Mass. 461, 8 Am. Dec. 146; Duncan v. Niles, 32 Ill. 532, 83 Am. Dec. 293; Union

§ 318. **No defense that agent received no benefit or acted under instructions.**—The fact that the agent derived no personal benefit or advantage from the wrong committed by him will be no justification of its commission;[100] as in the other instances named, he can not invoke the protection of his agency, and show that some one else received the benefit of his wrongful act. The principal could not have delegated any lawful authority to the agent to commit a wrong, and, whether he acted for himself or for some one else, he is none the less a wrongdoer; hence, that he acted within the scope of his instructions, or that his principal was present and directed him to do the act, will not exonerate him from personal responsibility;[101] if the principal could not with impunity have performed the act himself, he could not authorize the agent to do it, for he could not authorize another to do what he could not have done himself.[102]

School Township v. First Nat'l Bank, 102 Ind. 464; M'Henry v. Duffield, 7 Blackf. (Ind.) 41; Potts v. Henderson, 2 Ind. 327. There are cases, however, which hold that the agent in such a case may be made liable in an action on the case for deceit. Thus, it was said by the supreme court of Ohio, Williams, J., speaking for the court, in Trust Co. v. Floyd, 47 Ohio St. 525, 12 L. R. A. 346: "While, however, the authorities generally agree that a person who, without having in fact authority to make a contract as agent, yet does so under the *bona fide* belief that such authority is vested in him, is nevertheless personally responsible to those who contract with him in ignorance of his want of authority, a diversity of opinion is found in the cases in regard to the exact nature of the liability, and the character of the action by which it may be enforced. In Jenkins v. Hutchinson, 13 Q. B. (66 E. C. L.) 744, it is intimated by Erle, J., that an action of deceit would lie in such cases, notwithstanding the good faith of the agent, and some authorities may be found to that effect. Another class of cases hold that the liability is upon the contract; but it is believed that whether the agent is so liable depends upon the intention of the parties as discovered from the contract itself; and on this question the form of the agreement and the mode of signature may be quite conclusive. The rule on this subject as stated in Story on Agency is that an agent can not be sued on the very instrument itself, as a contracting party, unless there be apt words to charge him: Section 264a. Still another class of cases establish the rule, which we are inclined to adopt, that in cases like the one we are considering the agent is liable upon his implied promise that he possesses the authority he assumes to have."

[100] Weber v. Weber, 47 Mich. 569.

[101] Weber v. Weber, *supra;* Johnson v. Barber, 5 Gilm. (Ill.) 425, 50 Am. Dec. 416.

[102] Mali v. Lord, 39 N. Y. 381, 100 Am. Dec. 448. See Bocchino v. Cook (N. J. Sup.), 51 Atl. 487.

§ 319. **Agent of foreign principal—Former and modern rules.**— As to the agents of principals residing abroad,—as, where a merchant in Germany or France had his factor or other commercial agent to transact business for him in England or in this country,— the rule formerly was that the agent was liable on all contracts made by him for his principal, without regard to whether he described himself in the contract as agent or not; the presumption being that exclusive credit was given the agent, who resided at home, rather than to the principal, who resided abroad.[103] The reason for this rule was said to be the general convenience and usage of trade, and the fact that the principal was presumed to be unknown to the one extending the credit.[104] It would seem, therefore, that if the principal was in fact known and credit expressly and intentionally given him, instead of the agent, the reason for the rule would fail and the rule itself cease to operate. And this is believed to be true. The rule that the credit must be taken to have been extended to the agent was indeed only presumptive; and evidence was admissible to show that it was the intention to hold the principal liable nothwithstanding his business was in a foreign country;[105] although the presumption that exclusive credit was given to the agent was said to be so strong "as almost to amount to a conclusive presumption of law."[106] The rule, however, never applied to the states of the Union, as they were never considered foreign to each other in this sense.[107] According to the current of modern authority, the old doctrine is now practically exploded, and whether credit was given the principal or the agent is a question of fact and not of law.[108]

[103] Story Ag., §§ 268, 290, 400; Gonzales v. Sladen, Bull. N. P. 130; Peterson v. Ayre, 13 C. B. (76 E. C. L.) 353; Vawter v. Baker, 23 Ind. 63; Merrick's Estate, 5 W. & S. (Pa.) 9; Hochster v. Baruch, 5 Daly (N. Y.) 440; Pollock Conts. (6th ed.) 95; Kaulback v. Churchill, 59 N. H. 296.

[104] Wharton Ag., § 791; Story Ag., § 268.

[105] Vawter v. Baker, 23 Ind. 63; Maury v. Ranger, 38 La. Ann. 485, 58 Am. Rep. 197.

[106] Story Ag., § 290.

[107] Vawter v. Baker, 23 Ind. 63; Taintor v. Prendergast, 3 Hill (N. Y.) 72, 38 Am. Dec. 618.

[108] Green v. Kopke, 36 Eng. L. & Eq. 396; Kirkpatrick v. Stainer, 22 Wend. (N. Y.) 244; Taintor v. Prendergast, *supra;* Maury v. Ranger, 38 La. Ann. 485, 58 Am. Rep. 197; Oelricks v. Ford, 23 How. (U. S.) 49; Bray v. Kettell, 1 Allen (Mass.) 80; Murphy v. Helmrich, 66 Cal. 69.

CHAPTER IX.

DUTIES, OBLIGATIONS AND LIABILITIES OF PRINCIPAL TO THIRD PERSONS, AND RIGHTS OF THIRD PERSONS IN REGARD TO PRINCIPAL.

§ **320. Purpose of this chapter.**—In this chapter we shall consider the nature and extent of the duties and obligations a principal owes to those persons, generally designated as third persons or third parties, with whom the agent deals or transacts business for his principal; the principal's liability for failing to discharge those duties or obligations; and the rights of such persons out of which the duties and obligations of the principal arise.

§ **321. The doctrine of identity.**—As an agency is created mainly for the purpose of enabling the principal to enter into contract relations with persons with whom he can not conveniently deal in person, it becomes the duty of the principal to recognize and fulfill all the authorized lawful engagements into which his agent has entered for him, as well as those not authorized originally, but subsequently ratified by him. The agent, as Wharton expresses it, is absorbed in the principal, and he alone is liable upon such contracts as are legally executed for him by his agent.[1] Most, if not all, the liabilities of the principal for the acts of his agent grow out of the fiction of unity or identity: the contract, in contemplation of law, is entered into by the principal himself, for he and his agent are identical; whatever the agent does in the course of the agency is the same as if the principal had done it, and the principal receives all the benefits and must assume all the burdens of and liabilities for such acts, the same as if they were his own; from such a contract the agent, after its execution and delivery, becomes entirely eliminated, and thereafter the relation be-

[1] Wharton Ag., § 454.

tween the principal and other contracting party is the same as if it had been entered into by the principal individually. And this is true whether the authority was conferred upon the agent directly or by implication; for, if the principal has by his conduct suffered third parties to transact business with the agent on the assumption that he had authority from him, it is as fully his duty to make good the agreements thus made for him as if he had authorized them in the most solemn manner.[2] But the principal not only obligates himself by the assumption of the relation to perform the contracts made for him in pursuance of such authority as he has conferred or led others to believe he has conferred, and to perform those ratified by him, if originally unauthorized; but by force of the doctrine of identity he also becomes liable for the agent's torts. He tacitly warrants that the agent will so conduct himself, while in the performance of the duties of his employment, as not to cause any injury to those with whom he comes in contact as agent for him. The public, generally, have a right to assume that the principal will select no one to represent him who is not in every way fitted to discharge the trust imposed upon him, and if injury occurs by reason of the misconduct or negligence of the person so chosen, it is more in the interest of justice that the loss should be suffered by him who has set the cause thereof in motion than by another who had nothing whatever to do with inciting it. The principal may incur liabilities, then, for the agent's acts: (1) on contracts made by the agent, and (2) on torts committed by the agent.

§ 322. **Agent may bind principal on contract.**—We have already seen that an agent who is duly authorized to do so may bind his principal, *ex contractu*, if he execute the authority conferred upon him in the latter's name and on his behalf.[3] If the agent discloses both the fact of the agency and the name of the principal, and, in the execution of the contract, speaks for the principal only, it is the contract of the principal, and of him only, and he will be bound by it the same as if he had entered into it in person.[4] There can be no difficulty in establishing the obligation and liability of the principal, if the contract was duly authorized by and was entered into ostensibly for the principal. On the other hand, it is equally clear that if the contract was not authorized, and the principal had not by words or

[2] Wharton Ag., § 454.

[3] *Ante*, §§ 234, 301.

[4] *Ante*, § 207.

conduct led the third party to believe it was authorized, the alleged principal is under no obligation to carry out its terms; and in the absence of any ratification or estoppel on his part, he can not be bound by it. And so also, although the agent was fully authorized to enter into such a contract for the principal, yet if he did so on his own behalf, and for himself only, and not for and on behalf of the principal, the latter is not bound by it to the party with whom such agent contracted, if all the parties to the transaction were known. These are plain propositions and do not here require the citation of any authorities to confirm them.

I. Liability on Contracts.

§ **323. Principal bound on contract.**—It is well established by the authorities that the principal is bound by the contract of his agent, entered into on his behalf, not only when the same is within the real, but also when it is within the apparent scope of the agent's authority; provided, of course, that the terms employed are sufficiently apt, and that the third party acted in good faith.[5] If the authority exercised by the agent was fully authorized, or, in other words, if the agent acted within the actual scope of his authority, there is no doubt whatever of the principal's liability. But his liability is not confined to this. There are so many ways of conferring authority, and, in many cases, so much reason for believing it has been conferred, although it has not, that the policy of the law often is to imply such authority from the course of business or employment, or other circumstances indicating clearly that the acts performed have received the sanction of the principal. "The proof of such recognition [of authority], it may be admitted," say the supreme court of Iowa, "must be such as makes the belief of such authority strong and reasonable. The general rule is that the principal is bound if he has actually authorized the act or if he has authorized those with whom the agent dealt in his behalf to believe, as fair and reasonable men, that the authority had actually been given."[6] Akin to the doctrine we are now discussing is the rule that third parties will not be bound by secret in-

[5] Marsh v. Gilbert, 2 Hun (N. Y.) 58; Hunt v. Chapin, 6 Lans. (N. Y.) 139; Westfield Bank v. Cornen, 37 N. Y. 319, 93 Am. Dec. 573; Minor v. Mechanic's Bank, 1 Pet. (U. S.) 46; Whiting v. Western Stage Co., 20 Iowa 554; Wheeler v. McGuire, 86 Ala. 398; Story Ag., § 133; Crane v. Gruenewald, 120 N. Y. 274.

[6] Whiting v. Western Stage Co., 20 Iowa 554.

structions to an agent, of which such third parties have no knowledge. If a person delegates authority to an agent to perform certain acts or transact certain business for him, but restricts him in the exercise thereof by certain secret instructions or directions, the principal is nevertheless bound by the agent's act as authorized without such limitation, unless the third party had notice of such instructions or directions.[7] Any other rule would make innocent persons suffer who had nothing whatever to do with the appointment or holding out of the agent; whereas the equitable doctrine is that "where one of two or more innocent persons is to suffer, he ought to suffer who misled the other into the contract by holding out the agent as competent to act and as enjoying his confidence."[8] In harmony with these principles of the law, one who innocently pays money to an unauthorized agent for his supposed principal, when the latter has made it possible for the agent to mislead such innocent party, so as to repose confidence in him, will be protected by such payment. Thus, where one who had negotiated a loan of money through an agent, permitted the agent to retain the note and mortgage, and the mortgagor made payments to the agent while the papers were in his hands, it was held that such innocent third person would be protected and the mortgagee would be compelled to bear the loss.[9]

§ 324. **As to duty of third party to ascertain agent's authority.**— However, it is generally the duty of the third party to ascertain, in the first place, what the agent's authority is, and if it be in writing, to demand an inspection thereof. The mere fact that an agent assumes to act as such is not sufficient to render the principal liable to a third party with whom the agent has dealt;[10] but if the third party exercises due and proper care in ascertaining the agent's authority, he may safely act upon appearances; he can not be held bound by secret limitations upon the authority ostensibly given;[11] it is not his duty to inquire for private letters or secret instructions.[12]

[7] Rourke v. Story, 4 E. D. Smith (N. Y.) 54; Fatman v. Leet, 41 Ind. 133; Simonds v. Clapp, 16 N. H. 222; Walsh v. Hartford F. Ins. Co., 73 N. Y. 5.

[8] Story Ag., § 443; Crane v. Gruenewald, 120 N. Y. 274.

[9] Crane v. Gruenewald, 120 N. Y. 274.

[10] Hurley v. Watson, 68 Mich. 531.

[11] Markey v. Mutual, etc., Ins. Co., 103 Mass. 78; Cruzan v. Smith, 41 Ind. 288; Edwards v. Schaffer, 49 Barb. (N. Y.) 291; Murphy v. Southern L. Ins. Co., 3 Baxt. (Tenn.) 440, 27 Am. Rep. 761; Carmichael v. Buck, 10 Rich. Eq. (S. C.) 332, 70 Am. Dec. 226; Lister v. Allen, 31 Md. 543, 100 Am. Dec. 78.

[12] Story Ag., § 73.

§ 325. **Distinction between general and special agent.**—The distinction we have pointed out in the former chapters with respect to general and special agents is supposed by many of the older authorities to alter materially the conditions by which the principal's liability is determined.[13] Thus, if the agency be a general one, it is said to render the principal liable if the agent was acting within the general scope of his authority, notwithstanding the act was contrary to his private instructions; while in case of a special agency, the public is required to ascertain the precise extent of his authority, and the third party is bound even by private restrictions, unless the principal has held the agent out as possessing the authority exercised by him.[14] It is very doubtful, however, whether this distinction will hold in every case.[15] It may be conceded that if the agency be special, and the limitations be contained in the grant of authority itself, whether it be written or oral, the third party can not hold the principal liable beyond such authority: this, then, being the "scope" of the agent's authority.[16] But is not this true also of a general agency? Generally the scope of any agent's authority is determined by his commission or what is equivalent to it. In any agency the principal is bound by the acts of the agent, if they be within the apparent scope of authority; that is, the authority which the agent is held out to possess. "No man is at liberty to send another into the market to buy or sell for him as his agent, with secret instructions as to the manner in which he shall execute his agency, which are not to be communicated to those with whom he is to deal, and then when his agent has deviated from those instructions, to say that he was a special agent, that the instructions were limitations upon his authority, and that those with whom he dealt in the matter of his agency acted at their peril, because they were bound to inquire where inquiry would have been fruitless, and to ascertain that of which they were not to have knowledge. It would render dealing with a special agent a matter of great hazard. If the principal deemed the bargain a good one, the secret orders would continue sealed, but if his opinion were otherwise, the injunction of secrecy would be removed and the transaction avoided, leaving the party to such remedy as he might enforce against the agent."[17] If

[13] *Ante*, §§ 18, 192.

[14] Rossiter v. Rossiter, 8 Wend. (N. Y.) 495; Blackwell v. Ketcham, 53 Ind. 184; Cruzan v. Smith, 41 Ind. 288; Story Ag., § 126; Smith Mercantile Law (2d ed.) 59.

[15] See Fitzherbert v. Mather, 1 T. R. 12, 16.

[16] Munn v. Commission Co., 15 Johns. (N. Y.) 44, 8 Am. Dec. 219.

[17] Parker, C. J., in Hatch v. Taylor, 10 N. H. 538.

the limitation upon the authority of the agent be part and parcel of the authority conferred,—as where it is contained in the same written instrument, or stipulated orally in the contract of delegation of authority,—third parties must be bound by the limitation. Thus, if the owner of a horse send him to a market by a stranger with express directions not to warrant him, and the agent, contrary to such orders, sell him with a warranty, the owner will not be liable on the warranty.[18] In such a case as this the agency is special, and the third party must ascertain what the authority is at his peril, for it can not be maintained that there is anything about such an agency that carries with it an implication or appearance of authority to warrant. If the third party demands the agent's authority, and is shown an instrument containing the same, the principal would not be at liberty to show that the authority so delegated was in fact limited by private instructions that were not to be disclosed. And if the delegation of authority was oral, and the third party, upon demand, was informed of the nature thereof, the information being true and in harmony with the usages and customs of trade as to the extent to which an agent of his class generally exercises such authority, the principal can not show in defense that the agent had secret instructions contravening such ostensible authority.[19] If the authority is fairly inferable from the terms of the authority granted, the act of the agent in pursuance thereof, whether a general or special agent, is binding upon the principal as to all persons who act in good faith upon that assumption.[20]

[18] Fenn v. Harrison, 3 T. R. 757.

[19] Carmichael v. Buck, 10 Rich. L. (S. C.) 332, 70 Am. Dec. 226.

[20] Lister v. Allen, 31 Md. 543, 100 Am. Dec. 78; Westfield Bank v. Cornen, 37 N. Y. 320; Law v. Stokes, 3 Vroom (N. J.) 249, 90 Am. Dec. 655; Reynolds v. Davison, 34 Md. 662. In Lister v. Allen, *supra*, the court adopts the general rule as to special agents laid down by Chitty; namely:—"If the agent is appointed only for a particular purpose, and is invested with limited powers, or, in other words, is a special agent, then it is the duty of persons dealing with such agent to ascertain the extent of his authority, and the principal or master will not be bound by any act of the agent not warranted expressly by, or by fair and necessary implication from, the terms of the authority delegated to him,"—and then proceeds to say: "The general rule is correct; but in the application of it to cases affecting the rights of third persons who have dealt with the agent in good faith, care must be taken not to bind them by limitations placed on the authority of the agent by the private instructions of the principal, which are not known to such third persons, nor properly inferable from the nature of the agent's employment." Hence, it may

§ 326. Principal bound by authorized acts of agent, and the means of carrying such acts into execution.—Moreover, the agent having in all cases the implied authority to use all the means reasonably necessary to execute the powers actually conferred, it follows that the principal is bound by the acts of the agent performed in employing such means.[21] In accordance with this rule, it has been held that if a traveling salesman is sent out by his house to sell goods on samples he may bind the house for a livery bill contracted by him for the purpose of transporting himself and his samples; and this without regard to the fact that the principals had furnished him with money sufficient to pay all expenses, if the liveryman was ignorant of the fact of the agent's want of authority to have such bills charged to the principals.[22] Much depends also upon custom or usage. Thus, where it is

be stated upon the authority of the cases cited that even though the authority of the agent be a special one, yet if the principal placed in his hands such muniments of title as authorized the third party to deal with the agent as the owner of the article, or as having the power of disposition over it, and the third party dealt with the agent in good faith, he will be protected against the claim of the principal, although the agent may have violated his instructions; and in this regard there is no difference between a special and general agent.

[21] Huntley v. Mathias, 90 N. C. 101; Daylight Burner Co. v. Odlin, 51 N. H. 56.

[22] Bentley v. Doggett, 51 Wis. 224. "The real question is," said the court, "Can the agent, having the money of his principals in his possession for the purpose of paying such hire, by neglecting to pay for it, charge them with the payment to the party furnishing the same, such party being ignorant at the time of furnishing the same that the agent was furnished by his principals with money and forbidden to pledge their credit for the same? There can be no question that, from the nature of the business required to be done by their agent, the defendants held out to those who might have occasion to deal with him, that he had the right to contract for the use of teams and carriages necessary and convenient for doing such business, in the name of his principals, if he saw fit, in the way such service is usually contracted for; and we may, perhaps, take judicial notice that such service is usually contracted for, payment to be made after the service is performed. It would seem to follow that as the agent had the power to bind his principals by a contract for such service, to be paid for in the usual way, if he neglects or refuses to pay for the same after the service is performed, the principals must pay. The fault of the agent in not paying out of the money of his principals in his hands can not deprive the party furnishing the service of the right to enforce the contract against them, he being ignorant of the restricted authority of the agent. If the party furnishing the service knew that the agent had

customary to sell property with a warranty the authority to sell will generally imply authority to warrant, even though the agent have no actual authority to do so.[23] But the cases concerning which such custom prevails are usually limited to those in which the article sold and warranted was not present and subject to the purchaser's inspection.[24] Indeed, the authorities generally go so far as to hold that an authority to sell usually includes an authority to warrant the quality of the article sold, if such article is not present and subject to inspection of the purchaser.[25] An authority to sell does not usually imply authority to sell on credit.[26] A party who relies upon the authority of an agent to sell on credit, based upon commercial custom in a particular business, has the burden of showing such custom and proving that the credit given was not unreasonable.[27] And whenever a third party deals with an agent in a manner different from the general custom, it is the duty of such party to ascertain the extent of the agent's authority in such dealing.[28] Authority to collect is usually implied from the agent's possession of the paper; but evidence of this is indispensable, in the absence of proof of express authority.[29] In

been furnished by his principal with the money to pay for the service, and had been forbidden to pledge the credit of his principals for such service, he would be in a different position. Under such circumstances, if he furnished the service to the agent, he would be held to have furnished it upon the sole credit of the agent, and he would be compelled to look to the agent alone for his pay. We think the rule above stated as governing the case is fully sustained by the fundamental principles of law which govern and limit the powers of agents to bind their principals when dealing with third persons. . . . In this view of the case it was immaterial what the orders of the principal were to the agent, or that he furnished him money to pay these charges, so long as the person furnishing the service was in ignorance of such facts. In order to relieve himself from liability, the principal was bound to show that the plaintiff had knowledge of the restrictions placed upon his agent, or that the custom to limit the powers of agents of this kind was so universal that the plaintiff must be presumed to have knowledge of such custom."

[23] Andrews v. Kneeland, 6 Cow. (N. Y.) 354; Cooley v. Perrine, 41 N. J. L. 322; Edwards v. Dillon, 147 Ill. 14, 37 Am. St. 199. But a special agent to sell a horse has no such authority: Cooley v. Perrine, *supra*.

[24] Talmage v. Bierhause, 103 Ind. 270; Ahern v. Goodspeed, 72 N. Y. 108.

[25] Talmage v. Bierhause, 103 Ind. 270.

[26] Dyer v. Duffy, 39 W. Va. 148, 24 L. R. A. 339.

[27] Payne v. Potter, 9 Iowa 549.

[28] Tidrick v. Rice, 13 Iowa 214.

[29] Kohl v. Beach, 107 Wis. 409, 81 Am. St. 849.

a recent Illinois case it was held that a contract of guaranty against loss is not within the implied authority of a general salesman of goods.[30] And one who holds a claim for collection has no implied authority to receive anything in payment except money.[31]

§ 327. **Principal not bound if agent had adverse interest.**—The principal is not bound for the contracts or agreements of his agent if the latter had an adverse interest in the subject-matter of the agency, which was at the time of the transaction known to the third party, but unknown to the principal.[32] *A fortiori,* if the agent himself is the adverse party, his acts are not binding on his principal.[33]

§ 328. **Liability of undisclosed principal.**—What has been said thus far as to the liability of the principal on the contracts of his agent has reference to a principal who was disclosed by the agent and named by him in the contract on which it is sought to make the principal liable. The agent may, however, make a contract or perform an act for his principal, which he was authorized to make or perform, without naming or disclosing his principal, or even the fact of his agency, at the time he enters into the contract or performs the act, and the third party may deal with the agent in ignorance of the fact that there is a principal and of his identity. In such case the third party may, when he discovers the principal, elect to pursue him instead of the agent, and the former will be liable on the contract.[34] "It may certainly be now regarded as a point settled beyond all possible controversy that if an agent, duly authorized, makes a contract in his own name, without disclosing his principal, and even when such principal is entirely unknown to the other contracting party, he is nevertheless bound, and damages may be recovered of him in an action for its breach. By contracting in his own name the agent only adds his per-

[30] Braun v. Hess, 187 Ill. 283, 79 Am. St. 221. See to the same effect, Kinser v. Calumet Fire Clay Co., 165 Ill. 505.

[31] Cram v. Sickel, 51 Neb. 828, 66 Am. St. 478.

[32] See Wassell v. Reardon, 11 Ark. 705, 54 Am. Dec. 245; Harrison v. McHenry, 9 Ga. 164, 52 Am. Dec. 435; Herman v. Martineau, 1 Wis. 136, 151, 60 Am. Dec. 368.

[33] Harrison v. McHenry, *supra.*

[34] Taintor v. Prendergast, 3 Hill (N. Y.) 72, 38 Am. Dec. 618; Youghiogheny Iron, etc., Co. v. Smith, 66 Pa. St. 340; Hubbard v. Tenbrook, 124 Pa. St. 291, 10 Am. St. 585; Henderson v. Mayhew, 2 Gill (Md.) 393, 41 Am. Dec. 434; Merrill v. Kenyon, 48 Conn. 314, 40 Am. Rep. 174; Trueman v. Loder, 11 A. & E. 587, 39 E. C. L. 319; Smith v. Plummer, 5 Whart. (Pa.) 89, 34 Am. Dec. 530.

sonal obligation to that of the person who employs him."[35] Or the third party may knowingly prefer to deal with the agent on the latter's own responsibility and extend credit to him, whether he is aware of the agency or identity of the principal or not, in which case the agent, and not the principal, will be liable.[36] If the credit was given to the agent exclusively, the third party being in possession of all the facts with reference to the agency and the identity of the principal, no recourse can be had upon the principal.[37] The parties have a right to elect with whom they will deal, and another party can not be introduced into the contract, if they determine otherwise; and the election being once intelligently exercised, can not be abandoned thereafter by one of the contracting parties.[38] But if the facts of the agency or the identity of the principal be undisclosed, and there is no specific election to hold the agent instead of the principal, the latter is liable on the contract when discovered. The principal and agent are identical, so far as the effects of the contract are concerned. When the agent performs an act, the act is performed by the principal, and the results are the same unless there are intervening rights. When the agent enters into a contract, it is the principal entering into such contract; he receives the consideration for it and should, therefore, be subject to the corresponding liabilities. The doctrine of the identity of the principal and the agent, and that of holding one whose estate has been enriched at the expense of another liable to the extent of the benefits received, both unite in laying the foundation for the liability of an undisclosed principal, and give rise to the further (reciprocal) liability of third parties to the principal.[39] The rule that the undisclosed principal may be made liable to the third party, when discovered, is applicable even if the fact of the agency was known to such third party, provided the name or iden-

[35] Sharswood, J., in Youghiogheny Iron, etc., Co. v. Smith, 66 Pa. St. 340.

[36] Pope v. Meadow Spring Distilling Co., 20 Fed. 35; Schepflin v. Dessar, 20 Mo. App. 569.

[37] Henderson v. Mayhew, 2 Gill (Md.) 393, 41 Am. Dec. 434; Silver v. Jordan, 136 Mass. 319; Hyde v. Paige, 9 Barb. (N. Y.) 150; Jones v. Ætna Ins. Co., 14 Conn. 501. As to what constitutes an election to hold the agent, see Beymer v. Bonsall, 79 Pa. St. 298.

[38] Story Ag., § 447; Winchester v. Howard, 97 Mass. 303; Kingsley v. Davis, 104 Mass. 178.

[39] See Beymer v. Bonsall, 79 Pa. St. 298; Kayton v. Barnett, 116 N. Y. 625; Irvine v. Watson, L. R. 5 Q. B. D. 414; Thomson v. Davenport, 9 B. & C. 78, 3 Smith Ld. Cas. (9th ed.) 1648, 17 E. C. L. 45; Ford v. Williams, 21 How. (U. S.) 287; Merrill v. Kenyon, 48 Conn. 314, 40 Am. Rep. 174.

tity of the principal was unknown when the contract was made.[39a] In such case the third party may elect whether to hold the agent or the principal; but having once exercised the choice of election, he can not afterwards hold the party against whom he has abandoned his remedy. The difficult question is to determine when an election has been made.[40] It may be correctly laid down, then, as a rule, that where an authorized agent has entered into a simple contract with a third party, which was in fact made for his principal, but in which the name of the principal was not disclosed, and which contract was, on its face, in the name of the agent only, the third party may, when he discovers the principal, abandon his remedy against the agent and hold the principal.[41]

[39a] Merrill v. Kenyon, 48 Conn. 314, 40 Am. Rep. 174.

[40] Ferry v. Moore, 18 Ill. App. 135; Guest v. Burlington Opera House Co., 74 Iowa 457.

[41] See the citations in last note; also: Henderson v. Mayhew, 2 Gill (Md.) 393, 41 Am. Dec. 434; Mayhew v. Graham, 4 Gill (Md.) 339, 363; Borcherling v. Katz, 37 N. J. Eq. 150; Lovell v. Williams, 125 Mass. 439; Taintor v. Prendergast, 3 Hill (N. Y.) 72, 38 Am. Dec. 618; Episcopal Church of Macon v. Wiley, 2 Hill Eq. (S. C.) 584, 1 Riley Ch. (S. C.) 156, 30 Am. Dec. 386; Smith v. Plummer, 5 Whart. (Pa.) 89, 34 Am. Dec. 530; Higgins v. Senior, 8 M. & W. 834; Woodford v. Hamilton, 139 Ind. 481. "It has long been settled to be a general rule of law," said the supreme court of Texas, in Sanger v. Warren, 91 Tex. 472, 66 Am. St. 913, "that if A contracts with B, supposing him to be acting in his own behalf, but afterwards discovers that he was acting for C, A can thereupon elect to hold C upon the contract. The rule is held applicable to written contracts, and, by a process of reasoning not entirely satisfactory, even to those required by statute to be in writing. In the leading case of Higgins v. Senior, 8 M. & W. 834, Parke, B., said: 'The question in this case, which was argued before us in the course of the last term, may be stated to be, whether in an action on an agreement in writing, purporting on the face of it to be made by the defendant, and subscribed by him, for the sale and delivery by him of goods above the value of ten pounds, it is competent for the defendant to discharge himself, on an issue on the plea of *non assumpsit*, by proving that the agreement was really made by him by the authority of and as agent for a third person, and that the plaintiff knew those facts at the time when the agreement was made and signed. Upon consideration, we think it was not; and that the rule for a new trial must be discharged. There is no doubt that, where such an agreement is made, it is competent to show that one or both of the contracting parties were agents for other persons, and acted as such agents in making the contract, so as to give the benefit of the contract on the one hand to, and charge with liability on the other, the unnamed principals; and this, whether the agreement be or be not required to be in writing by the stat-

§ 329. **Parol evidence to establish liability of undisclosed principal.**—It is immaterial whether the contract is written or unwritten,

ute of frauds; and this evidence in no way contradicts the written agreement. It does not deny that it is binding on those whom, on the face of it, it purports to bind; but shows that it also binds another, by reason that the act of the agent, in signing the agreement, in pursuance of his authority, is in law the act of the principal. But, on the other hand, to allow evidence to be given that the party who appears on the face of the instrument to be personally a contracting party is not such would be to allow parol evidence to contradict the written agreement, which can not be done:' Beckham v. Drake, 9 M. & W. 79; Texas, etc., Co. v. Carroll, 63 Tex. 48; Heffron v. Pollard, 73 Tex. 96, 15 Am. St. 764. The exceptions to the rule, however, are so numerous, broad, and well defined, and rest upon principles of such a fundamental character, that the careful student of the law is driven to the conclusion that they are more important than the rule itself, and that the statement of the rule in such broad language has produced much confusion of thought and greatly embarrassed and probably has often misled the courts in their efforts to apply correct legal principles to particular cases. It is well settled that the rule never had any application to negotiable instruments, no one being chargeable thereon unless his name appears as a party to the paper in some relation: Authorities above cited. Again it has been said that this broad doctrine, that when an agent makes a contract in his own name only, the known or unknown principal may sue or be sued thereon, may be applied in many cases with safety, and especially in cases of informal commercial contracts. But it is certain that it can not be applied where exclusive credit is given to the agent, and it is intended by both parties that no resort shall be had by or against the principal: Story Ag., § 160a; nor does it apply to those cases where skill, solvency, or any personal quality of one of the parties to the contract is a material ingredient in it: Fry Spec. Perf., § 149; Kelly v. Thuey, 102 Mo. 522. And the court refused to allow the undisclosed principal to enforce specific performance of a contract to convey land on the ground that, the owner having contracted for the notes of the agent for deferred purchase-money, he could not be compelled to accept those of the principal. Again, it is well settled that the rule never had any application to sealed instruments, especially those which at common law must have been under seal, such as conveyances of land: Briggs v. Partridge, 64 N. Y. 357, 21 Am. Rep. 617; Tuthill v. Wilson, 90 N. Y. 423; Walters v. Northern Coal Co., 5 De G., M. & G. 629; Borcherling v. Katz, 37 N. J. Eq. 150; Farrar v. Lee, 10 App. Div. (N. Y.) 130, 41 N. Y. Supp. 672; Evans v. Wells, 22 Wend. (N. Y.) 324; Jones v. Morris, 61 Ala. 518. According to the weight of authority, if the deed from Bowser and others to Rees had been sealed and delivered by the grantors to Rees at common law, his acceptance thereof would have made it his deed to the same extent that it would have been if signed and sealed by him also, and that as to him it would or required to be in writing by the statute of frauds or not: the rule is applicable to all contracts not specialties or negotiable by the law

have been a sealed instrument. Therefore, an action of covenant could have been maintained against him, but not against his principals, Sanders and others, on the contract of assumption therein contained: Finley v. Simpson, 22 N. J. L. 311, 53 Am. Dec. 252, and authorities cited in briefs therein; Golden v. Knapp, 41 N. J. L. 215; Sparkman v. Gove, 44 N. J. L. 253; Atlantic Dock Co. v. Leavitt, 54 N. Y. 35, 13 Am. Rep. 556; Bowen v. Beck, 94 N. Y. 86, 46 Am. Rep. 124; Maynard v. Moore, 76 N. C. 158; Smith v. Pocklington, 1 Cromp. & J. 445; Vanmeter v. Vanmeter, 3 Gratt. (Va.) 148; and authorities *supra*. There are cases holding that it would not at common law have been considered Rees' deed, and that covenant could not have been maintained thereon against him: Maule v. Weaver, 7 Pa. St. 329; Johnson v. Muzzy, 45 Vt. 419, 12 Am. Rep. 214; Trustees v. Spencer, 7 Ohio (pt. 2) 149 (493); Goodwin v. Gilbert, 9 Mass. 510; Martin v. Drinan, 128 Mass. 515; Hinsdale v. Humphrey, 15 Conn. 431. Therefore, at common law the general rule above stated would have had no application to the conveyance to Rees, and his undisclosed principals would not have been liable. We are of opinion that the result is not affected by the following statute: 'No private seal or scroll shall be necessary to the validity of any contract, bond, or conveyance, whether respecting real or personal property, or any other instrument of writing, whether official, judicial or private, except such as are made by corporations, nor shall the addition or omission of a seal or scroll in any way affect the force and effect of the same:' Tex. Rev. Stats.., art. 4862. It is true the statute renders it unnecessary to place a seal upon a deed, but it does not undertake to give one executed without a seal a different *status* from what it would have had before if executed with a seal. On the contrary, it provides that the addition or omission of a seal shall not 'in any way affect the force and effect of the same.' In order for the omission of the seal not to in any way affect its force or effect, the deed must be allowed to retain the only *status* it had before. When we adopted the common law, its settled rules relating to the construction and effect of deeds became a part of our system. To them we were compelled to resort to determine the nature and extent of the estate conveyed by the deed as well as of the covenants therein contained, and who were bound or benefited thereby. It was not the intention of said statute to abolish them. As said in Jones v. Morris, 61 Ala. 518, in discussing a more comprehensive statute than ours: 'Though a seal may not now be necessary to a conveyance of a legal estate in lands, yet the instrument, the deed of conveyance, which it must still be termed, though shorn of its dignity of a seal, retains all the operation and effect of a deed sealed at common law. Its covenants may be as comprehensive, and, whatever they may be, are as obligatory, and its recitals are as incapable of being gainsaid, as if it were sealed with the greatest formality. The estoppel which a sealed instrument, or its covenants, merchant.[42] It may seem difficult to understand, at first, how one, not on the face of a written contract a party to it, can be brought into it without violating the rule that a written instrument can not be contradicted or varied by parol evidence. Parol testimony is admissible, however, to show that some one not named in the contract as the obligor was in fact the principal contracting party; and whatever may be the merits of the doctrine, it is now firmly settled that the admission of parol evidence is not in violation of the rule mentioned. The evidence is not admitted to vary or contradict the written contract; it is proposed in such case to prove by the testimony offered, not that the instrument is not binding upon those whom it purports to bind, but that it is binding also upon another, for the reason that when the agreement was entered into by the agent it was in law the act of the principal, the two being regarded as identical.[43]

§ 330. Qualification of doctrine of liability of undisclosed principal—English and American cases.—The doctrine of the liability of an undisclosed principal is to be qualified, however, by certain exceptions now to be mentioned. The English courts now hold that where the third party has by his words or conduct misled the principal so as to cause him to believe that the agent and third party have come to a settlement, and relying upon this the principal pays the agent or settles with him, the third party can not afterwards sue the prin-

created at common law it is now claimed by the appellee shall be attached to the conveyance by the agents of the appellant. And we can not doubt that the estoppel which at common law grew out of the covenants or the recitals of a sealed instrument attaches now to an unsealed conveyance of the legal estate in lands. The statute is not so broad in its sweep as to blot out the common-law principles which give security to conveyances of real estate. It would be fearful, indeed, if this was the operation of the statute, and the freehold in lands was not invested with greater dignity than the fleeting ownership of chattels.' Devlin Deeds, § 249, says: 'The effect of these statutes is simply to dispense with the necessity of affixing a seal to a deed; but in other respects,—as, for instance, with reference to the doctrine of estoppel,—the deed retains the incidents it possessed as a sealed instrument at common law.' The effect of the statute is different as to other contracts, for the placing of the seal thereon at common law raised them from parol to specialty contracts, which can not be done under the statute."

[42] See the cases in last note.

[43] Higgins v. Senior, 8 M. & W. 834; Watteau v. Fenwick, L. R. (1893) 1 Q. B. 346; Ford v. Williams, 21 How. (U. S.) 287; Byington v. Simpson, 134 Mass. 169, 45 Am. Rep. 314; Gates v. Brower, 9 N. Y. 205, 59 Am. Dec. 530; Chandler v. Coe, 54 N. H. 561.

cipal, his conduct in such case constituting an estoppel *in pais.*[44] According to these cases, an undiscovered principal would not be jus-

[44] Irvine v. Watson, L. R. 5 Q. B. D. 414; Davison v. Donaldson, L. R. 9 Q. B. D. 623; Heald v. Kenworthy, 10 Ex. 739, 24 L. J. (Ex.) 76. The modern English rule is so lucidly enunciated by Bramwell, L. J., in the case of Irvine v. Watson, just cited, that we deem it profitable to copy a portion of his opinion here. He says: "I am of opinion that the judgment must be affirmed. The facts of the case are shortly these: The plaintiffs sold certain casks of oil, and on the face of the contract of sale Conning appeared as the purchaser. But the plaintiffs knew that he was only an agent buying for principals, for he told them so at the time of the sale, therefore they knew that they had a right against somebody besides Conning. On the other hand, the defendants knew that somebody or other had a remedy against them, for they had authorized Conning, who was an ordinary broker, to pledge their credit, and the invoice specified the goods to have been bought 'per John Conning.' Then, that being so, the defendants paid the broker, and the question is whether such payment discharged them from their liability to the plaintiffs. I think it is impossible to say that it discharged them, unless they were misled by some conduct of the plaintiffs into the belief that the broker had already settled with the plaintiffs, and made such payment in consequence of such belief. But it is contended that the plaintiffs here did mislead the defendants into such belief, by parting with the possession of the oil to Conning without getting the money. The terms of the contract were 'cash on or before delivery,' and it is said that the defendants had a right to suppose that the sellers would not deliver unless they received payment of the price at the time of delivery. I do not think, however, that that is a correct view of the case. The plaintiffs had a perfect right to part with the oil to the broker without insisting strictly upon their right to prepayment, and there is, in my opinion, nothing in the facts of the case to justify the defendants in believing that they would so insist. No doubt if there was an invariable custom in the trade to insist on prepayment where the terms of the contract entitled the seller to it, that might alter the matter; and in such case non-insistence on prepayment might discharge the buyer if he paid the broker on the faith of the seller already having been paid. But that is not the case here; the evidence before Bowen, J., shows that there is no invariable custom to that effect. Apart from all authorities, then, I am of opinion that the defendants' contention is wrong, and upon looking at the authorities I do not think that any of them are in direct conflict with that opinion. It is true that in Thomson v. Davenport, 9 B. & C. 78, both Lord Tenterden and Bayley, J., suggest in the widest terms that a seller is not entitled to sue the undisclosed principal on discovering him, if in the meantime the state of the account between the principal and the agent has been altered to the prejudice of the principal. But it is impossible to construe the *dicta* of those learned judges in that case literally; it would operate most un-

tified in settling with his agent, and would be in danger of incurring liability to the third party also, unless such third party had, by his representations or conduct, or both, induced or misled the principal to settle with the agent. The majority of American decisions are to the effect that an undisclosed principal is not liable to the third party on a contract made by his agent, if the state of the accounts between the principal and his agent has been so altered that it would result in injury to the principal were he obliged to pay or settle again with the third party.[45] It can not be said, however, that the American decisions are uniform upon the subject. The courts of Louisiana and Maryland, and perhaps others, are disposed to follow the modern English rule.[46] It is thus seen that there is a manifest difference between what is generally spoken of as the American rule and that which is at present applied in England. According to the American rule, the principal may safely settle with the agent at any time before he is discovered, and he will not be liable. By the English rule, the duty of settling with the third party devolves upon the principal from the time the contract is entered into until it has been fully discharged, and he will only be justified in settling with the agent if he has been misled into doing so by the words or conduct of the third party. The American authorities are based upon the ruling of Lord Tenterden and Bayley, J., in the case of *Thomson* v. *Davenport*.[47] This ruling, or *dictum*, as it is now generally regarded, has been expressly repudiated by the English courts in the cases above cited, while the courts in this country have generally adhered to it,

justly to the vendor if we did. I think the judges who uttered them did not intend a strictly literal interpretation to be put on their words. But whether they did or not, the opinion of Parke, B., in Heald v. Kenworthy, 10 Ex. 739, 24 L. J. (Ex.) 76, seems to me preferable; it is this, that, 'If the conduct of the seller would make it unjust for him to call upon the buyer for the money, as, for example, where the principal is induced by the conduct of the seller to pay his agent the money on the faith that the agent and seller have come to a settlement on the matter, or if any representation to that effect is made by the seller either by words or conduct, the seller can not afterwards throw off the mask and sue the principal.' That is in my judgment a much more accurate statement of the law."

[45] Story Ag., § 449; Parsons Conts. 63; Thomas v. Atkinson, 38 Ind. 248; McCullough v. Thompson, 45 N. Y. Super. Ct. 449; Laing v. Butler, 37 Hun (N. Y.) 144; Knapp v. Simon, 96 N. Y. 284; Fradley v. Hyland, 37 Fed. 49. See Emerson v. Patch, 123 Mass. 541.

[46] Hyde v. Wolf, 4 La. 234, 23 Am. Dec. 484 and note on p. 486, citing other cases.

[47] 9 B. & C. 78. See note 44, *supra*.

and it has been approved by Story and Parsons. Mr. Mechem regards the present English doctrine as "eminently reasonable and just."[48] Whether our courts will eventually accept the views of Mr. Mechem and the later English cases, or those of Story and Parsons and the American decisions that have followed Lord Tenterden and Mr. Justice Bayley, remains to be seen. It may be said, therefore, that the right of the third party to proceed against the principal, when discovered, is subject to the exception that if the principal has in good faith paid or settled with the agent, in whole or in part, then to the extent of such payment or settlement he would be discharged from liability to the third party also. What constitutes good faith on the part of the principal is to be determined by the rule obtaining in the particular jurisdiction in which the question arises. If in such jurisdiction the old English rule is followed, then it is immaterial, it seems, whether the principal was misled into making such payment or settlement by the conduct of the third party or not, provided the payment or settlement was made before he was discovered as being the principal. If what we designate as the modern English rule governs, then the settlement will be no defense, unless the principal was misled into it by the conduct or representations of the third party. The former is believed to be the prevailing rule in this country.

§ 331. **Further exception—Election by third party.**—The liability of an undisclosed principal on the authorized contract of his agent is subject to the further exception that if, after such principal has been discovered, the third party knowingly elects to hold the agent liable, he is precluded from afterwards pursuing the principal; the liability to the third party is not a joint liability of the agent and principal. The third party may treat the contract as that of the principal, which it really was. It is only the agent's own conduct or concealment of the true principal, or the holding himself out as such principal, that renders such agent liable at the option of the third party. If, after discovering the real contracting party, he chooses to hold him to the contract that he has authorized his agent to make for him, his remedy is exhausted; provided, of course, the choice is made knowingly; but he can not hold them both liable.[49] The rule of election applies not

[48] Mechem Ag., § 697.

[49] Silver v. Jordan, 136 Mass. 319; Hyde v. Wolf, 4 La. 234, 23 Am. Dec. 484; Schepflin v. Dessar, 20 Mo. App. 569; Hyde v. Paige, 9 Barb. (N. Y.) 150; Ranken v. Deforest, 18 Barb. (N. Y.) 143; Meeker v. Claghorn, 44 N. Y. 349; Henderson v. Mayhew, 2 Gill (Md.) 393, 41 Am. Dec. 434; Addison v. Gan-

only to the case of an undisclosed, but to that of a known principal also.

§ **332. How question of election determined.**—Whether or not there has been an election made by the third person is a question that is not always free from doubt; for it must appear clearly that the choice was made with full knowledge of all the facts, and that full freedom of choice was exercised. Generally speaking, the question is one of fact for the jury, under the direction of the court.[50] There is in such case at least a *prima facie* presumption that the credit was given to the principal, and not to the agent; and if the plaintiff relies on the fact that credit was given to the agent, the plaintiff has the burden of establishing the fact by clear proof.[51] The mere fact that the third party has commenced an action against the agent, even after the discovery of the principal, is not conclusive evidence of an election, such as will discharge the principal;[52] nor is the fact, that, after discovery of the principal, demand was made upon the agent for the sum due.[53] Whether the taking of a judgment against the agent after the principal has been discovered is conclusive, is not certain; indeed, it has been held that nothing less than satisfaction of such a judgment would bar an action against the other party.[54] But the contrary has been held in England.[55] And so it has been ruled in Massachusetts that the prosecution of the claim to final judgment is a bar.[56] It is difficult to lay down a rule that will apply to all cases. Whether or not there has been an election must, of course, depend upon the peculiar circumstances of each case. There can not be said to be freedom of choice when the facts are not all known to the third party,

dassequi, 4 Taunt. 573, 3 Smith Ld. Cas. (9th ed.) 1641; Pope v. Meadow Spring Distilling Co., 20 Fed. 35; Ahrens v. Cobb, 9 Humph. (Tenn.) 643.

[50] Maryland Coal Co. v. Edwards, 4 Hun (N. Y.) 432; Cobb v. Knapp, 71 N. Y. 348, 27 Am. Rep. 51; Curtis v. Williamson, L. R. 10 Q. B. 57; Merrill v. Kenyon, 48 Conn. 314, 40 Am. Rep. 174.

[51] Meeker v. Claghorn, 44 N. Y. 349.

[52] Raymond v. Crown and Eagle Mills, 2 Metc. (Mass.) 319; Fery v. Moore, 18 Ill. App. 135; Beymer v. Bonsall, 79 Pa. St. 298.

[53] Calder v. Dobell, L. R. 6 C. P. 486.

[54] Beymer v. Bonsall, *supra;* Maple v. Railroad Co., 40 Ohio St. 313, 48 Am. Rep. 685.

[55] Paterson v. Gandassequi, 15 East 62, 3 Smith Ld. Cas. (9th ed.) 1634.

[56] Kingsley v. Davis, 104 Mass. 178.

or when the means of making such choice are not all in his possession; and in acting without such knowledge the act does not constitute an election. Nor is it sufficient, it seems, that the party acting has the means of ascertaining the facts, but does not make further inquiry, unless he knows who the real principal is. Though he be informed that there is a principal, and though he fail to pursue the inquiry, he will not be bound by the choice.[57]

§ 333. **Additional exception—Undisclosed principal can not be made liable on sealed instruments.**—Where the contract executed by the agent is a specialty,—that is, an instrument required by the common law to be under seal,—the general rule is that the principal can not be held bound by it unless it is executed in his name. This is an additional exception to the rule that the third party may hold the real principal when he discovers him. This exception is founded upon the inflexible common-law rule that forbids the introduction into such a contract of parties whose names do not appear upon the face of the same. On such a contract, therefore, no one is liable but the agent.[58] As to instruments in which a seal, though used, is not actually required, they may render the principal liable in *assumpsit* on the promise contained in the instrument, provided the principal's interest in the contract appear on the face thereof and he have received the benefits of its provisions.[59]

§ 334. **Another exception—Negotiable instruments.**—Still another exception to the liability of an undisclosed principal, when discovered, is in cases of negotiable instruments. Generally, by the strict rule of the law merchant, one who is not a party to a negotiable instrument is not bound by it; hence an undisclosed principal can not be made liable on such an instrument when the agent has contracted personally

[57] Thomson v. Davenport, 9 B. & C. 78, 3 Smith Ld. Cas. (9th ed.) 1648; Merrill v. Kenyon, 48 Conn. 314, 40 Am. Rep. 174.

[58] Briggs v. Partridge, 64 N. Y. 357, 21 Am. Rep. 617; Clarke v. Courtney, 5 Pet. (U. S.) 350; Borcherling v. Katz, 37 N. J. Eq. 150; Kiersted v. Orange, etc., R. Co., 69 N. Y. 343; Huntington v. Knox, 7 Cush. (Mass.) 371; Elwell v. Shaw, 16 Mass. 42, 8 Am. Dec. 126; Sanger v. Warren, 91 Tex. 472, 66 Am. St. 913. See note 33, *supra*, on this point.

[59] Dubois v. Delaware, etc., Canal Co., 4 Wend. (N. Y.) 285; Lawrence v. Taylor, 5 Hill (N. Y.) 107; Moore v. Granby Mining, etc., Co., 80 Mo. 86; Worrall v. Munn, 5 N. Y. 229, 55 Am. Dec. 330; Briggs v. Partridge, 64 N. Y. 357, 21 Am. Rep. 617; Randall v. Van Vechten, 19 Johns. (N. Y.) 60.

and in his own name.[60] By the rules of the law merchant each holder of the paper takes it upon what it purports to be on the face thereof, and parties not named in such contract can not be brought into it by parol. Such an instrument passes from hand to hand as money, and must be accepted in the character in which it appears and circulates.

II. Liability of Principal for Agent's Torts.

§ **335. Doctrine of identity the basis of principal's liability.**—Having now discussed the duties and liabilities of the principal upon the contracts of his agent, we pass to the consideration of his liability for the torts of the agent. It is a general principle of law, as well as of the social compact, that every one must so conduct himself in the enjoyment of the privileges of life and property as not to injure the person or property of others. But if a man can not with impunity perform an injurious act in person, neither can he do so by or through the instrumentality of another. In law the principal and his agent, or the master and his servant, are regarded as identical, at least in the performance of every authorized act. *"Qui per alium facit, per seipsum facere videtur"* is the maxim that applies here—"whatever a person does through another is the same as if he had done it himself." This identity of the principal and agent is sometimes spoken of as a fiction, but it conserves a rational public policy when properly applied. If a legal wrong is committed by an accountable being, the party injured may obtain redress therefor in damages. If the wrong was committed by his authorized agent, or servant, the result is the same. By "authorized agent" it is not meant to imply that the wrongful act itself must be authorized by the principal or master, or that any presumption of that nature must be indulged before the principal can be held responsible: it is sufficient if the agent was authorized to perform the act in the performance of which the wrong was committed; for the principal is responsible, not only for the act itself, but for the ways and means employed in the performance thereof. The principal may be perfectly innocent of any actual wrong or of any complicity therein, but this will not excuse him, for the party who was injured by the wrongful act is also innocent; and the doctrine is that where one of two or more innocent parties must suffer loss by the wrongful act of

[60] Evans Pr. & Ag. (Bedford's ed.) 517; Sturdivant v. Hull, 59 Me. 172; Powers v. Briggs, 79 Ill. 493; Brown v. Parker, 7 Allen (Mass.) 337; Huntington v. Knox, 7 Cush. (Mass.) 371; Slawson v. Loring, 5 Allen (Mass.) 340; Sparks v. Dispatch Transfer Co., 104 Mo. 531.

another, it is more reasonable and just that he should suffer it who has placed the real wrongdoer in a position which enabled him to commit the wrongful act, rather than the one who had nothing whatever to do with setting in motion the cause of such act.[61] "In such cases," says Story, "the rule applies (*respondeat superior*), and it is founded upon public policy and convenience, for in no other way could there be any safety to third persons in their dealings, either directly with the principal, or indirectly with him, through the instrumentality of agents. In every such case the principal holds out his agent as competent and fit to be trusted, and thereby, in effect, he warrants his fidelity and good conduct in all matters within the scope of the agency."[62]

§ 336. Principal liable for wrongful acts of agent done in course of employment.—Of course, if the master or principal authorized or ratified the tort, or participated in it himself, he will be liable for the damages occasioned by it.[63] But if he did not authorize or ratify it he will still be liable if it was done in the course of the agent's or servant's employment;[64] and this is so even if the master or principal had actually forbidden the act to be done.[65] The test is, whether the tort was committed in the course of the employment of the servant or agent: if the wrongful act complained of was outside of the course of such employment, the master or principal is not liable, unless it was subsequently ratified. Consequently, where an armed watchman was employed to guard a brewery and prevent breaches of the peace, and a person came about the premises intoxicated and disorderly, and was pursued, and while retreating, shot by the watchman, the shooting was held not to be in the line of the watchman's employment, and the owners of the brewery were held not liable.[66] But a railroad company is liable for the acts of its conductor or other servants having authority

[61] Lee v. Village of Sandy Hill, 40 N. Y. 442.

[62] Story Ag., § 452.

[63] Dempsey v. Chambers, 154 Mass. 330.

[64] Turner v. North Beach, etc., R. Co., 34 Cal. 594; Pittsburgh, etc., R. Co. v. Kirk, 102 Ind. 399, 52 Am. Rep. 675; Rounds v. Delaware, etc., R. Co., 64 N. Y. 129, 21 Am. Rep. 597; Oakland City, etc., Society v. Bingham, 4 Ind. App. 545; Quinn v. Power, 87 N. Y. 535; Howe v. Newmarch, 12 Allen (Mass.) 49; Merchants' Nat'l Bank v. Guilmartin, 88 Ga. 797; Moir v. Hopkins, 16 Ill. 313, 63 Am. Dec. 312.

[65] Turner v. North Beach, etc., R. Co., *supra;* Oakland City, etc., Society v. Bingham, *supra;* Moir v. Hopkins, *supra.*

[66] Golden v. Newbrand, 52 Iowa 59, 35 Am. Rep. 257.

to eject trespassers, if such conductor or other servant in ejecting such trespasser uses more force than is reasonably necessary to accomplish such ejection.[67] The test whether the act was committed in the line of employment or not is not applicable, generally, when such act consisted of an assault or other trespass upon or injury to a passenger while being carried on a train, boat or other vehicle operated by a carrier of passengers. In such case the carrier owes the passenger the duty of safe conduct and protection from all injury by any one, whether a servant of such carrier or not; it therefore makes no difference in the passenger's liability whether the injury is inflicted by a servant in the course of his employment or not.[68]

§ **337. Liability for agent's negligence.**—One of the classes of torts for which the principal is responsible in damages, if committed by the agent in course of the employment, is that of negligence. This class of torts arises most frequently in the relation of master and servant, though torts of this character also occur in the relation of principal and agent. If a locomotive-engineer, who is the servant of a railroad company, a common carrier of passengers and freight, so negligently run his train as to cause a derailment, and an injury result, the company will be liable in damages for the negligence of the engineer. This is a case of master and servant. The same rule applies in a case of principal and agent. Thus, if the owner of a certain estate place the same in charge of an agent or manager, and the latter negligently permit the houses thereon to go to decay; or if, in erecting a building on the premises, the work be done so negligently and unskillfully by the direction of the agent as to cause the building to fall over, in either of these cases there will be such negligence by the agent that a person injured in consequence thereof will have his remedy in an action of damages against the principal. In either case, however, the act negligently done or omitted must be within the scope or course of the employment of the agent or servant, or there will be

[67] Hoffman v. New York, etc., R. Co., 87 N. Y. 25, 41 Am. Rep. 337; Rounds v. Delaware, etc., R. Co., 64 N. Y. 129, 21 Am. Rep. 597; Chicago, etc., R. Co. v. Flexman, 103 Ill. 546; Craker v. Chicago, etc., R. Co., 36 Wis. 657, 17 Am. Rep. 504; McKinley v. Chicago, etc., R. Co., 44 Iowa 314, 24 Am. Rep. 748. See 3 Thompson Neg. (2d ed.), § 3302, *et seq.*

[68] See the exhaustive note in 41 Am. Rep., at p. 340. See also, Dwinelle v. New York, etc., R. Co., 120 N. Y. 117; Bryant v. Rich, 106 Mass. 180; Pittsburg, etc., R. Co. v. Hinds, 53 Pa. St. 512; Dillingham v. Russell, 73 Tex. 47; 3 Thompson Neg. (2d ed.), § 3162, *et seq.*

no liability on the part of the principal. Hence it may be correctly stated that if an agent or servant, while in the course of the employment of the principal or master, perform an act in a negligent or reckless manner, and an injury result to a third party, the principal will be liable in damages for such injury.[69]

§ 338. **Not necessary that act should have been authorized by principal if done in course of employment.**—The basis of liability in such cases is not the presumption that the tort has been committed with the assent or by the authority of the principal or master, for it is immaterial whether the principal assented or authorized the wrong or not, if it occurred in the course of the employment of the agent or servant.[70] It is rather on the ground of public policy that the principal is held responsible: he has introduced the agent to the business world, as it were, and he thereby vouches for the agent's skill and competency, and that he will exercise such skill as well as the requisite care in the transaction of his business. It is essential, however, that the injury occurred while the agent or servant was within the scope of his employment. When this is established or admitted, the principal's liability is clear, and it is immaterial whether the person who inflicted the injury was an agent or a servant.[71]

§ 339. **Meaning of scope or course of employment—Illustrative cases.**—Just what is meant by the scope or course of the employment is not always easy to determine; for a person may be within the scope of the employment for some purposes and not for others. In cases of negligence by a servant or agent, he is in the course of the employment when he is doing his master's work or performing the task of his principal. It is not necessary that he should be obeying the master's command at the moment when the injurious deed is committed, or the omission occurs, for then the agent could only bind the principal by authorized acts. He must, however, be engaged in the service of his employer or principal and must be in the prosecution of it when the wrong is committed, and there must be no willful departure from

[69] Garretzen v. Duenckel, 50 Mo. 104, 11 Am. Rep. 405; McKenzie v. M'Leod, 10 Bing. 385; Higgins v. Watervliet Turnpike Co., 46 N. Y. 23, 7 Am. Rep. 293; Pittsburg, etc., R. Co. v. Kirk, 102 Ind. 399, 52 Am. Rep. 675; Armstrong v. Cooley, 10 Ill. 509; Cosgrove v. Ogden, 49 N. Y. 255, 10 Am. Rep. 361; Cleveland v. Newsom, 45 Mich. 62.

[70] Higgins v. Watervliet Turnpike Co., *supra*.

[71] See Wilson v. Owens, 16 L. R. Ir. 225; Singer Mfg. Co. v. Rahn, 132 U. S. 518; Pollock Torts (4th ed.) 260; Maier v. Randolph, 33 Kan. 340.

such employment or service.[72] No inflexible rule can be laid down for determining whether or not the agent is within the scope of his employment when the injury was committed, and every case must be determined by its own peculiar facts. A few of the most frequently occurring instances may be cited in which the agent or servant would be within the course of his employment at the time of the injury. Thus, if a servant be set to cutting timber on his master's land, and he ignorantly cut trees on the land of another;[73] or if a father send his son in search of his (the father's) cattle, and the son ignorantly take with them other cattle belonging to a neighbor;[74] or where a man's servant, in the ordinary course of business, obstructs the public highway, by which a third person is injured;[75] or where a locomotive-engineer on a moving train fails to sound the whistle of his engine, as required by law, or according to custom, and a person is injured thereby;[76] or where a telegraph operator mistakenly or purposely sends a different message from the one delivered to him,[77]—in all these cases the master or servant is liable, the act being deemed in the course of the employment. Among the instances in which the agent or servant has been held not to be acting within the course of his employment, but independently thereof, may be mentioned the following:—Where a servant borrowed his master's team for his own private use, and while driving it injured another;[78] and where section men, employed to repair a railroad track, kindled a fire on the right of way for the purpose of cooking a meal, and left the fire unextinguished, and it spread and caused injury to adjoining property.[79] And it has been held that if a servant driving a carriage of his master, in order to effect some purpose of his own, wantonly strikes the horse of another person, producing an accident, the master is not liable; but if, in order to perform his master's orders, he strikes, but injudiciously, and in order to extricate himself from a difficulty,—that will be negligent and careless conduct, for which the master will be liable, being an act done in pursuance of the servant's authority.[80]

[72] Moir v. Hopkins, 16 Ill. 313, 63 Am. Dec. 312; Johnson v. Barber, 10 Ill. 425, 50 Am. Dec. 416; Armstrong v. Cooley, 10 Ill. 519; Tuller v. Voght, 13 Ill. 277; May v. Bliss, 22 Vt. 477; Luttrell v. Hazen, 3 Sneed (Tenn.) 20.

[73] Luttrell v. Hazen, *supra*.

[74] Andrus v. Howard, 36 Vt. 248, 84 Am. Dec. 680.

[75] Harlow v. Humiston, 6 Cow. (N. Y.) 189.

[76] Goodfellow v. Boston, etc., R. Co., 106 Mass. 461.

[77] New York, etc., Tel. Co. v. Dryburg, 35 Pa. St. 298.

[78] Bard v. Yohn, 26 Pa. St. 482.

[79] Morier v. St. Paul, etc., R. Co., 31 Minn. 351.

[80] Croft v. Alison, 4 B. & Ald. 590.

§ **340. Relation of principal and agent or master and servant must exist at time tort is committed.**—The question in such cases always is, whether at the time the injury was committed the agent or servant was serving the principal or master. The principal is not liable if the agent was at the time acting for himself, although this was but temporarily so: the relation of principal and agent or master and servant must subsist at the time.[81] Hence, if a person borrow a horse from the owner, and the borrower, by negligently driving, cause an injury to a third person, the owner of the horse will not be liable, for there is no relation of master and servant or principal and agent between the borrower and the owner.[82] And where the servant of a livery-stable keeper drove a horse immoderately and thereby killed the animal, such driving being entirely unauthorized by the keeper of the stable, and solely for purposes of the driver's own, the master was held not liable.[83]

§ **341. Liability for willful wrong of agent or servant.**—We pass now to consider whether a principal or master is liable for a tort committed willfully by his agent or servant. There is no doubt as to his liability, of course, if the wrongful act was done at his command or by his direction, connivance or acquiescence; in such a case, the fact that he stands to the perpetrator in the relation of principal or master does not render his accountability different from that of any other tort-feasor, if he is shown to have been a participant in the injurious deed. On the other hand, if the injury was done by the agent or servant while outside the scope of his employment, it is equally clear that there is no liability on the part of principal or master, unless the act was authorized by him.[84] The question that most concerns us, however, is whether, as in cases of negligence, he is also liable when the injury was perpetrated in the course of the employment of the agent or servant, but without knowledge or consent on his part, or in violation of his express direction. It was formerly thought that when the wrongful and unauthorized act of the servant or agent was done willfully or maliciously, that was

See also, McKenzie v. M'Leod, 10 Bing. 385.

[81] Joel v. Morison, 6 C. & P. 501; Bard v. Yohn, 26 Pa. St. 482; Mitchell v. Crassweller, 13 C. B. 237.

[82] Herlihy v. Smith, 116 Mass. 265.

[83] Adams v. Cost, 62 Md. 264, 50 Am. Rep. 211. See also, Stevens v. Woodward, L. R. 6 Q. B. D. 318.

[84] M'Manus v. Crickett, 1 East 106; Foster v. Essex Bank, 17 Mass. 479, 9 Am. Dec. 168.

of itself sufficient evidence of its not being done in the course of the employment; for in such circumstances the relation of master and servant or principal and agent could not be said to subsist, the act itself being a departure from the business of the master or principal; and there are many cases to support this doctrine.[85] The modern decisions, however, at least in this country, tend to support the rule that if the willful or intentional mischief was done by the agent or servant within the scope of the employment, the principal or master is liable.[86] "The test of the liability of the master is," say the supreme judicial court of Massachusetts, "that the act of the servant is done in the course of doing the master's work, and for the purpose of accomplishing it. If so done, it is the act of the master, and he is responsible whether the wrong done be occasioned by negli-

[85] Wright v. Wilcox, 19 Wend. (N. Y.) 343, 32 Am. Dec. 507; Richmond Turnpike Co. v. Vanderbilt, 1 Hill (N. Y.) 480; Whitaker v. Eighth Ave. R. Co., 51 N. Y. 295; Rounds v. Delaware, etc., R. Co., 64 N. Y. 129, 21 Am. Rep. 597; M'Manus v. Crickett, 1 East 106; Lyons v. Martin, 8 A. & E. 512; Peachey v. Rowland, 13 C. B. 182; Adams v. Cost, 62 Md. 264, 50 Am. Rep. 211; Croft v. Alison, 4 B. & Ald. 590.

[86] Williams v. Pullman, etc., Co., 40 La. Ann. 87, 8 Am. St. 512; Levi v. Brooks, 121 Mass. 501; Goddard v. Grand Trunk R. Co., 57 Me. 202, 2 Am. Rep. 39; Jeffersonville R. Co. v. Rogers, 38 Ind. 116, 10 Am. Rep. 103; McKinley v. Chicago, etc., R. Co., 44 Iowa 314, 24 Am. Rep. 748; Southern Kansas R. Co. v. Rice, 38 Kan. 398, 5 Am. St. 766; Sherley v. Billings, 8 Bush (Ky.) 147, 8 Am. Rep. 451; Stewart v. Brooklyn, etc., R. Co., 90 N. Y. 588, 43 Am. Rep. 185; Pennsylvania R. Co. v. Vandiver, 42 Pa. St. 365, 372; Dillingham v. Russell, 73 Tex. 47; Gilliam v. South, etc., R. Co., 70 Ala. 268; Chicago, etc., R. Co. v. Flexman, 103 Ill. 546; Chicago City R. Co. v. McMahon, 103 Ill. 485; Craker v. Chicago, etc., R. Co., 36 Wis. 657; Nashville, etc., R. Co. v. Starnes, 9 Heisk. (Tenn.) 52, 24 Am. Rep. 296; Mott v. Consumers' Ice Co., 73 N. Y. 543; Meyer v. Second Ave. R. Co., 8 Bosw. (N. Y.) 305; Quigley v. Central Pac. R. Co., 11 Nev. 350; Stewart v. Brooklyn, etc., R. Co., 90 N. Y. 588, 43 Am. Rep. 185. "The liability of the principal is not affected by the fact that the tort was willfully committed, for it is now firmly settled that whether the wrong results from negligence or is the product of willfulness, the principal is responsible if it was committed within the line of the agent's duty:" Elliott, J., in Evansville, etc., R. Co. v. McKee, 99 Ind. 519, 520. And on page 521 of the same case, the learned judge further says: "The rules we have stated lead to the conclusion that the principal is liable for the tort of the agent, where the particular act, although willful and not directly authorized, was within the line of the agent's duty; but if the act was an independent one, and not within the scope of the agency, the person injured can not compel the principal to respond in damages."

gence, or by a wanton and reckless purpose to accomplish the master's business in an unlawful manner."[87] And in a New York case it was said by Andrews, J., speaking for the court: "The master who puts the servant in a place of trust or responsibility, or commits to him the management of his business or the care of his property, is justly held responsible when the servant, through lack of judgment or discretion, or from infirmity of temper, or under the influence of passion aroused by the circumstances and the occasion, goes beyond the strict line of his duty or authority and inflicts an unjustifiable injury upon another."[88]

§ 342. **Rule is applicable to corporations.**—The rule applies to corporations that are principals as well as to individuals occupying a similar relation.[89] It has been held, however, that a corporation will not be liable for the malicious prosecution of a third person by one of its agents, unless the act has been expressly authorized or subsequently ratified.[90] In a Massachusetts case, decided in 1893, the action was for damages against an educational corporation for

[87] Levi v. Brooks, 121 Mass. 501.

[88] Rounds v. Delaware, etc., R. Co., 64 N. Y. 129, 21 Am. Rep. 597. "To constitute a willful injury the act which produced it must have been intentional, or must have been done under such circumstances as evinced a reckless disregard for the safety of others and a willingness to inflict the injury complained of. It involves conduct which is *quasi*-criminal:" Per Mitchell, J., in Louisville, etc., R. Co. v. Bryan, 107 Ind. 51. "Our decisions recognize the doctrine that where the act of the wrongdoer is so recklessly done, in disregard of the probable consequences, a willingness or intention to inflict the injury which results therefrom may be implied, and a distinction between an actual intention to do the injury and a constructive one is shown:" Per Jordan, J., in Cleveland, etc., R. Co. v. Miller, 149 Ind. 490, 500. "Willfulness does not consist in negligence. On the contrary, . . . the two terms are incompatible. Negligence arises from inattention, thoughtlessness, or heedlessness, while willfulness can not exist without purpose or design. No purpose or design can be said to exist where the injurious act results from negligence, and negligence can not be of such a degree as to become willfulness:" Parker v. Pennsylvania Co., 134 Ind. 673, quoted with approval in Cleveland, etc., R. Co. v. Miller, *supra*.

[89] Hanson v. European, etc., R. Co., 62 Me. 84, 16 Am. Rep. 404; Erie City Iron Works v. Barber, 106 Pa. St. 125, 51 Am. Rep. 508; Nims v. Mount Hermon Boys' School, 160 Mass. 177; Goodspeed v. East Haddam Bank, 22 Conn. 530, 58 Am. Dec. 439; Williams v. Planters' Ins. Co., 57 Miss. 759, 34 Am. Rep. 494.

[90] Dally v. Young, 3 Ill. App. 39; Carter v. Howe Machine Co., 51 Md. 290, 34 Am. Rep. 311.

personal injury occasioned to a passenger for hire, upon a boat used as a public ferry operated by the corporation, through the negligence of the ferryman in managing the boat. The defendant pleaded that the act was *ultra vires,* but the court held that this was not a good defense. The court said: "It is a general rule that corporations are liable for their torts as natural persons are. It is no defense to an action for a tort that the corporation is not authorized by its charter to do wrong. Recovery may be had against corporations for assault and battery, for libel and for malicious prosecution, as well as for torts resulting from negligent management of the corporate business. * * * If a corporation by its officers or agents unlawfully injures a person, whether intentionally or negligently, it would be most unjust to allow it to escape responsibility on the ground that its act is *ultra vires.* The only plausible ground on which the defendant in the present case can contend that it should be exempt from liability for the negligence of its servant in managing the ferryboat is that the contract to carry the plaintiff was *ultra vires,* and therefore invalid, and that the duty for neglect of which the plaintiff sues arose out of the contract, and disappears with it when the contract appears to be void." The court overruled the contention of counsel, however, and held the defendant liable upon the ground that the acts of such corporation were not different in kind from the ordinary acts of corporations in excess of the powers given them by their charter. "We are of opinion, therefore," the court continued, "that if the defendant, while running the ferryboat, accepted the plaintiff as a passenger to be transported for hire, and undertook to carry him across the river, he was in the boat as a licensee, and it owed him the duty to use proper care to carry him safely, and, whether an action could be maintained for a breach of contract or not, it is liable to the plaintiff in an action of tort for neglect of that duty.[91]

§ **343. Liability of principal for fraud of agent.**—A principal is liable also for the fraud of his agent in the transaction of the business intrusted to the agent by the principal, whether the fraud was author-

[91] Nims v. Mount Hermon Boys' School, 160 Mass. 177. See also, Vance v. Erie R. Co., 32 N. J. L. 334; Goodspeed v. East Haddam Bank, 22 Conn. 530, 58 Am. Dec. 439; Williams v. Planters' Ins. Co., 57 Miss. 759, 34 Am. Rep. 494; Philadelphia, etc., R. Co. v. Quigley, 21 How. (U. S.) 202; Gruber v. Washington, etc., R. Co., 92 N. C. 1; Merchants' Bank v. State Bank, 10 Wall. (U. S.) 604.

ized by him or not.[92] Thus, if an agent, appointed to sell property, in the course of the sale make false and fraudulent representations concerning its value and quality, and what the principal paid for it, the principal will be bound by such representations, if he accept the fruit of such sale.[93] And if an agent authorized to procure insurance fraudulently conceal from the underwriters a material fact within his knowledge, it will invalidate the insurance just as if it had been concealed by the principal himself. And here again the familiar rule is applicable, that "where one of two or more innocent persons must suffer, he ought to suffer who has misled the other into false confidence in his agent, by clothing him with apparent authority to act and speak in the premises; and who otherwise might receive an injury, for which he might have no adequate redress."[94] So, where an agent authorized to sell his principal's flock of sheep knew that some of them were diseased, but concealed such fact from the person to whom he sold the sheep for the principal, the latter was held liable for the damages sustained by the purchaser.[95] And where an agent fraudulently misappropriated collaterals deposited with him on a loan of his principal's money, the principal was held liable to the third party to the extent of the value of such collaterals.[96] Generally speaking, it is the duty of one who deals with an agent to ascertain what his authority is; and if the authority has been correctly ascertained, the principal will be bound by all the acts of his agent within the real or apparent scope of such authority. And if the act was originally unauthorized, but is subsequently ratified by the supposed principal, it becomes the act of the principal also, and he will be bound by it as if he had done it himself; and in ratifying such act, the principal should use proper diligence as to the scope of the matter about to be ratified; for when once he adopts the transaction as his own, it includes all the acts within the scope of the assumed authority.[97]

[92] Bank of Batavia v. New York, etc., R. Co., 106 N. Y. 195, 60 Am. Rep. 440; Friedlander v. Texas, etc., R. Co., 130 U. S. 416; Fifth Ave. Bank v. Forty-second St., etc., R. Co., 137 N. Y. 231; Fairchild v. McMahon, 139 N. Y. 290, 36 Am. St. 701; McKinnon v. Vollmar, 75 Wis. 82, 17 Am. St. 178.

[93] Fairchild v. McMahon, *supra*; Haskell v. Starbird, 152 Mass. 117.

[94] Story Ag., § 139.

[95] Jeffrey v. Bigelow, 13 Wend. (N. Y.) 518.

[96] Reynolds v. Witte, 13 S. C. 5, 36 Am. Rep. 678.

[97] Busch v. Wilcox, 82 Mich. 315, 326.

§ 344. **Whether it is necessary that fraud should be for principal's benefit.**—Whether the principal is responsible for the fraudulent acts of his agent which were for the agent's benefit only, is a question as to which there has not been complete uniformity in the adjudications. The English courts generally hold that the principal is liable only to the extent of the benefits or advantages received by him from the fraudulent contract or transaction.[98] "An attentive consideration of the cases has convinced me," says Benjamin, "that the true principle is that these corporate bodies, through whose agents so large a portion of the business of the country is now carried on, may be made responsible for the fraud of those agents to the extent to which the companies have profited from these frauds; but that they can not be sued as wrongdoers, by imputing to them the misconduct of those whom they have employed."[99] But while the more recent English cases are as stated by Mr. Benjamin, the king's bench decided in 1789 that the principal is liable in an action on the case for deceit for a false "affirmation" made by the agent with intent to defraud the third person, and that it is not necessary that the principal should be benefited by the deceit.[100] Many of the American cases, applying the rule that the principal is liable for all the acts and representations of his agent made in the course of the performance of the business confided to him, hold that if within these limits the agent has committed a fraud or other injury upon a third party, whether authorized by the principal or not, or whether it was for the benefit of the agent or of the principal, the principal is liable to such third party, if the latter dealt with the agent in good faith.[101] The theory upon which these cases proceed is that of estoppel: where the third party is ignorant of the facts misrepresented by the agent, and deals with such agent in good faith, and pursuant to the apparent power conferred upon him, the principal is estopped to deny the truth of the facts as represented by his agent, whom he has held out to the world as worthy of credence; the very fact of his authority being a sufficient warranty of the truth of all representations made by the agent in the course of the business for which he was employed.[102]

[98] Benjamin Sales, §§ 462-467, where the cases are cited.

[99] Benjamin Sales, § 466.

[100] Pasley v. Freeman, 3 T. R. 51, 2 Smith Ld. Cas. (9th ed.) 1300.

[101] Bank of Batavia v. New York, etc., R. Co., 106 N. Y. 195, 60 Am. Rep. 440.

[102] Bank of Batavia v. New York, etc., R. Co., *supra*; Germania Nat'l Bank v. Taaks, 101 N. Y. 442; Parker v. Board of Supervisors, 106 N.

§ 345. Elements requisite to bind principal.—Two elements seem to be necessary, according to the cases cited and others that might be mentioned, in order to bind the principal in such cases: 1. The agent must have been acting within the real or apparent scope of his authority; 2. The third party must have been acting in the utmost good faith in the matter. If either of these elements be wanting, there can be no liability on the part of the principal. Of course, the agent would not be acting within the apparent scope of his authority if he were a mere usurper, or one who had no authority whatever to perform the act in the course of which the fraud was committed: in that case, no one could be deceived by the agent's act; hence, where the agent is acting for himself, and that fact is known to third parties, both of these elements would be absent; for there could not be good faith on the part of the third person, nor could the agent be said to be acting within the apparent scope of his authority.[103]

§ 346. Basis of the doctrine of the American cases.—The doctrine of these American cases is more particularly applicable where the apparent authority of the agent is such as is calculated to deceive people of ordinary prudence and intelligence, and where the nature of the business for which the agent is employed is such that it bears the *indicia* of such apparent authority upon its face, so that it will naturally be relied upon by third persons. In such cases the power confided to the agent is such that it can not be executed by him without making some sort of representation to such party, although it may not have been contemplated by the principal that he should make a false or fraudulent one. But if he was authorized to make *some* representation, he is apparently authorized to make one that does not prove to be true. The principal has therefore enabled the agent to impose upon the third party, and must suffer the consequences.[104] The character of the fraud or deceit is immaterial, if it has produced an injury. The adjudications of this country have generally occurred in connection with the sale by agents of shares in some stock company,

Y. 392; New York, etc., R. Co. v. Schuyler, 34 N. Y. 30; Griswold v. Haven, 25 N. Y. 595; Fifth Ave. Bank v. Forty-second St., etc., R. Co., 137 N. Y. 231; Allen v. South Boston R. Co., 150 Mass. 200; Appeal of Kisterbock, 127 Pa. St. 601; Armour v. Michigan, etc., R. Co., 65 N. Y. 111; St. Louis, etc., R. Co. v. Larned, 103 Ill. 293; Wichita Sav. Bank v. Atchison, etc., R. Co., 20 Kan. 519.

[103] Moores v. Citizens' Nat'l Bank, 111 U. S. 156; Farrington v. South Boston R. Co., 150 Mass. 406.

[104] New York, etc., R. Co. v. Schuyler, 34 N. Y. 30.

or the issuing of false bills of lading by the agents of common carriers.[105] But the doctrine has been extended to many other classes of cases. Thus, a telegraph company has been held liable for the act of its agent in sending a false telegram and receiving money thereon;[106] and a bank for the act of its cashier in drawing checks falsely and using the money himself.[107] In a leading case in New York the agent of the defendants had sold to the plaintiff sheep infected with scab,—a fact at the time known to the agent but not to the defendants. The plaintiff sued the defendants in an action on the case for fraud, and the defendants were held liable not only for the loss of the sheep that were sold to him by defendants' agent, but also for others that had become infected by them.[108] The court in this case did not confine the damages to such as the principal derived profit from, but extended them so as to cover the entire injury sustained by the third parties.[109]

§ 347. **English doctrine adopted by federal courts.**—The federal courts have adopted the doctrine now prevailing in England. Thus, it is held by the supreme court of the United States that the agent of a railroad or steamship company can not bind the company by issuing a bill of lading for goods not actually placed in his possession or on board the conveyance; as, where a person in collusion with such agent fraudulently disposes of the goods represented therein instead of shipping the same to their destination.[110]

§ 348. **Public agents.**—The rules of liability of principals for the acts of their agents do not apply to public agencies: a public agent or officer can perform no act by which he can render his principal liable beyond the scope of his actual authority. Authority in such cases is generally conferred by law,—that is, by statute or other public acts, of which every one is presumed to have knowledge,—and hence no one can be heard to say that he dealt with the agent ignorantly. As a general rule, the government, whether state or federal, can not

[105] Armour v. Michigan, etc., R. Co., 65 N. Y. 111; New York, etc., R. Co. v. Schuyler, *supra*.

[106] McCord v. Western U. Tel. Co., 39 Minn. 181.

[107] Phillips v. Mercantile Nat'l Bank, 140 N. Y. 556.

[108] Jeffrey v. Bigelow, 13 Wend. (N. Y.) 518.

[109] See also, Bennett v. Judson, 21 N. Y. 238.

[110] St. Louis, etc., R. Co. v. Knight, 122 U. S. 79; Polland v. Vinton, 105 U. S. 7; Friedlander v. Texas, etc., R. Co., 130 U. S. 416. See also, Addison Torts, § 1209 and notes, and § 1213, *et seq.*

be sued without its consent; but assuming that this objection is waived or otherwise overcome, there is yet no liability. "In respect to the acts and declarations and representations of public agents," says Story, "it would seem that the same rule does not prevail, which ordinarily governs in relation to mere private agents. As to the latter (as we have seen), the principals are in many cases bound where they have not authorized the declarations and representations to be made. But in cases of public agents, the government or other public authority is not bound, unless it manifestly appears that the agent is acting within the scope of his authority, or he is held out as having authority to do the act, or is employed, in his capacity as a public agent, to make the declaration or representation for the government. Indeed, this rule seems indispensable, in order to guard the public against losses and injuries arising from the fraud or mistake, or rashness and indiscretion of their agents. And there is no hardship in requiring from private persons, dealing with public officers, the duty of inquiry as to their real or apparent power and authority to bind the government."[111] Hence, when third parties deal with public agents, in such matters as contracting with municipal authorities or city commissioners for public work, etc., they must know the powers of such agents or officials as they are contained in the city ordinances or other public law which contains the grant, and the legal effect thereof; and if they fail to do so, and trust to the representations of such agent or official, they do so at their peril, for the municipality will in no case be liable beyond the express authority of such agents and that necessarily incident thereto.[112] But the authority properly delegated to a public agent carries with it all the necessary incidental powers to execute such authority, and to this extent third parties are justifiable in trusting to appearances. Hence, where a county judge was empowered by statute to provide a public courthouse for the county, it was held that the performance of this duty involved the power to enter into all necessary contracts and to bind the county for the same, but that he would have no authority to issue negotiable bonds, bearing a high rate of interest, in discharge of such contract.[113] But a commissioner having authority to let a public contract has not the implied or incidental power to agree to changes or alterations, so

[111] Story Ag., § 307a.

[112] Mayor, etc., v. Eschbach, 18 Md. 276; Peirce v. United States, 1 N. & H. (Ct. of Cl.) 270; Hull v. County of Marshall, 12 Iowa 142; Missouri v. Bank of Missouri, 45 Mo. 528; Mayor, etc., v. Poultney, 25 Md. 18.

[113] Hull v. County of Marshall, *supra*.

as to render the municipality liable for additional work not embraced in the authorized contract, nor to agree to submit the matter to arbitration.[114] Public officers are not generally liable for the acts of their deputies or subalterns, though there are exceptions in some cases, such as those of sheriffs and constables, in which it is the policy of the law to make the superior officer responsible within certain limits for the official actions of the subordinate.[115]

§ 349. **Principal not liable when act was result of collusion between agent and third party.**—Nor will the principal in such a câse be held liable if the contract has been entered into through collusion or fraud between the agent and the third party; and this is true whether the agency be a public or a private one. Hence, where there is an agreement or understanding between the agent and a third person that the agent is to receive a commission or reward, if he will induce the principal to consent to a contract with such person, or enter into a contract with him for his principal, this being a fraud upon the latter, a contract so entered into can not be enforced against the principal, unless, with knowledge of the fraud, the principal elect to take the benefit of such contract.[116] The same doctrine applies where the agent is in reality the principal on the adverse side, or is secretly acting in the interest of the third party with the latter's knowledge or connivance: the principal may then avoid the contract.[117]

§ 350. **When principal bound by admissions of agent.**—The principal is bound also by the admissions and declarations, as well as the acts of his agent, when made while in the performance of the business of the employment;[118] but before the principal can be affected by such declarations it must be shown that the party making them was in fact the agent of the person sought to be so affected, or that he had authority to perform the act in relation to which the declarations were made.[119] It is also an essential requisite, to make

[114] Mayor, etc., v. Reynolds, 20 Md. 1, 83 Am. Dec. 535.

[115] Wharton Ag., § 550.

[116] City of Findlay v. Pertz, 66 Fed. 427.

[117] Wassell v. Reardon, 11 Ark. 705, 54 Am. Dec. 245.

[118] Vicksburg, etc., R. Co. v. O'Brien, 119 U. S. 99; Ball v. Bank of Alabama, 8 Ala. 590, 42 Am. Dec. 649; Dick v. Cooper, 24 Pa. St. 217, 64 Am. Dec. 652; White v. Miller, 71 N. Y. 118; Rowell v. Klein, 44 Ind. 290.

[119] Rowell v. Klein, *supra*; Coon v. Gurley, 49 Ind. 199; Wakefield v. South Boston R. Co., 117 Mass. 544.

such declarations binding upon the principal, that they should have been made so as to be a part of the *res gestae;* that is to say, so as to be a part of the transaction, or made in the course of the transaction, and not before or afterward.[120]

§ **351. When act is within res gestae.**—As to when an act or declaration is of the *res gestae* is not always clear. If the controversy be one growing out of a contract, it is not so difficult to determine; for the *res gestae* then covers the period of the negotiations only, and embraces but the time between the opening of the same and that of closing the contract.[121] If, however, the injury complained of be a tort, and the declarations of the agent or employe are claimed to be competent as being a part of the *res gestae,* the question is not so easy of solution. It must be borne in mind, in such cases, that the testimony can be admitted only if the declaration or statement is so connected and interwoven with the main transaction as to be spontaneous and not the result of design and afterthought, and pertains to and characterizes the main transaction: the statement must be one naturally accompanying the act or calculated to unfold its character or quality.[122] A statement made by an injured brakeman concerning the manner in which he received the injury, made ten minutes after the happening of the accident, and after he had been removed two hundred feet from the scene, was held by the appellate court of Indiana not a part of the *res gestae,* and, therefore, not admissible as evidence against the principal or master.[123] And on the same theory, it was held by the same court that the statements of a child injured by a street car, made ten minutes after the injury happened, and while the child was being taken to the hospital in an ambulance, were not parts of the *res gestae.*[124] But whenever what the agent did is admissible in evidence, what he said about the act while doing it will be admissible also; for what he said was but a verbal act, and is not regarded as hearsay. But whenever the right or power to act has ceased, the principal can no longer be affected by the declaration, and it becomes mere hearsay, and, consequently, incompetent as evidence against the principal.[125]

[120] Roberts v. Burks, Litt. Sel. Cas. (Ky.) 411, 12 Am. Dec. 325.

[121] Bolds v. Woods, 9 Ind. App. 657.

[122] Butler v. Manhattan R. Co., 143 N. Y. 417; Baker v. Gausin, 76 Ind. 317; Ohio, etc., R. Co. v. Stein, 133 Ind. 243.

[123] Cleveland, etc., R. Co. v. Sloan, 11 Ind. App. 401.

[124] Citizens', etc., R. Co. v. Stoddard, 10 Ind. App. 278.

[125] Greenleaf Ev. (16th ed.), § 184c; Story Ag., §§ 134–137.

§ 352. **Agent's statements need not have been made at precise moment of occurence of act to be of res gestae.**—There is considerable confusion in the decided cases as to the point of time, relative to the main transaction, at which the declaration must have been made, in order to be a part of the *res gestae.* The current of modern authority, however, seems to support the view that the statement need not have been made at the precise moment of the main act or occurrence: it is sufficient if it springs out of the principal transaction, tends to explain it, and is made "at a time so near it as to preclude the idea of deliberate design."[126] "Whether the declarations of an agent made in regard to transactions already past, but while the agency for similar objects still continues, will bind the principal, does not appear to have been expressly decided; but the weight of authority is in the negative."[127] The declaration, to bind the principal, must also have been made in relation to the subject-matter of the agency. "The mere idle, desultory, or careless talk of the agent, having no legitimate reference to or bearing upon the business of his principal, can not be binding upon the latter."[128]

§ 353. **Declarations of agent not admissible until proof of agency has been made.**—It is to be remembered, however, that the admission in evidence of the declarations of the agent is predicated on the assumption that proof of the agency, independently of the admissions, has been made sufficient to satisfy the jury, or court sitting as such, that the relation subsists; in the absence of such independent proof of the agency, the admissions are not competent. They are admissible only upon the theory of the legal identity of the principal and the agent, for otherwise they would be hearsay; and the *fact* of the agency must, therefore, be established before effect can be given to that theory. The agency itself—that is to say, the delegation of authority —can not, in such a case, be shown by the declarations or admissions

[126] People v. Vernon, 35 Cal. 49, 95 Am. Dec. 49; Com. v. McPike, 3 Cush. (Mass.) 181, 50 Am. Dec. 727; Illinois, etc., R. Co. v. Tronstine, 64 Miss. 834; Keyser v. Chicago, etc., R. Co, 66 Mich. 390; Cleveland v. Newsom, 45 Mich. 62; Toledo, etc., R. Co. v. Goddard, 25 Ind. 185; Louisville, etc., R. Co. v. Buck, 116 Ind. 566; Augusta Factory v. Barnes, 72 Ga. 217, 53 Am. Rep. 838; McLeod v. Ginther, 80 Ky. 399; Elkins v. McKean, 79 Pa. St. 493; O'Connor v. Chicago, etc., R. Co., 27 Minn. 166; Williamson v. Cambridge R. Co., 144 Mass. 148; Elledge v. National, etc., R. Co., 100 Cal. 282.

[127] Greenleaf Ev. (16th ed.), § 184c, note 5, by Wigmore.

[128] Mechem Ag., § 714.

of the agent.[129] The authority of the agent, or ratification of the act, must be shown, at least *prima facie,* before the principal can be bound by the agent's acts or statements. The agent himself is, however, a competent witness.[130]

§ 354. **Principal bound by notice to agent.**—It is, moreover, an old and well established rule that the principal is bound by any notice acquired by his agent during the course of the agency; "notice to the agent," it is said, "is notice to the principal."[131] If A, by his agent, B, purchase property of C, to which E claims an equitable title superior to the legal title of C, A would not be bound by the equity of E, unless he had knowledge or notice thereof; but if at the time of the purchase, B, the agent of A, had information as to E's equity, A is bound by it the same as if the information or knowledge had been possessed by A himself. This is upon the theory that A and B are identical, and that whatever notice or knowledge B, as such agent, has received concerning the matter, A is conclusively presumed to have received also, whether in point of fact this is true or not.[132] In the case supposed, had A and his agent, B, both been ignorant of E's equity, A would doubtless have obtained a clear title; and the same would be true had A contracted with C personally, and without the intervention of an agent; but having purchased through an agent who had knowledge, A will be affected with constructive notice.[133] The rule of constructive notice is based not only upon the doctrine of the identity of the principal and agent, but also upon the theory that whereas it is the duty of the agent to disclose to his principal all information which he may have respecting the subject-matter of the agency, it will be presumed that he has discharged that duty by giving the principal the information in question.[134]

[129] Greenleaf Ev. (16th ed.), § 184d.

[130] Smith v. Kron, 96 N. C. 392; Hatch v. Squires, 11 Mich. 185; Graves v. Horton, 38 Minn. 66; Howe Machine Co. v. Clark, 15 Kan. 492.

[131] Farmers', etc., Bank v. Butchers', etc., Bank, 16 N. Y. 125, 69 Am. Dec. 678; Hill v. Nation Trust Co., 108 Pa. St. 1, 56 Am. Rep. 189; Carpenter v. German, etc., Ins. Co., 135 N. Y. 298; Arff v. Star F. Ins. Co., 125 N. Y. 57; Evans Pr. & Ag. (Bedford's ed.) 194, *et seq.*; Corneille v. Pfeiffer, 26 Ind. App. 62.

[132] Mountford v. Scott, 3 Madd. 34, 40; Houseman v. Girard, etc., Ass'n, 81 Pa. St. 256.

[133] Per Pollock, C. B., in Dresser v. Norwood, 17 C. B. (N. S.) 466.

[134] Hyatt v. Clark, 118 N. Y. 563; Story Eq. Juris., § 408, note 2; Story Ag., § 140.

§ 355. Notice must have been received by agent in course of agency—Exceptions.—There can be no question of the correctness of the rule just stated, respecting constructive notice, provided the notice was received by the agent in the course of the agency. If, however, the notice came to him before the relation commenced, it is not so clear that it is the duty of the agent to disclose the information to the principal, or that a presumption can be predicated that such information has been communicated.[135] And as to the doctrine of identity, it can not apply but during the time of the agency. If, however, the knowledge was actually present in the mind of the agent at the time of the transaction in question, or if it had been acquired by him so recently as to raise a reasonable presumption that he must have had it in mind, it is now generally held that the principal is affected by it, although it was not acquired in the course of the agency, or was received prior to the commencement of the relation.[136] According to some authorities, however, it is the better doctrine that in order to bind the principal, the knowledge, if acquired outside of the course of the agency, must be actually present in the mind of the agent, and that the evidence must establish this in order to bind the principal.[137]

§ 356. When principal not bound by notice to agent.—If, however, the knowledge was such as the agent was in duty bound not to disclose, or such as it was reasonable to presume he would not disclose, or if there was between the agent and third party a collusion or conspiracy to defraud the principal, the latter will not be affected by the agent's knowledge, though it was received by the agent in the course of the agency.[138] And although the agent's knowledge was obtained in the course of the agency, if the agent is known to be adversely interested in the transaction, the principal is not affected by

[135] Willis v. Vallette, 4 Metc. (Ky.) 186; Martin v. Jackson, 27 Pa. St. 504; Yerger v. Barz, 56 Iowa 77; Shaffer v. Milwaukee, etc., Ins. Co., 17 Ind. App. 204.

[136] Brothers v. Bank, 84 Wis. 381; Lebanon Sav. Bank v. Hollenbeck, 29 Minn. 322; The Distilled Spirits, 11 Wall. (U. S.) 356; Fairfield Sav. Bank v. Chase, 72 Me. 226, 39 Am. Rep. 319; Dresser v. Norwood, 17 C. B. (N. S.) 466; Schwind v. Boyce (Md.), 51 Atl. 45.

[137] Constant v. University of Rochester, 111 N. Y. 604; Yerger v. Barz, 56 Iowa 77; Willis v. Vallette, 4 Metc. (Ky.) 186; Fairfield Sav. Bank v. Chase, *supra*.

[138] The Distilled Spirits, *supra*; Fairfield Sav. Bank v. Chase, *supra*; National Life Ins. Co. v. Minch, 53 N. Y. 144; Innerarity v. Merchants' Nat'l Bank, 139 Mass. 332, 52 Am. Rep. 710; Dillaway v. Butler, 135 Mass. 479.

such knowledge.[139] The reason for this exception to the general rule is that one who has an interest to act a certain way can not be presumed to act another way.[140]

§ 357. **Principal bound by knowledge actually in agent's mind at time of transaction.**—Whether knowledge was actually communicated to the principal or not seems to be immaterial; for the presumption, in the absence of the exceptions named, is conclusive, and can not be overcome by proof that the agent in fact did not transmit such notice to the principal.[141] And whether the time in which the information was received by the agent is so far past as to overcome the presumption that it was present in his mind is a question, it seems, to be decided by the circumstances of each case.[142] The burden of proof is upon the party alleging the existence of the knowledge or notice relied upon.[142a] Some of the cases hold, as has been said above, that the principal is never affected by the notice unless it was actually conveyed to the agent during the course of the agency; and, according to this view, if the notice was received before the agency began, it will, of course, have no binding effect upon the principal.[143] However, the weight of authority is believed to be that it is sufficient if the knowledge was actually in the mind of the agent at the time of the transaction, or was acquired so recently as to raise a presumption to that effect; unless, indeed, the agent is in duty bound not to reveal it, or the circumstances are such as to show collusion, personal interest or other matters which will exonerate the principal from being chargeable with such notice.[144] The knowledge must be of a matter so material to the transaction as to make it the agent's duty to communicate the fact to his principal;[145] if it concerns something else than the transaction in question, or is so vaguely connected with it that it would not bind the principal, if he were himself in possession thereof, it will not affect him. But if the knowledge is sufficient to put a prudent man upon inquiry, and which, if diligently pursued,

[139] Loring v. Brodie, 134 Mass. 453; Innerarity v. Merchants' Nat'l Bank, *supra*; Frenkel v. Hudson, 82 Ala. 158; Atlantic Nat'l Bank v. Harris, 118 Mass. 147.

[140] Frenkel v. Hudson, *supra*.

[141] The Distilled Spirits, *supra*.

[142] The Distilled Spirits, *supra*.

[142a] Mechem Ag., § 721.

[143] Houseman v. Girard, etc., Ass'n, 81 Pa. 256; Satterfield v. Malone, 35 Fed. 445.

[144] The Distilled Spirits, *supra*; Hunter v. Watson, 12 Cal. 363, 73 Am. Dec. 543; Wilson v. Minnesota, etc., Ins. Co., 36 Minn. 112, 1 Am. St. 659; Dresser v. Norwood, 17 C. B. (N. S.) 466; Chouteau v. Allen, 70 Mo. 290.

[145] Fairfield Sav. Bank v. Chase, 72 Me. 226, 39 Am. Rep. 319.

would place the principal in possession of actual knowledge, it will charge the latter with it, the same as if he had actually received it.[146]

§ 358. **Rule applies to corporations.**—Corporations are affected by such notice to their agents, the same as individual principals. The only way in which corporations act, or are acted upon, is through their agents. But the agent or officer who is thus capable of charging the corporation with knowledge through him must, as in cases of individuals, be one who is clothed with ample authority; hence, notice to a stockholder or a single director is generally not sufficient to charge the corporation.[147] If, however, the officer acts for the corporation in a capacity which authorizes him to bind the company in such matters, the latter is charged with the notice. Thus, where a note procured by fraud is discounted for a bank by one of its directors, concerned in or having knowledge of the fraud, his act is the act of the bank, and the bank is chargeable with his knowledge of such fraud.[148]

§ 359. **Notice to subagent.**—In cases where it is sought to charge the principal with notice to a subagent, no great difficulty can arise. If the subagent was appointed under circumstances which render him privy to the principal, or in other words, if the subagent was appointed by the authority, or with the assent, express or implied, of the principal, the latter will be bound by his acts, and consequently also by notice to such subagent. But if the subagent was appointed by the main agent, without authority, express or implied, of the principal, the latter is not responsible for his acts, and, consequently, is not bound by any notice to him.[149]

§ 360. **Liability of mercantile agencies for injuries resulting from false reports.**—Important questions frequently arise with regard to the liability of mercantile agencies for the reports they furnish their customers or subscribers of the commercial standing or ratings of merchants and others with whom such customers or subscribers desire to transact business. This subject might have been treated under the head of the liability of the agent to third persons for the acts

146 Baker v. Bliss, 39 N. Y. 70; Chapman v. Glassell, 13 Ala. 50, 48 Am. Dec. 41; Hood v. Fahnestock, 1 Pa. St. 470, 44 Am. Dec. 147.

147 Housatonic Bank v. Martin, 1 Metc. (Mass.) 294; Fairfield Sav. Bank v. Chase, 72 Me. 226, 39 Am. Rep. 319.

148 National Security Bank v. Cushman, 121 Mass. 490.

149 See Hoover v. Wise, 91 U. S. 308.

of the subagent; but as mercantile agencies are in one sense principals to those from whom they obtain their information, it is not inappropriate to regard them here in that light, and as ordinary contracting parties with their subscribers or customers. Should such an agency render a false report as to the standing of some one inquired about, and the subscriber or customer should sustain an injury by reason of such false information, would the agency be liable in damages? It is almost the universal custom of such agencies to contract with their subscribers that they will in no event be liable for the negligence of the agent or person who procures and reports the information, and that they do not guarantee the accuracy of the reports. When this is the contract between such an agency and its subscriber, the agency is, of course, not liable; its undertaking is simply that of transmitting the information it receives from the local agent to the subscriber; and if the report proves inaccurate, or false, or fraudulent, the agency can not be held accountable to him. Besides, even if we regard the subscriber as the principal, the rule applies that where the services demanded by the principal (the customer) can not be performed by the agent in person, the latter will not be liable for the negligence or misconduct of the subagent unless the chief agent himself be guilty of negligence.[150] Whether there is a liability on the part of the agency to the subscriber or not, therefore, depends on the nature of the contract between the two. If the agency has not expressly exonerated itself from liability, it is doubtless the implied undertaking that the information is accurate; and if it be not so, the agency is liable.

§ 361. **Principal not criminally liable for crimes of agent.**—The principal can not generally be held responsible, criminally, for the crimes or offenses of his agent, unless they were done by his command or with his assent, in which case he would himself be a party to the crime.[151] As was pointed out in a former portion of this work, the relation of principal and agent can not subsist in the commission of crimes or criminal offenses.[152] It is true, one person may aid and abet another in the commission of a crime, and the person who does this may, as to other matters, stand in the relation of agent to

[150] Dun v. City Nat'l Bank, 58 Fed. 174, 23 L. R. A. 687.

[151] Hipp v. State, 5 Blackf. (Ind.) 149, 33 Am. Dec. 463; City of Hammond v. New York, etc., R. Co., 5 Ind. App. 526, 533; Com. v. Putman, 4 Gray (Mass.) 16; United States v. Birch, 1 Cranch C. C. 571; Rex v. Huggins, 2 Stra. 883.

[152] *Ante*, § 68.

him at whose instance he so aids and abets; or one person may be an accessory and the other a principal in the commission of a criminal act; but the mere fact that one does an act of this nature at the request or command of another does not make the one a principal and the other an agent; and as no act can be criminal without a criminal intent, it would seem that there could be no criminal responsibility unless the party charged had in some way participated in the commission of such act,[153] and this is doubtless the general rule.[153a] But there is a class of offenses in which it it held that there may be a conviction even without any intent: these are usually such as arise under the revenue laws or pertain to police regulations. They may be and usually are acts intrinsically innocent, but prohibited by statute; or they may even be offenses under the common law. So, under the first class of cases, a person may be punished for the act of his agent in opening the doors of his saloon on Sunday and engaging in the unlawful sale of liquors;[154] and under the common law, book dealers and publishers have been held criminally liable for the publication and sale from their establishments of certain prohibited books, by their agents, of which the principals had no knowledge whatever.[155] As to prohibited sales of liquors, it was held in Illinois that a principal is criminally liable for the sale of intoxicants by his agent, though such sale was in violation of instructions by the principal.[156] The indictment in that case was predicated upon a statute providing that: "Whoever, by himself, clerk or servant, shall sell," etc., shall be liable. The evidence showed that the defendant kept intoxicating liquors for sale, and it was held by the supreme court that the defendant was responsible for the acts of his clerks, no matter what instructions he gave them. In Massachusetts it has been held that a sale of liquor by an agent is *prima facie* evidence of his authority to make such sale.[157] And in Michigan, a conviction of a saloon keeper for the violation of a statute requiring all saloons to be closed on Sunday, was affirmed, when the evidence showed that the saloon-keeper's clerk, without the knowledge or consent of his employer, but while the latter was on the premises, had opened the saloon on Sunday morning to

[153] Hipp v. State, *supra.*

[153a] People v. Parks, 49 Mich. 333; Com. v. Putman, 4 Gray (Mass.) 16; Nall v. State, 34 Ala. 262; Rex v. Huggins, 2 Stra. 883; United States v. Shuck, 1 Cranch C. C. 56.

[154] People v. Roby, 52 Mich. 577.

[155] Rex v. Walter, 3 Esp. 21; Rex v. Gutch, M. & M. 433, 22 E. C. L. 559.

[156] Noecker v. People, 91 Ill. 494.

[157] Com. v. Nichols, 10 Metc. (Mass.) 259.

have it cleaned out, and meanwhile sold a drink to a casual customer, who insisted on having it.[158] The case seems to have turned upon the point that the statute makes the offense in such a case to consist, "not in the affirmative act of any person," as Judge Cooley expresses it, "but in the negative conduct of failing to keep the saloon, etc., closed." This provision would make it the duty of the owner or proprietor not only to close the doors himself, but to keep a watch over them and see that no one else opens them or gives access to those desiring to purchase liquor. This is quite different from holding one accountable, however, for the affirmative act of another which he might not by the reasonable exercise of diligence have prevented. The learned court, however, did not base its conclusion solely upon the wording of the statute, but took the broad ground that in such cases no intent is necessary; although, in the case under consideration, the evidence was sufficient, the court said, to submit the question of intent to the jury, if intent were necessary to be found. Under a statute of Massachusetts prohibiting licensed liquor-sellers from maintaining a screen or curtain to cut off the public view of the premises, the court in that state ruled that it was no defense to a prosecution that the defendant had instructed his clerk not to draw the curtains, and that the clerk had done so in violation of such instructions.[159] And in the same state it was held that the proprietor of a saloon is criminally liable for a sale made by his clerk during prohibited hours.[160] But in Indiana the rule is to the contrary.[161] In Missouri it is held that proof of a sale of intoxicating liquors by an agent makes a *prima facie* case against the principal, which may, however, be rebutted by the latter by showing that the sale was forbidden by him.[162] In Connecticut, however, the court decided that a conviction for giving credit to college students, in violation of a statute, can not be upheld when the evidence shows that the sale was made by the barkeeper of the defendant without the knowledge and against the express directions of the latter, who was the proprietor of the saloon in which the sale was made, and that a subsequent ratification of the act would not render the defendant criminally responsible.[163]

§ **362. May be liable civilly for agent's crimes.**—But while, as a general rule, the principal can not be held criminally responsible for

[158] People v. Roby, 52 Mich. 577.

[159] Com. v. Kelley, 140 Mass. 441.

[160] Com. v. Wachendorf, 141 Mass. 270.

[161] Rosenbaum v. State, 24 Ind. App. 510.

[162] State v. McCance, 110 Mo. 398.

[163] Morse v. State, 6 Conn. 9.

the crimes of his agent, committed without his participation therein or knowledge of or consent to the same, he will be held liable in damages for any injury inflicted by his agent by means of such crime, either to the person or the property of another. Such crimes are also torts, and if committed by the agent in the course of his employment, the principal is civilly liable within the principles discussed in a previous section.[164] Many states have enacted statutes expressly providing that damages may be recovered by the injured party on account of the unlawful sales of intoxicating liquors to certain persons, either by the proprietor himself or by his agent;[165] and even without such statute the principal would doubtless be liable. If, however, the circumstances are such as to prove that the act was not done in the course of the business intrusted to the agent, or that he committed it by going outside of the lines of his employment, the principal is not liable;[166] but if the principal ratifies the act, or knowingly reaps a benefit from the same, he is liable.[167]

[164] *Ante*, § 342.

[165] George v. Gobey, 128 Mass. 289; Kreiter v. Nichols, 28 Mich. 496.

[166] Golden v. Newbrand, 52 Iowa 59, 35 Am. Rep. 257.

[167] Payne v. Newcomb, 100 Ill. 611 Erickson v. Bell, 53 Iowa 627, 36 Am. Rep. 246.

CHAPTER X.

DUTIES, OBLIGATIONS AND LIABILITIES OF THIRD PERSONS TO AGENT AND TO PRINCIPAL, AND RIGHTS OF AGENT AND PRINCIPAL, RESPECTIVELY, IN REGARD TO THIRD PERSONS.

A. Of Third Persons to Agent.

I. On Contracts.

§ 363. **Third party liable to agent in exceptional cases only.**— As a general rule, an agent, as such, has no claim upon a third party, nor right to hold him liable on a contract entered into by such agent on behalf of his principal.[1] As we have heretofore had occasion to state, an authorized agent who contracts in the name of his principal, in manner and form such as will bind the latter, can not be held liable to the other contracting party on such contract.[2] But if the agent can not be made personally liable to the third party, neither can the third party in such case become liable to the agent. The agent is but a middleman between the two, and as soon as the task of executing the contract for his principal is performed, the agent having acted in good faith, he is entirely eliminated from the transaction, and any consequences that follow are the same as if the principal and third party had entered into the contract in person; after that the principal can look only to the third party, and the third party to the principal. Thus, a clerk or shopman who sells his principal's goods can not maintain a suit against the purchaser for the price any more than a clerk or shopman who has purchased goods for the principal can be sued successfully by the vendor for the price of such goods.[3] This proposition is too plain to be misunderstood. Other cases to which the same rule applies do not appear so obvious, at least at first glance. Thus, in the case of the assignment or indorsement of a bill of lading to a person who is in reality but a mere agent of the shipper, the bill of lading not being a negotiable instrument in the sense that it vests title in an assignee or indorsee who has no general or special property in the goods, it is held that such agent can not maintain an action on such instrument for nondelivery of the goods by the carrier.[4] And so, an agent who, in pursuance of his principal's instructions, delivers money to a carrier, to be in turn delivered by the latter to a consignee, can not maintain an action against the carrier for failure to deliver the money, although the

[1] Commercial Bank v. French, 21 Pick. (Mass.) 486, 32 Am. Dec. 280. And generally, an agent can not maintain an action on a contract entered into by him on behalf of his principal: Taintor v. Prendergast, 3 Hill (N. Y.) 72, 38 Am. Dec. 618; Bayley v. Onondaga County Mut. Ins. Co., 6 Hill (N. Y.) 476, 41 Am. Dec. 759; Lineker v. Ayeshford, 1 Cal. 76.

[2] *Ante*, § 301.

[3] Story Ag., § 391.

[4] Lineker v. Ayeshford, 1 Cal. 76.

agent's money may have been substituted for that of the principal before delivery to the carrier.[5] The liability in these last-mentioned cases is based upon the same theory as in the cases of the clerk or shopman: the agent in neither case has any personal interest. It is only in exceptional cases, some of which we shall presently notice, that an agent who acts for his principal has a right to maintain in his own name an action on such a contract.

§ 364. **When agent contracts in his own name.**—But there are exceptional instances in which an agent may bring and maintain an action in his own name on a contract made with a third party by authority of his principal, and these we are now to consider. Though in fact acting for his principal, the agent may intentionally or unintentionally contract personally, or in his own name, as if he were the principal. If he do so intentionally, he will, of course, not disclose the principal's name nor make any reference to it in the contract. The general rule of the common law is that when an agent makes a contract in his own name, although in fact for his principal, the other contracting party binds himself personally to the agent, and may be sued by the latter in his (the agent's) own name.[6] In such case both the contracting parties assume obligations, the one to the other: the agent is personally bound to the third party, and the same is true of the third party to the agent.[7] Even if the third party knew

[5] Thompson v. Fargo, 63 N. Y. 479. In this case the plaintiff had collected a certain amount of money from the government of the United States for certain parties which was due them for back pay as soldiers in the army of the United States. The plaintiff had received the amount in a check, which he converted into United States treasury notes, and these, after deducting his fees for collecting the same, he inclosed in an envelope directed to J. & W. W., in care of M., at T., and delivered to the United States Express Company, at Springfield, Ill., for conveyance and delivery. The United States Express Company delivered the package to Fargo, another carrier, at Decatur, Ill., who conveyed it to its destination, but was unable to find the consignees at the place. The plaintiff—who had forwarded the money—sued Fargo for the money, but it was held by the New York court of appeals that the money became the property of the consignee the moment it was delivered to the express company, and that the consignor ceased to have any property in it whatever. See case between same parties in 49 N. Y. 188.

[6] Winters v. Rush, 34 Cal. 136; Murdock v. Franklin Ins. Co., 33 W. Va. 407; Colburn v. Phillips, 13 Gray (Mass.) 64; Rowe v. Rand, 111 Ind. 206.

[7] Story Ag., § 396; Beebe v. Robert, 12 Wend. (N. Y.) 413; Ludwig v. Gillespie, 105 N. Y. 653; Neal v. Andrews (Tex. Civ. App.), 60 S. W. 459; Rhoades v. Blackiston, 106 Mass. 334, 8 Am. Rep. 332; Evrit v. Ban-

that the agent was acting for another, and knew who that person was, the agent can not, in such case, be debarred from carrying on the suit in his own name whenever a right of action arises from such contract.[8] If, on the other hand, the agent unintentionally contracts in his own name, instead of the principal's, it may be the result of inadvertence or ignorance on his part in drawing the contract. In the latter case, if the promise runs to the agent *eo nomine,* although he may have described himself as "agent," or "agent of" some other person named, these words will not necessarily operate to place the right of action of the contract exclusively in his principal, and the word "agent," etc., may be regarded as descriptive merely,[9] leaving the legal title of the instrument in the name of such agent personally. The propositions here stated are, of course, subject to the rules concerning the rights and liabilities of undisclosed principals elsewhere considered.

§ 365. Under code provisions real party in interest must sue—Exceptions.—In states where the reformed or code procedure prevails, it is generally provided that actions must be brought in the name of the real party in interest. Where such is the rule the principal alone can sue, though the legal title of the chose in action or other matter in controversy be in the agent.[10] If, however, the agent be the trustee of an express trust, or a person with whom or in whose name a contract is made for the benefit of another, the codes usually make an exception by providing that such parties may sue in their own names, without joining their beneficiaries.[11] The provision by virtue of which the

croft, 22 Ohio St. 172; Rosser v. Darden, 82 Ga. 219, 14 Am. St. 152; DuBois v. Perkins, 21 Or. 189; Johnson v. Catlin, 27 Vt. 87, 62 Am. Dec. 622; Hately v. Pike, 162 Ill. 241, 44 N. E. 441; Stoll v. Sheldon (Ia.), 13 N. W. 201.

[8] Lowndes v. Anderson, 13 East 130; McHenry v. Ridgely, 3 Ill. 309, 35 Am. Dec. 110; Shepherd v. Evans, 9 Ind. 260; Winters v. Rush, 34 Cal. 136; McConnel v. Thomas, 3 Ill. 313; Clap v. Day, 2 Me. 305, 11 Am. Dec. 99; Bragg v. Greenleaf, 14 Me. 395; Considerant v. Brisbane, 22 N. Y. 389; Murdock v. Franklin Ins. Co., 33 W. Va. 407.

[9] Clap v. Day, 2 Me. 305, 11 Am. Dec. 99; Hately v. Pike, 162 Ill. 241, 44 N. E. 441; Goodman v. Walker, 30 Ala. 482, 68 Am. Dec. 134; Story Ag., § 394; *ante,* § 208.

[10] Phillips Code Pldg., § 450; Considerant v. Brisbane, 22 N. Y. 389.

[11] Coffin v. Grand Rapids Hydraulic Co., 136 N. Y. 655; Davis v. Harness, 38 Ohio St. 397; Close v. Hodges, 44 Minn. 204; Holmes v. Boyd, 90 Ind. 332; Landwerlen v. Wheeler, 106 Ind. 523; Weaver v. Trustees of Wabash & Erie Canal, 28 Ind. 112. See Bliss Code Pldg., § 57; Pomeroy Rem., §§ 171-182. In Rogers v. Gibson, 15 Ind. 218, the suit was upon a note payable to A., as school commissioner, and to his

trustee of an express trust is permitted to sue in his own name has been so liberally construed by the courts that the right of an agent to sue in his own name is quite as full and ample as it was under the common law, and the agent may therefore generally maintain the action notwithstanding the provision of the code giving the right of action to the real party in interest.[12] In the case of *Heavenridge* v. *Mondy,* just cited, the supreme court of Indiana said: "The meaning of the words the 'trustee of an express trust,' as used in section four above quoted, was not left to the interpretation and construction of the courts, but their signification and construction were so plainly and clearly defined by the legislature as to leave no room for doubt or construction. Any person is a 'trustee of an express trust' with whom, or in whose name, a contract is made for the benefit of another. The word 'contract' is not used in a limited or restricted sense, but is used and intended to be applied to all and any kinds of contracts. As the note sued upon was made for the use of William Mondy, this action might have been prosecuted in his name under the third section of article two of our code; but as it is payable to Alfred Mondy, for the use and benefit of William Mondy, it thereby makes Alfred Mondy the 'trustee of an express trust,' and the suit is properly prosecuted in his name under the fourth section above quoted." In the case of *Considerant* v. *Brisbane,* just cited, the court of appeals of New York, speaking of the section of the code in question, said: "It is intended, manifestly, to embrace, not only formal trusts, declared by deed *inter partes,* but all cases in which a person acting in behalf of a third party enters into a written express contract with another, either in

successors in office. The note was given for a loan of money belonging to the school fund, and a statute of the state made it the duty of county auditors to institute suits for the collection of such loans, in the name of the state. It was held that the action should have been prosecuted in the name of the state on the relation of the county auditor, although the code provided that every action must be brought in the name of the real party in interest, except that an executor, administrator, a trustee of an express trust, or a person expressly authorized by statute might sue without joining the beneficiary. In Vermont it is held that where an instrument is made payable to one as agent for a consideration advanced by the principal, the principal has a right of action on such instrument, and not the agent: Arlington v. Hinds, 1 D. Chip. (Vt.) 431, 12 Am. Dec. 704 and note, p. 709.

[12] Wolfe v. Missouri Pac. R. Co., 97 Mo. 473, 11 S. W. 49; Societa Italiana v. Sulzer, 138 N. Y. 168; West v. Crawford, 80 Cal. 19; Heavenridge v. Mondy, 34 Ind. 28; Considerant v. Brisbane, 22 N. Y. 389.

his individual name, without description, or in his own name, expressly in trust for, or on behalf of, or for the benefit of another, by whatever form of expression such trust may be disclosed. It includes not only a person with whom, but one in whose name a contract is made for the benefit of another." This is the general holding of the courts; and, as thus construed, the statute enlarges rather than limits the scope of cases in which an agent may sue in his own name on a contract made for his principal, for it includes cases in which the contract is made ostensibly in behalf of the principal, provided an express trust may be discovered in the relation between the principal and the agent.

§ 366. **Agent's right subordinated to that of principal, except when beneficially interested—Authority coupled with interest.**—In the cases covered by the last preceding section, the principal may sue in his own name also, unless the agent has an interest coupled with his authority, in which case he can sue to the extent of such interest. If the agent has no such interest, the principal, being the ultimate party in interest, should have the right to control the action, and he may, therefore, suspend or extinguish it by taking the agent's place in the suit, after it has been instituted, or by commencing the action in his own name before.[13] In such cases the agent and principal may both be made parties, especially in equity suits, so that full relief may be granted in a single suit.[14] If the agency has been terminated, the agent can no longer sue in his own name.[15] If, however, the agent has a beneficial interest in the subject-matter of the agency, the principal can not control the suit, at least to the extent of such agent's interest, and the agent may maintain the action thereupon in his own name to the exclusion of the principal. Thus, an auctioneer, who sells the goods of another in his (the auctioneer's) name, has such an interest in the contract that he may sue in his own name for the price of the goods sold.[16] The classes of agents generally regarded as having such an interest are factors, auctioneers, warehousemen, carriers, policy brokers, masters of ships and others who have a lien on the property for commissions, freights, etc., or a special property of any character in the subject-matter of the agreement.[17] In the case

[13] Rhoades v. Blackiston, 106 Mass. 334.

[14] 16 Encyc. Pl. & Pr. 895.

[15] Miller v. State Bank, 57 Minn. 319, 59 N. W. 309.

[16] Bogart v. O'Regan, 1 E. D. Smith (N. Y.) 590.

[17] See Grove v. Dubois, 1 T. R. 112; Johnson v. Hudson, 11 East 180; Brown v. Hodgson, 4 Taunt. 189;

of an auctioneer it is not necessary to prove that he has a special property or interest, for that follows as a matter of course from his position as an auctioneer; and "it is only where a party acts as a mere agent or servant that a special beneficial interest must be proved to maintain an action, or may be disproved, to defeat it."[18] With regard to auctioneers, "the doctrine stands upon the right of the auctioneer to receive, and his responsibility to his principal for the price of the property sold, and his lien thereon for his commissions, which give him a special property in the goods intrusted to him for sale and an interest in the proceeds. In case of real estate, he can have no special property, and would not ordinarily be held entitled to receive the price. But when the terms of his employment and of the authorized sale contemplate the payment of a deposit into his hands at the time of the auction and before the completion of the sale by the delivery of the deed, he stands, in relation to such deposit, in the same position as he does to the piece of personal property sold and delivered by him. He may receive and receipt for the deposit; his lien for commissions will attach to it; and we see no reason why he may not sue for it in his own name whenever an action for the deposit, separate from the other action for the purchase-money, may become necessary."[19] But an agent authorized to sell land for a commission, who makes such sale, does not thereby acquire the right to bring an action for a breach of the contract of sale.[20] The rule applies only to contracts made in the agent's name, or whether or not so made, when he has a special property or beneficial interest in the subject-matter;[21] and it is settled that a mere interest in the proceeds by way of a commission to be earned would not be sufficient.[22] A factor or commission merchant, having a special property in the goods consigned to him, is treated as a special owner of such property, and may sue in his own name for the price of goods sold by him for the principal.[23] A broker has, ordinarily, no authority to receive payment for property sold by him, and can not generally maintain an action for the breach of a contract made by him for his principal, he having no such interest in the subject-matter as brings him within the rule. There are excep-

Steamboat Co. v. Atkins, 22 Pa. St. 522; Neal v. Andrews (Tex. Civ. App.), 60 S. W. 459.

18 Minturn v. Main, 7 N. Y. 220.

19 Thompson v. Kelly, 101 Mass. 291, 3 Am. Rep. 353, per Wells, J.

20 Tinsley v. Dowell, 87 Tex. 23.

21 United States Tel. Co. v. Gildersleve, 29 Md. 232, 96 Am. Dec. 519.

22 Fairlie v. Fenton, L. R. 5 Ex. 169.

23 Graham v. Duckwall, 8 Bush (Ky.) 12.

tions, however, by the usages of trade; as in case of a policy broker, who usually has the policy written in his own name, and may then sue thereon.[24]

§ 367. **Instruments payable to cashier of bank, etc.**—It is now generally regarded as a settled rule that if a note or other instrument for the payment of money is made payable to the cashier of a bank,—and sometimes also when payable to the treasurer or other officer of a corporation,—the bank or corporation is deemed to be the real payee, and the action on the instrument may be maintained in its name as plaintiff.[25]

§ 368. **Undisclosed principal—Indorsements in blank.**—Where an agent contracts in his own name without any attempt to bind his principal, we have seen that he may be held liable on the contract thus entered into; although if it develops afterward that the contract was made for a principal who was at the time undisclosed or unknown in the transaction, the latter may also become liable at the option of the third party; and, conversely, the undisclosed principal may hold

[24] Story Ag., § 109.

[25] Commercial Bank v. French, 21 Pick. (Mass.) 486, 32 Am. Dec. 280; Crawford v. Dean, 6 Blackf. (Ind.) 181; Nave v. First Nat'l Bank, 87 Ind. 204; Erwin, etc., Co. v. Farmers' Nat'l Bank, 130 Ind. 367; Nave v. Hadley, 74 Ind. 155; Stamford Bank v. Ferris, 17 Conn. 258; Garton v. Union City Nat'l Bank, 34 Mich. 279; Bank of Genesee v. Patchin Bank, 19 N. Y. 312; First Nat'l Bank v. Hall, 44 N. Y. 395; Houghton v. First Nat'l Bank, 26 Wis. 663; Story Prom. Notes 127; Morse Banks and Banking, §§ 158h, 170; Horn v. Newton City Bank, 32 Kan. 518; 1 Daniels Neg. Instr., § 417. See *ante*, § 222. If the principal is named in such an instrument, the action may, of course, be maintained by him. If the principal, however, is not named in the instrument, extrinsic evidence is admissible to show who is the real principal. Hence, if a note or bill is made payable or is indorsed to "A. B. C., cashier, or order," the bank may sue upon it, although not named, and parol evidence would be admitted to show of what bank he was cashier. The suit, however, could also be maintained by the agent in his name. Even if the name of the cashier or agent is not given, the rule still holds good that the suit may be brought by the corporation, evidence *aliunde* being admissible to explain the ambiguity. While this is undoubtedly the tendency of modern decisions, there are authorities holding that only the agent can sue on such contracts. See Daniels Neg. Instr., §§ 1188, 1189. See also, in support of the doctrine of the text, Dutch v. Boyd, 81 Ind. 146; Folger v. Chase, 18 Pick. (Mass.) 63; Bank of New York v. Bank of Ohio, 29 N. Y. 619; Arlingtou v. Hinds, 1 D. Chip. (Vt.) 431, 12 Am. Dec. 704, and the exhaustive note on p. 709.

the third party liable, under certain conditions, on such contract.[26] The doctrine that the undisclosed principal is entitled to the benefits of the contract made by his agent on his behalf, though not in his name, is founded upon the fiction of the identity of the principal and agent; and the correlative doctrine that the third party may hold the principal liable when the latter is discovered is based upon the theory of reciprocity. As to the first part of this proposition, it may be stated that the principal's rights in the contract can not be due to the fact that they appear on the face of the contract, for they do not; these rights accrue to him only because the contract entered into by his agent is a result of the delegation of authority to the agent.[27] As between the principal and the agent, there can be no question that whatever benefits arise by reason of the agency inure to the principal's benefit. If they do not also inure to him when a third party is concerned, it must be because such third party has contracted without reference to the principal, and upon the sole credit of the agent. This can make no difference, however, if the third party has not been subjected to any loss by reason of the intervention of the principal; in other words, if the principal intervenes or asserts his rights before the third party has incurred a loss by settling with the agent, the third party is in just as good a position as if the principal had not intervened; all that the agent can be required to do in any event is to carry out the undertaking of the contract into which he has entered. The third party having lost nothing by the intervention of the principal, and the benefits of the contract in justice and equity belonging to the principal, the court will award such benefits to the principal upon the theory that the principal and the agent are one, and that what the agent has contracted for really belongs to the principal.[28] On the latter branch of the proposition stated, it is sufficient to say that if the principal is entitled to the benefits of the contract, he ought likewise to bear the burden thereof; and where it is shown that a party to a contract has received the benefits thereof, he will not be heard to say that he will not bear its corresponding burdens.[29] This is the doctrine of reciprocity or mutuality. Upon such a contract the agent

[26] See *ante*, §§ 328-334.

[27] Huntington v. Knox, 7 Cush. (Mass.) 371.

[28] Ford v. Williams, 21 How. (U. S.) 287. See Sims v. Bond, 5 B. & Ad. (27 E. C. L.) 389, per Lord Denman.

[29] See Louisville, etc., R. Co. v. Flanagan, 113 Ind. 488, 3 Am. St. 674; Vogel v. Pekoc, 157 Ill. 339; Stensgaard v. Smith, 43 Minn. 11, 19 Am. St. 205.

has the right to sue as long as the principal does not choose to do so himself.[30] "The law is that, where an agent acts for an undisclosed principal, he becomes personally bound on the contract. * * * And where the contract is made in his name, and he is individually liable thereon, the liability is reciprocal, and the party with whom the contract is made is bound to him for its performance, unless the principal is disclosed and asserts his rights."[31] The agent also has a

[30] Stewart v. Gregory, 9 N. D. 618, 84 N. W. 553.

[31] Per Templeton, J., in Neal v. Andrews (Tex. Civ. App.), 60 S. W. 459. Nor is it material that the agreement was required to be in writing by the statute of frauds; the recent case of Kingsley v. Siebrecht, 92 Me. 23, 69 Am. St. 486, contains a comprehensive statement of the law upon this subject; we quote a portion of the opinion of tne court by Salvage, J.: "Two questions arise: 1. May the undisclosed principal sue upon a contract made in the name of her agent? and 2. Is it competent for the undisclosed principal to show by parol that the party appearing in the memorandum to be the contracting party was her agent only, and contracted in her behalf, and thus be enabled to maintain an action on the contract? We think both questions must be answered in the affirmative. The authorities are numerous and decisive that the contract of the agent is in law the contract of the principal, and the latter can come forward and sue thereon, although at the time the contract was made the agent acted and appeared to be the principal. In Wilson v. Hart, 7 Taunt. 295, Parke, B., said: 'It is the constant course to show by parol evidence whether a contracting party is agent or principal.' In Eastern R. Co. v. Benedict, 5 Gray (Mass.) 561, 66 Am. Dec. 384, the court said that 'the rule that the principal may sue in his own name upon a contract made with his agent applies to cases of sales by written bills or other memoranda made by the agent, using his own name, and disclosing no principal,' the same as in cases of oral contracts: Tainter v. Lombard, 53 Me. 369; Barry v. Page, 10 Gray (Mass.) 398; Winchester v. Howard, 97 Mass. 303, 93 Am. Dec. 93; Sims v. Bond, 5 B. & Ad. 389; Huntington v. Knox, 7 Cush. (Mass.) 371; Exchange Bank v. Rice, 107 Mass. 37, 9 Am. Rep. 1; Byington v. Simpson, 134 Mass. 169, 45 Am. Rep. 314. And the weight of authority, we think, sustains the proposition that in case of a memorandum within the statute of frauds, where the name of the agent only appears, it may be shown by parol who the principal is, in support of an action by the latter. In Higgins v. Senior, 8 M. & W. 834, it is declared that 'there is no doubt that where such an agreement is made, it is competent to show that one or both of the contracting parties were agents for other persons, and acted as such agents in making the contract, so as to give the benefit of the contract on the one hand to, and charge with liability on the other, the unnamed principals; and this, whether the agreement be or be not required to be in writing by the statute of frauds; and this evidence in no way contradicts the written agreement. It does not deny that it is binding

right of action where a negotiable instrument is indorsed in blank and delivered to him for collection;[32] but if the agent holds the note merely as a depositary the right of action is in the principal.[33]

§ **369. Defenses by third party.**—When suit is brought by the agent upon a contract made by him for his principal, and which suit the agent has the right to maintain, the party sued may set up any defense

on those whom, on the face of it, it purports to bind, but shows that it also binds another by reason that the act of the agent, in signing the agreement, in pursuance of his authority, is in law the act of the principal. 'Parol evidence is always necessary to show that the party sued is the person making the contract and bound by it. Whether he does so in his own name, or in that of another, or in a feigned name, or whether the contract be signed by his own hand, of by that of an agent, are inquiries not different in their nature from the question who is the person who has just ordered goods in a shop. If he is sued for the price, and his identity is made out, the contract is not varied by appearing to have been made by him in a name not his own:' Trueman v. Loder, 11 Ad. & E. 589. The statute of frauds does not change the law as to the rights and liabilities of principals and agents, either as between themselves, or as to third persons. The provisions of the statute are complied witn if the names of the competent contracting parties appear in the writing, and, if a party be an agent, it is not necessary that the name of the principal shall be disclosed in the writing. Indeed, if a contract, within the provisions of the statute, be made by an agent, whether the agency be disclosed or not, the principal may sue or be sued as in other cases: Thayer v. Luce, 22 Ohio St. 62; Pugh v. Chesseldine, 11 Ohio 109, 37 Am. Dec. 414; Dykers v. Townsend, 24 N. Y. 57; Lerned v. Johns, 9 Allen (Mass.) 419; Hunter v. Giddings, 97 Mass. 41, 93 Am. Dec. 54; Williams v. Bacon, 2 Gray (Mass.) 387; Salmon Falls Mfg. Co. v. Goddard, 14 How. (U. S.) 446; Browne Statute of Frauds, § 373; 3 Parsons Conts. (5th ed.) 10. Judge Story, after stating the doctrine, said: 'The doctrine thus asserted has this title to commendation and support, that it not only furnishes a sound rule for the exposition of contracts, but that it proceeds upon a principle of reciprocity, and gives to the other contracting party the same rights and remedies against agent and principal which they possess against him:' Story Ag., § 160a. See also, cases cited in note to Wain v. Warlters, 2 Smith's Lead. Cas. 252. . .. There is no question but that the memorandum must name or describe two contracting parties, as in this case, a seller and a buyer, but the doctrine of the cases we have cited is to the effect that if one of the parties named is merely an agent, the undisclosed principal may be shown by parol. Accordingly, we hold that the plaintiff may show by parol that she was the real principal, although Moran appeared to be such in the memorandum."

[32] Guernsey v. Burns, 25 Wend. (N. Y.) 411.

[33] Hodge v. Comly, 2 Miles (Pa.) 286.

which would be good against the principal had he sued in his own name; unless the credit was extended to the agent exclusively, in which case the principal can not be brought into the transaction.[34] On the other hand, if the principal exercises his right to sue upon the contract, where he has the right, the third party may set up any defense he would have had against the agent, had the latter instituted the action in his name.[35] The third party is even entitled to a set-off against the agent for a debt which the agent previously owed him, unless such third person had reasonable grounds to believe that the agent was not dealing on his own account;[36] but if the third party dealt with the agent, knowing him to be such, he can not set up a defense that would be good against the agent alone, if the latter were the principal.[37]

§ 370. **Suit by principal who has represented himself as agent for another.**—An important question would be presented if a person who had represented himself as an agent were in reality the principal in the transaction. If, in such case, the performance of the contract involved some consideration of a personal nature, conditioned upon the identity of the parties as represented, such person could not maintain an action thereon, at least without notifying the other party

[34] Hayden v. Alton Nat'l Bank, 29 Ill. App. 458.

[35] Lime Rock Bank v. Plimpton, 17 Pick. (Mass.) 159, 28 Am. Dec. 286; Taintor v. Prendergast, 3 Hill (N. Y.) 72, 38 Am. Dec. 618; Judson v. Stilwell, 26 How. Pr. (N. Y.) 513.

[36] Baxter v. Sherman, 73 Minn. 434, 72 Am. St. 631. In this case the court, speaking of the right of the third party to set off an individual debt of the agent in a suit by the principal, says: "But this rule should not be extended beyond the reason or principle upon which it is founded. It was never intended to be so used as a shield as to make every right of the real owner subordinate to the right of a third party, dealing with the agent, to gain every possible advantage of the transaction. Hence, where an agent sells in his own name for an undisclosed principal, and the principal sues the buyer for the price, the buyer can not set off a debt due from the agent, unless, in making the purchase, he was induced by the conduct of the principal to believe, and did in fact believe, that the agent was selling on his own account. The rule of George v. Clagett, 7 T. R. 355, does not obtain where the purchaser knows that the agent is not the owner of the goods, or when circumstances are brought to his knowledge which ought to have put him upon inquiry, and by investigating which he would have ascertained that the agent was not the owner." See also, Belfield v. National Supply Co., 189 Pa. St. 189, 69 Am. St. 799; Powell v. Wade, 109 Ala. 95, 55 Am. St. 915.

[37] Bassett v. Lederer, 3 T. & C. (N. Y.) 671, 1 Hun (N. Y.) 274, 280.

of the true condition of things in sufficient time before suit to enable him to recede or to take steps to avoid the suit.[38] Every person has a just right to determine for himself with whom he will contract, and no one can be forced into a contract with another against his will.[39] If, however, the pretended agent—being the real principal—did not disclose or name any person for whom he professed to act, but merely assumed to contract for some unnamed person, or to be acting in the capacity of agent without stating for whom, it is held in England that the suit may be maintained by such assumed agent as the real principal.[40] In such a case, it is reasoned, it could not be well claimed that the other contracting party relied upon the credit or ability of the principal, for none such was named or disclosed; and he could have intended to rely upon no one but the party with whom he contracted,—namely, the one who assumed to act as agent; and his designation as agent will be disregarded as mere *discriptio personae.*

§ **371. Sealed instruments.**—Contracts under seal, or specialties, as we have seen, can not be varied or contradicted by parol, and hence no party not mentioned therein can be introduced into such a contract. If, therefore, a deed of conveyance of the principal's real estate is made by an authorized agent in his (the agent's) own name, it conveys nothing, and no action will lie against the principal on such instrument, for the deed can not be varied or explained by parol. On the other hand, if such a conveyance be made by a party to an agent in his (the agent's) name, as grantee, the principal can not maintain an action thereon for a breach of the covenants therein contained. And the same is true of an executory contract for the purchase of land.[41] And as parol evidence can not be received to explain the intention of the parties, even an attempt to execute such an instrument by an agent in the name of the principal could not be shown to be the act of another than the agent, and the fact that the party executing such instrument described himself as "agent," or "agent of" another party, will not change the character of the instrument or admit extrinsic evidence to show that it was in fact executed by such party as agent for some other person.[42] It is to this class of instruments that the common-law rule which forbids the contradiction of the contents of a writing by parol evidence is most rigidly applied. Instruments under seal, or specialties, were always regarded as possessing more

[38] Story Ag., § 78.

[39] Rayner v. Grote, 15 M. & W. 359.

[40] Schmaltz v. Avery, 16 Q. B. 655.

[41] Briggs v. Partridge, 64 N. Y. 357.

[42] *Ante*, § 333.

sacredness and solemnity than any other class of writings; and while a seal has lost much of its former importance, the distinction between simple contracts and specialties is still recognized, even in states where the requirement for the use of a seal has been entirely abrogated. A contract of this high character can not be turned into a simple contract, and a party can not be introduced into such contract who does not on its face appear to be interested in it.[43] If, therefore, an instrument under seal be executed by a third party to an agent by name, instead of his principal, the latter can not enforce the covenant therein contained, or sue the party who executed it for a breach thereof: such an action can be maintained only by the party to whom, on its face, the instrument purports to have been executed.[44] But if the instrument, though under seal, was not required to be so under the common law, the seal may be disregarded and the instrument treated as a simple contract.[45] In such a case the principal may be made liable in *assumpsit* upon the promise contained in the instrument, which may be resorted to in order to ascertain the terms of the agreement.[46] The same is doubtless true in case of a breach by the third party, in which case the action may be maintained by the principal, if he can show that such is his interest in the contract; for the same rules would then be applicable as in cases of other simple contracts in writing.

§ 372. **Money paid by mistake.**—In *Stevenson* v. *Mortimer*,[47] Lord Mansfield laid down the rule that "where a man pays money by his agent, which ought not to have been paid, either the agent or principal may bring an action to recover it back. The agent may, from the authority of the principal, and the principal may, as proving it to have been paid by the agent."[48] And the same doctrine has been applied where money has been paid by an agent for his principal on a contract which proved to be illegal, the agent being at the time ignorant of the facts which rendered it illegal. Thus, where an agent effected an insurance on a cargo of goods for his principal, who resided in another country, and hostilities had actually broken out between

[43] Briggs v. Partridge, 64 N. Y. 357. See also, Story Ag., § 422.

[44] Shack v. Anthony, 1 Man. & S. 573; Violett v. Powell, 10 B. Mon. (Ky.) 347.

[45] Lancaster v. Knickerbocker Ice Co., 153 Pa. St. 427.

[46] Lancaster v. Knickerbocker Ice Co., 153 Pa. St. 427.

[47] 2 Cowp. 805.

[48] Kent v. Bornstein, 12 Allen (Mass.) 342.

the country in which the insurance was effected and that of the owner of the goods, but news thereof had not reached the country where the insurance was taken out, the vessel with the goods being captured and confiscated, the court held the insurance void, but that the agent, being ignorant of the fact of hostilities when the premium was paid by him, was entitled to have the same returned as money had and received to the agent's use and without consideration.[49] It has been held, however, that if an agent, by mistake, sell the principal's goods for less than the scheduled price, an action by him against an innocent purchaser of the goods to recover the difference will not lie.[50] Where an agent lends his principal's money, taking a note therefor, payable to himself, the note belongs to the principal, who may maintain an action thereon; and if, after notice to him of the principal's superior right, the borrower pays the agent, he does so at his peril.[51] This is because of the privity between the parties, the principal simply asserting and obtaining the fruits of the contract entered into by his agent for him as an unknown principal. But where an agent collects money belonging to his principal and loans it to a third person, to whom the agent is indebted, without notice to the borrower that the money was that of another, the principal can not recover it, even after notice that it did not belong to the agent.[52] In the latter case, it could not be said that there was in the hands of the borrower money of the principal which in equity and good conscience should not be retained by the third party, for the latter, having obtained it from the agent without notice of the claim of the principal, and in view of the indebtedness of the agent to the borrower, had a legal right of set-off against the agent in order to secure his own debt, and could not be deprived of the same by the intervention of the principal's claim. This is so, as the court said in the case last cited, "not only because money has no ear-mark and can not easily be identified, but because a different doctrine would be productive of great mischief." Property other than money, however, stands upon different ground, and where an agent, without authority, disposes of the same to a third party, the latter receives no title.

II. In Tort.

§ **373. For injury to property of principal.**—An agent may maintain an action *ex delicto* against a third person for injury to goods

[49] Oom v. Bruce, 12 East 225.

[50] Hungerford v. Scott, 37 Wis. 341.

[51] Farmers', etc., Bank v. King, 57 Pa. St. 202, 98 Am. Dec. 215.

[52] Lime Rock Bank v. Plimpton, 17 Pick. (Mass.) 159, 28 Am. Dec. 286.

in which the agent had a special property or temporary ownership, with immediate possession. Thus, a bailor may maintain trover against all persons but the rightful owner if property in his possession be taken away from him;[53] and in such case the agent can recover damages for the full value of the property converted.[54] He holds the money over and above his own interest in trust for his principal.[55] He may maintain trover even against the absolute owner for a wrongful conversion by the latter, although he can then only recover damages to the extent of his interest.[56] So, the consignee of undelivered goods may maintain trover against one who has converted them.[57] And, generally, one who is entitled to the immediate possession of goods of which he is wrongfully deprived by another may maintain trover against the wrongdoer.[58] An agent may also maintain an action against a third person for a libel relative to business in which he is engaged for his principal, by reason of which he was injured in the loss of commissions on goods, etc.;[59] although this might not be true of an agent who works on a salary.

B. Of Third Persons to Principal.

§ **374. In general.**—While, as we have seen, those persons who engage in business transactions with an agent who is acting for his principal acquire certain well defined rights against him which he is in duty bound to recognize and live up to, it is true, on the other hand, that the principal also acquires certain reciprocal rights against such persons, and that they assume toward him certain obligations which he may enforce. Such obligations may arise out of contracts express or implied, into which the agent has entered for the principal, or out of torts committed by such third parties, to the injury of the principal, or out of certain conditions from which trusts are created, in equity, in favor of the principal.

I. On Contracts.

§ **375. Principal's right of action on authorized contracts or on unauthorized contracts subsequently ratified.**—The normal way in which an agent generally contracts is in the name of his principal.

[53] Faulkner v. Brown, 13 Wend. (N. Y.) 63.

[54] Finn v. Western R. Corp., 112 Mass. 524, 17 Am. Rep. 128.

[55] White v. Webb, 15 Conn. 302.

[56] Roberts v. Wyatt, 2 Taunt. 268; Pomeroy v. Smith, 17 Pick. (Mass.) 85; Schley v. Lyon, 6 Ga. 530.

[57] Fowler v. Down, 1 B. & P. 44.

[58] Cooley Torts 445-447.

[59] Weiss v. Whittemore, 28 Mich. 366.

When there is an express contract by an agent in the name of a disclosed principal, the latter may, of course, enforce the contract against the third party by suit in his own name the same as if he had entered into it in person.[60] But if the agent, at the time of entering into the contract, acts outside the real or apparent scope of his authority, and the contract is subsequently ratified by the principal, the latter may or may not be entitled to sue on the contract. This will depend upon the solution of the question whether or not the third party may recede from the contract before the principal has ratified it, and after the discovery that the agent's act was without original authority. This question was discussed in a former portion of this work.[61] If the contract is ratified by the principal, not having been previously receded from by the third party, the ratification relates back to the time the contract was entered into, and the rights of the parties are the same as if the contract had been authorized in the first instance. In such case the principal may, of course, maintain an action against the third party for a breach of such contract to the same extent as if the contract had been originally made by his authority; and the third party can not dispute the agent's authority.[62] But if the third party seasonably repudiates the transaction, the principal can not enforce the contract against him.[63] And, as we have hereinbefore pointed out, if any rights intervene in favor of strangers, subsequent to the original transaction, but prior to the ratification, the parties to the contract take subject to the rights of such strangers.[64]

§ 376. **Principal's rights subject to rights of third party.**—But while it is true that, by reason of such contract either originally authorized or subsequently ratified, the principal acquires the right to insist upon a performance and to sue for its breach, yet this right is subject to certain well-recognized qualifications. In the first place, the principal is bound by all the declarations, misrepresentations, concealments and fraud of the agent acting within the scope of his authority, and the principal can not claim any benefit from the contract made by the agent without at the same time making himself

[60] Barry v. Page, 10 Gray (Mass.) 398; Nicoll v. Burke, 78 N. Y. 581; Sharp v. Jones, 18 Ind. 314, 81 Am. Dec. 359; Destrehan v. Cypress Lumber Co., 45 La. Ann. 920; Donanoe v. McDonald, 92 Ky. 123.

[61] *Ante*, §§ 153, 154.

[62] Gold Mining Co. v. National Bank, 96 U. S. 640; Mayer v. McLure, 36 Miss. 389, 72 Am. Dec. 190.

[63] Dodge v. Hopkins, 14 Wis. 686; Wilkinson v. Heavenrich, 58 Mich. 574, 55 Am. Rep. 708.

[64] *Ante*, §§ 144, 285.

responsible for such agent's misconduct.[65] As was well said by the court of appeals of New York: "If an agent defrauds the person with whom he is dealing, the principal, not having authorized or participated in the wrong, may, no doubt, rescind, when he discovers the fraud, on the terms of making complete restitution. But so long as he retains the benefits of the dealing he can not claim immunity on the ground that the fraud was committed by his agent, and not by himself."[66] It is really immaterial whether the agent was acting within the exact scope of his authority or not: if the matter was entirely unauthorized by the principal, but he subsequently ratified it by appropriating the benefits thereof, he will be bound by the misconduct of the agent.[67]

§ 377. **Undisclosed principal.**—If the contract made by the agent for his principal was a simple contract, and either the fact of the agency or the name of the principal was undisclosed, the principal may, nevertheless, as we have seen, avail himself of the benefit of such contract and maintain a suit thereon for its breach;[68] and parol evidence may be introduced to prove such facts.[69] In such case, either the principal or the agent may be bound, at the option of the third party; the agent because he has expressly bound himself by his contract, and the principal because he has authorized the contract to be made for him;[70] it is analogous to the ordinary case of a dormant partner.[71] But this rule also must be taken with some qualification. Thus, if the principal exercises the privilege of appropriating the benefits of the contract to himself, and sues the third party, the latter has the right, as against the principal, to interpose every defense which would have existed in his favor had the agent been the principal and sued upon the contract; the principal's right, in other words, is subject to the equities of the third party.[72] However, if the third party has

[65] Evans Pr. & Ag. (Bedford's ed.) 469; Keough v. Leslie, 92 Pa. St. 424.

[66] Ewell v. Chamberlin, 31 N. Y. 611, 619.

[67] Du Souchet v. Dutcher, 113 Ind. 249; Sandford v. Handy, 23 Wend. (N. Y.) 260.

[68] *Ante*, § 366; Clark v. Smith, 88 Ill. 298; Butler v. Dorman, 68 Mo. 298, 302, 30 Am. Rep. 795.

[69] Salmon Falls Mfg. Co. v. Goddard, 14 How. (U. S.) 446.

[70] Paterson v. Gandasequi, 15 East 62, 3 Smith Ld. Cas. (9th ed.) 1634; Taintor v. Prendergast, 3 Hill (N. Y.) 72, 38 Am. Dec. 618.

[71] Huntington v. Knox, 7 Cush. (Mass.) 371.

[72] Taintor v. Prendergast, 3 Hill (N. Y.) 72, 38 Am. Dec. 618; Traub v. Milliken, 57 Me. 63; Ruiz v. Norton, 4 Cal. 355, 60 Am. Dec. 618; Nave v. Hadley, 74 Ind. 155.

paid the agent before discovering the real principal, or has acquired a set-off against him, the principal will generally be bound by such payment or set-off.[73] But this right of defense can not avail a third party, in case the agent is clothed with only a bare power to sell, without possession of the goods or other *indicia* of ownership; as, for example, in the case of a broker, who does not ordinarily have the possession of the property which he is authorized to sell: a party dealing with such an agent can not, without gross carelessness, be misled into the belief that the agent is really the principal, and can not therefore avail himself of the benefit of a set-off of a debt which the agent owes such third party.[74] But where a sale is made by a factor, instead of a broker, the purchaser can set off a debt owing him from the factor.[75]

§ **378. Third party's right of set-off.**—In a case decided by the English chancery division it was held that before a set-off will be available to the defendant, in case of a sale, the following conditions must be complied with: "1. That the sale should be made by a person intrusted with the possession of the goods; 2. That the agent should sell the goods as his own, and in his own name as principal, by the authority of the principal; and 3. That the purchaser dealt with the agent as, and believed him to be, the principal in the transaction up to the time when the set-off occurred."[76] And it is the duty of the third party to make reasonable efforts to ascertain whether the agent is dealing for himself or for an undisclosed principal; for "if, by due diligence, the buyer could have known in what character the seller acted, there would be no justice in allowing the former to set off a bad debt at the expense of the principal."[77] Where the third party has knowledge of the agency, but not of the principal's name, he is put upon his inquiry as to who the principal is.[78] But it has been held that the mere knowledge by the third party that the person with whom he is dealing is a factor, though he also carries on business on his own account, will not be sufficient notice unless such third party

[73] Peel v. Shepherd, 58 Ga. 365; Bernshouse v. Abbott, 16 Vroom (N. J.) 531, 46 Am. Rep. 789; Crosby v. Hill, 39 Ohio St. 100.

[74] Bernshouse v. Abbott, *supra;* Baring v. Corrie, 2 B. & Ald. 137.

[75] Bliss v. Bliss, 7 Bosw. (N. Y.) 339.

[76] Ex parte Dixon, L. R. 4 Ch. Div. 133.

[77] Miller v. Lea, 35 Md. 396, 6 Am. Rep. 417; Frame v. William Penn Coal Co., 97 Pa. St. 309.

[78] Whelan v. McCreary, 64 Ala. 319.

knew or had good reason to believe that the person was acting as agent for some one in that particular transaction.[79]

§ 379. Where contract is made on exclusive credit of agent.—The rule that an unknown principal may take the benefit of his agent's contract, when in fact it was made in behalf of such principal, has some well known exceptions. In the first place, where the contract between the agent and third person was made by the latter upon the basis of a personal trust or confidence in the agent, who was believed by him to be the principal, the undisclosed principal can not subsequently, without such third person's consent, take the benefit of such contract or maintain an action thereon.[80] No one can be forced to contract with any person contrary to his will; a party has a right to select the person with whom he will deal or enter into contracts. There may be special reasons why he should choose some particular person rather than another: the person to be employed may be an artist or an author, and the employer may prefer a painting from his hand, or a book of his composition, to that of another; or the third party may wish to engage the services of the person on account of his character or some particular traits or qualities: in all these cases the third party has the right to insist that the contract shall be performed by the party whom he had engaged to perform it. Moreover, there may be special reasons why the third party would not desire to deal with a particular person, and he might refuse to enter into a contract if the objectionable person were to be the other party to it; and if the undisclosed principal proves to be such a person he ought not to be permitted thus to thrust himself upon the other contracting party. In such case the undisclosed principal could not be heard to say that he was equally as skillful or competent as the one with whom the other party believed he was dealing or with whom he intended to deal; whether the person to be employed possesses the peculiar skill or ability desired by the other party is a question solely for the determination of the latter, and the freedom of contract can not be infringed by forcing upon one the services of another, contrary to the dictates of his own judgment; whether his reasons are good or bad is a question with which the courts have no concern whatever.[81] If, however, the contract or act

[79] Hogan v. Shorb, 24 Wend. (N. Y.) 458, 461.

[80] Boston Ice Co. v. Potter, 123 Mass. 28, 25 Am. Rep. 9; Winchester v. Howard, 97 Mass. 303, 93 Am. Dec. 93; King v. Batterson, 13 R. I. 117, 43 Am. Rep. 13.

[81] Boston Ice Co. v. Potter, *supra;* Winchester v. Howard, *supra.*

to be performed is of such a nature as not to depend upon any particular skill, ability, or other personal qualifications or traits, and the third party has received the benefit thereof, the law will require him to perform his part of the engagement also. And so, if the party for whose personal services the other stipulated actually performed the same, there is no good reason why the third party should not be required to render performance of his part of the contract to the unknown principal, if there be one. But where the third party deals with the agent upon the express understanding that the latter is the principal, the agent thus pledging his own credit for the performance of the contract, the unknown principal, if there be one, can not enforce performance of the contract from the other party.[82] In that case, the third party could not enforce performance against the principal, if the latter should fail to perform, and there being no mutuality in such contract, it can not be enforced on either side.

§ **380. Sealed instruments.**—Still another exception to the general rule that an undisclosed principal may avail himself of the benefits of a contract made for him by his agent by bringing suit in his own name, is in cases of sealed instruments. When an instrument is one that was required, at common law, to be under seal, we have seen that the courts will recognize only the parties whose names appear in the instrument itself, and will not admit parol evidence to prove that some other party was in fact the principal, obligor or obligee, grantor or grantee.[83] If the instrument was executed by an agent to a third party, and the agent failed to contract in the name of the principal, the agent alone can maintain an action for its breach; and this is true although the agent described himself as such, unless he acted ostensibly for and in the name of the principal.[84] The third party could not, in such case, maintain an action against the principal, because he does not on the face of the instrument stipulate for the performance of the contract; and it would be in violation of the rule that forbids such an instrument to be contradicted or varied by parol evidence, if the other contracting party were permitted to introduce extrinsic evidence to show that some one other than the ostensible obligor or grantor was the party intended to be bound.[85] This being true, and the contract being one of reciprocal obligations, the principal can not maintain an action on such a contract against the third

[82] Winchester v. Howard, *supra*.

[83] *Ante*, § 333.

[84] *Ante*, § 371.

[85] *Ibid*.

party.[86] In such case, however, the principal can generally avail himself of the benefits of the contract by suing in the name of the agent.[87]

§ 381. Implied or quasi-contract—Money paid by mistake.—The third party may also be liable to the principal in some cases on an implied contract, or *quasi*-contractual obligation. It is a general principle of equity that where a party in good faith has paid money to another under a mistake of fact, under circumstances that would render it unconscionable for the party to whom the money was paid to retain it, the person who has thus mistakenly paid such money may recover it from the party to whom it has been so paid.[88] While there is, in such case, no express promise to pay the money back, the courts have established the fiction of a promise by holding that the recipient can not be heard to say that although he has received the money, he has in fact never made any promise to repay it. And it can make no difference whether the money was thus paid by the principal himself or by his agent for him: under such circumstances, as we have seen, either the principal or the agent may sue to recover the money.[89]

§ 382. Money paid in violation of agent's duty—Bona fide recipient of money not affected.—The principle upon which money or property may be recovered, however, is not confined to cases in which money has been paid or property delivered by the agent under an honest mistake or in the belief that he had a right or that it was his duty to pay it: it extends to cases in which the agent pays such money or turns over such other property in violation of his duty; except, in some cases, where the party receiving it is a *bona fide* holder for value and without notice of the misapplication.[90] And it is not necessary that the third party should have known whose money or property it was that the agent was thus misapplying: it is sufficient if he knew that the party from whom he received it was holding it as an agent; and if he receives it with such knowledge he does so at his peril, and to

[86] Sims v. Bond, 5 B. & Ad. (27 E. C. L.) 389; Clarke v. Courtney, 5 Pet. (U. S.) 319; Briggs v. Partridge, 64 N. Y. 357, 21 Am. Rep. 617; Cocke v. Dickens, 4 Yerg. (Tenn.) 29, 26 Am. Dec. 214; Clap v. Day, 2 Greenl. (Me.) 305, 11 Am. Dec. 99.

[87] Violett v. Powell, 10 B. Mon. (Ky.) 347.

[88] Bispham Princ. of Eq. (6th ed.), § 190, *et seq.*

[89] *Ante*, § 372; Stevenson v. Mortimer, 2 Cowp. 806; Ancher v. Bank of England, 2 Doug. 637; Holman v. Frost, 26 S. C. 290.

[90] Rusk v. Newell, 25 Ill. 211; Farmers', etc., Bank v. King, 57 Pa. St. 202, 98 Am. Dec. 215; Mason v. Waite, 17 Mass. 560.

defeat a recovery by the principal he must show authority in the agent so to dispose of it.[91] If, however, the principal has invested the agent with the *indicia* of title to the property or with a semblance of authority to dispose of it, the third party, acting in good faith and paying value therefor, is protected, and the principal can not recover from him.[92]

§ **383. Distinction drawn between money and other property.**—Money or bank notes stand upon a different footing from other personal property, for as money has no ear-marks and can not well be identified, the third party usually acquires a good title to it if he obtains it for value and without notice. But one who buys or otherwise obtains from another personal property other than money generally obtains no better title than the person had from whom he obtained it, and hence the owner may recover either the specific property or its value from the party who has thus received it.[93]

§ **384. Money obtained from agent by fraud or duress.**—Where an agent is compelled to pay the money of his principal by duress, or it is obtained from him by fraud, either the principal or the agent may maintain an action against the wrongdoer for the money thus obtained.[94]

§ **385. Money obtained from agent by gambling, etc.**—A principal's money obtained from an agent on a wager or by gambling may be recovered from the winner by the principal in an action of *assumpsit* for money had and received, where the gambling or winning was unlawful.[95] In such cases the method of obtaining the money is illegal, and the third party can not shield himself behind the defense of innocence; he pays no value for the money, and he obtains it without the semblance of authority from the owner. The principal in such cases not being in *pari delicto,* the doctrine that the courts will not relieve the guilty parties from the consequences of their illegal transactions does not apply.[96] If by statute the losing party is enabled

[91] Gerard v. McCormick, 130 N. Y. 261.

[92] Brewster v. Sime, 42 Cal. 139; Levi v. Booth, 58 Md. 305, 42 Am. Rep. 332; McMahon v. Sloan, 12 Pa. St. 229, 51 Am. Dec. 601, 607; Saltus v. Everett, 20 Wend. (N. Y.) 267, 32 Am. Dec. 541.

[93] Levi v. Booth, 58 Md. 305, 42 Am. Rep. 332.

[94] Stevenson v. Mortimer, 2 Cowp. 805; Stevens v. Fitch, 11 Metc. (Mass.) 248; Holman v. Frost, 26 S. C. 290.

[95] Mason v. Waite, 17 Mass. 560.

[96] In Mason v. Waite, *supra*, the court, speaking through Parker, C. J., said: "The identical bills, paid by Sargent to the defendant, were proved to be the property of the

to recover the money so lost, it furnishes an additional reason for allowing the principal to recover it, although, in such case, the agent may maintain the action, if the principal does not choose to exercise the right.[97]

§ 386. Property wrongfully obtained from agent by barter, pledge or mortgage.—An agent who is authorized by the principal to sell the latter's property has no authority to barter, pledge, mortgage, or give away such property, and a transfer by any other method than that of a sale conveys no title to the purchaser where the agent has only the *indicia* of authority to sell such property. The principal has a right, therefore, to recover such property or its value from the person who has thus obtained it from the agent.[98] Nor has an agent any right or authority to pledge his principal's money or goods for the payment of his own debts; and if he does this, an action will lie by the principal against the party to whom the money was so paid or the property delivered, to recover the money or property or the value of the latter.[99]

plaintiff. They were committed to Sargent, as a carrier, to pay to the order of the plaintiff. They came into the hands of the defendant unlawfully; for gaming is unlawful by our statute. The defendant could have gained no property in them, even as against Sargent, who might have recovered them back within three months. Any other person might have recovered double the amount, without limitation of time; and the defendant was further liable to indictment. How then can he have a right to retain against the true owner, any more than he would a horse, or any other chattel, acquired in the same way? It is true, in such a case, trover would have been the proper action; and, perhaps, would have been the better action in this case, but for the difficulty of identifying bank notes. We do not see, however, why the action for money had and received will not lie. The notes were paid and received as money; and as to any want of privity, or any implied promise, the law seems to be, that where one has received the money of another, and has not a right conscientiously to retain it, the law implies a promise that he will pay it over. Had Sargent paid the money to an innocent person, for a valuable consideration, or to satisfy a debt of his own, the case might have been different; as it would be mischievous to require of persons, who receive money in the way of business, or in payment of debts, to look into the authority of him from whom they receive it."

97 See Allen v. Watson, 2 Hill (S. C.) 319.

98 Lowry v. Beckner, 5 B. Mon. (Ky.) 41; Bertholf v. Quinlan, 68 Ill. 297; Loring v. Brodie, 134 Mass. 453; Bott v. McCoy, 20 Ala. 578, 56 Am. Dec. 223; Hayes v. Colby, 65 N. H. 192.

99 Whitney v. State Bank, 7 Wis. 520; School Trustees v. McCormick, 41 Ill. 323.

§ **387. Demand not necessary before suit.**—No demand is generally necessary as a condition precedent to maintaining the action against the third party by the principal, where the third party has taken possession of the property and exercises acts of ownership over it. Thus, where a horse was let by the owner to another person, and the latter, without authority, bartered him to a third party, who took him and exercised acts of ownership over him, it was held that an action of trover and conversion would lie by the principal against such third party; and proof of a previous demand and refusal was held unnecessary, the exercise of dominion over the animal being sufficient evidence of a conversion.[100]

II. Pursuing Trust Funds.

§ **388. Constructive or resulting trusts.**—The relation of trustor and trustee may arise between parties without an express contract between them to that effect. Thus, where property belonging to a principal comes into the hands of his agent to be applied by him to certain objects, the property becomes stamped with the character of a trust, and can not subsequently be diverted from that purpose by the agent. These trusts are generally spoken of as constructive or resulting trusts.[101] They are so called because they arise not by virtue of any express contract, but result in or are construed as such by operation of law.[101a] Such trusts are created upon equitable principles, to prevent, as far as possible, the transmutation of property by fraudulent means. When such property has been wrongfully disposed of by the agent, the principal may follow it or the proceeds thereof so long as they are distinguishable.[102] It makes no difference whether the property is in its original or in an altered state as between the *cestui que trust* and the trustee and all parties claiming under him, nor even as to third parties, unless the latter be purchasers for a valuable consideration without notice.[103] Any subsequent holder will be affected by the trust, who has acquired the same as a gift, or without parting with value, or with actual or constructive notice of the trust.[104] There need be no active participation in any

[100] Gilmore v. Newton, 9 Allen (Mass.) 171, 85 Am. Dec. 749.

[101] Underhill Trusts & Trustees 12.

[101a] *Ibid.*

[102] Frith v. Cartland, 34 L. J. Ch. 301.

[103] Evans Pr. Ag. (Bedford's ed.) 141.

[104] Farmers', etc., Bank v. Sprague,

fraudulent transaction of the agent by the third party, or in any effort to defeat the trust: it is sufficient to affect him, if he be not an innocent holder for value.[105] So, where an agent loans his principal's money and takes a note therefor, payable to himself, such note belongs to the principal; and if the maker pays it to the agent after notice of the trust, he does so at his peril.[106] The general doctrine here involved is stated by Jordan, J., speaking for the supreme court of the state, in a recent Indiana case, thus: "The authorities generally affirm and support the right of a *cestui que trust* to pursue and recover trust funds wrongfully diverted, where their identity has not been lost, and where they have not passed into the hands of parties for value without notice of the trust. Whenever any property, or fund, in its original state, has once been impressed with the character or nature of a trust, no subsequent change of its original form, or the condition, can divest it of its trust character, so long as it is capable of being identified; and the beneficiary thereof may pursue and reclaim it, regardless of the form into which it may have been changed, provided it has not gone into the possession of a *bona fide* purchaser without notice. All that the law contemplates by requiring the property or fund to be identified is a substantial identification; and, in case the fund consists of money, the *cestui que trust* may reclaim it, although not able to trace the identical coins or bills, so long as its identity as a fund can be ascertained. It is a well settled principle that the abuse of a trust fund by a trustee, or fiduciary, confers no right upon him, nor upon those who claim in privity with him. Where the fund has been misapplied, or converted into other property, or mixed with the funds of the trustee, or those claiming through him, and can be traced and identified, courts will attribute the ownership to the *cestui que trust*, and will not permit the wrongful act of the trustee, or fiduciary, in mixing the trust fund with his own funds or those of a third party, to defeat a recovery, but, in general, in such cases, will separate the trust fund from the others with which it has been commingled, and restore it to the beneficiary entitled to receive it."[107] And if the trust property be other than money, the disposal thereof without

52 N. Y. 605; Drovers' Nat'l Bank v. O'Hare, 18 Ill. App. 182; Gerard v. McCormick, 130 N. Y. 261; Overseers of Poor v. Bank of Virginia, 2 Gratt. (Va.) 544, 44 Am. Dec. 399.

[105] Fifth Nat'l Bank v. Village of Hyde Park, 101 Ill. 595, 40 Am. Rep. 218.

[106] Farmers', etc., Bank v. King, 57 Pa. St. 202, 98 Am. Dec. 215.

[107] Pearce v. Dill, 149 Ind. 136, 142.

authority may be disavowed and set aside by the owner, even if it has found its way into the hands of an innocent purchaser.[108] And so, if the agent purchase property with the funds of his principal, it may be followed into the hands of a third person, though innocent, having no notice of the right of the principal, who purchases for value, for such third person can get no better title than has he from whom the third person derives it.[109] But if the money thus obtained be invested in the purchase of goods which are mixed with others so as to be incapable of identification, a court of equity will not enforce a trust.[110] And the property of the fund or article must be in the principal before the diversion takes place; for if an agent should fraudulently collect commissions from a third party and invest them in other property, the principal can not pursue the fund into the investments, since such fund was not the property of the principal, but only represented a debt due him from the agent for which an action for money had and received would lie.[111]

[108] Lime Rock Bank v. Plimpton, 17 Pick. (Mass.) 159, 28 Am. Dec. 286.

[109] Stevenson v. Kyle, 42 W. Va. 229, 57 Am. St. 854.

[110] Union Nat'l Bank v. Goetz, 138 Ill. 127, 32 Am. St. 119. See the elaborate note to this case at p. 125, *et seq.*, for a thorough review of the authorities upon the subject.

[111] Lister v. Stubbs, L. R. 45 Ch. Div. 1. In the case of Baker v. New York Nat'l Ex. Bank, 100 N. Y. 31, 53 Am. Rep. 150, some commission merchants had sold the goods of their principal and deposited the proceeds with the defendant bank in their own names, as agents. The agents were individually indebted to the bank, and the bank afterwards, upon the agents becoming insolvent, charged its own claim against the funds on deposit with it by said agents. The court, speaking through Andrews, J., said: "The relation between a commission agent for the sale of goods and his principal is fiduciary. The title to the goods until sold remains in the principal, and when sold, the proceeds, whether in the form of money, or notes, or other securities, belong to him, subject to the lien of the commission agent for advances and other charges. The agent holds the goods and the proceeds upon an implied trust to dispose of the goods according to the directions of the principal, and to account for, and pay over to him the proceeds from sales. The relation between the parties in respect to the proceeds of sales is not that of debtor and creditor simply. The money and securities are specifically the property of the principal, and he may follow and reclaim them, so long as their identity is not lost, subject to the rights of a *bona fide* purchaser for value. In case of the bankruptcy of the agent, neither the goods nor their proceeds would pass to his assignees in bankruptcy for general administration, but would be subject to the paramount claim of the principal: Chesterfield Mfg. Co. v. Dehon, 5 Pick. (Mass.) 7, 16 Am. Dec. 367; Merrill

III. In Tort.

§ 389. Injuries to property of principal.—Injuries to the property of the principal, while in the hands of an agent, or, as we have seen,

v. Bank of Norfolk, 19 Pick. (Mass.) 32; Thompson v. Perkins, 3 Mason (U. S.) 232; Knatchbull v. Hallett, L. R. 13 Ch. Div. 696; Duguid v. Edwards, 50 Barb. (N. Y.) 288; Story Ag., § 229. The relation between a principal and a consignee for sale is, however, subject to modification by express agreement, or by agreement implied from the course of business or dealing between them. The parties may so deal that the consignee becomes a mere debtor to the consignor for the proceeds of sales, having the right to appropriate the specific proceeds to his own use. In the present case the bank account against which the check was drawn represented trust moneys belonging to the principals for whom Wilson & Bro. were agents. The deposits to the credit of this account were made in the name of the firm, with the word "agents" added. They were the proceeds of commission sales. Wilson & Bro. became insolvent in October, 1878, and they opened the account in this form for the purpose of protecting their principals, which purpose was known to the bank at the time. The check in question was drawn on this account in settlement for a balance due to plaintiffs, upon cash sales made by the drawers as their agents. It is clear upon the facts that the fund represented by the deposit account was a trust fund, and that the bank had no right to charge against it the individual debt of Wilson & Bro. The bank, having notice of the character of the fund, could not appropriate it to the debt of Wilson & Bro., even with their consent, to the prejudice of the *cestuis que trustent.* The supposed difficulty in maintaining the action arising out of the fact that the money deposited was not the specific proceeds of the plaintiffs' goods, is answered by the case of Van Alen v. American Nat'l Bank, 52 N. Y. 1. Conceding that Wilson & Bro. used the specific proceeds for their own purposes, and their identity was lost, yet when they made up the amounts so used, and deposited them in the trust account, the amounts so deposited were impressed with the trust in favor of the principals, and became substituted for the original proceeds and subject to the same equities. The objection that the deposit account represented not only the proceeds of the plaintiff's goods but also the proceeds of goods of other persons, and that the other parties interested are not before the court, and must be brought in in order to have a complete determination of the controversy, is not well taken. The objection for defect of parties was not taken in the answer, and moreover, it does not appear that there are any unsettled accounts of Wilson & Bro. with any other person or persons for whom they were agents. The check operated as a setting apart of so much of the deposit account to satisfy the plaintiffs' claim. It does not appear tnat the plaintiffs are not equitably entitled to this amount out of the fund, or that there is any conflict of interest between them and any other person or persons for whom Wilson & Bro. acted as consignees. The a conversion of the same, renders the wrongdoer liable either to the owner or agent in damages to the extent of the injury or the value of the property converted,—the possession of the agent being regarded, in such cases, as the possession of the principal; and a judgment against one is a good bar to the action of the other.[112] And where the property of the owner has been taken by a writ of replevin from the possession of the agent, the principal may, even during the pendency of such action, retake it by replevin from the plaintiff in the first action.[113] But if the goods are in possession of an agent or bailee for a given time, by contract with the principal, the latter can not, during the life of such contract, maintain an action of trespass against one who has wrongfully taken the goods from the possession of the one lawfully entitled thereto.[114] If, however, the agent has wrongfully disposed of such property to a third party, the principal may recover the same or the value thereof from such party; as, in such case, the agent can not confer upon the purchaser a better title than he himself has.[115]

§ 390. **Conversion of principal's property by third party.**—The principal has his remedy against both the agent and the third party, when the agent, with the knowledge and consent of such third party, wrongfully converts the principal's property by selling or pledging it to the third party.[116] This is a case in which both the agent and third person participate in the wrong. It may be true, however, that the third person alone is blameworthy,—as, where he wrongfully converts or injures the principal's property, while in the agent's hands, without the knowledge or consent of the agent; or where he perpetrates a fraud upon the agent to the injury of the principal,—as, for example, in the purchase from or sale of goods to such agent for the principal.[117] In case there has been a conversion, the principal may sue in trover for the tort, or he may waive the tort and sue in *assumpsit*, for goods sold and delivered.[118] If the property

presumption, in the absence of any contrary indication, is that the fund was adequate to protect all interests, and that Wilson & Bro. appropriated to the plaintiffs only their just share."

[112] Faulkner v. Brown, 13 Wend. (N. Y.) 64; Thorp v. Burling, 11 Johns. (N. Y.) 285.

[113] White v. Dolliver, 113 Mass. 400, 18 Am. Rep. 502.

[114] Soper v. Sumner, 5 Vt. 274.

[115] Thompson v. Barnum, 49 Iowa 392; Clarke v. Shee, 1 Cowp. 197.

[116] Story Ag., § 437.

[117] Story Ag., § 438.

[118] Story Ag., § 439; Keener *Quasi* Conts. 170, *et seq.*

be other than money, and can be found in the possession of any third party, whether he had notice of the rights of the principal or not, it may be replevied from him by the principal; for the agent could give no better title than he had himself. If it has been changed into other property, the third party will be liable in trover for its value, for the conversion; equity, in such cases, impressing upon the property the character of a trust, and holding the party liable to account to the owner.[119] If the property converted be money or bank bills, the principal can waive the tort and maintain an action for money had and received; unless the third party was ignorant of the principal's rights, in which case no action whatever will lie against him, if he gave value for it.[120]

§ 391. **Fraud of third party in contracting with agent.**—A third party may also be liable to the principal, in a proper case, for a fraud perpetrated upon his agent in connection with a contract entered into between such agent and third person. The party dealing with the agent may, by misrepresentation, false warranty, or other wrongful methods, have overreached the agent and thereby obtained an unfair advantage to the injury of the principal The consequences of such wrongful conduct are, of course, the same as if they had been practiced by the third party in dealing with the principal directly: the latter may rescind or avoid the contract, or sue for damages in an action on the case, or, if the third person has thereby enriched his estate, may waive the tort and sue in general *assumpsit.*[121]

§ 392. **Fraud of third party in collusion with agent.**—The case supposed in the preceding section involves a wrong on the part of the third person only, without the participation therein of the agent. But the third party may enter into collusion with the agent and perpetrate a fraud upon the principal. In such case, the principal would have his remedy against the agent. But he is not confined to this. Public policy forbids the enforcement of a contract against the principal when such contract has been entered into as the result of a conspiracy between the principal's representative and the other party, by which it is intended that the agent and other contracting party

[119] 2 Pomeroy Eq. Jur., § 1047.

[120] *Ante,* § 382.

[121] See Tuckwell v. Lambert, 5 Cush. (Mass.) 23; Perkins v. Evans, 61 Iowa 35; Cushing v. Rice, 46 Me. 303, 71 Am. Dec. 579; Beebe v. Robert, 12 Wend. (N. Y.) 413, 417, 27 Am. Dec. 132.

shall gain an undue advantage over the principal; and it is immaterial whether any actual injury will result to the principal or not.[122] Hence, the principal may rescind the contract, or may avoid it by pleading the wrongful acts in defense of a suit upon such contract.[123] And so, where an agent receives from the third party a secret bonus with the view of being influenced by it to enter into a contract with the third party, and it is shown that he actually was improperly influenced thereby, the principal may rescind or avoid such contract.[124] Thus, in an Illinois case, the evidence disclosed that the owner of a city lot, who was a foreigner by birth and to a great extent ignorant of the English language and of business matters, was induced by frequent solicitations to sign a paper authorizing one who claimed to be acting as his agent to sell the lot for a price far below its real value, of which such owner was also ignorant; the person thus acting as agent being shown to be also the agent of and receiving pay from the purchaser and working for his interest and concealing important facts from such owner, the court refused to enforce specific performance, on the ground that the contract was not entered into with fairness and without misapprehension, but was inequitable and unjust. And as a further ground for refusing the relief, the court said that a contract made by one who acts as the agent of both parties may be avoided by either principal.[125] This was an executory contract. Were such a contract to be fully executed and a conveyance made, the latter would doubtless be set aside on the application of the injured party, or, if the rights of other parties had intervened, an action for damages for deceit would lie.[126] Or the principal may, in such case, if he act before other rights have intervened, and restore to the vendor what he has received from him, sue to rescind the contract and recover whatever property or rights he may have parted with in the transaction.[127]

§ 393. Enticing away or injuring servant.—A third person may also become liable to the principal, in an action of tort, for wrongfully inducing the agent or servant to abandon his employment, without the consent and against the will of the principal or master,

[122] *Ante*, § 72.

[123] Panama, etc., Tel. Co. v. India Rubber, etc., Co., L. R. 10 Ch. 515.

[124] Smith v. Sorby, L. R. 3 Q. B. D. 552, 28 Moak's Rep. 455.

[125] Fish v. Leser, 69 Ill. 394.

[126] See Panama, etc., Tel. Co. v. India Rubber, etc., Co., L. R. 10 Ch. 515; Glaspie v. Keator, 5 C. C. A. 474, 56 Fed. 203.

[127] Mechem Ag., § 798.

thereby causing loss of services and profits and advantages to the latter which he would have derived therefrom, if these can be determined from the facts in the case.[128] And in such a case, where the element of malice is an ingredient, even exemplary damages may be recovered.[129] "It is not necessary," said the supreme court of South Carolina, "to refer to authority to show that an action was maintainable at common law for enticing a servant from the service of his master. To sustain it there must be an actual binding contract of service, and where this exists, such an interference by a third person as results in its violation will render him liable to the master, not only for his actual loss, but for such further compensation in the way of damages as may be demanded by the character of the circumstances attending the injury through which the loss was inflicted."[130] An action in tort will also lie for an injury to the servant inflicted by the negligence of a third party; as, for example, where a carrier negligently injures an apprentice, while carrying him, from which injury a loss of services occur to the master.[131] The same liability will arise, of course, if the personal injury to the servant is from other causes than that of negligence; as, for example, the seduction of a man's daughter.[132] And upon the same ground, it has been held that a railroad company can maintain an action for damages against one who maliciously causes the arrest of its engineer while running a train, with intent to delay the train and injure the company.[133]

[128] Walker v. Cronin, 107 Mass. 555.

[129] Bixby v. Dunlap, 56 N. H. 456, 22 Am. Rep. 475, and note at p. 485.

[130] Daniel v. Swearengen, 6 S. C. 297, 24 Am. Rep. 471.

[131] Ames v. Union R. Co., 117 Mass. 541, 19 Am. Rep. 426. See also, Haskins v. Royster, 70 N. C. 601, 16 Am. Rep. 780.

[132] Kennedy v. Shea, 110 Mass. 147, 14 Am. Rep. 584.

[133] St. Johnsbury, etc., R. Co. v. Hunt, 55 Vt. 570, 45 Am. Rep. 639. In this case the supreme court of Vermont, in passing upon the question of what may be taken into consideration by the jury in assessing damages in such cases, said: "It is further insisted that the action can not be maintained because the damages are consequential and too remote. We think the injury and damages were direct. They were not only such as could reasonably have been contemplated at the time, which is one of the tests laid down in Sedgwick on Damages, vol. 1, marg. p. 66–67, but they were the damages actually contemplated. In Derry v. Flitner, 118 Mass. 131, the court say: 'A wrongdoer is liable not only for those injuries which are caused directly and immediately by his act, but also for such consequential injuries as, according to the common experience of men, are likely to result from his act.' Sedg-

wick, p. 88, says the disposition of courts is to include in the injurious consequences, flowing from the illegal act, those that are 'very remote.' No extreme view is required here. It can not be said that the stoppage and delay of the plaintiffs' train was a remote result of the defendant's act. It was the probable, if not necessary, result. And it was in fact the direct, proximate, immediate and contemplated result. Familiar cases, often cited as showing what damages are not too remote to be included in the recovery, are: McAfee v. Crofford, 14 How. (U. S.) 447; Gunter v. Astor, 4 Moore 12, 16 E. C. L. 357; Gribb v. Swan, 13 Johns. (N. Y.) 381; Vandenburgh v. Truax, 4 Denio (N. Y.) 464, 47 Am. Dec. 268; Burrows v. March Gas, etc., Co., L. R. 5 Ex. 67; Scott v. Kenton, 81 Ill. 96; Tarleton v. M'Gawley, Peake 205. In the latter case it was held by Lord Kenyon, at *nisi prius*, that an action lay for firing on negroes on the coast of Africa, and thereby deterring them from trading with the plaintiffs, so that the plaintiffs lost their trade. There the trespass was directly against the negroes, but the wrong intended and the injury actually done was to the plaintiffs. The defendant cites the case of Ashley v. Harrison, Peake 194, where the proprietors of a theater brought an action against the defendant for having written a libel upon one of the plaintiff's singers, by which she was deterred from appearing, whereby his profits were lost. Lord Kenyon held that the damages were too remote, but this was on the ground that the damages arose from the vain fears or caprice of the actress. She could have sung but would not. Her fears or caprice intervened between the wrongful act and the alleged result. To make the case parallel to this she should have been driven from the stage while performing her part, by unlawful interference of the defendant, for the purpose of injury to the plaintiff. See Hughes v. McDonough, 14 Vroom (N. J.) 459, 39 Am. Rep. 603."

CHAPTER XI.

ATTORNEYS AT LAW.

I. Qualification and Admission to Practice.

§ **394. Purpose of this chapter.**—We have heretofore given the definitions of the various terms by which practicing lawyers are known, such as attorneys at law, barristers, solicitors, proctors, sergeants, counselors, advocates, etc.[1] We now propose to consider this subject more in detail. We shall examine into the necessary qualifications of lawyers entitling them to practice their profession; the procedure incident to such admission; the relation which the practicing attorney sustains to the court and to the client; and the duties, obligations, rights and privileges owing by and to him by virtue of his office.

§ 395. Admission to practice, generally—Test oaths.—The admission to the practice of law, under the common law, is more in the nature of a privilege than a general right.[2] This is shown by the fact that it is required that, before any person shall be entitled to practice law, he must be *admitted* to the bar and thus *permitted* to practice law.[3] Moreover, in the absence of constitutional or statutory provisions, the power to admit to the practice of law rests entirely with the courts.[4] The admission of lawyers to the bar is generally regarded as a judicial function which can be exercised only by the courts; and grave doubts have been expressed whether the legislature has power even to prescribe the conditions upon which such admission may be made.[5] In the absence of constitutions or statutes to the contrary, and even supplementary to statutory rules of procedure, the admission of attorneys is generally regulated by rules of court.[6] But in the absence of constitutional regulations, it is generally conceded that the subject is within the legislative control, the same as in the case of other professions;[7] it is accordingly held that the legislature may prescribe such qualifications for admission as it may deem proper.[8] During

[1] *Ante*, 23.

[2] Cohen v. Wright, 22 Cal. 293; In re Day, 181 Ill. 73, 50 L. R. A. 519.

[3] Wharton Ag., § 557; Cobb v. Judge Sup. Ct., 43 Mich. 289; Bullard v. VanTassell, 3 How. Pr. (N. Y.) 401; In re Spicer, 1 Tuck. (N. Y.) 80; Newburger v. Campbell, 58 How. Pr. (N. Y.) 313, 9 Daly (N. Y.) 102; Rader v. Snyder, 3 W. Va. 413.

[4] Ex parte Secombe, 19 How. (U. S.) 9; In re Cooper, 22 N. Y. 67; In re Leach, 134 Ind. 665, 21 L. R. A. 701; In re Day, 181 Ill. 73, 50 L. R. A. 519.

[5] In re Goodell, 39 Wis. 232, 20 Am. Rep. 42; Splane's Petition, 123 Pa. St. 527, 16 Atl. 481; In re Day, 181 Ill. 73, 50 L. R. A. 519.

[6] Weeks Attys. at Law, § 42; In re Day, *supra*.

[7] Cohen v. Wright, 22 Cal. 293; Ex parte Yale, 24 Cal. 241, 85 Am. Dec. 62; In re Cooper, 22 N. Y. 67.

[8] Cohen v. Wright, 22 Cal. 293; Ex parte Yale, 24 Cal. 241, 85 Am. Dec. 62; In re Leach, 134 Ind. 665, 21 L. R. A. 701.

and immediately after the civil war, congress and several of the state legislatures prescribed as a test for the admission of attorneys to the practice in the courts of the United States and such states, respectively, an oath that the applicant had not aided or abetted the rebellion, etc. These acts were generally held void as being *ex post facto*, and in violation of the general pardon granted by the president;[9] but in some of the states the power of the legislature to exact such an oath was upheld;[10] and but for the objections named, the requirement for such an oath would doubtless be valid, except, perhaps, in jurisdictions where the power of the legislature to interfere is denied altogether. In some states an oath is required of an applicant for admission to the bar that he has not been concerned in any duel since a certain period, or at any time, and that he will not engage in one.[10a]

§ 396. Qualifications—Graduation from law school.—If it were not for constitutional provisions to the contrary, the legislature, according to many authorities, would have the power, within reasonable limits, to prescribe the qualifications necessary for admission to the bar.[11] Where the constitution required that every male person twenty-one years old and of good moral character, possessing the necessary qualifications to practice law, should be admitted to practice, it was held by the supreme court of New York that the legislature could not pass a valid law by which graduates of a certain law school should be deemed to possess sufficient learning, and be admitted to the bar without an examination;[12] but this decision was reversed by the court of appeals.[13] The validity of this act of the legislature was assailed partly upon the ground that it ignored the constitutional requirement that the applicant must be a male citizen of the age of twenty-one

[9] Ex parte Garland, 4 Wall. (U. S.) 333; Cummings v. Missouri, 4 Wall. (U. S.) 277; Ex parte Quarrier, 2 W. Va. 569, 4 W. Va. 210; Ex parte Law, 35 Ga. 285; Champion v. State, 3 Coldw. (Tenn.) 111.

[10] State v. Garesche, 36 Mo. 256; Cohen v. Wright, 22 Cal. 293; Ex parte Yale, 24 Cal. 241, 85 Am. Dec. 62.

[10a] See In re Blake, 1 Blackf. (Ind.) 483; Leigh's Case, 1 Munt. (Va.) 468; Ex parte Faulkner, 1 W. Va. 269; Ingersoll v. Howard, 1 Heisk. (Tenn.) 247. Such acts are not unconstitutional: In re Blake, *supra*. *Contra*, In re Dorsey, 7 Port. (Ala.) 293.

[11] In re Leach, 134 Ind. 665, 21 L. R. A. 701; In re Cooper, 22 N. Y. 67.

[12] In re Graduates, 19 How. Pr. (N. Y.) 97, 133, 10 Abb. Pr. (N. Y.) 348, 31 Barb. (N. Y.) 353.

[13] In re Cooper, 22 N. Y. 67.

years, and of good moral character. The court of appeals overruled this contention, however, by resorting to a liberal construction of the act in question, interpreting it to mean that the applicant must not only be a graduate of the law school named, but must possess all the other qualifications required by the constitution, as to age, sex, etc.; and with this construction the constitutionality of the law was upheld. In Indiana the constitution provides that every person of good moral character, being a voter, shall be entitled to admission to practice law in all courts of justice.[14] This provision has been by general consent interpreted to mean that no other qualifications than a good moral character and the right to vote shall be necessary in order to be admitted to the practice of law. An attempt was made, at the general election of 1900, so to amend the constitution of Indiana as to confer upon the general assembly the power to prescribe, by law, what qualifications should be necessary for admission to practice law in all courts of justice.[15] By a decision of the supreme court it was declared that the amendment had not received the required number of votes, and that it was, therefore, not adopted.[16] This case is the first authoritative construction of the constitutional provision as to the qualifications required of applicants for admission to practice; and it seems to hold that an applicant can not be denied admission on account of his unwillingness to submit to an examination as to his learning in the law. The legislature has sought to obviate the objectionable features of the constitutional provision which enables one not possessing any legal education whatever to practice law in all the courts of the state, by the enactment of a statute making it the duty of every court to keep a roll of attorneys, upon which shall be placed the names of all such attorneys, and only such, as have been admitted to practice after an examination by a committee of the bar appointed by the judge, touching the applicant's learning in the law. This statute has been practically a dead letter, however; and since the decision of *In re Denny* has been promulgated, it is questionable whether any one can be kept from being admitted to practice, and consequently from being treated in every way as a member in good standing at the bar, if he be a legal voter and have a good moral character. The legislature of Wisconsin enacted a law in 1849 containing substantially the same provisions as to the right to practice law as those

[14] Ind. Const., art. 7, § 21; Burns R. S. 1901, § 21.

[15] Acts 1900, p. 560.

[16] In re Denny, 156 Ind. 104, 59 N. E. 359.

contained in the constitution of Indiana, but the act was not generally enforced. Concerning that act the supreme court of that state, through Ryan, C. J., expressed its views in the following strong language:—"We do not understand that the circuit courts generally yielded to the unwise and unseemly act of 1849, which assumed to force upon the courts, as attorneys, any persons of good moral character, however unlearned or even illiterate; however disqualified by nature, education or habit, for the important trust of the profession. We learn from the clerk of this court that no application under that statute was ever made here. The good sense of the legislature has long since led to its repeal. And we have too much reliance on the judgment of the legislature to apprehend another such attempt to degrade the courts. The state suffers essentially by every such assault of one branch of the government upon another; and it is the duty of all the coördinate branches scrupulously to avoid even all seeming of such. If, unfortunately, such an attack on the dignity of the courts should again be made, it will be time for them to inquire whether the rule of admission be within the legislative or the judicial power. But we will not anticipate such an unwise and unbecoming interference in what so peculiarly concerns the courts, whether the power to make it exists or not."[17] Doubtless the general assembly of Indiana would long since have repealed the provision in question had it been in its power to do so; for it has repeatedly given expression of such intention by the proposal of constitutional amendments for its abrogation; but the process of changing the fundamental law is more tardy than that of ordinary legislation, and it is not easy to predict how long this obstruction to the judicial progress of a great state will continue to stand.

§ 397. Educational qualification—Examination—Diploma.—In all the states and territories,—except the state of Indiana,—as well as in the District of Columbia, applicants for admission to the bar are required to undergo some kind of an examination as to their learning in the law, etc., either before the court in session, a committee of attorneys appointed by the court, or a state board of examiners.[18]

[17] In re Goodell, 39 Wis. 232, 20 Am. Rep. 42.

[18] *Alabama:*—Written examination by the court, passed on by supreme court judges: Civ. Code 1896, ch. 12, §§ 579–587; Pamph. Acts 1897, p. 1482. *Alaska:*—Examination by judges of district court, or their appointees: 31 U. S. Stat. at Large, p. 448, §§ 731–736. *Arizona:*—Ex-

Many jurisdictions have adopted, in addition, a preliminary test of the general educational qualification of the applicant, in some in-

amination in open court before board of examiners of district court admits to district and inferior courts; admission to supreme court admits to all other courts in territory: Rev. St. 1901, §§ 391-399. *Arkansas:*—Public examination in state courts: Sand. & H. Stat. 1894, §§ 422-424; Sup. Ct. Rules, 52 S. W. v. *California:*—Examination in open court by justices of supreme court or by three or more supreme court commissioners appointed by supreme court: Desty Code Civ. Proc. 1899, §§ 275-279; Rules Supr. Ct., 64 Pac. vii. *Colorado:*—Examination by committee of law examiners appointed by supreme court: Mills Ann. Stat., p. 465, §§ 196-198; Rules Supr. Ct. 39-47, 49 Pac. v-vii. *Connecticut:*—Examination by commission of fifteen: Gen. Stat. 1888, §§ 784, 785, 3264; Rules Supr. Ct., 26 Atl. xviii, xix. *Delaware:*—Examination by judges: Rev. Stat. 1893, ch. 92, p. 698, § 6, ch. 24, p. 234, § 4; 13 Del. Laws, ch. 117, § 3. *District of Columbia:*—Examination by board of examiners: Rules Supr. Ct. & Ct. of App. *Florida:*—Examination in open court before judge and two members of bar: Laws 1899, ch. 4745; Rules Supr. Ct., 18 So. vi. *Georgia:*—Written examination by board of examiners appointed by supreme court: Act Dec. 19, 1898, p. 83; Rules Supr. Ct., 33 S. E. v-vii. *Idaho:*—Examination in open court by judges of supreme court admits to all courts; by district courts admits to them only: Rev. Stat. 1887, §§ 3990-3994; Supr. Ct. Rules, 32 Pac. v, vi. *Illinois:*—Written and oral test by state board of examiners, uniform throughout state: Hurd's Rev. Stat. 1899, ch. 13, §§ 1-4; Supr. Ct. Rules, § 39, 41 N. E. ix, x, 47 N. E. ix-xi. *Indian Territory:*—Examination in open court: Stat. 1899, § 419. *Iowa:*—Examination by supreme court or by board of examiners appointed by court: Ann. Code 1897, §§ 309-315; Act Apr. 16, 1900, p. 6. *Kansas:*—Examination by district court: Gen. Stat. 1901, §§ 388-392, 406; Supr. Ct. Rules, 58 Pac. vii. *Kentucky:*—Examination before two judges of court of appeals or commission of attorneys appointed by circuit court: Barb. & Carr. St. 1894, §§ 97-99. *Louisiana:*—Examination by committee of examiners appointed by supreme court: Rev. Laws 1897, §§ 111-115, 756; Supr. Ct. Rules, 20 So. v, 21 So. xi, xii, 26 So. vii. *Maine:*—Written and oral examination before state board appointed by governor on recommendation of chief justice: Act Mar. 17, 1899, p. 148. *Maryland:*—Written examination before state board of examiners appointed by court of appeals: Laws 1898, ch. 139; Rules of Ct. of App., 44 Atl. v, vi; 50 Atl. vii. *Massachusetts:*—Examination before state board of examiners for admission to supreme court: Acts 1897, ch. 508; Acts 1898, ch. 384; Rules Supr. Ct., 50 N. E. v. *Michigan:* — Written and oral examination for admission to supreme court before state board of examiners appointed by governor on recommendation of supreme court: Comp. Laws 1897, §§ 1119-1121, 1123, 1124. *Minnesota:*—Written and oral examination before state board of examiners: Stat. 1898, §§ 6172, 6174, 6175; Laws stances requiring the latter to pass an examination in certain branches, and in others to produce evidence of having taken the course in a high

1899, ch. 60; Rules Supr. Ct., 44 N. W. iv, 66 N. W. iv. *Mississippi:*—Written examination before chancery court of county of residence: Code 1892, §§ 202-209, 211. *Missouri:*—Oral examination in open court by judge or judges of court and by committee of three attorneys: Rev. Stat. 1899, §§ 4919-4921, 4937. *Montana:*—Examination — principally written — before supreme court: Code Civ. Proc. 1895, §§ 390-394, 396; Sup. Ct. Rule No. 17, in 13 Mont. 578; Supr. Ct. Rules, 57 Pac. ix, x. *Nebraska:*—Examination before supreme court or commission appointed by supreme court: Comp. Stat. 1901, ch. 7, §§ 2-9; Rules Supr. Ct., 83 N. W. vii, viii, 84 N. W. 611. *Nevada:*—Written examination in open court, at discretion of supreme court, by district judge and two attorneys, constituting board of examiners: Gen. Stat. 1885, §§ 2529-2535; Rules Supr. Ct., 62 Pac. vi. *New Hampshire:*—Examination by supreme court: Pub. Stat. 1901, ch. 213, §§ 1-5. *New Jersey:*—Examination before board of examiners: Gen. Stat., p. 1043, § 140, p. 2330, § 6, p. 2603, § 396; Rules Supr. Ct. 1885. *New Mexico:*—Examination by board of examiners for admission to supreme court: Gen. Laws 1897, § 1040a; Supr. Ct. Rules 1897. *New York:*—Oral or written examination before state board of examiners in any department of supreme court: Birdseye Stat. (2d ed.), pp. 167, 168, §§ 2-6; Supr. Ct. Rules, 48 N. E. vi-viii. *North Carolina:*—Written test before two or more justices of supreme court: Code, vol. 1, §§ 17-20; Supr. Ct. Rules, 39 S. E. v. *North Dakota:*—Examination before supreme court or committee: Laws 1901, ch. 23; Supr. Ct. Rules, 74 N. W. xii. *Ohio:*—Oral and written examination by "standing committee on examinations:" Bates Ann. Stat. (2d ed.), §§ 559-562; Supr. Ct. Rules, 35 N. E. vi, vii. *Oklahoma:*—Examination by court; by district court admits to practice in supreme court: Stat. 1893, §§ 316, 317; Supr. Ct. Rules, 43 Pac. ix. *Oregon:*—Examination by supreme court, in open court, for admission to same, which admits to all other courts: Hill's Ann. Laws 1892, §§ 1034-1036; *id.*, p. 1052a; Supr. Ct. Rules, 37 Pac. ix, x. *Pennsylvania:* — Examination by board of examiners: Pepper & L. Dig., p. 224, §§ 1, 3; Rule 8, Bd. of Exrs. *Rhode Island:*—Examination by board of examiners: Pub. Stat. 1882, ch. 192, § 7; Supr. Ct. Rules, 39 Atl. vi. *South Carolina:*—Written examination by supreme court: Rev. Stat. 1893, §§ 2288-2290; Supr. Ct. Rules. *South Dakota:*—Examination by supreme court or commission of examiners: Laws 1901, ch. 60; In re Applications for Admission to Practice, 14 S. Dak. 429, 85 N. W. 992. *Tennessee:*—Examination by two judges or chancellors or the faculty of any law school of the state: Shannon's Code 1896, §§ 5772, 5775-5779; Supr. Ct. Rules. *Texas:*—Examination before district court by committee appointed by court admitting to inferior courts; before supreme court admitting to all courts: Rev. Stat. 1895, §§ 255-260; Supr. Ct. Rules. *Utah:*—Examination by supreme court or by board of examiners: Rev. Stat. 1898, §§ 105-110; Supr. Ct. Rules, 49 Pac.

school in good standing.[19] In some states it is provided by law that a diploma from some particular law school or a law school in good standing shall admit the applicant without examination.[20] Such a

xiii. *Vermont:* — Examination by commission of attorneys, who report to supreme court: Stat. 1894, § 1003; Supr. Ct. Rules. *Virginia:*—Written and oral examination by three or more justices of supreme court of appeals: Code 1887, § 3193; Supp. Code 1898, §§ 3191, 3193; Supr. Ct. Rules, 27 S. E. xvii. *Washington:* —Written examination by committee; oral examination in addition before supreme court by court or committee: Ballinger's Code, §§ 4759–4764; Rules Supr. Ct., 40 Pac. xii, xiii. *West Virginia:*—Examination by committee appointed by supreme court: Acts 1901, ch. 62, amending sections 1 and 2 of ch. 119 of Code; Rules of Supr. Ct. & Bd. of Ex'rs. *Wisconsin:*—Examination by state board of examiners: Sanb. & B. Stat. 1898, § 2586. *Wyoming:* — Written examination by state board of examiners or district judge: Rev. Stat. 1899, §§ 3305, 3310; Supr. Ct. Rules, 58 Pac. viii, ix.

[19] This course was recommended by the committee on legal education of the American Bar Association in 1897. It has been adopted in Colorado, Connecticut, Illinois, Iowa, New Jersey, Ohio, Rhode Island and Vermont. See the citations of Statutes and Rules of Court under note 18, *supra*. *Delaware:*—Requires examination in Latin, higher mathematics, and in English and American history. *Minnesota:*—Applicant may be required to prove that he has passed examinations in one year's Latin, English and American history, English composition and rhetoric, and common school branches. *New York:*—Applicants not graduates of colleges of good standing must undergo examination under authority of the State University in English composition, advanced English, one year Latin, arithmetic, algebra, geometry, United States and English history, civics and economics or their equivalents. *Pennsylvania:* — Examination upon the branches of a good English education. See citations under note 18, *supra*.

[20] *Alabama:*—Diploma from University of Ala.—LL. B. degree. *Georgia:*—Graduates of law department of State University; of law school, Mercer University; of law department, Emory College, and of Atlanta Law School, without examination. *Kansas:*—Graduates of law school of Kansas University. *Louisiana:*—Diploma from law department of Louisiana University. *Michigan:*—Graduates of law department of University of Michigan. *Minnesota:*—Graduates of law department of University of Minnesota and St. Paul College of Law. *Mississippi:*—Graduates of law department of University of Mississippi. *Missouri:*—Graduates of law department of State University; Kansas City School of Law or Benton College of Law. *Nebraska:*—Graduate of College of Law of University of Nebraska. *North Dakota:* —Graduates from law department of State University. *Pennsylvania:* —Graduates from law department of University of Pennsylvania. *South Carolina:*—Graduates of law school of State University. *Tennessee:*—Faculty of any law school may grant license to practice. *Texas:*—Graduate of law school of

provision has been held constitutional.[21] But in a recent Illinois case the supreme court of that state asserts in strong language the inherent right of the courts to pass upon the question of admissibility of persons as members of the bar, as a judicial question, and denies the right of the legislature to override the rules of the court respecting admission to the bar, as an unconstitutional assumption by the legislature of judicial power.[21a] In this case the legislature had passed an act by virtue of which those who began the study of law prior to a certain period would be eligible to admission to the bar at the expiration of two years, while those who began afterward would be compelled to comply with the rules of the supreme court, which required three years. The supreme court declared the act unconstitutional as being special legislation; saying:—"The right to practice law is a privilege, and a license for that purpose makes the holder an officer of the court, and confers upon him the right to appear for litigants to argue causes, and to collect fees therefor, and creates certain exemptions, such as from jury service and arrest on civil process while attending court. The law conferring such privileges must be general in its operation. * * * Another fatal objection to the permission in question is that the legislature, in its enactment, overlooked the restraint imposed by

State University. *West Virginia:* —Diploma from law school of West Virginia University. *Wisconsin:*— Graduates of law department of State University. See the citations in note 18, *supra*, for statutes, etc.

[21] In re Cooper, 22 N. Y. 67, reversing s. c. sub nom. In re Graduates, 19 How. Pr. (N. Y.) 97, 10 Abb. Pr. (N. Y.) 348, 31 Barb. (N. Y.) 353. In Florida an act passed in 1897, entitled "An act to regulate admissions to the bar of this state, to create a board of legal examiners, and to provide for a uniform system of legal examinations," was held unconstitutional because it created state officers on the board of legal examiners and failed to provide for their election by the people or appointment by the governor, as required by the constitution, but made such officers appointive by the supreme court and fixed their terms of office for a term longer than the constitutional limit: State v. Hocker, 39 Fla. 477. In a recent case decided by the supreme court of Illinois a statute was declared unconstitutional which undertook to override the rules of the supreme court of that state respecting admission of attorneys to the bar, by requiring that any person who began to study law before a specified date, provided he had obtained a diploma from a law school of the state after a specified period of attendance, or passed a satisfactory examination before an examining board, should be admitted to practice. The court held the statute to be an unconstitutional assumption by the legislature of power properly belonging to the courts: In re Day, 181 Ill. 73, 50 L. R. A. 519.

[21a] In re Day, 181 Ill. 73, 50 L. R. A. 519.

the constitution, and assumed the exercise of a power properly belonging to the courts. A provision which has been incorporated in each successive constitution of this state is found in the present constitution as article 3, in the following language: "The powers of the government of this state are divided into three distinct departments,—legislative, executive and judicial; and no person or collection of persons, being one of these departments, shall exercise any power properly belonging to either of the others, except as hereinafter expressly directed or permitted.'" From this provision in the organic law of the state the court proceeds to discuss the relative powers of legislatures and courts upon the subject under consideration, reviewing the history of parliamentary legislation with reference to it, and holding that even if parliament could have exercised such powers, the state legislature can not do so, owing to its prescribed constitutional limitations. The court, after noticing the decisions of the courts in this country respecting this subject, and deploring the legislative enactments and constitutional provisions which declare that any male citizen of good moral character who is twenty-one years old may practice law, proceeds to say:—"This court has never acknowledged the power of the legislature to prescribe reasonable conditions which will exclude from the practice in our courts. * * * The effect of enforcing such a statute would be to degrade the profession and fill the ranks with those not qualified by our rules. * * * In any consideration of the question it must not be forgotten that restrictions upon the privilege of practicing law are created only in the interest of the public welfare, and neither for nor against the student. No one who has commenced preparation has any inchoate right on account of that fact, but is bound to furnish the test of fitness required when he asks to enter upon the practice. * * * The legislature may enact police legislation for the protection of the public against things hurtful or threatening to their safety and welfare. So long as they do not infringe upon the powers properly belonging to the courts, they may prescribe reasonable conditions which will exclude from the practice those persons through whom injurious consequences are likely to result to the inhabitants of the state. * * * It would be strange, indeed, if the court can control its own court-room and even its own janitor, but that it is not within its power to inquire into the ability of the persons who assist in the administration of justice as its officers. The function of determining whether one who seeks to become an officer of the courts, and to conduct causes therein, is sufficiently acquainted with the rules established by the legislature and the courts governing the rights of parties and under which justice is administered, pertains to the courts themselves. They must decide whether he has sufficient legal learning to enable him to apply those rules to varying conditions of fact, and to bring the facts and law before the court, so that a correct conclusion may be reached. The order of admission is the judgment of the court that he possesses the requisite qualifications, under such restrictions and limitations as may be properly imposed by the legislature for the protection and welfare of the public. The fact that the legislature may prescribe the qualifications of doctors, plumbers, horseshoers, and persons following other professions or callings, not connected with the judicial system, and may say what shall be evidence of such qualifications, can have no influence on this question. * * * The attorney is a necessary part of the judicial system, and his vocation is not merely to find persons who are willing to have lawsuits. He is the first one to sit in judgment on every case, and whether the court shall be called upon to act depends on his decision. * * * Whatever may have been the propriety of the rule admitting the holder of a diploma issued by a law school to practice, in view of the law schools existing at its adoption the rule had become an alarming menace to the administration of justice. The legislature of New York, by the statute above referred to, only sought to admit the graduates of a great university, who had been examined by eminent lawyers; but, under our rule, persons were admitted who had been only nominally in attendance for the stipulated period of time, upon schools of a very different grade. There was no state supervision of law schools, and any person who saw fit could organize a law school, and by advertising that the diplomas admitted to the bar, could obtain students. The language of the proviso, 'Any law school regularly organized under the laws of this state,' is mere sound, and means nothing. Anything in the form of a law school is regular, so far as the laws of this state are concerned. In view of the disastrous consequences to the profession and the public, the rule by which it was only a step from the diploma mill to the bar was changed, and, in an effort to discharge a duty to the public, the general standard of admission was raised. * * * It was a valid rule of the court, acting within its unquestionable jurisdiction, and the question is whether the legislature could rightfully encroach upon a power belonging to the judicial department, and set aside the rule. The constitution answers the question in the negative."

§ 398. **Moral character.**—In all jurisdictions applicants for admission to the bar are required to produce evidence of good moral character. This requirement has relation only to the character of the applicant for honesty and integrity such as fit him for the faithful and honest transaction of the business intrusted to him as a practicing attorney.[22] The courts are not limited in their inquiry as to the moral character of the applicant to the certificate produced by him, but may look behind it, and are bound to do so in cases attended with suspicious circumstances.[23] A finding that the applicant for readmission has been honest and upright in his business relations outside of his profession, is not equivalent to a finding that he is a person of good moral character.[24] In Indiana the statute provides that upon the question of the moral character of an applicant for admission, any citizen of the county may demand a jury;[25] but the supreme court of the state has decided that an application for readmission to practice is triable only by the court.[26] The words "good moral character," while general in their application, include all the elements essential to make up a good character, such as common honesty and veracity in professional intercourse;[27] and the collection of money and failure to pay it over to the proper person after repeated demands is such misconduct as will prevent an admission to the bar.[28]

§ 399. **Qualification as to age.**—In all the states except those mentioned below, statutes exist requiring that the person desiring to be admitted to the practice must be at least twenty-one years of age, or "of full age," as some of the statutes express it. The following states are exceptions to this general rule:—In Delaware the applicant need be but eighteen years old;[29] in Georgia the age is not mentioned and is, therefore, immaterial;[30] in Kansas he need only be a citizen of the United States;[31] in Maryland nothing is mentioned as to age.[32] A statute of Arkansas,[33] providing that the circuit court may remove disabilities of infants so as to enable them to do business as adults, is held by the supreme court of that state not to abrogate the provision of the prior statute requiring applicants for admission to the bar to be of the age of twenty-one years.[34] But under a similar statute in Florida, the court holds that a minor has a right to be

22 State v. Byrkett, 4 Ohio Dec. 89.

23 In re Attorney's License, 21 N. J. L. 345.

24 Ex parte Walls, 73 Ind. 95.

25 Burns Rev. Stat. 1901, § 974.

26 Ex parte Walls, 73 Ind. 95.

27 In re O——, 73 Wis. 602.

28 *Ibid.*

29 Del. R. S. 1874, ch. 92, § 6, ch. 24, § 4; Del. Laws, ch. 117, § 3.

30 Ga. Civ. Code 1895, §§ 4397-4412; Act Dec. 18, 1897, amended act Dec. 19, 1892.

31 Gen. Stat. 1899, §§ 388-392.

32 Pub. Gen. Laws 1888, art. 10, partly repealed; Laws 1898, ch. 139.

33 Mausf. Dig., § 1362.

34 Ex parte Coleman, 54 Ark. 235.

examined and admitted, if qualified, and that he may enforce such right by mandamus.[35]

§ 400. Qualification as to sex—Cases holding women ineligible.—Under the common law, according to the majority of the decisions, a woman has no right, even if otherwise properly qualified, to demand admission to the bar; and hence, in the absence of statutory or constitutional provisions, she is ineligible.[36] In *Bradwell's Case,* cited

[35] State v. Barnes, 25 Fla. 305.

[36] In re Bradwell, 55 Ill. 535, affirmed in 16 Wall. (U. S.) 130; In re Lockwood, 154 U. S. 116; Robinson's Case, 131 Mass. 376, 41 Am. Rep. 239; In re Leonard, 12 Or. 93, 53 Am. Rep. 323; In re Goodell, 39 Wis. 232, 48 Wis. 693, 20 Am. Rep. 42; Leighton v. Sargent, 27 N. H. 460. In Robinson's Case, above cited, Chief Justice Gray, speaking for the supreme judicial court of Massachusetts, said: "By the law of England, which was our law from the first settlement of the country until the American Revolution, the crown, with all its inherent rights and prerogatives, might indeed descend to a woman or to an infant; but under the degree of a queen, no woman, married or unmarried, could take part in the government of the state. Women could not sit in the house of commons or the house of lords, nor vote for members of parliament: 4 Inst. 5; Countess of Rutland's Case, 6 Coke 52b; Chorlton v. Lings, L. R. 4 C. P. 374, 391, 392. They could not take part in the administration of justice, either as judges or as jurors, with the single exception of inquiries by a jury of matrons upon a suggestion of pregnancy: 2 Inst. 119, 121; 3 Bl. Com. 262; 4 *id.* 395; Willes, J., in Chorlton v. Lings, L. R. 4 C. P. 390, 391. And no case is known in which a woman was admitted to practice as an attorney, solicitor or barrister. The only English instance of a woman lawyer, cited by the petitioner, is that stated in a note of Mr. Butler in Coke upon Littleton, as follows: 'The celebrated Anne, Countess of Pembroke, Dorset and Montgomery, had the office of hereditary sheriff of Westmoreland, and exercised it in person. At the assizes at Appleby, she sat with the judges on the bench:' Co. Litt. 326a, note 280. No authority is given for the statement. The office of sheriff of Westmoreland was granted by King John in the thirteenth century to Robert de Veteripont, or Vipont, and his heirs general, and after the death of his last heir male in 1265 descended to Isabella, wife of Roger de Clifford, and continued to be an hereditary office until 1850, when it was put by act of parliament on the footing of other like offices: 3 Selden's Works 1839; Co. Litt. 222; Collins Baronies 251, 317, 319, 321; Stat. 13 and 14 Vict., ch. 30. The Countess Anne was born in 1590, took the office by descent from her father, George, Lord Clifford and Earl of Cumberland, in 1605, and died in 1676, leaving a very full autobiography, a transcript of which is preserved among the Harleian manuscripts in the British Museum, in which she says of her ancestress, Isabella de Clif-

in the last note, the supreme court of Illinois reached the conclusion that under the statutes of that state no authority then existed to

ford, that 'in her widowhood she sat in person as sheriffess in the county of Westmoreland upon the bench with the judges, as appears by the pleas and records of her time;' and mentions the appointment of a deputy sheriff by herself in 1651. It is quite possible that as a matter of ceremony, or by way of asserting her title to the office, she (as well as her ancestress three centuries before) may sometimes herself have attended the judges, or that, in accordance with English usage, a person of her rank and distinction, when present in court, may have been invited by them to sit upon the bench. But that she habitually discharged the general duties of the office in person has been shown by an accomplished scholar, after careful research, to be highly improbable in fact: 4 Craik Romance of Peerage 162. And she could not have done so without violating the well-settled law. The office of sheriff was partly judicial and partly ministerial; the judicial functions could not be delegated; but the ministerial duties, including that of attendance upon the judges, might be performed by deputy: Dalton Sheriff, chs. 1, 4; Bandal's Case, Noy 21; Bacon Use of the Law, 4 Bacon's Works (ed. 1803) 97; Willes, J., in Chorlton v. Lings, L. R. 4 C. P. 390. When such an hereditary office descended to a woman, she might exercise the office by deputy (at least with the approval of the crown), but not in person; nor could it be originally granted to any woman, because of her incapacity of executing public offices: Duke of Buckingham's Case, Jenk. Cent. 6, pl. 14, Dyer, 285b, pl. 39, Keilw. 17; 4 Inst. 128; Co. Litt. 107b, 165a; Case of the Great Chamberlain of England, 2 Bro. P. C. (2d ed.) 146, 36 Lords' Journals 302. Women were permitted to hold the office of keeper of a castle or jail, governor of a workhouse, forester or constable, for the reason that each of those offices might be executed by a deputy: Lady Russell's Case, Cro. Jac. 17; 2 Inst. 382; Anonymous, 2 Ld. Raym. 1014; 3 Salk. 2; 4 Inst. 311; 2 Hawk., ch. 10, § 37; Willes, J., in Chorlton v. Lings, L. R. 4 C. P. 389. They were decided to be capable of voting for and of being elected to the office of sexton of a parish, upon the ground that this was not an office that concerned the public: Olive v. Ingram, 2 Stra. 1114, Vin. Abr., tit. Femme, A, pl. 7, 8; 7 Mod. 263, 273, 274. And we are not aware of any public office, the duties of which must be discharged by the incumbent in person, that a woman was adjudged to be competent to hold, without express authority of statute, except that of overseer of the poor, a local office of an administrative character, in no way connected with judicial proceedings: King v. Stubbs, 2 T. R. 395. An attorney at law is not indeed in the strictest sense a public officer. But he comes very near it. As was said by Lord Holt, "the office of an attorney concerns the public, for it is for the administration of justice:' White's Case, 6 Mod. 18; Ex parte Bradley, 7 Wall. 364, 378, 379. By our statutes he is required, upon his admission, to take and sub-admit women as attorneys. The court said: "Although an attorney is an agent * * * when he has been retained to act for another,

scribe in open court the oaths to support the constitutions of the United States and of this commonwealth, as well as the oath of office; this oath, the form of which has remained without substantial change since the time of Lord Holt, nearly a hundred and eighty years, pledges him to conduct himself 'in the office of an attorney within the courts' according to the best of his knowledge and discretion, and with all good fidelity as well to the courts as to his clients; and he becomes by his admission an officer of the court, and holds his office during good behavior, subject to removal by the court for malpractice: Gen. Stats., ch. 121, §§ 30, 31, 34; Rev. Stats., ch. 88, §§ 21, 22, 25, and commissioners' notes; Stats. 1785, ch. 23; Prov. St. 1701-2 (1 Anne), ch. 71; Prov. Laws (State ed.) 467; Randall's Case, 11 Allen (Mass.) 473; Randall v. Brigham, 7 Wall. (U. S.) 523; Ex parte Robinson, 19 Wall. (U. S.) 505, 512. There is nothing in the action of the legislature or of the judiciary of the commonwealth which has any tendency to prove such a change in the law and usage prevailing at the time of our separation from the mother country as to admit women to the exercise of any office that concerns the administration of justice. In 1871 the governor and council required the opinion of the justices of this court, under chapter 3, article 2, of the constitution of the commonwealth, upon the following questions: 'First. Under the constitution of this commonwealth, can a woman, if duly appointed and qualified as a justice of the peace, legally perform all acts pertaining to such office? Second. Under the laws of this commonwealth, would oaths and acknowledgments of deeds, taken before a married or unmarried woman, duly appointed and qualified as a justice of the peace, be legal and valid?' Although the provisions of the constitution and statutes of the commonwealth regarding the office of justice of the peace, while they do not mention women, are not in terms limited to men, yet the justices answered both the questions proposed in the negative, for the following reasons: 'By the constitution of the commonwealth, the office of justice of the peace is a judiclai office, and must be exercised by the officer in person, and a woman, whether married or unmarried, can not be appointed to such an office. The law of Massachusetts at the time of the adoption of the constitution, the whole frame and purport of the instrument itself, and the universal understanding and unbroken practical construction for the greater part of a century afterwards, all support this conclusion, and are inconsistent with any other. It follows that if a woman should be formally appointed and commissioned as a justice of the peace, she would have no constitutional or legal authority to exercise any of the functions appertaining to that office:' Opinion of Justices, 107 Mass. 604. Whenever the legislature has intended to make a change in the legal rights or capacities of women, it has used words clearly manifesting its intent and the extent of the change yet he is also much more than an agent. He is an officer of the court, holding his commission, in this state, from two members of

intended. The statutes permitting a married woman to hold and convey property, to make contracts, to sue and be sued, and to be an executrix, administratrix, guardian or trustee, have in no way enlarged the capacity of any woman, married or unmarried, to hold office, and have no application to single women or to legal disabilities to which married and unmarried women alike are subject: Gen. Stats., ch. 108; Stats. 1869, chs. 304, 409; 1871, ch. 312; 1874, ch. 184. The statute of 1869, ch. 346, providing that 'any parish or religious society may admit to membership women, who shall have all the rights and privileges of men,' would seem to imply a doubt, at least, whether they could previously have been admitted to such membership with equal privileges. The house of representatives in 1874 having taken the opinion of the justices of this court that there was nothing in the constitution itself to prevent women from being members of school committees, the legislature thereupon enacted that no person should be deemed to be ineligible to serve upon a school committee by reason of sex; and it has since expressly authorized women to vote at election of school committees: Opinion of Justices, 115 Mass. 602; Stats. 1874, ch. 389; 1879, ch. 223; 1881, ch. 191. We have not been referred to, and do not recall, any other statute respecting the legal capacity of women except those which require for their serving on certain public boards connected with the supervision of charitable or reformatory institutions or of prisons: Stats. 1877, ch. 195; 1879, chs. 291, 294. In making innovations upon the long-established system of law on this subject, the legislature appears to have proceeded with great caution, one step at a time; and the whole course of legislation precludes the inference that any change in the legal rights or capacities of women is to be implied, which has not been clearly expressed. The only statute making any provisions concerning attorneys, that mentions women, is the poor debtor act, which, after enumerating among the cases in which an arrest of the person may be made on execution in an action of contract, that in which 'the debtor is an attorney at law,' who has unreasonably neglected to pay to his client money collected, enacts, in the next section but one, that 'no woman shall be arrested on any civil process except for tort:' Gen. Stats., ch. 124, §§ 5, 7. If these provisions do not imply that the legislature assumed that women should not be attorneys, they certainly have no tendency to show that it intended that they should. The word 'citizen,' in the statute under which this application is made, is but a repetition of the word originally adopted with a view of excluding aliens, before the statutes of 1852, chapter 154, allowed those aliens to be admitted to the bar who had made the preliminary declaration of intention to become citizens: Rev. Stats., ch. 88, § 19; Gen. Stats., ch. 121, § 28. The re-enactment of the act relating to the admission of attorneys in the this court, and subject to be disbarred by this court for what our statute calls 'malconduct in his office.' He is appointed to assist in

same words without more, so far as relates to the personal qualifications of the applicant, since other statutes have expressly modified the legal rights and capacities of women in other important respects, tends rather to refute than to advance the theory that the legislature intended that these words should comprehend women. No inference of an intention of the legislature to include women in the statutes concerning the admission of attorneys can be drawn from the mere omission of the word 'male.' The only statute to which we have been referred, in which that word is inserted, is the statute concerning the qualifications of voters in town affairs, which, following the language of the article of the constitution that defines the qualifications of voters for governor, lieutenant-governor, senators and representatives, speaks of 'every male citizen of twenty-one years of age,' etc.: Gen. Stats., ch. 18, § 19; Const. Mass. Amendments, art. 3. Words which taken by themselves would be equally applicable to women and to men are constantly used in the constitution and statutes, in speaking of offices which it could not be contended, in the present state of the law, that women were capable of holding. The courts of the commonwealth have not assumed by their rules to admit to the bar any class of persons not within the apparent intent of the legislature as manifested in the statutes. The word 'person' in the latest rule of court upon the subject, was the word used in the rule of 1810 and in the statutes of 1785 and 1836, at times when no one contemplated the possibility of a woman's being admitted to practice as an attorney: Rules Sup. Jud. Ct., 121 Mass. 600; 6 Mass. 382; Stats. 1785, ch. 23; Rev. Stats., ch. 88, § 20; Gen. Stats., ch. 121, § 29. The United States court of claims, at December term, 1873, on full consideration, denied an application of a woman to be admitted to practice as an attorney, upon the ground 'that under the constitution and laws of the United States a court is without power to grant such an application, and that a woman is without legal capacity to take the office of an attorney:' Lockwood's Case, 9 Ct. of Cl. (U. S.) 346, 356. At October term, 1876, of the supreme court of the United States, the same petitioner applied to be admitted to practice as an attorney and counselor of that court, and her application was denied. The decision has not been officially reported, but upon the record of the court, of which we have an authentic copy, it is thus stated: 'Upon the presentation of this application, the chief justice said, that notice of this application having been previously brought to his attention, he had been instructed by the court to announce the following decision upon it: By the uniform practice of the court from its organization to the present time, and by the fair construction of its rules, none but men are admitted to practice before it as attorneys and counselors. This is in accordance with immemorial usage in England, and the law and practice in all the states until within a recent period; and the

the administration of justice, is required to take an oath of office, and is privileged from arrest while attending courts. * * * It is to be remembered that at the time this statute was enacted, we had, by express provision, adopted the common law of England, and, with three exceptions, the statutes of that country passed prior to the fourth year of James the First, so far as they were applicable to our condition. It is also to be remembered that female attorneys at law were unknown in England, and a proposition that a woman should enter the courts of Westminster Hall in that capacity, or as a barrister, would have created hardly less astonishment than one that she should attend the bench of bishops, or be elected to a seat in the house of commons. It is to be further remembered that when our act was passed, that school of reform which claims for women participation in the making and administering of the laws had not then arisen, or, if here and there a writer had advanced such theories, they were regarded rather as abstract speculations than as an actual basis for action. That God designed the sexes to occupy different spheres of action, and that it belonged to men to make, apply and execute the laws, was regarded as an almost axiomatic truth. It may have been a radical error, but that this was the universal belief certainly admits of no denial. A direct participation in the affairs of the government, in even the most elementary form,—namely, the right of suffrage,—was not then claimed, and has not yet been conceded, unless recently in one of the newly settled territories of the

court does not feel called upon to make a change until such a change is required by statute or a more extended practice in the highest courts of the states.' The subsequent act of congress of February 15, 1879, enables only those women to be admitted to practice before the supreme court of the United States who have been for three years members of the bar of the highest court of a state or territory, or of the supreme court of the District of Columbia. The conclusion that women can not be admitted to the bar under the existing statutes of the commonwealth is in accordance with judgments of the highest courts of the states of Illinois and Wisconsin: Bradwell's Case, 55 Ill. 535; In re Goodell, 39 Wis. 232, 20 Am. Rep. 42. The suggestion in the brief of the petitioner, that women have been admitted in other states, can have no weight here, in the absence of all evidence that (except under clear affirmative words in a statute) they have ever been so admitted upon deliberate consideration of the question involved, or by a court whose decisions are authoritative. It is hardly necessary to add that our duty is limited to declaring the law as it is, and that whether any change in that law would be wise or expedient is a question for the legislative and not for the judicial department of the government."

west. In view of these facts, we are certainly warranted in saying that when the legislature gave to this court the power of granting licenses to practice law, it was with not the slightest expectation that this privilege should be extended equally to men and women. Neither has there been any legislation since that period which would justify us in presuming a change in the legislative intent. Our laws to-day, in regard to women, are substantially what they have always been, except in the change wrought by the acts of 1861 and 1869, giving to married women the right to control their own property and earnings. * * * This step, if taken by us, would mean that, in the opinion of this tribunal, every civil office of this state may be filled by women; that it is in harmony with our constitution and laws that women should be made governors, judges and sheriffs. This we are not prepared to hold. * * * For us to attempt, in a matter of this importance, to inaugurate a practice at variance with all the precedents of the law we are sworn to administer, would be an act of judicial usurpation, deserving of the gravest censure. If we could disregard, in this matter, the authority of those unwritten usages which make the great body of our law, we might do so in any other, and the dearest rights of person and property would become a matter of mere judicial discretion. * * * If the legislature shall choose to remove the existing barriers, and authorize us to issue licenses equally to men and women, we shall cheerfully obey, trusting to the good sense and sound judgment of women themselves, to seek those departments of the practice in which they can labor without reasonable objection." In the state of Wisconsin the courts have always doubted the power of the legislature to determine the question as to who shall be allowed to practice law in the state courts. In *Goodell's Case*[37] the supreme court denied the right of women to practice, and refused to exercise the discretion to admit them, on the ground of public policy. And in *Lockwood's Case*.[38] the United States court of claims reached the same conclusion; giving, among other reasons why women should not be permitted to practice, the following: "In cases of misconduct by an attorney, he may be attached by the court, and imprisoned; but if the attorney were a married woman, then she might come in and say that the misconduct occurred in her husband's presence, and that, at common law, it was by his compulsion. She might misapply the funds of a client, or be guilty of gross neglect or

[37] 39 Wis. 232, 20 Am. Rep. 42.

[38] 9 Ct. of Cl. (U. S.) 346, affirmed in 154 U. S. 116.

fraud, and the husband be sued at common law, for the wrong." And so the general term of the supreme court of New York ruled that under the laws of that state a woman was not entitled to admission to the bar.[39] It has also been repeatedly held that the denial to a woman of the privilege of admission to the bar is not a violation of the provisions of the fourteenth amendment to the federal constitution.[40]

§ **401. Enabling statutes—Cases holding women eligible under common law.**—In many of the states of the Union statutes have been enacted enabling women to practice law; while in a few the courts hold that no enabling statute or constitutional provision is necessary to enable them to exercise that privilege,[41] if the courts see proper to admit them. Since the decision of the *Robinson Case*,[42] the legislature of Massachusetts has provided that women shall have the same right to be admitted to the practice as men;[43] and since the *Stoneman Case*[43a] was decided in New York, the legislature has amended the code of that state so that race or sex shall be no ground for excluding from admission to the bar;[44] and since the decision of the *Bradwell Case*,[45] the statutes of Illinois have been so amended that no person can be precluded or debarred from any occupation, profession or employment except military, on account of sex.[46] In Indiana the constitution permits any person to practice law who has a good moral character and is a legal voter.[47] There is no statute of the state by which women are given the right of admission to practice. The supreme court, in a somewhat recent case, has decided that neither the common law nor the constitution prohibits women from being admitted to the bar, and that the courts possess the inherent power to prescribe rules for the admission of women.[48] "Whatever the objections of the common law of England," said the court, "there is a law higher in this country, and better suited to the rights and liberties of

[39] In re Stoneman, reported in note to 53 Am. Rep. 323.

[40] Bradwell v. Illinois, 16 Wall. (U. S.) 130; Lockwood's Case, 9 Ct. of Cl. (U. S.) 346, affirmed in 154 U. S. 116; In re Taylor, 48 Md. 28, 30 Am. Rep. 451.

[41] See, as to the latter proposition, In re Thomas, 16 Colo. 441, 13 L. R. A. 538, 33 Cent. L. J. 416, 44 Alb. L. J. 358; In re Leach, 134 Ind. 665, 21 L. R. A. 701.

[42] 131 Mass. 376, 41 Am. Rep. 239.

[43] Act of April 10, 1882, p. 100.

[43a] Reported in note to 53 Am. Rep. 323.

[44] N. Y. Laws 1886, ch. 425, amending Code Civ. Proc., § 56.

[45] 55 Ill. 535.

[46] Starr & C. Ann. Stat., ch. 48, § 4.

[47] Ind. Const., art. 7, §§ 7, 21.

[48] In re Leach, 134 Ind. 665, 21 L. R. A. 701.

American citizens,—that law which accords to every citizen the natural right to gain a livelihood by intelligence, honesty, and industry in the arts, the sciences, the professions or other vocations. This right may not, of course, be pursued in violation of law, but must be held to exist as long as not forbidden by law. We are not unmindful that other states, notably Illinois, Wisconsin, Oregon, Maryland and Massachusetts, have held that in the absence of an express grant of the privilege, it may not be conferred upon women. In some instances the holding has been upon constitutional provisions unlike that of this state, and in others upon what we are constrained to believe an erroneous recognition of a supposed common-law inhibition. However, each of the states named made haste to create by legislation the right which it was supposed was forbidden by the common law, and thereby recognized the progress of American women beyond the narrow limits prescribed in Westminster Hall." The supreme court of Colorado takes the same advanced ground as that of Indiana.[49] In the case cited in the note, it is held that attorneys are not civil officers within the provision of the Colorado constitution that no person except a qualified elector shall be eligible to any civil or military office, and that there is nothing in the common law or in the statutes of that state prohibiting women from admission to the bar.[50] In New Hampshire

[49] In re Thomas, 16 Colo. 441, 13 L. R. A. 538.

[50] In the course of the opinion, Helm, C. J., takes occasion to say: "The written opinions [speaking of the decisions of courts taking the opposite view from the one here expressed] marshal all objections to conferring this privilege upon women, dwelling with special force and clearness upon those existing outside of constitutional and statutory provisions. They ably discuss questions of impropriety and inexpediency based upon the laws of nature, the bearing of historical customs and usages, and the impediments growing out of a woman's legal *status* at the common law. With all deference to those learned courts, we decline to imitate their example in the latter regard. We shall not indulge in speculation concerning the natural aptitude and physical ability of women to perform the duties of the profession, nor shall we dwell upon considerations of propriety or expediency in the premises. These are matters as to which wide differences of opinion exist; and we conceive that they have little, if any, bearing upon similar applications now presented in this state, however pertinent they may have been in the commonwealths referred to when the above rulings were made. We shall likewise decline to give controlling weight to historic custom or usage in England, in the American colonies, and in the republic during its infancy. Reasoning, predicated

it is held by the supreme court that the office of practicing attorney is not a public office within the common-law rule by which women are excluded from participating in the government of the state, as electors and office holders; and women are therefore not prevented by such rule from being licensed to practice law.[51] In Pennsylvania it is decided that the act of April 14, 1834, providing that judges of courts of record may admit a competent number of persons to practice, and that before any attorney shall enter upon the practice "he" shall take an oath, etc., does not prohibit a woman from being admitted to the bar as an attorney.[52] It may be safely stated, we think, that nearly all the states of the Union, and the several federal courts, now admit

upon the latter ground, possesses the inherent weakness of ignoring, to a greater or less extent, the marvelous changes throughout the country during the last fifty years in the legal *status* of woman. It is a significant circumstance, indicating the trend of popular sentiment on the subject, that each of the cases above referred to was speedily followed by a statute providing for the admission of women to the profession. The supreme court of the United States, and the courts of the district of Columbia, Massachusetts, Illinois and Wisconsin, no longer adhere to the rule of discrimination on the ground of sex. Women are now licensed without question to practice in these courts as well as in those of several other states upon the same conditions as men, save only that the act of congress requires three years' membership of the bar of the highest court in some state or territory as a condition precedent to their appearance before the supreme court of the United States. In this commonwealth, women of sufficient age, married or single, may make contracts, form partnerships, inherit, acquire and dispose of property, in all respects substantially the same as men. The policy of our legislative and judicial action has tended constantly towards conferring upon them the same property rights and business *status* as are enjoyed by men. They may undoubtedly pursue all vocations and enterprises of a business character. They may also become ministers, physicians, or educators, and if any limitation in regard to the learned professions exists, such limitation applies solely to the bar. The privilege of practicing this profession and sharing in its emoluments is alone questioned. Hence we contend with none of the difficulties encountered by the courts above mentioned arising from the disabilities of women, especially married women, at common law. Applications like the one before us may therefore be regarded with judicial favor, usually extended when equality of rights is involved, unless some restrictive provision be found in our statutes or constitution."

[51] In re Ricker, 66 N. H. 207, 24 L. R. A. 740.

[52] Richardson's Case (Com. Pl.), 3 Pa. Dist. Rep. 299. See also, In re Kilgore, 17 Wkly. Notes Cas. (Pa.) 562, 563.

women to practice, if they possess the necessary qualifications required by law or the rules of court.[52a]

§ **402. Race, residence and citizenship.**—It has been a custom of long standing in this country to permit a lawyer in good repute in another state to practice in particular cases without examination or without being sworn as a practicing attorney of the state into whose court he seeks admission; but an attorney has no right to compel such admission if refused, it being a mere matter of custom and comity, and being confined to the practice in "certain causes in which the attorney is retained for the time being." It does not include the right to a general license to practice.[53] In all save a few of the states, practicing attorneys in good standing in other states are admitted. In those states in which a contrary rule prevails it is generally provided by statute that such nonresident attorneys may be admitted if they have been practicing before the highest court of their own state for a number of years. Persons of good character may be admitted to the supreme court of the United States if they have practiced for three years in the supreme court of their own state.[54] Under the laws of California, a Chinaman will not be admitted to practice in the supreme court of that state, although he presents a license to practice in the supreme court of New York, and exhibits naturalization papers issued by a competent court, such papers being void under act of congress of May, 1882.[55] And in Maryland, under the act of 1876[56] of that state, a colored citizen of the state was held not eligible.[57] In North Carolina, aliens not naturalized can not be licensed to practice law.[58] But in Ohio, a foreigner who resides in the state and has declared his intention to become a citizen, and who possesses the other qualifications, may be admitted.[59] There is

[52a] It was recently decided in Maryland that under the statute of that state providing that "any male citizen" having certain qualifications shall be admitted to the practice of law, women are not entitled to admission, although the code provides that the masculine shall include all grades except where such construction would be absurd or unreasonable: In re Maddox, 93 Md. 727, 55 L. R. A. 298.

[53] In re Mosness, 39 Wis. 509, 20 Am. Rep. 55; In re Leonard, 12 Or. 93, 53 Am. Rep. 323; Matter of Henry, 40 N. Y. 560.

[54] Rule Supr. Ct., 3 Supr. Ct. Repr. v.

[55] In re Hong Yen Chang, 84 Cal. 163, 24 Pac. 156.

[56] Ch. 264, § 3.

[57] In re Taylor, 48 Md. 28, 30 Am. Rep. 451.

[58] In re Thompson, 10 N. C. 355.

[59] Ex parte Porter, 3 Ohio Dec. 333.

no natural right in favor of one not a citizen of the state, or of the United States, to be admitted to practice; and a statute or constitutional provision is generally regarded as necessary to warrant the admission of such person.[60] In some states resident aliens are expressly given the privilege of such admission by act of the legislature.[61]

§ **403. Requirement to serve clerkship.**—It is provided by statute in some jurisdictions that every applicant for admission to the bar must have served as a clerk in some lawyer's office for a prescribed period next before his examination for admission. Where this is the rule the candidate must have actually served such clerkship during the required period, and must have been actively engaged in assisting the attorney whom he serves as such clerk, with the business under his control.[62] It is not enough that he should simply have read law under the direction or tutelage of such lawyer: the requirement for service as clerk must be substantially complied with. "A clerkship to an attorney," said the supreme court of New Jersey, "imports the office of assistant to an attorney,—an actual occupation in and about the attorney's business and under his control. The service is to be rendered, not solely or mainly by the study of law books, but chiefly by attending to the work of the attorney under his direction. The purpose of the rule is that the clerk shall be actually engaged in the practice of law under the guidance of his master for the stated period, so that by direct contact with an attorney's duties he may acquire the skill and facility in the profession which are necessary for enabling him to protect and promote independently the interests that clients may afterward commit to him. This is the sole object of requiring the clerkship to be served with a practicing attorney. For the mere study of legal principles, a retired counselor or a professor would be an apter guide."[63] But it is doubtful whether this can be thought to be altogether the object of the provision, when it is held as it was in Pennsylvania, that a clerkship with a judge of the supreme court or the president of the common pleas, is a sufficient compliance with the requirement. As judges are not engaged in the practice of law, it can not in this case be deemed to be the purpose of the rule to enable the young attorney to acquire experience in the

[60] Matter of O'Neill, 90 N. Y. 584.

[61] Or. Laws 1891, p. 42.

[62] In matter of Dunn, 43 N. J. L. 359, 39 Am. Rep. 600; In re Taylor, 6 D. & R. 428; Ex parte Hill, 7 T. R. 452. See also, Commonwealth v. Judges, 1 S. & R. (Pa.) 187; Matter of Moore, 108 N. Y. 280; Ex parte Sayre, 7 Cow. (N. Y.) 368; In re A. B., 4 Johns. (N. Y.) 191.

[63] In matter of Dunn, *supra*.

practice by association with his preceptor.[64] The pursuit of classical studies was formerly deemed of sufficient importance in some jurisdictions to warrant the enactment of laws providing for a diminution of the term of the clerkship upon proof of the applicant's having to a certain extent pursued the study of the classics.[65]

§ 404. **Nonresident attorneys.**—Persons who are not residents of the state have, as stated above,[65a] no absolute right to practice therein, though possessed of all other qualifications.[66] Such attorneys are, indeed, admitted in most jurisdictions, *ex gratia;* but in the absence of a statutory or constitutional requirement, the courts are not bound by law to admit them. Even if the applicant can show that he has practiced his profession for the requisite number of years, if he is a resident of another state this will not give him the right of admission if he is not a citizen of the United States: he must be a citizen of this country when he makes application to be admitted.[67] Hence, a Chinaman can not be admitted, as of right, from the fact that he has been admitted in another state and has also been naturalized, the naturalization papers being void.[68] But statutes are frequently passed allowing nonresident attorneys to practice when otherwise properly qualified;[69] and as a general rule, attorneys from other states are admitted for the purpose of practicing in some particular case or cases, but not as permanent members of the bar.[70] They are sometimes admitted by statute upon the same terms on which nonresident attorneys are admitted in the state from which they have come.

[64] Commonwealth v. Judges, 1 S. & R. (Pa.) 187.

[65] See Anonymous, 3 Wend. (N. Y.) 456.

[65a] *Ante,* § 402.

[66] In re Henry, 40 N. Y. 560.

[67] Matter of O'Neill, 90 N. Y. 584.

[68] In re Hong Yen Chang, 84 Cal. 163, 24 Pac. 156.

[69] Or. Laws 1891, p. 42. See Splane's Petition, 123 Pa. St. 527; Ex parte Schaefer, 32 La. Ann. 1102; In re Mosness, 39 Wis. 509, 20 Am. Rep. 55.

[70] As said by Ryan, C. J., speaking for the supreme court of Wisconsin in the case last cited: "It is, we believe, the general practice of courts of record in the several states to permit gentlemen of the bar in other states to appear as counsel on the trial or argument of causes. Such has been the uniform practice of this court. And, under all ordinary circumstances, it will always be a pleasure to us to permit members of the bar of other states to argue causes here, whenever they may appear here to do so. No license to practice here is necessary or proper for that purpose; the usual and proper practice being to grant leave, *ex gratia,* for the occasion. But general license to practice here as attorney and counselor rests upon quite different considerations. The bar is no unimportant part of the court; and its members

§ **405. Mandamus to compel admission, etc.**—The question whether admission or readmission to the bar may be enforced by *mandamus* proceedings is one as to which there can not be much controversy: the great weight of authority being that *mandamus* will not lie to compel such admission. It is generally held that the act of admitting an attorney to the bar is a judicial one; and although the legislature may say what qualifications the applicant must possess, whether in fact he does possess these and other qualifications necessary, in the court's opinion, to admission, is a question for the court to which he applies, and can not be made the subject for a writ of *mandamus*.[71] But *mandamus* seems to be the proper remedy to compel the restoration of an attorney who has been disbarred or suspended; either where the act was without jurisdiction, or was an abuse of the court's discretion, or was unjust or unlawful.[72] *Mandamus* has been declared to be the proper remedy, also, to allow an applicant for admission to the bar to take the examination therefor, when refused though entitled to do so.[73] Where the facts are undisputed, the appellate tribunal may, perhaps, enforce admission by *mandamus*.

§ **406. Oath of office.**—Upon admission to the bar an attorney is required to take the oath of office, by which he promises to support the constitution of the United States and of his own state, and faithfully and honestly to discharge his duties as an attorney at law.[74]

are officers of the court, * * * and, if officers of the court, certainly, in some sense, officers of the state for which the court acts. * * * The state may have extraterritorial officers, as commissioners to take acknowledgments, etc. But these are exceptions; and the general business of the state must be performed by citizens or denizens of the state; and the officers charged with it must be resident in the state. * * * It would be an anomaly, dangerous to the safe administration of justice, that the office should be filled by persons residing beyond the jurisdiction of the court, and practically not subject to its authority. We take it that members of the bar of this state lose their right to practice here by removing from the state. After they become nonresidents, they can appear in courts of this state *ex gratia* only. Our courts can not have a nonresident bar."

71 Commonwealth v. Judges, 1 S. & R. (Pa.) 187; Ex parte Garland, 4 Wall. (U. S.) 333; Ex parte Secombe, 19 How. (U. S.) 9.

72 Ex parte Robinson, 19 Wall. (U. S.) 505; Walls v. Palmer, 64 Ind. 493.

73 State v. Baker, 25 Fla. 598. See Commonwealth v. Judges, 1 S. & R. (Pa.) 187.

74 This is the form of oath required in Indiana, under Burns Rev. Stat. 1901, § 977. There is no substantial difference in the forms

§ **407. License to practice.**—In many of the states an attorney at law is required to have a license or certificate before he is permitted to enter upon the practice of his profession. Such a license must be obtained in the manner prescribed by law or it will be revoked.[75] But it will be presumed, the contrary not appearing, that one actually practicing in court as an attorney has been duly licensed to practice.[76] The mere fact that the statute substitutes a diploma from a law school for an examination will not excuse the holder of such diploma from taking out a license; and one who undertakes to practice without such license is liable to be prosecuted, if to practice without a license constitutes an offense in the jurisdiction in which he so engages in the practice. But where the license is issued by the supreme court, an admission to the bar of that court, spread of record, is equivalent to the required license.[77] One can not represent another in a court of justice merely as an "agent." He must be a licensed attorney, and his license must be entered on the roll of the court in the clerk's office of the proper court.[78] A license from the supreme court of New York, stating that the holder has been admitted to the bar of the court of appeals of that state, is not a compliance with the rule of court in Pennsylvania which allows an attorney practicing in the highest court of a state to practice before the supreme court of Pennsylvania; as the supreme court of New York has no authority to certify to the

of the oaths in the different states. In Pennsylvania the applicant swears (or affirms) that he will support the constitution of the United States and the constitution of the commonwealth, "and that you will behave yourself in this court as to the client, and that you will use no falsehood, nor delay any person's cause for lucre or malice:" 1 Brightly's Purdon's Dig., ch. 189. The oath or affirmation required to be taken by the attorney or counselor on his admission to the supreme court of the United States is as follows: "I, ———, do solemnly swear (or affirm) that I will demean myself, as an attorney and counselor of this court, uprightly and according to law; and that I will support the constitution of the United States:" Rule 2, Supr. Ct. In the other federal courts a similar oath is required. In some of the states the oath of an attorney is that he will not violate the duties enjoined on him by law: Weeks Attys. at Law, § 67. In other jurisdictions the oath is that the applicant "will discharge the duties of attorney and counselor to the best of his knowledge and ability:" Weeks Attys. at Law, § 70.

[75] People v. Betts, 7 Colo. 453; In re Burchard, 27 Hun (N. Y.) 429.

[76] Ex parte Trippe, 66 Ind. 531.

[77] In re Villere, 33 La. Ann. 998.

[78] Robb v. Smith, 4 Ill. 46; Cobb v. Judge of Super. Ct., 43 Mich. 289; Weir v. Slocum, 3 How. Pr. (N. Y.) 397.

admission of attorneys to practice before the court of appeals.[79] And in Wisconsin it has been decided that a license to practice in the circuit courts will not entitle the holder thereof to practice in the supreme court of that state.[80] An attorney who has been licensed to practice in a state, before the formation of a new state out of a portion of the territory of the old state, will not be required to take out a new license in the new state.[81] In New Jersey, it is held to be within the discretion of a justice of the peace to admit an unlicensed attorney to appear and practice.[82] The requirement for a license to practice law usually applies only to the practice in courts of record.[83]

II. The Relation of the Attorney to the Court.

§ **408. Duty of attorney to court.**—An attorney at the bar is under obligations to deport himself with becoming respect to the court and its officers; and this duty requires him to refrain from abusive language toward both the court, counsel and parties.[84] But there must be a formal disbarment in order to justify a court in preventing a member of its bar from practicing before such court; and it is erroneous to exclude such a member from the practice, though he has been guilty of conduct that would be sufficient cause for disbarment, in the absence of a judgment of removal or suspension.[85]

§ **409. Summary jurisdiction—Disbarment.**—Attorneys may become liable to the summary jurisdiction of the court for various causes. This jurisdiction, as stated in a work of merit, extends "to cases when they [the attorneys] act without authority; to striking them from the rolls and suspending them from practice; to the offense of permitting others to use their names; to compelling in proper cases the disclosure of the client's abode or occupation, and to compelling them to produce the client, and to disclose a certain class of communications * * * ; to the paying of money and costs; to the answering of matters of affidavits; to contempts of court; and to

[79] Splane's Petition, 123 Pa. St. 527, 16 Atl. 481.

[80] In re Goodell, 39 Wis. 232, 20 Am. Rep. 42.

[81] Ex parte Faulkner, 1 W. Va. 269; Ex parte Quarrier, 2 W. Va. 569.

[82] M'Whorter v. Bloom, 3 N. J. L. 134.

[83] See Hall v. Sawyer, 47 Barb. (N. Y.) 116; Porter v. Bronson, 29 How. Pr. (N. Y.) 292, 19 Abb. Pr. (N. Y.) 236.

[84] Redman v. State, 28 Ind. 205; Dodge v. State, 140 Ind. 284; Bauer v. Betz, 1 How. N. S. (N. Y.) 344, affirmed in 99 N. Y. 672.

[85] Withers v. State, 36 Ala. 252.

professional misconduct generally."[86] It is generally conceded that courts, as a necessary part of their inherent power, and as incident to their power to admit attorneys to the bar, possess the right to suspend or disbar such attorneys for their misconduct.[87] It is not necessary that the attorney who is to be disbarred should have committed the offense or been guilty of the wrong conduct during the session of court or in its presence.[88] Appellate courts may take original jurisdiction and proceed against attorneys guilty of unprofessional conduct in such courts.[89] If, however, the misconduct occurred while the cause appealed was pending in the lower court, the appellate tribunal will not take cognizance, there being an adequate remedy in the lower court by contempt proceedings.[90] Where the supreme court has power to admit to practice generally, a proceeding to disbar is properly instituted by the attorney-general before that tribunal.[91] Where attorneys are admitted to practice in trial courts, such courts have power for proper cause to suspend an attorney from practicing therein.[92] Mutilation of a record by an attorney on appeal to the supreme court is such an offense as will warrant the supreme court to disbar such attorney; but it must be shown that he was connected with the act; and the mere fact that he argued the appeal from the record as filed is not in itself sufficient so to connect him with the improper act.[93] An attorney may also be proceeded against summarily for failing to pay over money belonging to his client; but only when it has come into his hands as attorney of the party claiming it, and not when he received it as a mere business agent.[94] The inherent power of courts to disbar an attorney may, however, be re-

[86] Weeks Attys. at Law, § 77. For other instances of misconduct for which an attorney may be disbarred, see Weeks Attys. at Law, § 81. An attorney may also be disbarred for contempt; but such an order should never be made unless tne offense is of such a nature as to render him unworthy of his office: Watson v. Citizens' Savings Bank, 5 S. C. 159.

[87] People v. Goodrich, 79 Ill. 148; Rice v. Commonwealth, 18 B. Mon. (Ky.) 472; In re Cooper, 22 N. Y. 67; Ex parte Secombe, 19 How. (U. S.) 9; Anonymous, 9 L. T. 299; State v. Mullins, 129 Mo. 231, 31 S. W. 744.

[88] In re O——, 73 Wis. 602.

[89] In re Whitehead, L. R. 28 Ch. Div. 614; People v. Green, 7 Colo. 237.

[90] People v. Berry, 17 Colo. 322.

[91] State v. Mullins, 129 Mo. 231, 31 S. W. 744.

[92] Mattler v. Schaffner, 53 Ind. 245.

[93] State v. Mullins, *supra*.

[94] In re Langslow, 167 N. Y. 314, 60 N. E. 591.

stricted by statute; and such power may be vested by the legislature in a particular court or courts, when the court from which the power is taken is one of limited or special jurisdiction or is of purely statutory origin.[95] And it seems to have been held in Indiana[96] that where specific causes are prescribed by statute for which an attorney may be disbarred, he can not be disbarred for any other;[97] but the general rule and weight of authority seem to be otherwise: statutes prescribing causes for disbarment are not usually regarded as limiting the common-law power of courts to disbar for causes not mentioned in the statute.[98] Where an indictment was pending against an attorney charging him with a crime, the court refused to disbar him before the indictment was disposed of.[99] In North Carolina it is declared by statute that no attorney shall be disbarred except upon a conviction for a criminal offense or after confession in open court; and this provision has been held valid and constitutional.[100]

§ 410. **Further as to disbarment of attorneys.**—It is not necessary that professional misconduct should amount to contempt of court in order to furnish grounds for disbarment proceedings. Thus, threats made to the judge, directly and personally and on account of his official action, even out of court, will constitute ground for a charge looking to disbarment.[101] But the court will not be justified in summarily striking an attorney's name from the rolls without the proceedings prescribed by statute, if such there be. A contempt of court may be such as to warrant disbarment, but here, too, there must be a charge and a hearing before there can be a judgment revoking the attorney's license.[102] In the federal courts it is held that an attorney may be disbarred for any act showing him to be unfit to practice in the court as one of the officers thereof,—such as shows bad moral character, commission of criminal, vicious, or other acts inconsistent with his official relation to the courts.[103] One of the acts which has

[95] State v. Laughlin, 73 Mo. 443. See also, State v. Harber, 129 Mo. 271, 31 S. W. 889.

[96] Ex parte Smith, 28 Ind. 47; Ex parte Trippe, 66 Ind. 531.

[97] This seems to be the rule also in North Dakota: In re Easton, 4 N. D. 514, 62 N. W. 597.

[98] Matter of Mills, 1 Mich. 392; Delano's Case, 58 N. H. 5, 42 Am. Rep. 555.

[99] People v. Comstock, 176 Ill. 192, 52 N. E. 67.

[100] Ex parte Schenck, 65 N. C. 353.

[101] State v. Root, 5 N. D. 487, 67 N. W. 590.

[102] State v. Root, *supra*.

[103] See Ex parte Cole, 1 McCrary (C. C.) 405; In re Wall, 13 Fed. 814.

been held sufficient ground for the disbarment of an attorney in Colorado is the advertising for divorce cases: notably the repeated insertion of such announcements as, "Divorces legally obtained very quietly, good everywhere."[104] Disbarments have been held justifiable on the following grounds:—libel;[105] purchasing demands for the purpose of instituting suits thereon;[106] retaining the funds of a client;[107] instituting divorce proceedings on behalf of a wife, at the instance of the husband, but without authority from the wife;[108] offering to sell information to the adverse party;[109] conviction of felony;[110] obtaining illegal fees in pension cases;[111] conviction of subornation of perjury;[112] falsifying records or documents;[113] abstracting record from files of court;[114] fraudulently altering a receipt;[115] forging and filing in court an affidavit for a change of venue;[116] appearing in court armed with a deadly weapon;[117] swearing falsely to an affidavit before the court;[118] bribing a witness;[119] threatening to chastise the judge of the court, though done outside of court.[120] Any matter showing an attorney's unfitness to practice in the court is sufficient ground for disbarment.[121]

§ 411. Practice in disbarment proceedings.—Proceedings to disbar an attorney may be instituted by the attorney-general, or by a member of the bar on his own motion, or the court may appoint an attorney

[104] People v. MacCabe, 18 Colo. 186, 36 Am. St. 270. See also, on the subject of advertising for divorce suits, People v. Goodrich, 79 Ill. 148.

[105] State v. Mason, 29 Or. 18, 43 Pac. 651.

[106] In re Bleakley, 5 Paige (N. Y.) 311.

[107] In re Titus, 66 Hun (N. Y.) 632, 21 N. Y. Supp. 724.

[108] Dillon v. State, 6 Tex. 55.

[109] In re Enright, 67 Vt. 351, 31 Atl. 786.

[110] In re McCarthy, 42 Mich. 71.

[111] Matter of ———, an Attorney, 86 N. Y. 563.

[112] State v. Holding, 1 McCord (S. C.) 379.

[113] People v. Leary, 84 Ill. 190; People v. Murphy, 119 Ill. 159; Rice v. Commonwealth, 18 B. Mon. (Ky.) 472; Ex parte Brown, 1 How. (Miss.) 303; State v. Mullins, 129 Mo. 231, 31 S. W. 744; State v. Harber, 129 Mo. 271, 31 S. W. 889; State v. Cadwell, 16 Mont. 119, 40 Pac. 176; Matter of Loew, 5 Hun (N. Y.) 462, 50 How. Pr. (N. Y.) 373; In re Goldberg, 29 N. Y. Supp. 972.

[114] In re Gates (Pa.), 2 Atl. 214.

[115] In re Serfass, 116 Pa. St. 455.

[116] Ex parte Walls, 64 Ind. 461.

[117] Sharon v. Hill, 24 Fed. 726.

[118] In re Houghton, 67 Cal. 511, 8 Pac. 52.

[119] Walker v. State, 4 W. Va. 749.

[120] Bradley v. Fisher, 13 Wall. (U. S.) 335.

[121] State v. Winton (Or.), 5 Pac. 337.

to prefer and prosecute the charges.[122] The proper practice then is to serve such attorney with notice, reciting the substance of the charge or information against him, and requiring him to appear and show cause why his name should not be stricken from the roll of attorneys.[123] No one can be legally prosecuted with a view to disbarment without having been given his day in court; and unless the misconduct is committed in view of the court, the accused must have due and sufficient notice; and judgment can only be rendered on the process, as otherwise the judgment against him can not be upheld; a mere motion, without notice, not being sufficient.[124] The offense must be clearly charged and proved, as it is but just that in an accusation of so grave a nature, and likely to lead to such serious consequences, great particularity should be required.[125] The accused can only be tried on the charges contained in the information; the court will not hear or consider evidence as to conduct not connected with the attorney's professional duties; and the prosecution should be instituted within a reasonable time after the commission of the alleged offense.[126] Disbarment is not a conviction of a crime, in the ordinary sense, and it is not within the power of the executive to pardon an attorney whose name has been stricken from the roll, so as to entitle him to restoration.[127] Even if the accused has been acquitted of the crime constituting the basis of the proceeding for disbarment, it will be no defense, if the facts proved sufficiently established his guilt.[128]

§ **412. Defenses.**—Disbarment proceedings for misconduct of an attorney toward the court are not barred by the statute of limitations.[129] Where the offense is a supposed contempt consisting of mere words capable of different constructions, the attorney may, under oath, disavow his intention to commit a contempt and thus purge himself so as to entitle him to have the proceedings discontinued;[130] but

[122] State v. Mullins, 129 Mo. 231, 31 S. W. 744; State v. Harber, 129 Mo. 271, 31 S. W. 889.

[123] Weeks Attys. at Law, § 83.

[124] Weeks Attys. at Law, § 83.

[125] People v. Allison, 68 Ill. 151; Dickinson v. Dustin, 21 Mich. 561.

[126] People v. Allison, *supra.*

[127] Matter of ———, an Attorney, 86 N. Y. 569. But in New York a statute authorizes the supreme court to vacate an order of disbarment on proof of a pardon: Laws 1890, ch. 258, p. 948.

[128] Matter of ———, an Attorney, *supra.*

[129] In re Lowenthal, 78 Cal. 427; Ex parte Tyler, 107 Cal. 78.

[130] In re Woolley, 11 Bush (Ky.) 95. See Ex parte Biggs, 64 N. C. 202.

when the matter is necessarily offensive and insulting, the disavowal can not justify the act, though it may tend to excuse it.[131] The fact that the client has condoned the offense of his attorney is no defense to the disbarment proceeding;[132] nor is the settlement of a criminal prosecution on the same charge.[133] That an appeal has been taken from the decision in the case constituting the basis of the disbarment proceedings, is no answer to the accusation.[134]

§ **413. Review of proceedings.**—Proceedings for disbarment of an attorney are generally reviewable, either on appeal[135] or on writ of error[136] or by *mandamus;*[137] and when an attorney has been suspended or disbarred without notice and opportunity to defend, a *mandamus* may issue to compel the trial court to restore the defendant to his rights as an attorney.[138]

§ **414. Contempts.**—An attorney at law may be guilty of a contempt of court for misconduct in the presence of the court or out of it. The former is said to be a direct contempt, or contempt *in facie curiae,*[139] and the latter an indirect or constructive contempt.[140] The refusal to pay over money to a client, upon order of court, will constitute a contempt of court for which an attachment may issue.[141] The attorney may place himself in contempt also by advising his client to violate an order of the court, for which the court may inflict proper punishment.[142] And so, it has been held to be a contempt

[131] In re Woolley, 11 Bush (Ky.) 95.

[132] Ex parte Orwig, 31 Leg. Int. (Pa.) 20.

[133] In re Davies, 13 Phila. (Pa.) 65.

[134] Matter of ———, an Attorney, 86 N. Y. 563.

[135] Winkelman v. People, 50 Ill. 449; Walls v. Palmer, 64 Ind. 493; Ex parte Trippe, 66 Ind. 531; Turner v. Com., 8 Ky. L. Rep. 350, 1 S. W. 475; In re Wool, 36 Mich. 299; In re Brown, 2 Okla. 590, 39 Pac. 469; In re H—— T——, 2 Penny. (Pa.) 84, 14 Lanc. Bar (Pa.) 127; Brooks v. Fleming, 65 Tenn. 331; Casey v. State, 25 Tex. 380. But no appeal can be taken by the prosecution from a judgment in defendant's favor: State v. Tunstall, 51 Tex. 81; In re Orton, 54 Wis. 379.

[136] Ex parte Biggs, 64 N. C. 202; Beene v. State, 22 Ark. 149.

[137] Ex parte Robinson, 86 U. S. 513.

[138] People v. Turner, 1 Cal. 143.

[139] Whittem v. State, 36 Ind. 196; Holman v. State, 105 Ind. 513; State v. Woodfin, 5 Ired. L. (N. C.) 199, 42 Am. Dec. 161.

[140] Hawkins v. State, 126 Ind. 294; In matter of Dill, 32 Kan. 668, 688, 49 Am. Rep. 505.

[141] Smith v. McLendon, 59 Ga. 523; Cotton v. Sharpstein, 14 Wis. 226, 80 Am. Dec. 774.

[142] King v. Barnes, 113 N. Y. 476, 655.

for an attorney to bring a fictitious suit.[143] Many of the things for which an attorney will be disbarred are contempts of court, and these, in the main, have already been noticed.[144] An attorney may be guilty of contempt by using indecent, defamatory, or other improper language in the court's presence;[145] filing an indecent petition;[146] and generally, for disobeying any order or process of court.[147] Contempts are punished by fine or imprisonment, or both, and by suspension, temporary or permanent, from practice. Direct contempts may be punished summarily, without previous proceedings; but indirect contempts can only be punished after notice and a hearing.[148] The power to punish for contempt is inherent in the courts, and can not be taken away by the legislature.[149] A distinction is also drawn by some courts between a civil and criminal contempt: proceedings in contempt instituted solely to vindicate the dignity of the court are criminal; while those instituted by private individuals to protect or enforce their rights are civil.[150] The first class, being an attack upon the dignity and power of the court, and thus threatening its very existence, are necessarily primitive and of a more aggravated character than the second; while the latter are such as do not directly affect the public business and have to do only with private controversies, though they, too, may be punished by the court.[151] At common law contempt proceedings were not reviewable by a higher court, the court in which they were had being the exclusive judge of whether the act was such an interference with its process or the exercise of its powers; and neither an appeal nor *habeas corpus* could be resorted to in such cases.[152] If, however, the court had no jurisdiction, its judgment could

[143] Smith v. Junction R. Co., 29 Ind. 546; Smith v. Brown, 3 Tex. 360, 49 Am. Dec. 748.

[144] *Ante*, § 410.

[145] State v. Root, 5 N. D. 487, 67 N. W. 590.

[146] Brown v. Brown, 4 Ind. 627, 58 Am. Dec. 641.

[147] Mowrer v. State, 107 Ind. 539; Baldwin v. State, 126 Ind. 24.

[148] Ex parte Bradley, 7 Wall. (U. S.) 364; Worland v. State, 82 Ind. 49; Whittem v. State, 36 Ind. 196.

[149] Little v. State, 90 Ind. 338; McKinney v. Frankfort, etc., R. Co., 140 Ind. 95, 97; Ex parte Terry, 128 U. S. 289; People v. Stapleton, 18 Colo. 568; Cartwright's Case, 114 Mass. 230; Arnold v. Commonwealth, 80 Ky. 300, 44 Am. Rep. 480; Yate's Case, 4 Johns. (N. Y.) 318.

[150] Thompson v. Pennsylvania R. Co., 48 N. J. Eq. 105. See People v. Court of Oyer, etc., 101 N. Y. 245, 54 Am. Rep. 691.

[151] Thompson v. Pennsylvania R. Co., *supra*.

[152] In re Swan, 150 U. S. 637; Ex parte Maulsby, 13 Md. 625; People v. Spalding, 10 Paige (N. Y.) 284, affirmed in Spalding v. People, 7

be reviewed by *certiorari*, or by appeal, or by *habeas corpus*.[153] It is held by some courts, however, that an appeal will lie in a case of punishment for contempt, though there be no statute authorizing it.[154] In most states, however, the proceedings in contempt cases are regulated by statutes, and provision is made for appeals.

III. Attorney's Relation to His Client.

§ **415. In general—The retainer.**—The relation of attorney and client, like that of any other principal and agent, generally grows out of a contract of employment, which in this case is called a "retainer."[155] As a general rule, the attorney must be retained before he can be considered authorized to appear in an action either to prosecute or to defend; but, of course, the employment may be established by implication, the same as in other cases of agency. "The payment of a fee is the most usual and weighty item of evidence to establish the relationship of client and attorney, but it is by no means indispensable. The essential feature of the professional relation is the fact of employment to do something in the client's behalf. There must be an agreement, expressed or implied, for compensation, but whether payment is made in part or in whole by retainer in advance is not material. Nor is it even indispensable that the compensation should be assumed by the client. Ordinarily, it is so from the nature of the employment, which in the vast majority of cases involves the guarding or enforcement of the client's interest against an adverse one, and is therefore exclusive. But even adverse interests, if to be amicably adjusted, may be represented by the same counsel, though the cases in which this can be done are exceptional and never entirely free from danger of conflicting duties."[155a] The appearance of an attorney in a case in court is, however, in itself *prima facie* evidence of his authority to appear; but this presumption may be rebutted by evidence of his non-employment or want of authority.[156] The court may, and upon proper showing, must call upon any attorney who appears in a

Hill (N. Y.) 301; Jordan v. State, 14 Tex. 436; In re Rosenberg, 90 Wis. 581.

[153] Ex parte Hollis, 59 Cal. 405; People v. Court of Oyer, etc., 101 N. Y. 245, 54 Am. Rep. 691.

[154] Commonwealth v. Newton, 1 Grant Cas. (Pa.) 453; Hawes v. State, 46 Neb. 149; In re Stokes, 5 S. C. 71.

[155] See Bouvier Law Dic., tit. Retainer.

[155a] Lawall v. Groman, 180 Pa. St. 532, 57 Am. St. 662.

[156] Great West. Min. Co. v. Woodmas, 12 Colo. 46, 20 Pac. 771.

case, to show his authority;[157] but in the absence of such a showing, authority of the attorney to make such appearance will be presumed.[158] And if a party desires to question the authority of an attorney to appear, such party should file a written motion verified by affidavit, stating not only the fact of such lack of authority, but the grounds for the belief that such is the case;[159] but the authority can not be contested by plea or answer.[160] An affidavit is, however, not always deemed essential: if the party go on the stand and testify as to such want of authority, this may take the place of an affidavit.[161] Nor can an attorney in regular practice be called upon to produce his authority to appear in a case unless he has received previous notice requiring him to do so.[162]

§ **416. Right of attorney to appear—By whom, how, and when it may be questioned.**—The question whether an attorney has the authority to appear may be raised by either party to a suit;[163] but the adverse party can raise the question only by showing that his rights are in some way prejudiced, or that he has been disturbed or vexed by being brought into litigation without the consent of the other party.[164] A mere stranger to the record has no right to question the authority of an attorney in a cause.[165] The adverse party can not

[157] Cartwell v. Menifee, 2 Ark. 556; State v. Houston, 3 Harr. (Del.) 15; Belt v. Wilson, 29 Ky. 495, 22 Am. Dec. 88; Roselius v. Delachaise, 5 La. Ann. 481, 52 Am. Dec. 597; Prentiss v. Kelley, 41 Me. 436; McKiernan v. Patrick, 5 Miss. 333; Allen v. Green, 1 Bailey (S. C.) 448; Ex parte Gillespie, 3 Yerg. (Tenn.) 325; Board of Com'rs, etc., v. Purdy, 36 Barb. (N. Y.) 266; Hollins v. St. Louis, etc., R. Co., 57 Hun (N. Y.) 139, 11 N. Y. Supp. 27.

[158] Osborn v. Bank of U. S., 9 Wheat (U. S.) 738; Wheeler v. Cox, 56 Iowa 36; Kerr v. Reece, 27 Kan. 469; Louisville, etc., R. Co. v. Newsome, 13 Ky. L. Rep. 174; Postal Tel. Cable Co. v. Louisville, etc., R. Co., 43 La. Ann. 522, 9 So. 119; Steffe v. Old Colony R. Co., 156 Mass. 262.

[159] Standefer v. Dowlin, 1 Hemp. (C. C.) 209; People v. Mariposa Co., 39 Cal. 683; Valle v. Picton, 16 Mo. App. 178, 91 Mo. 207; People v. Lamb, 32 N. Y. Supp. 584, 85 Hun (N. Y.) 171; Watrous v. Kerney, 79 N. Y. 496; Louisville, etc., R. Co. v. Newsome, 13 Ky. L. Rep. 174; Savery v. Savery, 8 Iowa 217.

[160] Robinson v. Robinson, 32 Mo. App. 88; North Brunswick v. Booream, 10 N. J. L. 305.

[161] Bender v. McDowell, 46 La. Ann. 393.

[162] Beckley v. Newcomb, 24 N. H. 359.

[163] People v. Mariposa Co., 39 Cal 683.

[164] M'Alexander v. Wright, 3 T. B. Mon. (Ky.) 189.

[165] Bryans v. Taylor, Wright (Ohio) 245.

raise the objection that the opposing counsel has not procured a license from the United States government.[166] The objection must always be raised before plea or answer, and at the earliest opportunity.[167] The question of authority or no authority may be determined by the court, if there be no jury, or by the jury if there be one; it being a question of fact such as a jury has the right to pass upon.[168] When the authority of an attorney is seasonably and appropriately questioned, it then devolves upon the party who questions such authority to produce some proof of the lack of such authority: the burden being on the attacking party to prove that the appearance is unauthorized.[169] The presumption in such cases is always in favor of the authority, as attorneys who are officers of the court must be presumed to have done their duty; for in such case the maxim applies that "all acts are presumed to have been rightly and regularly done."[170] But where the party represented by an attorney himself denies such attorney's authority under oath, it has been held that the burden is upon the attorney to prove such authority;[171] but where an appearance has been regularly entered by an attorney and an order made, if the party against whom such order was entered denies the authority of the attorney to enter such appearance, the burden is on such party to prove that the appearance by the attorney was without authority.[172] The authority may be shown by an express contract of employment, such as a letter or a power of attorney, or by any parol evidence raising a reasonable presumption of the existence of proper authority.[173] When considerable time has elapsed between the performance of the act and the denial of authority, the presumption in its favor is

[166] Harrington v. Edwards, 17 Wis. 604.

[167] Indianapolis, etc., R. Co. v. Maddy, 103 Ind. 200; People v. Lamb, 85 Hun (N. Y.) 171, 32 N. Y. Supp. 584; Beckly v. Newcomb, 24 N. H. 359; Rowland v. Gardner, 69 N. C. 53.

[168] Henderson v. Terry, 62 Tex. 281; Newhart v. Wolfe, 2 Penny. (Pa.) 295; Clark v. Holliday, 9 Mo. 711; Howard v. Smith, 33 N. Y. Super. 124.

[169] Bonnfield v. Thorp, 71 Fed. 924; Mutual Life Ins. Co. v. Pinner, 43 N. J. Eq. 52; Thomas v. Steele, 22 Wis. 207; Schlitz v. Meyer, 61 Wis. 418; Stubbs v. Leavitt, 30 Ala. 352; Holder v. State, 35 Tex. Cr. App. 19, 29 S. W. 793.

[170] Co. Litt. 6b, 332. See Rex v. Verelst, 3 Camp. 432, per Ld. Ellenborough, C. J.; Faulkner v. Johnson, 11 M. & W. 581.

[171] Dangerfield v. Thruston, 8 Mart. N. S. (La.) 119.

[172] Dey v. Hathaway, etc., Co., 41 N. J. Eq. 419.

[173] Rogers v. Park, 23 Tenn. 480.

strengthened by such lapse of time; and the proof of the want of such authority must be clear before it will overcome the opposing presumption. Thus where, after the lapse of six years, the authority of the attorney was questioned by the client, who refused to be bound by the attorney's appearance for him, and the attorney testified that he did not recollect whether he had authority to appear in the specific action, though it was unlikely he would have done so without such authority, and that he had previously been the counsel of the client; and the latter testified that he had no recollection whether he gave the authority or not,—it was held that the evidence was insufficient to overcome the presumption of authority furnished by the record itself.[174] And where the question was whether the attorney had sufficient authority to bind his client by a notice to take depositions served upon such attorney, it was held that proof of the fact that the attorney, who lived in the same town with the client, had previously represented him in a criminal prosecution, connected with the civil suit, was sufficient in the absence of rebutting testimony, to show that he was the authorized attorney and that the service of such notice was binding.[175] It must be remembered, however, that the mere fact of previous employment is not sufficient proof of the relation in the particular transaction in question, and only furnishes evidence of a presumption of such relation when there is no evidence to the contrary.[176] And a retainer in a case never authorizes or requires the attorney to appear for the client in collateral proceedings;[177] it does, however, give the attorney full power to transact all the business and perform all the acts incidentally necessary to the accomplishment of the main purpose.[178]

§ 417. **How far party bound by act of attorney.**—Generally speaking, and in the absence of fraud or collusion, the authorized acts of an attorney at law are binding upon the client, as in the case of any other agent, when such acts are within the scope of the authority.[179] The client, like any other principal, is responsible for such acts, the same as if they had been performed by him in person. If the attorney has been negligent in the conduct of legal proceedings, and the negligence has proved injurious to the client, the latter can not set up such neg-

[174] Fisher v. March, 26 Gratt. (Va.) 765.

[175] Coffin v. Anderson, 4 Blackf. (Ind.) 395.

[176] Ex parte Lynch, 25 S. C. 193; Hoover v. Greenbaum, 61 N. Y. 305.

[177] Jacobs v. Copeland, 54 Me. 503.

[178] See Scott v. Elmendorf, 12 Johns. (N. Y.) 315; Day v. Welles, 31 Conn. 344.

[179] Beck v. Bellamy, 93 N. C. 129; Wood v. Wood, 59 Ark. 441, 43 Am. St. 42.

ligence as an excuse, any more than if he had himself been guilty of it. Thus, where an attorney, with full authority in the premises, neglects to file and prosecute a claim against the estate of an insolvent debtor, the creditor can not be excused for the laches on account of the failure of his attorney to act.[180] And when an authorized attorney is present in court when an order is made granting a new trial as of right, under a statute, and fails to object, the client affected thereby is presumed to have consented to the order.[181] Not only is the client deprived of any relief from the injurious consequences naturally following from the negligent or other wrongful conduct of the attorney, but the client is personally liable to any third party who sustains an injury which proximately results therefrom,[182] as we had occasion to show when we considered the liability of the principal to third persons.[183]

§ **418. Duty of attorney to client—Fidelity—Confidential communications.**—We have already noticed the duties an attorney owes to the court, and the consequences that may result to him from a failure to discharge them.[184] An attorney also owes certain well-defined duties to his client, which we now propose to consider. Like any other agent, an attorney at law is bound to observe toward his principal, the client, the utmost good faith; the relation between them is one of the most sacred and confidential that may exist between one person and another; he must, therefore, in the language of one of the statutory provisions, "maintain inviolate the confidence, and at every peril to himself, preserve the secrets of his client."[185] He can not, as a general rule, be compelled to reveal his client's secrets, even in a court of justice. He violates the confidence reposed in him, by disclosing the confidential communications that have come to him in the course of the relation; and this is true whether such communications were made in a suit or in the course of private negotiations.[186] Such communications should never be disclosed except with the consent of the client.[187] Attorneys are liable for betraying confidence reposed in them, and especially for disclosing to the opponent in a cause the evidence in their client's case, or other secrets intrusted to them. In the

[180] Leo v. Green, 52 N. J. Eq. 1.

[181] Harvey v. Fink, 11 Ind. 249.

[182] Foster v. Wiley, 27 Mich. 244, 15 Am. Rep. 185.

[183] See *ante*, § 323, *et seq.*

[184] *Ante*, § 408, *et seq.*

[185] Burns Ind. Rev. Stat. 1901, § 979, cl. 5.

[186] Weeks Attys. at Law, § 310.

[187] Jenkinson v. State, 5 Blackf. (Ind.) 465; Bigler v. Reyher, 43 Ind. 112

first place, they are guilty of gross breach of moral duty; in the second, they are guilty of gross violation of professional duty and professional decency; and in the third place, they are civilly liable in damages to their clients. It is gratifying to find that the cases on this subject are exceedingly few.[188] After an attorney has been retained or consulted in a matter by a client, he can not consistently with professional duty act for the opposing party in the same matter, or in matters directly connected therewith.[189] If, in the course of his employment, he becomes cognizant of defects in his client's title, he can not take advantage of it to the latter's detriment without laying himself liable to him.[190] He should never attempt to represent conflicting interests, and if he does so, he may render himself liable to both his clients in damages. Thus, where an attorney is employed to borrow money and also assumes to act for the lender, by giving him advice, etc., though he receives no pay for the same, he will be liable for wrong advice to the lender, as to the sufficiency of the security, etc.[191]

§ 419. **Duty to exercise skill, care, etc.[191a]—Liability for negligence.**—An attorney, as agent of his client, is bound to exercise due and proper skill and care in the performance of his trust. He holds himself out as possessing, to a reasonable extent, the knowledge and skill required in the proper performance of his professional duties; and if he does not possess these, or fails to exercise proper skill and care, he will be liable in damages for any injury resulting to his client.[192] He is not liable, however, for every mistake that may occur in his practice, and if he has fair capacities and knowledge, and employs a reasonable degree of care and attention, he will not be liable.[193]

188 Weeks Attys. at Law, § 310.

189 Wilson v. State, 16 Ind. 392; Price v. Grand Rapids, etc., R. Co., 18 Ind. 137.

190 Ringo v. Binns, 10 Pet. (U. S.) 269; Cumberland Coal Co. v. Sherman, 30 Barb. (N. Y.) 553; Galbraith v. Elder, 8 Watts (Pa.) 81.

191 Donaldson v. Haldane, 7 Cl. & F. 762. See also, Taylor v. Blacklow, 3 Scott 614, 3 Bing. N. C. 235, 32 E. C. L. 116; Arnold v. Robertson, 3 Daly (N. Y.) 298.

191a See *ante*, § 342.

192 Gilbert v. Williams, 8 Mass. 51, 5 Am. Dec. 77; Watson v. Muirhead, 57 Pa. St. 161, 167, 98 Am. Dec. 213; Harter v. Morris, 18 Ohio St. 492; Walker v. Stevens, 79 Ill. 193; Von Wallhoffen v. Newcombe, 10 Hun (N. Y.) 236.

193 Kepler v. Jessup, 11 Ind. App. 241; Watson v. Muirhead, 57 Pa. St. 161, 98 Am. Dec. 213; Tuley v. Barton, 79 Va. 387; Cox v. Sullivan, 7 Ga. 144, 148, 50 Am. Dec. 386.

He is not required to possess a perfect knowledge of the law, and if doubt exists as to any legal proposition, or if well-informed lawyers may properly differ as to the same, he will not be held liable for his error, if such his advice or act should prove to be; nor would he be liable for any error of judgment as to new and undecided points.[194] He may, of course, assume the law to be correctly decided by the supreme court of his own state, even though such decision be subsequently overruled.[195] He must, however, know the settled rules of pleading and practice, and must use ordinary care in the preparation of his cases for trial.[196] In New York, where a statute regulating proceedings in attachment required an affidavit to be filed showing the existence of a cause of action and that the plaintiff was entitled to recover the sum stated over and above all counter claims; and an attachment was dissolved because the affidavit did not state the source of affiant's information,—it was held by the federal court that the attorney who prepared the affidavit was not liable to his client in damages for the omission: the decisions of the lower courts being conflicting as to the requirement of such statement in the affidavit, and the court of appeals not having passed upon the question.[197] And in a case in Indiana, a building and loan association was advised by its attorney that the title to a parcel of real estate was perfect and available to secure a loan applied for by one of its shareholders, and it was shown that the title to such real estate was held by the shareholder and his wife as tenants by the entireties. The borrower died before the loan was repaid, and his wife successfully resisted a suit for the foreclosure of the mortgage given to secure the loan: her defense being that she signed the note and mortgage merely as the surety of her husband. The supreme court decided that although, if the rule that in such cases a mortgage given by the husband and wife was void as to both had been clearly established by the decisions of the court before the advice was given, the attorney would have been liable for the damages sustained, yet that as such had never been the ruling of that court up to that time, the mistake of such advice was not such as

[194] Stevens v. Walker, 55 Ill. 151; Citizens' Loan, etc., Ass'n v. Friedley, 123 Ind. 143, 18 Am. St. 320; Babbitt v. Bumpus, 73 Mich. 331, 16 Am. St. 585.

[195] Marsh v. Whitmore, 21 Wall. (U. S.) 178; Citizens' Loan, etc., Ass'n v. Friedley, 123 Ind. 143, 18 Am. St. 320.

[196] Citizens' Loan, etc., Ass'n v. Friedley, 123 Ind. 143, 18 Am. St. 320.

[197] Ahlhauser v. Butler, 57 Fed. 121.

could be said to have resulted only from the want of ordinary knowledge and skill, or from the failure to exercise reasonable care and caution.[198] But an attorney must keep pace with the literature of the profession; and if a principle of law has been established by the decision of a court which has been reported and published a sufficient length of time to have become known to those who exercise reasonable diligence, and such attorney has failed to inform himself thereof, and his client has suffered from his ignorance, he will be liable for such damages as the client has sustained thereby.[199] An attorney must also know the statutes of his state, and the settled rules of pleading and practice of his court;[200] and if he undertakes to sue out a writ in a court of peculiar constitution, he must ascertain the machinery the court has with which to carry out the objects of the action.[201] But the skill and knowledge of an attorney must be considered with reference to the locality in which he practices, unless he undertakes that he has knowledge of the law of the jurisdiction with reference to which he is engaged to transact the business. Hence, if he fail to inform his client that under the law of a foreign state a building contract must be registered in order to be binding upon the parties to it, when the law of that state so requires, he will not be liable on account of his ignorance, although he was employed to draw a contract that would in all respects be binding on the parties; the mere acceptance of the employment not being a sufficient tacit agreement that he would draw the contract so as to make it binding by the laws of such foreign state.[202] In all cases, it is the client's duty to give the attorney a true statement of the facts of the case upon which he seeks advice or action; and there can be no liability on the part of the practitioner if the facts are wrongly stated to him.[203]

§ **420. Further as to attorney's liability for negligence.**—As in every other case of agency, it is the duty of an attorney at law to enter upon the performance of his undertaking as contemplated by his employment, and to pursue the task diligently until completed.[204] Hence, if an attorney who has a claim placed in his hands for collec-

[198] Citizens' Loan, etc., Ass'n v. Friedley, 123 Ind. 143, 18 Am. St. 320.

[199] Goodman v. Walker, 30 Ala. 482, 68 Am. Dec. 134.

[200] Godefroy v. Dalton, 6 Bing. 460, 19 E. C. L. 210.

[201] Cox v. Leech, 1 C. B. N. S. (87 E. C. L.) 617.

[202] Fenaille v. Coudert, 44 N. J. L. 286.

[203] Lee v. Dixon, 3 F. & F. 744.

[204] See *ante*, § 229.

tion, delays bringing suit beyond a reasonable time, a right of action arises against him for damages, if the claim is lost by reason of such negligence on his part.[205] But when the attorney has obtained judgment on a claim in favor of the client, and sued out execution, he will be justified in ceasing to take further steps—such as additional executions—whenever he is influenced, in good faith, by a prudent regard for the interest of his client, not to pursue the matter further, and will not be liable, though he has not asked for further instructions, unless he has disobeyed the positive directions of the client; but, as a general rule, it may be stated to be the duty of the attorney not only to sue out mesne and final process, but subsequent writs of execution, when the first proves inadequate.[206] He is not bound to institute new and collateral suits, such as actions against the sheriff or other officers for failing to do their duty, nor to attend to the levy of an execution, nor to search for property out of which to make the debt, as these are the duties of the sheriff.[207] But if there is a forthcoming bond with surety, it is incumbent upon him to pursue such surety thereon, and he is guilty of negligence for failing to do so.[208] And where an attorney has undertaken on behalf of a mortgagee to see that a mortgage is a first lien on the property of the mortgagor, he is liable to such mortgagee for a failure to use reasonable care and skill in performing that duty; and that without reference to the fact that he was the attorney of the mortgagor and that the latter paid the fees: the adverse interest not being such as to render the employment illegal.[209] And in such case the mortgagee need not wait until he has foreclosed his mortgage, but may, if he can establish the injury and damage, sue and recover from the attorney the difference between the value of the security contracted for and that actually received; the cause of action being the breach of duty, and not the damages, which are only an incident.[210] It is, of course, his duty, in cases in court, to prepare all the pleadings and take all necessary steps in the progress thereof; and, for a failure to perform this duty, in whole or in part, he will be liable to his client in such damages as the latter may have sustained.[210a] It seems that he is

[205] McArthur v. Baker, 7 Ky. L. Rep. 440.

[206] Pennington v. Yell, 11 Ark. 212, 52 Am. Dec. 262.

[207] *Ibid.*

[208] Lawall v. Groman, 180 Pa. St. 532, 57 Am. St. 662.

[209] *Ibid.*

[210] See Walker v. Goodman, 21 Ala. 647; Hunter v. Caldwell, 10 Q. B. (59 E. C. L.) 69.

[210a] Walsh v. Shumway, 65 Ill. 471.

not liable, however, for the result of any unskillful pleadings filed in a case by another attorney, and before his connection with it.[211] He is liable for negligence in failing to make proper preparations for the trial, such as the summoning of witnesses, etc.[212] Like other agents employed for the performance of a particular task, he must perform the same in person.[213] But the retainer of a member of a legal firm is equivalent to a retainer of all the members thereof, and, in the absence of an agreement to the contrary, any one of such members may conduct the case.[214] Whether an attorney has been negligent in any matter intrusted to him may be a question of fact for the jury; unless the facts are undisputed, in which case it is a question of law for the court.[215] The burden of establishing negligence is, of course, on the party asserting it.[216] To entitle the plaintiff to recover, however, it must be proved that some injury has resulted to the client.[217] Thus, where an attorney had a claim for collection, it was held in an action of negligence against the attorney that the plaintiff was required to show, not only that it was a valid debt, but that the debtor was solvent.[218] Where no injury is shown proof of negligence will entitle the plaintiff to nominal damages only.[219] The presumption is always in favor of the attorney having discharged his duty, and if the contrary be alleged, it devolves upon him who so alleges to prove the negligence charged. It is, moreover, the duty of the client, in case of negligence by the attorney, to do all he can to avert the injury; and hence, if a client discharge an attorney on account of his negligence, and the judgment taken by said attorney could then be collected by execution, it is the client's duty to have execution issued; and, on failure to do so, he can not recover the damages from the attorney if the debt be ultimately lost, the attorney being liable for nominal damages only; for, in that case, the client's own negligence must be regarded as the proximate cause of the loss.[220] And so, where the executors of a client sued an attorney for damages for

[211] Lowry v. Guilford, 5 C. & P. 234, 24 E. C. L. 542.

[212] Mercer v. King, 1 F. & F. 490.

[213] Eggleston v. Boardman, 37 Mich. 14, 19.

[214] *Ibid.*

[215] Hunter v. Caldwell, 10 Q. B. (59 E. C. L.) 69; Gambert v. Hart, 44 Cal. 542.

[216] See Pennington v. Yell, 11 Ark. 212, 52 Am. Dec. 262; Holmes v. Peck, 1 R. I. 242.

[217] Palmer v. Ashley, 3 Ark. 75; Spiller v. Davidson, 4 La. Ann. 171.

[218] Pennington v. Yell, 11 Ark. 212, 52 Am. Dec. 262.

[219] Nave v. Baird, 12 Ind. 318.

[220] Read v. Patterson, 11 Lea (Tenn.) 431.

improper advice, and the trial court refused to charge for the defendant that if the jury believed the plaintiff's testator had acted from other motives than the advice given him by the defendant, then the plaintiffs were not entitled to recover, it was held on appeal that the refusal so to charge was error, as there was some evidence to support this hypothesis.[221]

§ 421. **Duty of attorney to obey instructions.**—Except as to matters of minor detail, and those things about which the attorney possesses special and technical information, it is his duty to follow the instructions of his client; and, for a failure to do so, he renders himself liable to the latter for any damages sustained as a result thereof.[222] In case of doubt, it is the duty of counsel to advise his client what he believes is the best course to pursue; and if thereupon the client chooses to disregard the advice and pursue his own course, the attorney may safely follow the client's instructions, and it is perhaps safer for him to do so than otherwise.[223] In many things he is bound at his peril to obey implicitly. Thus, if an attorney be instructed to sue on a claim placed in his hands, it is not for him to determine as to the wisdom of such a course: his duty is to obey; and, for a failure to do so, he will be liable for any loss the client may suffer, without regard to whether or not the attorney acted in good faith and did what he regarded as being for the best interest of his client.[224] But, in the absence of specific instructions, the attorney always has a wide discretion, and where he acts in good faith and according to what his best judgment dictates as the wisest course to pursue, no liability attaches if loss should ensue.[225]

§ 422. **Attorney's duty to account and pay over.**[225a]—When an attorney has collected money or received other property belonging to his client, it becomes his duty to turn the same over to him at once. While it is true that the attorney will generally not be liable to an action for money thus collected until after a demand has been made

[221] Cochrane v. Little, 71 Md. 323, 18 Atl. 698.

[222] Read v. Patterson, 11 Lea (Tenn.) 431; Cox v. Livingston, 2 W. & S. (Pa.) 103, 37 Am. Dec. 486.

[223] Nave v. Baird, 12 Ind. 318.

[224] Cox v. Livingston, 2 W. & S. (Pa.) 103, 37 Am. Dec. 486.

[225] Webb v. White, 18 Tex. 572; Morrill v. Graham, 27 Tex. 646; Bennett v. Phillips, 57 Iowa 174; Pennington v. Yell, 11 Ark. 212, 52 Am. Dec. 262.

[225a] As to the duty of keeping an account, see Brigham v. Newton (La.), 30 So. 849.

upon and a refusal by him,[226] yet if he fails to use due care in preserving the money or property,—as by placing the funds in an insolvent bank, etc.,—the resulting loss will be the attorney's and not that of the client.[227] The only safe course for an attorney to pursue when he has collected money for his client is either to remit the amount collected, retaining any fees or commissions due him out of the same, or to place the same to the credit of the client in some solvent bank and advise him thereof without delay. Moreover, there may be circumstances under which the necessity for a demand will be dispensed with; as where the attorney has failed within a reasonable time to give notice of the collection to the client, or where he has shown a disposition to withhold the money.[228] He should use due care and diligence in making remittances, as forwarding by unauthorized or unusual modes is always at the risk of the attorney;[229] but he is always safe in remitting by the mode directed by his client.[230] Upon failure to remit or pay on demand, an action will lie against the attorney. The client may treat the attorney's failure to remit as a conversion and sue in trover,[231] or he may sue *ex contractu*, in *assumpsit*. The money in the hands of an attorney which has been collected for the client is a trust fund, and must be kept as such, separate and apart from the funds of the attorney. The statute of limitations does not begin to run in such case until after demand and refusal, or acts equivalent thereto.[232] But if the attorney denies his liability and sets up a cross-demand exceeding the amount of the funds in his hands. this would constitute a waiver of the demand.[233] And it is held that where an attorney fails to notify his client of the collection, suit may be maintained by the latter without a previous demand.[234] In Georgia it has been decided that no demand is necessary as a prerequisite to the maintenance of a suit in such case;[235] and in Iowa it was ruled

[226] Pierse v. Thornton, 44 Ind. 235; Claypool v. Gish, 108 Ind. 424; People v. Brotherson, 36 Barb. (N. Y.) 662; Beardslee v. Boyd, 37 Mo. 180.

[227] Grayson v. Wilkinson, 13 Miss. 268.

[228] Weeks Attys. at Law, §§ 308, 309.

[229] Grayson v. Wilkinson, 13 Miss. 268.

[230] See Kimmell v. Bittner, 62 Pa. St. 203.

[231] Houston v. Frazier, 8 Ala. 81.

[232] Sneed v. Hanly, Fed. Cas. No. 13,136, Hemp. 659; Roberts v. Armstrong, 64 Ky. 263, 89 Am. Dec. 624; Cord v. Taylor, 5 Ky. L. Rep. 852.

[233] Walradt v. Maynard, 3 Barb. (N. Y.) 584; Krause v. Dorrance, 10 Pa. St. 462, 51 Am. Dec. 496.

[234] Jett v. Hempstead, 25 Ark. 462; Denton v. Embury, 10 Ark. 228.

[235] Shepherd v. Crawford, 71 Ga. 458.

that the commencement of an action against the attorney was a sufficient demand upon him.[236] In Kansas the rule is laid down that in the absence of proof to the contrary, it will be presumed that the attorney notified the client of the collection and that the latter had demanded and been refused the money within a reasonable time.[237] In Pennsylvania it was held that where the money is not paid over within a reasonable time, it is culpable negligence for which an action will lie without a demand.[238]

§ **423. Client's obligations to attorney—Compensation—Contra for attorney's fees.**—As was shown in a previous portion of this work,[239] under the common-law system of jurisprudence, counsellors, advocates, barristers, etc., were not entitled to enforce the payment of compensation for their services by legal proceedings: such services being regarded as honorary, and presumed to have been rendered gratuitously; and this is still the law in England.[240] Ordinary attorneys, however, may recover fees by suit, even in England.[241] But in the United States it is now generally held, although some states formerly followed the English rule,[242] that lawyers stand upon the same footing as other persons who render services, and may, consequently, recover their fees on contracts, express or implied, to the same extent.[243] In states in which a license is required to practice law, an attorney can not usually recover for services until he has taken out such license.[244] Compensation may of course be fixed by express contract, as in other cases, where attorney's fees are recoverable; if not fixed thus, the attorney may recover the value of the services upon a *quantum meruit*.[245] And where the agreement is for a stipulated fee, but the attorney is discharged without fault of his own, he is entitled at least to payment for the services rendered, if not to the whole fee.[246] But if the attorney has abandoned his client's cause without just reason or ground, he can not

[236] Hollenbeck v. Stanberry, 38 Iowa 325.

[237] Voss v. Bachop, 5 Kan. 59.

[238] Glenn v. Cuttle, 2 Grant (Pa.) 273.

[239] *Ante*, § 253.

[240] 3 Bl. Com. 28; Kennedy v. Broun, 13 C. B. N. S. (106 E. C. L.) 677.

[241] Steadman v. Hockley, 15 M. & W. 553.

[242] *Ante*, § 253.

[243] Calvert v. Coxe, 1 Gill (Md.) 95, 123; Brackett v. Sears, 15 Mich. 244; Wilson v. Burr, 25 Wend. (N. Y.) 386.

[244] Hittson v. Browne, 3 Colo. 304; Tedrick v. Hiner, 61 Ill. 189.

[245] Weeks Attys. at Law, § 334.

[246] Myers v. Crockett, 14 Tex. 257; French v. Cunningham, 149 Ind. 632.

recover for services rendered.[247] In such case the contract for the stipulated amount of the fee may be treated as rescinded, by the client, and the attorney can recover nothing, or at most only as much as the services were reasonably worth, under the circumstances, and on the basis of a *quantum meruit.*[248] In case of the death, insanity or other disability of such attorney before the termination of the employment, his representative may recover what the attorney has earned.[249] And generally, in the absence of a specific agreement to the contrary, an attorney who is retained in a suit must serve to the end before his right to compensation attaches, the contract being regarded as entire;[250] but where he withdraws for a justifiable cause he can recover proportionately, at least.[251] In addition to the counsel fees, the attorney may recover from the client the reasonable expenses to which he has been put by reason of the litigation, and recover indemnity the same as other agents.[252] But the attorney can not recover fees for an undertaking which was immoral, illegal, or contrary to public policy;[253] nor for services that were entirely useless.[254] Attorneys' fees are often provided for in notes, mortgages, etc., the intention being that the debtor shall pay the expenses of the creditor in case the debt must be collected by suit. It is generally held that where a mortgage provides for the payment of reasonable attorneys' fees by the mortgagor to the mortgagee, in case of foreclosure, such provision is valid and may be enforced in the absence of prohibitory statutes.[255] As to whether such a stipulation may be enforced when contained in a note, is a question as to which the authorities are not entirely harmonious, although the weight of authority is in favor of the validity of such contracts.[256] As to the amount to be recovered, when the instrument

[247] Holmes v. Evans, 129 N. Y. 140.

[248] Morgan v. Roberts, 38 Ill. 65.

[249] Callahan v. Stotwell, 60 Mo. 398.

[250] Nichols v. Scott, 12 Vt. 47. See Sessions v. Palmeter, 75 Hun (N. Y.) 268.

[251] Tenney v. Berger, 93 N. Y. 524; Powers v. Manning, 154 Mass. 370.

[252] Helps v. Clayton, 17 C. B. N. S. 553; Vilas v. Bundy, 106 Wis. 168.

[253] See Treat v. Jones, 28 Conn. 334; Gammons v. Johnson, 76 Minn. 76, 78 N. W. 1035. See *ante*, § 264.

[254] French v. Cunningham, 149 Ind. 632, 639. See *ante*, § 264.

[255] Tallman v. Truesdell, 3 Wis. 443, 454; Smiley v. Meir, 47 Ind. 559; Walter v. Dickson, 175 Pa. St. 204; Hermes v. Vaughn, 3 Tex. Civ. App. 607.

[256] See in favor: Billingsley v. Dean, 11 Ind. 330; Stoneman v. Pyle, 35 Ind. 103; Sperry v. Horr, 32 Iowa 184; Wilson Sewing Mach. Co. v. Moreno, 6 Sawy. (C. C.) 35; Barton v. Farmers', etc., Bank, 122 Ill. 152; Dorsey v. Wolff, 142 Ill. 589; Smith v. Silvers, 32 Ind. 321. On the other hand, it has been decided that such a stipulation in a note is against public policy, usuri-

provides a stipulated sum or percentage it will be taken, *prima facie,* as the correct amount;[257] but the courts will not render judgment for excessive amounts though stipulated in the note or other instrument: the amount of the fee, though agreed upon in the contract, will be allowed only when reasonable; and the true value of the services may always be shown, although a larger sum has been agreed upon.[258] Where the amount is to be a percentage, it will be estimated on the principal and interest of the note.[259] When the debt is past due, no preliminary demand upon the debtor seems to be necessary in order that the plaintiff may be entitled to recover attorney's fees.[260] In all such cases the fees are recoverable only on the idea of indemnity; in principle, therefore, the plaintiff should not be allowed to recover more than he is required to pay to his attorney; and such fees belong to the client, and not to the attorney.[261] When the compensation is to be valued by *quantum meruit,* it is customary and proper to prove the value of such services by other attorneys at law, who, as professional experts, are acquainted with the value of such services.[262] But if such services were rendered under the eye of the court, the amount may be fixed by the court without hearing testimony;[263] and the court has a right to judge of the reasonableness of an attorney's charges without reference to the opinions of witnesses.[264] In estimating the value of the services, it is proper for plaintiff to prove his ability as a lawyer, in order to show the value of the services.[265] It is also proper to consider the amount that was recovered in the litigation, as a result of the attorney's services.[266] The amount in controversy, the ability of the party to pay, and the result of the effort, are proper circumstances to consider in fixing the compensation of an attorney in a

ous and invalid: Witherspoon v. Musselman, 14 Bush (Ky.) 214, 29 Am. Rep. 404; Boozer v. Anderson, 42 Ark. 167. There are statutory provisions in some states regulating contracts of this character.

[257] Dorsey v. Wolff, 142 Ill. 589.

[258] Moore v. Staser, 6 Ind. App. 364; Johnston v. Speer, 92 Pa. St. 227.

[259] Behrens v. Dignowitty, 4 Tex. Civ. App. 201.

[260] Walter v. Dickson, 175 Pa. St. 204. See Moore v. Staser, 6 Ind. App. 364.

[261] Moore v. Staser, 6 Ind. App. 364; Goss v. Bowen, 104 Ind. 207.

[262] Knight v. Russ, 77 Cal. 410; Stow v. Hamlin, 11 How. Pr. (N. Y.) 452; Vilas v. Downer, 21 Vt. 419; Blizzard v. Applegate, 61 Ind. 368.

[263] Dorsey v. Creditors, 5 Mart. N. S. (La.) 399; Baldwin v. Carleton, 15 La. 394.

[264] Gaylord v. Nelson, 7 Ky. L. Rep. 821.

[265] Lungerhausen v. Crittenden, 103 Mich. 173.

[266] Berry v. Davis, 34 Iowa 594.

case.[267] As to contingent fees and the doctrine of champerty and maintenance applicable thereto, they have been fully considered in another place in this work.[268]

§ 424. **Taxation of costs—Attorney's bill.**—As to those classes of legal practitioners known in England as solicitors and attorneys, the Roman *honorarium* theory has never been applied, and such solicitors or attorneys were consequently at liberty to enter into any contract as to fees upon which they and their clients could agree, provided such fees were not exorbitant; but under the judicature acts of 1873 and 1875, the fees which solicitors may charge are prescribed with great minuteness. And by statute it is also provided that suit for professional services of an attorney or solicitor shall not be commenced until the expiration of one calendar month after the delivery to the party charged, or sending to him by the post, or leaving at his last known place of abode, a bill of such fees, charges, and disbursements, subscribed by the attorney or his partner (if a firm), or his personal representative, if deceased, or inclosed in or accompanied by a letter subscribed in like manner referring to such bill.[269] It was the intention of this statute to give the client an opportunity to examine the bill and take advice upon it before any action is taken. In such case, it is not sufficient for the attorney to show the bill to the client: a copy must be left with him; and no action can be maintained for such services if this step is omitted.[270] If within the month allowed for examination no application is made to have the charges taxed by the taxing officer, the client can not question the reasonableness of the bill before a jury. The bill may, within a prescribed time, be submitted to a taxing officer by the client, who may refer any one or more items therein to the judge of the court, if he is in doubt as to its correctness.[271] It is also held that courts have the power to refer an attorney's bill to some officer for taxation independently of any statute.[272] Courts doubtless have inherent power to regulate the compensation of attorneys for services performed under their immediate supervision or observance. The matter of compensation of attorneys is now, in this country at least, generally left to the parties to settle

[267] Lombard v. Bayard, 1 Wall. Jr. (C. C.) 196.

[268] *Ante*, § 256, *et seq.*

[269] Weeks Attys. at Law, § 326.

[270] Weeks Attys. at Law, § 327.

[271] Weeks Attys. at Law, § 331.

[272] *Ibid.;* Filmore v. Wells, 10 Colo. 228.

by contract, although the courts may exercise a revisory power over these, so far as their reasonableness is concerned.

§ **425. Further as to fees of attorneys.**—Professional men, though they tacitly hold themselves out as possessing the required skill and knowledge to practice their professions successfully, are not insurers of their success as to the result of suits or proceedings in which they are retained, and hence an attorney may enforce the collection of his fee though unsuccessful.[273] But an attorney can not recover compensation for services upon a *quantum meruit* where the contract with the client was champertous, contrary to public policy, and the result of personal solicitation.[274] "To hold that a party can thus illegally stir up and instigate litigation," said Mitchell, J., speaking for the supreme court of Minnesota, in the case cited, "and yet obtain the benefits of it by ignoring the special contract and bringing suit upon a *quantum meruit* for services performed in prosecuting the litigation which he has unlawfully instigated, would be a travesty on justice, and to permit a party to do indirectly what he can not do directly." And Canty, J., in a concurring opinion said: "The great and crying evil which the courts should condemn most strongly is making a practice of soliciting such cases. An attorney who does this should, in my opinion, be disbarred; and surely he should not be rewarded by aiding him to recover remuneration for doing the very act, or one of the series of acts, for which he should be disbarred. On the plainest principles, the courts should condemn the practice of ambulance-chasers and prowling assignees who thus stir up litigation, and should refuse to aid them in recovering fees in such cases." As a general rule, however, the mere fact that the contract he has made with his client for fees is champertous, will not defeat the action for compensation upon the *quantum meruit*.[275] The court may also, in determining the value of counsel fees, take into consideration any negligence or other mistake of which the attorney was guilty during the progress of the suit or other matter in reference to which the fee is claimed.[276]

§ **426. Attorney's lien.**—An attorney, as we have previously seen,[277] at common law, had a lien on the property and papers of his

[273] See Fenner v. Succession of McCan, 49 La. Ann. 600.

[274] Gammons v. Johnson, 76 Minn. 76, 78 N. W. 1035.

[275] Gammons v. Johnson, 69 Minn. 488, 72 N. W. 563.

[276] Kruger v. Merguire, 130 Cal. 621, 63 Pac. 31.

[277] *Ante*, §§ 287-298.

client, in the hands of such attorney, for his fees. There are two kinds of common-law liens; namely, a general lien and a particular or special lien.[278] An attorney has a general lien upon the property and effects of his client, in his hands, for any balance due such attorney for any services as such attorney;[279] and he has a particular lien on any article of property or money for "labor bestowed or money expended in regard to that particular property."[280] To entitle the attorney to a general lien, the services for which the debt is owing must be of a professional character; and if papers have been delivered to him for a specific purpose, the lien can not usually extend beyond the purpose. The lien is frequently subject to the equitable right of set-off; and it may be waived by a contract inconsistent with that on which the lien is founded or by an express contract.[281] The particular or special lien of an attorney attaches to the fruits of a judgment or decree procured by the services of the attorney, as well as to deeds, insurance policies, and other documents in his hands which he has been employed to prepare and those he has been engaged to copy, abstract, peruse, consult, or exhibit to a witness on the trial;[282] it is limited, however, to the property or thing as to which or in connection with which the services have been performed, and in this respect it differs from the general lien, which attaches to all such articles generally on account of any balance due the attorney for professional services.[283] An attorney has an equitable (particular) lien on the judgment obtained by him for his client, and it only extends to such services as were performed in that particular suit.[284] Thus, an attorney who has in his hands a claim for collection can not hold the money arising out of such collection for a general debt due him from his client. And where an attorney received from an agency a claim for collection, it was held he could not retain from the proceeds thereof the amount of a debt owing to him for other services rendered such agency.[285] But where an attorney obtained a money judgment for his client, for damages, caused by the wrongful issuing of an injunction, such attorney having resisted the injunction proceedings and rendered

[278] *Ante*, § 288.

[279] McDonald v. Railroad, 93 Tenn. 281.

[280] Weeks Attys. at Law, § 369. See Finance Co. v. Charleston, etc., R. Co., 52 Fed. 526; Story Ag., § 383.

[281] Weeks Attys. at Law, § 369.

[282] *Ibid.*

[283] Matter of H., 87 N. Y. 521; Ward v. Craig, 87 N. Y. 550.

[284] Adams v. Fox, 40 Barb. (N. Y.) 442; Mansfield v. Dorland, 2 Cal. 507; McWilliams v. Jenkins, 72 Ala. 480.

[285] McMath v. Manns Bros., etc., Co. (Ky.), 15 S. W. 879.

other services in connection with the establishment of his client's right which culminated in the rendition of such judgment for damages, it was ruled that the attorney's lien on the judgment covered his fees in all the suits concerning the same matter, all being parts of a single litigation, though technically there were several suits.[286] As a general rule, however, the lien on the judgment extends only to fees in that particular case, although there may have been other suits intimately connected therewith.[287] An attorney also has an equitable lien on the distributive share of an heir, for services rendered the estate.[288] But there can be no lien by a prosecuting attorney on a judgment against a defaulting officer for money due the public, for the public funds can not be taken to satisfy the debts of individuals.[289] The English practice of taxing attorney's fees as costs once obtained in some of the American states.[290] When this was the rule, the attorney's lien extended only to such fees and disbursements as had been taxed as costs.[291] But this practice has been abandoned in nearly all if not all the states, and attorney's fees are not now taxed as costs any longer, while the matter of liens for fees is regulated largely by statutes.[292] A general lien can not be enforced by legal proceedings:

[286] Butchers' Naim Slaughter-house, etc., Co. v. Crescent City Fine Stock Lending, etc., Co., 41 La. Ann. 355.

[287] Massachusetts, etc., Const. Co. v. Gill's Creek Tp., 48 Fed. 145.

[288] Koons v. Beach, 147 Ind. 137.

[289] Wood v. State, 125 Ind. 219.

[290] See Ocean Ins. Co. v. Rider, 22 Pick. (Mass.) 210; Wright v. Cobleigh, 21 N. H. 339; Mansfield v. Dorland, 2 Cal. 507; Rooney v. Second Ave. R. Co., 18 N. Y. 368.

[291] Massachusetts, etc., Const. Co. v. Gill's Creek Tp., 48 Fed. 145; Forsythe v. Beveridge, 52 Ill. 268, 4 Am. Rep. 612; Miller v. Newell, 20 S. C. 123, 47 Am. Rep. 833, 836.

[292] See Warfield v. Campbell, 38 Ala. 527, 533, 82 Am. Dec. 724. In Indiana an attorney has a lien on a judgment only if he indorses on the margin of the order book a notice of his intention to hold such lien: Burns Rev. Stat. 1901, § 7238. Under this statute the supreme court holds that the notice must be entered within a reasonable time after the entry of judgment: Blair v. Lanning, 61 Ind. 499; Alderman v. Nelson, 111 Ind. 255. In Minnesota it is declared that an attorney has no lien except such as is given by statute: Forbush v. Leonard, 8 Minn. 303. In New Jersey the attorney's lien on the avails of a judgment can be satisfied only when he has received money on the judgment or has arrested it *in transitu*, or where the defendant has paid the judgment after receiving notice of the attorney's claim: Braden v. Ward, 42 N. J. L. 518. In New York the attorney has a lien on the judgment for his costs, and this can not be released by his client: Haight v. Holcomb, 16 How. Pr. (N. Y.) 173. In some cases it is held that

such a lien, which extends to all papers, documents and vouchers in his hands, depends wholly on possession, and gives the attorney the right to retain the same till his bill is paid;[293] in such cases, possession is indispensable, and hence, whenever it is parted with, the lien ceases.[294] Special liens on judgments may be enforced by equitable proceedings or according to the method pointed out by the statute in the jurisdiction where the judgment is taken. An attorney's lien on a judgment amounts to an equitable assignment,[295] and may be enforced by petition and reference.[296] The general mode, however, is by execution for the amount of the lien.[297] This is issued, of course, in the name of the client.[298] If an attorney accepts other security for his claim, he thereby waives his lien.[299] Such lien is a security for the debt due the lawyer for his services, and if he chooses to accept other security, he abandons his right to that given him by the law.[300] An attorney has no lien on real estate which may have been recovered in an action in which he has been retained.[301] An attorney's lien on a judgment was not a common-law right;[302] it exists, however, by statute in most of the American states, though not in all of them.

an attorney can have a lien on the judgment only when the amount of the compensation has been agreed upon,—never for a *quantum meruit:* In re Scoggin, 5 Sawy. (C. C.) 549; Ex parte Kyle, 1 Cal. 331; Pugh v. Boyd, 38 Miss. 326; Benedict v. Harlow, 5 How. Pr. (N. Y.) 347. In some jurisdictions it is held that an attorney has no lien on a judgment in an action for unliquidated damages: Swanston v. Morning Star Min. Co., 13 Fed. 215; Henchey v. Chicago, 41 Ill. 136; Abbott v. Abbott, 18 Neb. 503, 26 N. W. 361.

[293] In re Wilson, 12 Fed. 235.

[294] Eddinger v. Adams, 4 Kulp (Pa.) 401; Nichols v. Pool, 89 Ill. 491.

[295] Koons v. Beach, 147 Ind. 137; Weeks v. Wayne Circuit Judges, 73 Mich. 256; Marshall v. Meech, 51 N. Y. 140, 143; In re Wilson, 12 Fed. 235; Andrews v. Morse, 12 Conn. 444.

[296] Brown v. New York, 11 Hun (N. Y.) 21.

[297] Ackerman v. Ackerman, 11 Abb. Pr. (N. Y.) 256.

[298] See Albert Palmer Co. v. Van Orden, 64 How. Pr. (N. Y.) 79.

[299] See 13 Encyc. of Pl. & Pr. 151, *et seq.*

[300] Cowell v. Simpson, 16 Ves. Jr. 275.

[301] Smalley v. Clark, 22 Vt. 598. But see Smith v. Young, 62 Ill. 210.

[302] In re Wilson, 12 Fed. 235.

CHAPTER XII.

AUCTIONEERS.[1]

§ **426a. Authority of auctioneer.**—An auctioneer derives his authority principally from the vendor, whose agent he is primarily;[2] although from the time the hammer falls till the close of the bargain he is also the agent of the purchaser; though this is only for the purpose of making the memorandum of sale, so as to satisfy the statute of frauds.[3] His authority from the vendor may be conferred, as in the case of any other agency, by formal power of attorney, sealed or unsealed, by word of mouth, or by implication.[4] Such authority may be dissolved by the revocation of either party at any time before the fall of the hammer;[5] and it terminates by accomplishment of the purpose when the sale has been completed and the purchase-price paid. It has sometimes been doubted whether the authority of an auctioneer to sell land is not required to be in writing; but the rule is well established that such authority may be given verbally and will be sufficient.[6] But an auctioneer represents not only the vendor

[1] For definition, etc., see *ante*, § 24.

[2] Story Ag., § 27.

[3] Gill v. Hewett, 7 Bush (Ky.) 10; Meadows v. Meadows, 3 McCord (S. C.) 458, 15 Am. Dec. 645; Episcopal Church v. Wiley, 2 Hill Ch. (S. C.) 584, 30 Am. Dec. 386; Thomas v. Kerr, 3 Bush (Ky.) 619, 96 Am. Dec. 262; Simon v. Motivos, 3 Burr. 1921, 1 W. Bl. 599.

[4] Bateman Auctions 20–23.

[5] Bateman Auctions 30.

[6] Doty v. Wilder, 15 Ill. 407, 60 Am. Dec. 756; Yourt v. Hopkins, 24 Ill. 326.

at the sale, but, as we have seen, he is also the agent of the purchaser, for the purpose already stated. This relation between the auctioneer and purchaser is indeed a very unusual one, as generally an agent can not act for both principals in a sale when their interests are antagonistic.[7] The agency for the purchaser, while it can not be said to arise or be inferred from the official position of the auctioneer, is generally to be shown by the acts and conduct of the purchaser or bidder at the auction, such as standing by and bidding, either by means of words or by making signs or responding to signs given by the auctioneer;[8] slight evidence of assent being often sufficient.

§ **427. The statute of frauds—Duty of auctioneer.**—The seventeenth section of the English statute of frauds provides that "no contract for the sale of any goods, wares or merchandise, for the *price* of ten pounds sterling, or upwards, shall be allowed to be good, except the buyer shall accept part of the goods so sold, and actually receive the same, or give something in earnest to bind the bargain, or in part payment, or that some note or memorandum in writing of the said bargain be made, and signed by the parties to be charged by such contract, or their agents thereunto lawfully authorized."[9] By what is commonly known as "Lord Tenterden's Act,"[10] it was further provided, among other things, that the provisions of the seventeenth section "shall extend to all contracts for the sale of goods of the *value* of ten pounds sterling, and upwards, notwithstanding the goods may be intended to be delivered at some future time, or may not at the time of such contract be actually made, procured, or provided," etc.; and it is held that the effect of this supplementary statute is to substitute the word "value" for the word "price" in the seventeenth section.[11] The English statute of frauds has been generally adopted by the American states; but they do not all agree as to the amount necessary to bring a contract within its purview: in Indiana, New York and Massachusetts the amount being $50; while in other states the amount runs from $33.33 upward. Although it was at one time

[7] *Ante*, § 54.

[8] Mews v. Carr, 1 H. & N. 484; Bartlett v. Purnell, 4 A. & E. 792; Johnson v. Buck, 35 N. J. L. 338, 10 Am. Rep. 243; Hart v. Woods, 7 Blackf. (Ind.) 568; O'Donnell v. Leeman, 43 Me. 158; Smith v. Jones, 7 Leigh (Va.) 165, 30 Am. Dec. 498.

[9] 29 Charles II, ch. 3, § 17.

[10] 9 Geo. IV, ch. 14, § 7.

[11] Scott v. Eastern Counties R. Co., 12 M. & W. 33; Harman v. Reeve, 18 C. B. 587, 25 L. J. C. P. 257.

questioned whether auction sales were meant to be included within the seventeenth section of the statute of frauds, it is now universally recognized that they are within the statute.[12] And this applies to sales of land as well as personal property.[13] An auctioneer can not act as such at the sale of his own property and bind the purchaser by a memorandum without express authority: in that case, he would be acting as agent for a party to a contract to which he himself was the adverse party. "The great mischief intended to be prevented by the statute [of frauds]," said Bigelow, J., in *Bent* v. *Cobb*,[14] "would still exist if one party to a contract could make a memorandum of it which could absolutely bind the other. If such were its true construction, it would be a feeble security against fraud, or, rather, it would open a door for its easy commission. A vendor could fasten his own terms on his vendee. If it was a written contract binding on the purchaser, he could not show by parol evidence that the terms of the bargain were incorrectly or imperfectly stated. He could not vary or alter it by the testimony of those present at the sale. The publicity of a sale by auction would be no safeguard against false statements of the terms of sale made in a written memorandum signed by a party acting in the double capacity of auctioneer and vendor. The chief reason in support of the rule that an auctioneer, acting solely as such, may be the agent of both parties, to bind them by his memorandum, is, that he is supposed to be a disinterested person having no motive to misstate the bargain of both parties. But this reason fails, where he is the party to the contract and the party in interest also." If the seller is present in person, directing and controlling the sale, having simply employed a crier to cry the sale and knock the property off to the best bidder, the crier is not an auctioneer in the regular sense of the term, and has no authority as such to bind the purchaser by a memorandum; and the same is true as to the seller.[15] Nor does the fact that the vendor

[12] Hinde v. Whitehouse, 7 East 558; Kenworthy v. Schofield, 2 B. & C. 945; Morton v. Dean, 13 Metc. (Mass.) 385; People v. White, 6 Cal. 75; 2 Kent Com. 540; Hadden v. Johnson, 7 Ind. 394; Pike v. Balch, 38 Me. 302; Ruckle v. Barbour, 48 Ind. 274.

[13] People v. White, 6 Cal. 75; Ruckle v. Barbour, 48 Ind. 274; Episcopal Church v. Wiley, 2 Hill Ch. (S. C.) 584, 30 Am. Dec. 386; Gill v. Hewett, 7 Bush (Ky.) 10; Kenworthy v. Schofield, 2 B. & C. 945, per Bayley, J.; Buckmaster v. Harrop, 13 Ves. Jr. 456.

[14] 9 Gray (Mass.) 397, 69 Am. Dec. 295.

[15] Adams v. Scales, 1 Baxt. (Tenn.) 337, 25 Am. Rep. 772; Buckmaster v. Harrop, 13 Ves. Jr. 456.

is the owner only by virtue of a trust deed or in the capacity of trustee for another change the rule that he can not be auctioneer and vendor at once; this would only add another inconsistent function to those already exercised by him: it would make him at the same time the vendor, the auctioneer, and the agent of the purchaser, which are such incompatible positions that he could not justly discharge the duties of all of them in relation to the same subject-matter.[16] And so, a guardian, executor or administrator can not act as auctioneer of the property of his *cestui que trust* and bind the purchaser by a memorandum made at the sale, without express authority to do so.[17] The memorandum need not be signed by the auctioneer himself, but may be made by his clerk if done under the auctioneer's supervision. The rule applies, it is true, that delegated authority can not be again delegated;[17a] and unless the purchaser assents to such act of the clerk he can not be bound by it; but the assent may be shown by circumstantial evidence; and if the memorandum is made by such clerk, at the time of the sale, in the presence of the purchaser and auctioneer, it is sufficient to satisfy the statute.[18] The memorandum should contain the names of the parties, the articles sold, the price, terms of sale, and promise of the party to be charged.[19] Auctioneers usually keep a salesbook in which such memoranda are entered.[20] The memorandum, however, need not be kept in one paper or book, and may, if properly connected, be contained in two or more such papers, although parol evidence is not admissible to show the connection.[21] As to the time when the memorandum must be made, to satisfy the statute, the rule is that it must be done contemporaneously with the sale; that is, before the proceedings end.[22] The reason for the rule is that the bidder, when the

[16] Tull v. David, 45 Mo. 444, 100 Am. Dec. 385.

[17] See Bent v. Cobb, 9 Gray (Mass.) 397, 69 Am. Dec. 295; Tull v. David, *supra.*

[17a] Bateman Auctions 29.

[18] Doty v. Wilder, 15 Ill. 407, 60 Am. Dec. 756; Smith v. Jones, 7 Leigh (Va.) 165, 30 Am. Dec. 498.

[19] See Cherry v. Long, Phil. (N. C.) 466; McMullen v. Helberg, 6 L. R. Ir. Eq. 463; Lewis v. Wells, 50 Ala. 198; Ridgway v. Ingram, 50 Ind. 145; Norris v. Blair, 39 Ind. 90; Wilstach v. Heyd, 122 Ind. 574; Morton v. Dean, 13 Met. (Mass.) 385; O'Donnell v. Leeman, 43 Me. 158, 69 Am. Dec. 54. As to what constitutes a sufficient memorandum of the sale of land, see McBrayer v. Cohen, 92 Ky. L. 479, 18 S. W. 123.

[20] See Doty v. Wilder, 15 Ill. 407, 60 Am. Dec. 756; Bateman Auctions 159.

[21] Johnson v. Buck, 35 N. J. L. 338, 10 Am. Rep. 243; Bateman Auctions 157.

[22] Horton v. McCarty, 53 Me. 394.

article is knocked down to him, calls on the auctioneer or clerk to put his name down as the purchaser; and when this is done in his presence, it is presumed to be done with his consent, and there is but little danger of fraud or mistake; whereas, if the auctioneer or other person were permitted to make the entry afterwards, there might be danger of substituting other purchasers for the real ones, and upon different terms, thus defeating rights already vested and imposing liabilities never contracted.[23] But if a pencil memorandum be made at the time, and, as soon as possible after the sale, it be entered in the auctioneer's salesbook, the entry is considered an original one, and it is sufficient.[24]

§ 428. **Conduct of the sale.**—As shown in the last preceding section, an auctioneer can not, as a general rule, sell his own property at auction, and bind the purchaser by the memorandum, unless notice of the ownership has been publicly given by him at the sale. It sometimes happens that the vendor is obliged to reoffer the property for sale, where the former bidder has failed to comply with the conditions or to make good his bid. In the conduct of such a resale, it sometimes becomes a question whether the vendor may become the purchaser of the property. In a late New York case where the question was decided,[25] a majority of the court held that, in such a case, if the sale was fairly conducted, and due notice thereof given, with an opportunity for inspection of the property, the sale would be valid. Vann, J., speaking for the majority of the court, said: "While the courts below recognized this rule, they did not apply it, for they held that the sale at auction was no sale at all, because a man can not sell to himself. This would be true of an attempt to make a private sale to one's self, but it is not true of a sale at public auction, fairly conducted by a licensed auctioneer, and made at a reasonable time and place, after adequate opportunity to see the property, due advertisement to the public and personal notice to the vendee, when the real purpose is to ascertain the value of the property. The law is satisfied with a fair sale, made in good faith, according to established business methods, with no attempt to take advantage of the vendee; such as the jury might have found was the sale under consideration.

[23] Per Staples, J., in Walker v. Herring, 21 Gratt. (Va.) 678, 8 Am. Rep. 616.

[24] Episcopal Church v. Wiley, 2 Hill Ch. (S. C.) 584, 30 Am. Dec. 386. See also, McComb v. Wright, 4 Johns. Ch. (N. Y.) 659; Gill v. Bicknell, 2 Cush. (Mass.) 355.

[25] Ackerman v. Rubens, 167 N. Y. 405, 82 Am. St. 728.

The primary object of the sale was not to pass title from the vendor, but to lessen the loss of the vendee. The subject of the sale had no market value, and the amount for which it could be sold depended largely upon taste and fancy. A public competitive sale by outcry to the highest bidder, duly advertised and made upon notice to the vendee, is a safer method of measuring the damages than a sale by private negotiation, which has been held sufficient.[26] A fair public sale, in the absence of other evidence, is competent proof of value. The plaintiff did not conduct the sale himself, but placed the yacht in the hands of a public auctioneer for sale without reservation, on account of whom it might concern. While the auctioneer was his agent he could not lawfully control him so as to prevent an honest sale. The defendant had notice and an opportunity to protect himself, yet he asked for no postponement, made no request, gave no instruction, and did not even appear at the sale. If the plaintiff's agent had refrained from bidding, the property would have gone to a stranger for a less sum than it finally brought, and yet, in that event, even according to the defendant's theory, the sale would have been valid. The fact that the plaintiff outbid all competitors did not render the sale invalid, for he had a right to bid, provided he took no advantage by trying to prevent others from bidding or by disregarding any reasonable request of the defendant, or in any other way. If he had acted as auctioneer, or in collusion with the auctioneer, or there was any evidence of furtive effort on his part, or anything to challenge the fairness of the sale, the action of the trial court in virtually withdrawing the cause from the jury might have been justified, but the mere fact that he was the highest bidder at a public sale, the fairness of which is not questioned in any other respect, did not warrant the direction for nominal damages only. The object of the sale was to measure the damages caused by the default of the defendant, and they were diminished instead of being increased by the action of the plaintiff. We forbear further discussion, because the question is no longer open in this court, as it was involved in a case recently decided by us upon careful consideration after full discussion by counsel.[27] In that case, as in this, the property was sold at auction to a representative of the vendor, and the point was distinctly made on the argument before us that as the vendor was the real purchaser, 'the sale was colorable only and absolutely without effect upon the

[26] Citing Van Brocklen v. Smeallie, 140 N. Y. 70.

[27] Citing Moore v. Potter, 155 N. Y. 481, 63 Am. St. 692.

rights of the parties.' While we did not discuss the question in our opinion, it was necessarily involved, was passed upon in consultation, and decided. Both upon principle and authority we think that the amount for which the yacht was struck off to the vendor at an auction sale fairly conducted, upon notice to the vendee, with no suspicion of fraud or undue advantage, was lawful evidence of the value of the yacht and presented a case for the consideration of the jury." Haight, J., with whom concurred Gray and Werner, JJ., dissented on the ground that the vendor could not sell to himself. "Selling as agent," said Judge Haight, "he can not sell to himself. Selling involves contracting, and a person can not contract with himself and bind others thereby. If he could sell to himself publicly he could privately, and thus be able to perpetrate a fraud or an injustice which might be difficult to detect or prove.[28] In this case the sale was made by the seller to himself. It was made through the agency of an auctioneer, it is true, but the auctioneer was his agent and represented him in the transaction." The dissenting opinion considered that the question presented here was neither raised nor involved in the case of *Moore* v. *Potter.*[29] All auction sales should be open to full competition; and bids made in good faith by responsible parties should be accepted, as otherwise the auctioneer might subject himself to the imputation of fraud, for which he would be liable in damages. But he is not compelled to receive a bid from one whom he knows, or in good faith believes, to be irresponsible:[30] he may, for that reason, reject the bids of infants, lunatics, drunkards and others under disability. An auctioneer should not take it upon himself to become a bidder for others; as that would place him in the attitude of acting as agent for one whose interest is adverse to that of the seller; and, besides, would introduce into the transaction circumstances of suspicion which would tend to throw doubts upon its fairness.[31] It is the duty of the auctioneer to conduct the sale in an open manner, with fidelity to the seller and fairness to bidders. He has not the right to employ by-bidders simply to "puff" the property without the intention

[28] Citing Van Brocklen v. Smeallie, 140 N. Y. 70, 75; Pollen v. Le Roy, 30 N. Y. 549, 557; Dustan v. McAndrew, 44 N. Y. 78; Hayden v. Demets, 53 N. Y. 426; Bain v. Brown, 56 N. Y. 285.

[29] 155 N. Y. 481, 63 Am. St. 692.

[30] Hobbs v. Beavers, 2 Ind. 142, 52 Am. Dec. 500; Murdock's Case, 2 Bland (Md.) 461; Holder v. Jackson, 11 U. S. C. C. 546.

[31] See Randall v. Lantenberger, 16 R. I. 158; Veazie v. Williams, 8 How. (U. S.) 134; Brock v. Rice, 27 Gratt. (Va.) 812. But see Scott v. Mann, 36 Tex. 157.

of buying it, such an act being a fraud upon every genuine bidder, for which he may avoid the sale;[32] but by-bidding or "puffing" will not always avoid the sale, especially if the bid be a fair one and it be not the intention to enhance the price unreasonably.[33] At common law, "puffing" would avoid an auction sale, at the option of the bidder, unless notice was given.[34] Another thing which will make an auction sale voidable is what is known as "chilling," which is abstaining from bidding as the result of an agreement between two or more persons interested in having the property sell at a low price, not to bid against each other, and thus to stifle competition.[35] But not every agreement to abstain from bidding will necessarily render the sale voidable; thus, a number of interested parties may agree that one of them shall bid for the benefit of all, and the agreement is not illegal unless its purpose be to prevent competition.[36] Where an auctioneer discourages bidding so as to be able to secure the property himself, at a low value, it is such a fraud as will vitiate the sale.[37] Every sale at auction, unless notice be given to the contrary, means competition; and an agreement to run up the price unduly, on the one hand, by means of by-bidding, or to stifle competition on the other, is regarded as evidence of a fraud, and may avoid the sale at the option of the injured party.[38] Fraud, however, is a question of fact for the jury; and whether the intention was unduly to "puff" or to stifle competition, so as to amount to a fraud, must be left to them to determine.[39] Of course, fraud on the part of the auctioneer, in whatever manner

[32] Springer v. Kleinsorge, 83 Mo. 152; Davis v. Petway, 3 Head (Tenn.) 667, 75 Am. Dec. 789; Walsh v. Barton, 24 Ohio St. 28; Veazie v. Williams, 8 How. (U. S.) 134; Curtis v. Aspinwall, 114 Mass. 187; Towle v. Leavitt, 23 N. H. 360, 55 Am. Dec. 195; Peck v. List, 23 W. Va. 338, 48 Am. Rep. 398.

[33] Reynolds v. Dechaums, 24 Tex. 174, 76 Am. Dec. 101; Latham v. Morrow, 6 B. Mon. (Ky.) 630; Davis v. Petway, 3 Head (Tenn.) 667, 75 Am. Dec. 789.

[34] Towle v. Leavitt, 23 N. H. 360, 55 Am. Dec. 195.

[35] Pike v. Balch, 38 Me. 302, 61 Am. Dec. 248; Phippen v. Stickney, 3 Metc. (Mass.) 385; Hunter v. Pfeiffer, 108 Ind. 197.

[36] Goode v. Hawkins, 2 Dev. Eq. (N. C.) 393; Stout v. Voorhies, 4 La. 392. See also, Kearney v. Taylor, 15 How. (U. S.) 494.

[37] Brotherline v. Swires, 48 Pa. St. 68.

[38] See Smith v. Greenlee, 2 Dev. (N. C.) 126, 18 Am. Dec. 564; Veazie v. Williams, 8 How. (U. S.) 134, 137; Darst v. Thomas, 87 Ill. 222.

[39] Coxe v. Gibson, 27 Pa. St. 160, 67 Am. Dec. 454; Pike v. Balch, 38 Me. 302, 61 Am. Dec. 248; Hopkins v. Ensign, 122 N. Y. 144; Allen v. Stephanus, 18 Tex. 658.

it may be accomplished, will render the sale voidable on the part of the vendor.[40] And so, where an auctioneer, who saw a bidder approaching, at once knocked down the property to his brother, on a bid that was far less than the real value thereof, in order to prevent competition, it was held that the owner of the property could avoid the sale.[41] But a vendor who has employed "puffers" can not himself avoid the sale on that account, as that would be taking advantage of his own wrong.[42]

[40] Brock v. Rice, 27 Gratt. (Va.) 812; Myers v. Sanders, 7 Dana (Ky.) 506.

[41] Jackson v. Crafts, 18 Johns. (N. Y.) 110.

[42] Small v. Boudinot, 9 N. J. Eq. 381. The authorities are by no means agreed as to what constitutes "puffing" in the obnoxious sense, so as to render the sale voidable. In England, the law courts usually held that "puffing" was a fraud for which the sale might be avoided, while the chancery courts so modified the doctrine as to make puffing for the purpose of preventing a sacrifice legitimate: See Smith v. Clarke, 12 Ves. Jr. 477; Flint v. Woodin, 9 Hare 618. This difference in the decisions prompted parliament to enact a statute in 1867 declaring that whenever a contract would be invalid at law by reason of the employment of a "puffer" it should be deemed invalid also in equity. In the United States it is generally held that "puffing" is such evidence of fraud as will avoid the sale at the option of the purchaser. But even in this country the decisions upon the subject are not uniform. In a recent Georgia case, for example, it was held that an agreement by those entitled to the proceeds of land at an executor's sale, made with a third person, to run the property up to a certain price, so as to prevent a sacrifice, was not such as would avoid the sale, even though the parties interested agreed to take the property off his hands, in case it were knocked down to him: McMillan v. Harris, 110 Ga. 72, 48 L. R. A. 345. The opinion in this case, by Cobb, J., contains such an exhaustive review of the authorities that we think it useful to copy a large portion of it here. The learned justice said: "The controlling question to be determined is whether the conduct of Mr. Owen in entering into the arrangement with Mr. Seabrook to bid on the property in behalf of their respective clients so as to prevent its sacrifice, and bidding at the sale for that purpose without the expectation of becoming a purchaser himself, was of such a character as to authorize the court to declare that McMillan was misled, and that for that reason the sale was void, and should be set aside. To properly determine this it is necessary to investigate the law of sales at auction, and determine who is a puffer at an auction, and what conduct would amount to puffing so as to invalidate the sale. There is no decision of this court bearing directly upon this question. The presence at auction sales of persons who bid for the purpose of inflating the value of the property in behalf of those interested in the sale is a matter at the present time of very common

§ 429. **Nature of the contract of auction sale—Are separately accepted bids separate sales?**—Whether purchases of articles at an auc-

occurrence, and has been from the time that auction sales were first known. This practice has brought about many controversies which resulted in numerous cases, and the effect of such conduct has been discussed by many judges and text-writers. A person of the character referred to is usually denominated a 'puffer,' but he is sometimes referred to as a 'by-bidder,' capper,' 'decoy duck,' 'white bonnet,' or 'sham bidder.' The first time that this question seems to have come before the English courts, so far as the reported cases are concerned, was in the case of Walker v. Nightingale, 3 Bro. P. C. 263, which was decided in 1726. It was held by the house of lords in that case that a puffer could not recover compensation for his services, since they were contrary to good faith. The next case in point of time was Bexwell v. Christie, 1 Cowp. 395, which was decided by the court of king's bench in 1776. This was a decision by Lord Mansfield, and, as it was rendered prior to our adopting statute, it is controlling authority in this state: Thornton v. Lane, 11 Ga. 459, 500. For this reason it is necessary to examine that case with some care. An action was brought against an auctioneer for selling a horse at the highest price bid for him, contrary to the owner's express direction not to allow him to go under a larger sum named, and it was held that such an action would not lie, but that it would have been otherwise if the owner had directed the auctioneer to put the horse up at a particular price, and not lower. The opinion of Lord Mansfield in the case was as follows: 'The matter in question is in itself of small value, but in respect of the principles by which it must be governed it is a question of great importance. Since the trial I have mooted the point with many who are not lawyers upon the morality and rectitude of the transaction. The question is whether a bidding by the owner of goods at a sale under these conditions, namely, "that the highest bidder shall be the purchaser, and if a dispute arise, to be decided by a majority of the persons present," is a bidding within the meaning of such conditions of sale. There is no express undertaking on the part of the defendant, nor is it, as has been ingeniously said, a direction that there should be no bidding under £15, which might be fair; but the direction given to the defendant is "not to let the horse go under £15," which implies there might be a bidding under that sum. The question, then, is whether the owner can privately employ another person to bid for him. The basis of all dealing ought to be good faith; so, more especially in these transactions, where the public are brought together upon a confidence that the articles set up to sale will be disposed of to the highest real bidder. That could never be the case if the owner might privately and secretly enhance the price by a person employed for the purpose; yet tricks and practices of this kind daily increase, and grow so frequent that good men give in to the ways of the bad and dishonest in their own defense. But such a practice was never openly avowed.

tion, which have been made at different times, but which are delivered at the same time, constitute but a single sale, or more than one, is a

An owner of goods set up to sale at an auction never yet bid in the room for himself. If such a practice were allowed, no one would bid. It is a fraud upon the sale and upon the public. The disallowing it is no hardship upon the owner; for, if he is unwilling his goods should go at an under-price, he may order them to be set up at his own price and not lower. Such a direction would be fair. Or he might do as was done by Lord Ashburnham, who sold a large estate by auction. He had it inserted in the conditions of sale that he himself might bid once in the course of the sale, and he bid at once £15,000 or £20,000. Such a condition is fair, because the public are then apprised and know upon what terms they bid. In Holland it is the practice to bid downwards. The question, then, is, Is such a bidding fair? If not, it is no argument to say it is a frequent custom. Gaming, stock-jobbing and swindling are frequent. But the law forbids them all. Suppose there was an agreement to abate so much, which is the case where goods are sold by one person in the trade to another,—they abate sometimes 10 to 15 per cent. Such an agreement between the owner and the bidder at sale by auction would be a gross fraud. What is the nature of a sale by auction? It is that the goods shall go to the highest real bidder. But there would be an end of that if the owner might privately bid upon his own goods. There is no contract with the auctioneer. He is only an agent between the buyer and seller. He may fairly bid for a third person who employs him, but not for the owner. In this case there is another fraud put upon the public. For by the catalogue the goods are described to be "the goods of a gentleman deceased, and sold by order of the executor." Upon this representation many people would attend to bid on a supposition that the goods were necessarily to be sold at all events, whether valuable or not valuable; whereas they might have their suspicions if they were the property of persons living. Horses, or any other species of property, belonging to persons that are dead, are not so likely to be faulty as those which are parted with by persons in their life-time. We all remember the sale of a gentleman's wines, where vast quantities had been sent in belonging to other persons, and all sold at a very high price, under an idea they were his. The consequence was, most of the buyers were taken in. Therefore, upon full consideration, I am of opinion that a bidding by the owner in the manner contended for, and agreeable to the directions given in this case, would have been a fraud upon the sale; and, consequently, that this action against the defendant as auctioneer can not be maintained.' In Howard v. Castle, 6 T. R. 642, the decision of Lord Mansfield in Bexwell v. Christie was followed by Lord Kenyon. In Wheeler v. Collier, Moody & M. 123, a sale at which there were two puffers was held to be void; and Lord Tenterden stated that the inclination of his mind was that the employment of only one puffer would avoid a sale. In Crowder v. Austin, 3 Bing. 368, it appeared that the vendor of question as to which the English and American courts differ. This question may become important in cases in which some dispute has

a horse stationed his servant to join in the bidding at a public auction, and the servant bid up to £23 after a *bona fide* bidder had bid £12. It was held that the sale could not be enforced against a subsequent bidder. In Green v. Baverstock, 14 C. B. (N. S.) 204, it was held that upon a sale of goods by auction, where the highest bidder is to be the purchaser, the secret employment of a puffer on behalf of the vendor is a fraudulent act and vitiates the sale. In that case Byles, J., said: 'The sale is vitiated by the fraud, and void, unless the vendee, with knowledge of the fact, has acted upon it so as to deprive himself of the right to complain. This has been the law of England, and, indeed, of the whole of Europe, for a very long time indeed. It was a law of universal application even before the Christian era.' The decisions of the common-law courts of England have been almost without exception in line with the decision of Lord Mansfield in Bexwell v. Christie. The principle at the foundation of this decision was, that for one to offer his property at public outcry to the highest bidder, and then secretly arrange with another to bid on the property in his behalf, with the distinct understanding that he was not to incur any liability on his bid, was a fraud upon the right of those who attended the sale in good faith, expecting to come into competition with others like themselves who really desired to purchase the property on the best terms possible. The reason for the rule was the palpable fraud upon *bona fide* bidders. Strange as it may seem, the English court of chancery did not follow the rule laid down by Lord Mansfield, but, on the contrary, in a number of decisions this rule was criticized, and the fraud incident to puffing at auctions was not only tolerated, but approved of by that court. In Conolly v. Parsons, which will be found reported in a note in 3 Ves. Jr. 624,—a decision rendered in 1797,—Lord Chancellor Loughborough found great fault with the conclusion reached by Lord Mansfield, and also with the reasoning which led him to that conclusion. According to the rule in that case, unlimited puffing was allowable. While the decision last referred to was not followed by the court of chancery in all of its bearings, that court held on different occasions that the mere fact that one puffer was employed to prevent a sacrifice of the property would not be such a fraud as would vitiate the sale when it was otherwise free from infirmity. In Mortimer v. Bell, L. R. 1 Ch. 10, 5 Am. L. Reg. (N. S.) 310, it was held by Lord Chancellor Cranworth that the rule said to exist in equity, allowing one puffer to be employed, without notice, to prevent a sale at an undervalue, is abstractly less sound than the rule at law, which declares such employment to be fraudulent, and rests only on the authority of decisions in lower branches of the court. See also, in this connection, Flint v. Woodin, 9 Hare 618; Robinson v. Wall, 2 Phill. Ch. 372; Smith v. Clarke, 12 Ves. Jr. 477. The conflict between the rule laid down by the common-law and the chancery courts of England was finally set-arisen as to the validity of the sale or sales, owing to the operation of the statute of frauds. Thus, if purchases were made in different lots,

tled by an act of parliament which provided that, 'whenever a sale by auction of land would be invalid at law by reason of the employment of a puffer, the same shall be deemed invalid in equity as well as at law.' In the case of Peck v. List, 23 W. Va. 338, 48 Am. Rep. 398, which is one of the leading American cases on the subject, the English decisions above referred to, as well as many others by the common-law and chancery courts, are collected and commented on in the opinion of Mr. Justice Green. We have referred to such of those decisions as we deem necessary to the present discussion. The decision of Lord Mansfield must be treated as binding authority in this state, as there are none of our own decisions in conflict with the rule he there lays down. Attention was called in the argument to the fact that the record in the case of Locke v. Willingham, 99 Ga. 297, 25 S. E. 693, disclosed that certain charges of the trial judge bearing upon the subject under consideration in the present case were under review, and that the effect of the ruling in that case, which was merely a head-note, that no error of law was committed, was to approve of the charges made by the trial judge. We have examined the record in that case, and we find that the charges of the judge under review were not only not in conflict with the rule laid down by Lord Mansfield, but seem to have been in accord therewith. The following decisions and authorities will show the ruling of some of the American courts on this subject: 2 Pomeroy Eq. Jur., § 934, pp. 1336, 1337; 3 Am. & Eng. Encyc. of Law (2d ed.) 304, 305; Benjamin Sales (7th ed.), § 70, *et seq.;* 1 Warvelle Vendors 254; 1 Story Eq. Jur., § 293; Bispham Eq., § 209; Tiedeman Sales, § 165; Rorer Judicial Sales 44; Bateman Auctions 131; 1 Wait Act. & Def. 482; Story Sales 482; Veazie v. Williams, 8 How. (U. S.) 134, 12 L. ed. 1018; Flannery v. Jones, 180 Pa. St. 338, 36 Atl. 856; Bowman v. McClenahan, 20 App. Div. (N. Y.) 346, 46 N. Y. Supp. 945; Pennock's Appeal, 14 Pa. St. 446, 53 Am. Dec. 561; Hartwell v. Gurney, 16 R. I. 78; Nightingale v. Nightingale, 13 R. I. 113; Reynolds v. Dechaums, 24 Tex. 174, 76 Am. Dec. 101; Davis v. Petway, 3 Head (Tenn.) 667, 75 Am. Dec. 789; Miller v. Baynard, 2 Houst. (Del.) 559, 83 Am. Dec. 168; Jenkins v. Hogg, 2 Treadway Const. (S. C.) 821; East v. Wood, 62 Ala. 313; Woods v. Hall, 1 Dev. Eq. (N. C.) 411; National Bank &c. v. Sprague, 20 N. J. Eq. 159; Hinde v. Pendleton, Wythe (Va.) 354; Curtis v. Aspinwall, 114 Mass. 187, 19 Am. Rep. 332; Springer v. Kleinsorge, 83 Mo. 152; Towle v. Leavitt, 23 N. H. 360, 55 Am. Dec. 195; Staines v. Shore, 16 Pa. St. 200, 55 Am. Dec. 492. An examination of the authorities above cited, as well as of many others which might be cited, will show that the conclusions reached by the American courts on this question are far from being uniform. Some have followed the rule laid down by Lord Mansfield, others the rule announced by Lord Loughborough, and still others are not in exact accord with either, but are modifications of one or the other. It is not possible to reconcile the some of which were bidden in under circumstances which would render the transaction void under the statute, a delivery and accept-

American decisions on this subject, and it would not be profitable to undertake to do this, even if it were possible. We may lay it down as a rule without exception that the employment of a puffer at an auction sale is such a fraud as will vitiate the sale. Such being the rule, the question now to be determined is, Who is a puffer? Mr. Justice Green, in Peck v. List, cited above, thus defines a puffer: 'A puffer, in the strictest meaning of the word, is a person who, without having any intention to purchase, is employed by the vendor at an auction to raise the price by fictitious bids, thereby increasing competition among the bidders, while he himself is secured from risk by a secret understanding with the vendor that he shall not be bound by his bids.' This definition will be found to have been approved by several of the text-writers and many of the judges in the authorities and decisions above cited. It is directly in line with the ruling made by Lord Mansfield in Bexwell v. Christie. In order to constitute one who bids at a sale a puffer it is not only necessary that he shall be employed by the owner of the property which is being sold, or by some person having an interest therein, but it must appear that the person employing the puffer was so interested in the auction or act of selling that there could be made with him a binding agreement by which the person bidding incurs not the slightest risk of being called upon to comply with the terms of any bid that he may make. If he be employed by the owner of the property, and the owner has complete control of the auction and the auctioneer, as was the case in Bexwell v. Christie, then no one would question that he was a puffer, within the meaning of the law, and his employment would amount to a fraud upon the real bidder. If he be employed by a person interested in the property, although not the sole owner, and such person has complete control over the auction, so that he could entirely relieve him from all responsibility for the bid he would make, then a person employed under such circumstances would be a puffer, within the principle of the ruling made in Bexwell v. Christie. The rule is thus stated by Mr. Justice Green in Peck v. List, before referred to: 'But it is obviously unimportant whether the by-bidder is employed by the owner of the land or by some one else having a pecuniary interest in the auction about to be made, and who stands in such a relation to it that he can make good his assurance to the by-bidder that he shall not be held responsible for his bid if it happen to be the highest bid made. The real essence of the fraud is not that the owner is bidding for the property, but it consists in the fact that a by-bidder, pretending to be a *bona fide* bidder, deceives honest bidders, raises the price of the property by fictitious bids increasing competition, while he himself has good reason to believe and does believe that he is secure from any risk of being held personally liable for his bids. It is immaterial from whom he derives this assurance of immunity, provided the party giving the assurance expressly or imance of the whole might take the entire purchase out of the operation of the statute, if it constituted but a single sale. The courts in Eng-

pliedly has the power, either legally or practically, to make good the assurance. It makes no difference that such puffer or by-bidder was employed to prevent a sacrifice of the property, and was directed to bid it up, to a fixed price only; nor does it make any difference that the property only sold at a reasonable price.' In many of the cases it is said that a person employed by the owner to secretly bid upon the property would be a puffer; in still others it is said that a person so employed by the vendor would be a puffer; in still others it is stated that a person so employed by the seller would be a puffer; and in still others it is declared that a person employed by those who are pecuniarily interested in the property would be a puffer. In dealing with this subject the terms 'owner,' 'vendor,' 'seller,' and 'person pecuniarily interested in the property or its proceeds' are to be given the same meaning, and they all refer to one who, without regard to what may be his peculiar interest in the property, must have absolute control of the auction sale, and is at liberty of his own volition to discharge any bidder from liability on account of his bid. If the person conducting the sale can, notwithstanding the agreement of one who has a larger interest in the proceeds of the sale, hold the bidder responsible for the amount of his bid, then a person employed by the person having such larger interest in the proceeds would not be a puffer within the meaning of the law. Bidding by such a person would not be fraudulent, and therefore the sale would not be affected by the employment of such a person. An auctioneer is the agent of the person who directs him to make the sale. The sale is, therefore, controlled by one who directs the auctioneer. When an auction sale is declared by the auctioneer to be without reserve, this is, in effect, a statement that the person who directs the auctioneer to make the sale, no matter what his interest in the property may be, has empowered the auctioneer to sell the property to the highest bidder, and that the person directing the auctioneer will not himself bid upon the property, or employ others to do so in his behalf. Where the auctioneer puts up property without any statement as to the conditions of sale, the bidders have a right to presume that the sale is to be without reserve. The owner, vendor, seller, or person interested in the sale, whatever we may call him,—that is, the person who has directed the auctioneer to sell the property, and who will be compelled to make good to the bidder the acceptance of a bid by the auctioneer,—is not allowed to secretly bid at the sale. He may bid, however, if public notice be given of the fact, so that other bidders may know that they are coming into competition with the person who has control of the sale. The mere fact that a person is pecuniarily interested in the property which is being sold at auction does not preclude him from becoming a bidder, and this is true of judicial sales as well as private sales. No matter what interest a person may have in the proceeds land hold that the making and acceptance of each bid constitute a

of the sale, or in the property which is going to be sold at public outcry, either at private auction or judicial sale, his right to become a bidder at the sale is well recognized by numerous decisions of this court, as well as of other courts in this country, provided the sale is not under his control. See, in this connection, Freeman v. Cooper, 14 Ga. 238; White v. Crew, 16 Ga. 416; Buckner v. Chambliss, 30 Ga. 652; Kilgo v. Castleberry, 38 Ga. 512, 95 Am. Dec. 406; Kearney v. Taylor, 15 How. (U. S.) 493, 14 L. ed. 787; Richards v. Holmes, 18 How. (U. S.) 143, 15 L. ed. 304; Pewabic Min. Co. v. Mason, 145 U. S. 349, 36 L. ed. 732, 12 S. Ct. Rep. 887; Blossom v. Railroad Co., 3 Wall. (U. S.) 196, 18 L. ed. 43; Smith v. Black, 115 U. S. 308, 29 L. ed. 398, 6 S. Ct. Rep. 50; Allen v. Gillette, 127 U. S. 589, 32 L. ed. 271, 8 S. Ct. Rep. 1331; Baird v. Baird, 1 Dev. & B. Eq. (N. C.) 524, 31 Am. Dec. 399; Gulick v. Webb, 41 Neb. 706, 60 N. W. 13; Phippen v. Stickney, 3 Met. (Mass.) 384; Pennsylvania Transp. Co.'s Appeal, 101 Pa. St. 576; Thames v. Miller, 2 Woods 564, Fed. Cas. No. 13,860; Twin Lick Oil Co. v. Marbury, 91 U. S. 587, 23 L. ed. 328. Such being the right of one who is interested in the property sold or in the próceeds of the sale, who is himself not conducting the sale, and who has not such control over the sale as that he can make a binding agreement with a bidder that he will not be held responsible for his bid, it can not be a fraud for such person to employ one to bid at a sale in his behalf, even though the fact that the bidder is bidding in behalf of one interested in the property is not disclosed to the other bidders. The law charges one who attends an auction sale, no matter what its character, whether resulting from a private agreement or from a judgment of a court, that any one interested in the proceeds of the sale or in the property, and who has no absolute control over the sale, may become a competitor with any other person at the sale, and bid for the property, and such a person is under no obligation to disclose to others his intention to bid; and therefore the employment by such a person of another to bid in his behalf, without disclosing that he is representing the person so interested, could not, in any sense, be a fraud upon other bidders. It is true that the law prohibits certain persons from acting as agents of such a person. A sheriff can not become a bidder at his own sale as agent for another: Harrison v. McHenry, 9 Ga. 164, 52 Am. Dec. 435; Coleman v. Maclean, 101 Ga. 303, 28 Ga. 861; though it has been held that a sheriff acting as auctioneer at an administrator's sale may make one bid for a person interested in the property to be sold, if he discloses the fact that he is bidding for another, and if his authority is limited to making one bid, and he have no discretion to do otherwise: James v. Kelley, 107 Ga. 446, 33 S. E. 425. The matter may thus be summed up: If a person who has such control of an auction sale that he, of his own volition, can release a bidder from all responsibility for his bid, employs another, upon an understanding of that character, to bid at the sale, without disclosing for whom separate contract;[43] unless, indeed, the several articles purchased are so related that one article can not be used or enjoyed except in connection with the others, in which case only may the purchasing of the several articles constitute but a single contract.[44] But in the United States the rule seems to be otherwise: here it is held that if one person obtains a number of articles as the result of separate bids, all the purchases together constitute but one sale.[45] "When the purchase is made at an auction sale of goods, at one and the same time, and from the same vendor, although the articles purchased are numerous, and are struck off separately at separate and distinct prices, the whole constitutes but one entire contract; and the prices of the different articles fixed on are but part and parcel of it."[46]

§ 430. **Rights and liabilities of purchaser and seller.**—A purchaser of property at auction sale has the right to the possession of the same as soon as he has complied with the terms of the sale; the title vesting in the bidder *eo instante,* on being adjudicated to him;[47]

he is bidding, for the purpose of preventing the property from selling at a sacrifice, or for the purpose of making the same bring more than its actual value, the bidding by one or more persons under such employment is such a fraud upon the real bidders that the sale will be declared void at their instance. The only lawful way in which such a person can prevent a sacrifice of the property sold is to fix a minimum price, of which public notice shall be given, or make public the fact that he, either by himself or by others, will be a bidder at the sale. On the other hand, the mere fact that the person is interested in the property to be sold, or in the proceeds of the sale, will not preclude him from either bidding himself or from procuring another to bid, either openly or secretly, in his behalf, without regard to what the agreement may be with such bidder, if the one employing such bidder has not himself such control of the sale that he could absolutely release the bidder from all responsibility growing out of his having participated in the sale in that capacity. Applying the principles above announced to the facts of the present case, Mr. Owens was in no sense a puffer, and the sale was not, for any reason set up by the plaintiff in error, invalid."

[43] Emmerson v. Heelis, 2 Taunt. 38; Roots v. Dormer, 4 B. & Ad. 77, 24 E. C. L. 43.

[44] Chambers v. Griffiths, 1 Esp. 150; Gibson v. Spurrier, 2 Peake 49.

[45] Mills v. Hunt, 17 Wend. (N. Y.) 333; Coffman v. Hampton, 2 W. & S. (Pa.) 377, 37 Am. Dec. 511; Tompkins v. Haas, 2 Pa. St. 74; Jenness v. Wendell, 51 N. H. 63, 12 Am. Rep. 48.

[46] Per Sergeant, J., in Coffman v. Hampton, *supra.*

[47] Succession of Boudousquie, 9 Rob. (La.) 405; Noah v. Pierce, 85 Mich. 70.

hence, if property so purchased is destroyed by fire, before it is removed by the purchaser, it will be at his loss.[48] But as long as the conditions remain unfulfilled, the purchaser has no right to the possession of the property; hence, if the chattel is offered on a credit, the purchaser to give his note with good security, drawing interest, etc., the purchaser is not entitled to the possession of the property until such note has been tendered to the seller, or a sum of money equal to the principal and interest which would have been due upon the note at maturity.[49] The conditions prerequisite to a delivery may be waived, however; and if the seller delivers the property without a previous compliance with conditions, the delivery passes a good title.[50] As to the right of retraction of a bid, it may be said that a bidder is not bound to receive the property and pay the price, if he withdrew his bid before the hammer fell; and this is true, although it is provided in the terms of sale that bids shall not be withdrawn.[52] A bid is nothing more than an offer or proposal to purchase at such a price, and, if not immediately accepted, may be withdrawn, provided the withdrawal be made before acceptance; the retraction, however, must be made publicly, or at least so the crier can hear it, the same as the bid. On the other hand, if the purchaser does not comply with the conditions of the sale, the property having been knocked down to him, and fails or refuses to take the property thus purchased by him on the conditions of the sale, he is liable to the vendor for the purchase price, the vendor holding himself ready to turn the property over to him.[53] The vendor may, however, treat the contract as rescinded, and resell the property and sue for damages for a breach of the contract; the measure of his damages then being the difference between the sale price and the net proceeds of the resale.[54] Before a resale, however,

[48] Jenness v. Wendell, 51 N. H. 63, 12 Am. Rep. 48.

[49] Wainscott v. Smith, 68 Ind. 312; Mazoue v. Caze, 18 La. Ann. 31.

[50] Burt v. Kennedy, 3 Penny. (Pa.) 238; Mitchell v. Zimmerman, 109 Pa. St. 183, 58 Am. Rep. 715; Sweeney v. Vaughn, 94 Tenn. 534.

[52] Fisher v. Seltzer, 23 Pa. St. 308, 62 Am. Dec. 335; Payne v. Cave, 3 T. R. 148.

[53] Corlies v. Gardner, 2 N. Y. Super. 345; Girard v. Taggart, 5 S. & R. (Pa.) 19, 9 Am. Dec. 327.

[54] Mount v. Brown, 33 Miss. 566, 69 Am. Dec. 362; Bowser v. Cessna, 62 Pa. St. 148; Waples v. Overaker, 77 Tex. 7, 19 Am. St. 727; Grist v. Williams, 111 N. C. 53, 32 Am. St. 782. The rule seems to be different in case of judicial sales. For example, if the sale is by a commissioner appointed by the court, the purchaser is not bound to pay until the deed is confirmed; and if the purchaser refuses to pay, and the commissioner resells the property, without reporting the first sale, the

the vendor should give the original purchaser reasonable notice of his intention to do so; and the resale must be at public auction.[55] Or he may keep the property as his own and sue for the difference between the market value and the price at which the property was struck off to the purchaser.[56] If the purchaser refuse to take the property on account of fraud at the sale, or in the conditions, he must, if he has taken the property, return it as soon as he discovers the fraud; but if he does not discover it till too late to return it before suit, he can plead the fraud as a defense, although he has not returned the property.[57] In case a right of action exists against the purchaser, it may be exercised by either the auctioneer or the seller; for the auctioneer has such a special property in the articles sold that he may bring the action in his own name without joining his principal, the seller.[58] When a purchaser has given bond for the performance of his contract, and the sale is invalid on account of the statute of frauds, he is not liable on the bond, as in such case this is also invalid.[59] The purchaser is entitled to all he has purchased at the sale, and unless the vendor has title to some portion of such property, however small, the vendor can not force him to accept the remainder, even though he offer to secure him in the part to which he has no title.[60] Nor can the vendee be compelled to accept a title which is encumbered, unless he had notice of such encumbrance.[61] But at a judicial sale there is no warranty, either of title or that the property is free from encumbrances; and the purchaser at such sale takes only what title

purchaser at the first sale is not liable: Campe v. Saucier, 68 Miss. 278.

[55] Mount v. Brown, *supra;* Bowser v. Cessna, *supra;* Hill v. Hill, 58 Ill. 239; Riggs v. Pursell, 74 N. Y. 370.

[56] Ackerman v. Rubens, 167 N. Y. 405, 82 Am. St. 728. "When the vendee of personal property, under an executory contract of sale, refuses to complete his purchase, the vendor may keep the article for him and sue for the entire purchase price; or he may keep tne property as his own and sue for the difference between the market value and the contract price; or he may sell the property for the highest sum he can get, and, after crediting the net amount received, sue for the balance of the purchase-money: Moore v. Potter, 155 N. Y. 481, 63 Am. St. 692, 50 N. E. 271; Dustan v. McAndrew, 44 N. Y. 72."

[57] Staines v. Shore, 16 Pa. St. 200, 55 Am. Dec. 492.

[58] Hulse v. Young, 16 Johns. (N. Y.) L

[59] Thomas v. Trustees, 3 A. K. Marsh. (Ky.) 298, 13 Am. Dec. 165.

[60] Pontchartrain R. Co. v. Durel, 6 La. 481.

[61] Porter v. Liddle, 7 Mart. O. S. (La.) 23.

the former owner had. If there was fraud or mistake at the sale, it may be set aside; but the objection must be made before confirmation, if then discovered; but in the absence of fraud, the sale will stand after it has been confirmed.[62] As a general rule, there is no warranty in an auction sale, in the absence of special authority given to the auctioneer; and where an auctioneer, in the absence of the owner, at the sale, stated publicly that a horse he was about to offer was sound, and no authority was shown in the auctioneer to make such statement, it was held not to be a warranty for which the seller was liable.[63] And so the statement by an auctioneer as to sheep offered for sale, that "here is a nice lot of young, sound sheep," is not a warranty that the sheep are in good health.[64]

§ **431. Duties and liabilities of auctioneer to the vendor.**—As previously stated, the auctioneer is primarily the agent of the vendor, and the rules applicable to principals and agents generally, with regard to the duty of the agent to the principal, are applicable to auctioneers. It is the duty of the auctioneer to obey the instructions of the vendor, when not contrary to law or public policy; hence, where an auctioneer is instructed not to sell certain goods below a certain price, he must start the sale at such price, and has no right to close such sale if the goods will not bring it;[65] and if he sell for less than the price authorized, it has been held that he will be liable to the owner for the difference.[66] Generally it is the duty of an auctioneer to conduct the sale in a manner that will make it binding on the vendee; and if he fail to do so, and on a resale the property sell for less, he will be liable for the difference. But he is said to be answerable only for "gross" negligence; and hence, where he failed to comply with a recent statutory regulation which was of doubtful construction, it was held that he was not liable.[67] Concerning funds in his hands derived from sales of the vendor's property, he is in duty bound to account for these, as any other agent,[68] and keep them separate from his

[62] See Farmers' Bank v. Peter, 13 Bush (Ky.) 591; Hickson v. Rucker, 77 Va. 135; Hunting v. Walter, 33 Md. 60; Wood v. Winings, 58 Ind. 322; Weaver v. Guyer, 59 Ind. 195.

[63] Court v. Snyder, 2 Ind. App. 440.

[64] McGrew v. Forsythe, 31 Iowa 179.

[65] Williams v. Poor, 3 Cranch (C. C.) 251, Fed. Cas. No. 17,732; Hazul v. Dunham, 1 N. Y. Super. 655.

[66] Steel v. Ellmaker, 11 S. & R. (Pa.) 86. Compare Pennock's Appeal, 14 Pa. St. 446, 451.

[67] Hicks v. Minturn, 19 Wend. (N. Y.) 550.

[68] Gray v. Haig, 20 Beav. 219.

own. But where he mingles them with his own funds and those belonging to other parties, the seller becomes his general creditor, and has no preference over other creditors.[69] As a general rule, he is not liable for interest on money received, unless fraudulently withheld,[70] or withheld after demand. When it is his duty to insure goods, and he neglects to do so, the risk is his own.[71] If, for any reason, he can not insure, it is his duty to notify his principal thereof. But if he insure in a solvent company, he will not be liable for any loss that may occur, though the company subsequently fail to pay the insurance.[72] It is his duty to exercise reasonable care over the property in his hands which he is to sell; and for any loss caused by his negligence, he is liable in damages to the owner or vendor.[73]

§ **432. Duties and liabilities of auctioneer to purchaser.**—As in the case of making a contract for an undisclosed principal, by an agent, an auctioneer is personally liable as vendor if he fails to disclose the name of the party for whom he is selling.[74] And where the names of the principals were disclosed in the notices and advertisements, yet if the bills were made out in the names of the auctioneers, and they undertook to deliver the goods, it was held they were personally liable for their non-delivery.[75] So, also, where the auctioneer has sold the goods without disclosing the name of the owner, and the property is afterward claimed by a superior title, the auctioneer will be liable to the purchaser for the purchase-money, in an action for money had and received.[76] The same was true where the auctioneer signed the contract for a sale of land, but did not disclose the principal: he was held personally liable for the purchase-money, including his fees, and the interest.[77] The auctioneer is also liable to the purchaser for misrepresentation or fraud perpetrated on the purchaser and resulting in injury to him. Thus, if he received from the purchaser a deposit, knowing that the vendor's title is defective, and fail to disclose that

[69] Levy v. Cavanagh, 2 Bosw. (N. Y.) 100.

[70] Turner v. Burkinshaw, L. R. 2 Ch. 488.

[71] Shoenfeld v. Fleisher, 73 Ill. 404.

[72] Johnson v. Campbell, 120 Mass. 449.

[73] Maltby v. Christie, 1 Esp. 340.

[74] Mills v. Hunt, 17 Wend. (N. Y.) 333, 20 Wend. (N. Y.) 431; Thomas v. Kerr, 3 Bush (Ky.) 619, 96 Am. Dec. 262.

[75] Elison v. Wulff, 26 Ill. App. 616.

[76] Seemuller v. Fuchs, 64 Md. 217, 54 Am. Rep. 766.

[77] Bush v. Cole, 28 N. Y. 261, 84 Am. Dec. 343.

fact to him, the auctioneer will be liable to the purchaser for the deposit, though he have already paid it over to the vendor.[78]

§ 433. **Duties and liabilities of auctioneer to third persons.**—An auctioneer, like any other agent, is never liable to a third party for a violation of his duty to his principal. But if he commit an injury to such third person, unless it be a mere nonfeasance, he will be liable. Thus, if he sell the property of a third party and pay over the proceeds to the party who has delivered the property to the auctioneer, the latter will be liable to the owner for its value in an action of trover.[79] But while this is the weight of authority, there are cases holding the contrary.[80] He has recourse, however, upon his principal for any loss he may thus sustain.[81] He is also liable for goods that were fraudulently obtained, provided he had notice of the fraud.[82] Even if he had no notice of the fraud originally, but was notified thereof subsequently to the sale, he will be personally liable for such proceeds as he may thereafter turn over to his principal; but if he turn the proceeds over without notice of the fraud, he will not be liable; and for any money advanced by him without notice of such fraud, he may hold the goods until he is reimbursed.[83] In a Massachusetts case the facts were that A, the owner of certain goods, sold them conditionally to B, the latter agreeing to pay for them in installments and not to sell or mortgage them as long as any payments were due. B mortgaged them to C, who took without notice and for value. The mortgagee had the goods sold at auction to satisfy the mortgage, which had been duly recorded. At the time of the execution of the mortgage, B was in default according to the agreement, and A had a right to the immediate possession of the goods without demand or notice. A sued the auctioneer in trover, and the supreme court held that he was liable, and that his ignorance and good faith constituted no defense to the action.[84] But, in a Tennessee case, it was held that the

[78] Edwards v. Hodding, 1 Marsh. (C. P.) 377.

[79] Kearney v. Clutton, 101 Mich. 106, 45 Am. St. 394; Hills v. Snell, 104 Mass. 173, 6 Am. Rep. 216; Coles v. Clark, 3 Cush. (Mass.) 399; Davis v. Artingstall, 49 L. J. Ch. 609, 42 L. T. 507.

[80] Rogers v. Huie, 2 Cal. 571, 56 Am. Dec. 363; Frizzell v. Rundle, 88 Tenn. 396, 17 Am. St. 908.

[81] Adamson v. Jarvis, 4 Bing. 66, 13 E. C. L. 403.

[82] Morrow Shoe Mfg. Co. v. New England Shoe Co., 57 Fed. 685.

[83] Higgins v. Lodge, 68 Md. 229, 6 Am. St. 437; Lewis v. Mason, 94 Mo. 551; Baugh v. Kirkpatrick, 54 Pa. St. 84, 93 Am. Dec. 675.

[84] Robinson v. Bird, 158 Mass. 357, 35 Am. St. 495.

registration of a chattel mortgage is not notice to an auctioneer, and he is not liable to the mortgagee even though the mortgagor acted fraudulently, where he has sold the property at the instance of the mortgagor and turned the proceeds over to him.[85]

§ **434. Duties and liabilities of vendor to auctioneer—Compensation.**—One of the duties the vendor or principal of the auctioneer owes the latter is to compensate him for his services. Where the compensation is fixed by the agreement between the two this will, of course, control;[86] when no compensation has been agreed upon, the auctioneer will be entitled to recover on the *quantum meruit;* that is to say, such commissions as are customarily paid for such services.[87] Auctioneer's fees are sometimes fixed by statute; when this is the case, the statutory compensation covers only the services he performs as auctioneer. Where he performs other services he is entitled to reasonable compensation for these, or for services beyond the mere selling in public to the highest bidder.[88] An auctioneer can not recover compensation unless he has actually sold the property; and this is true although the owner sold it himself, at private sale, the day before the day on which it was advertised to be sold at auction.[89]

[85] Frizzell v. Rundle, 88 Tenn. 396, 17 Am. St. 908.

[86] Cochran v. Johnson, 2 McCord L. (S. C.) 21; Carpenter v. Le Count, 93 N. Y. 562.

[87] Griffin v. Helmbold, 72 N. Y. 437.

[88] Russell v. Miner, 61 Barb. (N. Y.) 534.

[89] Girardey v. Stone, 24 La. Ann. 286.

CHAPTER XIII.

BANK OFFICERS.

§ **435. In general.**—The banking system in the United States and in England is conducted mostly by corporations chartered or organized for that purpose. There is no reason, however, why a firm or even a private person should not engage in the business of banking; and in point of fact a considerable portion of the banking business is still transacted by such firms and individuals, although this is not nearly so much the case now as it was formerly. But whether the banking concern be a corporation, a firm or an individual party, the business is necessarily transacted by certain agents or officers of the banks, whose duties are generally defined by the laws and usages relative to banks and banking. It would be far beyond the scope of this work to enter upon a discussion of banks and banking generally, and the student is referred to the special treatises upon those topics. We shall here confine ourselves, as the subject indicates, to a consideration of bank officers as agents of banks and banking institutions; and whatever may be said as to the latter subjects will be merely incidental to or in elucidation of our discussion of the rights and liabilities of such officers or agents.

§ **436. Bank directors.**—Ordinarily the general management and supervision of the affairs of a bank—at least when it is a corporation—devolves upon a board of directors. When the stockholders are not more numerous than the membership of the board of directors, such board may consist of all the stockholders, they having elected themselves to their positions as directors. If the bank is constituted of a firm or an individual, instead of a corporation, such firm or individual may discharge in person the business which would usually devolve upon the board of directors in case the bank were a corporation. The ordinary duties devolving upon such board are found in both the common law and the usage governing banks and banking officers in that connection; but the duties may be modified or enlarged by the provisions of the charter or the general statutes under which the incorporation may have taken place. The directors are elected by the stockholders at their annual meeting; and it has been held that all of them must be elected at one and the same time and place; and each stockholder has a right to vote for the entire directory.[90] This statement must, of course, be qualified to the extent that if all the directors are, by the law, not to be selected at the same time, all need not be voted for at the same time and place; and the same is true with regard to filling vacancies caused by death, resignation, etc.[91] The duties devolving upon the board of directors are those which devolve upon the bank itself; for the law requires the directors to have the general superintendence and active management of the concerns of the corporation. We have already pointed out some of the duties of bank directors.[92] Bank directors are in duty bound to use such care and diligence as is usually exercised by good business men of the same kind.[93] The corporate functions of the organization exercised by the board may be and in many instances are delegated to individual agents for execution, but these are under the immediate control and supervision of the board. They are, in a general way, required to know the system and rules by which the business of the bank is transacted, and also to perform many duties with regard to the same in person.[94] One of the functions which they are required to perform in person is the making of discounts: they may say to the cashier or other financial officer to make such loans as he may wish or as he may see proper, within a certain time and at certain sums, or at such sums as he may call for, up to a certain amount at certain rates of interest and upon designated conditions, and upon specified security; but while in this manner the responsibility of making the loans and discounts is to some extent shifted, and while they thus avoid making each discount or loan in person, they nevertheless are made on the authority of the

[90] State v. Ashley, 1 Ark. 513.

[91] See Jordy v. Hebrard, 18 La. 455; Prieur v. Commercial Bank, 7 La. 509.

[92] *Ante*, § 232.

[93] Hargroves v. Chambers, 30 Ga. 580.

[94] Morse Banks & Banking, § 116.

board and on the discretion of its members.[95] But the directors, like any other agents, can bind the bank only by acts that are within the scope or apparent scope of their authority.

§ 437. **Bank president.**—The president of a bank is its chief executive officer, and he has certain responsible duties to perform. He is generally elected by the directors and is usually one of them.[96] His duties and functions are determined by the charter of the corporation, if the bank be a corporation, or by the general law, or by usage among bankers, or by the actions of the directors. He can bind the bank by any act or declaration which is within the scope of his duties, but not beyond that.[97] It would be difficult to state, in a general way, the nature and extent of all the duties devolving upon this officer, and we can not hope to do more than to give a faint outline of the same; indeed, as a well-known authority informs us, "ordinarily the position is one of dignity and of an indefinite general responsibility, rather than of any accurately known powers;"[98] but, as the same authority observes, "the president is usually expected to exercise a more constant, immediate and personal supervision over the daily affairs of the bank than is required from any other director."[99] As to the validity of his election, it has been held that a majority of the board of directors constitute a quorum, and that, consequently, if a majority of such quorum vote for a candidate for president, he is elected.[100] And as to his duties, there is much in common with the chief executive officer of other private corporations. It is not always necessary that express authority be shown for his acts in order to render them binding upon the corporation: as a general rule, whatever is customary or necessary to be done by the executive officer, if done by him, will bind the corporation:[101] but if the act of the president of a private corporation is beyond the usual scope of his authority, and yet within the powers of the board of directors to authorize him to perform, then such authority must be shown.[102] Owing to the difficulty of calling the directors together so often, necessity requires

[95] See Bank of U. S. v. Dunn, 6 Pet. (U. S.) 51.

[96] Morse Banks & Banking, § 143.

[97] Wharton Ag., § 683.

[98] Morse Banks & Banking, § 143.

[99] *Ibid.*

[100] Booker v. Young, 12 Gratt. (Va.) 303.

[101] Kennedy v. Otoe Co. Nat'l Bank, 7 Neb. 59; First Nat'l Bank v. Hoch, 89 Pa. St. 324.

[102] Farmers' Bank v. McKee, 2 Pa. St. 318; Marine Bank v. Clements, 3 Bos. (N. Y.) 600.

that the president have some general authority to represent and transact business for them in their absence, and this the law accords him freely. Even when authority from the directors is required it is not essential that it should be conferred before the act is performed, but it may as well be subsequently ratified; and this may be done not only by formal resolution, but by continued acquiescence; provided, of course, the act be within the powers of the bank and not *ultra vires* or illegal.[103] But the president has no authority to bind the bank outside of the ordinary course of the company's business;[104] for example, the president of a private corporation has no power to sell the company's property;[105] nor to assign choses in action except in the usual course of business.[106] He may appear and answer in a lawsuit against the bank and employ counsel to defend.[107] In case of emergency or where the ordinary course of business warrants, the president of a private corporation may bring suits on behalf of the company as necessity or good business judgment dictates.[108] He may call together the board of directors in special session whenever he desires to place before them any matter of business requiring their attention.[109] When he has the general authority to certify checks conferred upon him, he is not thereby authorized to certify his own checks;[110] nor has he any implied authority to use the funds of the bank with which to pay his individual obligations.[111]

§ **438. The cashier.**—The cashier of a bank is its chief financial agent, who has the immediate charge of its currency and bullion as well as the securities and paper of the bank generally. It is his duty, under the direction of the board of directors, to loan money of the bank, discount notes on its behalf, collect its debts, and do whatever is necessary and proper to receive or pass away the funds of the bank

[103] Planters' Bank v. Sharp, 4 S. & M. (Miss.) 75, 43 Am. Dec. 470; Kelsey v. Nat'l Bank of Crawford Co., 69 Pa. St. 426; Neiffer v. Bank of Knoxville, 1 Head (Tenn.) 162; Minor v. Mechanics' Bank, 1 Pet. (U. S.) 46; Rich v. State Nat'l Bank, 7 Neb. 201, 29 Am. Rep. 382.

[104] Farmers' Bank v. McKee, 2 Pa. St. 318.

[105] Crump v. United States Mining Co., 7 Gratt. (Va.) 352.

[106] Hoyt v. Thompson, 5 N. Y. 320.

[107] Savings Bank v. Benton, 2 Metc. (Ky.) 240.

[108] Reno Water Co. v. Leete, 17 Nev. 203.

[109] Union Gold Mining Co. v. Rocky Mt. Nat'l Bank, 1 Colo. 531.

[110] Claflin v. Farmers', etc., Bank, 25 N. Y. 293.

[111] Chrystie v. Foster, 61 Fed. 551.

for banking purposes.[112] The cashier, like the president, is selected by the board of directors, but need not be and usually is not a member of such board. He may be elected for a term as fixed in the charter, by-laws, or by the vote of the directors, and usually holds until his successor is elected or until he is removed or dies, or the bank goes out of existence. He is usually required to give bond for the faithful performance of his duties.[113] The cashier has power to bind the bank by all his acts and conduct that are within the general scope of his authority; and whether the act is or is not within such scope is considered to be a question of law, for the decision of the court, and not for the determination of the jury.[114] The cashier has power to draw on the funds of the bank deposited to its credit in other banks, for the purpose of paying its debts, or selling drafts, or discounting notes, etc. When such a check or draft is ambiguous, parol evidence may be introduced to show that the instrument was drawn by the cashier as such, and also the purpose for which the draft was made or the check given.[115] The cashier has also the inherent power to certify checks,[116] and to buy and sell bills of exchange, when the bank engages in this branch of business;[117] he may also, as a part of his usual business, bind the bank by indorsing negotiable paper for collection or discount or for payment of the debts of the bank;[118] and he has the general power to pay the debts and obligations of the bank by executing its paper or using its funds. Although a cashier be forbidden to do certain acts by the directors, such restriction is not binding on innocent third parties, unless they have notice thereof, or unless the act be *ultra vires*;[119] he has no power to bind the bank outside the usual course of business, however.[120] As to the forms of contract by which he may bind his principal, the subject has already been touched upon

[112] Wharton Ag., § 684.

[113] Morse Banks & Banking, § 16.

[114] Peninsular Bank v. Hanmer, 14 Mich. 208. But see Merchants' Bank v. State Bank, 10 Wall. (U. S.) 604; Martin v. Webb, 110 U. S. 7, 14; Gale v. Chase Nat'l Bank, 104 Fed. 214.

[115] Mechanics' Bank v. Bank of Columbia, 5 Wheat. (U. S.) 326.

[116] Farmers', etc., Bank v. Butchers', etc., Bank, 16 N. Y. 125; Clarke Nat'l Bank v. Bank of Albion, 52 Barb. (N. Y.) 592; Merchants' Bank v. State Bank, 10 Wall. (U. S.) 604; Muth v. St. Louis Trust Co., 88 Mo. App. 596, 4 Bank Cas. 416, 67 S. W. 978.

[117] Fleckner v. Bank of U. S., 8 Wheat. (U. S.) 338, 360; Robb v. Ross Co. Bank, 41 Barb. (N. Y.) 586.

[118] See West St. Louis Sav. Bank v. Shawnee Co. Bank, 95 U. S. 557.

[119] Merchants' Bank v. State Bank, 10 Wall. (U. S.) 604.

[120] Lamb v. Cecil, 25 W. Va. 288.

in connection with that of an agent's execution of authority.[121] It may be added here that he may make a valid written contract for his principal, either as maker or indorser of paper, by acting ostensibly in the name of such principal; as, "——— bank, by ———, cashier."[122] But other forms, showing the intention to bind the bank as such, and not the cashier individually, have been held good for that purpose; as simply "A. B., cashier," or "A. B., cashier of ——— bank:"[123] his signature as "cashier" being generally interpreted to imply an intention to bind the bank.[123a] The cashier of a bank may also, as an incident of his power to collect the debts of the bank, turn over to an attorney, for collection, the notes and claims of the bank, representing debts due to it by others, if it becomes necessary to do so.[124] He may borrow money for the bank and execute the company's paper for the same.[125] The directors may, indeed, deprive the cashier of this power by placing it in the hands of some other officer, or one especially appointed for that purpose; but it being a common usage among banks for the cashier to discharge that duty, in the absence of notice of the deprivation of such power third parties would be protected in dealing with the cashier on the assumption that he had such authority.[126] Such are a few of the most generally-recognized inherent powers of bank cashiers, but they are by no means even the greater portion of these. A cashier may also perform many acts for his bank which are not a portion of his inherent authority, but which he has been especially authorized to do by the charter, or by the vote of the directors, or even by the custom of bankers in the particular community. He can only bind the bank by acts within the scope of his employment: he can not, for example, bind his principal by official indorsement of his, the cashier's, individual note;[127] and he can not render the bank liable for any acts or declarations done or made in the pursuit of his private business.[128]

§ **439. Tellers.**—Cashiers of all but very small banks have under them as assistants certain officers called "tellers." These are the

[121] *Ante*, § 207.

[122] Spear v. Ladd, 11 Mass. 94.

[123] Bank of Genesee v. Patchin Bank, 13 N. Y. 309; Robb v. Ross Co. Bank, 41 Barb. (N. Y.) 586; Houghton v. First Nat'l Bank, 26 Wis. 663. See *ante*, § 222.

[123a] See *ante*, § 222.

[124] Eastman v. Coos Bank, 1 N. H. 23.

[125] Chemical Nat'l Bank v. Kohner, 58 How. Pr. (N. Y.) 267.

[126] Crain v. First Nat'l Bank, 114 Ill. 516.

[127] West St. Louis Sav. Bank v. Shawnee Co. Bank, 95 U. S. 557.

[128] Allen v. First Nat'l Bank, 127 Pa. St. 51, 14 Am. St. 829.

cashier's subordinates, but they are not subagents in the sense of rendering him liable for their defaults. Tellers, where the business justifies it, are divided into paying tellers and receiving tellers; and, as the respective terms indicate, the one is engaged in paying out and the other in taking in the moneys of the bank. These officers are but the cashier's arms, so to speak, by which different portions of his own functions are performed.[129] They only perform such portions of the business as would otherwise be intrusted to the cashier, but is not because he has not the time to do such business himself; and hence, their functions can not be said to be independent of, but rather are concurrent with, those of the cashier. Where a statute authorized a "bank" to receive money on deposit, it was held that the cashier, as the agent of such bank, was authorized to receive money on deposit, receipt for the same, and enter it upon the books of the bank, and that the bank would be bound by his act.[130] Generally, a person desiring to make a deposit in a bank should place it with the receiving teller, as the paying teller is not authorized to receive money for the bank; and if he receives it nevertheless, he thereby becomes the agent of the depositor, and renders the bank liable only in the event he pays the money over to the proper officer and it becomes a portion of the funds of the bank.[131]

§ **440. Liability of bank for acts of officers.**—As between the bank and its officers, the former is liable for their acts only when they have been duly authorized or ratified. If an act is done outside the authority conferred on such officer or agent, the latter is responsible to the injured party in person, and may also be liable in damages to the bank, if any loss has been incurred by it. As between the bank and third persons, the former is liable for all the acts of its agents or officers performed in the course of the business in which they are employed, the same as in the case of any other agent.[132] Even if the act is outside the real and apparent authority of the officer, but is subsequently ratified by the bank,—as, for example, by retaining the benefits derived from it,—the bank will be bound by such act.[133] And so, the bank will also be bound by notice to or knowledge of its

[129] Merchants' Bank v. State Bank, 10 Wall. (U. S.) 604.

[130] State Bank v. Kain, 1 Ill. 75; Squires v. First Nat'l Bank, 59 Ill. App. 134.

[131] Thatcher v. Bank of State of New York, 5 Sandt. (N. Y. Super.) 121. See East River Nat'l Bank v. Gove, 57 N. Y. 597, 602, 603.

[132] West v. First Nat'l Bank, 20 Hun (N. Y.) 408.

[133] *Ante*. § 96, *et seq.*

officers or agents, unless the knowledge or information was obtained outside the scope of the agent's authority.[134]

§ **441. Liability of third persons to bank on contracts made with officer.**—As to the liability of third persons to the bank on contracts made on its behalf by its officers or agents, with its authority, or without such authority and subsequently ratified, it is much the same as in case of individuals or other corporations.[135] Thus, if a cashier or other officer of a bank use the bank's money in payment of his own obligations, the third party will be liable to the principal for the money thus obtained by him, unless such third party be an innocent holder of such fund, for value, without notice.[136]

[134] Bank of Columbia v. Patterson, 7 Cranch (U. S.) 299; Fleckner v. Bank of U. S., 8 Wheat. (U. S.) 338.

[135] See chap. 10, *ante*.

[136] Bank of Metropolis v. New England Bank, 6 How. (U. S.) 212; May v. LeClaire, 11 Wall. (U. S.) 217; United States v. State Bank, 96 U. S. 30.

CHAPTER XIV.

BROKERS.

§ **442. Their authority.**—We have previously given the definition of a broker and pointed out the various classes. A broker derives his authority from his principal, the same as other agents, either by express appointment or by implication; and it is proved in the same manner.[136a] A letter to a broker by his principal stating that he had paid a specified price for certain property and would not sell it for less than a certain other sum, and that the broker could have all over that sum, is at most an authority to find a buyer, but not to make the sale.[137] When it is conceded that the broker has a general authority, the particular authority claimed for him may be shown by the usages and customs of the business in which he is employed. Thus, where one employs a broker in some particular line of business, he has such implied authority as usage and custom of the business in that particular community sanction. But usage can never take the place of positive instructions;[138] and where such instructions are in writing and understood by the parties, the law will not tolerate any deviation from them so as to affect the rights of the parties.[139] Nor will usage authorize any contract which is illegal or contrary to public policy.[140] Whatever is necessary to effect the purpose of his employ-

[136a] See Jesson v. Texas Land & Loan Co., 3 Tex. Civ. App. 25.

[137] Campbell v. Galloway, 148 Ind. 440.

[138] *Ante*, § 193; Riday v. Oil, etc., Pub. Co., 7 N. Y. St. 31.

[139] Parsons v. Martin, 11 Gray (Mass.) 111.

[140] Wheeler v. Newbould, 16 N. Y. 392. See Barnard v. Kellogg, 10 Wall. (U. S.) 383.

ment is included in his implied powers, unless he has instructions to the contrary: the authority to sign "bought" and "sold" notes being one of the implied powers of a broker.[141] And where a broker sells by sample, he impliedly warrants that the bulk shall correspond to the sample; and this power is included in his general authority. In such case, the article itself not being open to inspection, the rule *caveat emptor* does not apply.[142] And so, a loan-broker has implied authority to bind his principal to the party who is to loan the money, that "full brief of title and searches, with opinion of counsel will be required;"[143] for as said by Mitchell, J., in the case cited in the note, "Any owner * * * was bound to know that a loan would not in the ordinary course of business be made on mortgage without an examination of title, and finding it marketable for mortgage purposes, and this was a matter for the opinion of counsel." A broker ordinarily has no authority to receive payment, not having the goods in his possession;[144] and this is so if he sells by sample.[145] As we have already seen, a broker can not, as a general rule, act for both parties to a sale, where there is a conflict of interest such as there usually is between the purchaser and seller of property;[146] if, however, the injured principal, with a full knowledge of all the facts, subsequently ratifies the transaction, the contract is binding on him.[147] But in respect of points in which their interests are not antagonistic, such as making the memorandum of sale, etc., the broker may lawfully represent both parties;[148] and certainly he may do so, if both principals have knowledge of the fact that he is acting for both and make no objections:[149] after he has brought the parties together, his

[141] Saladin v. Mitchell, 45 Ill. 79.

[142] Boorman v. Jenkins, 12 Wend. (N. Y.) 566, 27 Am. Dec. 158.

[143] Middleton v. Thompson, 163 Pa. St. 112.

[144] Story Ag., §§ 61, 106; Higgins v. Moore, 34 N. Y. 417. Hence a payment to a broker will not release the party who pays to him, from liability: Wharton Neg., § 714; Crosby v. Hill, 39 Ohio St. 100. See also, Law v. Stokes, 32 N. J. L. 249.

[145] Butler v. Dorman, 68 Mo. 298, 30 Am. Rep. 795.

[146] *Ante*, § 244; Farnsworth v. Hemmer, 1 Allen (Mass.) 494, 79 Am. Dec. 756; Borie v. Satterthwaite, 12 Montg. Co. L. Rep. (Pa.) 194; Marsh v. Buchan, 46 N. J. Eq. 595.

[147] *Ibid.*

[148] Story Ag., § 31. Where a memorandum is required by the statute of frauds, the broker's entry of the sale is sufficient to satisfy the statute, and is binding on both parties: Wharton Ag., § 718.

[149] Alexander v. North Western, etc., University, 57 Ind. 466.

employment ends, and he may then act for either or both principals.[150] Neither can a broker who is employed to sell purchase of himself.[151] A broker, like any other agent, should contract in the name of his principal; and if he contracts in his own name, without disclosing his principal, he makes himself personally liable; although the third party may elect to hold the principal when he discovers him.[152] When he is authorized to sell, he has no implied power to sell on credit.[153] The authority of a broker may be revoked at any time, as in other cases of agency; and the revocation may be implied from the circumstances; as, from the employment of another broker and the accomplishment by the latter of the object of the employment.[154] But where the authority is to sell within a certain time, the principal can not revoke the authority sooner and escape liability, if the broker finds a purchaser within such time.[154a]

§ 443. **Duty of broker to principal.**—It is the duty of a broker, with reference to the subject-matter of the agency, to obey the principal's instructions, to act in good faith, to exercise reasonable skill and diligence in the performance of his undertaking, and to account for all the proceeds arising from the business intrusted to him. Respecting the duty of obedience, it may be stated as an axiomatic proposition that the broker, like any other agent, engages to execute the will and judgment of his principal, and not his own; and if the broker is instructed to pursue a certain course, it is his duty to follow such instruction substantially, or give notice that he will not continue longer in the principal's employment.[155] Hence, if he has instructions to sell the principal's property at a certain price, and he sells for a less price, he will be liable to the principal for the difference;[156] and when he is directed to sell for cash, he has no discretion to sell on credit.[157] A broker is, of course, not an insurer of the success of the business in which he engages for his principal: if he follows the directions of the principal *bona fide*, this is all he

[150] See Woods v. Rocchi, 32 La. Ann. 210.

[151] Stewart v. Mather, 32 Wis. 344; Hughes v. Washington, 72 Ill. 84; Taussig v. Hart, 58 N. Y. 425.

[152] Graham v. Duckwall, 8 Bush (Ky.) 12.

[153] Illinois v. Delafield, 8 Paige (N. Y.) 527.

[154] Ahern v. Baker, 34 Minn. 98.

[154a] Blumenthal v. Goodall, 89 Cal. 251.

[155] Galigher v. Jones, 129 U. S. 193.

[156] See Dufresne v. Hutchinson, 3 Taunt. 117.

[157] Boorman v. Brown, 3 A. & E. (N. S.) 511, 43 E. C. L. 843.

is required to do; and he is not responsible for any loss that may follow.[158] The broker is not acting in good faith, if, when he is employed by one to purchase certain land, he fails to disclose to such person that he is already employed to sell the same land,[159] and if he fails to account for a surplus remaining over and above the amount given him with which to purchase.[160] It is likewise the duty of a broker to possess reasonable skill and exercise proper care in the transaction of the business intrusted to him;[161] thus, if a broker who is employed to sell real estate, through want of skill or diligence, sell the same for less than its real value, he will be liable to his principal in damages; and he will not be excused because he believed in good faith he was receiving the full value of the property;[162] and if he neglects to take sufficient security when he sells on credit, he is liable to the principal for the loss.[163] He will, of course, be liable for the difference if he sell property for less than the authorized price;[164] but if he exercise reasonable skill and care under the circumstances, and act in good faith, he will not be liable although he should make a mistake.[165] It is also the duty of a broker to account to his principal for all the proceeds of any sale he has made for him; and he is not permitted to make any profits out of such sale, even though the principal was willing to sell for a smaller amount.[166] But it has been held that where the broker was employed to buy property at a fixed sum, with the understanding that he should receive this price without reference to what he might pay for it, he can not be made to account for the difference unless the transaction is, in some way, tinctured with fraud.[167]

[158] Matthews' v. Fuller, 123 Mass. 446.

[159] Marsh v. Buchan, 46 N. J. Eq. 595.

[160] Cottom v. Holliday, 59 Ill. 176. See further, as to what is in violation of good faith of a broker, Turnbull v. Gadsden, 2 Stroh. Eq. (S. C.) 14; Taylor v. Guest, 45 How. Pr. (N. Y.) 276; Lewis v. Denison, 2 App. D. C. 387; Love v. Hoss, 62 Ind. 255; Salsbury v. Ware, 183 Ill. 505.

[161] Boorman v. Brown, 3 A. & E. (N. S.) 511, 43 E. C. L. 843; Stewart v. Muse, 62 Ind. 385.

[162] Price v. Keyes, 62 N. Y. 378.

[163] Harlow v. Bartlett, 170 Mass. 584.

[164] Taylor v. Ketchum, 28 N. Y. Super. 507.

[165] Matthews v. Fuller, 123 Mass. 446.

[166] Bassett v. Rogers, 165 Mass. 377; Merryman v. David, 31 Ill. 404; Tilleny v. Wolverton, 46 Minn. 256; Kerfoot v. Hyman, 52 Ill. 512; Stearns v. Hochbrunn, 24 Wash. 206.

[167] Anderson v. Weiser, 24 Iowa 428.

§ **444. Principal's obligations to broker—Compensation, reimbursement, etc.**—The rights of the broker, as between him and his employer, are to be found in the contract entered into between them. The chief obligation of the principal to the broker is to compensate him for his services. If the contract specifies the amount or rate of compensation the broker is to receive, that will be the amount to which he will be entitled. A broker's compensation is usually made by way of commissions; that is, by a percentage on each dollar's worth of property sold or purchased by him for the principal. If the compensation is not specified, and the services have been fully performed, the broker will be entitled to such compensation as the usages of the business in the particular community entitle him to receive under the particular circumstances. But even where the contract is express, and stipulates for a certain commission, its construction is not always free from difficulty. Thus, if the right to receive commissions be qualified, by providing that no commissions shall be paid if the property be "sold to a party sent by Mr. R."; or if the time within which sales to such persons might be made be limited,—the broker may or may not be entitled to commissions, owing to whether or not the conditions have been fulfilled.[168] Commissions are payable whenever the broker has produced a party who is ready, willing and able to buy or sell, as the case may be;[169] and the fact that the sale was actually made or not is immaterial, if the broker has done his part;[170] when a bringing together of the parties has thus been effected by the broker, his commissions are earned; and a subsequent modification of the contract, without a new consideration, would not deprive the broker of the right to recover. Thus, where a building-lot that had been placed with a broker for sale was withdrawn from market, after it had been sold by the broker, but he was laboring under the erroneous belief that the lot to be withdrawn was not the one sold, it was held that he was entitled to his commissions.[171] And a subsequent agreement that no commission is to be paid unless a deed is executed, is without consideration, and can not be enforced against the broker.[172] Where

[168] Gaty v. Clark, 28 Mo. App. 332.

[169] See *ante*, § 265; McFarland v. Lillard, 2 Ind. App. 160; Pape v. Wright, 116 Ind. 502; Cheatham v. Yarbrough, 90 Tenn. 77; Oullahan v. Baldwin, 100 Cal. 648; Telford v. Brinkerhoff, 45 Ill. App. 586.

[170] See cases in last note.

[171] Sayre v. Wilson, 86 Ala. 151.

[172] Moskowitz v. Hornberger, 38 N. Y. Supp. 114; McComb v. VonEllert, 27 N. Y. Supp. 372.

a broker acts without, or in excess of, authority, he can not generally recover commissions, unless the act be subsequently ratified.[173] Commissions are generally the kind of compensation to which brokers are entitled; but it has been held that where one renders services in assisting a broker in bringing about a sale, while, in a proper case, he may recover compensation for the services, it is not by way of commissions.[174] Compensation can generally only be collected by a broker for services when the object of his appointment has been accomplished; and when the broker, or his agent, notifies the principal of his, the broker's, inability to perform the service for which he was employed, there is an abandonment of the contract, and the principal will not be liable for the services.[175] When there is such an abandonment, the broker can collect no commissions, although the principal afterward sell the property to the person who was introduced by the broker to the owner.[176] The mere fact that the owner of the property has employed a broker to sell it will not prevent him from negotiating the sale himself, any more than it will prevent him from placing the property for sale in another agency; and in case of sale by the owner, without the assistance of such broker, and before any sale by the latter, the owner is not liable for commissions.[177] While a real-estate broker is not entitled to compensation by either party when, without their consent, he undertakes to represent two principals adversely interested,[178] it has been held that where he has a farm for sale for one principal, and is employed by another to effect an exchange of city property for the farm, and he brings the owners together, who make an exchange, there being no fraud on his part, he is entitled to collect compensation also from the party who employed him to make the exchange.[179] A broker is not complying with the terms of his employment to sell his principal's real estate by becoming the purchaser himself or selling to a syndicate of which he is a member;

[173] Hansen v. Boyd, 161 U. S. 397; Nesbitt v. Helser, 49 Mo. 383; Smith v. Schiele, 93 Cal. 144.

[174] Hawkins v. Chandler, 8 Houst. (Del.) 434, 32 Atl. 464.

[175] Everett v. Farrell, 11 Ind. App. 185.

[176] Bouscher v. Larkins, 84 Hun (N. Y.) 288, 32 N. Y. Supp. 305; Fairchild v. Cunningham, 84 Minn. 521, 88 N. W. 15.

[177] Dolan v. Scanlan, 57 Cal. 261; Waterman v. Boltinghouse, 82 Cal. 659; Doonan v. Ives, 73 Ga. 295; Stewart v. Murray, 92 Ind. 543, 47 Am. Rep. 167; Vandyke v. Walker, 49 Mo. App. 381.

[178] Chapman v. Currie, 51 Mo. App. 40; Strawbridge v. Swan, 43 Neb. 781; Cannell v. Smith, 142 Pa. St. 25, 12 L. R. A. 395.

[179] Cox v. Haun, 127 Ind. 325.

and he is not entitled to any commissions in such case, in the absence of an express agreement with full knowledge of his interest, to pay such commissions.[180] But where there was an agreement that the broker might himself become the purchaser, and the broker found a purchaser to whom the owner refused to convey, and the broker, taking a deed on his own option, conveyed to the purchaser, it was held that the broker was entitled to his commissions.[181] It is sometimes difficult to decide whether a broker has rendered such services as, under his contract, entitle him to compensation; the mere fact that he has contributed somewhat to a sale or purchase is not sufficient: he must be the efficient or procuring cause of the same.[182] And a broker can not be deprived of his commission, if he has introduced the purchaser to the seller, although the latter make the sale himself, voluntarily reducing the price of the property.[183] In addition to his compensation, a broker is also entitled to be reimbursed by his principal for any expenses, losses, or outlays on account of the business he was employed to transact, such as expenses and services in bringing the property to market, etc.;[184] but he is entitled to reimbursement only if he effects a sale or purchase, as the case may be;[185] and he can not recover compensation if he was guilty of such negligence as rendered his services worthless.[185a]

§ **445. Broker's remedies against principal.**—A broker has the same remedies as other agents, to enforce his right to compensation against the principal. The common-law remedies of *assumpsit* and debt are, of course, open to him; while in code states he may bring his action on account, or on the special contract for services, for compensation due him.[186] The broker, besides these ordinary remedies, also has a lien on the fund or subject-matter of the agency, if the same be in his possession; and he may retain his commissions, etc.,

[180] Hammond v. Bookwalter, 12 Ind. App. 177.

[181] Riemer v. Rice, 88 Wis. 16, 59 N. W. 450.

[182] Whitcomb v. Bacon, 170 Mass. 479; Tombs v. Alexander, 101 Mass. 255, 3 Am. Rep. 349; Sussdorff v. Schmidt, 55 N. Y. 319; Zeimer v. Antisell, 75 Cal. 509; Platt v. Johr, 9 Ind. App. 58; Hoadley v. Savings Bank, 71 Conn. 599, 44 L. R. A. 321.

[183] Hafner v. Herron, 165 Ill. 242.

[184] Sentance v. Hawley, 13 C. B. (N. S.) (106 E. C. L.) 458; Chilton v. Butler, 1 E. D. Smith (N. Y.) 150; Bennett v. Covington, 22 Fed. 816; Wisehart v. Deitz, 67 Iowa 121; Esser v. Linderman, 71 Pa. St. 76.

[185] Didion v. Duralde, 2 Rob. (La.) 163.

[185a] Fisher v. Dynes, 62 Ind. 348.

[186] Lockwood v. Rose, 125 Ind. 588; Wright v. Beach, 82 Mich. 469.

out of such fund;[187] but brokers, having usually no possession of the property which they buy or sell for their principals, have no general lien; and can enforce a particular lien only when they do have possession of the property or thing on which it is asserted.[188]

§ 446. **Liability of principal to third parties.**—The principal is liable on all contracts entered into in his behalf by the broker which were actually or apparently authorized, but not on contracts that were either unauthorized or in excess of the actual authority, unless they were within its apparent scope.[189] Thus, where a broker who was authorized to sell stock, without special authority to sell it on credit, nevertheless did sell it on credit, it was held that the owner of the stock was not bound by the contract.[190] And so, where a broker deviated from his instructions by taking notes and payments for a sale different from those mentioned in such instructions, of which the purchaser had knowledge, the principal was held not bound by the sale.[191] Where a broker was directed to sell cotton and deliver a bill of lading for it only upon payment of a draft drawn on the purchaser for the goods, but the broker delivered up such bill of lading upon the acceptance by the purchaser of such draft for such amount, and without receiving any money for the same,—it was held that the purchaser took no title to the property, and that an action would lie by the owner against the third party for the conversion of

[187] Vinton v. Baldwin, 95 Ind. 433; Barry v. Boninger, 46 Md. 59. An insurance broker, at common law, has a general lien on policies for any balance due him. He is usually intrusted with the possession of policies so as to enable him to make adjustment of losses; and if a policy thus in his possession was effected by him, he may retain it to secure any balance due him by his principal on their mutual accounts concerning the business: Wharton Ag., § 707.

[188] Barry v. Boninger, 46 Md. 59. "Where a broker is intrusted with possession of the property in respect to which he negotiates, thus combining with his character as a broker certain of the characteristics of a factor, he is entitled to a lien upon such property, or on the proceeds thereof, if in his possession, for his commissions:" Per Collins, J., in Peterson v. Hall, 61 Minn. 268, 63 N. W. 733. A real-estate broker has no general lien upon title papers in his hands, unless he is an attorney at law, and the relation of attorney and client subsists between him and his principal: Carpenter v. Momsen, 92 Wis. 449.

[189] Wanless v. McCandless, 38 Iowa 20; Lawrence v. Gallagher, 42 N. Y. Super. 309; Smith v. Allen, 101 Iowa 608.

[190] Wiltshire v. Sims, 1 Campb. 258.

[191] Siebold v. Davis, 67 Iowa 560.

the goods. The facts in the case show that the agency was but a special one, and the purchaser was bound to know the broker's authority.[192] Indeed, the agency of a broker is generally a limited one; and in the absence of circumstances showing that he has a general authority, parties who deal with a broker are bound to ascertain what the real extent of his authority is; and if there are letters they should ascertain their contents.[193] But the third party may safely act upon appearances, if the vendor has created these.[194] When a sale has once been completed between a broker and purchaser, and the goods shipped and bill of lading forwarded directly to the latter, it is not within the general authority of the broker to rescind the contract; and if in such case the broker receives from the purchaser the bill of lading indorsed by the latter, and thus obtains possession of the goods from the carrier or causes them to be delivered to another, the purchaser is not relieved from liability to the seller for the price at which the goods were sold on the original contract; and this is true notwithstanding a custom by which such dealings between the broker and purchaser are recognized and upheld, unless the custom was known to the seller, so that his assent to the usage could reasonably be inferred.[195] The principal is liable for the acts of a broker even though the latter had no express authority from the former, but only did some act or acts from which a holding out could be properly inferred; but the mere fact that a broker erects a sign upon property advertising it for sale by him, as agent, but without stating who is the principal or owner, does not constitute such a holding out by the principal of the broker to the public as will justify a third party to purchase the property of the broker.[196] If authority has been properly granted the broker, and in pursuance thereof he sells property and receives the required deposit, the purchaser can sue the seller and recover from him the deposit, if the conditions are broken; and he need not, in such case, sue the broker.[197] A vendor is also liable to a purchaser who has incurred loss thereby for fraud or misrepresentation in a sale by the broker who made it; but the purchaser must have relied upon the fraudulent or false representations, and

[192] Stollenwerck v. Thacher, 115 Mass. 224.

[193] Merritt v. Wassenich, 49 Fed. 785.

[194] See Association v. Miller, 1 W. N. C. (Pa.) 120.

[195] Kelly v. Kauffman Milling Co., 92 Ga. 105, 18 S. E. 363.

[196] Davis v. Gordon, 87 Va. 559.

[197] Malone v. Ruffino, 129 Cal. 514.

not upon some other fact as an inducement.[198] However, in such case, if the sale was to a firm of which the broker was a member, the firm can not recover damages from the principal for the agent's wrong; for the other members of such firm were parties to the broker's violation of his trust.[199] Where goods have been sold by sample, by the broker, there is, as we have heretofore seen, an implied warranty that the bulk of the goods will correspond with the sample; and, in such case, if they do not correspond, the seller is liable to the purchaser for the damage.[200] As a general rule, however, a broker has no implied power, by the usages of trade, to warrant the goods to be of a merchantable quality; and his principal will therefore incur no liability on account of such warranty.[201] The principal may, of course, render himself liable for the unauthorized acts of the broker by a subsequent ratification; and such ratification will, as in other cases, relate back to the time the act was performed;[202] and this is true whether the broker acted altogether without authority or simply exceeded his powers. The ratification need not be made by the principal in person, but may be effected by another agent. Hence, where a real-estate broker undertook to sell the owner's land without sufficient authority; and the owner sent another agent to make investigation, instructing him that if he found the contract price was a proper one, and it was to the principal's interest to carry it into effect, to do so in his name; and such agent, upon satisfying himself that the sale would be beneficial to the principal, agreed in writing to carry out the broker's contract,—it was held that this was a sufficient ratification to bind the principal, and that the latter might, in a proper case, be decreed to make specific performance.[203] A principal may also estop himself from denying the broker's authority, although not actually conferred. Thus, where a vendee of a mine accepted title and made part payment according to the terms agreed upon between the vendor of the mine and the broker through whom the sale was made, the court ruled that the vendor could not successfully deny the broker's authority to make the agreement and that the vendee had rendered himself liable on such agreement.[204] And where

[198] Pineville, etc., Co. v. Hollingsworth, 21 Ky. L. 899, 53 S. W. 279.

[199] *Ibid.*

[200] Boorman v. Jenkins, 12 Wend. (N. Y.) 566, 27 Am. Dec. 158; Beebe v. Robert, 12 Wend. (N. Y.) 413.

[201] Dood v. Farlow, 93 Mass. 426, 87 Am. Dec. 726.

[202] Roby v. Cossitt, 78 Ill. 638; Rowan v. Hyatt, 45 N. Y. 138.

[203] Hoyt v. Tuxbury, 70 Ill. 331.

[204] Seymour v. Slide & Spur Gold Mines, 42 Fed. 633.

a person bought apples through a broker, who examined and accepted them, it was held that the purchaser was estopped, in an action for the purchase price, to claim that the quality of such apples was not what had been bargained for.[205] "Whatever may have been the kind and quality of the apples received by the appellee," said the court, "they were the ones purchased by him through his agent, with full knowledge of their quality and condition, under an agreement to pay for them the price sued for. Therefore, if the apples were not as the appellee ordered, and he has been injured by having put off on him apples of less value, he must look to his agent, and not to appellants, for the damages." A principal, in dealing through a broker, may even estop himself from pleading usury by permitting his broker to represent that a note offered for sale by such broker for the principal is "business paper." Thus, where one was indebted to a note-broker, and, for the purpose of reducing such indebtedness, placed in the broker's hands his own promissory note to be sold by the broker at a discount of twelve per cent., the proceeds to be applied on such indebtedness; and the broker sold the note at such discount, representing that it was first-class business paper; and the maker of the note subsequently brought suit against the holder to cancel the note, as usurious,—it was decided that, the broker being the agent of the maker of the note, in the sale thereof, the maker was estopped to set up the usury.[206] "It appears," said the court, "that Ahern knew that the first note made by him was to be sold by Bound & Co. [the brokers]. He also knew, as his testimony shows, that it was to be sold in pursuance of a prior negotiation, at a discount of twelve per centum per annum. He knew that the note was not business paper. He had been a large purchaser of Bound & Co., and hence knew their mode of effecting sales of paper. It is to be inferred that he knew that in the purchase of paper at a greater rate of discount than seven per centum per annum, the buyer usually exacted a representation that the paper sold was business paper, so that he might rely upon the fact, if indeed the paper was such, or upon the estoppel if it was not."

§ **447. Bought and sold notes.**—By the usage of trade, when a broker has negotiated a sale, he makes an entry in his book and gives each party a copy thereof; or he may give out such memoranda with-

[205] Killough v. Cleveland (Tex. Civ. App.), 33 S. W. 1040.

[206] Ahern v. Goodspeed, 72 N. Y. 108.

out an entry in the book. Such memorandum, when delivered to the purchaser, is called the "bought note," and when delivered to the seller, the "sold note."[207] Although there is some conflict in the authorities, it seems to be the weight of opinion that the bought and sold notes do not constitute the original contract, but that the best evidence of this is to be found in the book entry; the bought and sold notes being sent by the broker to the vendor and vendee more in the way of information that he has acted upon their instructions.[208] But if it be the custom to make no book entry, and to use the bought and sold notes, as such, these will be sufficient, and the best evidence of the contract.[209] When a book entry has been made and signed by the broker for both parties, it is always the best evidence of the contract; and if there be a conflict between its statements and those of the bought and sold notes, the contents of the entry will be taken as the evidence of the contract.[210] If there is no entry, or it is not signed, and the bought and sold notes contain all the terms of the contract, and there is no variance between them, they are sufficient to satisfy the statute.[211] But if, in the absence of a signed entry, there is a material conflict between the bought and sold notes, the notes will not be taken to establish the existence of the contract, and the sale is invalid, or at least may be avoided;[212] the variance, however, must be a material one, or it will not render the contract invalid;[213] a mere difference in language is not a variance if the meaning be practically the same.[214] And where the vendee himself signed such a note and through the broker delivered it to the vendor, it was held that he was bound by it, though it was at variance with the note sent to the vendee.[215] To prove a variance when one note has been introduced in evidence, the other party may give in evidence the signed entry or

[207] Wharton Ag., § 719; Benjamin Sales, § 276.

[208] Sievewright v. Archibald, 20 L. J. Q. B. 529, 17 Q. B. (79 E. C. L.) 103, per Ld. Campbell, C. J.; Maclean v. Dunn, 4 Bing. 722, 13 E. C. L. 710.

[209] Hawes v. Foster, 1 Mood. & Rob. 368.

[210] Benjamin Sales, § 294.

[211] Hawes v. Foster, 1 Mood. & Rob. 368; Parton v. Crofts, 16 C. B. (N. S.) (111 E. C. L.) 11.

[212] Sievewright v. Archibald, 20 L. J. Q. B. 529, 17 Q. B. (79 E. C. L.) 103; Davis v. Shields, 26 Wend. (N. Y.) 341; Butters v. Glass, 31 Up. Can. Q. B. 379.

[213] Phippen v. Hyland, 19 Up. Can. C. P. 416; Sievewright v. Archibald, 20 L. J. Q. B. 529, 17 Q. B. (79 E. C. L.) 103.

[214] Benjamin Sales, § 304.

[215] Rowe v. Osborne, 1 Stark. 112, 2 E. C. L. 61.

the note held by himself.[216] The authority of the broker may be revoked at any time before his task has been performed; but when the broker has once signed the entry or the notes constituting the bargain, it is too late to revoke his authority, although this might have been done at any time prior to such signing.[217]

§ **448. Liability for torts.**—Both the principal and the broker are liable for torts, as in case of other agencies. The principal is only liable, of course, when the wrongful act was committed in the course of the broker's employment; while the broker is responsible for his wrongful acts whether they were committed within the scope of his employment or not. If a broker wrongfully converts a third person's goods to his own use, he is answerable to him in an action of trover, or, in a proper case, an action of *assumpsit;* and this is true, even if the conversion take place under the direction of his principal.[218]

[216] Benjamin Sales, § 298.

[217] *Idem*, § 305.

[218] Wharton Ag., § 731.

CHAPTER XV.

FACTORS.

§ **449. Who is a factor—Factors' acts.**—A factor, as was said in a previous place, is an agent who, for a commission, sells goods for his principal which the latter has consigned to him; and he is also called a "commission merchant" and a "consignee."[219] To constitute a factor the agent must pursue the business as a trade: a person who makes a single sale for the principal of some particular thing not being a factor unless it is a part of his vocation. But he need not be confined to the sale of property in the condition in which it is consigned to him: the property may undergo change by manufacturing, etc., before it is offered for sale; thus, a person who kills hogs and sells the products thereof for others is a factor.[220] A factor usually transacts his business in some locality other than that of the principal, and frequently in a different country, though not necessarily so. Ordinarily the factor must have the goods in his possession, though he may sell by sample only; and he must be clothed with the power to sell, but has at common law no incidental power to pledge or barter the goods.[221] What are known as "factors' acts" are statutory enactments designed for the protection of persons who in good faith buy goods of factors or other agents and pay for them without knowing that they are the property of some other person than the agent.[222] These acts being in derogation of the common law

[219] *Ante*, § 22.

[220] Shaw v. Ferguson, 78 Ind. 547.

[221] See Wharton Ag., § 735.

[222] Benjamin Sales, § 19.

must be strictly construed.[223] The protection is confined to cases of agents or factors who have possession of the goods and who, from the nature of their employment, possess the right to sell.[224] So, where a valuable opal table was intrusted to one who, as a part of his known business, also sold such things for other people in his own name, having them in possession,—but in this particular instance directions having been given him not to sell the article without first obtaining authority from the owner, and that the check that might be received in payment be delivered to the principal intact, the commission to be paid to the principal thereafter,—it was decided by the English queen's bench that the purchaser was not protected by the factors' acts.[225] The court, by Wills, J., said: "Do the factors' acts protect the defendant? I think not. I think it is an essential condition of validity of a sale protected by them that the goods should have been intrusted to the agent for sale. I think the factors' acts would apply, so far as relates to the business which Geddes was carrying on, the nature of the article dealt in, and what was usually in such a trade. But the defect that the article never was intrusted to him for sale is fatal. I think there is another difficulty. In order to validate payment to the agent under 6 Geo. IV., ch. 94, § 4, it must be made in the ordinary course of business; that is, by cash or check or bill, as the case may be. I do not think that buying up a judgment from some one else, partly by delivery of a diamond of the defendant's own, can be considered as payment in the ordinary course within the section. And there is good reason for it. If the agent gets cash, he may be able to hand it to his principal; but if he does not get cash, and there is only a transaction of this kind, he can not, if impecunious, pay the principal; it is out of his power to do so." That the agent occasionally sells goods, although he generally acts in some other capacity, does not entitle the person dealing with him to protection under the statute. These statutes are in part confirmatory of the common law and in part alterations of that law.[226] It is generally held that the statutes are applicable only to mercantile transactions.[227] But under the present English act a sale by one

[223] Victor Sewing Mach. Co. v. Heller, 44 Wis. 265.

[224] Benjamin Sales, § 19; Thacker v. Moors, 134 Mass. 156; H. A. Prentice Co. v. Page, 164 Mass. 276.

[225] Biggs v. Evans, L. R. (1894) 1 Q. B. 88.

[226] Evans Pr. & Ag. (Bedford's ed.) 487, 488.

[227] Levi v. Booth, 58 Md. 305, 42 Am. Rep. 332; Lamb v. Attenborough, 1 B. & S. (101 E. C. L.) 831; Bush v. Fry, 15 Ont. 122.

who holds possession under an agreement to purchase shall have the same effect as if he were a mercantile agent in possession of the goods.[227a] By the weight of authority one buying in good faith from a conditional vendor gets no title unless the rule has been changed by statute.[228] The common law did not recognize in the agent any power to pledge the goods consigned to him, whether he had actual possession or possession constructively by means of documents, such as bills of lading, etc.; for he could not give any greater title than he had. This entailed great hardship upon innocent purchasers and proved injurious to commerce, and these factors' acts were intended to remedy such evils. Factors' acts were first passed in England in 1823, and as late as 1889; the latter repealing all former acts upon the subject and embodying many of the provisions of the former ones. Similar enactments were adopted in many of the states of the Union.

§ 450. **Factor's authority—How conferred and exercised.**—The authority of a factor from his principal must be by appointment, and there must be an acceptance on the part of the factor.[229] But the appointment and acceptance need not be shown by positive evidence, but may be implied from the circumstances; as, where one sends goods to a broker of the kind which he generally sells: the presumption in such case being that they were sent to be sold, and such act being held to give implied authority to the agent to sell.[230] The principal may show, however, how the goods came into the factor's possession, and that they were not consigned to him for sale.[231] It is not necessary to the validity of the factor's authority that it be conferred in writing.[232] The sale, in order to bind the principal, must be made in the ordinary course of business. "Such a construction of his power," said the court of appeals in a New York case, speaking of the construction of a factor's power to sell outside the ordinary course of

[227a] Lee v. Butler, L. R. (1893) 2 Q. B. 318.

[228] Story Sales, § 313; Armour v. Pecker, 123 Mass. 143; Lanman v. McGregor, 94 Ind. 301; National Bank of Commerce v. Chicago, etc., R. Co., 44 Minn. 224, 20 Am. St. 566.

[229] See Rapp v. Livingston, 14 Daly (N. Y.) 402.

[230] Dows v. McCleary, 14 Ill. App. 137; Smith v. Clews, 105 N. Y. 283.

[231] Cook v. Beal, 1 Bosw. (N. Y.) 497; H. A. Prentice Co. v. Page, 164 Mass. 276.

[232] Deshler v. Beers, 32 Ill. 368, 83 Am. Dec. 274.

business, "would be inçonvenient and might lead to great abuses. It would enable the factor to put his principal's property out of his hands before any default on the part of his principal, thereby depriving the latter of the right to the possession of his property on discharging the factor's claim. Assuming that the transferee would himself be held to account, it subjects the principal to the embarrassment of calling third parties into the settlement of his transaction with his agent. The transaction in this case was out of the ordinary course of business and has all the earmarks of an irregular proceeding."[233] A general usage or custom may, if not contrary to law or to the express provisions of the broker's instructions or authority, confer authority upon the factor which has not been expressly delegated; indeed, the larger portion of the authority exercised by factors is that derived by implication from the usages of trade. Such a usage, however, must be so notorious as to raise the presumption that it was generally known.[234] A factor's authority is always governed by the law of the place where the sale or contract of disposition is made by him.[235] But where the parties themselves place a construction upon the contract, as to whether it is a consignment or a sale, it is conclusive, without reference to what it actually was under the law.[236] A factor's business being to sell, all the powers properly incident thereto are necessarily implied. It is not deemed necessary to enumerate all or any considerable number of the powers implied in a factor's authority to sell. It has been held that he may employ counsel to defend any suits that may be brought against him concerning the goods consigned to him, and his principal is bound to reimburse him for the expenses incurred;[237] that where the factor is employed to sell the goods of a manufacturing company and to buy stock, he has power to buy on credit, but not to give the note of the corporation;[238] and that he may give bond when necessary to carry out the instructions of the principal.[239] But a factor has no authority to compromise a suit;[240] nor to sell a debt due his principal in

[233] Per Andrews, J., in Commercial Nat'l Bank v. Heilbronner, 108 N. Y. 439.

[234] Wootters v. Kaufman, 73 Tex. 395; Lyon v. Culbertson, 83 Ill. 33.

[235] Frank v. Jenkins, 22 Ohio St. 597; Harbert v. Neill, 49 Tex. 143.

[236] Pam v. Vilmar, 54 How. Pr. (N. Y.) 235.

[237] Monnet v. Merz, 127 N. Y. 151, 158.

[238] Emerson v. Providence Mfg. Co., 12 Mass. 237.

[239] Hardee v. Hall, 12 Bush (Ky.) 327.

[240] See Monnett v. Merz, 127 N. Y. 151; Greenleaf v. Moody, 13 Allen (Mass.) 363.

order to reimburse himself for advances: the party buying such claim getting no title to the same.[241] A factor has no implied authority to sell property not in his possession.[242] The power to sell does not, under common-law rules, include the power to barter or exchange the property for other goods.[243] Neither has the factor any power at common law to pledge such property except to the extent of his lien for compensation, advances, etc.[244] Unless the factor has instructions to the contrary, or the usage of trade is otherwise, he may sell his principal's goods on a reasonable credit;[245] but in such case it is the duty of the broker to use due care in selling to responsible parties. He has also the implied authority to warrant the condition and quality of the goods sold by him;[246] but he has no authority to warrant the goods as to future conditions, etc.[247] A factor has implied authority to insure the goods consigned to him, and his interest in them is such that he may do so in his own name.[248] He may receive payment for goods sold.[249] A factor, like any other agent, is generally prohibited from delegating his authority to another or others: he is a specialist in the business intrusted to him,

[241] Commercial Nat'l Bank v. Heilbronner, 108 N. Y. 439.

[242] Harbert v. Neill, 49 Tex. 143. And where a factor has learned that the property intrusted to him for sale has been sold by his principal, his authority to sell the same is revoked, and he can not sell the property even to the extent of satisfying his lien for advances or for liabilities incurred by him in the attempt to sell such property, unless the sale becomes necessary to protect his interest: Walker Co. v. Dubuque Fruit, etc., Co., 106 Iowa 245, 53 L. R. A. 775.

[243] Haas v. Damon, 9 Iowa 589; Kauffman v. Beasley, 54 Tex. 563; Victor Sewing Mach. Co. v. Heller, 44 Wis. 265; Trudo v. Anderson, 10 Mich. 357, 81 Am. Dec. 795.

[244] Mechanics', etc., Ins. Co. v. Kiger, 103 U. S. 352; Merchants' Nat'l Bank v. Pope, 19 Or. 35; Allen v. St. Louis Bank, 120 U. S. 20; Commercial Bank v. Lee, 99 Ala. 493, 19 L. R. A. 705; National Exch. Bank v. Graniteville Mfg. Co., 79 Ga. 22.

[245] Burton v. Goodspeed, 69 Ill. 237; Roosevelt v. Doherty, 129 Mass. 301, 37 Am. Rep. 356; Daylight Burner Co. v. Odlin, 51 N. H. 56, 12 Am. Rep. 45; Walker Co. v. Dubuque Fruit, etc., Co., 106 Iowa 245, 53 L. R. A. 775; Foster v. Waller, 75 Ill. 464.

[246] Nelson v. Cowing, 6 Hill (N. Y.) 336; Flash v. American Glucose Co., 38 La. Ann. 4.

[247] Upton v. Suffolk Co. Mills, 11 Cush. (Mass.) 586, 59 Am. Dec. 163.

[248] Shoenfeld v. Fleisher, 73 Ill. 404; DeForest v. Fulton Fire Ins. Co., 1 Hall (N. Y.) 84, 110.

[249] Pickering v. Busk, 15 East 38; Butler v. Dorman, 68 Mo. 298, 30 Am. Rep. 795; Corlies v. Cumming, 6 Cow. (N. Y.) 181; Graham v. Duckwall, 8 Bush (Ky.) 12.

and is required to act in person;[250] but as in other cases of agency, mere ministerial and mechanical duties may be redelegated;[251] and the usages of trade or commerce frequently sanction a redelegation of authority.[252]

§ **451. Factor's obligations to principal.**—The general duties and obligations of a factor to his principal are much the same as in other agencies. He must, first and foremost, act in the utmost good faith in the discharge of his duties.[253] He can not, without the consent of the principal, sell to himself,[254] such sale being *prima facie* invalid.[255] Such a sale, however, is not absolutely void, and may, therefore, be ratified at the principal's election.[256] He is required to render implicit obedience to the instructions of his principal;[257] but he is not in duty bound to follow directions which require him to go outside of the scope of his employment, and he is not liable to the principal if he refuses to do so.[258] He may, of course, make a subsequent agreement to do this; but it is no part of his original undertaking; and he can not be said to be disobeying instructions for failure to take upon himself such additional obligations: if he obeys the legitimate instructions of his principal, it is all he can be required to do; but as to this he has no discretion. If injury results from the obedience it is the principal's loss and not his. He must obey if he can do so;[259] he is only required to use reasonable diligence, and if by so doing he is unable to comply, he will be exonerated.[260] And it has been held that a factor may sell his principal's goods even in

[250] McMorris v. Simpson, 21 Wend. (N. Y.) 610; Kauffman v. Beasley, 54 Tex. 563; Terry v. Bamberger, 44 Conn. 558; Warner v. Martin, 11 How. (U. S.) 209; Sparks v. Flannery, 104 Ga. 323.

[251] McMorris v. Simpson, *supra*.

[252] Warner v. Martin, *supra*; Terry v. Bamberger, *supra*; Strong v. Stewart, 9 Heisk. (Tenn.) 137, 147; Trueman v. Loder, 11 A. & E. 589, 39 E. C. L. 319.

[253] Govan v. Cushing, 111 N. C. 458; Rice v. Brook, 20 Fed. 611; Babcock v. Orbison, 25 Ind. 75.

[254] Wadsworth v. Gay, 118 Mass. 44.

[255] Tilleny v. Wolverton, 46 Minn. 256.

[256] Sims v. Miller, 37 S. C. 402, 34 Am. St. 762.

[257] Wilkinson v. Campbell, 1 Bay (S. C.) 169; Maggoffin v. Cowan, 11 La. Ann. 554; Strong v. Stewart, 9 Heisk. (Tenn.) 137; Maynard v. Pease, 99 Mass. 555; Rollins v. Duffy, 18 Ill. App. 398.

[258] Thompson v. Woodruff, 7 Coldw. (Tenn.) 401.

[259] Evans v. Root, 7 N. Y. 186, 57 Am. Dec. 512.

[260] DeTastett v. Crousillat, 2 Wash. (U. S.) 132.

violation of instructions, to reimburse himself for advances: provided he has made reasonable demand therefor of the principal without obtaining payment from him;[261] in such case the agent has a special property in the goods, which gives him such an interest therein as enables him to make the sale, after proper demand. The English courts deny the agent's right to make such a sale, however.[262] It is also the factor's duty to inform the principal of everything which is proper for the principal to know relating to the business intrusted to the factor, and a failure to do so will render the agent liable in damages.[263] Thus, where goods are sold by a factor on credit, and the purchaser subsequently becomes insolvent, it is the duty of the factor, if he have information of such insolvency, to notify the principal thereof within a reasonable time.[264] And where it was the duty of a factor to insure, and he was unable to do so for any reason, it was held to be his duty to notify the principal of his inability, and that a failure to do so would make the factor liable in damages.[265] It is furthermore the duty of such agent to exercise ordinary care as to the time and manner of selling the goods and transacting the business of his principal generally.[266] He is not an insurer of the safety of the goods in his custody, however, and if they are injured without his negligence he can not be held liable.[267] He is required to use such skill and diligence as persons usually exercise in that kind of business.[268] So, if the goods naturally depreciate while in his possession, the factor being without instructions to sell in his discretion, he is not required to notify the principal of the depreciation and can not be held responsible for it.[269] It is his duty to keep the goods of his principal separate from his own and those of other owners;[270] but by usage or custom he may be justified in storing them with other

[261] Parker v. Brancker, 22 Pick. (Mass.) 40; Davis v. Kobe, 36 Minn. 214, 1 Am. St. 663; George Campbell Co. v. Angus, 91 Va. 438; Dalby v. Stearns, 132 Mass. 230.

[262] Raleigh v. Atkinson, 6 M. & W. 670; DeComas v. Prost, 3 Moo. P. C. (N. S.) 158.

[263] Howe v. Sutherland, 39 Iowa 484; Callander v. Oelrichs, 5 Bing. N. C. 58, 35 E. C. L. 41; DeTastett v. Crousillat, 2 Wash. (U. S.) 132.

[264] Forrestier v. Bordman, 1 Story (U. S.) 43.

[265] DeTastett v. Crousillat, 2 Wash. (U. S.) 132.

[266] Milbank v. Dennistown, 10 Bosw. (N. Y.) 382; Eaton v. Welton, 32 N. H. 352; Atkinson v. Burton, 4 Bush (Ky.) 299.

[267] Dunbar v. Gregg, 44 Ill. App. 527.

[268] See Foster v. Bush, 104 Ala. 662; Vincent v. Rather, 31 Tex. 77, 98 Am. Dec. 516.

[269] Adams v. Capron, 21 Md. 186, 83 Am. Dec. 566.

[270] Clarke v. Tipping, 9 Beav. 284.

goods of the same grade.[271] He is not required, as a general rule, to insure goods that have been consigned to him;[272] but when he is intrusted to do so he will be liable if he does not and there is a loss.[273] Where it is the custom or habit of a factor to insure, or where the usage of the community requires it, the agent renders himself liable for any loss that may occur by reason of his failure to effect such insurance as will reasonably protect the property.[274] Of course, a factor is in duty bound to account to his principal for all sales made and for goods in his possession.[275] The duty to account includes that of remitting the proceeds of sales when requested;[276] but he need not remit until demand is made; and generally, if he does so, the remittance will be at his own risk.[277]

§ **452. Obligations of principal to factor.**—Like other agents, a factor is entitled from his principal to be compensated for his services and to be reimbursed for proper expenditures and indemnified against all losses properly incurred. He may, however, forfeit his right to compensation and even to reimbursement, on account of his misconduct or negligence in the discharge of his duties.[278] The principal is also liable to the factor for advances made by him to the principal. Advances are moneys paid by the factor to his principal on the consignment of goods, and in anticipation of the debt that will become due to the principal when the goods are sold;[279] and these, it is held, are made both on the faith of the goods consigned to the factor and on the principal's personal credit.[280] The fact that the goods have been destroyed will not prevent the factor from recovering of the principal his advances.[281] The principal is liable to the

[271] Davis v. Kobe, 36 Minn. 214, 1 Am. St. 663.

[272] Shoenfeld v. Fleisher, 73 Ill. 404; Lee v. Adsit, 37 N. Y. 78.

[273] Shoenfeld v. Fleisher, *supra*; Gordan v. Wright, 29 La. Ann. 812.

[274] Shoenfeld v. Fleisher, *supra*; Lee v. Adsit, *supra*; Burbridge v. Gumbel, 72 Miss. 370.

[275] See Fish v. Seeberger, 154 Ill. 30; Terwilliger v. Beals, 6 Lans. (N. Y.) 403.

[276] See Ferris v. Paris, 10 Johns. (N. Y.) 285; Cooley v. Betts, 24 Wend. (N. Y.) 203; Middleton v. Twombly, 125 N. Y. 520.

[277] Johnson v. Martin, 11 La. Ann. 27, 66 Am. Dec. 193.

[278] White v. Chapman, 1 Stark. 113, 2 E. C. L. 51; Fordyce v. Peper, 16 Fed. 516; Fish v. Seeberger, 154 Ill. 30; Norman v. Peper, 24 Fed. 403.

[279] Balderston v. National Rubber Co., 18 R. I. 338, 49 Am. St. 772.

[280] Stewart v. Lowe, 24 Up. Can. Q. B. 434; Perin v. Parker, 126 Ill. 201, 9 Am. St. 571; Balderston v. National Rubber Co., 18 R. I. 338, 49 Am. St. 772.

[281] Kufeke v. Kehlor, 19 Fed. 198.

factor for all losses sustained by the latter without his own fault, by reason of the agency. Thus, where a factor, after having accounted to his principal, is compelled to refund to a purchaser the price of goods, on account of negligent packing, he can recover the amount thus paid by him from his principal.[282] But he is not entitled to indemnity if the transaction from which the loss arose was unauthorized by the principal,[283] unless such transaction was subsequently ratified. A factor has a lien for his compensation or for advances and other expenses legitimately incurred, upon the goods consigned to him;[284] if the goods have been sold, the lien is upon the proceeds or securities for the price of the goods sold.[285] A factor has a general lien for any balance due him on the accounts between him and his principal;[286] but before such a lien accrues to the factor it must be shown that the goods were delivered to him as factor:[287] a delivery to him of goods as agent for his principal by a third person does not give him a lien, as such possession is the possession of the principal.[288] The factor must have possession of the goods or he can claim no lien.[289]

§ 453. **Rights of factor as to third parties.**—A factor can maintain an action in his own name against a third party to whom he has sold and delivered goods for his principal, for their price.[290] The provision, found in the varying codes, by which the real party in interest is required to prosecute every civil action in his own name, does not stand in the way of the factor's right to maintain the action; for there is generally contained in the codes the further provision, which forms an exception to that already mentioned, requiring any "trustee of an express trust" to bring such action in his own name without

[282] Beach v. Branch, 57 Ga. 362. See also, Randall v. Kehlor, 60 Me. 37, 11 Am. Rep. 169.

[283] Rogers v. Kneeland, 10 Wend. (N. Y.) 219.

[284] Fourth Nat'l Bank v. American Mills Co., 29 Fed. 611; Shaw v. Ferguson, 78 Ind. 547; Jonnson v. Campbell, 120 Mass. 449; Harrison v. Mora, 150 Pa. St. 481.

[285] Vail v. Durant, 7 Allen (Mass.) 408, 83 Am. Dec. 695; Commercial Nat'l Bank v. Heilbronner, 108 N. Y. 439.

[286] Drinkwater v. Goodwin, 1 Cowp. 251; Baker v. Fuller, 21 Pick. (Mass.) 318; Martin v. Pope, 6 Ala. 532, 41 Am. Dec. 66; McGraft v. Rugee, 60 Wis. 406, 50 Am. Rep. 378; Comer v. Way, 107 Ala. 300, 54 Am. St. 93.

[287] Dixon v. Stansfeld, 10 C. B. (70 E. C. L.) 398.

[288] Gurney v. Sharp, 4 Taunt. 242.

[289] Warren v. First Nat'l Bank, 149 Ill. 9, 36; Baker v. Fuller, 21 Pick. (Mass.) 318.

[290] Toland v. Murray, 18 Johns.

joining the person for whose benefit the action is prosecuted.[291] These provisions are usually made applicable, by express statutory enactment, to any person with whom, or in whose name, a contract is made for the benefit of another: such enactments being designed to preserve the modern common-law right of action which exists by reason of such conditions.[292] But, as in other suits of this character by agents, the principal has the right to intervene and control the suit: his claim being, of course, superior to that of the factor;[293] but the principal can not by such intervention defeat the factor's right to recover to the extent of his lien.[294] In such suits by the factor, the defendant can always interpose any defense that would have been proper had the action been brought by the principal.[295] Besides the factor's right to sue for the price of goods sold by him for his principal, he may also maintain an action in his own name against any wrongdoer for any injury to the goods, or for a breach of the contract of sale;[296] thus, he may bring suit in his own name against the carrier of the goods for loss or injury caused by its negligence.[297] But he can not maintain such suit in his own name if he has no lien.[298] And to the extent of his lien on such goods for advances, etc., he may even maintain an action against an attachment creditor of his principal who has taken the goods under a writ of attachment, and recover from him the value of the special property.[299]

§ 454. **Rights of principal as to third parties.**—Notwithstanding the factor's right to sue in his own name on matters growing out of contracts made in the principal's behalf, the latter also has the right, indeed, he has the primary right, to do so, except so far as the factor has an interest in the subject-matter of the agency: he may sue, as any other principal may, on contracts made for him by the factor,

(N. Y.) 24; Graham v. Duckwall, 8 Bush (Ky.) 12.

[291] Wolfe v. Missouri Pac. R. Co., 97 Mo. 473, 10 Am. St. 331. The factor, by reason of his lien, has such interest as will entitle him to sue in his own name: Dows v. Greene, 32 Barb. (N. Y.) 490.

[292] *Ibid.*

[293] Jackson Ins. Co. v. Partee, 9 Heisk. (Tenn.) 296.

[294] Drinkwater v. Goodwin, 1 Cowp. 251.

[295] Gibson v. Winter, 5 B. & Ad. 96, 27 E. C. L. 50.

[296] Groover v. Warfield, 50 Ga. 644; Allen v. Steers, 39 La. Ann. 586.

[297] Boston, etc., R. Co. v. Warrior Mower Co., 76 Me. 251; Vose v. Allen, 3 Blatchf. (U. S.) 289.

[298] Cobb v. Illinois Cent. R. Co., 88 Ill. 394.

[299] Heard v. Brewer, 4 Daly (N. Y.) 136.

the same as if made by himself;[300] and this is true although the factor be a *del credere* agent.[301] While the principal can not defeat the just claim himself, he has the right to make collections of the remaining portion of such claim.[302] And if the factor improperly disposes of the goods,—as by pawning or selling them on his own credit,—the third party having no knowledge of his being a factor or agent, the principal may forbid the payment to be made to the factor; and a subsequent payment to the latter would be no protection to the purchaser, unless he had given the factor some negotiable security which had actually been negotiated before notice.[303] The rule just stated does not apply, however, where the factor sells in his own name, being himself responsible to the principal for the price of the goods sold, whether collected or not; nor where he sells them to his own creditor, where there are mutual dealings:[304] in these instances the principal can look to the factor alone for payment. Where the factor disposes of the goods consigned, taking in exchange for them shares of stock in a company in which he is a stockholder, the purchaser obtains no title, and the consignor may recover the goods from such third party.[305] If the principal was not disclosed when the sale was made, and the transaction was in the factor's own name, the principal may nevertheless assert his rights against the third party if the factor did not by his agreement with the principal assume the responsibility for the price of the goods sold; in such case he may recover from the third party; and it is not necessary that the principal first make a demand of the third party.[306] The principal's claim in such cases is always subject to any defenses, however, which the third party would have had against the factor.[307] And where the principal was unknown at the time of the sale, the third party can set off an antecedent debt which he held against the factor prior to the time of the transaction by which such third party himself became indebted.[308] "Where a factor," said Lord Mansfield, "dealing for a principal, but concealing that principal, delivers goods in his own name, the person contracting with him has the right to consider him, to all intents

[300] Burton v. Goodspeed, 69 Ill. 237.

[301] Moore v. Hillabrand, 37 Hun (N. Y.) 491.

[302] Morris v. Cleasby, 1 M. & S. 576.

[303] Kinder v. Shaw, 2 Mass. 398.

[304] Kelley v. Munson, 7 Mass. 319.

[305] Wyeth v. Renz-Bowles Co. (Ky.), 66 S. W. 825.

[306] Foster v. Smith, 2 Coldw. (Tenn.) 474, 88 Am. Dec. 604.

[307] George v. Clagett, 7 T. R. 355, 2 Sm. L. C. (8th ed.) 118; Gardner v. Allen, 6 Ala. 187, 41 Am. Dec. 45.

[308] Hogan v. Shorb, 24 Wend. (N. Y.) 458.

and purposes, as the principal. And though the real principal may appear and bring an action upon that contract against the purchaser of the goods, yet the purchaser may set off any claim he may have against the factor in answer to the demand of the principal."[309] But if the principal be known, or if the third party have good reason to suspect that the vendor of the goods is but an agent for some other person, he must make inquiry and ascertain, if he can, in what capacity or character the seller acts; otherwise he will not be entitled to a set-off.[310] It is not sufficient in such case, to entitle the debtor to a set-off, that he was ignorant of the identity of the real principal: he must have been unaware also that the seller was acting as agent.[311] The mere fact that the seller was in the commission business would not of itself be notice to the purchaser, however, that he was a factor in that particular transaction, if he also carried on business on his own account.[312] Even where the factor takes a note for the purchase-money payable to himself individually, the principal may sue for the price unless the same was taken as a payment or amounted to such in law.[313] As the title to the goods consigned to a factor remains in the principal,[314] the latter can always maintain an action against the purchaser for the same unless the proceeds have already been paid to the factor under circumstances justifying such payment. The factor holds the goods as trustee of the principal, and the principal may follow them into the hands of any person except a *bona fide* purchaser, where they can be identified.[315] Under the common law, one who acquires the principal's goods from a factor by barter gets no title to them, and the principal may recover them in specie.[316] In such case, the want of knowledge of the third party affords no protection; for the factor can give no title to the property, to which he has none himself, except in the usual course of business.[317] If

[309] Rabone v. Williams, 7 T. R. 356 *n.*

[310] Miller v. Lea, 35 Md. 396, 6 Am. Rep. 417; Baring v. Corrie, 2 B. & Ald. 137; Cooke v. Eshelby, L. R. 12 App. Cas. 271.

[311] Miller v. Lea, *supra.*

[312] Hogan v. Shorb, 24 Wend. (N. Y.) 458.

[313] Corlies v. Cumming, 6 Cow. (N. Y.) 181.

[314] Baker v. National Exch. Bank, 100 N. Y. 31.

[315] National Cordage Co. v. Sims, 44 Neb. 148; Union Stock Yards Bank v. Gillespie, 137 U. S. 411; Baker v. National Exchange Bank, 100 N. Y. 31; Clemmer v. Drovers' Nat'l Bank, 157 Ill. 206; Cady v. National Bank, 46 Neb. 756.

[316] Guerreiro v. Peile, 3 B. & Ald. 616, 5 E. C. L. 354.

[317] Potter v. Dennison, 10 Ill. 590; Romeo v. Martucci, 72 Conn. 504, 77 Am. St. 327.

the factor thus dispose of the goods of his principal, even to an innocent purchaser, the principal may maintain against the latter an action of trover.[318] The principal may, however, estop himself from denying the factor's authority, by clothing him with the apparent muniments of absolute title.[319] The third party is also liable to the principal in tort for injury to his property, and he may maintain an action therefor. Thus, a sheriff or other officer who wrongfully levies upon or attaches the principal's goods while in the possession of the factor, for a debt of the factor or other person, is liable to the principal in trespass.[320]

§ **455. Rights of third parties as to principal and factor.**—It is scarcely necessary to discuss at any length the duties and obligations of the principal and factor to third parties, and the rights which flow from these to such third parties. Some of these have been noticed in connection with the defenses of third persons to actions by the principal or the factor. They are in all essential regards the same as those concerning other agents, and have been heretofore fully considered. To repeat what has been said before, in substance, we may state the general rule to be that the principal is responsible to third parties for all the acts of his factor which have been performed within the scope of the latter's employment, either in contract or in tort.[321] If, however, credit was given to the agent knowingly and exclusively, the principal can not be held liable.[322] And where the factor is guilty of having committed a fraudulent transaction in behalf of his principal, and the latter ratifies it or knowingly reaps a benefit therefrom, such principal is responsible to the party injured for such damages as he may have sustained.[323] In all cases of tort, the obligation is both joint and several, and the third party may therefore sue both principal and factor or either alone.

§ **456. Del credere factors.**—A *del credere* commission was defined by Lord Ellenborough in *Morris* v. *Cleasby*,[324] as "the premium or price given by the principal to the factor for a guaranty."[325] The

[318] *Ibid.*; 2 Kent Com. 625. See also, Neill v. Billingsley, 49 Tex. 161.

[319] Dunlap's Paley Ag., § 212.

[320] Holly v. Huggeford, 8 Pick. (Mass.) 73.

[321] Higgins v. McCrea, 116 U. S. 671.

[322] McCullough v. Thompson, 45 N. Y. Super. 449.

[323] Story Ag., § 179 n.

[324] 4 M. & S. 566.

[325] See *ante*, § 22.

duties of a *del credere* agent are not materially different from those of an agent who does not guarantee the risk incident to the sale of goods. A *del credere* factor practically insures the collection of the debts arising from sales of his principal's goods; for which he receives an extra consideration called a "*del credere* commission."[326] Whether the relation of a *del credere* factor to the principal exists may be implied from the course of dealing between the parties.[327] The cases have not been altogether harmonious as to whether such a factor is liable to the principal as an original debtor or a surety would be, or only after a failure on the part of the debtor to pay, as a guarantor would be. The English cases now hold that the factor is only a guarantor, and can be rendered liable only after the debt has become due and there has been a default by the debtor, and the remedy against him exhausted.[328] The American decisions generally hold to the other view: they make the position of the factor one more in the nature of a suretyship, and render him liable in the first instance, after the debt has become due.[329] "Although the factor is absolutely liable, he is not bound to pay until the money becomes due from the purchaser."[330] There is, under either view, no liability until the debt has become due.[331] The extent of the agent's liability to his principal is, of course, the full amount of the debt; and if the agent has accepted depreciated currency or other articles of some or no value therefor, he must account for the entire sum.[332] And, although the factor becomes liable to the principal upon the expiration of the credit, the main debtor is still liable to the principal also, and may be sued by him when the right of action has accrued.[333]

[326] Grove v. Dubois, 1 T. R. 112; Morris v. Cleasby, 4 M. & S. 566.

[327] Shaw v. Woodcock, 7 B. & C. 73, National Cordage Co. v. Sims, 44 Neb. 148; Balderston v. National Rubber Co., 18 R. I. 338, 49 Am. St. 772.

[328] Morris v. Cleasby, 4 M. & S. 566; Hornby v. Lacy, 6 M. & S. 166; Peele v. Northcote, 7 Taunt. 478, 2 E. C. L. 456.

[329] Lewis v. Brehme, 33 Md. 412; Greentree v. Rosenstock, 61 N. Y. 583; Balderston v. National Rubber Co., 18 R. I. 338, 49 Am. St. 772; Leverick v. Meigs, 1 Cow. (N. Y.) 645.

[330] Wordsworth, J., in Leverick v. Meigs, *supra*.

[331] Bradley v. Richardson, 2 Blatchf. (U. S.) 343; Wallace v. Castle, 14 Hun (N. Y.) 106; Lewis v. Brehme, 33 Md. 412; Leverick v. Meigs, 1 Cow. (N. Y.) 645.

[332] Dunnell v. Mason, 1 Story (U. S.) 543; Muller v. Bohlens, 2 Wash. (U. S.) 378.

[333] Leverick v. Meigs, 1 Cow. (N. Y.) 645; Balderston v. National Rubber Co., 18 R. I. 338, 49 Am. St. 772.

The relation between a principal and a *del credere* factor is, in many respects, a peculiar one. If he becomes primarily indebted to the principal by virtue of the sale, is he also the owner of the goods, when the matter is considered in view of his relation to the purchaser? If he is only a guarantor, or even a surety, is his undertaking not one by which he answers for the debt of another, and therefore within the purview of the statute of frauds? These are important questions, and the answers that have been given to them are not based upon the most satisfactory reasoning. True, it is held that the undertaking is not within the statute;[334] and the reason given for this conclusion is that it is in the nature of an original undertaking, though it has also some of the elements of a guaranty, but that guaranties do not always have to be in writing.[335] The factor may

[334] Wolff v. Koppel, 5 Hill (N. Y.) 458, affirmed in 2 Den. (N. Y.) 368, 43 Am. Dec. 751; Sherwood v. Stone, 14 N. Y. 267; Swan v. Nesmith, 7 Pick. (Mass.) 220.

[335] Wolff v. Koppel, 5 Hill (N. Y.) 458, affirmed in 2 Den. (N. Y.) 368, 43 Am. Dec. 751. In this case Cowen, J., states the reasons as follows: "It is objected that the contract of a factor, binding him in the terms implied by a *del credere* commission, is within the statute of frauds and should, therefore, be in writing. Such is the opinion expressed by Theobald Princ. & Surety 64, 65, and in Chitty Conts. (Am. ed., 1842) 209, 210. The question was also mooted in Gall v. Comber, 1 J. B. Moore 279; but not decided as seems to be implied in the careless manner in which the case is quoted by Chitty: S. C. 7 Taunt. 558. All the authority presented on the argument grows out of the nature of the contract as held by the king's bench in Morris v. Cleasby, 4 Mau. & S. 566, 574, 575. That case certainly defines the liability of the factor somewhat differently from what several previous cases seem to have done. The effect of acting under the commission is said to be, that the factor becomes a guarantor of the debts which are created; that is to say, they are debts due to the merchant, and the factor's engagement is secondary and collateral, depending on the fault of the debtors, who must first be sought out and called upon by the merchant. See also, Hornby v. Lacy, 6 Mau. & S. 166, 171, 172; Peele v. Northcote, 7 Taunt. 478, 484, 1 J. B. Moore 178; Leverick v. Meigs, 1 Cow. (N. Y.) 645, 664. On this we have the opinion of learned writers that if the agreement *del credere* be made without writing the case comes within the statute. On the other hand, approved writers assert that this is not so: 1 Beawes 46; 3 Chit. Com. L. (6th Lond. ed.) 220, 221. It is true, these latter go on the more stringent obligation supposed by Lord Mansfield; that of a principal debtor on the part of the factor, the accessorial obligation lying rather on the purchaser. This view of the matter was no longer correct after the cases I have mentioned were decided. The consequence sought to be derived, however, by writers, is merely spec-

collect from the purchaser in his own name, not because he was the owner of the goods sold, but by reason of his peculiar relation to the

ulative; and the contrary has of late been directly held by the supreme court of Massachusetts, in Swan v. Nesmith, 7 Pick. (Mass.) 220. It is said this was without the court being aware of Morris v. Cleasby. Be that as it may, they seem to have been fully aware of the rule laid down in that case, and to have recognized it as correct. They considered the obligation as a guaranty. But a guaranty, though by parol, is not always within the statute. Perhaps, after all, it may not be strictly correct to call the contract of the factor a guaranty, in the ordinary sense of that word. The implied promise of the factor is merely that he will sell to persons in good credit at the time; and in order to charge him, negligence must be shown. He takes an additional commission, however, and adds to his obligation that he will make no sales unless to persons absolutely solvent; in legal effect, that he will be liable for the loss which his conduct may bring upon the plaintiff, without the *onus* of proving negligence. The merchant holds the goods, and will not part with them to the factor without this extraordinary stipulation, and a commission is paid to him for entering into it. What is this after all, but another form of selling the goods? Its consequences are the same in substance. Instead of paying cash, the factor prefers to contract a debt or duty which obliges him to see the money paid. This debt or duty is his own, and arises from an adequate consideration. It is contingent, depending on the event of his failing to secure it through another—some future vendee, to whom the merchant is first to resort. Upon non-payment by the vendee, the debt falls absolutely on the factor. As remarked by Parker, C. J., in Swan v. Nesmith, 7 Pick. (Mass.) 220, the form of the action does not seem to be material in such case; that is to say, whether the merchant sue for goods sold, or on the special engagement. The latter is perhaps the settled form; but still the action is, in effect, to recover the factor's own debt. In the late case of Johnson v. Gilbert, 4 Hill (N. Y.) 178, the defendant, in consideration of money paid for him by the plaintiff, assigned a chattel note and guaranteed its payment. In such a case the declaration must be on the guaranty to pay the debt of another; but this is so in form merely. We held that the contract was to pay the defendant's own debt; that it was not a contract to pay as the surety of another. All such contracts and many others are, in form, to pay the debt of another, and so literally within the statute, but without its intent. A promise by A to B, that the former will pay a debt due from the latter, is not within the meaning, though it is within the words: Conkey v. Hopkins, 17 Johns. (N. Y.) 113; Eastwood v. Kenyon, 11 Ad. & E. 438. So are a numerous class of cases, where the promise is made in consideration of the creditor relinquishing some lien, fund or security: Theobald Princ. & Surety 45, and cases cited. The merchant gives up his goods to be sold, and pays a premium. Is not this in truth as much and more than many of those principal and of the special property he has in them. In this way only can the doctrine be explained which permits the principal to intervene if he chooses to exercise that privilege:[336] the property never becomes that of the factor absolutely; and his right over it, except to the extent of his vested interests, continues until after sale, to be followed only by his right to collect the proceeds. The *del credere* factor has a lien upon the goods and proceeds for advances, commissions, etc., the same as any other factor.[337] While such factor guarantees the solvency of the purchaser to whom he sells, the debt is not extinguished as to such purchaser until actually paid in money to the factor or principal. He does not, on the other hand, warrant the payment of the remittance, if under the contract with his principal he undertakes to remit to him. As to collection and remittance, a *del credere* factor is under the same obligations as any other agent whose duty it is to collect and remit: in this regard he is only required to use proper care and diligence in purchasing the remittance: he does not insure its payment.[338]

cases require which go on the relinquishment of a security? Suppose a factor agrees by parol to sell for cash but gives a credit. His promise is virtually that he will pay the amount of the debt he thus makes. Yet who would say his promise is within the statute? The amount of the argument for the defendant would seem to be, that an agent for making sales, or indeed, a collecting agent, can not, by parol, undertake for extraordinary diligence, because he may thus have the debt of another thrown upon him. But the answer is, that all such contracts have an immediate respect to his own duty or obligation. The debt of another comes incidentally as a measure of damages."

[336] See Miller v. Lea, 35 Md. 396, 6 Am. Rep. 417.

[337] Miller v. Lea, *supra*; Holbrook v. Wight, 24 Wend. (N. Y.) 169, 35 Am. Dec. 607; Merrill v. Thomas, 7 Daly (N. Y.) 393.

[338] Story Ag., § 215.

CHAPTER XVI.

INSURANCE AGENTS.

§ 457. **Who are insurance agents—Their authority.**—The term "insurance agents" is usually applied to those agents of insurers and insurance companies who solicit applications for risks, issue and deliver policies, collect premiums, and generally transact some portion of the business in which the insurers or companies engage. Such agent's appointment may be in writing, but need not be, and may rest in parol.[339] It may also be established, as other agencies are, by the conduct of the principal in holding the agent out as such,[340] or in ratifying his acts though they had not been originally authorized.[341] Whether the agent is acting for the insured or the insurer, in a given case, depends, of course, upon the facts; but when the facts are admitted, the question is one of law, for the decision of the court.[342] It is frequently stipulated in the printed application for insurance that the statements therein, if made to an agent, shall not be binding on the insurer, and that for the purpose of the application, he shall

[339] See Lumberman's Mut. Ins. Co. v. Bell, 166 Ill. 400, 57 Am. St. 140.

[340] List v. Commonwealth, 118 Pa. St. 322; Hardin v. Alexandria Ins. Co., 90 Va. 413.

[341] Terry v. Provident Fund Society, 13 Ind. App. 1.

[342] Indiana Ins. Co. v. Hartwell, 123 Ind. 177; Phenix Ins. Co. v. Lorenz, 7 Ind. App. 266; Sellus v. Commercial Fire Ins. Co., 105 Ala. 282; Murphy v. Southern Life Ins. Co., 3 Baxt. (Tenn.) 440, 27 Am. Rep. 761; National Bank v. Knoxville Fire Ins. Co., 85 Tenn. 76, 4 Am. St. 744.

be deemed the agent of the applicant; but it is generally held that the company can not thus escape the consequences of the acts of its agents. In some jurisdictions, however, the rule appears to be that the question as to whose agent one is is a mixed question of law and fact;[343] while in other jurisdictions still, it has been ruled that the question is one of fact for the jury.[344] Of course, the agent's declarations out of court can not be taken as proof of the agency, when made in the absence of the principal or without its authority; and before such declarations will bind the insurer, the fact of the agency must be established by the proper evidence.[345] Where an agent has a written commission from an insurance company authorizing him to receive applications for insurance, moneys for premiums, and to countersign, issue and renew policies signed by the president, etc., subject to the rules and regulations of the company, he is a general and not a special agent; and if he has private instructions, not attached to the policy, restricting his authority to take certain risks, such instructions do not render his agency a special one, and third parties are not bound by the limitations;[346] but if the agent's written commission expressly excludes certain risks, third persons are bound by it.[347] And the fact that his agency is limited to a certain locality does not prevent him from being a general agent with regard to soliciting and accepting risks and agreeing upon settlements of terms of insurance, etc.[348] And any evidence is competent which tends to show that the agent had general authority: such as the possession of policies issued in blank;[349] the fact that the agent made and filed an affidavit for a continuance in a cause to which the company was a party, etc.[350] And generally, a limitation upon the agent's authority will not be binding upon the insured unless he had notice thereof, if the agent was one who possessed general authority.[351] But an insurance broker who has authority only to deliver a policy of

[343] Lumberman's Mut. Ins. Co. v. Horton, 166 Ill. 400, 57 Am. St. 140; Partridge v. Commercial Fire Ins. Co., 17 Hun (N. Y.) 95.

[344] Davis v. Ætna Fire Ins. Co., 67 N. H. 335.

[345] Rahr v. Manchester Fire Ins. Co., 93 Wis. 355.

[346] Germania Fire Ins. Co. v. Columbia Encaustic Tile Co., 15 Ind. App. 623.

[347] Reynolds v. Continental Ins. Co., 36 Mich. 131.

[348] Continental Ins. Co. v. Ruckman, 127 Ill. 364, 11 Am. St. 121.

[349] Continental Ins. Co. v. Ruckman, 127 Ill. 364, 11 Am. St. 121.

[350] Parker v. Citizens' Ins. Co., 129 Pa. St. 583.

[351] Germania Fire Ins. Co. v. Columbia Encaustic Tile Co., 15 Ind. App. 623.

insurance to the insured and receive the premium therefor has no authority to alter the provisions of the policy; and if he receives from the insured an application for such change and undertakes to procure it, he is in that connection the agent of the insured and not of the company.[352] A local insurance agent appointed by the insurance company to solicit applications can not, at the same time, be the agent of the applicant for insurance, and he is generally held to be the agent of the insurer; and any mistake made by the agent who writes or directs the application is chargeable to the company and not to the insured;[353] and a stipulation in such application that the policy agent is the agent of the insured and not of the company is not binding on the insured;[354] and if the agent writes down false answers without the knowledge of the insured, after he has been truthfully informed of the matter by the applicant, the applicant is not bound by it although he signs the application and the policy makes the statements warranties.[355] There are cases, however, which hold that the question as to whose agent the solicitor is depends upon the facts and circumstances of each case.[356]

§ 458. **Liability of insurer for acts of agent.**—The insurer, or insurance company, like any other principal, is liable for the acts and representations of its agents, whether on contract or in tort, if made within the scope, apparent or real, of the agent's authority.[357] If, however, the authority of the agent was special, or if limited, and the insured had notice of such limitation,—the company is not liable beyond the agent's actual authority.[358] In practice the question

[352] Duluth Nat'l Bank v. Knoxville Fire Ins. Co., 85 Tenn. 76, 4 Am. St. 744.

[353] Woodbury Sav. Bank v. Charter Oak Ins. Co., 31 Conn. 517.

[354] Commercial Union Assur. Co. v. State, 113 Ind. 331; Indiana Ins. Co. v. Hartwell, 100 Ind. 566, 123 Ind. 177; Sprague v. Holland Purchase Ins. Co., 69 N. Y. 128; Pierce v. People, 106 Ill. 11, 46 Am. Rep. 683; Eilenberger v. Protective Mut. Fire Ins. Co., 89 Pa. St. 464.

[355] Continental Ins. Co. v. Pearce, 39 Kan. 396, 7 Am. St. 557; Hingston v. Ætna Life Ins. Co., 42 Iowa 46; Kausal v. Minnesota Farmers' Mut. Fire Ins. Co., 31 Minn. 17, 47 Am. Rep. 776; Deitz v. Providence &c. Ins. Co., 31 W. Va. 851, 13 Am. St. 909.

[356] Davis v. Ætna Mut. Fire Ins. Co., 67 N. H. 335.

[357] Van Werden v. Equitable Life Assur. Soc., 99 Iowa 621; Continental Ins. Co. v. Kasey, 25 Gratt. (Va.) 268, 18 Am. Rep. 681; New York Life Ins. Co. v. McGowan, 18 Kan. 300.

[358] Paine v. Pacific Mut. Life Ins. Co., 51 Fed. 689; Shaffer v. Milwaukee Mech. Ins. Co., 17 Ind. App. 204. See Sun Fire Office v. Wich, 6 Colo. App. 103.

frequently arises as to the company's responsibility for the acts of its agents with regard to effecting insurance. If an agent has no authority to issue policies, can he bind the insurer by an agreement to insure, if based upon a sufficient consideration? This question has generally been answered in the negative. Where a special agent of a fire-insurance company has been commissioned to solicit and receive proposals for insurance and collect premiums, subject to the rules and regulations of the company and "such instructions as may be given from time to time by the general agent of the western department" of the company in this country, a parol contract entered into by him and an applicant for a policy, sanctioned by such general agent, is binding upon the company.[359] But where a local agent, who was not authorized to make contracts of insurance, but only to receive and forward applications and to deliver policies sent to him and collect the premiums thereon, entered into an agreement with an applicant for fire-insurance, the understanding being that on receipt of the policy the applicant should pay the premium; whereupon the applicant was informed by the agent that his insurance would take effect from the date of the application; which agreement he was authorized to make with reference to certain property, but subject to the approval of the general agent, the insured property not falling within that class, and the general agent not accepting the same, but rejecting it after the property was burned, but before he had any notice of the fact,—the supreme court of Wisconsin held that the jury had no right to find that there was any valid contract for insurance between the parties, especially as the company never held the agent out as possessing authority to take such risks for it, or that it had notice that he was violating his instructions or acting in any way not authorized about its business.[360] And where, under similar circumstances, an application was forwarded, accompanied by the cash premium, to be approved by the directors, and nearly six months' time elapsed before any reply was made to the proposition for insurance, the court ruled that it did not constitute an authority to make a contract of insurance, and that an acceptance could not be presumed by lapse of time, although the company had agreed that the money was to be returned if the application was rejected.[361] The mere fact

[359] Harron v. City of London Fire Ins. Co., 88 Cal. 16.

[360] Fleming v. Hartford Fire Ins. Co., 42 Wis. 616.

[361] Insurance Co. v. Johnson, 23 Pa. St. 72.

that the company furnished its agent with an advertising card as a part of his agency supplies, upon which his name was printed as agent and that he was authorized to countersign policies, where the agent had no power to issue policies, and was not supplied with such, —would not confer upon him authority to bind the company to a contract of insurance before any policy was issued.[362] But when an insurance company clothes an agent with all the *indicia* of authority, it is bound by his acts, whether the same were actually authorized or not: provided the insured had no notice of any limitation of the agent's authority; and the company is bound by any waiver made by such agent of conditions in the policy which might otherwise avoid it.[363] And so, where an adjuster was specially employed to adjust one of two losses resulting from the same fire and sustained by the same person, but under different policies and upon different property; and having adjusted the loss as to which he was employed, agreed with the owner of the property that he need not make proofs of loss under the other policy, but that the claim should abide the result of arbitration with other companies, etc.,—the supreme court of Iowa decided that this amounted to a waiver of the proofs of loss which bound the company.[364] And where the agent of a company

[362] Armstrong v. State Ins. Co., 61 Iowa 212. See also, O'Brien v. New Zealand Ins. Co., 108 Cal. 227.

[363] Manhattan Life Ins. Co. v. Carder, 82 Fed. 986.

[364] Slater v. Capital Ins. Co., 89 Iowa 628. In that case the court, speaking through Granger, C. J., said: "What, then, as between the plaintiff and the defendant, is the legal effect of the authority granted to Philbrook? The company had sent him to Slater & Eller as their adjuster. Neither the company nor Philbrook intimated that his authority as an adjuster was limited, but, on the contrary, he in the one case authoritatively exercised the usual powers of such an agent. The company had said to both Slater and Eller: "This is my authorized agent. Deal with him as such." In view of the finding of the jury, we may say that Philbrook assumed the same authority for adjustment under one policy as under another. The rule of the appellants' contention would require us to hold that Slater, after dealing with him as an authorized adjuster with him and Eller in regard to the loss on the contents of the barn on one policy, could not recognize him as an adjuster on a loss on another policy from the same company to him, resulting from the same fire. We think that such a rule should not obtain. Looking to the manner in which the insurance business of the country is transacted, through agents, distant from the home offices of the companies, by which patrons neither see nor know any other than the soliciting agent, who, upon a written application, either issues or procures and delivers the policy, and, after loss, the adjuster, through whom the business of ad-

collected the renewal premium on a policy, and informed the party who paid it that he was insured for another year; and the company or

justment is carried on, and the consequences of the rule contended for will be apparent. The rules of law are designed to be in harmony with the natural and reasonable conduct of parties in their business intercourse, and with the changed condition in the business intercourse of the country from time to time must come such changes in the laws governing legal rights as will maintain such harmony. Philbrook had been sent to Slater as an adjuster. It is the law that Slater must, at his peril, know Philbrook's authority to act as such; but with his knowledge that he was an adjuster came the legal right to assume that his power was commensurate with the duties of adjustment between the persons to whom he was sent and the company, as to all matters that should reasonably be considered as intended by the company. We think, that after the adjustment of the Slater & Eller loss by Philbrook, no reasonable person would have doubted his pretended authority to adjust the loss on the barn, particularly in view of the close identity of the losses as to parties and circumstances. It was the act of the company that gave rise to this reasonable belief on the part of Slater by sending Philbrook as adjuster. If an insurance company does not wish to be bound up by so broad a presumption as to the authority of an adjuster, a reasonable and very just rule, as applied to the present method of insurance business, would require that it should impart to the assured the limitations upon his authority, by which means the parties could act upon an equality, a condition absolutely forbidden by the rule contended for. The general importance of the rule we are considering will justify a somewhat extended quotation from Insurance Co. v. Wilkinson, in 13 Wall. (U. S.) 22, where the United States supreme court has adopted reasoning somewhat similar to ours, with like conclusions. We quote therefrom as follows: 'It is well known,' said the court, '(so well that no court would be justified in shutting its eyes to it), that insurance companies organized under the law of one state, and having in that state their principal business office, send these agents all over the land, with directions to solicit and procure applications for policies, furnishing them with printed arguments in favor of the value and necessity of the life insurance, and of the special advantages of the corporation which the agents represent. They pay these agents large commissions on the premiums thus obtained, and the policies are delivered at their hand to the assured. The agents are stimulated by letters and instructions to activity in procuring contracts, and the party who is in this manner induced to take out a policy rarely sees or knows anything about the company or its officers by whom it is issued, but looks to and relies upon the agent who has persuaded him to effect insurance as the full and complete representative of the company in all that is said or done in making the contract. Has he no right to so regard him? It is quite true that the reports of judicial decisions are agent retained the premium but failed to issue a renewal policy thereon as was the custom of the company, until after a loss by fire

filled with the efforts of these companies, by their counsel, to establish the doctrine that they can do all this, and yet limit their responsibility for the acts of these agents to the simple receipt of the premium and delivery of the policy; the argument being that, as to all other acts of the agent, he is the agent of the assured. The proposition is not without support in some of the earlier decisions on the subject; and at a time when insurance companies waited for parties to come to them to seek assurance, or to forward applications on their own motion, the doctrine had a reasonable foundation to rest upon. But to apply such a doctrine, in its full force, to a system of selling policies through agents, which we have described, would be a snare and a delusion, leading, as it has done in numerous instances, to the grossest frauds, of which the insurance corporations receive the benefits, and the parties supposing themselves insured are the victims. The tendency of the modern decisions in this country is steadily in the opposite direction. The powers of the agent are *prima facie* coextensive with the business intrusted to his care, and will not be narrowed by limitations not communicated to the person with whom he deals. An insurance company establishing a local agency must be held responsible to the parties with whom they transact business for the acts and declarations of the agent, within the scope of his employment, as if they proceeded from the principal.' The arguments in that case apply with strong, if not with equal, force to the business of fire insurance, and to the duties and authority of agents acting for the companies after losses occur. In view of the business zeal and competition of the times, with insurance companies we may say 'no stone is left unturned' to secure applications, and to this end agents wait upon desired customers in field and shop and home, to urge their superior claims for patronage. After a loss occurs, agents are promptly on the ground for investigation, conference, and adjustment. Under the business education of the times they are factors by and through which patrons may know and deal with the companies. The agent is the representative of the company. Now, it is certainly a reasonable rule that when an agent approaches a patron who has met with a loss, he may know to what extent he can safely act or deal with him as such agent. The company has that knowledge. If they are to do business upon equal terms, the patron should also have it. It is hardly to be expected that the business of adjustment must await a correspondence between the assured and the company to know the fact. But two other methods are open: First, that the company shall give notice of the authority possessed by its agent: or, second, that the assured may lawfully assume that the agent has authority to transact the business in hand as if possessing general powers for that purpose. Such a rule has full support in Insurance Co. v. Wilkinson, *supra*. and also in considerations of both public and private good. See also, as bearing on had occurred,—the company was held bound by the renewal contract; although the first policy provided that "the company should not be liable for contracts of its agents before the contract had been approved and certified to in writing by the secretary."[365] So, where a party obtained a policy of insurance on his building from the recognized agent of a company, and paid him the premium, and the agent reported to the home office and forwarded the premium; and after waiting the usual time and receiving no reply he delivered the policy to the owner of the property, which was in accordance with the usual course of dealing of the company,—it was ruled that the company was liable on the contract.[366] An insurance company can not escape the result of an agreement by its general agent to waive the condition of a policy that the payment of the premium in cash shall be a condition precedent to the validity of the policy, if the agent had real or apparent authority to make insurance contracts.[367] But where the policy contains an express limitation upon the agent's power and is accepted with it, the agent can not change or waive it so as to bind the company.[368] In such case the holder of the policy, by accepting it, is estopped to rely upon any authority of the agent in opposition to

this question, Silverberg v. Insurance Co., 67 Cal. 36, 7 Pac. 38, and, to some extent, Insurance Co. v. Gallatin, 48 Wis. 36, 3 N. W. 772. There are very many cases in which other, but somewhat kindred subjects are discussed, wherein, from the reasoning, this position receives support. Of those, see Morrison v. Insurance Co., 69 Tex. 353, 6 S. W. 605; Cleaver v. Insurance Co., 71 Mich. 414, 39 N. W. 571; Schoener v. Insurance Co., 50 Wis. 575, 7 N. W. 544; Alexander v. Insurance Co., 67 Wis. 422, 30 N. W. 727, and cases therein cited. It should be stated that the state of Wisconsin has a general statute on the subject, which controls the decisions of that state to some extent. We think the facts of the case justify the application of such a rule, and that the company is responsible for failure to make the proofs of loss. The evidence and admissions were such that, under the law as we have expressed it, it was not error to refuse the motion to instruct the jury to return a verdict for the defendant." See also, Weidert v. State Ins. Co., 19 Or. 261, 20 Am. St. 809; Russell v. Insurance Co., 80 Mich. 407; Hoge v. Dwelling-House Ins. Co., 138 Pa. St. 66; California Ins. Co. v. Gracey, 15 Colo. 70, 22 Am. St. 376.

365 King v. City of Oshkosh, 75 Wis. 517.

366 Mullen v. McKinney, 138 Pa. St. 69.

367 Home Ins. Co. v. Gilman, 112 Ind. 7; Willcuts v. Northwestern, etc., Co., 81 Ind. 300.

368 Robinson v. Fire Ass'n, 63 Mich. 90; Cleaver v. Traders' Ins. Co., 65 Mich. 527.

the limitation.[369] But even an act done in violation of the agent's authority may be ratified by the company, or the proper officer thereof; and this may be done expressly or it may be implied by the conduct of the company or of such qualified agent.[370]

§ **459. Liability of agent to the insured.**—The insured may avoid the contract of insurance, if it was induced by the false and fraudulent representations of the agent, if they were material. Thus, where a person executed a premium note to an insurance company for a policy, on the false and fraudulent representation of the agent that certain persons named by him and who were well known to the insured would constitute the board of directors, the insured may interpose this as a defense to the note, the representations being more than the mere expression of an opinion as to the legal effect of the contract.[371] But he may also, if he has paid any premium, sue and recover from such agent the amount of such premium paid, as the measure of his damages.[372] And where an applicant for insurance has paid to an agent the premium for a policy to be issued, on the false and fraudulent promise to have a policy issued on said application, which is not done, the agent is liable to the applicant for the premium;[373] unless the agent had authority from the company and the latter failed to issue such a policy as the applicant contracted for, in which case the remedy is against the company and not against the agent.[374] Where a policy prohibited the keeping of petroleum on the insured premises, and the applicant declined to accept it on that condition, saying he was bound to keep a little, and asked that the fact be noted in the policy, but was told by the agent that he should have the privilege of keeping one barrel of petroleum in connection with the stock of goods insured, and that it was unnecessary to mention the fact in the policy, and there was a loss by fire for which the insured, owing to the violation of the provision of the policy relating to the keeping of oil on the premises, was not permitted to recover, the court held that the agent was liable to the

[369] Cleaver v. Traders' Ins. Co., *supra*.

[370] Keith v. Globe Ins. Co., 52 Ill. 518; Niagara Ins. Co. v. Lee, 73 Tex. 641; Howard Ins. Co. v. Owen, 94 Ky. 197.

[371] Penn Mut. Life Ins. Co. v. Crane, 134 Mass. 56.

[372] Hedden v. Griffin, 136 Mass. 229, 49 Am. Rep. 25.

[373] Collier v. Bedell, 39 Hun (N. Y.) 238.

[374] Bleau v. Wright, 110 Mich. 183. See also, Bryan v. Viele, 4 N. Y. St. 872.

assured to the extent of the injury sustained by the misrepresentations.[375] Failure or neglect to procure insurance on the part of the agent, if based upon a sufficient consideration, such as the payment to such agent of the advance premium, is such a breach of duty as will render the agent liable to the applicant for all damages resulting from the loss;[376] but where there is no premium paid, and consequently no consideration passed, it is doubtful whether the agent can be held liable.[377] An agent may also render himself personally liable for doing business for a foreign company not authorized to operate within the state by reason of non-fulfilment of the statutory requirements, if injury result from his act. Thus, if such agent issue an insurance policy in such a company, and, in case of loss, the assured is defeated in collecting the proceeds of the policy by reason of the company's insolvency, the agent is personally liable to the policy-holder for the loss; the agent in such case being held impliedly to warrant the company's solvency.[378] The agent may render himself liable to the assured in other cases of negligence; as where, for example, he receives from an applicant the premium for a policy, but before it is paid over to the company the latter becomes insolvent, and the applicant demands of the agent the return of his premium, and informs him that he does not rely on the policy issued to him: in such case the insured may doubtless recover the premium from the agent, and this is true although the policy has not been returned or tendered back before suit.[379]

§ **460. Liability of insurance agent to his principal.**—For any violation of his duty to his principal, an insurance agent is, of course, liable to such principal in damages to the extent of the injury. For the purpose of enforcing the more positively the obligations of their agents to them, insurance companies usually require such agents to give bond, with surety or sureties, for the faithful performance of their duties; and a liability will arise on such bond as well as individually whenever there has been a breach of such duty. Thus, where an agent had been directed by his company to cancel a policy

[375] Kroeger v. Pitcairn, 101 Pa. St. 311, 47 Am. Rep. 718.

[376] Haight v. Kremer, 9 Phila. (Pa.) 50, 29 Leg. Int. (Pa.) 30.

[377] See Fraunthal v. Derr, 13 W. N. C. (Pa.) 485; Stadler v. Trever, 86 Wis. 42.

[378] Morton v. Hart, 88 Tenn. 427.

[379] Smith v. Binder, 75 Ill. 492. But see Farrow v. Cochran, 72 Me. 309, as to the necessity of returning or offering to return the policy.

which contained a stipulation for its cancelation, and the agent failed to do so within a reasonable time, and the company suffered a loss thereby, it was held that the agent was liable to the company for the damages;[380] and he is not excused in such case by the fact that he notified the broker who had placed the insurance to cancel it: the broker being in that case but the agent of the agent.[381] The question of what is a reasonable time and effort to have the policy canceled is usually a question of fact, for the jury;[382] but where the facts are undisputed it is a question of law, for the court.[383] But if the duty of seeing to the cancelation of policies is not contained in the agent's written contract of appointment, and there is no evidence that he assumed that duty independently thereof, evidence of his failure to have a policy canceled is not admissible against him, when the suit is on such written contract of appointment.[384] It is otherwise, of course, if the performance of that duty is within the scope of the undertaking, though not expressly enumerated in the written appointment; as where he engages to perform such duties as he is requested to do. And where an agent himself effects insurance which the principal declines to accept, it is his duty to have the policy canceled when directed to do so; and upon failure to obey such orders, he is liable to the company for negligence;[385] in such case he must obey the instructions of his principal, and he has no right to set himself up to pass judgment as to the wisdom or expediency of the orders given him. He must obey the orders and directions of his principal with reasonable promptness and fidelity.[386] Moreover, an insurance agent, like any other agent, being required to act with fidelity to his principal, must not act for himself in connection with the business of his principal: he can not be agent for the company and deal with himself as principal; and hence, he is without power to make a contract with himself for the insurance of his individual property;[387] and hence, if an agent forwards an application for insur-

[380] Kraber v. Union Ins. Co., 129 Pa. St. 8, 24 W. N. C. (Pa.) 547; Sun Fire Office v. Ermentrout, 2 Pa. Dist. R. 77.

[381] Franklin Ins. Co. v. Sears, 21 Fed. 290; Sun Fire Office v. Ermentrout, *supra*.

[382] American Cent. Ins. Co. v. Hagerty, 92 Hun (N. Y.) 26, 36 N. Y. Supp. 558.

[383] Franklin Fire Ins. Co. v. Sears, *supra*.

[384] Norwood v. Alamo Fire Ins. Co., 13 Tex. Civ. App. 475.

[385] Kraber v. Union Ins. Co., 129 Pa. St. 8, 24 W. N. C. (Pa.) 547.

[386] *Ibid.*

[387] Bentley v. Columbia Ins. Co., 19 Barb. (N. Y.) 595; May Ins., § 125.

ance on a vessel of which he is a part owner, which fact he conceals from the company, and procures a policy on the property, and delivers it to the insured, the policy is void.[388] The agent is also liable for the acts of his subagents appointed by himself, when such acts are within the scope of their employment; and the sureties on the agent's bond are responsible for losses occurring from the default of such subagents.[389] And so, the bondsmen are liable also for a loss on account of the agent's failure to cancel a policy when directed to do so.[390] When the action on the bond is for failure to account for premiums as stipulated therein, the sureties are liable, as well as the principal, for all the premiums collected by the agent, less his commissions thereon; but the liability would not include a premium for which he had improperly given credit to the insured, if he had not received it.[391]

§ 461. **Liability of insurer to agent—Compensation.**—Like any other principal, an insurance company is, by its contract, express or implied, bound to compensate its agents for their services. Many of the officers and higher classes of agents of insurance companies receive their remuneration in stipulated salaries; but those agents who solicit applications for policies are customarily paid in commissions, or salary and commissions, and these frequently extend to the annual premiums that accrue subsequently to that paid by the insured when he receives the policy; but an agent who voluntarily leaves the service of the company thereby forfeits his commissions on subsequently-accruing premiums, unless his contract with the company provides otherwise.[392] When an agent is wrongfully discharged before his contract is terminated, he has his remedy for a breach of contract as other agents have: if his compensation consists of commissions on future premiums, he may recover the amount of probable loss on such commissions, less what he might have reasonably earned during the unexpired period, and it is competent to prove by witnesses in such cases the probable value of renewals during that time.[393] A contract providing that an agent shall receive commissions on renewal premiums will

[388] Ritt v. Washington, etc. Ins. Co., 41 Barb. (N. Y.) 353.

[389] Phenix Mut. Life Ins. Co. v. Holloway, 51 Conn. 310, 50 Am. Rep. 20.

[390] Royal Ins. Co., etc., v. Clark, 61 Minn. 476.

[391] Byrne v. Ætna Ins. Co., 56 Ill. 321.

[392] May Ins., § 576. See Spaulding v. New York Life Ins. Co., 61 Me. 329.

[393] May Ins., § 576.

terminate with the period of service for which the agent was employed, where the commissions are limited to "business procured by the agent under this appointment."[394] But where the contract gave the agent authority to effect life-insurance and appoint subagents throughout the state, for which he was to receive a certain salary and office expenses; and it was provided that in addition thereto he was to receive a percentage upon original and renewal premiums upon all policies procured by him, the expenses of collection to be deducted when the premiums were collected by other agents; either party having the privilege to terminate the agency upon three months' notice, and the company having given the notice required and thus dissolved the relation,—it was held by a majority of the court that the right to commissions on policies procured by the agent continued as long as the policies were kept in force by renewals, if the renewal premiums were collected by the company.[395] Usage becomes a part of every contract for the compensation of an agent, when from all the circumstances it appears that it was so intended by the parties, but not otherwise; for the parties have a right, by their contract, to exclude the usage. Where this is the case, proof of usage is inadmissible, and an unreasonable usage does not enter into the contract.[396] The parties can not by parol evidence of custom or usage establish the existence of a different contract from that to which they expressly agreed;[397] but where the usage is reasonable and it is not in conflict with the contract, it will properly enter into the contract for compensation. The principal may, of course, be liable to the agent in many other particular instances,—as, for a premature discharge and other breaches of the contract; but the obligation in such instances is not different from that of other principals to their agents and requires no special consideration.

[394] Spaulding v. New York Life Ins. Co., 61 Me. 329. See also, Moses v. Union Cent. Life Ins. Co., 7 Ohio Dec. R. 609, 4 Wkly. Law Bull. 214.

[395] Hercules, etc., Society v. Brinker, 77 N. Y. 435.

[396] Castleman v. Southern Mutual Life Ins. Co., 14 Bush (Ky.) 197.

[397] Partridge v. Phenix Mut. Ins. Co., 15 Wall. (U. S.) 573.

CHAPTER XVII.

TRAVELING SALESMEN.

§ 462. **Definitions.**—Traveling salesmen include commercial travelers, or "drummers," and pedlers and hawkers. Commercial travelers or drummers are a large class of modern commercial agents whose business it is to travel about the country for wholesale houses and take orders from retail dealers for merchandise to be shipped to the latter by the respective firms or concerns which such drummer or agent represents. "The term 'drummer' has acquired a common acceptation, and is applied to commercial agents who are traveling for wholesale merchants, and supplying the retail trade with goods, or rather, taking orders for goods to be shipped to the retail merchant, upon which merchandise the state collects her revenue."[398] Definitions of the terms "drummer," "commercial traveler," etc., are often called into requisition by the courts in construing statutes assessing a license tax on these or on "pedlers," "hawkers," etc. It often happens in such cases that distinctions are to be drawn between pedlers and drummers, as the latter are not usually required to procure a license. Ordinarily a municipal corporation has power to impose such a tax upon pedlers and hawkers, because they carry their goods with them and the same constitute a portion of the bulk of the taxable property of the state; while drummers, or commercial travelers, usually sell from samples and generally for firms or corporations in other states; and a license fee or tax imposed upon such goods as they sell, if from another state or states, would be taxing interstate com-

[398] Per Turney, J., in Singleton v. Fretch, 4 Lea (Tenn.) 93. See also, State v. Miller, 93 N. C. 511, 53 Am. Rep. 469; Ex parte Taylor, 58 Miss. 478, 38 Am. Rep. 336.

merce, which under the federal constitution can not be legally done.[399] So, it has been held that a person who solicits and takes orders for books issued or published by his principal, who is a resident of another state, without delivering such books at the time the orders are taken, is not a hawker or pedler, but a drummer or canvasser, within the meaning of a statute giving municipal corporations the power "to license, tax, regulate, suppress and prohibit 'hawkers' and 'pedlers.' "[400] Pedlers and hawkers are those who travel from city to city or from house to house, and sell commodities which they ordinarily carry with them, and deliver at once upon sale, as opposed to those who sell at an established shop,[401] or by sample for future delivery. If one thus goes from house to house to sell goods, though it be on the installment plan, delivering them as sold, he is a pedler.[402] One may, however, under exceptional circumstances, be a pedler, although he does not deliver at once when the order is taken. Thus, butchers who take orders for meat from house to house, and then deliver it to the consumers, are pedlers.[403] A person who carries jewelry from county to county to sell is a pedler.[404] The terms "hawkers," "pedlers" and "traveling merchants" are in some sense synonymous, meaning those who go about with goods making or attempting to make sales, and making delivery.[405] It seems that hawkers were in ill favor at the common law; and Jacob designates them as "those deceitful fellows who went from place to place buying and selling brass, pewter and other merchandise which ought to be uttered in open market, * * * and the appellation seems to grow from their uncertain wandering, like persons that with hawks seize their game where they can find it."[406] Generally, selling goods by sample is not pedling.[407] But "any method of selling goods, wares or merchandise by outcry on the

[399] Emmons v. City of Lewiston, 132 Ill. 380, 22 Am. St. 540; Village of Cerro Gordo v. Rawlings, 135 Ill. 36.

[400] *Ibid.* See to the same effect, City of Kansas v. Collins, 34 Kan. 434.

[401] Emmons v. City of Lewiston, 132 Ill. 380, 22 Am. St. 540; Commonwealth v. Gardner, 133 Pa. St. 284, 19 Am. St. 645, 7 L. R. A. 666.

[402] City of South Bend v. Martin, 142 Ind. 31, 29 L. R. A. 531; People v. Sawyer, 106 Mich. 428; City of St. Paul v. Briggs (Minn.), 88 N. W. 984.

[403] Davis v. City of Macon, 64 Ga. 128, 37 Am. Rep. 60; City of Duluth v. Krupp, 46 Minn. 435.

[404] Wynne v. Wright, 18 N. C. 19.

[405] Commonwealth v. Edson, 2 Pa. Co. Ct. 377.

[406] Jacob Law Dic.

[407] Commonwealth v. Jones, 70 Ky. 502; State v. Hoffman, 50 Mo. App. 585; Commonwealth v. Eichenburg, 140 Pa. St. 158; City of Davenport v. Rice, 75 Iowa 74.

streets or public places in a city, or by attracting persons to purchase goods exposed for sale at such places, by placards or signals, or by going from house to house selling or offering goods for sale at retail to individuals not dealers in such commodities, whether the goods be carried along for delivery promptly, or whether the sales be made for future delivery, constitutes the person so selling a hawker or pedler within the meaning of the statute."[408] Soliciting orders for the making of shirts[409] or clothing[410] or sewing-machines[411] or beer in bottles[412] to be delivered in the future, is not pedling or hawking, although an article is occasionally delivered at the time of sale.[413]

§ **463. Commercial travelers or drummers.**—This class of agents have certain duties, obligations and rights in connection with the relation to their principals and to third parties not essentially different from those of other agents. As a general rule, a drummer's duties are confined to the soliciting of orders for goods.[414] He has no implied authority to collect money, not being in possession of the goods or having other *indicia* of authority; and if the purchaser pays such an agent, he does so at his peril, and the burden is upon him to prove that the agent possessed such authority.[415] This is one exception to the general rule that the power to sell includes the power to collect payment on account of the sale:[416] the rule does not apply when the agent has not the possession of the goods. Traveling salesmen have become such a numerous class of agents that their duties and powers have become a matter of common knowledge in the business world, and parties who deal with them must be presumed to know at least the general scope of these. In the absence of actual authority to collect payment for goods sold in such cases, by traveling salesmen who solicit orders, the principal can only be made liable in the event he holds out the

[408] Per Mitchell, J., in Graffty v. City of Rushville, 107 Ind. 502, 57 Am. Rep. 128.

[409] City of Elgin v. Picard, 24 Ill. App. 340.

[410] Radebaugh v. City of Plain City, 11 Ohio Dec. 612.

[411] Commonwealth v. Farnum, 114 Mass. 267; State v. Moorehead, 42 S. C. 211, 46 Am. St. 419, 26 L. R. A. 585.

[412] DuBoistown v. Rochester Brewing Co. (Com. Pl.), 9 Pa. Co. Ct. 442.

[413] See also, City of Stuart v. Cunningham, 88 Iowa 191, 29 L. R. A. 439; Village of Stamford v. Fisher, 140 N. Y. 187; Hewson v. Inhabitants, etc., 55 N. J. L. 522, 21 L. R. A. 736.

[414] Ex parte Taylor, 58 Miss. 478; Chambers v. Short, 79 Mo. 204.

[415] Butler v. Dorman, 68 Mo. 298; Chambers v. Short, 79 Mo. 204, 207.

[416] Story Ag., § 102.

agent as possessing such power: it is not implied in the authority to take orders for goods.[417] The purchaser can not with safety rely upon the statement of the agent that he possesses such authority: a holding out by the principal can generally be shown only by admissions or conduct on the part of such principal.[418] Where the agent is intrusted with the possession of goods, or sells over the counter, authority to receive payment will generally be implied, unless forbidden by the seller; in such case, the rule is directly opposite from what it is in case of a mere solicitor for orders.[419] Nor is it within the implied powers of such an agent to cancel his contracts for and take back goods previously sold to the customer which are not satisfactory to him.[420] The sale between the customer and the principal, when made by a traveling salesman, unless it be in writing, is complete only from the time the goods are shipped, provided the principal ships within a reasonable time the amount and quality of the goods ordered, and in the manner directed. From that time on, if the contract be valid and binding, and the delivery is to be "f. o. b.," the title to the goods vests in the purchaser, subject only to stoppage *in transitu.* If a different kind or quantity be shipped from those ordered, or if shipment be delayed an unreasonable time, the purchaser is not bound to receive the shipment, and may avoid liability therefor by notifying the seller, within a reasonable time, that he declines to receive the goods. But if he receive and appropriate the goods, he is liable for them the same as if he had ordered them, and he must pay what they are reasonably worth.[421] On the other hand, if the agent exceed his authority, by agreeing to certain conditions not within the scope of his powers, the principal may reject them; but if he accept the contract of the agent, he will be bound by it; and he can not accept it in part and repudiate it in part.[422] So, where a drummer made an unauthorized arrangement with a customer to discount a bill ten per cent. off list price, the principal was held not bound by the arrangement; and since the agreement was beyond the apparent scope of the agent's authority, the purchaser was held liable

[417] Kornemann v. Monaghan, 24 Mich. 36; Chambers v. Short, 79 Mo. 204, 207.

[418] Holland v. Van Beil, 89 Ga. 223; Kornemann v. Monaghan, *supra*; McKinly v. Dunham, 55 Wis. 515.

[419] Law v. Stokes, 3 Vroom (N. J.) 249, 90 Am. Dec. 655.

[420] Diversby v. Kellog, 44 Ill. 114, 92 Am. Dec. 154.

[421] Diversby v. Kellog, *supra*.

[422] Babcock v. Deford, 14 Kan. 408.

for the list prices.[423] In that case, however, the purchaser had notice that the agent had no such authority, from the fact that the latter agreed to make good the discount himself, if the principal did not do so; otherwise it would seem that the purchaser had the right to dictate his own terms of the purchase; and if such terms were not agreeable to the seller, he should decline to forward the goods. It is within the implied powers of such an agent, who is paid a certain salary and traveling expenses for his compensation, to bind his principal for the use of horses and carriages used by him in his principal's business;[424] the reason for this, as we have seen in a previous place in this work,[425] is that the agent's power to do a thing includes all the necessary means of doing it; and where an agent is sent by his house with large trunks and sample-cases, it is but natural that he should have the means of transporting these over the route of his travels. Inasmuch as even an agent who has the goods which he is to sell in his possession has no implied authority to barter or exchange them for other goods, or articles, or pledge them for his own debt,[426] it follows that an agent of the character now under consideration has no such implied powers. And a commercial traveler, even though he have authority to collect accounts and receive money and checks payable to his principal, has no implied authority to indorse his principal's name on such checks; and if a bank pay such checks on his indorsement, it will be responsible to the principal.[427] Established

[423] Taylor Mfg. Co. v. Brown (Tex. App.), 14 S. W. 1071.

[424] Bentley v. Doggett, 51 Wis. 224, 37 Am. Rep. 827; Huntley v. Mathias, 90 N. C. 101, 47 Am. Rep. 516. 59 Am. Dec. 331.

[425] *Ante*, § 326.

[426] Wheeler & Wilson Mfg. Co. v. Givan, 65 Mo. 89.

[427] Jackson v. National Bank, 92 Tenn. 154 The court in that case, speaking through Holman, J., said: "No authority will be implied from an express authority. Whatever powers will be conceded to the effectual exercise of the express powers will be conceded to the agent by implication. In order, therefore, that the authority to make or draw, accept, and indorse commercial paper as the agent of another may be implied from some other express authority, it must be shown to be strictly necessary to the complete execution of the express power. The rule is strictly enforced that the authority to execute and indorse bills and notes as agent will not be implied from an express authority to transact some other business, unless it is absolutely necessary to the exercise of express authority: Tiedeman Com. Paper, § 77. Possession of a check payable to order, by one claiming to be agent of the payee, is not *prima facie* proof of authority to demand payment in the name

usage will, however, as in the case of any other agent's authority, enter into the contract of agency of a drummer, if there be nothing in that instrument to the contrary; so, where there is a general and well-known usage that an agent to solicit orders may collect payment, the agent in the given case will be presumed to possess such authority, in the absence of evidence to the contrary.[428] Nor has a drummer an implied authority to sell his samples and take pay for them; and if he does, the owner may recover their value from the purchaser, in a proper action.[429] A drummer's samples are not included in the ordinary baggage of a passenger for which a common carrier becomes liable in case of loss or injury to the baggage, unless the baggage became injured or lost by the "gross" negligence of the carrier; but the company is liable, even for ordinary negligence, or as an insurer, where the railroad-agent having control of the receipt of the baggage had knowledge of what was contained in such baggage, and no misrepresentation as to such contents was made to such railroad agent

of the true owner: *Idem*, § 312. A bank is obliged by custom to honor checks payable to order, and pays them at its peril to any other than the person to whose order they are made payable: *Idem*, § 431. It must see that the check is paid to the payee therein named upon his genuine indorsement, or it will remain responsible: Pickle v. Muse, 88 Tenn. 380, 12 S. W. 919. An authority to receive checks in lieu of cash in payment of bills placed in the hands of an agent for collection does not authorize the agent to indorse and collect the check: Graham v. Institution, 46 Mo. 186; 1 Wait Act. & Def. 284; 1 Daniel Neg. Inst. 294. The indorsement of the check was not a necessary incident to the collection of accounts: Graham v. Institution, 46 Mo. 186. It follows that a drummer or commercial traveler, employed to sell and take orders for goods, to collect accounts, and receive money, and checks payable to the order of his principal, is not by implication authorized to indorse such principal's name to such checks. No equitable considerations can be invoked to soften seeming hardships in the enforcement of the laws and rules fixing liability on persons handling commercial paper. These laws are the growth of ages, and the result of experience, having their origin in necessity. The inflexibility of these rules may occasionally make them seem severe, but in them is found general security."

[428] Meyer v. Stone, 46 Ark. 210, 55 Am. Rep. 577; Janney v. Boyd, 30 Minn. 319. Some courts have indeed held that a commercial traveler or drummer whose business it is to solicit orders, has implied authority to collect payment also: Trainor v. Morison, 78 Me. 160, 57 Am. Rep. 790; Collins v. Newton, 7 Baxt. (Tenn.) 269. But the great weight of authority is to the contrary.

[429] Kohn v. Washer, 64 Tex. 131, 53 Am. Rep. 745.

by the drummer having it in charge.[430] In such case, the contract is a personal one between the drummer and the carrier, and the owner of the samples (the drummer's principal) has no right of action.[431]

§ **464. Pedlers and hawkers.**—Statutes and municipal ordinances requiring pedlers and hawkers to procure a license for the privilege of selling their commodities, and imposing a penalty for failure to procure such license, are constitutional as a proper exercise of the police power: occupations of this character, if not restrained, are liable to become nuisances, and a license fee may be imposed which is large enough to act as a restraint, or to limit the number of persons to engage in it.[432] But such statutes or ordinances must make no distinction between classes of citizens or residents of different states or of subdivisions of the same states.[433] An apparent exception with regard to some classes of citizens is upheld by the courts in sustaining provisions granting the exclusive privilege of a community or neighborhood to physically disabled soldiers and sailors, or conferring such privilege without pay upon such of these as are not able to make a livelihood by manual labor, or upon crippled or disabled persons without reference to whether or not they were formerly soldiers or sailors.[434] Such statutes have been held constitutional although the effect is to exclude all able-bodied persons from the privilege.[435] The holder of a license to peddle can not delegate

[430] Humphreys v. Perry, 148 U. S. 627; Dibble v. Brown, 12 Ga. 217, 56 Am. Dec. 460; Stimson v. Connecticut River R. Co., 98 Mass. 83, 93 Am. Dec. 140.

[431] Dibble v. Brown, *supra.*

[432] City of Duluth v. Krupp, 46 Minn. 435; Morrill v. State, 38 Wis. 428, 20 Am. Rep. 12.

[433] Commonwealth v. Gardner, 133 Pa. St. 284, 19 Am. St. 645, 7 L. R. A. 666.

[434] In re Fisher, 3 Lanc. Bar. 391; In re Morris, 5 Pa. Co. Ct. 193.

[435] Commonwealth v. Brinton, 132 Pa. St. 69. "Especially is it urged," said the court in this case, "that the discrimination in favor of those under physical disability, is unauthorized, unjust and oppressive While the argument of the appellant on this subject is ingenious, and shows research and learning, we do not regard the subject as fairly debatable. The recital in the earlier acts shows by the express declaration of the lawmakers, what is quite apparent from the nature of the several provisions they contain, that the purpose of the legislation was the protection of society from the lawless, able-bodied wanderer, whose presence is a source of apprehension in any community. To refuse a license which would serve as an excuse for visiting private houses and securing access thereto, to the able-bodied stranger,

the rights and privileges thereunder to another, nor is the same transferable, the rights conferred being of a personal nature; and, in such cases as these, the license would be no protection to the transferee, even though he were an agent or servant of the licensee, unless the employment of an agent or servant were permitted by statute.[436] In England, it seems that the licensed party may, by virtue of the statute, employ a servant to drive the wagon and sell the goods, and the license is a protection to both.[437] A license to peddle may not be conferred upon a corporation, unless there is a statute which permits it.[438] A statute authorizing municipalities of a certain grade to collect license fees, etc., from pedlers, etc., is not obnoxious to the constitutional provision requiring uniformity of legislation for the entire state;[439] such a fee being held not to be a tax within the strict sense of the word, but simply a license charge. Under modern authority pedling and hawking are not considered immoral in themselves, or contrary to the public interests; and, hence, they may be regulated or restricted only on the theory of preventing a nuisance.[440] Some courts hold that it is immaterial whether the license is required upon the theory of a police power, as a means of restraining certain occupations, or whether it comes properly within the taxing power of the legislature, as a means of raising revenue; that in either case it is a constitutional exercise of the legislative function, and is accomplished by means of issuing a license.[441] The better opinion, however, seems to be that the imposing of a license tax upon pedlers and hawkers for the purpose of raising revenue would be unconstitutional, and that the power may be exercised only as a police regulation.[442] Under this view the license fee must not be unreasonable or oppressive in amount.[443] Hence, a city ordinance requiring hawkers or pedlers who travel on foot to take out a license, paying therefor a fee of ten dollars for the first day,

was an exercise of police power, as clearly as the laws regulating the granting of liquor licenses or the rule of fire-arms."

[436] Gibson v. Kauffield, 63 Pa. St. 168; Temple v. Sumner, 51 Miss. 13, 24 Am. Rep. 615.

[437] 51 & 52 Vict., ch. 33.

[438] Wrought Iron Bridge Co. v. Johnson, 84 Ga. 754.

[439] Johnson v. Asbury Park, 60 N. J. L. 427, 431.

[440] State v. Wagener, 69 Minn. 206, 65 Am. St. 565.

[441] Johnson v. Asbury Park, 60 N. J. L. 427, 431.

[442] Van Hook v. Selma, 70 Ala. 361, 45 Am. Rep. 85; Easterly v. Irwin, 99 Iowa 694.

[443] State v. Glavin, 67 Conn. 29; State Center v. Barenstein, 66 Iowa 249.

and five dollars for each subsequent day, if traveling on foot; and, if traveling with one horse, twenty dollars the first day and fifteen dollars for each subsequent day; but if traveling with two or more horses, twenty-five dollars for the first day and fifteen dollars for each subsequent day,—was held invalid by the supreme court of Michigan, as being unreasonable and amounting to practical prohibition.[444] But the same court held a license fee of five dollars per week from all classes of hawkers and pedlers reasonable and valid.[445] There is in a municipality no inherent power to exact a license fee for pedling or hawking, and such power can be exercised only when granted by the legislature;[446] and statutes delegating such power to municipalities should not be construed beyond the natural import of their language; and when this is doubtful, as to whether or not the power has been conferred, the statute should be interpreted so as to relieve the citizen of the burden.[447] Neither can such power, when properly delegated, be redelegated by the municipality to a board or committee or other person, unless the power of redelegation is expressly mentioned or clearly implied in such statute. This is upon the familiar principle that delegated authority which involves the exercise of discretion and judgment can not be redelegated.[448] The state, within its constitutional sphere, may prohibit some occupations entirely, and the courts will not interfere with the legitimate exercise of such right.[449] And it is immaterial whether the commodities as to which the license fee is imposed be manufactured in the same state in which they are to be sold or not; but there must be no interference with interstate or foreign commerce, or the statute requiring a license will be unconstitutional.[450]

§ 465. Sales of goods by drummers and other agents—Statute of frauds.—The 17th section of the English statute of frauds, and equivalent sections enacted by the legislatures of different states in this

[444] Brooks v. Mangan, 86 Mich. 576, 24 Am. St. 137.

[445] People v. Baker, 115 Mich. 199, 73 N. W. 115.

[446] Smith Munic. Corp., § 1477; Shelton v. Mobile, 30 Ala. 540, 68 Am. Dec. 143; Van Hook v. Selma, 70 Ala. 361, 45 Am. Rep. 85.

[447] Ex parte Taylor, 58 Miss. 478, 38 Am. Rep. 336. See also, Kennedy v. People, 9 Colo. App. 492.

[448] State v. Glavin, 67 Conn. 29, 34.

[449] Cooley Const. Lim. (6th ed.) 742.

[450] Brennan v. Titusville, 153 U. S. 289; City of Huntington v. Mahan, 142 Ind. 695; City of Bloomington v. Bourland, 137 Ill. 534; Ex parte Thomas, 71 Cal. 204; Ex parte Rosenblatt, 19 Nev. 439, 3 Am. St. 901.

country, are generally applicable to a contract for the sale of goods by a drummer or other traveling agent who does not deliver on sale.[451] As the rule of law differs in different states with respect to the question whether such a sale falls within the statute at all, and if so, what will be its construction, etc., the governing rule of law must always be sought in the jurisdiction where the contract was made or attempted to be made, and the principles here stated are of general application only. Under the 17th section of the English statute, a contract or order for goods of the value of ten pounds sterling ($50.00) or more can not be enforced unless it is in writing, or unless there has been a delivery, receipt and acceptance of the goods, in whole or in part, or payment or part payment of the purchase price, or of some earnest-money.[452] Whether the amount is sufficient or not to bring the case within the statute depends sometimes upon the question whether the sale of different articles of goods of various kinds, the value of each of which is less than $50.00 (or whatever the statutory amount may be), is an entire contract within the meaning of the statute, or whether each article constitutes a separate sale: if it was all one sale, it of course comes within the provisions of the statute, unless the value or price of all the articles was less than $50.00; but if each article was sold separately, and its price or value was less than $50.00, the statute will not apply.[453] Whether the subject-matter of a contract falls within the purview of the statute also depends upon whether or not the object to be accomplished is a sale of personal property or a contract for work and labor or material; for if an article is contracted for which has as yet no existence, and, when manufactured and delivered according to the contract, would not be a sale of personal property, but might simply be work and labor and material furnished, the statute does not apply. It has been held in England that "if the contract be such that when carried out it would result in the sale of a chattel, the party can not sue for work and labor; but if the result of the contract is that the party has done work and labor, which ends in nothing that can become the subject of a sale, the party can not sue for goods sold and delivered."[453a] But the weight of authority in this country is that an order to manufacture and deliver is not a sale. To employ a person to manufacture and furnish ironwork for a building, for example, is not a contract within the statute of frauds for the sale of goods;[454] but where the essence of the contract is the sale

[451] See Hausman v. Nye, 62 Ind. 485, 30 Am. Rep. 199; Winner v. Williams, 62 Mich. 363.

[453] Allard v. Greasert, 61 N. Y. 1.

[453a] Lee v. Griffin, 1 Best & S. 272.

[454] Heintz v. Burkhard, 29 Or. 55.

of goods, though they do not exist in the form in which they are to be delivered, having yet to undergo a process of manufacture, the contract is within the scope of the statute.[455] In other words, the contract must be essentially for the sale of goods, and not for the manufacture of an article or articles or for the employment of labor.[456] A sale requiring a delivery, whether present or future, is within the letter and spirit of the statute; and hence, executory contracts are as fully within its meaning as others;[457] but when the delivery is made at the time of the sale, followed by an aceptance, the requirement of the statute is fulfilled, and no written memorandum is necessary.[458] On the other hand, when the contract is in writing, or there is a cash payment, in whole or in part, of the purchase-money, no delivery is necessary under the statute to complete the sale.[459] A delivery of a portion of the goods is enough, if accepted by the purchaser;[460] but the delivery and acceptance of samples as mere specimens is not sufficient to take the transaction out of the statute.[461] When a sale is relied upon and no written memorandum is produced, the burden of proving a delivery and acceptance is upon the party alleging it; the question being for the jury.[462] If there was no memorandum made or earnest-money paid, three things are necessary to make the contract binding: (1) a delivery by the seller; (2) a receipt by the buyer; (3) an acceptance by the buyer.[463] There must be an actual receipt of the goods or what is equivalent to it:[464] it will not be sufficient for the seller to show that the goods were as represented and that he had otherwise fully complied with his agreement;[465] hence, the purchaser may refuse to accept the goods

31 L. R. A. 508. See also, Mattison v. Westcott, 13 Vt. 258; Winship v. Buzzard, 9 Rich. L. (S. C.) 103.

[455] Prescott v. Locke, 51 N. H. 94, 12 Am. Rep. 55; Pitkin v. Noyes, 48 N. H. 294, 2 Am. Rep. 218.

[456] Wharton v. Missouri Car Foundry Co., 1 Mo. App. 577; Passaic Mfg. Co. v. Hoffman, 3 Daly (N. Y.) 495; Heintz v. Burkhard, 29 Or. 55, 31 L. R. A. 508; Meincke v. Falk, 55 Wis. 427.

[457] Bennett v. Hull, 10 Johns. (N. Y.) 364; Ide v. Stanton, 15 Vt. 685, 40 Am. Dec. 698; Hooker v. Knab, 26 Wis. 511; Edwards v. Grand Trunk R. Co., 48 Me. 379.

[458] Houghtaling v. Ball, 19 Mo. 84, 59 Am. Dec. 331.

[459] Pierce v. Gibson, 2 Ind. 408.

[460] Austin v. Boyd, 23 Mo. App. 317; Garfield v. Paris, 96 U. S. 557.

[461] Moore v. Love, 57 Miss. 765.

[462] Johnson v. Watson, 1 Ga. 348.

[463] Browne Stat. of Frauds, § 316, *et seq.;* Benjamin Sales, § 138, *et seq.*

[464] Shepherd v. Pressey, 32 N. H. 49; Jones v. Mechanics' Bank, 29 Md. 287, 96 Am. Dec. 533.

[465] Stone v. Browning, 68 N. Y. 598.

and repudiate the sale at any time; but he must do so before or within a reasonable time after he receives the goods,[466] or he will be held to have accepted them. Where the purchaser takes possession of the goods merely for the purpose of inspection, this is not an acceptance, and he may, within a reasonable time thereafter, repudiate the contract, upon giving timely notice;[467] but if the purchaser, having the right of inspection, sells the goods without exercising such right, he thereby waives the right to inspect, and the act amounts to an acceptance.[468] Whether a delivery to a common carrier constitutes an acceptance is a question of great importance in the construction of the section. If nothing were required but a delivery, to complete the sale, it would be sufficient to deliver to a public carrier, and especially so if the carrier had been designated by the purchaser: such a delivery constituting a receipt of the goods by the purchaser;[469] but a delivery and receipt, as we have seen, are not enough, under the statute: there must also be an acceptance by the purchaser, for the two are not identical. The buyer has the right of inspection, and this continues until he has had an opportunity to ascertain whether he desires to receive the goods or not;[470] hence the delivery to a carrier, though designated by the purchaser, is not an acceptance of the goods, unless such carrier has been specially appointed with that end in view, his general designation to transport the goods not being sufficient.[471] The true rule would seem to be then, that delivery to a carrier designated by the purchaser is a receipt but not an acceptance of the goods: the carrier being the purchaser's agent for the one but not for the other purpose; and that the right to repudiate the contract continues until the goods arrive at their destination and have been taken into custody by such purchaser, either actually or constructively. The buyer may refuse to accept

[466] Spencer v. Hale, 30 Vt. 314, 73 Am. Dec. 309.

[467] Hill v. McDonald, 17 Wis. 97.

[468] Benjamin Sales, § 181; Liggett & Myers Tob. Co. v. Collier, 89 Iowa 144; Sullivan v. Sullivan, 70 Mich. 583; Spencer v. Hale, 30 Vt. 314, 73 Am. Dec. 309.

[469] Bacon v. Eccles, 43 Wis. 227.

[470] Lloyd v. Wright, 25 Ga. 215; Browne Stat. of Frauds, § 327.

[471] Allard v. Graesert, 61 N. Y. 1; Smith v. Brennan, 62 Mich. 349; Grimes v. Van Vechten, 20 Mich. 410; Johnson v. Cuttle, 105 Mass. 447, 7 Am. Rep. 545; Jones v. Mechanics' Bank, 29 Md. 287, 96 Am. Dec. 533; Billin v. Henkel, 9 Colo. 394; Keiwert v. Meyer, 62 Ind. 587, 30 Am. Rep. 206; Lloyd v. Wright, 25 Ga. 215; Cross v. O'Donnell, 44 N. Y. 661; Rodgers v. Phillips, 40 N. Y. 519; Wilcox Silverplate Co. v. Green, 72 N. Y. 17.

the goods for any reason satisfactory to himself; for it is not a question of what he ought to do, but of what has been done.[472] The question of acceptance, like that of receiving, is generally a question of fact for the jury;[473] if, however, the facts are not in dispute, and but one conclusion may be drawn from them, it is a question of law for the court.[474] It is not necessary, however, that there should be a manual taking possession of the goods by the buyer in person; for the acceptance may be constructive—although it must be clear and unequivocal.[475] What we have said on the subject of the statute of frauds applies, of course, to the 17th section of the English statute and to the similar sections adopted by American states; wherever the provisions vary from this section, they may not be subject to the same construction. In ordinary sales, not within the provisions of this section, a delivery to a public carrier without condition is sufficient to pass the title to the property to the vendee; the carrier being the bailee of the vendee, and not of the vendor, subject to the right of inspection.[476] Payment of earnest-money or part payment of the price of the goods ordered, and written memoranda by the purchaser, are such rare occurrences in sales of goods by commercial travelers or drummers that we do not regard these topics of sufficient importance to enter upon a discussion of them in a work of this character; and the reader is referred to works on sales and the statute of frauds for further information.

[472] Gibbs v. Benjamin, 45 Vt. 124, 131; Pope v. Allis, 115 U. S. 363, 372; Fogel v. Brubaker, 122 Pa. St. 7; Johnson v. Cuttle, 105 Mass. 447.

[473] Per Coleridge, J., in Bushel v. Wheeler, 15 Q. B. 442 n.; Tibbetts v. Morton, 15 Q. B. 428, 19 L. J. Q. B. 382; Borrowsdale v. Bosworth, 99 Mass. 378.

[474] Shepherd v. Pressey, 32 N. H. 49, 56; Denny v. Williams, 5 Allen (Mass.) 1, 5.

[475] Benjamin Sales, § 144, *et seq.;* Shepherd v. Pressey, *supra;* Clark v. Labreche, 63 N. H. 397; Stone v. Browning, 68 N. Y. 598. What is a sufficient symbolic delivery,—see Parker v. Jervis, 3 Keyes (N. Y.) 271; Sahlman v. Mills, 3 Strob. L. (S. C.) 384, 51 Am. Dec. 630; Dixon v. Buck, 42 Barb. (N. Y.) 70.

[476] State v. Wingfield, 115 Mo. 428, 37 Am. St. 406; Scharff v. Meyer, 133 Mo. 428, 54 Am. St. 672; Kuppenheimer v. Wertheimer, 107 Mich. 77, 61 Am. St. 317; Barton v. Kane, 17 Wis. 38, 84 Am. Dec. 728.

CHAPTER XVIII.

PUBLIC AGENTS AND OFFICERS.

§ 466. **Definitions and classifications.**—Public agents are those persons who are chosen to perform the duties of the public,—that is, the government or municipality. They may be divided into two principal classes; namely, employes and officers. It is true the term "employe," in a sense, applies also to officers, for it may be said that every officer is an employe; but, on the other hand, a public employe is not necessarily a public officer; thus, a mere janitor of county or state buildings, a county physician, and other employes who do not take an official oath nor file an official bond, are not officers but employes.[1] An employe of the government usually owes his position to some officer whose duty it is to make the employment, and it is based entirely upon contract.[2] On the other hand, an officer owes his selection to a source fixed by the constitution or statute,[3] and not by contract.[4] Moreover, the term "public office" embraces the idea of tenure and duration, while a mere public employment may involve only transient or incidental duties.[5] An office is an entity which may continue even after the death or withdrawal of

[1] Trainor v. Board of County Auditors, 89 Mich. 162, 15 L. R. A. 95; Hall v. Wisconsin, 103 U. S. 5; Opinion of Judges, 3 Maine 481.

[2] See Hall v. Wisconsin, *supra*.

[3] Herrington v. State, 103 Ga. 318, 68 Am. St. 95.

[4] State v. Hocker, 39 Fla. 477, 63 Am. St. 174; Water Commissioners v. Cramer, 61 N. J. L. 270.

[5] In re Oaths, 20 Johns. (N. Y.) 492; Olmstead v. Mayor, 42 N. Y. Supr. 481; United States v. Hartwell, 6 Wall. (U. S.) 385.

the incumbent.[6] A public office involves the delegation to the incumbent of a portion of the sovereign power of the state, either to make, administer, or execute the laws; and it signifies that the incumbent is to exercise some functions of that nature, and take the fees and emoluments belonging to the position.[6a] On the other hand, there may be and are many employments by the national, state, city or town government which do not constitute the employe a public officer. "The work of the commonwealth," said the supreme judicial court of Massachusetts, "and of the cities and towns must be done by agents or servants, and much of it is of the nature of an employment. It is sometimes difficult to make the distinction between a public office and an employment, yet the title of 'public officer' is one well known to the law, and it is often necessary to determine what constitutes a public office. Every copying-clerk or janitor of a building is not necessarily a public officer."[7] A mere employe may, of course, be engaged by the appointing power for a definite time, or to accomplish a definite purpose, and in that sense his position may involve the nature of duration also; while, on the other hand, his employment may be altogether for an indefinite period, and he be subject to removal at any time. An employe under contract may be discharged without cause, unless the statute or constitution directs otherwise, but a public officer can not generally be removed without cause, although the power of removal is inherent in the appointing power: the reason being that the power of removal is generally restricted by constitutional or statutory provisions.[8] The English notion that an office is hereditary does not obtain in this country, though it is true that the rights and privileges of an officer are the rights and privileges of the incumbent; in this country both the power of appointment and that of removal inhere in the people and are subject to their control by constitutions and statutes.[9] An office not being the creature of a contract, but simply a delegation of a portion of the sovereign power, it follows, according to the

[6] State v. Wilson, 29 Ohio St. 347; People v. Stratton, 28 Cal. 382.

[6a] See the opinion of Marshall, C. J., in United States v. Maurice, 2 Brock. 96, 102; State v. Jennings, 57 Ohio St. 415.

[7] Brown v. Russell, 166 Mass. 14.

[8] Trainor v. Board of County Auditors, 89 Mich. 162, 15 L. R. A. 95; State v. Hewitt, 3 S. D. 187, 16 L. R. A. 413; Jacques v. Little, 51 Kan. 300; Board of Com'rs v. Johnson, 124 Ind. 145, 19 Am. St. 88; State v. Walbridge, 119 Mo. 383, 41 Am. St. 788; State v. Johnson, 57 Ohio St. 429.

[9] State v. Davis, 44 Mo. 129.

weight of authority, that the incumbent has no right of property in the office.[10]

§ 467. **Classification of officers according to nature of duties.**—For the purposes of our presentation public officers may be divided into ministerial, executive, legislative, and judicial officers. Those public servants of the government who have only or mainly ministerial duties to perform are denominated "ministerial officers." Ministerial duties and functions are those performed in obedience to the dictates or directions of superiors, and which involve the exercise of no discretion on the part of those charged with their performance or execution.[11] An executive officer is one whose chief duties consist in the execution of the laws,[12]—such as the president of the United States, the governors of the states and territories, sheriffs, constables, marshals and police officers. Legislative officers are those who enact the laws,—such as members of congress, of the state legislatures, councilmen, etc., of cities, etc. Judicial officers are intrusted with the duties of hearing and deciding private judicial controversies in litigated cases called lawsuits, and in public controversies where accusations are preferred and tried for the commission of public offenses.[13] It is not within the scope of this work to enter upon any discussion as to the mode of selection of these various officers, or their tenures and the duration and termination thereof: what we are chiefly concerned with is in respect of their duties and the performance thereof, and the effect upon the officers themselves and upon others.

§ 468. **Right of officer to compensation.**—An office may or may not be accompanied by emolument, though it is a usual element thereof.[14] The compensation of an officer is usually provided for by statute or city ordinance. When no compensation is fixed the office may be a merely honorary one and the officer will not be entitled to receive any. When the statute fixes the compensation, it is usually by way of fees or a specified salary, and when that is the case the compensation laid down in the statute will, of course,

[10] State v. Hawkins, 44 Ohio St. 98.

[11] Pennington v. Streight, 54 Ind. 376.

[12] Bouvier Law Dic.

[13] See Bouvier Law Dic.; People v. Keeler, 99 N. Y. 463.

[14] State v. Hocker, 39 Fla. 477, 63 Am. St. 174; State v. Kennon, 7 Ohio St. 546; State v. Stanley, 66 N. C. 59, 8 Am. Rep. 488.

govern.[15] If there is no dispute as to the title of the incumbent to the particular office, and the fees or salary is fixed by statute, no difficulty can occur with regard to the officer's compensation; but when a controversy arises over the right to hold an office, the question as to who is entitled to the salary may also become involved. In this connection it may be well to point out a distinction between a *de jure* and a *de facto* officer. An officer is said to be *de jure* when he is legally entitled to hold the office although some other claimant of the office may be actually in possession thereof; while a *de facto* officer is one actually in the exercise of the power and functions of the office under color of right, without having the legal title thereto.[16] Whether a *de facto* officer who has in good faith and without fraud or dishonesty in connection with the title and possession of the office discharged some of the duties thereof is entitled to its fees and emoluments, is a question as to which the decisions are not in entire harmony. In some of the states it is held than an officer *de facto* who is not tainted with fraud or dishonesty is entitled to the emoluments of the office as long as he actually discharges the duties thereof;[17] and that if during the incumbency of the *de facto* officer his salary is paid to him, before any judgment of ouster has been rendered against him, the officer *de jure* has lost his right to such compensation: the reasons given being that the right to compensation depends, not upon the title to the office, but upon the performance of the services, and that while the *de facto* officer is in possession the officer making payment can not be expected to determine who has the actual title to the office, but has a right to assume the legality of the title of the occupant.[18] But, on the other hand, it has been repeatedly decided that an officer *de facto* can not maintain an action for the salary of the office;[19] that if the salary is actually paid to such officer, such payment constitutes no defense to a claim for the same by the officer *de jure*;[20] and that

[15] Hall v. Wisconsin, 103 U. S. 5.

[16] Hamlin v. Kassafer, 15 Or. 456, 3 Am. St. 176; Wilcox v. Smith, 5 Wend. (N. Y.) 231.

[17] Erwin v. Jersey City, 60 N. J. L. 141, 64 Am. St. 584.

[18] Auditors of Wayne Co. v. Benoit, 20 Mich. 176, 4 Am. Rep. 382; McVeany v. Mayor, 80 N. Y. 185, 36 Am. Rep. 600; Steubenville v. Culp, 38 Ohio St. 18; State v. Milne, 36 Neb. 301.

[19] McCue v. Wapello Co., 56 Iowa 698, 41 Am. Rep. 134; Dolan v. Mayor, 68 N. Y. 274, 36 Am. Rep. 168.

[20] State v. Carr, 129 Ind. 44, 13 L. R. A. 177; McVeany v. Mayor, 80 N. Y. 185, 36 Am. Rep. 600.

the officer *de jure* may recover of the officer *de facto* the fees and salaries collected by the latter, after it has been determined judicially that the former is the party entitled to the office.[21] These cases proceed upon the theory that an office is property, and that the right to enjoy the proceeds thereof is not dependent upon the performance of its duties, but upon the title to the office. The difficulty arises from the variety of judicial views as to the nature of the right enjoyed by one who has been chosen to fill a public office,—whether such right is one of property which he has a right to secure to himself as in other cases where property rights are invaded, or whether it is a mere inchoate right which does not become absolute until he has actually performed the services. The latter view would seem to be the better one, or at least the one more in harmony with the theory upon which the right to hold office in this country rests.[22]

§ **469. Ministerial officers.**—Many public officers have duties to perform which are of a mixed nature, having the elements of ministerial, judicial, executive and legislative duties; but in the main the separation of the various functions and powers into departments is one of the distinguishing features of our American form of government. Nevertheless, it is often the case even in this country, that the duties of a public officer are so near the dividing line that it is very difficult to determine upon which side to place them. Where the duties are prescribed and defined by law or by the mandate of a superior officer, leaving no room for the exercise of judgment or discretion, they are ministerial; and so it is held that if the time, mode and occasion of the performance of the act or acts are prescribed with such certainty that nothing remains for judgment or discretion, the act is ministerial.[23] As we have several times pointed out, duties which are strictly ministerial, as well as those which are mechanical, may be delegated to be performed by some one else than the person selected to perform them;[24] hence, a ministerial

[21] Mayfield v. Moore, 53 Ill. 428, 4 Am. Rep. 52; Douglas v. State, 31 Ind. 429; Hunter v. Chandler, 45 Mo. 452.

[22] See also, Romero v. United States, 24 Ct. of Cl. 331, 5 L. R. A. 69; Andrews v. Portland, 79 Maine 484, 10 Am. St. 280, and note on p. 284.

[23] Grider v. Tally, 77 Ala. 422, 54 Am. Rep. 65.

[24] See Birdsell v. Clark, 73 N. Y. 73, 29 Am. Rep. 105; Hope v. Sawyer, 14 Ill. 254; Williams v. Woods, 16 Md. 220.

officer may, without express authority to do so, appoint a deputy to perform any or all of the functions of the office.[25] Powers and functions not in themselves ministerial may, however, be delegated by legislative authority; thus, legislative and judicial duties are frequently conferred upon the subordinate branches of government by laws enacted by the state and national legislatures,—thus conferring upon municipal and other public corporations such powers as the general legislative body can not conveniently execute itself.[26] Where the implied power of an officer exists to appoint a deputy, the latter must perform all acts as such in the name of his principal; otherwise the performance is by some courts held to be a nullity;[27] as in such case the authority rests nominally in the principal officer, and must therefore be executed in his name.[28] If, however, the office of deputy is created by express provision of law, the deputy may act in his own name, and use his own official signature, and designation, instead of that of his principal officer.[29] The better view would seem to be, however, that the use of the deputy's name is a mere matter of form; and whether the act is done in the name of the principal or agent, it will in neither event, perhaps, vitiate the act.[30] A ministerial officer, like any other, must perform his duties with fidelity to his principal (the government or municipality); and he can not, as a general rule, lawfully act at all, if he is adversely interested.[31] When an office is purely ministerial its duties may be enforced by *mandamus*.[32] Any violation of duty on the part of a ministerial officer resulting in injury to the public, as such, may be redressed only by a public prosecution, either at common law or under statutory provisions;[33] but if the officer owes a duty to some person individually, which he neglects to perform, he is liable for any injury proximately resulting from such negli-

[25] Abrams v. Ervin, 9 Iowa 87; Hope v. Sawyer, *supra;* Attorney-General v. Detroit, 58 Mich. 213, 55 Am. Rep. 675; Roberts v. People, 9 Colo. 458.

[26] Tilley v. Savannah, etc., R. Co., 5 Fed. 641; Richland Co. v. Lawrence Co., 12 Ill. 1; Cincinnati, etc., R. Co. v. Clinton Co., 1 Ohio St. 77.

[27] Glencoe v. Owen, 78 Ill. 382; Arnold v. Scott, 39 Tex. 378.

[28] Talbot v. Hooser, 12 Bush (Ky.) 408.

[29] Westbrook v. Miller, 56 Mich. 148; Eastman v. Curtis, 4 Vt. 616.

[30] Westbrook v. Miller, *supra.*

[31] Woods v. Gilson, 17 Ill. 218; Mills v. Young, 23 Wend. (N. Y.) 314; Boykin v. Edwards, 21 Ala. 261.

[32] Grider v. Tally, 77 Ala. 422, 54 Am. Rep. 65.

[33] Bartlett v. Crozier, 17 Johns. (N. Y.) 439, 8 Am. Dec. 428.

gence.[34] If, however, the officer acts with due care, and within the scope of his authority, he is not liable to an individual for any resulting injury.[35] If a ministerial officer execute the process of a court, regular on its face, he will be protected although it was issued without jurisdiction as to person and place;[36] but if the want of jurisdiction is of the subject-matter,[37] or even of parties, but apparent on the face of the process,[38] or if the process was based on an unconstitutional statute,[39]—it furnishes no protection. The officer is not liable for the acts of his subordinates where they are appointed by virtue of a statute and are thus created independent public officers.[40] The office of sheriff seems to be an exception to this rule; and that officer is liable for the official acts of his deputies, as at common law the deputy was considered the private servant of the officer, and officers were liable for the acts of such servants.[41] We have already seen that a public officer is not generally liable individually on contracts entered into on behalf of his principal, unless it be the intention to bind him individually;[42] this exemption, of course, includes ministerial offices as well as others. A ministerial officer may, in the commission of some wrongful act, so far depart from the line of his office as to be entirely outside of any official relation; and where this is the case, while he will doubtless be individually liable for the consequences of such act, he can not be said to be officially responsible, and therefore the sureties on his official bond will not be answerable therefor.[43] If the negligent act or failure occurred in the line of the officer's employment, the officer may be liable civilly, notwithstanding the same act or omission also constituted a criminal offense for which he may be indicted and prosecuted criminally.[44] A public officer is generally indictable as for a crime for any omission or failure in the performance

[34] Bennett v. Whitney, 94 N. Y. 302; State v. Harris, 89 Ind. 363, 46 Am. Rep. 169; Hayes v. Porter, 22 Maine 371.

[35] Mechem Pub. Off., § 661.

[36] Young v. Wise, 7 Wis. 128; Cannon v. Sipples, 39 Conn. 505; Taylor v. Alexander, 6 Ohio 144.

[37] Smith v. Shaw, 12 Johns. (N. Y.) 257; Wilmarth v. Burt, 7 Met. (Mass.) 257; Griffin v. Wilcox, 21 Ind. 370.

[38] Davis v. Wilson, 65 Ill. 525; Parker v. Walrod, 16 Wend. (N. Y.) 514, 30 Am. Dec. 124.

[39] Sumner v. Beeler, 50 Ind. 341, 19 Am. Rep. 718.

[40] Foster v. Metts, 55 Miss. 77, 30 Am. Rep. 504.

[41] 1 Bl. Com. 344, 346; 3 Minor's Inst. (3d ed.) 254.

[42] *Ante*, § 299.

[43] McLendon v. State, 92 Tenn. 520, 21 L. R. A. 738.

[44] Raynsford v. Phelps, 43 Mich. 342, 38 Am. Rep. 198.

of his duties,—particularly those duties which are purely ministerial and leave the officer no discretion in their performance.[45] If the officer has the privilege of exercising judgment or discretion in the case, and he follows such judgment or discretion honestly, and does not act maliciously or wantonly or corruptly,[46] he is not indictable.

§ 470. **Judicial and quasi-judicial officers.**—Judicial officers represent that division in our governmental system known and designated as the judicial department of government of the state or nation. Judicial officers necessarily have the largest share of discretionary powers confided to them. Such an officer necessarily has other powers also, as executive and legislative, but he is called a judicial officer because his main functions are judicial. Such officers have many privileges and immunities not common to other officers, varying with the degrees of importance of the courts which they respectively represent. Thus, a justice of the supreme court of the United States is entitled to the protection of the government from personal violence, not only while on the bench or holding court, but while traveling through the country to and from the place where his court may be in session.[46a] Such functionaries, like legislative and executive officers, are privileged from arrest and from civil process while holding their courts and traveling to and from the same.[47] At common law a judicial officer may excuse himself from testifying as a witness in a case in which he is the presiding judge.[48] He can not be arrested on common-law process issued out of his own court, but must be proceeded against by bill, if at all.[49] But while they are entitled to many privileges, as such officers, they are also placed by the law under certain restraints and disabilities in consequence of their official positions; thus, a judge who has ordered the sale of a piece of land, subject to his confirmation or disapproval, can not become a purchaser at such sale, as he comes within the reason of the rule that trustees and other fiduciaries can not purchase at a sale

[45] State v. Glasgow, Cam. & N. (N. C.) 38, 2 Am. Dec. 628; Stone v. Graves, 8 Mo. 148, 40 Am. Dec. 131.

[46] State v. Williams, 12 Ired. (N. C.) 172; People v. Coon, 15 Wend. (N. Y.) 277.

[46a] In re Nagle, 135 U. S. 1.

[47] Lyell v. Goodwin, 4 McLean (U. S.) 44.

[48] Welcome v. Batchelder, 23 Maine 85; People v. Miller, 2 Parker Cr. (N. Y.) 197.

[49] In re Livingston, 8 Johns. (N. Y.) 351.

in connection with which they have official duties to perform.[50] Judges and judicial officers are generally prohibited by statute or constitutional provisions from acting as attorneys during their terms of office or from holding any other office, though this inhibition is limited in some states to other than judicial offices. Constitutional provisions are also made by which the compensation of judges may not be reduced during their terms of office; and in the federal courts and in the courts of Massachusetts the tenure of office is for life or during good behavior. As to their liabilities, it may be laid down as the general rule that such an officer is not liable to any individual for damages for any erroneous decision or judgment he may render, if at the time he was within the jurisdiction as to person and subject-matter.[51] The officer may go far astray in the exercise of his functions and not render himself liable, for the law has a tender regard for the imperfections of men's judgments and decisions. Public policy forbids that any one should be punished for every mistake, as in that event no one could be secured who would be willing to fill such places.[52] A judge or justice of the peace may innocently commit an injury upon some individual without being liable; thus, where such an officer wrongfully but innocently orders a person ejected from the court-room, which order is obeyed, there can be no liability on the part of the judge, if he acted under the erroneous belief that the case was one in which he had a right to sit with closed doors.[53] If the officer is actually within his jurisdiction when the act is committed there can be no doubt that he is exempt from liability; but it does not necessarily follow that when a judicial officer acts without jurisdiction, he is always liable, as is seen by the case last cited. Much depends upon the intention of the officer, and if he believes in good faith that he has jurisdiction, having reasonable grounds for so believing, he is exempt from liability.[54] The act, however, must be a judicial one; for if it be ministerial only, the good faith of the officer will not protect him; thus, if a police officer order the arrest of a person for an act which does not constitute a crime at

[50] Tracy v. Colby, 55 Cal. 67. See also, Hopkinson v. Jacquess, 54 Ill. App. 59.

[51] Chickering v. Robinson, 3 Cush. (Mass.) 543; Walker v. Hallock, 32 Ind. 239; Jordan v. Hanson, 49 N. H. 199, 6 Am. Rep. 508; Cooley Torts 408.

[52] See opinion of Lord Tenterden, in Garnett v. Ferrand, 6 B. & C. 611.

[53] Williamson v. Lacey, 86 Maine 80, 25 L. R. A. 506.

[54] Thompson v. Jackson, 93 Iowa 376; Scott v. Fishplate, 117 N. C. 265.

law, or is not punishable by arrest and imprisonment, he is liable to the party arrested for damages sustained, his motives being immaterial.[55] If he were a judicial officer he would not be liable in such a case if he believed he was acting within his jurisdiction and had reasonable grounds for such belief; for the mere assertion of good faith without reasonable grounds therefor is no defense to an act committed even by a judicial officer who is palpably without jurisdiction; thus, if the judge of a court should, without any color or semblance of jurisdiction, sentence a person to imprisonment for an offense which he had never committed, such officer would doubtless be liable. Courts do not always discriminate between judicial and non-judicial acts in determining an officer's liability; hence, an elective officer who refuses to receive an elector's vote is in some states held liable regardless of his motive;[56] but in other courts the act has been regarded as purely judicial and the officer exempt.[57] An officer who is guilty of corruption while in office, or who acts from any unlawful motives, may be held accountable by the state or other government in a proceeding to impeach him, or in a public prosecution for such an offense; but even in that case he would not necessarily be liable to an individual who suffered by reason of his infamy. An officer having quasi-judicial powers is entitled to the same immunity as those exercising purely judicial functions, if the act complained of was done within the limits of authority conferred upon the officer.[57a] And if a judicial officer himself has to determine whether or not he has jurisdiction, and in determining the facts relied upon to give jurisdiction he makes an erroneous decision in reference thereto, an action will not lie against him.[58] But it has been held that this rule does not apply to a judicial officer of an inferior court.[59] Where a judicial officer also has ministerial duties to perform, he may render himself liable for a wrongful exercise of the latter.[60] Thus, a county judge whose duty it is to appoint guardians, administrators, etc., and approve their bonds, while not liable for erroneously determining that an insolvent bond is good, when such determination is made after a judicial investiga-

[55] Bolton v. Vellires, 94 Va. 393, 64 Am. St. 737.

[56] Larned v. Wheeler, 140 Mass. 390, 51 Am. Rep. 43; Jeffreys v. Ankeny, 11 Ohio 372.

[57] Chrisman v. Bruce, 1 Duv. (Ky.) 63, 85 Am. Dec. 603.

[57a] East River Gaslight Co. v. Donnelly, 93 N. Y. 557.

[58] Busteed v. Parsons, 54 Ala. 393, 25 Am. Rep. 688.

[59] Craig v. Burnett, 32 Ala. 728.

[60] Grider v. Tally, 77 Ala. 422, 54 Am. Rep. 65.

tion of the facts as to solvency, is liable civilly to the injured party, where he has accepted such a bond without first properly determining its sufficiency, unless he knows the bond to be sufficient without investigation.[61] A probate judge upon whom devolves the duty of accepting such a bond can not escape liability for any omission of a ministerial duty,—such as requiring a bond to be filed when the law enjoins that he shall have this done;[62] or the ordering of a renewal of such bonds every two years, when the failure to order a renewal is the result of willful or malicious negligence.[63]

§ **471. Executive and legislative officers.**—Many of the privileges and immunities granted by law to judicial officers are also accorded to executive and legislative officers; such, for instance, as freedom from arrest or from service of civil process while actively engaged in the discharge of their duties are common to all public officers.[64] As to the liabilities of such officers for injury caused by their official acts it may be truly stated that they are not generally liable if the act performed was within the scope of the official business. Such officers have a large discretion in determining whether their acts are wise or unwise, proper or improper; and when exercised within the limits mentioned the officer is not liable, nor even subject to have his motives questioned, in a suit by an individual for damages, although it be asserted that he acted corruptly or maliciously.[65] And a legislator can not be held accountable in a civil action for what he does or says on the floor of the legislative hall,—such immunity being guaranteed to him upon grounds of public policy.[66] "It would be a doctrine fraught with consequences of incalculable mischief," said Frazer, C. J., in the case cited in the last note, "if a public officer could be held personally responsible, either civilly or criminally, for his judgment upon such questions." If that were the rule men of character and responsibility would refuse to serve as members of public deliberative bodies, and the public business of the community would fall into the hands of irresponsible administrators.

§ **472. Liability of the public for the acts of its officers and agents.**—No contract executed by a public officer or agent will bind

[61] Colter v. McIntyre, 74 Ky. 565; McIntyre v. Gritton, 5 Ky. L. Rep. 686.

[62] State Bank v. Davenport, 19 N. C. 45; Boggs v. Hamilton, 2 Mill Const. (S. C.) 382.

[63] Boyd v. Ferris, 29 Tenn. 406.

[64] Miner v. Markham, 28 Fed. 387; Secor v. Bell, 18 Johns. (N. Y.) 52.

[65] Cooley Torts 376.

[66] Walker v. Hallock, 32 Ind. 239.

his principal unless it is within the scope of his actual authority;[67] the government can only be bound in the manner it has agreed to be bound, and its agents must follow the prescribed formalities to make it liable;[68] hence, where the law requires a contract for government supplies to be in writing, the requirement is mandatory, and there can be no recovery on such contract if it is oral.[69] If the supplies have been furnished, however, in whole or in part, the claimant may recover their fair value upon the implied contract.[70] A private agent might render his principal liable upon mere appearances, or the principal might estop himself from denying the agent's authority by acts *in pais;* but this is not true of public agents; and the state or government can not be bound by an estoppel *in pais* or by laches.[71] The state or federal government can not be sued without its consent, as we learned in a former place;[72] but when it permits itself to be brought into court by legislative enactment, or voluntarily appears to an action against it, it will be subject to the same rules as other defendants and will be bound by the judgment, although the orders of a court may not be enforced by execution against it. A public principal, such as a state or municipality, or the general government, may ratify the act of its agent and thus render itself liable the same as if it had authorized it in the first instance.[73] The government, whether national or state, can not be held liable, however, for the torts of its agents.[74] Municipal corporations are not generally liable for the acts of their servants except when they were committed in connection with some ministerial duty, in which case they stand upon the same footing as private corporations or individuals.[75]

[67] Brady v. Mayor, etc., 20 N. Y. 312; Clark v. Des Moines, 19 Iowa 199, 87 Am. Dec. 423; Sutro v. Pettit, 74 Cal. 332, 5 Am. St. 442; McCaslin v. State, 99 Ind. 428. See also, *ante*, §§ 299, 348.

[68] Camp v. United States, 113 U. S. 648.

[69] Clark v. United States, 95 U. S. 539.

[70] *Ibid.*

[71] Bishop Conts., § 993; United States v. Kirkpatrick, 9 Wheat. (U. S.) 720.

[72] *Ante*, § 348.

[73] Cook Co. v. Harms, 108 Ill. 151; Rock Creek v. Strong, 96 U. S. 271.

[74] Story Ag., § 319; Gibbons v. United States, 8 Wall. (U. S.) 269.

[75] See Richmond v. Long, 17 Gratt. (Va.) 375, 94 Am. Dec. 461; Cooley Torts 122.

CHAPTER XIX.

MASTER AND SERVANT.

§ **473. General statement.**—It must have been noticed by the reader of this work that the terms "principal and agent" and "master and servant" have often been used interchangeably, and that many of the rules governing the one relation have sometimes been applied without discrimination to the other. This was necessarily so because many of the modern rules controlling these respective relations are practically identical, albeit the two systems are traceable to different origins. Indeed, it is certain that our modern law of principal and agent is largely the result of two main influences; namely, (a) the Roman law of *mandatum,* modified and molded by the usages of modern commerce, and (b) the ancient English law of master and servant. Anciently the servant was a slave; his services were completely at the disposal and under the control of the master; and the master was responsible for the servant's acts. The idea of contract did not enter into the relation between the two; it was essentially a relation of *status.* Even in the old Roman law of agency the idea of a contract was of only minor importance.[1] Gradually slavery became extinct, and in its place was adopted the system of hired service; but many of the ancient rules applying to slavery remained: men and women were no longer owned by their masters permanently, but they would, for a consideration, sell their services, and with them largely their freedom and discretion; the master continuing to control the services and conduct of the servant and to be responsible for his acts. As the desire for liberty of action was enforced by the influence which the laboring-man came to exert, the idea of *status* gave way to that of contract. On the other hand, as commerce grew and men needed assistants to aid them in carrying on their business, agents were employed by them for that purpose. These were necessarily men of higher mental endowments than the mere servants whose chief occupation was manual labor, performed under the immediate direction of the master. The agent was accorded a large share of discretion and judgment, for to him was left in a degree the management of his principal's business. While these fundamental principles still inhere in these respective systems, it is only so in a relative measure. Commerce and labor have come to travel hand in hand, and the employes of one have many things in common with those of the other. The conductor of a railroad-train is in many respects a servant, for he has to perform many duties that are but menial and as to which he has no discretion whatever. But he is also an agent, for his menial duties are by no means the only ones: he represents the company he serves in many transactions requiring a high degree of skill, judgment and discretion; and much is left to his independent determination with which a mere servant would not be intrusted. And this is true of numerous other employes. It must be obvious that as time advances the laws governing the subjects of "principal and agent" and "master and servant" will become still more

[1] Story Ag., § 4.

homogeneous, and the distinctions now obtaining in many of the rules acting upon these respective relations will become less apparent as well as less important.

§ 474. **The relation of master and servant.**—Whether the relation between an employer and employe is that of master and servant or not is still a matter of considerable importance. The importance is not so much, however, in tracing the distinction between a servant and an agent as it is in ascertaining the distinction between a servant and a contractor. The doctrine of *respondeat superior* renders the master liable for those acts of his servant which have been committed in the course of the service he was employed to render; and the same liability obtains on the part of the principal for the acts of his agent done in the line of such agent's employment. But a contractor, being neither a servant nor an agent, sustains no such relation to his employer as will render the latter liable for his acts, whether they be performed in or out of the scope of the employment. The rule *respondeat superior* has no application to an independent contractor who is employed, for instance, to do a piece of work for the employer, during the performance of which a third party is injured.[2] The distinction between a servant and an agent, however, or between a master and a principal, is not without moment. "Master and servant expresses the relation in private life, founded in convenience, whereby a man calls in the assistance of others when his own skill and labor is not sufficient to answer the cares incumbent upon him." [3] "A master is one who stands to another in such a relation that he not only controls the results of the work of that other, but also may direct the manner in which such work shall be done." [4] A servant is a person hired or employed by another to work and labor for him, either at so much per hour, day, week, month, year or other period, or at some agreed price for the entire piece of work, though the latter idea is more in the nature of a contract than of hiring. The term "servant" ordinarily indicates a person hired for wages, to work as the employer may direct; and the control which thus exists in a superior over the subordinate is the principal feature which distinguishes between him and a contractor.[5] "The relation of master and servant exists whenever the

[2] Robinson v. Webb, 11 Bush (Ky.) 464; Bailey v. Troy, etc., R. Co., 57 Vt. 252, 52 Am. Rep. 129.

[3] Anderson Law Dic., tit. Master.

[4] 20 Am. & Eng. Encyc. L. 10.

[5] Morgan v. Bowman, 22 Mo. 538; 1 Thompson Neg. (2d ed.), §§ 578, 579.

employer retains the right to direct the manner in which the business shall be done, as well as the result to be accomplished, or, in other words, not only what shall be done, but how it shall be done."[6] "One may be employed without being a servant, and have an employer who is nevertheless not the master. * * * The relation exists where the employer selects the workman, may remove or discharge him for misconduct, and may order not only what work shall be done, but the mode and manner of performance."[7] The

[6] Per Gray, J., in Singer Mfg. Co. v. Rahn, 132 U. S. 518.

[7] Per Finch, J., in Butler v. Townsend, 126 N. Y. 105. The controlling question in determining the existence of the relation is that the employe is so far under the immediate direction of the master, with reference to the work in which the employe is engaged, as to be altogether subject to the former's will or approval. He must have the right to give direction in the method and manner of the execution of the work and to employ and discharge workmen of that class: Wood Master & Serv., § 306; Cooley Torts 533; Mound City Paint & Color Co. v. Conlon, 92 Mo. 221; Fell v. Rich Hill, etc., Co., 23 Mo. App. 216; Wiltse v. State Road Bridge Co., 63 Mich. 639. "He is to be deemed the master who has the superior choice, control, and direction of the servant, and whose will the servant represents, not merely in the ultimate result of his work, but in all its details:" Shearman & Redf. Neg. 83. It is not necessary that the servant be in the regular employment of the master. Thus, the porter of a palace-car company, though regularly employed by the latter to serve on its cars, is yet regarded for some purposes as the servant of the railroad company of whose train the Pullman car is a part; and such company is liable for the wrongful acts of such porter in all matters pertaining to the safety of passengers: Williams v. Pullman Palace-Car Co., 40 La. Ann. 417, 8 Am. St. 538. And where a person hired a team and a driver, the latter being sent with the team by the owner, at the special request of the person hiring the team, and there was an injury to a third party, due to the driver's negligence, it was held that the owner was not liable, as the driver was the servant of the hirer and not of the owner: Joslin v. Grand Rapids Ice Co., 50 Mich. 516, 45 Am. Rep. 54. But where a horse and driver were hired by the owner of the horse to a city by the day to work at improving the streets, it being the duty of such driver, who had the exclusive management of the horse, to see that he was properly shod, and to have him shod at all times when it was needed; and the horse, being violently struck by the driver, kicked a loose shoe through a large plate-glass window to the damage of the owner of the building,—it was ruled that the driver was the servant of the owner of the horse, and that such owner was responsible for any acts of negligence committed by the driver: Huff v. Ford, 126 Mass. 24, 30 Am. Rep. 645. And where a railroad company operates a road over the tracks of another company, which owns it, the lessee

relation is now always established by contract, express or implied.[8] The contract may be in writing, but it need not be. In such a contract the master obligates himself to supply the servant with work of a certain character and to pay him a certain compensation therefor, the nature and amount of which may or may not be expressly stipulated; while the servant agrees on his part to render services.[9] As to who is competent to enter into the relation, it may be stated as the general rule that those who are competent to become principals and agents may assume the relation of master and servant.[10]

I. Duties, Obligations and Liabilities of Master to Servant.

§ **475. Duty to furnish employment.**—One of the master's obligations to the servant is to furnish him employment so long as his contract requires it. If he has hired the servant for a definite time, it is his duty, unless the servant by his misconduct has merited a prior discharge, to supply him with work of the character of that which he was employed to perform, during that time, at the contract rate.[11] It is no excuse that the master has discontinued the business for which the servant was employed;[12] nor that the business if continued would be unprofitable;[13] nor that the master's building, the place in which the servant had been at work, was partially destroyed by fire:[14] his undertaking being an absolute one, nothing but the fault of the servant will excuse him from performing it. Where the contract is indefinite as to the duration of the employment, the courts in this country generally hold that it is terminable, *prima facie* at least, at the will of either party. Thus, a contract by which a party was to secure the services of another "during the term of not exceeding three years" was held to be terminable by

company that uses the tracks accepting the services of the gatemen employed by the company owning the road, instead of employing gatemen of its own, the lessee company sustains the relation of master to such gatemen while working under its direction, and is responsible for their negligence: Railway Co. v. Schneider, 45 Ohio St. 678.

[8] 2 Kent Com. 258; Growcock v. Hall, 82 Ind. 202. For definitions of "principal" and "agent," see *ante*, §§ 11, 12.

[9] 2 Kent Com. 258.

[10] See *ante*, § 30, *et seq.*

[11] Goddard v. Morrissey, 172 Mass. 594; Wright v. C. S. Graves Land Co., 100 Wis. 269.

[12] Vail v. Jersey Little Falls Mfg. Co., 32 Barb. (N. Y.) 564.

[13] Standard Oil Co. v. Gilbert, 84 Ga. 714.

[14] Eastman v. Eastman, etc., Co., 1 N. Y. Supp. 16.

the employer at any time by giving the other reasonable notice.[15] And where an insurance company employed an officer in its real-estate department at a salary of so much per year, payable monthly, it was decided by the court of appeals of New York that this was a hiring at will, which either party might terminate at any time.[16] The mere fact that the agreement provides for the payment of services by the year or other period will not conclusively prove a hiring by the year or such other period,[17] but it is a circumstance strongly indicative of the period of service contracted for; and if the agreement to pay periodically is the only evidence as to the duration of the period of employment, it will be taken to be a hiring for that time.[18] Where a contract based upon a sufficient consideration provides for "steady and permanent employment" at a stated compensation, the agreement is not terminable as long as the employe is ready, willing and able to perform such work as the employer may have to give him.[19] In England, however, the rule seems to be that a hiring as to which no time is fixed is a hiring by the year;[20] but the English rule is founded on usage, and there being no such usage in the United States, the rule does not operate.[21] Like any other fact in the case, the hiring and length of time of the employment may be proved by circumstantial evidence. Thus, if an employe is hired for a year and continues in the service without a new arrangement, the presumption is that he was employed for the next year on the same terms;[22] which presumption may, however, be rebutted by evidence to the contrary.[23] And where a merchant em-

[15] Harper v. Hassard, 113 Mass. 187.

[16] Martin v. New York Life Ins. Co., 148 N. Y. 117. See, to the same effect, Coffin v. Landis, 46 Pa. St. 426; Franklin Min. Co. v. Harris, 24 Mich. 115; East Line, etc., R. Co. v. Scott, 72 Tex. 70, 13 Am. St. 758.

[17] Prentiss v. Ledyard, 28 Wis. 131.

[18] Beach v. Mullin, 34 N. J. L. 343.

[19] Pennsylvania Co. v. Dolan, 6 Ind. App. 109; Harrington v. Kansas City, etc., R. Co., 60 Mo. App. 223; Hobbs v. Brush Elec. Light Co., 75 Mich. 550; Thomas v. Hammond, 47 Tex. 42.

[20] King v. Worfield, 5 T. R. 506; Foxall v. International Land Credit Co., 16 L. T. N. S. 637; Wood Master & Serv. (2d ed.), § 136.

[21] Kansas Pac. R. Co. v. Roberson, 3 Colo. 142. See Harnwell v. Parry Sound Lumber Co., 24 Ont. App. 110, 115.

[22] Wright v. Elk Rapids Iron Co. (Mich.), 89 N. W. 335; Tatterson v. Suffolk Mfg. Co., 106 Mass. 56; Adams v. Fitzpatrick, 125 N. Y. 124; Ingalls v. Allen, 132 Ill. 170; Thompson v. Detroit, etc., Copper Co., 80 Mich. 422.

[23] Ingalls v. Allen, *supra;* Ewing v. Janson, 57 Ark. 237.

ployed a clerk at so much per month, and the clerk, after a time, expressed a desire to have his employment made more permanent, whereupon an agreement was made by which he was to receive so much a year, it was held that the jury would have a right to infer that this constituted a contract for a year.[24] A hiring for a certain sum per month is a hiring for at least one month, which may be terminated by either party at the end of any month.[25] When an employe has been hired for a definite period of time provided his services are satisfactory to the employer, it is held that the employer may exercise the right to discharge him whenever he, in good faith, becomes dissatisfied with the services, whether he have good reasons for it or not.[26] Some of the courts hold, however, that upon such a contract the master may not, at his mere whim and caprice, discharge the servant, whether he has any ground for it or not, but that he must be dissatisfied in good faith and for good reason before he will be warranted to exercise that privilege.[27] It seems the courts are not in entire harmony as to whether a contract for "permanent employment" is a definite contract or not. Some tribunals have ruled that a contract for permanent employment does not mean for life or for any fixed or certain period, but only that it shall continue until one of the parties shall wish, for good reason, to terminate it.[28] On the other hand, it is held that where the contract stipulates for "steady and permanent" employment, at a fixed price,[29] or for "steady and constant" employment as long as the employe shall properly do the work assigned to him,[30] or for whatever length of time the employe may desire to serve,[31] the contract is not indefinite, and, if based upon a sufficient consideration, may be enforced as long as the employe is ready and able to perform the services and presents himself for that purpose.

[24] Bascom v. Shillito, 37 Ohio St. 431.

[25] Tennessee Coal, Iron & R. Co. v. Pierce, 26 C. C. A. 632, 81 Fed. 814.

[26] Koehler v. Buhl, 94 Mich. 496; Crawford v. Mail, etc., Pub. Co., 163 N. Y. 404; Alexis Stoneware Mfg. Co. v. Young, 59 Ill. App. 226.

[27] See Rhodes, etc., Furn. Co. v. Frazier (Tex. Civ. App.), 55 S. W. 192; Grinnell v. Kiralfy, 55 Hun (N. Y.) 422; Hotchkiss v. Gretna Ginnery, etc., Co., 36 La. Ann. 517.

[28] Louisville, etc., R. Co. v. Offutt, 99 Ky. 427, 59 Am. St. 467; Lord v. Goldberg, 81 Cal. 596, 15 Am. St. 82.

[29] Pennsylvania Co. v. Dolan, 6 Ind. App. 109, 51 Am. St. 289.

[30] Harrington v. Kansas City, etc., R. Co., 60 Mo. App. 223.

[31] East Line, etc., R. Co. v. Scott, 72 Tex. 70, 13 Am. St. 758.

§ 476. **Duty to compensate servant.**—As in the case of an agent, so a servant is entitled to receive compensation from his employer. Where the contract expressly provides for the nature and amount of compensation, that must, of course, control; otherwise the servant or employe is entitled to recover on a *quantum meruit,* or what the services are reasonably worth.[32] The contract may stipulate that the amount of the compensation shall be determined and fixed by the employer, after the services have been performed; and, when this is the agreement, the amount fixed by him is conclusive, unless there is fraud or bad faith on the part of the master in fixing the amount.[33] But it has been held that an agreement to pay the servant what the master thinks he is worth to him does not mean that the master shall fix the compensation at any low rate he chooses, after the services have been rendered, although such an agreement would be upheld if clearly proved; it amounts to no agreement at all, and the law implies that the master shall pay what the services are reasonably worth.[34] The law as to the duty of a master to compensate his servant is in most all respects identical with that which determines the compensation of a principal to his agent, and it is unnecessary to repeat what has been said upon the subject.[35]

§ 477. **Master's duty to provide and maintain safe place for employe in which to work, and suitable and safe machinery and appliances with which to work.**—This is one of the duties peculiar to the relation of master and servant which, from the nature of the employment, does not apply to the relation of principal and agent. The master being entitled to the services of his servant, and to control and direct him in the performance thereof, assumes the reciprocal obligation of exercising reasonable care in providing for his safety. As a branch of this obligation he must use reasonable diligence in seeing that the place set apart for him to work in is safe;[36] but the master does not insure the safety of

[32] Ruckman v. Bergholz, 38 N. J. L. 531; Kent Furniture Mfg. Co. v. Ransom, 46 Mich. 416.

[33] Butler v. Winona Mill Co., 28 Minn. 205, 41 Am. Rep. 277.

[34] Millar v. Cuddy, 43 Mich. 273, 38 Am. Rep. 181.

[35] See *ante,* §§ 253–278.

[36] Vanesse v. Catsburg Coal Co., 159 Pa. St. 403; Richmond, etc., R. Co. v. Norment, 84 Va. 167, 10 Am. St. 827, and note on p. 835; Cadden v. American Steel Barge Co., 88 Wis. 409; Williams v. St. Louis, etc., R. Co., 119 Mo. 316; Gustafsen v. Washburn, etc., Mfg. Co., 153 Mass. 468; Kelley v. Ryus, 48 Kan. 120; O'Neal v. Chicago, etc., R. Co., 132

the place, and is required to use only ordinary care and diligence in making it safe.[37] What is ordinary care and diligence must depend upon the circumstances of each particular case: the care must be commensurate with the apparent danger. The rule is aptly stated by Circuit Judge Sanborn in a case decided by the circuit court of appeals of the eighth circuit;[38] he says: "The care and diligence required of the master is such as a reasonably prudent man would exercise under like circumstances in order to protect his servants from injury. It must be commensurate with the character of the service required, and with the dangers that a reasonably prudent man would apprehend under the circumstances of each particular case. Obviously, a far higher degree of care and diligence is demanded of the master who places his servant at work digging coal beneath overhanging masses of rock and earth in a mine, than of him who places his employe on the surface of the earth, where danger from superincumbent masses is not to be apprehended. A reasonably prudent man would exercise greater care and watchfulness in the former than in the latter case, and, throughout all the varied occupations of mankind, the greater the danger that a reasonably intelligent and prudent man would apprehend, the higher is the degree of care and diligence the law requires of the master in the protection of the servant. For a failure to exercise this care, resulting in the injury of the employe, the employer is liable; and this duty and liability extend, not only to the unreasonable and

Ind. 110; Cheeney v. Ocean Steamship Co., 92 Ga. 726, 44 Am. St. 113; St. Louis, etc., R. Co. v. Eggmann, 161 Ill. 155; Bethlehem Iron Co. v. Weiss, 40 C. C. A. 270, 100 Fed. 45; Mellors v. Shaw, 1 B. & S. (101 E. C. L.) 437; Seymour v. Maddox, 16 Q. B. (71 E. C. L.) 326; Caldwell v. Mills, 24 Ont. 462.

[37] Union Pac. R. Co. v. O'Brien, 161 U. S. 451, 457. "The general rule undoubtedly is," said Chief Justice Fuller, in this case, "that a railroad company is bound to provide suitable and safe materials and structures in the construction of its road and appurtenances, and if, from a defective construction thereof, an injury happen to one of its servants, the company is liable for the injury sustained. The servant undertakes the risks of the employment as far as they spring from defects incident to the service, but he does not take the risks of the negligence of the master itself. The master is not to be held as guaranteeing or warranting absolute safety under all circumstances, but it is bound to exercise the care which the exigency reasonably demands in furnishing proper road-bed, track and other structures, including sufficient culverts for the escape of water collected and accumulated by its embankments and excavations."

[38] Union Pac. R. Co. v. Jarvi, 53 Fed. 65.

unnecessary risks that are known to the employer, but to such as a reasonably prudent man in the exercise of ordinary diligence—diligence proportionate to the occasion—would have known and apprehended." What is due and proper care under the circumstances is usually a question of mixed law and fact; but if the facts are undisputed and the inferences to be drawn from them are unequivocal, then the question is generally one of law for the determination of the court;[39] the court, however, always determines the law of the case, and in proper circumstances must charge the jury or decide the case upon the facts specially found. If the injury to the employe was the result of a pure accident, or was not attributable to the failure of the master to provide against probable danger, the master is not liable. That it was possible for such an injury to happen is not enough to charge the master with negligence in failing to guard against it: it must appear that the injury was likely to occur if not properly guarded against;[40] the master is not bound to guard against all possible dangers, but only to exercise ordinary and reasonable care against those which are probable. The servant has a right to rely upon the fact that the master will do his duty in making reasonable inspection of the place and seeing that it is free from danger, and to assume that this has been done; for it is the master's duty to make reasonable inspection, and the servant is not required to do so.[41] And this is true also as to machinery and appliances. But where the servant knows of the danger or has an opportunity of knowing it equal to that of the master, he can not recover, as he would then be guilty of contributory negligence or would be assuming the risk.[42] Whether the defect was thus obvious to the employe is, in doubtful cases at least, a question for the jury.[43] The duty to protect the servant in his place of work is a continuing one, and requires the master to use ordinary care and diligence to keep it safe; and if

[39] See Cincinnati, etc., R. Co. v. Grames, 8 Ind. App. 112, where the authorities are collected and reviewed.

[40] McKee v. Chicago, etc., R. Co., 83 Iowa 616.

[41] Ross v. Shanley, 185 Ill. 390; National Syrup Co. v. Carlson, 155 Ill. 210; Soltenberg v. Pittsburg, etc., R. Co., 165 Pa. St. 377.

[42] Vincennes Water Supply Co. v. White, 124 Ind. 376; Big Creek Stone Co. v. Wolf, 138 Ind. 496; Island Coal Co. v. Greenwood, 151 Ind. 476; Fisk v. Central Pac. R. Co., 72 Cal. 38, 1 Am. St. 22; Sullivan v. Simplex Elec. Co., 178 Mass. 35, 59 N. E. 645; Clark v. St. Paul, etc., R. Co., 28 Minn. 128; De Forest v. Jewitt, 88 N. Y. 264.

[43] Amato v. Northern Pac. R. Co., 46 Fed. 561; Lasch v. Stratton, 101 Ky. 672; De Maio v. Standard Oil Co., 74 N. Y. Supp. 165.

he neglects to do so he is answerable in damages;[44] and he can not delegate this duty to another and escape liability if the party thus delegated fails to perform the duty.[45] But the employe must exercise his senses of observation; and if he had notice of the defects, or if the dangers were so obvious and patent that a man of his experience and understanding ought to have noticed them, he will be held to have assumed the risk; and the question is then one of law for the court, and not one of fact for the jury.[46] All varieties of manual labor are attended with some danger, some more and some less than others. The servant or employe assumes the risk of many dangers incident to the employment, and this is especially true when they are obvious or apparent; but he does not assume the risk of defects that are latent or of dangers that are hidden and that could not with the exercise of ordinary care have been observed, but which it is the duty of the master to know or use ordinary diligence to discover.[47] It is always the duty of the employer to warn the employe of the danger of the place or the work about which he is engaged; and the former can not relieve himself from responsibility by delegating the performance of that duty to a foreman, who is in a sense a fellow servant of the injured party.[48] But when the employe has once been notified as to the danger and instructed how to avoid it, the employe, by accepting or continuing in the employment, assumes the risk, and the employer is not liable in case he is injured;[49] but the warning must be given in such plain and comprehensive language as to enable the servant to comprehend the dangers of the situation.[50] And if the servant

[44] Nall v. Louisville, etc., R. Co., 129 Ind. 260; Racine v. New York Cent., etc., R. Co., 70 Hun (N. Y.) 453.

[45] Elliott Railroads, § 1268.

[46] Lindsay v. New York, etc., R. Co., 50 C. C. A. 298, 112 Fed. 384; Bethlehem Iron Co. v. Weiss, 40 C. C. A. 270, 100 Fed. 45; Money v. Lower Vein Coal Co., 55 Iowa 671; Andrews v. Tamarack Min. Co., 114 Mich. 375. See Judkins v. Maine Cent. R. Co., 80 Me. 417, and note at end of case; McGuirk v. Shattuck, 160 Mass. 45, 39 Am. St. 454; Illick v. Flint, etc., R. Co., 67 Mich. 632; Huda v. American Glucose Co., 154 N. Y. 474; Throckmorton v. Missouri, etc., R. Co., 14 Tex. Civ. App. 222; Williamson v. Sheldon Marble Co., 66 Vt. 427; Herold v. Pfister, 92 Wis. 417; Dillenberger v. Weingartner, 64 N. J. L. 292.

[47] Union Pac. R. Co. v. O'Brien, 161 U. S. 451; Millard v. West End St. R. Co., 173 Mass. 512.

[48] Tedford v. Los Angeles Elec. Co., 134 Cal. 76, 54 L. R. A. 85.

[49] Hill v. Meyer Bros. Drug Co., 140 Mo. 433; Daester v. Mechanics' Planing Mill Co., 11 Mo. App. 593.

[50] Yeager v. Burlington, etc., R.

has knowledge or information of the danger, though latent, and though his information was not derived from the master, the servant can not recover damages.[51] In case the servant, by reason of his youth, or for other reasons, is unable, after instruction, to appreciate the danger, the master has no right to keep him in his employment, and will be liable thereafter for any injury incident to the employment, although the servant has been warned of such danger.[52] The master's duty also requires him to make proper and reasonable inspection for such defects as are likely to arise and endanger the employe's safety; and it is not sufficient that competent inspectors have been employed by the master, but the inspection must actually be made, when the circumstances are such as to require it.[53] The presumption always is that the master has performed his duty in this respect, and the burden is on the plaintiff who sues for damages to prove the master's negligence.[54] The term "place," in connection with the work of the employe, indicates the locality of the employment; it is very comprehensive, and embraces a great variety of objects; thus, the rule applies to buildings and objects within them, in and about which the servant is employed;[55] to walks and ways about buildings;[56] to mines;[57] to excavations of various kinds, such as ditches, sewers, quarries, etc.;[58] to railway-tracks and road-beds;[59] to railroad-bridges;[60] to switch-yards or yards where

Co., 93 Iowa 1; Sullivan v. India Mfg. Co., 113 Mass. 396; Tinkham v. Sawyer, 153 Mass. 485.

[51] Taylor v. Wootan, 1 Ind. App. 188, 50 Am. St. 200.

[52] Hinckley v. Horazdowsky, 133 Ill. 359, 23 Am. St. 618; Taylor v. Wootan, 1 Ind. App. 188, 50 Am. St. 200; Louisville Bagging Co. v. Dolan, 13 Ky. L. Rep. 493.

[53] Pittsburg, etc., R. Co. v. Thompson, 27 C. C. A. 333, 82 Fed. 720. See also, Ford v. Fitchburg R. Co., 110 Mass. 240, 14 Am. Rep. 598; Pennsylvania, etc., Canal & R. Co. v. Mason, 109 Pa. St. 296, 58 Am. Rep. 722.

[54] Snodgrass v. Carnegie Steel Co., 173 Pa. St. 228; Sappenfield v. Main St., etc., R. Co., 91 Cal. 48.

[55] Sansol v. Compagnie Generale Transatlantique, 101 Fed. 390; The Saratoga, 87 Fed. 349; W. C. De Pauw Co. v. Stubblefield, 132 Ind. 182; Harding v. Railway Transfer Co., 80 Minn. 504.

[56] United States Rolling Stock Co. v. Weir, 96 Ala. 396.

[57] Linton Coal, etc., Co. v. Persons, 11 Ind. App. 264.

[58] Taylor v. Star Coal Co., 110 Iowa 40; Hancock v. Keene, 5 Ind. App. 408; Fitzsimmons v. Taunton, 160 Mass. 223.

[59] Union Pac. R. Co. v. O'Brien, 161 U. S. 451; Lake Erie, etc., R. Co. v. Morrissey, 177 Ill. 376; Torian's Adm'r v. Richmond, etc., R. Co., 84 Va. 192; Elliott Railroads, § 1268.

[60] Elliott Railroads, § 1270.

trains are made up;[61] and to many other places and things which we can not undertake to enumerate. Wherever the employe is at work, whether the place be stationary,—as a building, mine, quarry, yard, street or walk, etc.,—or moving,—as a steamboat, railway-car, or other vehicle,—the master must use due care in protecting the servant, or he will be liable for damages, if injury results. Not only does the law require the master to provide the servant with a safe place in which to work, but also to furnish him with reasonably safe appliances and machinery. This duty is not absolute in the case of machinery and appliances, any more than it is with regard to the place designed for the servant in which to work: all he is required to do is to use ordinary care in the selection and repairs thereof.[62] The appliances need not be of the latest invention: if the master employs those in general use, and keeps them in reasonably safe condition and repair, he is not guilty of negligence because of the use of defective machinery and appliances.[63] It is held, however, that if the occupation is attended with great and unusual danger, the master is bound to use all appliances known to science which are readily attainable, in order to prevent accidents;[64] indeed, it may be stated as a rule without any exceptions, that the degree of diligence and precaution required in the selection and keeping of appliances, like that of furnishing and maintaining a place to work in, must always be proportionate to the danger involved.[65] And in all cases of negligence, before there can be any recovery by the servant on account of the unsafe condition of the place of work or the machinery or appliances, the injured party must show that such negligence was the proximate cause of the injury.[66] The statutory obligation of railroad companies to fence in their tracks, it seems, is not one of the duties they owe to their employes, unless

[61] Elliott Railroads, § 1272.

[62] Atchison, etc., R. Co. v. Napole, 55 Kan. 401.

[63] Pennsylvania Co. v. Congdon, 134 Ind. 226, 236, 39 Am. St. 251; Sappenfield v. Main St., etc., R. Co., 91 Cal. 48; Smith v. St. Louis, etc., R. Co., 69 Mo. 32, 33 Am. Rep. 484; Sisco v. Lehigh, etc., R. Co., 145 N. Y. 296; Kern v. De Castro, etc., Sugar Ref. Co., 125 N. Y. 50; Burns v. Chicago, etc., R. Co., 69 Iowa 450, 58 Am. Rep. 227; Lloyd v. Hanes, 126 N. C. 359.

[64] Mather v. Rillston, 156 U. S. 391.

[65] Union Pac. R. Co. v. Daniels, 152 U. S. 684; Mather v. Rillston, *supra*.

[66] Kauffman v. Maier, 94 Cal. 269; Carr v. North River Const. Co., 48 Hun (N. Y.) 266; Avery v. Meek, 96 Ky. 192; Galveston, etc., R. Co. v. Lynch, 22 Tex. Civ. App. 336; Youngbluth v. Stephens, 104 Wis. 343.

the statute in terms so provides.[67] There is some conflict of authority, however, upon this point, and there are well-considered cases which hold to the opposite view.[68]

§ 478. **Master's obligation to furnish medical and surgical aid to servant.**—As a general rule, no obligation rests upon the master to provide surgical or medical aid for his employes, who become ill or injured while in his employment.[69] Many of the modern cases decide, as we have heretofore seen, that a railroad company may, in cases of great emergency, render itself liable for the employment of a surgeon by one of its principal officers, to wait upon an injured employe of the company, although no express authority has been conferred upon such officer to make the employment.[70] Railroad companies and other corporations who thus provide surgical aid for an employe are not liable for negligence on account of malpractice on the part of a physician or surgeon, if due and proper care has been exercised in the selection of such surgeon or physician. When the company voluntarily undertakes to procure surgical aid for an injured servant, it is required to use only ordinary care and diligence in the selection of a competent physician or surgeon: it is not required to select one possessing the highest skill or longest experience.[71] And it was held by the supreme court of Tennessee that the company is not liable even for the malpractice of its regularly-employed surgeon who treats one of its employes under the circumstances alluded to, because the relation of master and servant does not exist between the railroad company and such surgeon.[72] This ruling, it seems to us, rests upon sound principles. "If it be," said Beard, J., speaking for the court in that case, "* * * that the decisive test of this relationship, or even one of its decisive tests, is that the master has the right to select the end of the servant's employment, and that the master's uncontrolled will is

[67] Cowan v. Union Pac. R. Co., 35 Fed. 43; Patton v. Central Iowa R. Co., 73 Iowa 306; Sweeney v. Central Pac. R. Co., 57 Cal. 15.

[68] Dickson v. Omaha, etc., R. Co., 124 Mo. 140, 25 L. R. A. 320; Blair v. Milwaukee, etc., R. Co., 20 Wis. 254; Atchison, etc., R. Co. v. Reesman, 60 Fed. 370.

[69] Pittsburg, etc., R. Co. v. Sullivan, 141 Ind. 83, 50 Am. St. 313; Davis v. Forbes, 171 Mass. 548; Denver, etc., R. Co. v. Iles, 25 Colo. 19; Cairo, etc., R. Co. v. Mahoney, 82 Ill. 73; Elliott Railroads, § 222.

[70] *Ante*, § 85.

[71] Pittsburgh, etc., R. Co. v. Sullivan, 141 Ind. 83, 50 Am. St. 313; Ohio, etc., R. Co. v. Early, 141 Ind. 73.

[72] Quinn v. Railroad, 94 Tenn. 713, 45 Am. St. 767.

the law of the servant, 'in the means and methods' by which this end is to be reached, then it can not be maintained that these surgeons were the servants of the corporation. They were not employed to do ordinary corporate work, but to render services requiring special training, skill and experience. To perform these services so as to make them effectual for the saving of life and limb it was necessary that those surgeons should bring to their work not only their best skill, but the right to exercise it in accordance with their soundest judgment and without interference. Not only was this the right of these surgeons, but it was as well a duty that the law imposed. If the railroad authorities had undertaken to direct them as to the method of treatment of the injured man, and this method was regarded by them as unwise, they would have been 'bound to exercise their own superior skill and better judgment, and to disobey their employers, if, in their opinion, the welfare of the patient required it.'[73] In accordance with this view it has been uniformly held, so far as we have been able to discover, that, having selected surgeons skilled and competent in their profession, the corporation has discharged every duty that humanity or sound morals impose, and that it is to no extent liable for the mistakes they may subsequently commit." If a company or individual were to carry on a hospital for the treatment of injured persons for profit, such company or person would doubtless be liable for any malpractice committed by the surgeons therein employed; and the same is perhaps true where for a sufficient consideration a railroad company or other employer of laborers agrees to see that these have proper surgical treatment in case of injury.[74] But where the treatment is voluntarily furnished by a corporation or individual gratuitously, or even where it is required to be done by the law, the master is required to do no more than to exercise ordinary care in the selection and retention of the surgeon, and is not responsible for his negligence if it has fulfilled its own obligation in employing and keeping such surgeon. Thus, a steamship company required by law to provide a surgeon for its ship is not liable even to a passenger, for the negligent setting of a fractured limb received on board the ship, if such company exercised reasonable care in the selection and retaining of the surgeon; nor is it required to employ men of the highest skill and widest

[73] Citing Union Pac. R. Co. v. Artist, 60 Fed. 365.

[74] See Richardson v. Carbon Hill Coal Co., 10 Wash. 648, 20 L. R. A. 338.

experience.[75] The company is responsible only for its own negligence in employing and keeping an incompetent surgeon, but is not responsible for such surgeon's negligence, the relation of master and servant not existing between the company and the surgeon.[76] But where a railroad company maintained a hospital for the care and treatment of those of its employes who might be injured while in its service, by means of funds raised in assessments upon its employes and deduction of the sum from their wages, it was held liable for the malpractice of one of its surgeons, rendered incompetent by habits of intoxication and the use of narcotics, of which the company had notice.[77] And where the company, by reason of deducting certain amounts from the wages of its employes, derives a profit, in consideration of which it undertakes to furnish surgical treatment to its injured servants, the company will be liable for an injury incurred by an employe by reason of improper treatment administered by its surgeon.[78] This liability, however, can not be said to arise out of the relation of master and servant, but doubtless by force of the contract entered into between the employer and employe, providing for the treatment of the latter. A hospital maintained by a railroad corporation for the free use of its servants who have been injured in its employment is a charitable institution; and this is true although the company derives a portion of the maintenance fund by receiving contributions from the employes; and unless the company derives a profit out of such maintenance, it will not be liable for injuries caused by the negligence of hospital attendants, unless the company failed to use ordinary care in their selection.[79]

§ 479. **Liability of master to servant for negligence of fellow servant.**—As a general rule, every person is responsible only for his own wrongs and not for those of others. If a person is guilty of a tort, he is responsible for all its proximate injurious consequences, to any one to whom he owed the duty of protection, or, at least the duty of not doing or omitting to do that which would injure him. One may render himself liable, however, for the conduct or omission of another than himself, when there is such a relation be-

[75] Laubheim v. De Koninglyke N. S. Co., 107 N. Y. 228, 1 Am. St. 815.

[76] Allan v. State Steamship Co., 132 N. Y. 91, 28 Am. St. 556; Louisville, etc., R. Co. v. Foard, 104 Ky. 456, 47 S. W. 342.

[77] Wabash R. Co. v. Kelley, 153 Ind. 119.

[78] Texas, etc., Coal Co. v. Connaughten, 20 Tex. Civ. App. 642.

[79] Union Pac. R. Co. v. Artist, 60 Fed. 365.

tween him and that other person that the rule *respondeat superior* is applicable. Thus, as we have seen, the master is responsible to third parties for the torts of his servant, and the principal for those of his agent, when committed within the scope or course of the business or labor in which such servant or agent was employed. And while the master is personally responsible for any wrongful act committed by himself and resulting in injury to his servant, he is not liable, as a general rule, for an injury inflicted by one of his servants upon another or fellow servant, although the wrongful act resulting in such injury was committed in the performance of the master's work. If, when the master employed the coservant, he was not guilty of negligence in selecting him, or, in other words, if he exercised reasonable care in securing a servant who was competent and qualified to do the work for which he was chosen, he has done all the law requires him to do; unless, indeed, he retains the employe in his service after he discovers the incompetency.[80] It is as much the duty of the master to employ and keep in his service competent coservants as it is to furnish his employe a safe place in which to work and proper and adequate machinery and appliances for his work:[81] if he fails in this he is guilty of negligence. But the negligence of coemployes is not the master's negligence; the doctrine of *respondeat superior* does not apply between the master and coservant. The general rule is that he who engages in the service of another to perform certain specified duties for compensation assumes the natural and ordinary perils and risks that are incident to such employment, including those which result from the negligence of other persons engaged in the performance of the same work with him. It is said that these rules rest upon a basis of sound public policy and general convenience, and tend to promote the safety and security of all parties concerned.[82] The rule and reasons therefor are very ably and tersely stated by Chief Justice Shaw in an early and leading Massachusetts

[80] "Nor is the master who uses due diligence in the selection of his servants answerable to one of them for an injury received by him in consequence of another's carelessness while both were engaged in the same service. There is no express or implied contract or principle of policy applicable to the case as between two servants in the same service, and giving an action against the master for an injury by one to the other:" 2 Kent Com. (13th ed.) 260, note.

[81] Laning v. New York Cent. R. Co., 49 N. Y. 521.

[82] Norfolk, etc., R. Co. v. Donnelly, 88 Va. 853.

case,[83] in which he says, among other things, that "one who enters the

[83] Farwell v. Boston, etc., R. Corp., 4 Met. (Mass.) 49, 38 Am. Dec. 339. We deem the opinion of the learned Chief Justice of sufficient importance to give it here practically in its entirety. He says: "This is an action of new impression in our courts, and involves a principle of great importance. It presents a case where two persons are in the service and employment of one company, whose business it is to construct and maintain a railroad, and to employ their trains of cars to carry persons and merchandise for hire. They are appointed and employed by the same company to perform separate duties and services, all tending to the accomplishment of one and the same purpose,—that of the safe and rapid transmission of the trains; and they are paid for their respective services according to the nature of their respective duties, and the labor and skill required for their proper performance. The question is, whether, for damages sustained by one of the persons so employed, by means of the carelessness and negligence of another, the party injured has a remedy against the common employer. It is an argument against such an action, though certainly not a decisive one, that no such action has before been maintained. It is laid down by Blackstone, that if a servant, by his negligence, does any damage to a stranger, the master shall be answerable for his neglect. But the damage must be done while he is actually employed in the master's service; otherwise, the servant shall answer for his own misbehavior: 1 Bl. Com. 431; M'Manus v. Crickett, 1 East 106. This rule is obviously founded on the great principle of social duty, that every man, in the management of his own affairs, whether by himself or by his agents or servants, shall so conduct them as not to injure another; and if he does not, and another thereby sustains damage, he shall answer for it. If done by a servant, in the course of his employment, and acting within the scope of his authority, it is considered, in contemplation of law, so far the act of the master, that the latter shall be answerable *civiliter.* But this presupposes that the parties stand to each other in the relation of strangers, between whom there is no privity; and the action, in such case, is an action sounding in tort. The form is trespass on the case, for the consequential damages. The maxim *'respondeat superior'* is adopted in that case, from general considerations of policy and security. But this does not apply to the case of a servant bringing his action against his own employer to recover damages for an injury arising in the course of that employment, where all such risks and perils as the employer and the servant respectively intend to assume and bear may be regulated by the express or implied contract between them, and which, in contemplation of law, must be presumed to be thus regulated. The same view seems to have been taken by the learned counsel for the plaintiff, in the argument; and it was conceded, that the claim could not be placed on the principle indicated by the maxim *'respondeat superior,'* which binds the master to indemnify a stranger for the dam-

service of another takes upon himself the ordinary risks of the em-

age caused by the careless, negligent or unskillful act of his servant in the conduct of his affairs. The claim, therefore, is placed, and must be maintained, if maintained at all, on the ground of contract. As there is no express contract between the parties, applicable to this point, it is placed upon the footing of an implied contract of indemnity, arising out of the relation of master and servant. It would be an implied promise, arising from the duty of the master to be responsible to each person employed by him in the conduct of every branch of business where two or more persons are employed, to pay for all damage occasioned by the negligence of every other person employed in the same service. If such a duty were established by law,—like that of a common carrier, to stand all losses of goods not caused by the act of God, or of a public enemy—or that of an innkeeper, to be responsible, in like manner, for the baggage of his guests,—it would be a rule of frequent and familiar occurrence, and its existence and application, with all its qualifications and restrictions, would be settled by judicial precedents. But we are of opinion that no such rule has been established; and the authorities, as far as they go, are opposed to the principle: Priestley v. Fowler, 3 M. & W. 1; Murray v. South Carolina R. Co., 1 McMull. L. (S. C.) 385. The general rule, resulting from considerations as well of justice as of policy, is, that he who engages in the employment of another for the performance of specified duties and services, for compensation, takes upon himself the natural and ordinary risks and perils incident to the performance of such services; and, in legal presumption, the compensation is adjusted accordingly. And we are not aware of any principle which should except the perils arising from the carelessness and negligence of those who are in the same employment. These are perils which the servant is as likely to know, and against which he can as effectually guard, as the master. They are perils incident to the service, and which can be as distinctly foreseen and provided for in the rate of compensation as any others. To say that the master shall be responsible because the damage is caused by his agents, is assuming the very point which remains to be proved. They are his agents to some extent, and for some purposes; but whether he is responsible, in a particular case, for their negligence, is not decided by the single fact that they are, for some purposes, his agents. It seems to be now well settled, whatever might have been thought formerly, that underwriters can not excuse themselves from payment of a loss by one of the perils insured against, on the ground that the loss was caused by the negligence or unskillfulness of the officers or crew of the vessel in the performance of their various duties as navigators, although employed and paid by the owners, and, in the navigation of the vessel, their agents: Copeland v. New England, etc., Ins. Co., 2 Met. (Mass.) 432, 440-443, and cases there cited. I am aware that the maritime law has its own rules and analogies, and that we can not always safely rely upon them in apployment in which he engages, including the negligent acts of his fel-

plying them to other branches of law; but the rule in question seems to be a good authority for the point, that persons are not to be responsible, in all cases, for the negligence of those employed by them. If we look from considerations of justice to those of policy, they will strongly lead to the same conclusion. In considering the rights and obligations arising out of particular relations, it is competent for courts of justice to regard considerations of policy and general convenience, and to draw from them such rules as will, in their practical application, best promote the safety and security of all parties concerned. This is, in truth, the basis on which implied promises are raised, being duties legally inferred from a consideration of what is best adapted to promote the benefit of all persons concerned, under given circumstances. To take the well-known and familiar cases already cited: A common carrier, without regard to actual fault or neglect in himself or his servants, is made liable for all losses of goods confided to him for carriage, except those caused by the act of God or of a public enemy, because he can best guard them against all minor dangers, and because, in case of actual loss, it would be extremely difficult for the owner to adduce proof of embezzlement, or other actual fault or neglect on the part of the carrier, although it may have been the real cause of the loss. The risk is therefore thrown upon the carrier, and he receives, in the form of payment for the carriage, a premium for the risk which he thus assumes. So of an innkeeper; he can best secure the attendance of honest and faithful servants, and guard his house against thieves; whereas, if he were responsible only upon proof of actual negligence, he might connive at the presence of dishonest inmates and retainers, and even participate in the embezzlement of the property of the guests, during the hours of their necessary sleep, and yet it would be difficult, and often impossible, to prove these facts. The liability of passenger-carriers is founded on similar considerations. They are held to the strictest responsibility for care, vigilance and skill, on the part of themselves and all persons employed by them, and they are paid accordingly. The rule is founded on the expediency of throwing the risk upon those who can best guard against it: Story Bailm., § 590, *et seq.* We are of opinion that these considerations apply strongly to the case in question. Where several persons are employed in the conduct of one common enterprise or undertaking, and the safey of each depends much on the care and skill with which each other shall perform his appropriate duty, each is an observer of the conduct of the others, can give notice of any misconduct, incapacity, or neglect of duty, and leave the service, if the common employer will not take such precautions, and employ such agents, as the safety of the whole party may require. By these means, the safety of each will be much more effectually secured, than could be done by a resort to the common employer for indemnity in case of loss by the negligence of each other. Regarding it in this light, it is the low workmen in the course of the employment." For further cases

ordinary case of one sustaining an injury in the course of his own employment, in which he must bear the loss himself, or seek his remedy, if he have any, against the actual wrongdoer. In applying these principles to the present case, it appears that the plaintiff was employed by the defendants as an engineer, at the rate of wages usually paid in that employment, being a higher rate than the plaintiff had before received as a machinist. It was a voluntary undertaking on his part, with a full knowledge of the risks incident to the employment; and the loss was sustained by means of an ordinary casualty, caused by the negligence of another servant of the company. Under these circumstances, the loss must be deemed to be the result of a pure accident, like those to which all men, in all employments, and at all times, are more or less exposed; and, like similar losses from accidental causes, it must rest where it first fell, unless the plaintiff has a remedy against the person actually in default, of which we give no opinion. It was strongly pressed in the argument, that although this might be so where two or more servants are employed in the same department of duty, where each can exert some influence over the conduct of the other, and thus, to some extent, provide for his own security, yet that it could not apply where two or more are employed in different departments of duty, at a distance from each other, and where one can in no degree control or influence the conduct of another. But we think this is founded upon a supposed distinction; on which it would be extremely difficult to establish a practical rule. When the object to be accomplished is one and the same, when the employers are the same, and the several persons employed derive their authority and their compensation from the same source, it would be extremely difficult to distinguish what constitutes one department and what a distinct department of duty. It would vary with the circumstances of every case. If it were made to depend upon the nearness or distance of the persons from each other, the question would immediately arise, How near or how distant must they be, to be in the same or different departments? In a blacksmith's shop, persons working in the same building, at different fires, may be quite independent of each other, though only a few feet distant. In a rope-walk, several may be at work on the same piece of cordage, at the same time, at many hundreds feet distant from each other, and beyond the reach of sight and voice, and yet acting together. Besides, it appears to us that the argument rests upon an assumed principle of responsibility which does not exist. The master, in the case supposed, is not exempt from liability because the servant has better means of providing for his safety when he is employed in immediate connection with those from whose negligence he might suffer, but because the implied contract of the master does not extend to indemnify the servant against the negligence of any one but himself; and he is not liable in tort,—as, for the negligence of his servant,—because the person suffering does not stand towards him in the relation of a stranger, but is one whose rights are regulated by stating and illustrating the rule as laid down by Chief Justice

contract express or implied. The exemption of the master, therefore, from liability for the negligence of a fellow servant, does not depend exclusively upon the consideration, that the servant has better means to provide for his own safety, but upon other grounds. Hence the separation of the employment into different departments can not create that liability, when it does not arise from express or implied contract, or from a responsibility created by law to third persons and strangers, for the negligence of a servant. A case may be put, for the purpose of illustrating this distinction. Suppose the road had been owned by one set of proprietors, whose duty it was to keep it in repair and have it at all times ready and in fit condition for the running of engines and cars, taking a toll, and that the engines and cars were owned by another set of proprietors, paying toll to the proprietors of the road, and receiving compensation from passengers for their carriage; and suppose the engineer to suffer a loss from the negligence of the switch-tender. We are inclined to the opinion that the engineer might have a remedy against the railroad corporation; and, if so, it must be on the ground that, as between the engineer, employed by the proprietors of the engines and cars, and the switch-tender, employed by the corporation, the engineer would be a stranger, between whom and the corporation there could be no privity of contract, and not because the engineer would have no means of controlling the conduct of the switch-tender. The responsibility which one is under for the negligence of his servant, in the conduct of his business, towards third persons, is founded on another and distinct principle from that of implied contract, and stands on its own reasons of policy. The same reasons of policy, we think, limit this responsibility to the case of strangers, for whose security alone it is established. Like considerations of policy and general expediency forbid the extension of the principle so far as to warrant a servant in maintaining an action against his employer for an indemnity which, we think, was not contemplated in the nature and terms of the employment, and which, if established, would not conduce to the general good. In coming to the conclusion that the plaintiff, in the present case, is not entitled to recover, considering it as in some measure a nice question, we would add a caution against any hasty conclusion as to the application of this rule to a case not fully within the same principle. It may be varied and modified by circumstances not appearing in the present case, in which it appears, that no willful wrong or actual negligence was imputed to the corporation, and where suitable means were furnished and suitable persons employed to accomplish the object in view. We are far from intending to say that there are no implied warranties and undertakings arising out of the relation of master and servant. Whether, for instance, the employer would be responsible to an engineer for a loss arising from a defective or ill-constructed steam-engine; whether this would depend upon an implied warranty of its goodness and sufficiency, or upon the fact of willful

Shaw, see the cases cited in the foot-note.[84] The first reported case which declared the fellow-servant doctrine in this country was decided by the supreme court of South Carolina.[85] The enunciation, in that case, by Evans, J., of the principle that the servant assumes the risk of injury resulting from the negligence of a co-servant, was concurred in only by a majority of the court. The action was by the fireman of a locomotive-engine, for an injury received by him by reason of the engine being thrown from the track, in consequence of the negligent conduct of the engineer. The same doctrine was declared shortly afterward by the supreme judicial court of Massachusetts in the case already cited and quoted from.[86] The opinion in the Massachusetts case by Chief Justice Shaw is pronounced by able law-writers[87] as "one of the most profound and masterly that ever emanated from the pen of that distinguished jurist." Mr. Freeman further says of it: "It has commanded the admiration and elicited the encomiums of judges and text-writers alike, and has been cited and approved by the courts of justice of two continents. The learning, ability and reputation of Chief Justice Shaw, and the surpassing strength and force of his deductions in that case, together with the circumstance that it was a very early one involving the principle, have rather overshadowed the opinion of Judge Evans in *Murray* v. *South Carolina R. Co.*;[87a] and the Massachusetts case, though of later date, has attained the dignity of a leading case upon this subject, and has by some writers been regarded,

misconduct or gross negligence on the part of the employer, if a natural person, or of the superintendent or immediate representative and managing agent, in case of an incorporated company,—are questions on which we give no opinion."

[84] Coombs v. New Bedford Cord. Co., 102 Mass. 572; Grimsley v. Hankins, 46 Fed. 400; Blondin v. Oolitic Quarry Co., 11 Ind. App. 395; Chicago, etc., R. Co. v. Kneirim, 152 Ill. 458, 43 Am. St. 259; Schaub v. Hannibal, etc., R. Co., 106 Mo. 74; Dallas v. Gulf, etc., R. Co., 61 Tex. 196; Johnson v. Portland Stone Co. (Or.), 67 Pac. 1013; Shugard v. Union Traction Co. (Pa.), 51 Atl. 325; Brady v. Western Union Tel. Co., 113 Fed. 909; New Pittsburgh, etc., Coke Co. v. Peterson, 136 Ind. 398, 43 Am. St. 327; Spees v. Boggs, 198 Pa. St. 112, 82 Am. St. 792; Maltbie v. Belden, 167 N. Y. 307, 54 L. R. A. 52.

[85] Murray v. South Carolina R. Co., 1 McMull. L. (S. C.) 385, 36 Am. Dec. 268.

[86] See note 83, *supra*.

[87] See the note of Mr. Freeman, in 36 Am. Dec. 280. See also, the article of John F. Dillon, on "American Law Concerning Employers' Liability" in 24 Am. L. Rev. 175.

[87a] 1 McMull. L. (S. C.) 385, 36 Am. Dec. 268.

although erroneously, as being the first case in which the doctrine was declared." A still earlier case containing what is frequently claimed as the first promulgation of the fellow-servant rule, was decided by Lord Abinger in 1837.[88] In this case the plaintiff, who was a servant of the defendant, was sent by the latter with certain goods in a van, in charge of another servant. The van, being overloaded, broke down, and the plaintiff, who was riding in it, was injured, and it was held that under these circumstances the defendant was not liable. But as Mr. Dillon points out in an article in the *American Law Review,* the case was really not one involving the fellow-servant doctrine, and therefore can not be claimed as the pioneer case upon the subject.[89] But whatever may have been the origin of the fellow-servant doctrine, it is now universally recognized, in its general scope, in all common-law jurisdictions. The reason for the fellow-servant rule is usually given, as we have seen, as being the assumption of the risk by the servant injured. When the injured servant entered into the contract with the master and agreed to the compensation he was to receive, he must have done so with reference to the risks of the employment, not the least of which was the probable or possible negligence of the servants who were to work with him in the same employment.[90] "The bed-rock of that doctrine is," say the supreme court of North Dakota, in speaking of the basis of the fellow-servant rule, "that every employe assumes the risk of his coemploye's negligence as one of the ordinary risks of his work."[91] "The reason usually given in the cases for the rule, as we have stated it," said Niles, J., speaking for the supreme court of California, "is that a servant, in bargaining with his employer, is presumed to know the ordinary risks of the business in which he is to engage, and can obtain a compensation in accordance with the risks, or, at his option, decline the employment. Among the ordinary perils of the service are those arising from the carelessness or negligence of colaborers, and they are presumed to be provided for in the bargain which he makes. He assumes the risk as a part of his contract of service. The duty of the employer in this regard extends no further than to the use of due care and prudence in the selection of competent servants in the several departments of the business."[91a]

[88] Priestley v. Fowler, 3 M. & W. 1.

[89] See "American Law Concerning Employers' Liability," 24 Am. L. Rev. 175.

[90] Anderson v. Bennett, 16 Or. 515, 8 Am. St. 311; Lewis v. Seifert, 116 Pa. St. 628, 2 Am. St. 631.

[91] Ell v. Northern Pac. R. Co., 1 N. Dak. 336, 26 Am. St. 621.

[91a] Yeomans v. Contra Costa S. N. Co., 44 Cal. 71, 81.

To these reasons may doubtless be added that of public policy; for, as said by the supreme court of Iowa, "the moral effect of devolving these risks upon the employes themselves, would be to induce a greater degree of caution, prudence and fidelity, than would in all probability be otherwise exercised by them."[92] The fellow-servant rule, however, does not apply to cases in which the master owed the injured servant a positive duty which the law imposed on him and which he failed to discharge; for in such cases, the master can not escape liability by shifting the duty upon a colaborer of the employe to whom such duty is owing; and if he undertakes to do so, and the servant intrusted with the discharge of the duty either fails to do it or does it in a wrongful manner, from which injury results, the master is liable. Thus, it is the duty of the master, as has been seen, to provide the servant with a reasonably safe place in which to work and with reasonably safe appliances and machinery, as well as a sufficient number of competent coservants; and if he omits to do this, the law will hold him accountable, and he could not be heard to say that he had directed another servant to do it, but that the latter had forgotten the task, or had performed it in such a manner as to result in injury to the complaining servant. Hence, it is held that where it is the duty of a railroad company suitably to prepare its car, whether passenger or freight, for the use to which it has been assigned, and the company fails to do this, but leaves the matter to a fellow servant of the one who is injured by the defect in such car, the company is liable to the injured servant.[93] And so, the duty of furnishing a locomotive-engineer with a safe track upon which to operate his engine can not be delegated by the master so as to exonerate him; and if a rail be removed and the engineer not notified of the fact, and an injury occur to the engineer, the company will be liable, notwithstanding, under different circumstances, the servant guilty of the wrongful act might have been only a fellow servant of the one injured.[94] Without enumerating individual cases, we may summarize by stating that whenever a positive duty devolves upon the master to one of his servants, the master's obligation is either to perform the task himself or to see that it is actually performed; and he will be liable for all negligence in connection therewith, if it be the proximate cause of the injury complained of.[95]

[92] Sullivan v. Mississippi, etc., R. Co., 11 Iowa 421.

[93] Bushby v. New York, etc., R. Co., 107 N. Y. 374, 1 Am. St. 844.

[94] Chicago, etc., R. Co. v. Eaton, 194 Ill. 441, 62 N. E. 784.

[95] See Myers v. Hudson Iron Co., 150 Mass. 125, 15 Am. St. 176; Pull-

§ 480. **Master's liability for employment and retention of incompetent coservants.**—In the previous section we showed the rule to be that if the master exercised reasonable care in securing competent servants, he would not generally be liable to any of them for injury resulting from the negligence of any other of such servants. But the duty of employing and retaining competent colaborers is one he owes to each of his employes, and for a failure to perform it with proper and reasonable care he is answerable to the injured servant in damages, except in cases in which such injured servant has assumed the risk.[96] The rule is universally recognized in this country. Judge Thompson, in his work on Negligence, states it as follows: "If the master has failed to exercise ordinary or reasonable care in the selection of his servants, in consequence of which he has in his employ a servant who, by reason of habitual drunkenness, negligence or other vicious habits, or by reason of want of the requisite skill to discharge the duties which he is employed to perform, or for any other cause, is unfit for the service in which he is engaged, and if, in consequence of such unfitness, an injury happens to another servant, the master must answer for the damages suffered by such servant."[97] The master is not an insurer of the competency of his servants:[98] he is required to exercise only ordinary or reasonable care and diligence. "The exceptional cases," said the supreme court of Illinois, "are only * * * where the injury is imputable directly

man Palace-Car Co. v. Laack, 143 Ill. 242; Young v. New Jersey, etc., R. Co., 46 Fed. 160; Tedford v. Los Angeles Elec. Co. (Cal.), 54 L. R. A. 85; Chicago, etc., R. Co. v. Eaton, 96 Ill. App. 570, affirmed in 194 Ill. 441.

[96] Farwell v. Boston, etc., R. Corp., 4 Met. (Mass.) 49, 38 Am. Dec. 339 (see note 83, *supra*); McPhee v. Scully, 163 Mass. 216; Huntsinger v. Trexler, 181 Pa. St. 497; Campbell v. Cook, 86 Tex. 630, 40 Am. St. 878, and note; Fast Line, etc., R. Co. v. Scott, 71 Tex. 703, 10 Am. St. 804; Western Stone Co. v. Whalen, 151 Ill. 472, 42 Am. St. 244; Slater v. Chapman, 67 Mich. 523, 11 Am. St. 593; Davis v. Detroit, etc., R. Co., 20 Mich. 105, 124; Conrad v. Gray, 109 Ala. 130; Colorado Midland R. Co. v. O'Brien, 16 Colo. 219; Norfolk, etc., R. Co. v. Nuckols, 91 Va. 193; Anderson v. New York, etc., S. S. Co., 47 Fed. 38; Northern Pac. R. Co. v. Mares, 123 U. S. 710; Evansville, etc., R. Co. v. Guyton, 115 Ind. 450; Hall v. Bedford Stone Co., 156 Ind. 460; Indianapolis Frog, etc., Co. v. Boyle, 18 Ind. App. 169; Chicago, etc., R. Co. v. Beatty, 13 Ind. App. 604; Union Pac. R. Co. v. Young, 19 Kan. 488.

[97] 2 Thompson Neg. (1st ed.) 974.

[98] Keith v. Walker Iron, etc., Co., 81 Ga. 49, 12 Am. St. 296; Reiser v. Pennsylvania Co., 152 Pa. St. 38, 34 Am. St. 620; Stephens v. Doe, 73 Cal. 26.

to the personal negligence of the defendant [the master] in the selection of the servant, or in retaining him in service after the incompetency was known. The master does not warrant the competency of any of his servants, to the others. The extent of the undertaking is, the company will exercise reasonable care in the selection of an employe, and if his incompetency is discovered, it will dismiss him from its service."[99] The court further said: "The case of *Wright* v. *New York Cent. R. Co.*[100] is a well-considered case on this subject. It is there distinctly declared the employer does not undertake with his employes for the skill and competency of the other employes in and about the same service. The liability is placed on the ground of personal negligence of the company in the selection of its servants. In cases of injury to passengers, the fault of the agent is imputed to the company on grounds of public policy, but the rule is different where it is sought to make the company responsible for an injury to one of its own employes, unless the case can be brought within the exception to the general doctrine. The principle is certainly sustained by the weight of authority."[100a] "The master, in relation to fellow servants, is bound to exercise diligence and care that he brings into his service only such as are capable, safe, and trustworthy, and for any neglect in exercising that diligence he is liable to his servant for injuries sustained from that neglect."[101] The incompetency of the servant may be shown by the testimony of witnesses who know the fact to be true. If the master knew of the unfitness of the servant for the particular work in hand, this is of course the strongest evidence of his culpability. But it is not essential that actual notice of the servant's incapacity be brought home to the master; it is sufficient if he might by the exercise of ordinary and reasonable diligence have discovered the incompetency; and ignorance of the fact, if he had sufficient opportunity to be informed, is itself evidence of negligence on the part of the mas-

[99] Columbus, etc., R. Co. v. Troesch, 68 Ill. 545, 18 Am. Rep. 578, citing Shearman & Redf. Neg., § 86.

[100] 25 N. Y. 562.

[100a] Columbus, etc., R. Co. v. Troesch, *supra*.

[101] Isham, J., in Noyes v. Smith, 28 Vt. 59, 65 Am. Dec. 222. See, to the same effect, McLean v. Blue Point Gravel Min. Co., 51 Cal. 255; Jungnitsch v. Michigan Malleable Iron Co., 105 Mich. 270; Ohio, etc., R. Co. v. Collarn, 73 Ind. 261, 38 Am. Rep. 134; Norfolk, etc., R. Co. v. Hoover, 79 Md. 253, 47 Am. St. 392; Tyson v. South, etc., R. Co., 61 Ala. 554, 32 Am. Rep. 8.

ter.[102] The incompetency or unfitness of the servant may be proved by the latter's general reputation for intemperance or whatever is the peculiar trait rendering him disqualified or unfit for the discharge of the particular duties of the employment.[103] "Want of ordinary care" is defined as want of ordinary attention to the business in hand.[104] "The decisions, with few exceptions not important to mention," said Justice Harlan, in a carefully-considered case,[105] "are to the effect that the corporation must exercise ordinary care. But according to the best-considered adjudications, and upon the clearest grounds of necessity and good faith, ordinary care in the selection and retention of servants and agents implies that degree of diligence and precaution which the exigencies of the particular service reasonably require. It is such care as, in view of the consequences that may result from negligence on the part of the employes, is fairly commensurate with the perils and dangers likely to be encountered."[106] It must not be inferred, however, that the servant who labors with an incompetent coservant does not assume some risk, even where the master was negligent in employing or retaining the incompetent servant; for if the servant who asks for damages had knowledge of the incompetency of the fellow servant and continued in the common service of the master with the other servant, without complaint, he can not recover, as in such case he is held to have assumed the risk, just the same as if he had continued in the employment after having discovered the unsafe condition of his place of work or his appliances, machinery, etc.[107] Some courts hold, especially where the injured servant held a position above that of the incompetent

[102] Davis v. Detroit, etc., R. Co., 20 Mich. 124, 4 Am. Rep. 364; Western Stone Co. v. Whalen, 151 Ill. 472, 42 Am. St. 244; Baltimore, etc., R. Co. v. Henthorne, 19 C. C. A. 623, 73 Fed. 634; Harper v. Indianapolis, etc., R. Co., 47 Mo. 567, 4 Am. Rep. 353.

[103] Norfolk, etc., R. Co. v. Hoover, 79 Md. 253, 47 Am. St. 392; Western Stone Co. v. Whalen, *supra*; Baltimore, etc., R. Co. v. Henthorne, 19 C. C. A. 623, 73 Fed. 634.

[104] White v. Dresser, 135 Mass. 150, 46 Am. Rep. 454.

[105] Wabash R. Co. v. McDaniels, 107 U. S. 454.

[106] See, to the same effect, Baltimore, etc., R. Co. v. Henthorne, 19 C. C. A. 623, 73 Fed. 634; Haworth v. Seevers Mfg. Co., 87 Iowa 765; Kansas, etc., Coal Co. v. Brownlie, 60 Ark. 582; Evansville, etc., R. Co. v. Guyton, 115 Ind. 450.

[107] Hatt v. Nay, 144 Mass. 186; Spencer v. Ohio, etc., R. Co., 130 Ind. 181; Chicago, etc., R. Co. v. Champion, 9 Ind. App. 570; Bolton v. Georgia Pac. R. Co., 83 Ga. 659.

servant, that where the injured servant and the master had equal means of ascertaining the incompetency of the coemploye, the injured employe can not recover;[108] but this doctrine is not recognized by all the courts, and is expressly repudiated by some.[109]

§ **481. Vice-principal and superior agent or servant.**—As has already been stated, the master can not exonerate himself from responsibility to his servants where a positive duty rests upon him requiring him to do or omit to do something concerning the servant, or his work, —such as supplying him with safe places in which to work, safe and suitable appliances, competent fellow workmen, etc.,—by delegating such duty to another. Of course, it frequently happens that the master can not discharge that duty in person,—as, for example, in the case of a corporation, which can act only through the instrumentality of an agent; and it is not meant that the duty must be performed by the principal in person; the meaning of the rule is that it is incumbent on the master to see that such duty is actually performed, whether by himself or by some one else to whom he may see proper to intrust the matter; and for the failure to discharge such duty, or negligence in its performance, the master is liable in damages, whether the duty is undertaken by the master in person, or by some other person to whom he has delegated the performance of the duty.[110] Great confusion exists among the decided cases concerning the terms "vice-principal," "superior agent," or "manager." We can not undertake, within our limits, to attempt a review of the numerous decisions upon the subject; but we think that, according to the great weight of modern authority, a vice-principal is an employe of the master to whom has been intrusted by the latter the performance of some duty which the master owes to his servant

[108] Davis v. Detroit, etc., R. Co., 20 Mich. 105, 4 Am. Rep. 364. See Indiana, etc., R. Co. v. Dailey, 110 Ind. 75.

[109] Louisville, etc., R. Co. v. Kelly, 63 Fed. 407; Western Stone Co. v. Whalen, 151 Ill. 472, 42 Am. St. 244.

[110] Davis v. Central Vermont R. Co., 55 Vt. 84, 48 Am. Rep. 590; Harrison v. Detroit, etc., R. Co., 79 Mich. 409, 19 Am. St. 180; Mobile, etc,. R. Co. v. Godfrey, 155 Ill. 78; Nord Deutscher Lloyd S. S. Co. v. Ingebregsten, 57 N. J. L. 400; Randall v. Baltimore, etc., R. Co., 109 U. S. 478, 483; Prevost v. Citizens' Ice, etc., Co., 185 Pa. St. 617; Dwyer v. American Express Co., 82 Wis. 307, 33 Am. St. 44; Colorado, etc., R. Co. v. Naylon, 17 Colo. 501, 31 Am. St. 335; Sweeney v. Gulf, etc., R. Co., 84 Tex. 433, 31 Am. St. 71; Louisville, etc., R. Co. v. Hanning, 131 Ind. 528, 31 Am. St. 443; Cole Bros. v. Wood, 11 Ind. App. 37.

or servants.[111] It is immaterial whether the servant to whom the duty had been intrusted was superior in rank to the injured employe or not: the only question is whether the master owed the duty in the performance of which the negligent act was committed. If he did, then the employe so selected was a vice-principal, although he represented the employer only in that single task and not in a general way.[112] If, however, the servant who committed the negligent act was not in the performance of a duty which the master owed directly to the injured servant, then the negligence was that of a fellow servant, and there is no liability on the part of the master, even if the injured servant was inferior and acting in obedience to the command of the negligent servant, who was the superior in rank, in the sense of having authority to direct and control the other with regard to such service. This is what is sometimes denominated the English doctrine, and is severely criticised by some text-writers as being founded upon some early cases of inferior English courts, which were "ill-considered and ill-reasoned."[113] However that may be, the doctrine seems to be firmly established in Great Britain by numerous modern decisions, only a few of which are cited in the note.[114] The rule referred to seems to prevail with more or less variation and with many dissenting opinions by individual judges, in the states of Massachusetts, Indiana, Michigan, Minnesota, Pennsylvania, Wisconsin, Maine, Maryland, New York, New Jersey, North Dakota, Iowa, Connecticut, and perhaps other states.[115] To this array of state

[111] See the cases cited in last note; also, Mobile, etc., R. Co. v. Godfrey, 155 Ill. 78.

[112] See Elliott Railroads, § 1317.

[113] Shearman & Redf. Neg., § 227.

[114] Wilson v. Merry, L. R. 1 Sc. App. 326; Wigmore v. Jay, 5 Ex. 354; Lovegrove v. London, etc., R. Co., 16 C. B. N. S. (111 E. C. L.) 669, 33 L. J. C. P. 329.

[115] Moody v. Hamilton Mfg. Co., 159 Mass. 70, 38 Am. St. 396; New Pittsburgh Coal, etc., Co. v. Peterson, 136 Ind. 398, 43 Am. St. 327; Beesley v. Wheeler, etc., Co., 103 Mich. 196; Brown v. Winona, etc., R. Co., 27 Minn. 162, 38 Am. Rep. 285; Ross v. Walker, 139 Pa. St. 42, 23 Am. St. 160; Dwyer v. American Express Co., 82 Wis. 307, 33 Am. St. 44; Blake v. Maine Cent. R. Co., 70 Me. 60, 35 Am. Rep. 297; Norfolk, etc., R. Co. v. Hoover, 79 Md. 253, 47 Am. St. 392; Kimmer v. Weber, 151 N. Y. 417; O'Brien v. American Dredging Co., 53 N. J. L. 291; Ell v. Northern, etc., R. Co., 1 N. Dak. 336, 12 L. R. A. 97, 26 Am. St. 621; Houser v. Chicago, etc., Co., 60 Iowa 230, 46 Am. Rep. 65; Darrigan v. New York, etc., R. Co., 52 Conn. 285, 52 Am. Rep. 590. See also, McMaster v. Illinois Cent. R. Co., 65 Miss. 264, 7 Am. St. 653; McBride v. Union Pac. R. Co., 3 Wyo. 183, 21 Pac. 687; Anderson v. Bennett, 16 Or. 515, 8 Am. St. 311; Deserant v. Cerrillos Coal R. Co., 9 N. Mex. 495, 55 Pac. 290.

courts of final jurisdiction must now be added, with its great weight and influence, the supreme court of the United States. Although that tribunal and all the other federal courts were, up to the time of the decision of what is generally known as the *Ross Case*,[116] regarded as being on the side of those courts which hold to the superior-servant doctrine, the more recent decisions have practically overthrown the rule asserted in the earlier cases, so far as the federal tribunals are concerned, which now recognize and assert, in substance, the fellow-servant doctrine as administered by the greater number of the state courts.[117] Over against this doctrine stands what is generally known as the Ohio rule, applied in its fullest and most liberal scope by the supreme court of that state, and followed, in a more limited measure, by the courts of Kentucky, Tennessee, Missouri, Texas, Louisiana, North Carolina, Kansas, Illinois, and perhaps other states. The Ohio rule is stated by the supreme court of that state as follows: "Where one servant is placed by his employer in a position of subordination to, and subject to the orders and control of another, and such inferior servant, without fault, and while in the discharge of his duties, is injured by the negligence of the superior servant, the master is liable for such injury."[118] And the fact that the superior servant was then performing the services of a common workman and not those strictly pertaining to the duties of a foreman or superior officer, the court declares, in no wise relieves the master from liability.[119] It must be confessed that the courts which have generally applied the Ohio doctrine have not always been consistent in their rulings upon the subject, and many of their decisions are difficult to reconcile; which is perhaps to be explained upon the ground of frequent changes in the personnel of the respective courts. We cite only a few of the cases which, in a general way, apply the Ohio rule.[120] It

[116] Chicago, etc., R. Co. v. Ross, 112 U. S. 377.

[117] See Northern Pac. R. Co. v. Peterson, 162 U. S. 346; Northern Pac. R. Co. v. Charless, 162 U. S. 359; Baltimore, etc., R. Co. v. Baugh, 149 U. S. 368; Alaska Min. Co. v. Wheelan, 168 U. S. 86; Martin v. Atchison, etc., R. Co., 166 U. S. 399.

[118] Per Boynton, J., in Berea Stone Co. v. Kraft, 31 Ohio St. 287.

[119] *Ibid.*, citing Little Miami, etc., R. Co. v. Stevens, 20 Ohio 415; Cleveland, etc., R. Co. v. Keary, 3 Ohio St. 201; Mad River, etc., R. Co. v. Barber, 5 Ohio St. 541; and other Ohio decisions.

[120] Louisville, etc., R. Co. v. Cavens, 9 Bush (Ky.) 559; Louisville, etc., R. Co. v. Bowler, 9 Heisk. (Tenn.) 886; Coal Creek Min. Co. v. Davis, 90 Tenn. 71; Sweeney v. Gulf, etc., R. Co., 84 Tex. 433, 31

must be admitted that the tendency of recent adjudications, under the common law, is clearly to the effect that mere difference in rank between the injured and the offending servant does not determine the master's liability, although the inferior employe's injury was received as a result of obedience to the superior servant's commands, which the latter had a right to give, and which it was the duty of the former to obey. All the cases agree that the master is liable for the negligence of a fellow servant, whether superior or not, if such negligence consisted in the careless performance of some act which the master was in duty bound to perform, or in the omission of such act entirely. There is also practically unanimous agreement that if, as to the particular service in the performance of which the injury was received, the negligent and the injured servant were of equal rank, and were engaged in a common employment, and if the negligent servant was not at the time undertaking to perform a duty which the master owed to the injured servant, there is no liability on the part of the master. The greatest difference of opinion is as to the superior-agent rule. Many of the cases confuse the terms "vice-principal" and "superior agent" or "servant." But a vice-principal is not necessarily a superior agent or servant; for a servant may be a vice-principal without holding any superior rank over the other employes of the master. According to the superior-servant doctrine, a superior agent or servant must exercise control and direction over the other employes. It is not essential that he should be intrusted with the performance of duties which the master owes to other employes, except the general duty of protection. The master is responsible for the general management of the business as to which the superior agent or servant has been appointed. "When the servant by whose acts of negligence or want of skill other servants of the common employer have received injury is the *alter ego* of the master, to whom the employer has left everything, then the middleman's negligence is the negligence of the employer, for which the latter is liable. The

Am. St. 71; Missouri Pac. R. Co. v. Williams, 75 Tex. 4; Houston, etc., R. Co. v. Stuart (Tex. Civ. App.), 48 S. W. 799; Van Amburg v. Vicksburg, etc., R. Co., 37 La. Ann. 650; Miller v. Missouri Pac. R. Co., 109 Mo. 350, 32 Am. St. 637; Dowling v. Allen, 74 Mo. 13; Hutson v. Missouri Pac. R. Co., 50 Mo. App. 300; Dobbin v. Richmond, etc., R. Co., 81 N. C. 446 (but see Turner v. Goldsboro Lumber Co., 119 N. C. 387); Missouri Pac. R. Co. v. Peregoy, 36 Kan. 424; Walker v. Gillett, 59 Kan. 214; Chicago, etc., R. Co. v. May, 108 Ill. 288; Wabash, etc., R. Co. v. Hawk, 121 Ill. 259, 2 Am. St. 82.

servant in such case represents the master, and is charged with the master's duty."[121] If the master were himself in control of the workmen and guilty of negligence in giving directions, he would doubtless be liable for any proximately-resulting injury to the servant if the latter used due care.[122] "The servant does not stand on the same footing with the master. His primary duty is obedience, and if, when in the discharge of that duty, he is damaged through the neglect of the master, it is but meet that he should be recompensed."[123] What the master may do himself, he may do by another; he is therefore liable for the conduct of his representative. If the master is not, or from the nature of the case, can not be present in person, but has intrusted the particular business to a superintendent, who has power to employ and discharge the workmen, the superintendent is not a fellow servant, but a representative of the master, sometimes improperly called a "vice-principal."[124] Where the superintending servant is in charge of a distinct department, this is also true.[125] The fellow-servant rule does not prevent a faithful and obedient employe from yielding obedience to the orders of the master or his representative who is urging him to hurry his work and directs him suddenly to assume a position of great danger; and the employe will not be guilty of contributory negligence for obeying the command, although he had some knowledge of the additional danger, but, owing to the suddenness of the order, had not time nor opportunity to deliberate upon it.[126]

§ 482. **Statutory enactments.**—While the tendency of the courts of this country and England in the application of common-law principles is to exonerate the principal from liability for the negligent acts of superior servants, the legislatures of the different states as well as that of England have shown a disposition to counteract these adjudications by the adoption of statute-laws holding the employer to a more strict accountability for the negligence of fellow servants who are intrusted with power to superintend, though they

[121] Per Allen, J., in Malone v. Hathaway, 64 N. Y. 5.

[122] Haley v. Case, 142 Mass. 316; Kehler v. Schwenk, 151 Pa. St. 505.

[123] Per Gordon, J., in Patterson v. Pittsburgh, etc., R. Co., 76 Pa. St. 389.

[124] Mitchell v. Robinson, 80 Ind. 281; Atlas Engine Works v. Randall, 100 Ind. 293; Foley v. Chicago, etc., R. Co., 64 Iowa 644; Willis v. Oregon, etc., R. Co., 11 Or. 257.

[125] Denver, etc., R. Co. v. Driscoll, 12 Colo. 520, 13 Am. St. 243.

[126] Lee v. Woolsey, 109 Pa. St. 124; Indiana Car Co. v. Parker, 100 Ind. 181; Pittsburgh, etc., R. Co. v. Adams, 105 Ind. 151.

may also be fellow servants.[126a] These so-called "employers'-liability acts" frequently apply only to railroad corporations and sometimes to these and other corporations, except municipal; and render the employer liable in damages when an employe is injured while in the exercise of due care, where the injury results from the negligence of any servant of the corporation to whose orders the injured employe is bound to conform and does conform. Though considerable difference exists in many of these statutes, many of them are modeled after that of England adopted in 1880.[127] These acts also contain provisions rendering the employer liable for defects in machinery, tools, etc., due to the negligence of the master or the servant intrusted with the duty of keeping them in proper condition; for injuries to servants received by them while acting in obedience to the rules or particular instructions of any person to whom such duty has been delegated; and for injuries due to the negligence of those having charge of signals, telegraph-offices, switch-yards, etc.[128] Some of the provisions of these statutes are but reassertions of common-law principles, and add little, if anything, to the liability of masters to servants for the negligence of their coservants, while others make radical changes in the rules. Among the important provisions of such statutes are those pertaining to the master's responsibility for injuries due to the negligence of coemployes who are at the time acting as superintendents or superior servants, and whose commands the injured employe is bound to obey; and it is generally held by the courts, in construing such provisions, that the negligent employe must be engaged in an act of superintendency when the negligent act is committed by him which results in the injury of the servant under him.[129] "We think there can be no doubt," said Hackney, J., in a recent Indiana case, "that it was intended by the third subdivision to make corporations liable where the servant does an act or omits action in obedience to the command of the corporation given by rule, regulation or by-law, or through any person delegated with

[126a] See Appendix for a few of these acts.

[127] 43 & 44 Vict., ch. 42; Appendix, p. 605, *post*.

[128] See Burns R. S. Ind. 1901, § 7083; Code of Ala. 1896, §§ 1749, 1751; Stat. Mass. 1887, ch. 270; Gen. Laws Minn. 1895, ch. 173. See these acts in the Appendix, *post*.

[129] Whelton v. West End St. R. Co., 172 Mass. 555; Cashman v. Chase, 156 Mass. 342; Fitzgerald v. Boston, etc., R. Co., 156 Mass. 293; Whittaker v. Bent, 167 Mass. 588; Dantzler v. De Bardeleben Coal, etc., Co., 101 Ala. 309; Baltimore, etc., R. Co. v. Little, 149 Ind. 167; Kellard v. Rooke, 21 Q. B, Div. 367.

authority from the corporation to make the command, and such act or omission results in injury to another."[130] These statutes are doubtless intended to enlarge the common-law liability of the master for the negligence of his superintending servants, or at least to render definite and certain the answer to the much-mooted question, Who are superintendents or superior servants? but the same tendencies toward liberal or narrow construction of the common law with reference to the master's liability for injuries which prevailed in the courts of particular states prior to the enactment of these various statutes obviously continue to manifest themselves in connection with their construction, and hence the answer to the question, What is a "superintendence"? according to the views of one court might not be the same as in the judgment of another.[131] The employers'-liability acts were doubtless intended to limit the common-law exemption of the master for negligence of one of his servants who was in a common employment with another. Some of the statutes enacted by state legislatures providing for the liability of corporations for the negligence of fellow servants apply exclusively to railroad companies. Such statutes are held not to be in violation of those constitutional inhibitions against class legislation contained in the organic law of many states, inasmuch as they supply a necessity for protection to employes whose employers expose them to peculiar hazards and dangers.[132] By the construction usually given these provisions, when the superintendent voluntarily performs the act resulting in the injury of the coemploye, without the direction or approval of the employer, the latter is not liable.[133] The law is not changed with reference to the assumption of the risk by those servants who know of the danger and voluntarily continue in the service, or are guilty of contributory negligence:[134] they can not recover damages for injuries thus sustained.

[130] Baltimore, etc., R. Co. v. Little, *supra.*

[131] Compare, for example, Kansas City, etc., R. Co. v. Burton, 97 Ala. 240, with Cashman v. Chase, 156 Mass. 342, and O'Neil v. O'Leary, 164 Mass. 387.

[132] Schus v. Powers-Simpson Co. (Minn.), 89 N. W. 68; Johnson v. St. Paul, etc., R. Co., 43 Minn. 222, 8 L. R. A. 419; Chicago, etc., R. Co. v. Pontius, 157 U. S. 209; Missouri Pac. R. Co. v. Mackey, 33 Kan. 298, affirmed in 127 U. S. 205; Campbell v. Cook, 86 Tex. 630; Herrick v. Minneapolis, etc., R. Co., 31 Minn. 11.

[133] Shea v. Willington, 163 Mass. 364.

[134] Louisville, etc., R. Co. v. Stutts, 105 Ala. 368; Larkin v. New York, etc., R. Co., 166 Mass. 110; Cassaday

§ 483. **Duty to promulgate rules and regulations and to give warning to employes—Duty of inspection.**—As a part of the general obligation of the master to afford reasonable protection to his servants, it is his duty to adopt and promulgate rules and regulations for carrying on the business in which his servants are engaged. This duty is incumbent more particularly upon persons, firms, and corporations having a large number of employes and carrying on a specially hazardous business, such as railroading, manufacturing, etc. If in such instances the employer fails to discharge the duty incumbent upon him, and there is a resulting injury to a servant, he is liable in damages.[135] This duty, like that of furnishing safe places in which to work, etc., is one which the employer must perform or see that it is performed; and he can not exonerate himself by the plea that he had delegated the duty to a servant who had failed to discharge it, or had discharged it negligently. But, before the injured servant can recover, he must prove that the failure to promulgate such rules and regulations was the proximate cause of the injury.[136] The master, in this respect, as in others relating to his business, must guard against probable and not against possible casualties: if the rules are such as are usually adopted by prudent employers in the same line of business, they are sufficient to meet the requirement:[137] the master can not be expected to anticipate every emergency, and is required to make only such reasonable rules and regulations as an ordinarily prudent person would make under the circumstances, ordinary care being all he is required to exercise.[138] Where the business is not specially hazardous or complicated, failure to promulgate rules and regulations is not negligence in the master.[139] The rules and regulations must be promulgated in such manner as to afford employes

v. Boston, etc., R. Co., 164 Mass. 198; Trinity, etc., R. Co. v. Mitchell, 72 Tex. 609; Murphy v. Chicago, etc., R. Co., 45 Iowa 661; Weblin v. Ballard, 17 Q. B. Div. 122.

[135] Lewis v. Seifert, 116 Pa. St. 628, 2 Am. St. 631; Reagan v. St. Louis, etc., R. Co., 93 Mo. 348, 3 Am. St. 542; Doing v. New York, etc., R. Co., 151 N. Y. 579; Ford v. Lake Shore, etc., R. Co., 124 N. Y. 493, 12 L. R. A. 454; Chicago, etc., R. Co. v. Taylor, 69 Ill. 461; Lake Shore, etc., R. Co. v. Lavalley, 36 Ohio St. 222; Missouri, etc., R. Co. v. McElyea, 71 Tex. 386, 10 Am. St. 749; Evansville, etc., R. Co. v. Holcomb, 9 Ind. App. 198; Smith v. Oxford, etc., Co., 42 N. J. L. 467.

[136] Doing v. New York, etc., R. Co., 26 N. Y. Supp. 405.

[137] Abel v. Delaware, etc., Canal Co., 128 N. Y. 662.

[138] Berrigan v. New York, etc., R. Co., 131 N. Y. 582; Atchison, etc., R. Co. v. Caruthers, 56 Kan. 309.

[139] Texas, etc., R. Co. v. Echols, 87 Tex. 339.

a reasonable opportunity to acquaint themselves with them;[140] but if the employe obtains knowledge of such rules, however it may be acquired, it will be sufficient to absolve the employer.[141] Failure to enforce such rules is likewise culpable negligence on the part of the master; and proof that it is customary on his part to disregard the rules is evidence of the failure to enforce them.[142] It is the duty of the servant, however, to obey such rules, whether others do so or not, and a failure to do so on the servant's part will generally excuse the employer from liability: he does not insure their observance.[143] It is also the duty of the employer to warn the employe of the dangers of the employment, particularly those not in open view, but which are known to the employer, or could with reasonable diligence have been ascertained by him, and which the employe, on account of his ignorance, inexperience or youth, may not be able to appreciate readily.[144] The duty to warn the employe applies with particular force to cases where a change has taken place in machinery or appliances, and the hazard has thereby been increased to which the servant will be exposed and which he would not probably observe.[145] If, however, the defects are obvious and patent to a person of ordinary intelligence, the master is not in duty bound generally to give warning, as in such cases the employe assumes the risks,[146] unless he is so inexperienced or ignorant, or young, as not to appreciate the danger.[147] The employer is invariably bound to

[140] Abel v. Delaware, etc., Canal Co., 103 N. Y. 581, 57 Am. Rep. 773; Little Rock, etc., R. Co. v. Leverett, 48 Ark. 333, 348, 3 Am. St. 230; Fay v. Minneapolis, etc., R. Co., 30 Minn. 231; Evansville, etc., R. Co. v. Holcomb, 9 Ind. App. 198.

[141] Grady v. Southern R. Co,. 92 Fed. 491.

[142] Northern Pac. R. Co. v. Nickels, 50 Fed. 718; Chicago, etc., R. Co. v. Flynn, 154 Ill. 448.

[143] Richmond, etc., R. Co. v. Thomasson, 99 Ala. 471; Abend v. Terre Haute, etc., R. Co., 111 Ill. 202; Rutledge v. Missouri Pac. R. Co., 123 Mo. 121, 133.

[144] Consolidated, etc., R. Co. v. Haenni, 146 Ill. 614; Smith v. Peninsular Car Works, 60 Mich. 501; Erickson v. St. Paul, etc., R. Co., 41 Minn. 500, 5 L. R. A. 786; Sullivan v. India Mfg. Co., 113 Mass. 396; Salem Stone, etc., Co. v. Griffin, 139 Ind. 141; Atlas Engine Works v. Randall, 100 Ind. 293; Reisert v. Williams, 51 Mo. App. 13; Gates v. State, 128 N. Y. 221; Louisville, etc., R. Co. v. Hall, 87 Ala. 708, 13 Am. St. 84; Norfolk Beet Sugar Co. v. Hight, 56 Neb. 162; Fisk v. Central Pac. R. Co., 72 Cal. 38, 1 Am. St. 22; Hayes v. Colchester Mills, 69 Vt. 1.

[145] Cincinnati, etc., R. Co. v. Gray, 101 Fed. 623.

[146] Kohn v. McNulta, 147 U. S. 238.

[147] Wallace v. Standard Oil Co., 66 Fed. 260. This was a case decided by the United States circuit court

instruct new and inexperienced employes as to the nature of the work upon which they are about to enter and the dangers to which they

for the district of Indiana, where a boy, seventeen years of age, was employed in the business of handling, transporting and selling coal oil, turpentine, gasoline and other inflammable oils. One of the negligent acts charged against the employer was that he failed to instruct the boy, who was ignorant and inexperienced, as to the dangers incident to such employment. The boy's clothes had become saturated with the oils, and, being cold and chilly, he was directed by the employer's agent, who was in charge of the business, to go into the office, where there was a stove containing a hot fire, and warm himself. He did so, and while there his clothing caught fire from the stove and he received such injuries as resulted in his death. Speaking of the duty of the master to instruct such a servant, the learned district judge (Baker) observed: "This duty is not discharged so as to exonerate the master from liability by mere general instructions, but they must be so full, plain and specific as to bring to the knowledge and understanding of such infant the dangers incident to and growing out of his employment. This duty is the master's; and the agent, employe, or servant who may be delegated to perform it stands in the master's place, and his negligence is the master's negligence. In the performance of that duty, the servant, whatever his grade, is a vice-principal, and speaks and acts for the master. The defendant owed the decedent the duty of instruction, so that he might fully understand and avoid the danger from fire arising from the nature of his employment, and, instead of performing that duty, he misled the decedent by the false assurance that there was no danger from fire. This was a plain breach of duty, and, if the injury complained of resulted from such breach of duty, the complaint must be held sufficient. If his clothes had taken fire from exposure to it while the decedent was actually engaged at work for the defendant, there could be no serious dispute concerning its liability under the circumstances. It is said the accident was one which ought not to have been anticipated by the defendant, and was not a probable result of the saturation of his clothes with oils and gases. It seems to me that this contention is unfounded. The danger of the ignition of clothes, when saturated with oils and gases as alleged, by exposure to fire, is obvious, and is one which the defendant was bound to take notice of. It is equally obvious that the decedent, in the cold days of winter and spring, would be likely to be about fires, and in dangerous proximity to them, while his clothes were impregnated with oils and gases, especially if he was told by his employer that there was no danger in so doing, and he believed what he was told. The decedent was guilty of no negligence in acting on the direction of the representative of the defendant in going dangerously near to the hot stove in question. He went where he had a lawful right to be. His danger in so acting arose from conditions incident to the service, which conditions continued to be will probably be exposed. After the servant has been sufficiently instructed as to the dangers of the employment, and how to avoid them, he assumes the risk if he enters upon or continues in it.[148] The duty to furnish safe working-places and appliances carries with it the further duty of the master to make proper and adequate inspection from time to time, for defects in such places and appliances, such as are likely to occur as incidents of the business.[149] But the duty of making inspection is not extended to the ordinary appliances and tools with which employes are generally familiar; and the master has a right to assume that the servant who makes use of these will discover the defects and cease using them or apprise the master of their unfitness for further use.[150] Another limitation of the rule requiring the master to make inspection is in respect of defects that arise "in the constant use of the appliances, for which proper and suitable materials are supplied, and which may easily be remedied by the workmen, and are not of a permanent character, or requiring the help of skilled mechanics."[151] The mere fact that the servant might have avoided the accident by the use of special care in the operation of a defective machine will not excuse the master.[152] The workman has a right to assume, generally, that the employer has per-

present with him, and caused the burning of his clothes and subsequent death. This ignition of his clothes, and injury therefrom, were the direct result of the condition of his clothes incident to his employment. While the boy was sent to warm himself by his employer, he did not cease to be in its service, and he was, it seems to me, as much entitled, under the circumstances, to charge the defendant for its failure of duty to instruct, as though, at the time of the accident, he had been actually at work in the room. His clothes, saturated with the dangerous and inflammable substances mentioned, continued to be a source of danger, while unremoved, after, as well as during, his hours of actual service; and, in my opinion, it was actionable negligence to direct the decedent to go into the room containing the hot stove, even if the direction were only permissive, without instructing him in regard to the danger from a too near approach to it."

148 Daester v. Mechanics' Planing Mill Co., 11 Mo. App. 593.

149 Union Pac. R. Co. v. Daniels, 152 U. S. 684; Pennsylvania Co. v. White, 15 Ind. App. 583; Rogers v. Ludlow Mfg. Co., 144 Mass. 198, 59 Am. Rep. 68.

150 Wachsmuth v. Shaw Elec. Crane Co., 118 Mich. 275.

151 Per Finch, J., in Cregan v. Marston, 126 N. Y. 568, 572. See also, McGee v. Boston Cordage Co., 139 Mass. 445; Whittaker v. Bent, 167 Mass. 588.

152 Stringham v. Stewart, 100 N. Y. 516; McGee v. Boston Cordage Co., *supra*.

formed his duty as to inspection and repairs, as well as other duties; and if he relies upon this and is injured, he can not be held guilty of contributory negligence. "It has been often said that the master is not liable for defects in such things to a servant whose means of knowledge thereof were equal to those of the master. But this is an erroneous statement. The master has no right to assume that the servant will use such means of knowledge, because it is not part of the duty of the servant to inquire into the sufficiency of these things. The servant has a right to rely upon the master's inquiry, because it is the master's duty to inquire; and the servant may justly assume that all these things are fit and suitable for the use he is directed to make of them."[153] If, however, the defect was of such a character that its dangerous condition could not reasonably have been anticipated, the master can not be held accountable for it, and it becomes simply a case of assumption of the risk by the servant.[154] The defect must be such, in order to render the master liable for failing to remedy it, as could by the exercise of ordinary care have been detected by him.[155] If the master has promised the servant to repair or remedy the defect, the servant may rely upon the fact that the former will do so within a reasonable time; and if, within such time, he is injured therefrom, he will not generally be charged with contributory negligence;[156] but if, with a full knowledge of the defect, and without any promise or probability on the part of the master to make the repair or supply other instruments, the servant continues in the work, he assumes the risks, and can not recover if an accident occurs.[157]

[153] Shearman & Redf. Neg., § 287, quoted with approval in Magee v. North Pac., etc., R. Co., 78 Cal. 430, 12 Am. St. 69. See also, Western Stone Co. v. Musical, 96 Ill. App. 288.

[154] Morris v. Gleason, 1 Ill. App. 510.

[155] Pennsylvania Co. v. Congdon, 134 Ind. 226, 39 Am. St. 251; Reed v. Boston, etc., R. Co., 164 Mass. 129; Lanza v. LeGrand Quarry Co. (Iowa), 88 N. W. 805.

[156] Missouri Furnace Co. v. Abend, 107 Ill. 44; Donley v. Dougherty, 174 Ill. 582; Atchison, etc., R. Co. v. Sadler, 38 Kan. 128, 5 Am. St. 729; New Jersey, etc., R. Co. v. Young, 49 Fed. 723.

[157] Indianapolis, etc., R. Co. v. Watson, 114 Ind. 20, 5 Am. St. 578; Hunt v. Kane, 100 Fed. 256; Houston, etc., R. Co. v. Myers, 55 Tex. 110.

II. Liability of Master to Third Persons for Acts of Servant.

§ **484. In general.**—The liability of a principal to a third party for the acts of his agents, and incidentally some instances of accountability of the master for the acts of his servants, have already been presented.[158] It is proper now that we should notice more specifically the duties and liabilities of those persons whose principal attributes in the relation existing between them and their employes are those of masters. As a general rule, a servant, who, in the main, possesses none of the authority of an agent, can not render his master liable on any contract he may undertake to enter into for him: the master's only liability, as a general rule, for the acts of his servants is the liability for his torts. The master may be liable to a third party (a) for the negligence of the servant,[158a] and (b) for the willful, wanton or intentional wrongs of the latter.[158b] Before there can be any liability in either case, the relation of master and servant must actually exist; that is, the servant must be in the employment of the alleged master;[159] and there must be present the right to select, control and discharge the servant or employe. "The liability of any one, other than the party actually guilty of any wrongful act, proceeds on the maxim, '*Qui facit per alium facit per se.*' The party employing has the selection of the party employed; and it is reasonable that he who has made choice of an unskillful or careless person to execute his orders should be responsible for any injury resulting from the want of skill, or want of care, of the person employed; but neither the principle of the rule nor the rule itself can apply to a case where the party sought to be charged does not stand in the character of employer to the party by whose negligent act the injury has been occasioned."[160] "The relation," said Field, J., speaking for the supreme court of California, " * * * must be that of superior and subordinate, or, as it is generally expressed, of master and servant, in which the latter is subject to the control of the former. The responsibility is placed where the power exists. Having the power to control, the superior or master is bound to exercise it to the prevention of injuries to third

[158] *Ante*, Chapter VIII.

[158a] See 1 Thompson Neg. (2d ed.), ch. 15.

[158b] See 1 Thompson Neg. (2d ed.), ch. 16.

[159] Kueckel v. Ryder (N. Y.), 62 N. E. 1096; Aldritt v. Gillette-Herzog Mfg. Co. (Minn.), 88 N. W. 741.

[160] Per Baron Rolfe, in Hobbit v. London, etc., R. Co., 4 Exch. 254.

parties, or he will be held liable. The responsibility attaches to the latter, upon the principle, '*Qui facit per alium facit per se.*' To determine the responsibility, therefore, it is necessary to ascertain whether the relation existing between the party charged and the party committing the injury be in fact that of superior and subordinate, or master and servant."[161] "The distinction on which all the cases turn is this: If the person employed to do the work carries on an independent employment, and acts in pursuance of a contract with his employer, by which he has agreed to do the work on certain specified terms, in a particular manner, and for a stipulated price, then the employer is not liable. The relation of master and servant does not exist between the parties, but only that of contractor and contractee. The power of directing and controlling the work is parted with by the employer, and given to the contractor. But, on the other hand, if work is done under a general employment, and is to be performed for a reasonable compensation, or for a stipulated price, the employer remains liable, because he retains the right and power of directing and controlling the time and manner of executing the work, or of refraining from doing it, if he deems it necessary or expedient."[162] If there be not the relation of master and servant, however, the master may still make himself liable for the torts of his servant, where by a subsequent adoption or sanctioning of the acts he renders himself a legal participator in them.[163] The offending party need not, however, be actually in the employ of the alleged master, under contract of employment for wages, before the latter can be held liable: if he hold the person out to the public as his servant, and the wrong is committed within the apparent scope of such employment, or the alleged master receive the benefits of the other's labor, he may be liable, although there is no actual employment or contract between the two.[164] "It is enough that, at the time of the accident, he was in charge of the defendant's property by his assent and authority, engaged in his business, and, in respect to that property and business, under his control."[165]

[161] Boswell v. Laird, 8 Cal. 469, 68 Am. Dec. 345.

[162] Bigelow, C. J., in Brackett v. Lubke, 4 Allen (Mass.) 140. See also, Miller v. Minnesota, etc., R. Co., 76 Iowa 655, 14 Am. St. 258; Robinson v. Webb, 11 Bush (Ky.) 464; Samuelian v. American Tool, etc., Co., 168 Mass. 12, 46 N. E. 98; and the note to Brown v. Smith, 86 Ga. 274, in 22 Am. St. 459.

[163] McGuire v. Grant, 25 N. J. L. 356, 67 Am. Dec. 49; 1 Thompson Neg. (2d ed.), § 539.

[164] Denver, etc., R. Co. v. Gustafson, 21 Colo. 393.

[165] Per Wells, J., in Kimball v. Cushman, 103 Mass. 194, 4 Am. Rep.

§ 485. Master's liability for servant's negligence—Scope of employment—Contributory negligence—Proximate cause.—It is an elementary principle, coming down to us from the Roman law as a branch of the doctrine of *respondeat superior,* that the master is liable for the negligent acts or omissions of his servants, whereby the person or property of a third party is injured, if the servant was at the time acting within the scope of the employment.[166] "There is no material difference whether the party committing the injury is a servant or agent of the defendant. A servant is an agent. The principal is responsible for the act of his agent, and this case is only an application of the doctrine of *respondeat superior.*"[167] The modern decisions make the doctrine rest upon public necessity or expediency:[168] its hardships having often been appreciated and deplored by courts, but its enforcement being necessary to the reasonable security of society.[169] One who makes use of dangerous agencies in his business owes a duty to the public to exercise the greatest care in keeping and using them, and this duty he can not devolve from himself upon his servant so as to avoid liability.[170] The act, however, must be done within the scope

528, citing Wood v. Cobb, 13 Allen (Mass.) 58.

[166] 2 Kent Com. (12th ed.) 260, n. 1; Alserver v. Minneapolis, etc., R. Co. (Iowa), 88 N. W. 841; Tuel v. Weston, 47 Vt. 634; Hays v. Millar, 77 Pa. St. 238; Schulte v. Holliday, 54 Mich. 73; Conlon v. Eastern R. Co., 135 Mass. 195; Stephenson v. Southern Pac. R. Co., 93 Cal. 558, 27 Am. St. 223; Chicago, etc., R. Co. v. Bryant, 65 Fed. 969; Garretzen v. Duenkel, 50 Mo. 104; Stephens v. Chausse, 15 Can. Sup. 359; Milner v. Great Northern R. Co., 50 L. T. N. S. 367; Waters v. Pioneer Fuel Co., 52 Minn. 474, 38 Am. St. 564; Gaines v. Bard, 57 Ark. 615, 38 Am. St. 266; Gray v. Boston, etc., R. Co., 168 Mass. 20.

[167] Per Dowse, B., in Wilson v. Owens, 16 L. R. Ir. 225.

[168] Siegrist v. Arnot, 10 Mo. App. 197, per Thompson, J.

[169] Shea v. Reems, 36 La. Ann. 966; Hall v. Smith, 2 Bing. 160; McDonald v. Snelling, 14 Allen (Mass.) 290, 92 Am. Dec. 768; Pittsburgh, etc., R. Co. v. Shields, 47 Ohio St. 387, 8 L. R. A. 464.

[170] Pittsburgh, etc., R. Co. v. Shields, *supra.* "And it stands to reason," said the court in this case, "that one charged with a duty of this kind can not devolve it upon another, so as to exonerate himself from the consequences of injury being caused to others by the negligent manner in which the duty in regard to the custody of such an instrument may be performed. Speaking of the absolute duty imposed by statute in certain cases, or, also, the duty required by common law of common carriers, of owners of dangerous animals, or other things involving by their nature or position special risk or harm to neighbors, Pollock observes: 'The question is not by whose hand an unsuccessful attempt was made, whether that of the party itself, or

of the employment or the master will not be bound; for otherwise the rule *respondeat superior* does not apply. It is not always an easy matter to determine whether an act was or was not within the course of the business in which the employe was engaged for the employer. Where the facts are in dispute upon the question it is generally for the jury to determine.[171] Thus, where a corporation, by its agent, sold to a party by a parol contract a cooking-range, and sent its servant to deliver it and set it up ready for use, and the servant set it up in a defective and dangerous manner, and the servant took from the purchaser what was claimed to be a receipt, but which proved to be a written contract at variance with the parol agreement upon which the purchaser relied, the court held that it was for the jury to decide upon the terms of the agreement, and whether, under such terms, the servant was acting within the scope of the master's business.[172] So, where a party was taking treatment in a bath-house, and the baths were administered by servants, who received their compensation from the bathers, but were selected by and under the control and direction of the manager of the bath-house, the court held that this was sufficient to authorize the conclusion that the attendants were the servants of the owner and that he was liable for an injury to one of the patrons caused by their negligence.[173] *Primâ facie,* when a person is found doing service for another he is in that other's employ; and the fact that the one so employed carried on another business or employment separate and distinct from the one in which the negligent act was committed does not change the rule.[174] In an action against a railway company for the alleged negligence of its employe in attempting to stop a runaway

of his servant, or of an independent contractor, but whether the duty has been adequately performed or not:' Pollock Torts 64. We in no way limit nor question the soundness of the general rule which exonerates the master from liability for the acts of his servant done outside of his employment. What has been stated is strictly within the reason and principle of the rule, which is that whatever the servant is intrusted by the master to do for him must be done with the same care and prudence that would be required of the master acting in that regard for himself; if it be the custody of dangerous instruments, he must observe the utmost care."

171 Ritchie v. Waller, 63 Conn. 155, 27 L. R. A. 161; 1 Thompson Neg. (2d ed.), § 615.

172 Wrought Iron Range Co. v. Graham, 42 C. C. A. 449, 80 Fed. 474.

173 Gaines v. Bard, 57 Ark. 615, 38 Am. St. 266; 1 Thompson Neg. (2d ed.), § 604.

174 Perry v. Ford, 17 Mo. App. 212.

horse, whereby the occupant of the vehicle to which the animal was attached sustained an injury, the court of civil appeals of Texas held that the company was not liable, as the efforts of the employe to stop the horse were not acts within the scope of his employment.[175] And where a grocer sued a street-railroad company for damages because its foreman, by words and conduct, persuaded and induced the men whom he employed, controlled and had the power to discharge not to deal with the grocer, whereby the latter's business was injured and he sustained losses, the court held that the company was not liable, such acts and conduct not being within the scope of the foreman's employment.[176] In an action for negligence against a railroad company on account of permitting fire to escape from its right of way, the complaint or declaration should charge that the negligent act was done by the company, and not its servants; at least, it must appear from the averments that the acts of the servants were done while they were in the employ of the company; and where there is an allegation that the "workingmen and employes of the defendant" committed the act, the pleading is insufficient on demurrer.[177] The good motives or intentions of the master constitute no defense to the action; and he is not excused because the wrongful act or omission was without his consent or even against his express orders:[178] the liability is not grounded upon the master's supposed acquiescence, but, as stated above, he is held responsible for reasons of public policy.[179] The mental condition of the servant at the time of the wrongful act does not affect the employer's liability, if the servant was acting in the line of the employment, such condition, if it was the cause or occasion of the act complained of, being regarded simply as the misfortune of the master.[180] Before the master can be ren-

[175] San Antonio, etc., R. Co. v. Belt (Tex. Civ. App.), 46 S. W. 374.

[176] Graham v. St. Charles St. R. Co., 47 La. Ann. 1656.

[177] Louisville, etc., R. Co. v. Palmer, 13 Ind. App. 161. See further, on the point of the scope of employment, Singer Mfg. Co. v. Rahn, 132 U. S. 518; Driscoll v. Scanlan, 165 Mass. 348, 52 Am. St. 523; Morris v. Brown, 111 N. Y. 318; Mayer v. Thompson-Hutchison Bldg. Co., 104 Ala. 611, 53 Am. St. 88; Keating v. Michigan Cent. R. Co., 97 Mich. 154, 37 Am. St. 328; First Nat'l Bank v. Marietta, etc., R. Co., 20 Ohio St. 259, 5 Am. Rep. 655.

[178] Heinrich v. Pullman Palace-Car Co., 20 Fed. 100; Garretzen v. Duenkel, 50 Mo. 104; Consolidated Ice Machine Co. v. Keifer, 134 Ill. 481, 23 Am. St. 688; Pittsburgh, etc., R. Co. v. Kirk, 102 Ind. 399, 52 Am. Rep. 675; Powell v. Deveney, 3 Cush. (Mass.) 300, 50 Am. Dec. 738; Wood Master & Serv. 593, 594.

[179] See note 165, *supra*.

[180] Thus, where an intoxicated

dered liable there must, of course, be negligence on the part of the servant, and the negligent act or omission must be the proximate cause of the injury.[181] Negligence is variously defined as the omission of that which a reasonable man would do, or the doing of something a reasonable man would not do; the neglect to use ordinary care towards one to whom a duty is owing to use such care; the absence of due care; the omission of a duty, etc.[182] The authors last cited themselves define it as "an omission, by a responsible person, to use that degree of care, diligence and skill which it was his legal duty to use for the protection of another person from injury, as in a natural and continuous sequence causes unintended damage to the latter."[183] "Negligence," said the supreme court of Nebraska, "is the failure to exercise such care, prudence and forethought as, under the circumstances, duty requires should be given and exercised. It is the omission to do something which a reasonable man, guided by those considerations which ordinarily regulate the conduct of human affairs, would do, or doing something which a prudent and reasonable man would not do."[184] But not only must the injured party prove such actionable negligence, on the part of the servant engaged in the master's business, as was the proximate cause of the plaintiff's injury, but the latter can not recover damages unless he himself was free from contributory negligence.[185] Contributory negligence is the want of due and proper care by the injured person such as contributed proximately to his injury.[186] It is "such an act or omission," says Beach, "on the part of the plaintiff, amounting to a want of

employe of a railway corporation negligently left down the bars of a fence, whereby the plaintiff's horses escaped and were killed by a passing train, the corporation was held liable for such servant's negligence: Chapman v. New York Cent. R. Co., 33 N. Y. 369, 88 Am. Dec. 392. But in Christian v. Columbus, etc., R. Co., 79 Ga. 460, 7 S. E. 216, it was said that if the act of the servant was the result of insanity, and the master was faultless in regard to the employment of the servant, anything that would excuse the latter criminally from the act would excuse the master civilly.

[181] Kelsey v. Jewett, 28 Hun (N. Y.) 51; Jackson v. St. Louis, etc., R. Co., 87 Mo. 422; Chicago, etc., R. Co. v. Bell (Kan.), 41 Pac. 209.

[182] 1 Thompson Neg. (2d ed.), §§ 1-3; Shearman & Redf. Neg., § 1, note.

[183] Shearman & Redf. Neg., § 2.

[184] Brotherton v. Manhattan, etc., Co., 50 Neb. 214, 33 L. R. A. 598.

[185] Shearman & Redf. Neg., § 61; 1 Thompson Neg. (2d ed.), § 168, *et seq.*

[186] 1 Thompson Neg. (2d ed.), § 169.

ordinary care, as, concurring or co-operating with the negligent act of the defendant, is a proximate cause or occasion of the injury complained of. To constitute contributory negligence there must be a want of ordinary care on the part of the plaintiff, and a proximate connection between that and the injury."[187] If, then, the injured party could have avoided the injury by the exercise of ordinary care, he can not recover, although the defendant was guilty of negligence which was, in part, the proximate cause of the plaintiff's injury; for the common law, out of considerations of public policy, refuses to apportion the damages arising from the negligence of the parties combined;[188] although what is known as the doctrine of "comparative negligence" has been recognized in at least one American state; by which doctrine, if the negligence of the defendant was "gross," and that of the plaintiff but slight, the plaintiff could still recover, notwithstanding the plaintiff's negligence also contributed to the injury.[188a] To support an action for negligence these two things must concur: there must have been a negligent act or omission by the defendant (or his servant), which was a proximate cause of the injury complained of, and there must have been such ordinary care by the complaining party as would have avoided the injury had the defendant also acted with ordinary care.[189] Not every act or omission showing a want of ordinary care on the part of the plaintiff will defeat his right of action, any more than every act or omission showing a want of ordinary care on the part of the defendant will give the plaintiff a right of action. The plaintiff's negligence, to defeat his right of recovery, must have been a proximate cause of the injury; and the defendant's negligence, to give the plaintiff a right to recover, must have been a proximate cause of the injury.[190] Nor is it necessary that the defendant's negligence should have been the sole cause of the injury; for it is generally held that where the injury was caused by the concurrent negligence of the defendant and a stranger, the defendant is not excused.[191]

[187] Beach Contr. Neg., § 7.

[188] 1 Thompson Neg. (2d ed.), §§ 176, 177; Beach Contr. Neg., §§ 7-14.

[188a] Chicago, etc., R. Co. v. Dimick, 96 Ill. 43, 47. But the doctrine is now abandoned in Illinois: City of Lanark v. Dougherty, 153 Ill. 163, 165. See discussion of this doctrine in 1 Thompson Neg. (2d ed.), ch. 10.

[189] Butterfield v. Forrester, 11 East 60.

[190] 1 Thompson Neg. (2d ed.), §§ 85, 86; Davies v. Mann, 10 M. & W. 546; Smithwick v. Hall, etc., Co., 59 Conn. 261, 12 L. R. A. 279.

[191] Louisville, etc., R. Co. v. Lucas, 119 Ind. 583, 6 L. R. A. 193; Carterville v. Cook, 129 Ill. 152, 16 Am. St. 248; Atkinson v. Goodrich

§ 486. **Master's liability for willful or wanton wrongs of servant.**—The rule *respondeat superior,* in its logical application, has originated the modern doctrine that a master is liable to a third party for the intentional and malicious acts of his servant, if committed within the scope of the employment, as well as for his acts of mere negligence.[192] Formerly it was the view of the interpreters of the law that the very fact that the servant had so far departed from the master's presumed direction to do his business in a right and proper manner as to commit a willful or wanton wrong was in itself sufficient evidence that the act could not have been committed within the scope of such business; and that, therefore, the injured party could look only to the servant for redress;[193] but this is no longer the law. According to the modern rule, a shopkeeper was held liable for an assault and battery by a clerk upon a woman at the time in the shop, in an attempt to take away from her an article which the clerk believed had been stolen by her from the shop, such act being within the scope of the employment.[194] And so, it is now held to be within the scope of the employment of a salesman to cause the arrest and search of a person suspected by him of having stolen property in her possession which had been taken from the store, and the master is liable therefor.[195] And a master who sent his servant to take possession of furniture forfeited to him on account of non-payment of the price is liable for the willful assault of such servant committed by

Transportation Co., 60 Wis. 141, 50 Am. Rep. 352; 2 Thompson Neg. (2d ed.), §§ 68, 75; Shearman & Redf. Neg., § 66; Bishop Non-Contract Law, §§ 39, 450.

[192] Pioneer Fireproof Constr. Co. v. Sunderland, 188 Ill. 341; Lucas v. Michigan Cent. R. Co., 98 Mich. 1, 39 Am. St. 517; St. Louis, etc., R. Co. v. Hackett, 58 Ark. 381, 41 Am. St. 105; Moore v. Fitchburg R. Corp., 4 Gray (Mass.) 465, 64 Am. Dec. 83; Texas, etc., R. Co. v. Scoville, 62 Fed. 730; Golden v. Newbrand, 52 Iowa 59, 35 Am. Rep. 257; Pennsylvania Co. v. Weddle, 100 Ind. 138; Nelson Bus. Coll. Co. v. Lloyd, 60 Ohio St. 448, 46 L. R. A. 314; Maryland Consol. R. Co. v. Pierce, 89 Md. 495, 45 L. R. A. 527; Van Den Eynde v. Ulster R. Co., Ir. R. 5 C. L. 6, 328; 1 Thompson Neg. (2d ed.), § 552, *et seq.*

[193] For cases holding that the master is not liable for the willful wrong of his servant, see Wright v. Wilcox, 19 Wend. (N. Y.) 343, 32 Am. Dec. 507; Moore v. Sanborne, 2 Mich. 519, 59 Am. Dec. 209; Illinois Cent. R. Co. v. Downey, 18 Ill. 259; Church v. Mansfield, 20 Conn. 284; Lyons v. Martin, 8 A. & E. 512; Story Ag., § 456. And see 1 Thompson Neg. (2d ed.), § 552 and cases cited.

[194] McDonald v. Fanchere, 102 Iowa 496, 71 N. W. 427.

[195] Staples v. Schmid, 18 R. I. 224, 19 L. R. A. 824; 1 Thompson Neg. (2d ed.), § 567.

him in obtaining possession of such furniture, such act being within the course of the transaction of the master's business.[196] In a case decided in New York the facts were that the plaintiff went into the defendant's store and tried on an article of clothing, when he was accused by defendant's floor-walker as being a spy from a rival store, and by the direction of such floor-walker a saleswoman took the garment from the plaintiff. The court held that an assault was committed for which the defendant was liable.[197] Where a street-railway conductor wrongfully and maliciously ejects a passenger from a car for alleged non-payment of fare, the conductor acts within the course of his employment, and the company is liable for the wanton and malicious act.[198] The same is true where a trespasser is ejected with unnecessary force from a railway train by a servant in the employ of the carrier.[199] A master is generally liable for any trespass committed by a servant in the scope of the employment,[200] and the fact that the act was willful and malicious is no defense.[201] If the act was not within the scope of the employment, the master may still be liable therefor if he knowingly receives a benefit therefrom or otherwise ratifies or approves of it.[202]

III. Obligations and Liabilities of Servants.

§ 487. Liability of servant to master for the servant's own wrongs. —In a previous chapter we discussed the duties and liabilities of the agent to his principal, and the rights and remedies of the principal against the agent for their violations.[203] Wherever the employe is both an agent and a servant, the duties under which he rests to the principal are much the same as those owing by an agent to his principal.[203a] It is only necessary to point out specifically a few of the wrongs for which the servant may be rendered liable to the master. If he entails a loss upon his master on account of his negligence or willful misconduct to a third person, he thereby renders himself liable to indemnify the master for whatever damage the latter has to pay.

[196] Levi v. Brooks, 121 Mass. 501.

[197] Meehan v. Morewood, 52 Hun (N. Y.) 566.

[198] North Chicago, etc., R. Co. v. Gastka, 128 Ill. 613.

[199] St. Louis, etc., R. Co. v. Hendricks, 48 Ark. 182, 3 Am. St. 220; 3 Thompson Neg. (2d ed.), § 3304.

[200] 1 Thompson Neg. (2d ed.), § 560.

[201] 1 Thompson Neg. (2d ed.), § 561.

[202] Dempsey v. Chambers, 154 Mass. 330, 26 Am. St. 249.

[203] See Chapter VI, *ante*.

[203a] See *ante*, § 243.

This liability is not grounded upon the doctrine of *respondeat superior,* although that doctrine applies when it is sought to establish the master's liability for the wrongful act of the servant for which the master had to pay damages: the liability of the servant to the master arises out of his obligation to serve the latter faithfully, and to exercise care and diligence in the performance of the work undertaken by him; if he fails to fulfill this obligation, he violates his contract with the master, and becomes liable to him on account of the breach.[204] It is immaterial whether the injury is inflicted by the servant directly upon the property of the master, or indirectly by an injury to the property or person of a stranger, for which the master must respond in damages: the principle upon which the master can recover from the servant is the same in either case: in either case it is, as between the master and the servant, a violation of the duties

[204] See Zulkee v. Wing, 20 Wis. 408, 91 Am. Dec. 425, in which Dixon, C. J., delivering the opinion of the court, said: "If the injury is done by a servant in the course of his employment, it is, in contemplation of law, so far the act of the master, that the latter is civilly responsible therefor. '*Qui facit per alium facit per se.*' But this maxim is applicable only as between the master or principal and third persons. It presupposes that the parties stand to each other in the relation of strangers, between whom there is no privity; and has no application as between the master and his negligent servant, and the principal and his agent who has so unskillfully or carelessly conducted his business as to cause him damage. As between the master and a stranger, the servant represents the master, and the master is responsible; but as between the master and the servant who has committed the wrong, or violated his duty no less to the master than to the stranger, no such rule prevails. A servant is directly liable to his master for any damage occasioned by his negligence or misconduct, whether such damage be direct to the property of the master, or arise from the compensation which the master has been obliged to make to third persons for injuries sustained by them. To apply the maxim in such a case would be an utter perversion of it, and destructive of all liability on the part of servants. The servant in such case represents, not the master, but himself. It is his own negligence and misconduct for which he is required to answer; and in this respect he stands upon the same footing as any other wrongdoer. In the case above supposed, the master, having paid the damage caused by the negligence of his servant in running over a stranger, may sue the servant for the same act of negligence, to recover back the money paid. It would be strange if the servant, in answer to such an action, could say: '*Respondeat superior.* I was your servant at the time of the injury; my act was your act, my negligence your negligence; and therefore you can not recover.' Such an answer would be absurd enough."

the servant has undertaken to perform, resulting in an invasion of the property-rights of the master. Hence, where a hired servant sued his master for wages, it was held that the latter could recoup the damages he had sustained by reason of the servant's seduction of the master's minor daughter.[205] The court said in this case: "The plaintiff seeks to recover the wages on the contract of hiring. The cases cited show that the seducer broke that contract, and these damages resulted to the defendant in consequence of the breach. This gives the defendant the same right to recoup the damages that he would have had if the servant had intentionally killed the defendant's horse, or burned his dwelling, for in such cases the contract of hiring would have been broken. The law is now well established that whenever a party seeeks to recover on a contract which he has broken, the defendant in the suit has the right to recoup the damages he has sustained in consequence of the breach." Of course, the master is not confined to the remedy of recoupment, but may maintain an action against the servant for any such breach of his contract, or violation of duty growing out of the contract. Where the baggage-master of a railroad-train negligently carried a trunk belonging to a passenger beyond the proper station, and placed it in charge of the station-agent there, to be sent back by the latter to the station at which the baggage-master was directed to deliver it, and the trunk was stolen from the custody of the agent to whom it had been delivered,—the court held that the baggage-master was liable to the company for the damages for the loss of the trunk which it had to pay, and that the company could set off such damages in a suit by such employe for his wages.[206] And where, by the fault and negligence of a freight-conductor, one of the cars on his train was run into by another train and the company suffered a loss, it was held that the damages could be set off to a claim of the conductor for compensation.[207] So, an officer of a corporation, whose duty it is to receive its moneys and pay them over to another officer, is liable to the corporation for money stolen from him if he was negligent in paying it over.[208] In short, the servant is responsible to his master for all damages suffered by the latter through the servant's failure to exer-

[205] Bixby v. Parsons, 49 Conn. 483, 488, 44 Am. Rep. 246.

[206] Georgia, etc., R. Co. v. Jossey, 105 Ga. 271, 31 S. E. 179.

[207] Mobile, etc., R. Co. v. Clinton, 59 Ala. 392, 31 Am. Rep. 15.

[208] Odd Fellows' Mut. Aid Ass'n v. James, 63 Cal. 598, 49 Am. Rep. 107.

cise ordinary care or through want of proper skill, and which are the proximate results of such negligence.[209]

§ 488. **Servant's liability to third persons.**—As seen in a previous place, an agent is generally under no obligations to perform any affirmative act to any one but his principal, and is therefore not liable to a third person for nonfeasance, or for a failure to discharge a duty which he owes only to such principal.[210] The failure of an agent to act for his principal, when duty to the latter compels him to act, may give rise to an action by a third party against the principal, who was under obligation to perform such act. The principal could certainly not excuse himself by pleading that he had shifted the obligation to his agent; neither could the third party sue the agent for such failure, because the latter owes the former no duty and there is no privity between them. In such a case it might become desirable for the third party to proceed against the agent for various reasons, chief among which might be the principal's insolvency and the agent's solvency; but the injured third party has no legal remedy against the agent, and his only recourse is upon the principal, the party who by the contract between them owed him the duty. These principles are equally applicable to masters and servants. No duty is owing, no obligation exists, which holds a servant responsible to a third party for his mere failure to act, however serious the consequences may be to such party. If A enter into a contract with B in which B agrees to build a house for A within a certain time; and B employ C, D and E to work upon such house as carpenters, stonecutters, plumbers, etc., and by the failure of C, D and E, or either of them, the house is not completed within the time, or, in consequence of B's compulsion to employ other servants, the house is poorly constructed and A is damaged, A must look to B, and to B alone, for his indemnity.[211] But this doctrine can be accepted only with the qualification that the servant owes the third party no duty; for if he does, the mere fact that he is a servant or agent will not excuse him. And, generally, a servant or agent, because he happens to be such, is under just as many obligations as any other person so to conduct

[209] Shearman & Redf. Neg., § 242.

[10] *Ante*, §§ 300, 312.

[211] That the mere nonfeasance of a servant will not give a right of action to a stranger to whom no duty was owing by the servant, see Bristol, etc., R. Co. v. Collins, 7 H. L. Cas. 194; Blackstock v. New York, etc., R. Co., 20 N. Y. 48; Carey v. Rochereau, 16 Fed. 87; Feltus v. Swan, 62 Miss. 415; Shearman & Redf. Neg., § 241.

himself and to use the instruments in his custody and under his control as to avoid injury to his neighbors; and if he fails to do this he is guilty of such misconduct as will render him personally liable to one who sustains an injury or loss. This is usually denominated "misfeasance," and for that and any affirmative malicious or willful and wrongful act, called "malfeasance," he is equally liable. Even misfeasance may sometimes consist partly in non-action, as was well decided by the supreme court of Michigan.[212] Thus, where a servant, who was hauling wood for his master, and obtained permission of a neighbor to open a gap in his fence, but with directions to close it up after he went in and after he came out, left the gap open, and the hogs of the owner of the field escaped and one was killed and the other injured on a railroad-track, it was held that the leaving down of the bars was a misfeasance, and that the fact that he was a servant would not exempt him from liability.[213] It is sometimes erroneously stated that a servant can not be held liable to a third party for mere negligence. But negligence is not necessarily nonfeasance; and if it be misfeasance in any given case, the servant is liable to the injured party just as he would be if he had been acting for himself instead of his master. And this is none the less true because the master is also liable, for the master and servant are, in such cases, joint tort-feasors; as where a servant negligently drives his master's team over a stranger and injures him.[214] A servant is liable jointly with the principal, or separately, for other torts committed on behalf of his master; as for a trespass on land;[215] and for a conversion of the property of a third party.[216] The mere keeping of goods, however, for the master, and refusal to surrender them, is perhaps not sufficient to create a liability on the part of the servant: he must commit some active wrong, such as converting the property to his own use, or aiding another in doing so;[217] but if, after having due notice of the title

[212] Ellis v. McNaughton, 76 Mich. 237.

[213] Homer v. Lawrence, 37 N. J. L. 46.

[214] Phelps v. Wait, 30 N. Y. 78; Hewitt v. Swift, 3 Allen (Mass.) 420. See also, Wright v. Compton, 53 Ind. 337; Blue v. Briggs, 12 Ind. App. 105; Hill v. Caverly, 7 N. H. 215, 26 Am. Dec. 735; Welsh v. Stewart, 31 Mo. App. 376.

[215] McNichols v. Nelson, 45 Mo. App. 446; Hazen v. Wight, 87 Me. 233, 32 Atl. 887.

[216] Cook v. Monroe, 45 Neb. 349; Shearer v. Evans, 89 Ind. 400; Porter v. Thomas, 23 Ga. 467.

[217] See Nelson v. Iverson, 17 Ala. 216; Mount v. Derick, 5 Hill (N. Y.) 455.

of a person demanding the property, he persists in refusing to deliver it, this may amount to a conversion, such as will render him liable to the party entitled to such property.[218]

§ 489. **Servant's liability to fellow servants.**—The fact that fellow servants do not stand in privity of contract the one to the other has led some of the text-writers to lay down the doctrine that there can be no liability of a servant to his coservant for negligence.[219] This also seems to be the holding of some of the earlier decisions.[220] But there is no good reason why a person who occupies to another the position of a fellow servant, or who is engaged with him in the employment of a common master, should not be required so to conduct himself and so use the instruments in his custody as not to injure such other person, or, in other words, to exercise such reasonable and ordinary care as he is required to exercise toward any other person. Such fellow servant can not be held to have assumed the risks—as between him and the other servant—which result from the other's negligence; and it is now the universally-accepted rule that an employe or servant is in duty bound to exercise ordinary care in the performance of the work intrusted to him; and that for a failure to do so he is liable to his coemploye or fellow servant for any injury which the latter may suffer by the former's negligence.[221] If the master himself assumes the position of a workman or superintendent in the prosecution of the work, he is of course likewise liable for an injury sustained by another workman or employe through his negligence or tortious conduct.[222]

[218] Singer Mfg. Co. v. King, 14 R. I. 511.

[219] Wharton Neg., § 245; Wood Master & Serv., § 335.

[220] Southcote v. Stanley, 1 H. & N. 247; Albro v. Jaquith, 4 Gray (Mass.) 99, 64 Am. Dec. 56.

[221] Hare v. McIntire, 82 Maine 240, 8 L. R. A. 450; Hinds v. Overacker, 66 Ind. 547, 32 Am. Rep. 114; Rogers v. Overton, 87 Ind. 410; Kenney v. Lane, 9 Tex. Civ. App. 150; Griffiths v. Wolfram, 22 Minn. 185; Osborne v. Morgan, 130 Mass. 102 (overruling Albro v. Jaquith, *supra*); Warax v. Cincinnati, etc., R. Co., 72 Fed. 637; Shearman & Redf. Neg., § 245; 2 Thompson Neg. (1st ed.) 1062.

[222] Ashworth v. Stanwix, 3 El. & El. (107 E. C. L.) 701; Leonard v. Collins, 70 N. Y. 90.

APPENDIX.

EMPLOYERS' LIABILITY ACTS.

I.

ENGLISH EMPLOYERS' LIABILITY ACT.

(43 & 44 Vict., ch. 42.)

An act to extend and regulate the liability of employers to make compensation for personal injuries suffered by workmen in their service. [7th September, 1880.]

Be it enacted by the queen's most excellent majesty, by and with the advice and consent of the lords spiritual and temporal, and commons, in this present parliament assembled, and by the authority of the same, as follows:

1. Where, after the commencement of this act, personal injury is caused to a workman

(1) By reason of any defect in the condition of the ways, works, machinery, or plant connected with or used in the business of the employer; or

(2) By reason of the negligence of any person in the service of the employer who has any superintendence entrusted to him whilst in the exercise of such superintendence; or

(3) By reason of the negligence of any person in the service of the employer to whose orders or directions the workman at the time of the injury was bound to conform, and did conform, where such injury resulted from his having so conformed; or

(4) By reason of the act or omission of any person in the service

of the employer done or made in obedience to the rules or by-laws of the employer, or in obedience to particular instructions given by any person delegated with the authority of the employer in that behalf; or

(5) By reason of the negligence of any person in the service of the employer who has the charge or control of any signal, points, locomotive engine, or train upon a railway, the workman, or in case the injury results in death, the legal personal representatives of the workman, and any persons entitled in case of death, shall have the same right of compensation and remedies against the employer as if the workman had not been a workman of nor in the service of the employer, nor engaged in his work.

2. A workman shall not be entitled under this act to any right of compensation or remedy against the employer in any of the following cases; that is to say,

(1) Under sub-section one of section one, unless the defect therein mentioned arose from, or had not been discovered or remedied owing to the negligence of the employer, or of some person in the service of the employer, and entrusted by him with the duty of seeing that the ways, works, machinery, or plant were in proper condition.

(2) Under sub-section four of section one, unless the injury resulted from some impropriety or defect in the rules, by-laws, or instructions therein mentioned; provided that where a rule or by-law has been approved or has been accepted as a proper rule or by-law by one of her majesty's principal secretaries of state, or by the board of trade, or any other department of the government, under or by virtue of any act of parliament, it shall not be deemed for the purposes of this act to be an improper or defective rule or by-law.

(3) In any case where the workman knew of the defect or negligence which caused his injury, and failed within a reasonable time to give, or cause to be given, information thereof to the employer or some person superior to himself in the service of the employer, unless he was aware that the employer or such superior already knew of the said defect or negligence.

3. The amount of compensation recoverable under this act shall not exceed such sum as may be found to be equivalent to the estimated earnings, during the three years preceding the injury, of a person in the same grade employed during those years in the like employment and in the district in which the workman is employed at the time of the injury.

4. An action for the recovery under this act of compensation for an injury shall not be maintainable unless notice that injury has been sustained is given within six weeks and the action is commenced within six months from the occurrence of the accident causing the injury, or, in case of death, within twelve months from the time of death: provided always, that in case of death the want of such notice shall be no bar to the maintenance of such action if the judge shall be of opinion that there was reasonable excuse for such want of notice.

5. There shall be deducted from any compensation awarded to any workman, or representatives of a workman, or persons claiming by, under, or through a workman in respect of any cause of action arising under this act, any penalty or part of a penalty which may have been paid in pursuance of any other act of parliament to such workman, representatives, or persons in respect of the same cause of action; and where an action has been brought under this act by any workman, or the representatives of any workman, or any persons claiming by, under, or through such workman, for compensation in respect of any cause of action arising under this act, and payment has not previously been made of any penalty or part of a penalty under any other act of parliament in respect of the same cause of action, such workman, representatives, or person shall not be entitled thereafter to receive any penalty or part of a penalty under any other act of parliament in respect of the same cause of action.

6. (1) Every action for recovery of compensation under this act shall be brought in a county court, but may, upon the application of either plaintiff or defendant, be removed into a superior court in like manner and upon the same conditions as an action commenced in a county court may by law be removed.

(2) Upon the trial of any such action in a county court before the judge without a jury one or more assessors may be appointed for the purpose of ascertaining the amount of compensation.

(3) For the purpose of regulating the conditions and mode of appointment and remuneration of such assessors, and all matters of procedure relating to their duties, and also for the purpose of consolidating any actions under this act in a county court, and otherwise preventing multiplicity of such actions, rules and regulations may be made, varied, and repealed from time to time in the same manner as rules and regulations for regulating the practice and procedure in other actions in county courts.

"County court" shall, with respect to Scotland, mean the "sheriff's court," and shall, with respect to Ireland, mean the "civil bill court."

In Scotland any action under this act may be removed to the court of session at the instance of either party, in the manner provided by, and subject to the conditions prescribed by, section nine of the Sheriff Courts (Scotland) Act, 1877.

In Scotland the sheriff may conjoin actions arising out of the same occurrence or cause of action, though at the instance of different parties and in respect of different injuries.

7. Notice in respect of an injury under this act shall give the name and address of the person injured, and shall state in ordinary language the cause of the injury and the date at which it was sustained, and shall be served on the employer, or, if there is more than one employer, upon one of such employers.

The notice may be served by delivering the same to or at the residence or place of business of the person on whom it is to be served.

The notice may also be served by post by a registered letter addressed to the person on whom it is to be served at his last known place of residence or place of business; and, if served by post, shall be deemed to have been served at the time when a letter containing the same would be delivered in the ordinary course of post; and, in proving the service of such notice, it shall be sufficient to prove that the notice was properly addressed and registered.

Where the employer is a body of persons corporate or unincorporate, the notice shall be served by delivering the same at or by sending it by post in a registered letter addressed to the office, or if there be more than one office, any one of the offices of such body.

A notice under this section shall not be deemed invalid by reason of any defect or inaccuracy therein unless the judge who tries the action arising from the injury mentioned in the notice shall be of opinion that the defendant in the action is prejudiced in his defense by such defect or inaccuracy, and that the defect or inaccuracy was for the purpose of misleading.

8. For the purposes of this act, unless the context otherwise requires,—

The expression "person who has superintendence entrusted to him" means a person whose sole or principal duty is that of superintendence, and who is not ordinarily engaged in manual labor:

The expression "employer" includes a body of persons corporate or unincorporate:

The expression "workman" means a railway servant and any person to whom the Employers and Workmen Act, 1875, applies.

9. This act shall not come into operation until the first day of January, one thousand eight hundred and eighty-one, which date is in this act referred to as the commencement of this act.[1]

10. This act may be cited as the Employers' Liability Act, 1880, and shall continue in force till the thirty-first day of December, one thousand eight hundred and eighty-seven, and to the end of the then next session of parliament, and no longer, unless parliament shall otherwise determine, and all actions commenced under this act before that period shall be continued as if the said act had not expired.[2]

II.

ALABAMA EMPLOYERS' LIABILITY ACT.

(Civil Code Ala. 1896, §§ 1749-1751.)[3]

1749 (2590). *Liability of master or employer to servant or employe for injuries.*—When a personal injury is received by a servant or employe in the service or business of the master or employer, the master or employer is liable to answer in damages to such servant or employe, as if he were a stranger, and not engaged in such service or employment, in the cases following:

1. When the injury is caused by reason of any defect in the condition of the ways, works, machinery, or plant connected with, or used in the business of the master or employer.

2. When the injury is caused by reason of the negligence of any person in the service or employment of the master or employer, who has any superintendence intrusted to him, whilst in the exercise of such superintendence.

3. When such injury is caused by reason of the negligence of any person in the service or employment of the master or employer, to whose orders or directions the servant or employe, at the time of

[1] This section, 9, is repealed by 57 & 58 Vict., cap. 56, Statute Law Revision Act, 1894.

[2] The Employers' Liability Act, 1880, was continued in force until December 31, 1889, by 51 & 52 Vict., cap. 58, and has been continued annually since then by the Expiring Laws Continuance Act.

[3] Found also in Code 1886, §§ 2590-2592.

the injury, was bound to conform, and did conform, if such injuries resulted from his having so conformed.

4. When such injury is caused by reason of the act or omission of any person in the service or employment of the master or employer, done or made in obedience to the rules and regulations or by-laws of the master or employer, or in obedience to particular instructions given by any person delegated with the authority of the master or employer in that behalf.

5. When such injury is caused by reason of the negligence of any person in the service or employment of the master or employer, who has the charge or control of any signal, points, locomotive, engine, switch, car, or train upon a railway, or of any part of the track of a railway.

But the master or employer is not liable under this section, if the servant or employe knew of the defect or negligence causing the injury, and failed in a reasonable time to give information thereof to the master or employer, or to some person superior to himself engaged in the service or employment of the master or employer, unless he was aware that the master or employer, or such superior, already knew of such defect or negligence; nor is the master or employer liable under subdivision one, unless the defect therein mentioned arose from, or had not been discovered or remedied owing to the negligence of the master or employer, or of some person in the service of the master or employer, and intrusted by him with the duty of seeing that the ways, works, machinery, or plant, were in proper condition.

1750 (2592). *Damages exempt.*—Damages recovered by the servant or employe, of and from the master or employer, are not subject to the payment of debts, or any legal liabilities incurred by him.

1751 (2591). *Personal representative may sue, if injury results in death.*—If such injury results in the death of the servant or employe, his personal representative is entitled to maintain an action therefor, and the damages recovered are not subject to the payment of debts or liabilities, but shall be distributed according to the statute of distributions.

III.

INDIANA EMPLOYERS' LIABILITY ACT.

(Burns' Rev. St. Ind. 1901, §§ 7083-7087.)[1]

7083. *Liability for personal injuries.*—1. That every railroad or other corporation, except municipal, operating in this state, shall be liable in damages for personal injury suffered by any employe while in its service, the employe so injured being in the exercise of due care and diligence, in the following cases:

First. When such injury is suffered by reason of any defect in the condition of ways, works, plant, tools and machinery connected with or in use in the business of such corporation, when such defect was the result of negligence on the part of the corporation, or some person entrusted by it with the duty of keeping such ways, works, plant, tools or machinery in proper condition.

Second. Where such injury resulted from the negligence of any person in the service of such corporation, to whose order or direction the injured employe at the time of the injury was bound to conform, and did conform.

Third. Where such injury resulted from the act or omission of any person done or made in obedience to any rule, regulation or by-law of such corporation, or in obedience to the particular instructions given by any person delegated with the authority of the corporation in that behalf.

Fourth. Where such injury was caused by the negligence of any person in the service of such corporation who has charge of any signal, telegraph-office, switch-yard, shop, round-house, locomotive-engine, or train upon a railway, or where such injury was caused by the negligence of any person, coemploye, or fellow servant engaged in the same common service in any of the several departments of the service of any such corporation, the said person, coemploye, or fellow servant, at the time acting in the place, and performing the duty of the corporation in that behalf, and the person so injured, obeying or conforming to the order of some superior at the time of such injury, having authority to direct; but nothing herein shall be

[1] Acts Ind. 1893, ch. 130.

construed to abridge the liability of the corporation under existing laws.

7084. [Repealed by acts 1895, chapter 64, section 1.]

7085. *Measure of damages.*—3. The damages recoverable under this act shall be commensurate with the injury sustained unless death results from such injury, when, in such case, the action shall survive and be governed in all respects by the law now in force as to such actions: *provided,* that where any such person recovers a judgment against a railroad or other corporation, and such corporation takes an appeal, and, pending such appeal, the injured person dies, and the judgment rendered in the court below be thereafter reversed, the right of action of such person shall survive to his legal representative.

7086. *Laws of other states not a defense.* 4. In case any railroad corporation which owns or operates a line extending into or through the state of Indiana and into or through another or other states, and a person in the employ of such corporation, a citizen of this state, shall be injured as provided in this act, in any other state where such railroad is owned or operated, and a suit for such injury shall be brought in any of the courts of this state, it shall not be competent for such corporation to plead or prove the decisions or statutes of the state where such person shall have been injured as a defense to the action brought in this state.

7087. *Contracts of release void.*—5. All contracts made by railroads or other corporations with their employes, or rules or regulations adopted by any corporation releasing or relieving it from liability to any employe having a right of action under the provisions of this act are hereby declared null and void. The provisions of this act, however, shall not apply to any injuries sustained before it takes effect, nor shall it affect in any manner any suit or legal proceedings pending at the time it takes effect.

IV.

MASSACHUSETTS EMPLOYERS' LIABILITY ACT.

(Rev. Laws 1902, ch. 106, §§ 71-79.)

If personal injury is caused to an employe, who, at the time of the injury, is in the exercise of due care, by reason of:

SECTION 71. First, a defect in the condition of the ways, works or machinery connected with or used in the business of the employer, which arose from, or had not been discovered or remedied in consequence of, the negligence of the employer or of a person in his service who had been intrusted by him with the duty of seeing that the ways, works or machinery were in proper condition; or,

Second, the negligence of a person in the service of the employer who was intrusted with and was exercising superintendence and whose sole or principal duty was that of superintendence, or, in absence of such superintendent, of a person acting as superintendent with the authority or consent of such employer; or,

Third, the negligence of a person in the service of the employer who was in charge or control of a signal, switch, locomotive-engine or train upon a railroad; the employer, or his legal representatives, shall, subject to the provisions of the eight following sections, have the same rights to compensation and of action against the employer as if he had not been an employe, nor in the service, nor engaged in the work, of the employer.

A car which is in use by, or which is in possession of, a railroad corporation shall be considered as a part of the ways, works or machinery of the corporation which uses or has it in possession, within the meaning of clause one of this section, whether it is owned by such corporation or by some other company or person. One or more cars which are in motion, whether attached to an engine or not, shall constitute a train within the meaning of clause three of this section, and whoever, as a part of his duty for the time being, physically controls or directs the movements of a signal, switch, locomotive-engine or train shall be deemed to be a person in charge or control of a signal, switch, locomotive-engine or train within the meaning of said clause.

SECTION 72. If the injury described in the preceding section results in the death of the employe, and such death is not instantaneous or is preceded by conscious suffering, and if there is any person who would have been entitled to bring an action under the provisions of the following section, the legal representatives of said employe may, in the action brought under the provisions of the preceding section, recover damages for the death in addition to those for the injury.

SECTION 73. If, as a result of the negligence of an employer himself, or of a person for whose negligence an employer is liable under the provisions of section seventy-one, an employe is instantly killed, or dies without conscious suffering, his widow or, if he leaves no widow, his next of kin, who, at the time of his death, were dependent upon his wages for support, shall have a right of action for damages against the employer.

SECTION 74. If, under the provisions of either of the two preceding sections, damages are awarded for the death, they shall be assessed with reference to the degree of culpability of the employer or of the person for whose negligence the employer is liable. The amount of damages which may be awarded in an action under the provisions of section seventy-one for a personal injury to an employe, in which no damages for his death are awarded under the provisions of section seventy-two, shall not exceed four thousand dollars. The amount of damages which may be awarded in such action, if damages for his death are awarded under the provisions of section seventy-two, shall not exceed five thousand dollars for both the injury and the death, and shall be apportioned by the jury between the legal representatives of the employe and the persons who would have been entitled, under the provisions of section seventy-three, to bring an action for his death if it had been instantaneous or without conscious suffering. The amount of damages which may be awarded in an action brought under the provisions of section seventy-three shall not be less than five hundred nor more than five thousand dollars.

SECTION 75. No action for the recovery of damages for injury or death under the provisions of sections seventy-one to seventy-four, inclusive, shall be maintained unless notice of the time, place and cause of the injury is given to the employer within sixty days, and the action is commenced within one year after the action which causes the injury or death. Such notice shall be in writing, signed by the person injured or by a person in his behalf; but if from physical or mental incapacity it is impossible for the person injured to give the notice within the time provided in this section, he may give it within ten days after such incapacity has been removed, and if he dies without having given the notice and without having been for ten days at any time after his injury of sufficient capacity to give it, his executor or administrator may give such notice within sixty days after his appointment. A notice given under the provisions of this section shall not be held invalid or insufficient solely by reason of an inaccuracy in stating the time, place or cause of the injury, if it is shown that there was no intention to mislead, and that the employer was not in fact misled thereby. The provisions of section twenty-two of chapter fifty-one shall apply to notices under the provisions of this section.

SECTION 76. If an employer enters into a contract, written or verbal, with an independent contractor to do part of such employer's work, or if such contractor enters into a contract with a subcontractor to do all or any part of the work comprised in such contractor's contract with the employer, such contract or subcontract shall not bar the liability of the employer for injuries to the employes of such contractor or subcontractor, caused by any defect in the condition of the ways, works, machinery or plant, if they are the property of the employer or are furnished by him and if such defect arose, or had not been discovered or remedied, through the negligence of the employer or of some person intrusted by him with the duty of seeing that they were in proper condition.

SECTION 77. An employe or his legal representatives shall not be entitled under the provisions of sections seventy-one to seventy-four, inclusive, to any right of action for damages against his employer if such employe knew of the defect or negligence which caused the injury, and failed within a reasonable time to give, or cause to be given, information thereof to the employer, or to some person superior to himself in the service of the employer who was intrusted with general superintendence.

SECTION 78. An employer who shall have contributed to an insurance fund created and maintained for the mutual purpose of indemnifying an employe for personal injuries for which compensation may be recovered under the provisions of sections seventy-one to seventy-four, inclusive, or to any relief society formed under the provisions of sections seventeen, eighteen and nineteen of chapter one hundred and twenty-five, may prove in mitigation of the damages recoverable by an employe under the provisions of said sections, such proportion of the pecuniary benefit which has been received by such employe from any such fund or society on account of such contribution of said employer, as the contribution of such employer to such fund or society bears to the whole contribution thereto.

SECTION 79. The provisions of the eight preceding sections shall not apply to injuries caused to domestic servants or farm laborers by fellow employes.

V.

MISSISSIPPI EMPLOYERS' LIABILITY ACT.

(Acts Spec. Sess. 1898, ch. 66.)

FELLOW-SERVANT RULE.

SECTION 1. Every employe of any corporation shall have the same rights and remedies for an injury suffered by him from the act or omission of the corporation or its employes, as are allowed by [law to] other persons not employes where the injury results from the negligence of a superior agent or officer, or of a person having the right to control or direct the services of the party injured; and also when the injury results from the negligence of a fellow servant engaged in another department of labor from that of the party injured, or of a fellow servant on another train of cars, or one engaged about a different piece of work. Knowledge by an employe injured of the defective or unsafe character or condition of any machinery, ways, or appliances, or of the improper loading of cars, shall not be a defense to an action for injury caused thereby, except as to conductors or engineers in charge of dangerous or unsafe cars or engines voluntarily operated by them.

When death ensues from an injury to an employe an action may be brought in the name of the widow of such employe for the death of the husband, or by the husband for the death of his wife, or by the parent for the death of a child, or in the name of the child for the death of an only parent, for such damages as may be suffered by them respectively by reason of such death, the damages to be for the use of such widow, husband or child, except that in case the widow should have children the damages shall be distributed as personal property of the husband. The legal or personal representative of the person injured shall have the same rights and remedies as are allowed by law to such representatives of other persons. In every such action the jury may give such damages as shall be fair and just with reference to the injury resulting from such death to the persons suing. Any contract or agreement, express or implied, made by an employe to waive the benefit of this section shall be null and void; and this section shall not deprive an employe of a corporation or his legal [or] personal representative of any right or remedy that he now has by law.

VI.

NEW YORK EMPLOYERS' LIABILITY ACT.

(Laws 1902, ch. 600.)

SEC. 1. Where, after this act takes effect, personal injury is caused to an employe who is himself in the exercise of due care and diligence at the time:

1. By reason of any defect in the condition of the ways, works or machinery connected with or used in the business of the employer which arose from or had not been discovered or remedied owing to the negligence of the employer or of any person in the service of the employer and intrusted by him with the duty of seeing that the ways, works or machinery were in proper condition;

2. By reason of the negligence of any person in the service of the employer intrusted with and exercising superintendence whose sole or principal duty is that of superintendence, or in the absence of such superintendent, of any person acting as superintendent with the authority or consent of such employer;

3. The employe, or in case the injury results in death, the executor or administrator of a deceased employe who has left him surviving a husband, wife or next of kin, shall have the same right of compensation and remedies against the employer as if the employe had not been an employe of nor in the service of the employer nor engaged in his work. The provisions of law relating to actions for causing death by negligence, so far as the same are consistent with this act, shall apply to an action brought by an executor or administrator of a deceased employe suing under the provisions of this act.

SEC. 2. No action for recovery of compensation for injury or death under this act shall be maintained unless notice of the time, place, and cause of the injury is given to the employer within one hundred and twenty days and the action is commenced within one year after the occurrence of the accident causing the injury or death. The notice required by this section shall be in writing and signed by the person injured or by some one in his behalf, but if from physical or mental incapacity it is impossible for the person injured to give notice within the time provided in said section, he may give the same within ten days after such incapacity is removed. In case of his death without having given such notice, his executor or administrator may give such notice within sixty days after his appointment, but no notice under the provisions of this section shall be deemed to be invalid or insufficient solely by reason of any inaccuracy in stating the time, place or cause of the injury if it be shown that there was no intention to mislead and that the party entitled to notice was not in fact misled thereby. The notice required by this section shall be served on the employer, or if there is more than one employer, upon one of such employers, and may be served by delivering the same to or at the residence or place of business of the person on whom it is to be served. The notice may be served by post, by letter addressed to the person on whom it is to be served, at his last known place of residence or place of business, and if served by post shall be deemed to have been served at the time when the letter containing the same would be delivered in the ordinary course of the post. When the employer is a corporation, notice shall be served by delivering the same or by sending it by post addressed to the office or principal place of business of such corporation.

SEC. 3. An employe, by entering upon or continuing in the service of the employer, shall be presumed to have assented to the necessary risks of the occupation or employment and no others. The necessary risks of the occupation or employment shall, in all cases arising after this act take effect, be considered as including those risks, and those only, inherent in the nature of the business which remain after the employer has exercised due care in providing for the safety of his employes, and has complied with the laws affecting or regulating such business or occupation for the greater safety of such employes. In an action maintained for the recovery of damages for personal injuries to an employe received after this act takes effect, owing to any cause for which the employer would otherwise be liable, the fact that the employe continued in the service of the employer in the same place and course of employment after the discovery by such employe, or after he had been informed of, the danger of personal injury therefrom, shall not, as a matter of law, be considered as an assent by such employe to the existence or continuance of such risks of personal injury therefrom, or as negligence contributing to such injury. The question whether the employe understood and assumed the risk of such injury, or was guilty of contributory negligence, by his continuance in the same place and course of employment with knowledge of the risk of injury shall be one of fact, subject to the usual powers of the court in a proper case to set aside a verdict rendered contrary to the evidence. An employe, or his legal representative, shall not be entitled under this act to any right of compensation or remedy against the employer in any case where such employe knew of the defect or negligence which caused the injury and failed, within a reasonable time, to give or cause to be given, information thereof to the employer, or to some person superior to himself in the service of the employer who had intrusted to him some general superintendence, unless it shall appear on the trial that such defect or negligence was known to such employer, or superior person, prior to such injuries to the employe.

SEC. 4. An employer who shall have contributed to an insurance fund created and maintained for the mutual purpose of indemnifying an employe for personal injuries, for which compensation may be recovered under this act, or to any relief society or benefit fund created under the laws of this state, may prove in mitigation of damages recoverable by an employe under this act such proportion of the pecuniary benefit which has been received by such employe from such fund or society on account of such contribution of employer, as the contribution of such employer to such fund or society bears to the whole contribution thereto.

SEC. 5. Every existing right of action for negligence or to recover damages for injuries resulting in death is continued, and nothing in this act contained shall be construed as limiting any such right of action, nor shall the failure to give the notice provided for in section two of this act be a bar to the maintenance of a suit upon any such existing right of action.

INDEX

[References are to Sections.]

[*References are to Sections.*]

[*References are to Sections.*]

[*References are to Sections.*]

[*References are to Sections.*]

[*References are to Sections.*]

[*References are to Sections.*]

[*References are to Sections.*]

[*References are to Sections.*]

[*References are to Sections.*]

[*References are to Sections.*]

[*References are to Sections.*]

[*References are to Sections.*]

[*References are to Sections.*]

[*References are to Sections.*]

[*References are to Sections.*]

[*References are to Sections.*]

[*References are to Sections.*]

[*References are to Sections.*]

[*References are to Sections.*]

[*References are to Sections.*]

[*References are to Sections.*]

[*References are to Sections.*]

[*References are to Sections.*]

[*References are to Sections.*]

[*References are to Sections.*]

[*References are to Sections.*]

P

[*References are to Sections.*]

[*References are to Sections.*]

[*References are to Sections.*]

R

[*References are to Sections.*]

[*References are to Sections.*]

[*References are to Sections.*]

[*References are to Sections.*]

[*References are to Sections.*]

[*References are to Sections.*]

U

Whole number of pages, 767.

Spotted something that isn't quite right?

Let us know and we'll fix it for future reprints. And as a thank you for your diligence, we'll send you a free Sothis book of your choice.

publisher@sothis.press

This page intentionally left blank

Except of course for that line above. And this one.
And whilst we have your attention, perhaps you'd
like to follow us on Instagram @sothis.press. Go on.

Made in the USA
Monee, IL
08 November 2026

68028681R00454